PRENTICE HALL
LITERATURE

Grevy's Zebra, **Endangered Species Series, 1983, Andy Warhol**
Grevy's Zebra by Andy Warhol (1928–1987) demonstrates the Pop Art movement's embrace of commercial and popular culture during the 1960s. Warhol and other pop artists drew their subject matter and artistic techniques from television, advertisements, comic books, and popular social issues. This painting is part of Warhol's Endangered Species Series, which reflects popular culture's interest in wildlife conservation. For this series, Warhol used a technique called silk-screening to impose photo images onto canvas.

P E N G U I N **E D I T I O N**

Upper Saddle River, New Jersey

Boston, Massachusetts

ISBN: 0-13-131714-8

3 4 5 6 7 8 9 10   10 09 08 07 06

ACKNOWLEDGMENTS

Grateful acknowledgment is made to the following for copyrighted material:

Miriam Altshuler Literary Agency "Treasure of Lemon Brown" by Walter Dean Myers from *Boy's Life Magazine, March 1983*. Copyright © 1983, by Walter Dean Myers. Reprinted by permission of Miriam Altshuler Literary Agency, on behalf of Walter Dean Myers.

American National Red Cross "How to Recognize Venomous Snakes in North America" by American Red Cross and Kathleen A. Handal, M.D. from *The American Red Cross First Aid And Safety Handbook*. Copyright © 1992 by The American National Red Cross. Reprinted by courtesy of the American National Red Cross. All rights reserved in all countries.

Americas Magazine "Mongoose on the Loose" reprinted from *Americas*, a bimonthly magazine published by the General Secretariat of the Organization of American States in English and Spanish. Reprinted by permission.

Arte Público Press "Bailando" by Pat Mora from *Chants*. Reprinted with permission from the publisher of *Chants* (Houston: Arte Publico Press-University of Houston, 1985.) "Maestro" by Pat Mora from *Borders*. Reprinted with permission from the publisher of *Borders* (Houston: Arte Publico Press-University of Houston, 1986).

Bantam Books, a division of Random House, Inc. "The Eternal Frontier" from *Frontier* by Louis L'Amour. Photographs by David Muench, copyright © 1984 by Louis L'Amour Enterprises, Inc. Used by permission of Bantam Books, a division of Random House, Inc.

Elizabeth Barnett, literary executor for the Edna St. Vincent Millay Society "The Courage That My Mother Had" by Edna St. Vincent Millay from *Collected Poems*, HarperCollins. Copyright © 1954, 1982 by Norma Millay Ellis. All rights reserved. Used by permission of Elizabeth Barnett, literary executor.

Susan Bergholz Literary Services "Four Skinny Trees" by Sandra Cisneros from *The House On Mango Street*. Copyright © 1984 by Sandra Cisneros. Published by Vintage books, a division of Random House, Inc., and in hardcover by Alfred A. Knopf in 1994. "My First Free Summer" by Julia Alvarez Copyright © 2003 by Julia Alvarez. First published in *Better Homes and Gardens, August 2003*. "Something to Declare (Introduction)" by Julia Alvarez Copyright © 1998 by Julia Alvarez. From *Something to Declare*, published by Plume, an imprint of Penguin Group (USA), in 1999 and originally hardcover by Algonquin Books of Chapel Hill. Reprinted by permission of Susan Bergholz Literary Services, New York. All rights reserved.

Acknowledgments continue on p. R61, which constitutes an extension of this copyright page.

CONTRIBUTING AUTHORS

The contributing authors guided the direction and philosophy of *Prentice Hall Literature: Penguin Edition.* Working with the development team, they helped to build the pedagogical integrity of the program and to ensure its relevance for today's teachers and students.

Kevin Feldman

Kevin Feldman, Ed.D., is the Director of Reading and Intervention for the Sonoma County Office of Education and an independent educational consultant. He publishes and provides consultancy and training nationally, focusing upon improving school-wide literacy skills as well as targeted interventions for struggling readers, special needs students, and second language learners. Dr. Feldman is the co-author of the California Special Education Reading Task Force report and the lead program author for the 2002 Prentice Hall secondary language arts program *Timeless Voices: Timeless Themes.* He serves as technical consultant to the California Reading and Literature Project and the CalSTAT State Special Education Improvement Project. Dr. Feldman has taught for nineteen years at the university level in Special Education and Masters' level programs for University of California, Riverside, and Sonoma State University.

Dr. Feldman earned his undergraduate degree in Psychology from Washington State University and has a Masters Degree from UC Riverside in Special Education, Learning Disabilities, and Instructional Design. He has an Ed.D. from the University of San Francisco in Curriculum and Instruction.

Sharon Vaughn

Sharon Vaughn, Ph.D., is the H.E. Hartfelder/The Southland Corporation Regents Professor at the University of Texas and also director of the Vaughn Gross Center for Reading and Language Arts at the University of Texas (VGCRLA). As director of the VGCRLA, she leads more than five major initiatives, including The Central Regional Reading First Technical Assistance Center; the Three-Tier Reading Research Project; a bilingual-biliteracy (English/Spanish) intervention research study; the first through fourth grade Teacher Reading Academies that have been used for teacher education throughout Texas and the nation; and the creation of online professional development in reading for teachers and other interested professionals.

Dr. Vaughn has published more than ten books and over one hundred research articles. She is Editor in Chief of the *Journal of Learning Disabilities* and serves on the editorial boards of more than ten research journals, including the *Journal of Educational Psychology,* the *American Educational Research Journal,* and the *Journal of Special Education.*

Kate Kinsella

Kate Kinsella, Ed.D., is a teacher educator in the Department of Secondary Education at San Francisco State University. She teaches coursework addressing academic language and literacy development in linguistically and culturally diverse classrooms. She maintains secondary classroom involvement by teaching an academic literacy class for adolescent English learners through the University's Step to College Program. She publishes and provides consultancy and training nationally, focusing upon responsible instructional practices that provide second language learners and less proficient readers in Grades 4–12 with the language and literacy skills vital to educational mobility

Dr. Kinsella is the program author for *Reading in the Content Areas: Strategies for Reading Success,* published by Pearson Learning, and the lead program author for the 2002 Prentice Hall secondary language arts program *Timeless Voices: Timeless Themes.* She is the co-editor of the *CATESOL Journal* (California Teachers of English to Speakers of Other Languages) and serves on the editorial board for the *California Reader.* A former Fulbright scholar, Dr. Kinsella has received numerous awards, including the prestigious Marcus Foster Memorial Reading Award, offered by the California Reading Association in 2002 to a California educator who has made a significant statewide impact on both policy and pedagogy in the area of literacy.

Differentiated Instruction Advisor
Don Deshler

Don Deshler, Ph.D., is the Director of the Center for Research on Learning (CRL) at the University of Kansas. Dr. Deshler's expertise centers on adolescent literacy, learning strategic instruction, and instructional strategies for teaching content area classes to academically diverse classes. He is the author of *Teaching Content to All: Evidence-Based Inclusive Practices in Middle and Secondary Schools,* a text which presents the instructional practices that have been tested and validated through his research at CRL.

UNIT AUTHORS

An award-winning contemporary author hosts each unit in each level of Prentice Hall Litera-*ture. Serving as a guide for your students, these authors introduce literary concepts, answer questions about their work, and discuss their own writing processes, using their works as models. Following are the featured unit authors for Grade 7.*

Richard **Peck (b. 1934)**

Unit 1: Fiction and Nonfiction Richard Peck, recipient of a 2001 National Humanities Medal for his distinguished fiction and nonfiction, is the perfect guide for this unit. In novels like *A Year Down Yonder* (Newbery award) and *A Long Way from Chicago* (National Book Award Finalist), he brings the past to life for young readers. These and similar works combine strong and humorous characterizations with settings grounded in historical fact.

Walter Dean **Myers (b. 1937)**

Unit 2: Short Stories Walter Dean Myers is well suited as a guide for the short story unit, having won acclaim for his own short stories and novels. Some of his best stories appear in *145th Street: Short Stories,* which focuses on a particular street in Harlem, New York City. Among the many prizes Mr. Myers has won for his work are the Coretta Scott King Award for Fiction, a Newbery Honor Book citation, and the Parents' Choice Award.

Richard **Mühlberger (b. 1938)**

Unit 3: Types of Nonfiction The art historian Richard Mühlberger, who spent many years working as an educator in museums, is a master of nonfiction writing. While on the staff of the Metropolitan Museum of Art, he wrote a number of books that introduce young adults to the work of great artists. This highly praised series includes such titles as *What Makes a Van Gogh a Van Gogh?* and *What Makes a Rembrandt a Rembrandt?*

Pat **Mora (b. 1942)**

Unit 4: Poetry Pat Mora, the guide for the poetry unit, has won acclaim both for her poetry and for her skill in teaching poetry. Her many verse collections include *Agua Santa: Holy Water, Borders, Chants, Communion,* and *My Own True Name: New and Selected Poems for Young Adults.* Among the prizes given to her for her verse are the Southwest Book Award and the Pellicer-Frost Bi-national Poetry Award.

Laurence **Yep (b. 1948)**

Unit 5: Drama Laurence Yep is well suited as a guide for the drama unit because he has written plays such as *Pay the Chinaman* and adapted his award-winning novel *Dragonwings* for the theater. His many books include such popular young adult novels as *Child of the Owl* and *Dragon's Gate.* Mr. Yep is the winner of the 2005 Laura Ingalls Wilder Medal for a substantial and lasting contribution to literature for children.

Jon **Scieszka (b. 1954)**

Unit 6: Themes in the Oral Tradition The ideal guide for this unit, Jon Scieszka is highly knowledgeable about the oral tradition. He would not be able to "mess up" traditional stories in his uniquely comic ways if he did not understand and love them. His most famous book of "fractured fairy tales," *The Stinky Cheese Man and Other Fairly Stupid Tales,* is a Caldecott Honor Book and appears on the Publishers Weekly Top-Selling Kids' Books of All Time List.

PROGRAM ADVISORS

The program advisors provided ongoing input throughout the development of *Prentice Hall Literature: Penguin Edition.* Their valuable insights ensure that the perspectives of the teachers throughout the country are represented within this literature series.

Sherice Alford
Language Arts Instructor
Cape Fear Senior High School
Fayetteville, North Carolina

Leslie Ballard
State Director
North Central Association CASI
Indiana State University
Terre Haute, Indiana

Heather Barnes
Language Arts Instructor
Central Crossing High School
Grove City, Ohio

Kathryn Shelley-Barnes
District Support Specialist
Traverse City Central High School
Traverse City, Michigan

Karen C. Lilly-Bowyer
Instructional Services Assessment Team
Winston-Salem Forsyth County Schools
Winston-Salem, North Carolina

Lee Bromberger
English Department Chairperson
Mukwonago High School
Mukwonago, Wisconsin

Shawn L. Brumfield
Literacy Coach
Horace Mann Middle School
Los Angeles Unified School District
Local 3
Los Angeles, California

Susanne Buttrey
Librarian
Sycamore Middle School
Pleasant View, Tennessee

Denise Campbell
K-12 Literacy Content Coordinator
Cherry Creek School District
Centennial, Colorado

Patricia A. Cantrowitz
Language Arts Instructor (Retired)
Union-Endicott High School

Holly Carr
Language Arts Instructor
Central Crossing High School
Grove City, Ohio

Melody Renee Chalmers
Language Arts Instructor
E. E. Smith High School
Fayetteville, North Carolina

Susan Cisna
Language Arts Instructor
East Prairie Junior High School
Tuscola, Illinois

Barbra Evans-Thompson
English Department Chairperson
Westover High School
Fayetteville, North Carolina

Ebony Forte
Language Arts Instructor
Pine Forest Senior High School
Fayetteville, North Carolina

Linda Fund
Reading Specialist
Ezra L. Nolan Middle School #40
Jersey City, New Jersey

Karen Gibson, Ph.D.
Communication Arts Program Leader
Appleton Area School District
Appleton, Wisconsin

Gail Hacker
Language Arts Instructor, Retired
North Charleston High School
North Charleston, South Carolina

Kimberly Hartman
Language Arts Instructor
Franklin Heights High School
Columbus, Ohio

Doris Sue Hawkins
Language Arts Instructor
C. W. Otto Middle School
Lansing, Michigan

Darby Holley
Language Arts Instructor
Henry L. Sneed Middle School
Florence, South Carolina

Helen Hudson
Language Arts Instructor
Crawfordsville High School
Crawfordsville, Indiana

Kathleen Keane
English Department Chairperson
Foxborough High School
Foxborough, Massachusetts

John Kiser
English Curriculum Specialist (Retired)
Charlotte-Mecklenburg Schools
Charlotte, North Carolina

Cheryl W. Lee
Language Arts Instructor
Douglas Byrd High School
Fayetteville, North Carolina

Carrie Lichtenberg
Language Arts Instructor
Highlands High School
Ft. Thomas, Kentucky

Catherine Linn
Language Arts Instructor
Palm Springs High School
Palm Desert, California

Agathaniki Locklear
District Technology Resource Teacher
Kenton County Schools
Ft. Wright, Kentucky

John Ludy
Language Arts Instructor
Fremont High School
Fremont, Indiana

Leigh L. Matthewson
Language Arts Instructor
Albuquerque Public Schools
Albuquerque, New Mexico

Sherrie McDowell
Language Arts Instructor
Central High School
Cheyenne, Wyoming

Suzanne Mitoraj
English/Language Arts Consultant
Berlin, Connecticut

Nancy Monroe
Language Arts Instructor
Bolton High School
Alexandria, Louisiana

Gail Phelps
Language Arts Instructor
Northwood Middle School
North Little Rock, Arkansas

Matthew Scanlon
K-12 Humanities Supervisor
Hackettstown Public Schools
Hackettstown, New Jersey

John Scott
Language Arts Instructor (Retired)
Hampton City Schools
Hampton City, Virginia

Jean Shope
Language Arts Instructor
Grant Middle School
Albuquerque, New Mexico

Margaret St. Sauver
Staff Development-English/Language Arts
St. Paul Public Schools
St. Paul, Minnesota

Steve Thalheimer
Language Arts Instructor
Lawrenceburg High School
Lawrenceburg, Indiana

Cathy Robbs Turner
Director of Academies
Chattanooga Central High School
Harrison, Tennessee

Sandra VanBelois
Language Arts Instructor
Jack Britt High School
Fayetteville, North Carolina

Martha Lee Wildman
Language Arts Instructor
Lynn Middle School
Las Cruces, New Mexico

Melissa Williams
Language Arts Instructor
Delsea Regional High School
Franklinville, New Jersey

Charles Youngs
HS Language Arts Curriculum Facilitator
Bethel Park High School
Bethel Park, Pennsylvania

CONTENTS IN BRIEF

Unit 1 Fiction and Nonfiction

From the Author's Desk

Part One
Reading Skills Focus: Context Clues

Part Two
Reading Skills Focus: Author's Purpose

Unit 2

Short Stories

From the Author's Desk

Part One
Reading Skills Focus: Predicting

Part Two
Reading Skills Focus: Making Inferences

Part Two
Reading Skills Focus: Fact and Opinion

Unit 4 · Poetry

From the Author's Desk

Pat Mora

Part One
Reading Skills Focus: Drawing Conclusions

Part Two
Reading Skills Focus: Paraphrasing

Unit 5 Drama

From the Author's Desk

Part One
Reading Skills Focus: Purpose for Reading

Part Two
Reading Skills Focus: Summarizing

Unit 6 — Themes in the Oral Tradition

Part Two
Reading Skills Focus: Comparison and Contrast

Resources

SELECTIONS BY READING SKILL

Unit 1

Unit Two

Unit Four

Part Two: Paraphrasing

Unit Five

Part One: Purpose for Reading

Part Two: Summarizing

Unit Six

Part One: Cause and Effect

Part Two: Comparison and Contrast

SELECTIONS BY THEME

■ Independence and Identity

■ Common Threads

What Matters

Meeting Challenges

Just for Fun

Deciding What Is Right

NONFICTION AND INFORMATIONAL TEXTS

■ Reading Informational Materials—Instructional Workshops

■ Additional Nonfiction

■ Literature in Context—Reading in the Content Areas

A wealth of expository nonfiction is found throughout this program.
Nonfiction is shown in red in the index

COMPARING LITERARY WORKS

SKILLS WORKSHOPS

■ Writing Workshops

■ Spelling Workshops

■ Communications Workshops

Unit 1

Fiction and Nonfiction

Unit 1 Overview

Introduction
Exploring Fiction
and Nonfiction

Part 1: Context Clues

Part 2: Author's Purpose

Introduction:
Fiction and Nonfiction

Richard
Peck

Richard Peck
Talks About the Forms

I write **fiction**—made-up stories—because of two boys I met when I was only a kid myself. I didn't meet them in school; I'm not sure I'd have sat next to them at school. I met them in the library: Tom Sawyer and Huckleberry Finn.

I'd already met their creator, Mark Twain, in his book *Life on the Mississippi*. It appeared to be **nonfiction**, a factual account, and so I believed every word of Mark Twain's apprenticeship as a Mississippi riverboat pilot.

▲ **Richard Peck** has written many novels in which teenage characters show independence and individuality.

Reading Needed To Be Real

At the time, it seemed to me that reading needed to be real. I even talked my parents into driving us the eighty-five miles to Hannibal, Missouri, to see the house they said Mark Twain had lived in and the remains of the pier where the riverboats had put in. I needed to know.

I read nonfiction and dreamed of writing it. But then I came across Tom and Huck. On the next page, you can read an account of Tom running into Huck on a dusty Hannibal street, just about a century before I was born.

▼ **Critical Viewing** How does this picture dramatize Richard Peck's assertion that "nobody but a reader ever becomes a writer"? **[Connect]**

Hooked on Fiction

I was hooked. Tom and Huck helped me make the journey from nonfiction to fiction. I wanted to be there with them in all their adventures. After all, I was growing up with neither a cave nor a raft. I began to see that in fiction, just as in nonfiction, you can go anywhere and be anybody.

But what I liked best about Huck and Tom was how they spoke because a story is only as strong as the voices telling it.

Huck and Tom's **dialogue** blended in my mind with the stories my dad told me of growing up at the end of Twain's nineteenth century. In fact I could see and hear Huck and Tom in my own dad: the country talk, the sly wit, the outrageous pranks, the remembering of old times.

Tom hailed the romantic outcast.
"Hello, Huckleberry!"
"Hello yourself, and see how you like it."
"What's that you got?"
"Dead cat."
"Lemme see him Huck. My, he's pretty stiff. Where'd you get him?"
"Bought him off'n a boy."
"What did you give?"
"I give a blue ticket and a bladder that I got at the slaughter-house."
from The Adventures of Tom Sawyer
—Mark Twain

And so my fate was decided. I turned to the fiction shelves of the library, in the hope that one day my own books would be there because nobody but a reader ever becomes a writer.

More About the Author

Richard **Peck** (b. 1934)

Richard Peck says that a writer has to be a good listener: "I was born listening—eavesdropping, if you like." He prepares dialogue by keeping a notebook with him at all times and recording different dialects. His books have won critical acclaim for their realism and emotional power.

Fast Facts

▶ Richard Peck has written, "I read because one life isn't enough, and in the page of a book I can be anybody."

▶ He thinks that his experience as a junior high school teacher made him a writer—he found his audience among the students he taught.

Learning About Fiction and Nonfiction

Elements of Fiction

Fiction writing can be inspired by fact or based entirely on the fantastic. All works of fiction, regardless of their content, share certain basic elements.

- Fictional works include made-up people or animals, called **characters,** and a made-up series of events, called the **plot.**
- They take place in a time and location, or **setting,** which may or may not be real.
- Fictional writing is narrated or told by a speaker, called the **narrator.**
- Fiction is told from a certain perspective, or **point of view. First-person point of view** is the perspective of a character in the story. **Third-person point of view** is the perspective of a narrator outside the story.
- Works of fiction often include a **theme,** or message, about life.

PEANUTS reprinted by permission of United Feature Syndicate, Inc.

Types of Fiction

Novels are long works of fiction. They contain such elements as characters, plot, conflict, and setting. In addition to its main plot, a novel may contain one or more **subplots,** or independent, related stories.

Novellas are works of fiction that are shorter than novels but longer than short stories.

Short Stories are brief works of fiction. Short stories contain the same basic elements as novels and novellas but tend to focus on one main plot structured around a single conflict. Short stories are meant to be read in one sitting.

Elements of Nonfiction

Nonfiction works differ from fiction works in a few important ways.

- Nonfiction deals only with real people, events, or ideas.
- Works of nonfiction are narrated from the **point of view,** or perspective, of the author, who is a real person.
- Nonfiction presents facts or discusses ideas.
- It may reflect the **historical context** of the time period, including references to major social and cultural information.

Types of Nonfiction

Biographies tell the story of someone's life and are told from the perspective of another writer.

Autobiographies and memoirs tell the story of the author's life and reflect the writer's thoughts and feelings about events.

Letters are written forms of communication from one person to another. A letter might share information, thoughts, or feelings.

Journals and diaries are records of daily events and the writer's thoughts and feelings about them. They are meant to be either public or private.

Essays and articles are brief written works about a specific topic. The purpose of an essay or article might be to explain, persuade, or inform.

Informational texts are written documents commonly found in everyday life. Examples of these documents include textbooks, applications, instructions, and articles.

▼ **Critical Viewing**
How does this photograph show historical context? **[Analyze]**

Check Your Understanding

Indicate whether each literary work described here is an example of fiction or nonfiction.

1. a book about the life of a famous person
2. an essay on a controversial issue
3. a story told from the point of view of a dog

From the Author's Desk
Richard Peck Introduces "The Three-Century Woman"

As the twenty-first century approached, it occurred to me to write a story about someone who'd been born in 1899 and was still here to see in the new year of 2001. Thus, Great-grandma Breckenridge came to be, with plenty of fight left in her to start her third century.

Weaving History Into Narratives

Great-grandma Breckenridge has the whole sweep of the twentieth-century to look back upon. That suited me because I like weaving history into **narratives**, or stories, of my own. When she's being interviewed (and annoyed) by a slick television anchor man, she recalls two famous events: the San Francisco earthquake and the explosion of the Hindenburg airship.

I didn't live through the San Francisco earthquake or personally survive the Hindenburg explosion. But like Great-grandma I can read.

I'd already written a novel for adult readers set during the earthquake of 1906 (*This Family of Women*), and so my shelves are still ranked with good reference books.

Setting a Tone Through the Narrator

Since the Hindenburg was destroyed, as Great-grandma reminds us, in May of 1937, research is as near as the volumes of *Time* magazine for that year at my local library. We don't write what we know. We write what we can find out.

But including two such famous disasters poses a problem for a story meant to be light and funny. To linger over these events and their terrible loss of life could damage the tone of my narrative, so the story treads lightly and moves quickly.

But what of Megan, the **narrator,** who is only fourteen? The story is told from her viewpoint, and her vision improves on every page. In the serious heart of a humorous story, she finds a role model for her own twenty-first-century future.

The Three-Century Woman

Richard Peck

"I guess if you live long enough," my mom said to Aunt Gloria, "you get your fifteen minutes of fame."

Mom was on the car phone to Aunt Gloria. The minute Mom rolls out of the garage, she's on her car phone. It's state-of-the-art and better than her car.

We were heading for Whispering Oaks to see my great-grandmother Breckenridge, who's lived there since I was a little girl. They call it an Elder Care Facility. Needless to say, I hated going.

The reason for Great-grandmother's fame is that she was born in 1899. Now it's January 2001. If you're one of those people who claim the new century begins in 2001, not 2000, even you have to agree that Great-grandmother Breckenridge has lived in three centuries. This is her claim to fame.

We waited for a light to change along by Northbrook Mall, and I gazed fondly over at it. Except for the Multiplex, it was closed because of New Year's Day. I have a severe mall habit. But I'm fourteen, and the mall is the place without homework. Aunt Gloria's voice filled the car.

Fiction
Plot and Conflict
This paragraph introduces a **conflict:** the speaker's unhappiness about visiting her great-grandmother.

"If you take my advice," she told Mom, "you'll keep those Whispering Oaks people from letting the media in to interview Grandma. Interview her my foot! Honestly. She doesn't know where she is, let alone how many centuries she's lived in. The poor old soul. Leave her in peace. She's already got one foot in the—"

"Gloria, your trouble is you have no sense of history." Mom gunned across the <u>intersection</u>. "You got a C in history."

"I was sick a lot that year," Aunt Gloria said.

"Sick of history," Mom mumbled.

"I heard that," Aunt Gloria said.

They bickered on, but I tuned them out. Then when we turned in at Whispering Pines, a sound truck from IBC-TV was blocking the drive.

"Good grief," Mom murmured. "TV."

"I told you," Aunt Gloria said, but Mom switched her off. She parked in a frozen rut.

"I'll wait in the car," I said. "I have homework."

"Get out of the car," Mom said.

If you get so old you have to be put away, Whispering Oaks isn't that bad. It smells all right, and a Christmas tree glittered in the lobby. A real tree. On the other hand, you have to push a red button to unlock the front door. I guess it's to keep the inmates from escaping, though Great-grandmother Breckenridge wasn't going anywhere and hadn't for twenty years.

When we got to her wing, the hall was full of camera crews and a woman from the suburban newspaper with a notepad.

Mom sighed. It was like that first day of school when you think you'll be okay until the teachers learn your name. Stepping over a cable, we stopped at Great-grandma's door, and they were on to us.

"Who are you people to Mrs. Breckenridge?" the newspaperwoman said. "I want names."

These people were seriously pushy. And the TV guy was wearing more makeup than Mom. It dawned on me that they couldn't get into Great-grandma's room without her permission. Mom turned on them.

"Listen, you're not going to be interviewing my grandmother," she said in a quiet bark. "I'll be glad to tell you anything you want to know about her, but you're not going in there. She's got nothing to say, and . . . she needs a lot of rest."

Vocabulary Builder
intersection (in´ tər sek´ shən) *n.* the place where two or more roads cross

Fiction
Point of View The narrator's use of the pronouns *I* and *we* shows that the story is being told from the perspective of one character.

Richard Peck
Author's Insight By comparing a trip to an elder care facility to school, I'm showing how Megan would view things.

"Is it Alzheimer's?"[1] the newswoman asked. "Because we're thinking Alzheimer's."

"Think what you want," Mom said. "But this is as far as you get. And you people with the camera and the light, you're not going in there either. You'd scare her to death, and then I'd sue the pants off you."

They pulled back.

But a voice came wavering out of Great-grandma's room. Quite an eerie, echoing voice.

"Let them in!" the voice said.

It had to be Great-grandma Breckenridge. Her roommate had died. "Good grief," Mom muttered, and the press surged forward.

Mom and I went in first, and our eyes popped. Great-grandma was usually flat out in the bed, dozing, with her teeth in a glass and a book in her hand. Today she was bright-eyed and propped up. She wore a fuzzy pink bed jacket. A matching bow was stuck in what remained of her hair.

"Oh, for pity's sake," Mom said. "They've got her done up like a Barbie doll."

Great-grandma peered from the bed at Mom. "And who are you?" she asked.

"I'm Ann," Mom said carefully. "This is Megan," she said, meaning me.

"That's right," Great-grandma said. "At least you know who you are. Plenty around this place don't."

The guy with the camera on his shoulder barged in. The other guy turned on a blinding light.

Great-grandma blinked. In the glare we noticed she wore a trace of lipstick. The TV anchor elbowed the woman reporter aside and stuck a mike in Great-grandma's face. Her claw hand came out from under the covers and tapped it.

"Is this thing on?" she inquired.

"Yes, ma'am," the TV anchor said in his broadcasting voice. "Don't you worry about all this modern technology. We don't understand half of it ourselves." He gave her his big, five-thirty news smile and settled on the edge of the bed. There was room for him. She was tiny.

---

1. Alzheimer's (älts´ hï´ mərz) *n.* a progressive disease in which brain cells degenerate, leading to severe dementia.

Fiction
Character Mom's words show her fierce loyalty to Great-grandma.

Richard Peck
Author's Insight
I added the lipstick in a later draft, as visual proof that Great-grandma has prepared with more care for this interview than the anchorman has.

Reading Check

Why is the interview worrying Mom?

"We're here to congratulate you for having lived in three centuries—for being a Three-Century Woman! A great achievement!"

Great-grandma waved a casual claw. "Nothing to it," she said. "You sure this mike's on? Let's do this in one take."

The cameraman snorted and moved in for a closer shot. Mom stood still as a statue, wondering what was going to come out of Great-grandma's mouth next.

"Mrs. Breckenridge," the anchor said, "to what do you attribute[2] your long life?"

"I was only married once," Great-grandma said. "And he died young."

The anchor stared. "Ah. And anything else?"

"Yes. I don't look back. I live in the present."

The camera panned around the room. This was all the present she had, and it didn't look like much.

"You live for the present," the anchor said, looking for an angle, "even now?"

Great-grandma nodded. "Something's always happening. Last night I fell off the bed pan."

Mom groaned.

The cameraman pulled in for a tighter shot. The anchor seemed to search his mind. You could tell he thought he was a great interviewer, though he had no sense of humor. A tiny smile played around Great-grandma's wrinkled lips.

"But you've lived through amazing times, Mrs. Breckenridge. And you never think back about them?"

Great-grandma stroked her chin and considered. "You mean you want to hear something interesting? Like how I lived through the San Francisco earthquake—the big one of oh-six?"

Beside me, Mom stirred. We were crowded over by the dead lady's bed. "You survived the 1906 San Francisco earthquake?" the anchor said.

Great-grandma gazed at the ceiling, lost in thought.

"I'd have been about seven years old. My folks and I were staying at that big hotel. You know the one. I slept in a cot at the foot of their bed. In the middle of the night, that room gave a shake, and the chiffonier walked right across the floor. You know what a chiffonier is?"

---

2. **attribute** (ə trib′ yо̄ot) *v.* think of as caused by.

▶ Critical Viewing
What event in the story does this image likely illustrate? How do you know? [Make Connections]

Richard Peck
Author's Insight
A running joke is that Great-grandma knows modern media jargon; another warning the anchor doesn't heed.

Fiction
Character Comments like this one reveal that Great-grandma has a lively sense of humor.

"A chest of drawers?" the anchor said.

"Close enough," Great-grandma said. "And the pictures flapped on the walls. We had to walk down twelve flights because the elevators didn't work. When we got outside, the streets were ankle-deep in broken glass. You never saw such a mess in your life."

Mom nudged me and hissed: "She's never been to San Francisco. She's never been west of Denver. I've heard her say so."

"Incredible!" the anchor said.

"Truth's stranger than fiction," Great-grandma said, smoothing her sheet.

"And you never think back about it?"

Great-grandma shrugged her little fuzzy pink shoul-

ders. "I've been through too much. I don't have time to remember it all. I was on the Hindenburg when it blew up, you know."

Mom moaned, and the cameraman was practically standing on his head for a close-up.

"The Hindenburg!"

"That big gas thing the Germans built to fly over the Atlantic Ocean. It was called a zeppelin.[3] Biggest thing you ever saw—five city blocks long. It was in May of 1937, before your time. You wouldn't remember. My husband and I were coming back from Europe. No, wait a minute."

Great-grandma cocked her head and <u>pondered</u> for the camera.

"My husband was dead by then. It was some other man.

Vocabulary Builder
pondered (pän´ dərd)
v. thought about deeply; meditated

Reading Check

Why are the reporters eager to interview Great-grandma?

---

3. zeppelin (zep´ ə lin) n. a large, cigar-shaped airship with separate compartments filled with gas; used from 1900 to 1937.

Anyway, the two of us were coming back on the Hindenburg. It was smooth as silk. You didn't know you were moving. When we flew in over New York, they stopped the ball game at Yankee Stadium to see us passing overhead."

Great-grandma paused, caught up in the memories.

"And then the Hindenburg exploded," the anchor said, prompting her.

Literature in Context   Social Studies Connection

The New York Times.

"All the News That's Fit to Print."

LATE CITY EDITION
Fair today, temperature unchanged. Tomorrow fair, little change in temperature.

NEW YORK, FRIDAY, MAY 7, 1937.

VOL. LXXXVI....No. 28,958.

TWO CENTS

HINDENBURG BURNS IN LAKEHURST CRASH; 21 KNOWN DEAD, 12 MISSING; 64 ESCAPE

▲ The Hindenburg crash was reported nationwide.

Tragedy Strikes

The gas inside the balloon was highly flammable. However, no one is sure how it caught fire. ▶

Lakehurst, NJ

ATLANTIC OCEAN

D-LZ129

Connect to the Literature What do these graphics suggest about the scope of the tragedy Great-grandmother Breckenridge describes?

3 football fields

She nodded. "We had no complaints about the trip till then. The luggage was all stacked, and we were coming in at Lakehurst, New Jersey. I was wearing my beige coat—beige or off-white, I forget. Then whoosh! The gondola[4] heated up like an oven, and people peeled out of the windows. We hit the ground and bounced. When we hit again, the door fell off, and I walked out and kept going. When they caught up to me in the parking lot, they wanted to put me in the hospital. I looked down and thought I was wearing a lace dress. The fire had about burned up my coat. And I lost a shoe."

"Fantastic!" the anchor breathed. "What detail!" Behind him the woman reporter was scribbling away on her pad.

"Never," Mom muttered. "Never in her life."

"Ma'am, you are living history!" the anchor said. "In your sensational span of years you've survived two great disasters!"

"Three." Great-grandma patted the bow on her head. "I told you I'd been married."

"And before we leave this <u>venerable</u> lady," the anchor said, flashing a smile for the camera, "we'll ask Mrs. Breckenridge if she has any predictions for this new twenty-first century ahead of us here in the Dawn of the <u>Millennium</u>."

"Three or four predictions," Great-grandma said, and paused again, stretching out her airtime. "Number one, taxes will be higher. Number two, it's going to be harder to find a place to park. And number three, a whole lot of people are going to live as long as I have, so get ready for us."

"And with those wise words," the anchor said, easing off the bed, "we leave Mrs. B—"

"And one more prediction," she said. "TV's on the way out. Your network ratings are already in the basement. It's all websites now. Son, I predict you'll be looking for work."

And that was it. The light went dead. The anchor, looking shaken, followed his crew out the door. When TV's done with you, they're done with you. "Is that a wrap?" Great-grandma asked.

But now the woman from the suburban paper was moving in on her. "Just a few more questions, Mrs. Breckenridge."

"Where you from?" Great-grandma blinked pink-eyed at her.

---

4. **gondola** (gän´ dō lə) *n.* a cabin attached to the underside of an airship to hold the motors, instruments, passengers, etc.

Fiction
Plot Why is Great-grandma able to adjust the events of the Hindenburg crash?

Vocabulary Builder
venerable (ven´ ər ə bəl) *adj.* worthy of respect or reverence by reason of age

Millennium (mi len´ ē əm) *n.* the year 2000 or, some people say, the year 2001

**Reading Check**

What historical events does Great-grandma claim to have witnessed?

"The Glenview Weekly Shopper."

"You bring a still photographer with you?" Great-grandma asked.

"Well, no."

"And you never learned shorthand[5] either, did you?"

"Well, no."

"Honey, I only deal with professionals. There's the door."

So then it was just Mom and Great-grandma and I in the room. Mom planted a hand on her hip. "Grandma. Number one, you've never been to San Francisco. And number two, you never saw one of those zeppelin things."

Great-grandma shrugged. "No, but I can read." She nodded to the pile of books on her nightstand with her spectacles folded on top. "You can pick up all that stuff in books."

"And number three," Mom said, "Your husband didn't die young. I can remember Grandpa Breckenridge."

"It was that TV dude in the five-hundred-dollar suit who set me off," Great-grandma said. "He dyes his hair, did you notice? He made me mad, and it put my nose out of joint. He didn't notice I'm still here. He thought I was nothing but my memories. So I gave him some."

Now Mom and I stood beside her bed.

"I'll tell you something else," Great-grandma said. "And it's no lie."

We waited, holding our breath to hear. Great-grandma Breckenridge was pointing her little old bent finger right at me. "You, Megan," she said. "Once upon a time, I was your age. How scary is that?"

Then she hunched up her little pink shoulders and winked at me. She grinned and I grinned. She was just this little withered-up leaf of a lady in the bed. But I felt like giving her a kiss on her little wrinkled cheek, so I did.

"I'll come and see you more often," I told her.

"Call first," she said. "I might be busy." Then she dozed.

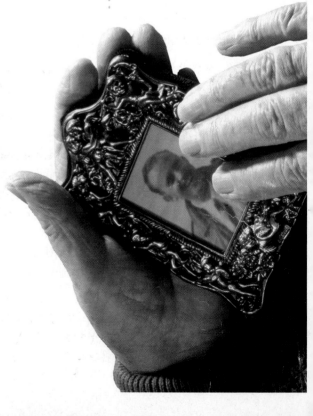

Fiction
Character This conversation alters the first impression that Great-grandma might not think clearly because of her age.

---

5. shorthand (shôrt′ hand′) *n.* a system of speed writing using symbols to represent letters, words, and phrases.

Q. Why did you tell this story from Megan's point of view?

A. Megan is the readers' representative in the story, someone near their age who shares their viewpoint. Almost all my stories are told in the voices of young characters whom the readers can befriend.

Q. Does even a funny story like this one have a conflict?

A. All stories are based on conflict. This one starts with Megan's mother and her aunt wrangling over the car phone. Then after a brief conflict between Mom and Megan ("'Get out of the car.'"), there is Great-grandma's true battle with the media people. Conflicts can be fun.

Q. Great-grandma is surprising. Do you like surprising readers?

A. I especially enjoy surprising young readers with elderly characters unlike those in younger children's books. I don't like sweet old folks; I like them tough. They'd have to be, or they wouldn't still be here.

StudentCorner

Q. Did you have a relative that you based the story on?
—Ahsan Ford, Covington, Kentucky

A. I have a ninety-eight-year-old mother who lives in a nursing home. But, no, real people don't fit into stories. You create characters by taking traits from lots of different people and putting them together in a character who will play the role. You also read and reread other writers' works to see how they do it. Charles Dickens has some excellent old ladies.

 Writing Workshop: *Work in Progress*

Descriptive Essay

For a description of a setting you may write, think of a memorable place. List five qualities or features that make it memorable. Save this Place List in your portfolio.

"The Fall of the Hindenburg" is a clear example of the sort of **informative article** writers use to give their stories **historical context.** Nonfiction is the bedrock of fiction, and the Hindenburg's last moments are as dramatic and terrifying as any fiction.

Details Enrich a Narrative Account

This famous disaster was filmed by a newsreel camera, bringing it alarmingly alive to every generation since. It was also recorded on radio. We can still hear Herb Morrison crying into his microphone: "Oh, the humanity!" All authors after that time can use these pictures and voices to enrich their **narrative accounts**.

Like the Titanic before it, the Hindenburg's end took on mythical meaning. The sinking of the Titanic seemed to be the end of an entire way of life shortly before World War I. The Hindenburg's destruction foreshadowed World War II.

Mystery still hangs over both the Titanic and the Hindenburg. New theories about their destruction keep arising, inspiring more stories yet to be woven from their remains.

Using Nonfiction to Write Fiction

The Hindenburg explodes in one of my short stories, "The Three-Century Woman." The Titanic sinks in not one, but two of my novels: *Amanda Miranda* and *The Dreadful Future of Blossom Culp.*

Fiction writers always use real events for the same purpose: to show characters more clearly. In "The Three-Century Woman," Great-grandma remembers the San Francisco earthquake and the Hindenburg's explosion. These events give a sense of the length of her lifetime. More to the point, they tell something about her personality. She appears to remember disasters, not sweet and sentimental events.

Fictional characters are woven from the facts of their times and those eternal truths about people, whenever they've lived.

The Fall of the Hindenburg

Michael Morrison

On May 6, 1937, the German airship Hindenburg burst into flames 200 feet over its intended landing spot at New Jersey's Lakehurst Naval Air Station. Thirty-five people on board were killed (13 passengers and 22 crewmen), along with one crewman on the ground.

803 Feet Long and 242 Tons The giant flying vessel measured 803.8 feet in length and weighed approximately 242 tons. Its mostly metal frame was filled with hydrogen. It came complete with sleeping quarters, a library, dining room, and a magnificent lounge, but still managed a top speed of just over 80 miles per hour. The zeppelin had just crossed the Atlantic Ocean after taking off from Frankfurt, Germany 2 1/2 days prior on its first transatlantic voyage of the season. Thirty-six passengers and a crew of 61 were on board.

Disaster Strikes As it reached its final destination in New Jersey, it hovered over its landing spot and was beginning to be pulled down to the ground by landing lines by over 200 crewmen when disaster struck. A burst of flame started

Nonfiction Exposition The facts in this paragraph identify the features of the Hindenburg.

✔ **Reading Check**

Where did the journey of the Hindenburg begin?

just forward of the upper fin, then blossomed into an inferno that engulfed the Hindenburg's tail.

"Oh, the Humanity!" Many jumped from the burning craft, landed on the soft sand of the naval base below, and lived to tell about it; others weren't so lucky. Herb Morrison, a reporter for WLS Radio in Chicago, happened to be covering the event and cried out the now famous words, "Oh, the Humanity!" The majestic ship turned into a ball of flames on the ground in only 34 seconds.

Unknown Cause The cause of the disaster is still uncertain. At the time, many thought the ship had been hit by lightning. Many still believe that the highly flammable hydrogen was the cause. Some Germans even cried foul play, suspecting sabotage intended to sully the reputation of the Nazi regime. NASA research, however, has shown that the highly combustible varnish treating the fabric on the outside of the vessel most likely caused the tragedy.

Nonfiction
Cause and Effect
This paragraph discusses possible causes of the fall of the Hindenburg.

▲▶ **Critical Viewing** How do these images help you understand the Hindenburg disaster? **[Make Connections]**

Q. Do you read articles like this when you write your fiction?

A. All fiction is based on research, and I especially like looking up and including real events. Referring to actual history gives the story someplace to stand.

Q. How do you know that the facts in an article are true?

A. All famous events, from wars to earthquakes, are covered and recounted by many journalists and historians. Some are more accurate than others. The fiction writer has the advantage of being able to pick the most interesting accounts, not necessarily the most accurate.

Q. Do you use the Internet for your research?

A. I never use the Internet. There's too much at the library that isn't on the Net. Besides, I like being in the library. Every book begins in the library in the hope it will end there. In other words, writers begin their books with library research, hoping to produce a book that will end up on a library shelf!

StudentCorner

Q. How did you first become interested in the Hindenburg disaster?
—Nicole McBride, Torrington, Connecticut

A. I must have first heard about the Hindenburg from grownups recalling it. I spent my childhood eavesdropping on adults, so I expect that's where I first heard the story.

 Writing Workshop: *Work in Progress*

Descriptive Essay
Choose three features from the Place List in your writing portfolio. For each, write down words that capture the look, smell, sound, or feel of the place. Save this work in your writing portfolio.

Fiction and Nonfiction

Thinking About the Selections

1. **Respond:** Would you want someone like Great-grandmother Breckenridge as a friend? Why or why not?

2. **(a) Recall:** In the first column of a chart, like the one shown, write three of Great-grandma's comments or reactions to the reporters. **(b) Infer:** In the second column, explain what these comments or reactions reveal about Great-grandma's character and her ideas about herself. **(c) Interpret:** In the third column, explain what theme or message these ideas might convey.

Her Comments	Her Character	Message/Theme

Fiction and Nonfiction Review

3. **(a)** Who is the **narrator** of "The Three-Century Woman"? **(b)** Based on what you know about Richard Peck, how can you tell the story is a work of **fiction**?

4. **(a)** How does the fictional account of the Hindenburg differ from the **nonfiction** article? **(b)** Which one is a more accurate source of facts?

Research the Author

Using the Internet and library resources, create an **annotated bibliography** of five or more works by Richard Peck. Follow these steps:

- From Peck's many award-winning works, choose the ones that you think will be most interesting for your classmates.
- Annotate, or explain and summarize, each work in a paragraph that will motivate students to read the work.
- Present your annotated bibliography to your class.

Academic Vocabulary: Words for Discussing Context Clues

The following words will help you write and talk about context clues as you read the selections in this part.

Word	Definition	Example Sentence
clarify *v.*	make clear	The clues will help me *clarify* the meaning of the word.
context *n.*	surrounding text or information	In this *context,* the word timidly means "with shyness."
reveal *v.*	make known	He will *reveal* his plan later.
significance *n.*	meaning, importance	Explain the *significance* of the details.
verify *v.*	prove to be true	Can he *verify* his claim?

Vocabulary Skill: Etymology

▶ The origin, or **etymology,** of a word is the history of the word.

In Part 1 you will learn the Latin origins shared by these words:
- *significance* and *signify* (p. 44)
- *reveal* and *revelation* (p. 44)
- *context* (p. 66)
- *verify* (p. 66)

Many dictionaries give etymology in the entry for a word. Look at the sample entry for the word *clarify.*

clarify (klar' ə fī') [[ME *clarifien* <OFr *clarifier* <LL(Ec) *clarificare*, to make illustrious <L *clarus*, famous, CLEAR + *facere*, to make, DO¹]]

ME = Middle English
OFr = Old French
LL = Late Latin
L = Latin
< means "coming from"

Activity Look up the words from the vocabulary chart in a dictionary. Explain how the origin of each word helps you to remember the meaning of the word.

These skills will help you become a better reader. Practice them with either "Papa's Parrot" (p. 26) or "mk" (p. 33).

Reading Skill

Context, the words and phrases surrounding a word, can help you understand a word you do not know. When you come across an unfamiliar word, **use context clues to unlock the meaning.** Look for a word or words that might mean the same thing or have the opposite meaning of the unfamiliar word. In addition, you may find definitions, examples, or descriptions of the unfamiliar word.

As you read, use context clues to find possible meanings for unfamiliar words. Check the words in a dictionary after you read.

Literary Analysis

Narrative writing is any type of writing that tells a story. The act or process of telling a story is also called **narration.**

- A narrative is usually told in chronological order—the order in which events occurred in time.
- A narrative may be fiction, nonfiction, or poetry.

Use a graphic organizer like the one shown to record events from the story you are reading.

Sequence of Events
Beginning
↓
Middle
↓
End

Vocabulary Builder

Papa's Parrot

- **ignored** (ig nôrd´) *v.* paid no attention to (p. 27) *I ignored his rude comment and went on talking.*
- **resumed** (ri zōōmd´) *v.* began again, continued (p. 29) *The hikers resumed hiking after stopping for lunch.*

mk

- **quest** (kwest) *n.* a long search for something (p. 34) *The pirates were on a quest for lost treasure.*
- **adequate** (ad´ i kwət) *adj.* enough (p. 35) *The food supply was not adequate for the crowd.*

- **deceive** (dē sēv´) *v.* make someone believe something that is not true (p. 37) *The criminal tried to deceive the jury with a confusing list of false explanations.*
- **transformation** (trans´ fər mā´ shən) *n.* change (p. 37) *After we painted it, the dining room underwent a dramatic transformation.*
- **ignorant** (ig´ nə rənt) *adj.* not knowing facts or information (p. 40) *The traveler was ignorant of the country's customs and had to ask a lot of questions.*

Build Understanding • *Papa's Parrot*

Background

Parrots Parrots can learn to say words that are repeated over and over to them. Most of a parrot's "vocabulary" is taught on purpose, but a parrot may learn words accidentally. In "Papa's Parrot," the bird's accidental vocabulary plays a key part in the story.

Connecting to the Literature

Reading/Writing Connection In "Papa's Parrot," a boy's behavior changes when he enters middle school. Write several sentences that describe ways in which young people's behavior or attitudes might change as they get older. Use at least three of the following words: *react, appreciate, communicate, mature.*

Meet the Author

Cynthia **Rylant** (b. 1954)

Growing up in a small mountain town in West Virginia, Cynthia Rylant never thought about becoming a writer. Aside from comic books, she did not do much reading, and the only writing she did was for school assignments. A future career as an author was the farthest thing from her mind.

A Change of Plans When Rylant entered college, her plan was to become a nurse. Then, in a required English course, she read a story by Langston Hughes. The story "just knocked me off my feet," Rylant has said. She decided to change her major to English. It was a good choice, as she has found great success as a writer.

Fast Facts

▶ Inspired by childhood memories, Rylant wrote *When I Was Young in the Mountains* in 1982.

▶ She has written picture books, novels, short stories, and biographies.

▶ An animal lover with many dogs in her home, Rylant often includes animals in her stories.

Author Link

For: More about the author
Visit: www.PHSchool.com
Web Code: eme-9102

Papa's Parrot

Cynthia Rylant

Though his father was fat and merely owned a candy and nut shop, Harry Tillian liked his papa. Harry stopped liking candy and nuts when he was around seven, but, in spite of this, he and Mr. Tillian had remained friends and were still friends the year Harry turned twelve.

For years, after school, Harry had always stopped in to see his father at work. Many of Harry's friends stopped there, too, to spend a few cents choosing penny candy from the giant bins or to sample Mr. Tillian's latest batch of roasted peanuts. Mr. Tillian

▲ **Critical Viewing** Based on the picture and the background, why might people find parrots appealing as pets? [**Apply Prior Knowledge**]

looked forward to seeing his son and his son's friends every day. He liked the company.

When Harry entered junior high school, though, he didn't come by the candy and nut shop as often. Nor did his friends. They were older and they had more spending money. They went to a burger place. They played video games. They shopped for records.[1] None of them were much interested in candy and nuts anymore.

A new group of children came to Mr. Tillian's shop now. But not Harry Tillian and his friends.

The year Harry turned twelve was also the year Mr. Tillian got a parrot. He went to a pet store one day and bought one for more money than he could really afford. He brought the parrot to his shop, set its cage near the sign for maple clusters, and named it Rocky.

Harry thought this was the strangest thing his father had ever done, and he told him so, but Mr. Tillian just <u>ignored</u> him.

Rocky was good company for Mr. Tillian. When business was slow, Mr. Tillian would turn on a small color television he had sitting in a corner, and he and Rocky would watch the soap operas. Rocky liked to scream when the romantic music came on, and Mr. Tillian would yell at him to shut up, but they seemed to enjoy themselves.

The more Mr. Tillian grew to like his parrot, and the more he talked to it instead of to people, the more embarrassed Harry became. Harry would stroll past the shop, on his way somewhere else, and he'd take a quick look inside to see what his dad was doing. Mr. Tillian was always talking to the bird. So Harry kept walking.

At home things were different. Harry and his father joked with each other at the dinner table as they always had— Mr. Tillian teasing Harry about his smelly socks; Harry teasing Mr. Tillian about his blubbery stomach. At home things seemed all right.

But one day, Mr. Tillian became ill. He had been at work, unpacking boxes of caramels, when he had grabbed his chest and fallen over on top of the candy. A customer had found him, and he was taken to the hospital in an ambulance.

---

1. **records** (rek´ erdz) *n.* thin grooved discs on which music is recorded and played on a phonograph, or record player.

Literary Analysis
Narration What details make this fictional narrative seem realistic?

Vocabulary Builder
ignored (ig nôrd´)
v. paid no attention to

✔ **Reading Check**

Why is Harry embarrassed by his father?

Mr. Tillian couldn't leave the hospital. He lay in bed, tubes in his arms, and he worried about his shop. New shipments of candy and nuts would be arriving. Rocky would be hungry. Who would take care of things?

Harry said he would. Harry told his father that he would go to the store every day after school and unpack boxes. He would sort out all the candy and nuts. He would even feed Rocky.

So, the next morning, while Mr. Tillian lay in his hospital bed, Harry took the shop key to school with him. After school he left his friends and walked to the empty shop alone. In all the days of his life, Harry had never seen the shop closed after school. Harry didn't even remember what the CLOSED sign looked like. The key stuck in the lock three times, and inside he had to search all the walls for the light switch.

The shop was as his father had left it. Even the caramels were still spilled on the floor. Harry bent down and picked them up one by one, dropping them back in the boxes. The bird in its cage watched him silently.

Harry opened the new boxes his father hadn't gotten to. Peppermints. Jawbreakers. Toffee creams. Strawberry kisses. Harry traveled from bin to bin, putting the candies where they belonged.

"Hello!"

Harry jumped, spilling a box of jawbreakers.

"Hello, Rocky!"

Harry stared at the parrot. He had forgotten it was there. The bird had been so quiet, and Harry had been thinking only of the candy.

"Hello," Harry said.

"Hello, Rocky!" answered the parrot.

Harry walked slowly over to the cage. The parrot's food cup was empty. Its water was dirty. The bottom of the cage was a mess.

Literary Analysis
Narration What does Harry do after school to help his father?

Reading Skill
Context Clues What clues point to the meaning of the word *bin*?

Harry carried the cage into the back room. "Hello, Rocky!"

"Is that all you can say, you dumb bird?" Harry mumbled. The bird said nothing else.

Harry cleaned the bottom of the cage, refilled the food and water cups, and then put the cage back in its place and <u>resumed</u> sorting the candy.

"Where's Harry?"

Harry looked up.

"Where's Harry?"

Harry stared at the parrot.

"Where's Harry?"

Chills ran down Harry's back. What could the bird mean? It was something from "The Twilight Zone."[2]

"Where's Harry?"

Harry swallowed and said, "I'm here. I'm here, you stupid bird."

"You stupid bird!" said the parrot.

Well, at least he's got one thing straight, thought Harry.

"Miss him! Miss him! Where's Harry? You stupid bird!"

Harry stood with a handful of peppermints.

"What?" he asked.

"Where's Harry?" said the parrot.

"I'm here, you stupid bird! I'm here!" Harry yelled. He threw the peppermints at the cage, and the bird screamed and clung to its perch.

Harry sobbed, "I'm here." The tears were coming.

Harry leaned over the glass counter.

"Papa." Harry buried his face in his arms.

"Where's Harry?" repeated the bird.

Harry sighed and wiped his face on his sleeve. He watched the parrot. He understood now: someone had been saying, for a long time, "Where's Harry? Miss him."

Harry finished his unpacking and then swept the floor of the shop. He checked the furnace so the bird wouldn't get cold. Then he left to go visit his papa.

---

2. **"The Twilight Zone"** science-fiction television series from the 1960s.

Literature in Context

Science Connection

Do parrots like Rocky understand language? Here are two sides of the scientific debate:

- Birds just mimic the sounds they hear without demonstrating thought or logic. In the wild, parrots develop their own songs to communicate with other parrots.

- Parrots can be taught language. A Harvard University researcher taught a parrot named Alex to recognize items by name and to identify seven different colors. Alex can understand concepts like bigger versus smaller.

Connect to the Literature

Which side of the debate do you think the story supports? Explain your answer.

Vocabulary Builder
resumed (ri zoomd´)
v. began again;
continued

Apply the Skills

Papa's Parrot

Thinking About the Selection

1. **Respond:** Do you think Harry should tell his father what he learned from Rocky? Why or why not?
2. **(a) Recall:** In the past, why did Harry and his friends visit Mr. Tillian after school? **(b) Infer:** Why have Harry and his friends stopped visiting Harry's father?
3. **(a) Recall:** Who is Rocky? **(b) Analyze Cause and Effect:** Why does Mr. Tillian buy Rocky?
4. **(a) Recall:** Explain how Harry reacts when Rocky says "Where's Harry?" and "Miss him!" **(b) Analyze:** Why does Harry react as he does?
5. **(a) Analyze:** What does each main character need to understand about the other? **(b) Make a Judgment:** Which character has a greater responsibility to be understanding? Why? **(c) Discuss:** Share your response with a partner. Then, explain how looking at someone else's response did or did not change your opinion.

Reading Skill

6. In a chart like this, write the italicized word in the left column. Then, write the **context clues** from the passage and decide what the word means. Check your response in a dictionary. **(a)** Harry would *stroll* past the pet shop on his way to somewhere else . . . Mr. Tillian was always talking to the bird. So Harry kept on walking. **(b)** He checked the *furnace* so the bird wouldn't get cold.

Unfamiliar Word	Context Clues	Possible Meaning

Literary Analysis

7. Identify a reason that the story is called a **narrative**.
8. The order of events is important in **narration**. **(a)** Did Mr. Tillian buy his parrot before or after Harry stopped coming to the store? **(b)** Why is this important to the story?
9. Briefly summarize the major events in "Papa's Parrot" in chronological order.

QuickReview

Who's Who in the Story

Harry: a young man

Mr. Tillian: Harry's father

Rocky: Mr. Tillian's parrot

Go Online
Assessment

For: Self-test
Visit: www.PHSchool.com
Web Code: ema-6103

Context: the words and phrases surrounding a word. Context clues can help clarify an unfamiliar word.

Narrative Writing: any type of writing that tells a story

Vocabulary Builder

Practice Answer each of the following questions based on your knowledge of the italicized words.

1. Would you *resume* a meeting before or after taking a break? Explain.

2. If you *ignored* what your brother said to you, would you respond to him? Explain.

Writing

Write a **brief essay** in which you compare and contrast Harry's behavior before and after he entered junior high school. Gather details from the story in a two-column chart.

- In the first column, list details that show what Harry was like before junior high school.
- In the second column, list details that show his behavior and thoughts once he entered junior high school.

Use details from your chart as you draft your essay.

For *Grammar, Vocabulary,* and *Assessment,* see **Build Language Skills,** pages 44–45.

Extend Your Learning

Listening and Speaking With a partner, perform a **dramatic reading** of "Papa's Parrot." Divide the text so that everyone can present a portion. As you rehearse, focus on these points:

- Speak clearly so that each word can be heard.
- Raise and lower your voice to express emotion where appropriate.
- Slow down and stress certain words for effect.

Research and Technology Use the Internet and library resources to find information about the process that enables parrots to learn to speak. Use the information in a brief **report** that explains the following:

- why the parrot knows how to say "Where's Harry?"
- why the parrot continues to ask, even though Harry is in the room.

Build Understanding • *mk*

Background

Overseas Schools When American parents live and work outside the United States, their children often attend American schools overseas. At most of these schools, students are taught in English and study many of the things that students study in the U.S. International schools, like the one described in this selection, are located all over the world.

Connecting to the Literature

Reading/Writing Connection Jean Fritz, the author of "mk," was the child of American missionaries, people who do religious work in a foreign land. Because of her parents' work, Jean went to school in China until the seventh grade. Describe the possible differences between growing up in another country and growing up in the United States. Use at least three of these words: *discover, explore, imitate, observe.*

Review

For **Reading Skill, Literary Analysis,** and **Vocabulary Builder,** see page 24.

Meet the Author

Jean **Fritz** (b. 1915)

Missionary Kid An only child of missionary parents, Jean Fritz grew up in China. Although she had not yet been in the United States, she read and heard from her father about American heroes, such as George Washington and Teddy Roosevelt. Her fascination with these heroes inspired her career as a writer of American history.

Fast Facts

▶ As a child, Fritz kept a journal to help her feel less lonely.

▶ As an adult, she wrote an autobiography, called *Homesick.*

▶ Fritz fills her biographies with unusual but true details about her subjects, which she researches thoroughly. "History is full of gossip; it's real people and emotion," she says. The details make her books about historical figures such as Pocahontas or Sam Adams come alive.

Go **Online**
Author Link
For: More about the author
Visit: www.PHSchool.com
Web Code: eme-9103

mk

Jean Fritz

I suspect for most of us MKs[1] China not only sharpened our sense of time but our sense of place. We always knew where we were in relation to the rest of the world. And we noticed. Perhaps because we knew we would be leaving China sometime (we wouldn't be MKs or even Ks forever), we developed the habit of observing our surroundings with care. We have strong memories, which explains why as an adult, walking along a beach in Maine, I suddenly found myself on the verge of tears. In front of me, pushing up from the crevice of a rock, was a wild bluebell[2] like the wild bluebells I had known in my summers at Kuling.[3] Suddenly I was a child again. I was back in China, welcoming bluebells back in my life.

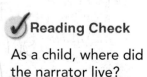 **Reading Check**

As a child, where did the narrator live?

---

1. MKs (em′ kāz′) *n.* Missionary Kids; the children of missionaries.
2. bluebell (bloo′ bel′) *n.* plant with blue, bell-shaped flowers.
3. Kuling (kool′ iŋ) *n.* now called Lushan, a hill resort south of the Yangtze River in China.

For a long time it was hard for me to unscramble the strings that made up my quest. I have noticed, however, that those MKs who were born in China and stayed there through their high school years were more likely to commit their lives in some way to China. After finishing their higher education in the States, they would return to China as consuls, as teachers, as businessmen and women, as writers, as historians.

I wouldn't be staying through high school. My family planned to return to America when I had finished seventh grade, whether I was finished with China or not. Of course I knew I had to become an American, the sooner the better. So far away from America, I didn't feel like a real American. Nor would I, I thought, until I had put my feet down on American soil.

I had just finished sixth grade at the British School in Wuhan,[4] so I would have one more year to go. Nothing would change that. I knew that there was fighting up and down the Yangtze River, but the Chinese were always fighting— warlord against warlord.[5] That had nothing to do with me. But as soon as I saw the servant from next door racing toward our house with a message for my mother, I knew something was happening. Since we had no phone, we depended on our German neighbors for emergency messages. My father had called, the servant explained. All American women and children had to catch the afternoon boat to Shanghai.[6] The army, which had done so much damage to Nanjing (just down the river), was on its way here.

As I helped my mother pack, my knees were shaking. I had only felt this once before. My mother and I had been in a ricksha on the way to the racecourse when farmers ran to the road, calling hateful words at us and throwing stones.

Reading Skill
Context Clues
Identify examples in this paragraph that help you define *commit*.

Vocabulary Builder
quest (kwest) *n.* a long search for something

▲ Critical Viewing
Does a ricksha offer much protection to the riders? [Speculate]

---

4. **Wuhan** (wōō´ hän´) *n.* city in the central part of China, near the Yangtze River.
5. **warlord** (wôr´ lôrd´) *n.* local leader.
6. **Shanghai** (shaŋ´ hī´) *n.* seaport in E. China.

The ricksha-pullers were fast runners, so we weren't hurt, but I told myself this was like Stephen in the Bible who was stoned to death. He just didn't have a ricksha handy. By the time we reached the boat that afternoon, my knees were normal. So was I. And I knew what our plans were. My father and other American men would work in the daytime, but for safety at night they would board one of the gunboats anchored in the river. The women and children going to Shanghai would be protected from bullets by steel barriers erected around the deck. And when we reached Shanghai, then what? I asked my mother.

We would be staying with the Barretts, another missionary family, who had one son, Fletcher, who was two years younger than I and generally unlikable. Mr. Barrett met us in Shanghai and drove us to their home, where his wife was on the front porch. My mother greeted her warmly but I just held out my hand and said, "Hello, Mrs. Barrett," which I thought was <u>adequate</u>. She raised her eyebrows. "Have you become so grown up, Jean," she said, "that I'm no longer your 'Auntie Barrett'?"

I didn't say that I'd always been too grown up for the "auntie" business. I just smiled. In China all MKs called their parents' friends "auntie" or "uncle." Not me. Mrs. B. pushed Fletcher forward.

"Fletcher has been so excited about your visit, Jean," she said. "He has lots of games to show you. Now, run along, children."

Fletcher did have a lot of games. He decided what we'd play—rummy, then patience, while he talked a blue streak. I didn't pay much attention until, in the middle of an Uncle Wiggley game, he asked me a question.

"Have you ever been in love, Jean?" he asked.

What did he think I was? I was twelve years old, for heaven's sakes!

Ever since first grade I'd been in love with someone. The boys never knew it, of course.

Fletcher hadn't finished with love. "I'm in love now," he said. "I'll give you a hint. She's an MK."

"Naturally."

"And she's pretty." Then he suddenly shrieked out the answer as if he couldn't contain it a second longer. "It's you," he cried. "Y-O-U."

Vocabulary Builder
adequate (ad´ i kwət) *adj.* enough

Reading Skill
Context Clues
Which word restates the meaning of *shrieked* in the last paragraph?

Reading Check

Why is it necessary for Jean and her mother to travel to Shanghai?

Well, Fletcher Barrett was even dumber than I'd thought. No one had ever called me "pretty" before. Not even my parents. Besides, this conversation was making me sick. "I'm tired," I said. "I think I'll get my book and lie down."

At the last minute I had slipped my favorite book in my suitcase. It was one my father and I had read last year—*The Courtship of Miles Standish*[7]—all about the first settlers in America. I knew them pretty well now and often visited with Priscilla Alden.

Settled on the bed in the room I'd been told was mine, I opened the book and let the Pilgrims step off the Mayflower into Shanghai. Priscilla was one of the first.

"You're still a long way from Plymouth," I told her, "but you'll get there. Think you'll like it?"

"I know I will," she answered promptly. "Everything will be better there."

"How do you know?"

"It's a new country. It will be whatever we make it."

"It may be hard," I warned her.

"Maybe," she admitted. "But I'll never give up. Neither will John," she added.

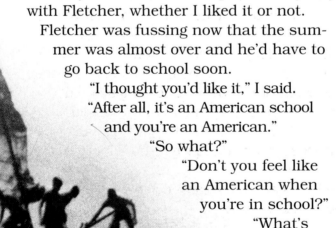

I was being called for supper. I waited for the Pilgrims to get back on the Mayflower. Then I closed the book and went downstairs.

The days that followed, I spent mostly with Fletcher, whether I liked it or not.

Fletcher was fussing now that the summer was almost over and he'd have to go back to school soon.

"I thought you'd like it," I said. "After all, it's an American school and you're an American."

"So what?"

"Don't you feel like an American when you're in school?"

"What's there to feel?"

7. *The Courtship of Miles Standish* n. narrative poem by Henry Wadsworth Longfellow, written in 1858. One character is Priscilla Alden.

Literary Analysis
Narration What problems does reading help Jean solve?

◄ **Critical Viewing** Jean probably saw boats like this on the Yangtze River. What purpose do you think a boat like this might serve? **[Hypothesize]**

He was impossible. If he had gone to a British school, the way I had all my life, he might realize how lucky he was. The Shanghai American School was famous. Children from all over China were sent there to be boarders. Living in Shanghai, Fletcher was just a day student. But even so!

Then one day my mother got a letter from my father. The danger was mostly over, he thought, but some foreign businesses were not reopening. The British School had closed down. (Good news!)

The Yangtze River boats went back in service the next week, so my mother went downtown to buy our tickets back to Wuhan. Fletcher was back in school now, and as soon as he came home, he rushed to see me, his face full of news.

"Your mother is only buying one ticket," he informed me. "You're not going. You're going to the Shanghai American School as a boarder."

"My mother would never do that. You're crazy," I replied. "Where did you get such an idea?"

"I overheard our mothers talking. It's true, Jean."

"Yeah, like cows fly."

When my mother came back, I could see that she was upset. Fletcher did a disappearing act; I figured he didn't want to be caught in a lie.

"Oh, I'm sorry, Jean," my mother said, her eyes filling with tears. She put her arms around me. "Since the British School is closed," she said, "I've arranged for you to be a boarder at the American School. It won't be for long. We may even go back to America early. At least I'll know you're safe."

I knew my mother was worried that I'd be homesick, so I couldn't let on how I really felt. (Just think, I told myself, I'd have almost a year to practice being an American.) I buried my head on her shoulder. "I'll be okay," I said, sniffing back fake tears. Sometimes it's necessary to <u>deceive</u> your parents if you love them, and I did love mine.

After my mother left on the boat, Mr. Barrett took me to the Shanghai American School (SAS for short). I guess I expected some kind of immediate <u>transformation</u>. I always felt a tingling when I saw the American flag flying over the American consulate. Surely it would be more than a tingling now; surely it would overwhelm me. But when we went through the iron gates of the school grounds, I didn't feel a thing. On the football field a group of high school girls were practicing cheerleading. They were jumping,

Literary Analysis
Narration What world events affect the author of this nonfiction narrative?

Vocabulary Builder
deceive (dē sēv´) v. make someone believe something that is not true

transformation (trans´fər mā´shən) n. change

Reading Check

Why is Jean excited about going to the American school?

standing on their hands, yelling rah, rah, rah. It just seemed like a lot of fuss about football. What was the matter with me?

The dormitory where I'd be living was divided in half by a swinging door. The high school girls were on one side of the door; the junior high (which included me) were on the other. On my side there were two Russian girls and two American MKs, the Johnson sisters, who had long hair braided and wound around their heads like Sunday school teachers. And there was Paula, my American roommate, who looked as though she belonged on the other side of the door. Hanging in our shared closet I noticed a black velvet dress. And a pair of high heeled shoes. She wore them to tea dances, she explained, when one of her brother's friends came to town. She was squinting her eyes as she looked at me, sizing up my straight hair and bangs.

"I happen to know you're an MK," she said, "but you don't have to look like one." The latest style in the States, she told me, was a boyish bob.[8] She'd give me one, she decided.

So that night she put a towel around my shoulders and newspaper on the floor, and she began cutting. This might make all the difference, I thought, as I watched my hair travel to the floor.

It didn't. My ears might have felt more American, but not me. After being in hiding all their lives, my ears were suddenly outdoors, looking like jug handles on each side of my face. I'd get used to them, I told myself. Meanwhile I had to admit that SAS was a big improvement over the British School. Even without an American flag feeling, I enjoyed the months I was there.

What I enjoyed most were the dances, except they weren't dances. There were too many MKs in the school, and the Ms didn't approve of dancing. Instead, we had "talk parties." The girls were given what looked like dance cards and the boys

▼ Critical Viewing
In what ways do the children in this picture look similar to and different from children of today? [Compare and Contrast]

Literary Analysis
Narration What is the first thing Jean's roommate decides to do for Jean?

---

8. bob (bäb) *n.* woman's or child's short haircut.

were supposed to sign up for the talk sessions they wanted. Of course a girl could feel like a wallflower[9] if her card wasn't filled up, but mine usually was. These parties gave me a chance to look over the boys in case I wanted to fall in love, and actually I was almost ready to make a choice when my parents suddenly appeared. It was early spring. Just as my mother had suspected, we were going to America early.

I knew that three weeks crossing the Pacific would be different from five days on the Yangtze but I didn't know how different. My father had given me a gray-and-green plaid steamer rug that I would put over me when I was lying on my long folding deck chair. At eleven o'clock every morning a waiter would come around with a cup of "beef tea." I loved the idea of drinking beef tea under my steamer rug but it didn't happen often. The captain said this was the roughest crossing he'd ever made, and passengers spent most of their time in their cabins. If they came out for a meal, they were lucky if they could get it down before it came back up again. I had my share of seasickness, so of course I was glad to reach San Francisco.

I couldn't wait to take my first steps on American soil, but I expected the American soil to hold still for me. Instead, it swayed as if we were all still at sea, and I lurched about as I had been doing for the last three weeks. I noticed my parents were having difficulty, too. "Our heads and our legs aren't ready for land," my father explained. "It takes a little while." We spent the night in a hotel and took a train the next day for Pittsburgh where our relatives were meeting us.

It was a three-day trip across most of the continent, but it didn't seem long. Every minute America was under us and rushing past our windows—the Rocky Mountains, the Mississippi river, flat ranch land, small towns, forests, boys dragging school bags over dusty roads. It was all of America at once splashed across where we were, where we'd been, where we were going. How could you not feel American? How could you not feel that you belonged? By the time we were settled at my grandmother's house, I felt as if I'd always been a part of this family. And wasn't it wonderful to have real aunts and uncles, a real grandmother, and yes, even a real bathroom, for heaven's sakes?

---

9. wallflower (wôl′ flou′ ər) *n.* person who stands against the wall and watches at a dance, due to shyness or lack of popularity.

Literary Analysis
Narration Why is Jean excited about the end of the crossing?

Reading Check

How does Jean feel about living in the United States?

I wanted to talk to Priscilla, so I took my book outside, and when I opened it, out tumbled the Pilgrims, Priscilla first. I smiled. Here we were, all of us in America together, and it didn't matter that we came from different times. We all knew that America was still an experiment and perhaps always would be. I was one of the ones who had to try to make the experiment work.

"You'll have disappointments," Priscilla said. "But it will help if you get to know Americans who have spent their lives working on the experiment."

I wasn't sure just what she meant, but I knew it was important. "I'll try," I said.

"Try!" Priscilla scoffed. "If you want to be a real American, you'll have to do more than that." Her voice was fading. Indeed, the Pilgrims themselves were growing faint. Soon they had all slipped away.

I learned about disappointment as soon as I went to school. Of course I was no longer an MK, but I was certainly a curiosity. I was the Kid from China. "Did you live in a mud hut?" one boy asked me. "Did you eat rats and dogs? Did you eat with sticks?"

I decided that American children were <u>ignorant</u>. Didn't their teachers teach them anything? After a while, as soon as anyone even mentioned China, I shut up. "What was the name of your hometown?" I was asked, but I never told. I couldn't bear to have my hometown laughed at.

"Not all American children are ignorant," my mother pointed out. "Just a few who ask dumb questions."

Even in high school, however, I often got the same questions. But now we were studying about the American

Reading Skill
Context Clues
Which clues in the paragraph help you to understand the meaning of *fading*?

Vocabulary Builder
ignorant (ig´ nə rənt)
adj. not knowing facts or information

Revolution and George Washington. Of course I'd always known who Washington was, but knowing history and understanding it are two different things. I had never realized how much he had done to make America into America. No matter how much he was asked to do for his country, he did it, even though he could hardly wait to go back home and be a farmer again. Of course there were disappointments on the way; of course he became discouraged. "If I'd known what I was getting into," he said at the beginning of the Revolution, "I would have chosen to live in an Indian teepee all my life." He never took the easiest way. When he thought his work was over at the end of the Revolution, he agreed to work on the Constitution. When the country needed a president, he took the oath of office. When his term was over, he was persuaded to run once again. Everyone had confidence that as long as he was there, the new government would work.

Although Washington was the first, there were many more like him who were, as Priscilla would say, "real" Americans. As I went through college and read about them, I knew I wanted to write about them someday. I might not talk to them in the same way I talked to Priscilla, but I would try to make them as real as they were when they were alive.

I had the feeling that I was coming to the end of my quest. But not quite. One day when someone asked me where I was born, I found myself smiling. I was for the moment standing beside the Yangtze River. "My hometown," I said, "was Wuhan, China." I discovered that I had to take China with me wherever I went.

Literary Analysis
Narration What does Jean learn in high school that she had not understood before then?

▼ **Critical Viewing** How does this landscape of the United States compare with Jean's descriptions of where she lived in China? [**Compare and Contrast**]

Apply the Skills

mk

Thinking About the Selection

1. **Respond:** What questions do you have about the narrative? Write them in the first column of a three-column chart. Trade charts with a partner.
   - In the second column, answer your partner's questions. Discuss your responses.
   - In the third column, explain how the discussion affected your understanding of the work.
2. **(a) Recall:** Why do Jean and her mother travel to Shanghai? **(b) Infer:** Does the American School in Shanghai live up to Jean's expectations? Why or why not?
3. **(a) Recall:** What is Jean's favorite book? **(b) Interpret:** Why do you think Jean relates to the main character, Priscilla Alden?
4. **Take a Position:** What are the pros and cons of living outside the United States? Choose a position and support your answer.

Reading Skill

5. In a chart like this, write the italicized word in the left column. Then, write the **context clues** from the passage and decide what the word means. Check your response in a dictionary.
   (a) I always felt a tingling when I saw the American flag flying over the American consulate. Surely it would be more than a tingling now; surely it would *overwhelm* me. **(b)** I expected the American soil to hold still for me. Instead, it *swayed* as if we were all still at sea.

Unfamiliar Word	Context Clues	Possible Meaning

Literary Analysis

6. Identify the main reason that "mk" is classified as a **narrative**.
7. The order, or sequence, of events is important in any type of **narration**. **(a)** What is the first thing Jean sees as she goes through the iron gates of the Shanghai American School? **(b)** Why is this information important to the story?

QuickReview

Story at a Glance
Jean Fritz describes some of her experiences growing up as a missionary kid in China.

Go Online
Assessment
For: Self-test
Visit: www.PHSchool.com
Web Code: ema-6104

Context: the words and phrases surrounding a word. Context clues can help clarify an unfamiliar word.

Narrative Writing: any type of writing that tells a story

Vocabulary Builder

Practice Rewrite each sentence, replacing each underlined word with a **synonym**, or word with a similar meaning.

1. The travelers were on a <u>quest</u> for adventure.
2. They brought <u>adequate</u> supplies for a week of camping.
3. When you smile, your face undergoes a <u>transformation</u>.
4. Do not try to <u>deceive</u> me with that silly mask and fake voice!
5. The children were <u>ignorant</u> about the rules of the new game.

Writing

Write a **brief essay** in which you compare and contrast Jean's feelings about America before and after she arrives in the United States. Gather details from the story in a two-column chart.

- In the first column, list details that show her thoughts and feelings about America while she is still living in China.
- In the second column, list details that show her thoughts and feelings when she lives and goes to school in the United States.

Use details from your chart as you draft your essay.

For *Grammar, Vocabulary,* and *Assessment,* see **Build Language Skills,** pages 44–45.

Extend Your Learning

Listening and Speaking Review the narrative and decide which part of "mk" is especially moving or funny. Then, perform a **dramatic reading** of that passage for the class. Rehearse your presentation, keeping these points in mind:

- Speak clearly so that each word can be heard.
- Raise and lower your voice to express emotion where appropriate.
- Slow down and stress certain words for effect.

Research and Technology Use library resources and the Internet to write a **report** about children who go to American schools overseas. Include information about what countries have the most American children, reasons why the children are overseas, and the kinds of schools that they attend.

Build Language Skills

Papa's Parrot • mk

Vocabulary Skill

Word Origins The words *signify* and *significance* share a common Latin origin—*signum,* or sign. Words that have this origin have meanings related to showing or indicating, like a sign. For example, the *significance* of something is its meaning or importance.

▶ **Example:** The historian explained the *significance* of the ancient writing.

The word **reveal** comes from the Latin word *revelare,* which means "to draw back the veil." This word origin is helpful in visualizing what the word *reveal* means. *Reveal* means "to make known" or "show."

▶ **Example:** Jonna drew back the curtain to *reveal* the famous painting.

Practice Using your dictionary, look up *signal, signify,* and *revelation.* Explain how the meanings of the words are related to the origin they share with *significance* and *reveal.* Then, use each word in a sentence that illustrates the meaning of the word.

Grammar Lesson

Common and Proper Nouns All nouns can be classified as either **common nouns** or **proper nouns.** A common noun names a person, place, or thing. A proper noun names a specific person, place, or thing. Common nouns are not capitalized unless they begin a sentence or a title. Proper nouns are always capitalized.

MorePractice

For more practice with common and proper nouns, see the Grammar Handbook, p. R31.

Common Nouns	singer	city	dog
Proper Nouns	Jennifer Johnson	Phoenix	Prince

Practice Underline the common nouns and circle the proper nouns in each sentence.

1. Bethany drove to the store on Wednesday.
2. Will John feed the puppy in September?
3. The woman phoned Ralph on Tuesday.
4. Mr. Fineman carried the flag down First Street.
5. Thousands of people visited the Lincoln Memorial in July.

WG Prentice Hall Writing and Grammar Connection: Chapter 14, Section 1

Reading: Context Clues

Directions: *Read the selection. Then answer the questions.*

Robert Louis Stevenson was a <u>puzzle</u>. He grew up a <u>frail</u> boy in Scotland and was <u>troubled</u> by poor health throughout his life. However, this sickly author wrote stirring tales of adventure, including *Treasure Island.*

Tall and thin, with a storklike walk, Stevenson looked as if he could be <u>toppled</u> by a gust of wind. Yet he was secretly tough and traveled all over the world.

1. What does the word *puzzle* mean in this selection?
   - **A** difficult
   - **B** mystery
   - **C** complicated
   - **D** game

2. In the selection, which words are clues to the meaning of the word *frail*?
   - **A** Scotland, poor health
   - **B** stirring tales, Scotland
   - **C** poor health, sickly
   - **D** troubled, adventure

3. In this selection, the word *troubled* means
   - **A** instructed
   - **B** blessed
   - **C** bothered
   - **D** freed

4. What does the word *toppled* mean in this selection?
   - **A** knocked over
   - **B** sickened
   - **C** turned
   - **D** irritated

Timed Writing: Narrative [Cognition]

Review "Papa's Parrot" or "mk." Briefly summarize the story using the correct order of events. In your summary, include one important event from the beginning, the middle, and the end of the story. **(20 minutes)**

 ## Writing Workshop: *Work in Progress*

Descriptive Essay
Refer to the list of qualities and features of a memorable place, in your writing portfolio. Pick one or two items from this list and jot down sensory details that you associate with them. Describe the sight, sound, and smell of the places or events.

Reading Informational Materials

Reference Materials

In Part 1, you are learning about using context clues in literature. This skill is also useful in reading informational materials such as reference books, encyclopedias, and atlases. If you read "mk," about Jean Fritz's experiences in China, you may have wanted to check an atlas to learn more about that country.

About Reference Materials

The most common reference materials are almanacs, encyclopedias, Internet resources, and maps. These materials can be useful when you are researching information for reports. Maps are typically found in large books, called **atlases,** such as the one featured here.

The maps in an atlas provide an overview of various geographic locations. They are often accompanied by brief articles that provide more detailed information. Map keys, called **legends,** explain the symbols and colors used to show information on the map.

Reading Skill

When you conduct research, you may face unfamiliar words and terms. Context, the words and phrases surrounding a word, can help you understand an unfamiliar word in a reference source. You may find context clues that follow these patterns:

- **Restatement:** The *population*, or <u>number of people in the country</u>, is stable.
- **Opposite:** Average rainfall has not *declined*; it has <u>increased</u>.
- **Example:** *Modes* of transportation, such as <u>car, train</u>, and <u>airplane</u>, are available.

As you read the atlas entry, jot down any unfamiliar words in a chart like the one shown. Then, reread or read ahead to find clues. Use those clues to determine the word's meaning. If you cannot understand a word from its context, look in a dictionary.

Word	Location	Context Clues	Pattern	Meaning
Populous	Introductory text	"Over one billion people"	Restatement	Full of people; heavily populated

EAST ASIA

China, Mongolia, Taiwan

China is the world's third-largest country and its most populous—over one billion people live there. Under its communist government, which came to power in 1949, China has become a major industrial nation, but most of its people still live and work on the land as they have for thousands of years. Taiwan also has a booming economy and exports its products around the world. Mongolia is a vast, remote country with a small population, many of whom are nomads.

A small distance on a map represents a larger distance in real life. The scale bar shows this relationship.

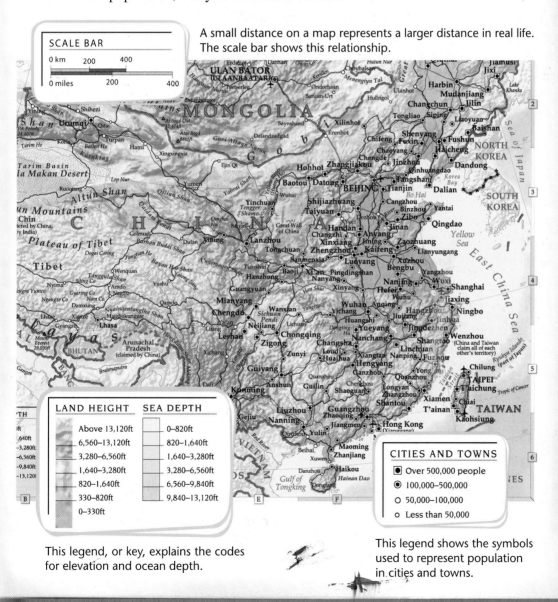

This legend, or key, explains the codes for elevation and ocean depth.

This legend shows the symbols used to represent population in cities and towns.

Reading Informational Materials

Population

Most of China's people live in the eastern part of the country, where climate, landscape and soils are most favorable. Urban areas there house more than 250 million people, but almost 75% of the population lives in villages and farms the land. Taiwan's lowlands are very densely populated. In Mongolia, about 50% of the people live in the countryside.

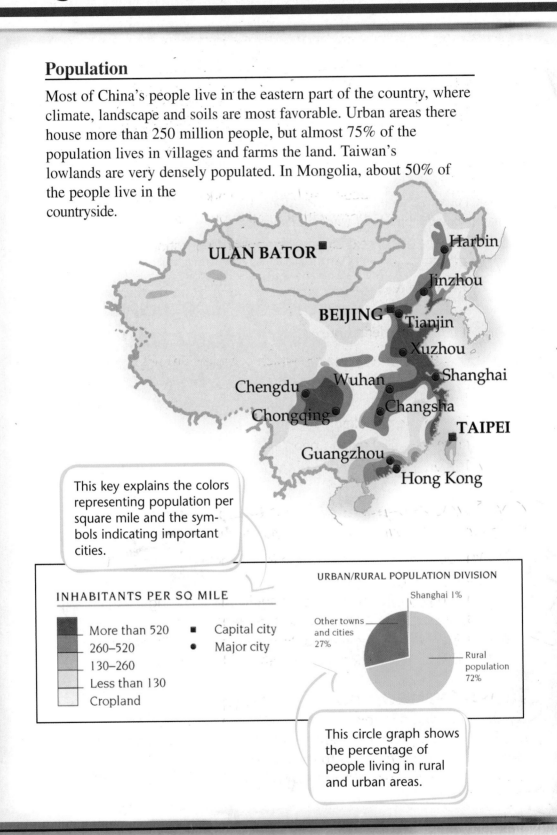

This key explains the colors representing population per square mile and the symbols indicating important cities.

INHABITANTS PER SQ MILE

- More than 520
- 260–520
- 130–260
- Less than 130
- Cropland

- ■ Capital city
- ● Major city

URBAN/RURAL POPULATION DIVISION

Shanghai 1%

Other towns and cities 27%

Rural population 72%

This circle graph shows the percentage of people living in rural and urban areas.

Reading: Context Clues

Directions: *Choose the letter of the best answer to each question.*

1. In the introduction on page 47, which words help you determine the meaning of *industrial*?
   A most populous
   B came to power in 1949
   C but most of its people still live and work on the land
   D vast, remote country with a small population

2. What type of context clue is the answer to question 1?
   A a restatement
   B an opposite
   C an example
   D a dictionary definition

3. In "Population" on page 48, which context clues help you determine the meaning of *urban*?
   A farms the land
   B 75% of the population
   C more than 250 million people
   D Taiwan's lowlands

Reading: Comprehension and Interpretation
Directions: *Write your answers on a separate sheet of paper.*

4. Why do most of China's people live in the eastern part of the country? **[Knowledge]**
5. How do you think people in Mongolia make a living? Support your answer with details from the text. **[Generating]**
6. Use the map and legends to describe the city of Shanghai in terms of location, population, and elevation. **[Analyzing]**

Timed Writing: Description [Interpretation]
Use the information in this atlas entry to plan a mountain-climbing expedition to East Asia. Describe the route that would take you into the most mountainous areas and to the highest peaks. Include the names of countries you would pass through as well as specific mountains and rivers.
(15 minutes)

These skills will help you become a better reader. Practice them with either the excerpt from *An American Childhood* (p. 52) or "The Luckiest Time of All" (p. 61).

Reading Skill

Context clues are the examples, descriptions, and other details in the text around an unfamiliar or unusual word or expression. When you come across an unfamiliar word, use context clues to figure out what the word probably means. Then, **reread and read ahead to confirm the meaning.** The chart shows an example of how to do this.

Context
The doll's small feet wore *miniscule* shoes.

Function in Sentence
It is an adjective that describes the shoes.

Meaning
Miniscule probably means "tiny."

Literary Analysis

Point of view is the perspective from which a narrative is told. Point of view affects what kinds of details are revealed to the reader.

- **First-person point of view:** The narrator is a character who participates in the action of the story and uses the first-person pronouns *I* and *me.* The narrator can reveal only his or her own observations, thoughts, and feelings.
- **Third-person point of view:** The narrator is not a character in the story. He or she uses third-person pronouns such as *he, she,* and *they* to refer to the characters. The narrator may know and reveal the observations, thoughts, and feelings of more than one character.

Vocabulary Builder

from An American Childhood

- **strategy** (strat´ ə jē) *n.* set of plans used to gain success or achieve an aim (p. 53) *The general presented his* strategy *for the attack.*
- **compelled** (kəm peld´) *v.* forced (p. 56) *Honesty* compelled *him to tell the truth.*
- **improvising** (im´ prə vīz´ iŋ) *v.* making up or inventing on the spur of the moment (p. 56) *The cooking contest called for* improvising *with on-hand ingredients.*

The Luckiest Time of All

- **twine** (twīn) *n.* strong string or cord of two or more strands twisted together (p. 63) *We tied the newspaper bundle with* twine.
- **acquainted** (ə kwānt´ əd) *adj.* familiar (p. 63) *Until he met them at the football game, Jake was not* acquainted *with his new friend's sisters.*

Autobiography

Background

The American Suburbs The events in this narrative take place in a suburban neighborhood. The word *suburban* refers to a residential area on or near the outskirts of a city, or "urban" area. After World War II, more people had cars and were able to leave crowded cities. Suburban living has some of the conveniences of a city—such as shopping and entertainment—in a quieter environment.

Connecting to the Literature

Reading/Writing Connection In this excerpt from *An American Childhood,* Annie Dillard recalls how a childhood chase transformed her quiet neighborhood into the setting for an exciting adventure. Write a short description of a time when you gave all your effort to a physical task and ended up tired but exhilarated. Use at least three of the following words: *accelerate, challenge, exert, exceed, invest.*

Meet the Author

Annie **Dillard** (b. 1945)

Growing up in Pittsburgh, Pennsylvania, Annie Dillard loved reading, drawing, and observing the natural world. During high school, Dillard began reading and writing poetry. Her favorite book, however—which she still reads once a year—is *The Field Book of Ponds and Streams.*

Pulitzer Prize–Winning Book While attending college in Virginia, Dillard lived near a creek in a valley of the Blue Ridge Mountains. In 1974, she published *Pilgrim at Tinker Creek,* which describes her explorations of that environment. During the writing of the book, she would sit for hours watching a praying mantis lay its eggs, then she would return home and think about her observations, mixing them with her readings from science and philosophy.

Dillard gives this advice to aspiring writers: "You have enough experience by the time you're five years old. What you need is the library. What you have to learn is the best of what is being thought and said."

Go **Online**
Author Link

For: More about the author
Visit: www.PHSchool.com
Web Code: eme-9104

from An American Childhood

Annie Dillard

Some boys taught me to play football. This was fine sport. You thought up a new <u>strategy</u> for every play and whispered it to the others. You went out for a pass, fooling everyone. Best, you got to throw yourself mightily at someone's running legs. Either you brought him down or you hit the ground flat out on your chin, with your arms empty before you. It was all or nothing. If you hesitated in fear, you would miss and get hurt: you would take a hard fall while the kid got away, or you would get kicked in the face while the kid got away. But if you flung yourself wholeheartedly at the back of his knees—if you gathered and joined body and soul and pointed them diving fearlessly—then you likely wouldn't get hurt, and you'd stop the ball. Your fate, and your team's score, depended on your concentration and courage. Nothing girls did could compare with it.

Boys welcomed me at baseball, too, for I had, through enthusiastic practice, what was weirdly known as a boy's arm. In winter, in the snow, there was neither baseball nor football, so the boys and I threw snowballs at passing cars. I got in trouble throwing snowballs, and have seldom been happier since.

On one weekday morning after Christmas, six inches of new snow had just fallen. We were standing up to our boot tops in snow on a front yard on trafficked Reynolds Street, waiting for cars. The cars traveled Reynolds Street slowly and evenly; they were targets all but wrapped in red ribbons, cream puffs. We couldn't miss.

I was seven; the boys were eight, nine, and ten. The oldest two Fahey boys were there—Mikey and Peter—polite blond boys who lived near me on Lloyd Street, and who already had four brothers and sisters. My parents approved Mikey and Peter Fahey. Chickie McBride was there, a tough kid, and Billy Paul and Mackie Kean too, from across Reynolds, where the boys grew up dark and furious, grew up skinny, knowing, and skilled. We had all drifted from our houses that morning looking for action, and had found it here on Reynolds Street.

◄ Critical Viewing Do you think that children and adults would have the same reaction to this snow scene? Explain. [**Compare and Contrast**]

Vocabulary Builder
strategy (strat´ ə jē)
n. set of plans used to gain success or achieve an aim

Literary Analysis
Point of View Which words and details in the first two paragraphs indicate that this narrative is told from the first-person point of view?

✔ **Reading Check**

What are Annie and her friends doing?

from *An American Childhood* ■ 53

It was cloudy but cold. The cars' tires laid behind them on the snowy street a complex trail of beige chunks like crenellated castle walls.[1] I had stepped on some earlier; they squeaked. We could have wished for more traffic. When a car came, we all popped it one. In the intervals between cars we reverted to the natural solitude of children.

I started making an iceball—a perfect iceball, from perfectly white snow, perfectly spherical, and squeezed perfectly translucent so no snow remained all the way through. (The Fahey boys and I considered it unfair actually to throw an iceball at somebody, but it had been known to happen.)

I had just embarked on the iceball project when we heard tire chains come clanking from afar. A black Buick was moving toward us down the street. We all spread out, banged together some regular snowballs, took aim, and, when the Buick drew nigh, fired.

A soft snowball hit the driver's windshield right before the driver's face. It made a smashed star with a hump in the middle.

Often, of course, we hit our target, but this time, the only time in all of life, the car pulled over and stopped. Its wide black door opened; a man got out of it, running. He didn't even close the car door.

He ran after us, and we ran away from him, up the snowy Reynolds sidewalk. At the corner, I looked back; incredibly, he was still after us. He was in city clothes: a suit and tie, street shoes. Any normal adult would have quit, having sprung us into flight and made his point. This man was gaining on us. He was a thin man, all action. All of a sudden, we were running for our lives.

Wordless, we split up. We were on our turf; we could lose ourselves in the neighborhood backyards, everyone for himself. I paused and considered. Everyone had vanished except Mikey Fahey, who was just rounding the corner of a yellow brick house. Poor Mikey, I trailed him. The driver of the Buick sensibly picked the two of us to follow. The man apparently had all day.

He chased Mikey and me around the yellow house and up a backyard path we knew by heart: under a low tree, up a bank, through a hedge, down some snowy steps, and across the grocery store's delivery driveway. We smashed through a gap in

---

1. **like crenellated** (kren´ əl āt´ əd) **castle walls** in rows of squares like the notches along the top of castle walls.

▼ Critical Viewing
In what two ways is this photograph of a snow-covered bicycle a good image for this narrative? [Support]

Reading Skill
Context Clues
What clues clarify the meaning of the expression "gaining on us" in the sixth paragraph?

another hedge, entered a scruffy backyard and ran around its back porch and tight between houses to Edgerton Avenue; we ran across Edgerton to an alley and up our own sliding wood-pile to the Halls' front yard; he kept coming. We ran up Lloyd Street and wound through mazy backyards toward the steep hilltop at Willard and Lang.

He chased us silently, block after block. He chased us silently over picket fences, through thorny hedges, between houses, around garbage cans, and across streets. Every time I glanced back, choking for breath, I expected he would have quit. He must have been as breathless as we were. His jacket strained over his body. It was an immense discovery,

Reading Check

Why are Annie and her friends being chased?

pounding into my hot head with every sliding, joyous step, that this ordinary adult evidently knew what I thought only children who trained at football knew: that you have to fling yourself at what you're doing, you have to point yourself, forget yourself, aim, dive.

Mikey and I had nowhere to go, in our own neighborhood or out of it, but away from this man who was chasing us. He impelled us forward; we <u>compelled</u> him to follow our route. The air was cold; every breath tore my throat. We kept running, block after block; we kept <u>improvising</u>, backyard after backyard, running a frantic course and choosing it simultaneously, failing always to find small places or hard places to slow him down, and discovering always, exhilarated, dismayed, that only bare speed could save us—for he would never give up, this man—and we were losing speed.

He chased us through the backyard labyrinths of ten blocks before he caught us by our jackets. He caught us and we all stopped.

We three stood staggering, half blinded, coughing, in an obscure hilltop backyard: a man in his twenties, a boy, a girl. He had released our jackets, our pursuer, our captor, our hero: he knew we weren't going anywhere. We all played by the rules. Mikey and I unzipped our jackets. I pulled off my sopping mittens. Our tracks multiplied in the backyard's new snow. We had been breaking new snow all morning. We didn't look at each other. I was cherishing my excitement. The man's lower pants legs were wet; his cuffs were full of snow, and there was a prow of snow beneath them on his shoes and socks. Some trees bordered the little flat backyard, some messy winter trees. There was no one around: a clearing in a grove, and we the only players.

It was a long time before he could speak. I had some difficulty at first recalling why we were there. My lips felt swollen; I couldn't see out of the sides of my eyes; I kept coughing.

"You stupid kids," he began perfunctorily.

We listened perfunctorily indeed, if we listened at all, for the chewing out was redundant, a mere formality, and beside the point. The point was that he had chased us passionately without giving up, and so he had caught us. Now he came down to earth. I wanted the glory to last forever.

But how could the glory have lasted forever? We could have run through every backyard in North America until we got to

Vocabulary Builder
compelled (kəm peld´) *v.* forced

improvising (im´ prə vīz´ iŋ) *v.* making up or inventing on the spur of the moment

Reading Skill
Context Clues
Which words in this paragraph verify the meaning of *redundant* by restating it?

Panama. But when he trapped us at the lip of the Panama Canal, what precisely could he have done to prolong the drama of the chase and cap its glory? I brooded about this for the next few years. He could only have fried Mikey Fahey and me in boiling oil, say, or dismembered us piecemeal, or staked us to ant-hills. None of which I really wanted, and none of which any adult was likely to do, even in the spirit of fun. He could only chew us out there in the Panamanian jungle, after months or years of exalting pursuit. He could only begin, "You stupid kids," and continue in his ordinary Pittsburgh accent with his normal righteous anger and the usual common sense.

If in that snowy backyard the driver of the black Buick had cut off our heads, Mikey's and mine, I would have died happy, for nothing has required so much of me since as being chased all over Pittsburgh in the middle of winter—running terrified, exhausted—by this sainted, skinny, furious red-headed man who wished to have a word with us. I don't know how he found his way back to his car.

Literary Analysis
Point of View Why are the man's thoughts not revealed in this narrative?

◄ **Critical Viewing** What details of a snowy scene like this one might the narrator have found exciting? **[Speculate]**

Apply the Skills

from *An American Childhood*

Thinking About the Selection

1. **Respond:** Would you want the young Annie Dillard as a friend? Why or why not?
2. **(a) Recall:** What are Dillard and her friends doing "On one weekday morning after Christmas"? **(b) Describe:** Describe the way the man chases Dillard and her friend. **(c) Interpret:** Why does Dillard call the man who chased her "our hero"?
3. **(a) Recall:** What does the man do when he catches Dillard and her friend? **(b) Infer:** How do his actions cause this "hero" to come "down to earth"?
4. **(a) Analyze:** In general, what does the young Dillard value and not value in people? **(b) Evaluate:** Do you think this episode from Dillard's early life has a larger meaning, or is it just an entertaining story? Explain.

Reading Skill

Read these lines from the narrative: *"You stupid kids," he began* <u>*perfunctorily*</u>*. We listened perfunctorily indeed, if we listened at all, for the chewing out was redundant, a mere formality, and beside the point.*

5. What is the underlined word's function in the sentence?
6. What **context clues** suggest a possible meaning?
7. What is a possible meaning for *perfunctorily*?
8. Does your possible meaning make sense when you reread the passage and when you read ahead?

Literary Analysis

9. Using a chart like the one shown, give two examples from the story in which the narrator shares her thoughts or feelings about a situation.

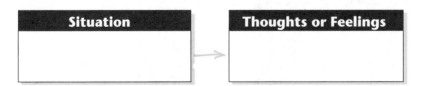

Situation	Thoughts or Feelings

10. What are three details that could have been included if the **first-person narrator** had been the man?

QuickReview

Story at a Glance
After they hit a car with a snowball, a girl and her friends lead a wild chase through their neighborhood.

Go Online
Assessment
For: Self-test
Visit: www.PHSchool.com
Web Code: ema-6105

Context clues: the examples, descriptions, and other details surrounding an unfamiliar word

Point of View: the perspective from which a narrative is told. A narrative may be told in *first-* or *third-person point of view.*

Vocabulary Builder

Practice Decide whether each statement is true or false. Explain your response to each item.

1. Few doctors feel *compelled* to help others.

2. We are *improvising* by using garbage bags for rain ponchos.

3. Studying hard is a good *strategy* for passing a test.

Writing

In the excerpt from *An American Childhood,* Annie Dillard uses **hyperbole,** an exaggeration for effect. She describes how a chase might have turned out: "We could have run through every back-yard in North America until we got to Panama."

Think of three circumstances or situations, such as being very hungry, very tired, or very cold. For each one, write a **description** that includes hyperbole. For example, if you are describing being very cold, you might write, "I felt like my blood was frozen solid in my veins. If I had cut myself, I would have bled icicles."

For *Grammar, Vocabulary,* and *Assessment,* see **Build Language Skills,** pages 66–67.

Extend Your Learning

Listening and Speaking Prepare and present a **persuasive speech** about the dangers of throwing snowballs at cars.
- Cite examples to show what could happen.
- Find facts and statistics to back up your opinion.

Present your speech to the class.

Research and Technology Use the Internet and library resources to research Annie Dillard's life. Gather information about the following:
- her childhood
- major events in her life
- her writing career

Present your findings in a **biographical report.**

Short Story

Background

Dialect is a form of language spoken by people in a specific region or group. Dialects differ from standard formal language in pronunciation, grammar, and word choice. In "The Luckiest Time of All," Lucille Clifton uses a dialect of the rural South. The informal language contributes to the feeling that readers are listening to a story told aloud.

Connecting to the Literature

Reading/Writing Connection In this story, a character's great-grandmother tells how an event that seems to be "bad luck" can really be "good luck." Describe what you think "luck" is. Use at least three of the following words: *define, confirm, demonstrate, interpret*.

Review

For **Reading Skill, Literary Analysis,** and **Vocabulary Builder,** see page 50.

Meet the Author

Lucille **Clifton** (b. 1936)

Lucille Sayles Clifton was born into a large, working-class family in Depew, New York. Although her parents were not formally educated, they taught their children to appreciate books and poetry. During her childhood, Clifton also developed a deep respect for her African American culture and its storytelling tradition.

A Life of Achievement After becoming the first member of her family to graduate from high school, Clifton entered college. Two years later, she left school and began her writing career. Her first collection of poems was published in 1969, and the *New York Times* called it one of the best books of the year.

Fast Facts

▶ From 1979 to 1982, Clifton served as Poet Laureate of Maryland.

▶ She won an Emmy Award from the Academy of Television Arts & Sciences.

Author Link

For: More about the author
Visit: www.PHSchool.com
Web Code: eme-9105

The Luckiest Time of All

Lucille Clifton

Mrs. Elzie F. Pickens was rocking slowly on the porch one afternoon when her Great-granddaughter, Tee, brought her a big bunch of dogwood blooms, and that was the beginning of a story.

"Ahhh, now that dogwood reminds me of the day I met your Great-granddaddy, Mr. Pickens, Sweet Tee.

"It was just this time, spring of the year, and me and my best friend Ovella Wilson, who is now gone, was goin to join the Silas Greene. Usta be a kinda show went all through the South, called it the Silas Greene show. Somethin like the circus. Me and Ovella wanted to join that thing and see the world. Nothin wrong at home or nothin, we just wanted to travel and see new things and have high times. Didn't say nothin to nobody but one another. Just up and decided to do it.

"Well, this day we plaited our hair and put a dress and some things in a crokasack[1] and started out to the show. Spring day like this.

Reading Skill
Context Clues Read ahead. Then, tell what clues show you that Silas Greene is not the name of a person in this context.

---

1. **crokasack** (krō´ kər sak) *usually spelled croker sack, n.* bag made of burlap or similar material.

"We got there after a good little walk and it was the world, Baby, such music and wonders as we never had seen! They had everything there, or seemed like it.

"Me and Ovella thought we'd walk around for a while and see the show before goin to the office to sign up and join.

"While we was viewin it all we come up on this dancin dog. Cutest one thing in the world next to you, Sweet Tee, dippin and movin and head bowin to that music. Had a little ruffly skirt on itself and up on two back legs twistin and movin to the music. Dancin dancin dancin till people started throwin pennies out of they pockets.

"Me and Ovella was caught up too and laughin so. She took a penny out of her pocket and threw it to the ground where that dog was dancin, and I took two pennies and threw 'em both.

"The music was faster and faster and that dog was turnin and turnin. Ovella reached in her sack and threw out a little pin she had won from never being late at Sunday school. And me, laughin and all excited, reached in my bag and threw out my lucky stone!

"Well, I knew right off what I had done. Soon as it left my hand it seemed like I reached back out for it to take it back. But the stone was gone from my hand and Lord, it hit that dancin dog right on his nose!

"Well, he lit out after me, poor thing. He lit out after me and I flew! Round and round the Silas Greene we run, through every place me and Ovella had walked before, but now that dancin dog was a runnin dog and all the people was laughin at the new show, which was us!

"I felt myself slowin down after a while and I thought I would turn around a little bit to see how much

Culture Connection

A Matter of Luck Most people believe that hard work contributes more than luck to a person's success. However, there is scientific evidence that a positive attitude increases a person's chances for success. In this sense, any action or object that contributes to a person's positive attitude could be considered lucky. Here is how some accomplished Americans approach the issue:

- Basketball superstar Michael Jordan always wore his blue University of North Carolina shorts under his Chicago Bulls uniform when he played.

- When she is on the ice, skating star Michelle Kwan wears a Chinese good luck charm around her neck. Featuring a symbol like the one shown here, it was a gift from her grandmother.

Connect to the Literature

Why do you think Elzie considers the stone to be lucky?

gain that cute little dog was makin on me. When I did I got such a surprise! Right behind me was the dancin dog and right behind him was the finest fast runnin hero in the bottoms of Virginia.

"And that was Mr. Pickens when he was still a boy! He had a length of <u>twine</u> in his hand and he was twirlin it around in the air just like the cowboy at the Silas Greene and grinnin fit to bust.

"While I was watchin how the sun shined on him and made him look like an angel come to help a poor sinner girl, why, he twirled that twine one extra fancy twirl and looped it right around one hind leg of that dancin dog and brought him low.

"I stopped then and walked slow and shy to where he had picked up that poor dog to see if he was hurt, cradlin him and talkin to him soft and sweet. That showed me how kind and gentle he was, and when we walked back to the dancin dog's place in the show he let the dog loose and helped me to find my stone. I told him how shiny black it was and how it had the letter A scratched on one side. We searched and searched and at last he spied it!

"Ovella and me lost heart for shows then and we walked on home. And a good little way, the one who was gonna be your Great-granddaddy was walkin on behind. Seein us safe. Us walkin kind of slow. Him seein us safe. Yes." Mrs. Pickens' voice trailed off softly and Tee noticed she had a little smile on her face.

"Grandmama, that stone almost got you bit by a dog that time. It wasn't so lucky that time, was it?"

Tee's Great-grandmother shook her head and laughed out loud.

"That was the luckiest time of all, Tee Baby. It got me <u>acquainted</u> with Mr. Amos Pickens, and if that ain't luck, what could it be! Yes, it was luckier for me than for anybody, I think. Least mostly I think it."

Tee laughed with her Great-grandmother though she didn't exactly know why.

"I hope I have that kind of good stone luck one day," she said.

"Maybe you will someday," her Great-grandmother said.

And they rocked a little longer and smiled together.

Vocabulary Builder
twine (twīn) *n.* strong string or cord of two or more strands twisted together

Literary Analysis
Point of View In Elzie's narrative, why are Mr. Pickens's thoughts not revealed?

Vocabulary Builder
acquainted (ə kwānt′ əd) *adj.* familiar

Literary Analysis
Point of View How does the writer indicate that the point of view changes from a first-person narrative by Elzie to a third-person narrative about Elzie and Tee?

Apply the Skills

The Luckiest Time of All

Thinking About the Selection

1. **Respond:** Have you ever met someone "by chance," the way Elzie met Mr. Pickens? What happened?
2. **(a) Recall:** Why do Ovella and Elzie go to the Silas Greene show? **(b) Infer:** What does this tell you about Elzie as a young woman? **(c) Connect:** In what ways is Elzie similar or different as an older woman?
3. **(a) Recall:** When does Elzie first see Mr. Pickens? **(b) Infer:** Why does he save Elzie from the dog? **(c) Analyze:** How does Elzie know that Mr. Pickens is a good man?
4. **(a) Speculate:** Would you say that Elzie has been happy with her life? Support your opinion with examples. **(b) Synthesize:** What might Tee learn from her great-grandmother's story?

Reading Skill

Read the following lines from the story: *Well, he <u>lit out</u> after me, poor thing. He lit out after me and I flew! Round and round the Silas Greene we run . . . but now that dancing dog was a runnin dog. . . .*

5. What is the underlined word's function in the sentence?
6. What **context clues** suggest a possible meaning?
7. What is a possible meaning for *lit out*?
8. Does your possible meaning make sense when you reread the passage and when you read ahead?

Literary Analysis

9. Using a chart like the one shown, give two examples from Elzie's story in which she shares her thoughts or feelings about a situation.

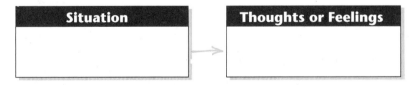

Situation	Thoughts or Feelings

10. What are three details that could have been included if the **first-person narrator** had been Mr. Pickens?

QuickReview

Story at a Glance
A girl meets her future husband when he rescues her by capturing the dog that is chasing her.

Go **O**nline
Assessment
For: Self-test
Visit: www.PHSchool.com
Web Code: ema-6106

Context clues: the examples, descriptions, and other details surrounding an unfamiliar word

Point of View: the perspective from which a narrative is told. A narrative may be told in *first-* or *third-person point of view.*

Vocabulary Builder

Practice **Analogies** show the relationships between pairs of words. In the exercise below, *harmed* and *hurt* are synonyms. *Thread* is used for *sewing.* Use a word from the vocabulary list on page 50 to complete each analogy. Your choice should make a word pair that matches the relationship between the first two words.

1. harmed : hurt : : _____ : known
2. thread : sewing : : _____ : tying

Writing

Mrs. Elzie Pickens uses **hyperbole**—an exaggeration for effect—to describe how impressed she was with Mr. Pickens: "right behind him was the finest fast running hero in the bottoms of Virginia."

Think of three qualities or skills a person could have, such as being very tall, very funny, or very shy. Choose one, and write a **description** that includes hyperbole. For example, if you are describing someone very smart, you might write, "She knew more than all the professors at the university. She had answers to questions that hadn't even been thought of yet."

For *Grammar, Vocabulary,* and *Assessment,* see **Build Language Skills,** pages 66–67.

Extend Your Learning

Listening and Speaking Prepare and present a **persuasive speech** about the dangers of teasing animals.
- Cite examples to show what could happen.
- Find facts and statistics to back up your opinion.

Present your speech to the class.

Research and Technology Use the Internet and library resources to research Lucille Clifton's life. Gather information about the following:
- her childhood
- major events in her life
- her writing career

Present your findings in a **biographical report.**

Build Language Skills

from *An American Childhood* • *The Luckiest Time of All*

Vocabulary Skill

Word Origins The word *context* comes from the Latin *com-,* meaning "together," and *textere,* meaning "to weave." *Context* is the connection or weaving together of the words and phrases surrounding a word to construct meaning.

➤ **Example:** In this *context, desert* means "abandon."

The word *verify* comes from the Latin word *verus* meaning "true." If you verify something, you prove whether it is true.

➤ **Example:** He brought a doctor's note to *verify* that he had been sick.

Practice Answer the following questions in complete sentences.

1. If you were asked to *verify* your identity, how would you do it?
2. If you were asked to give the *context* of an unfamiliar word, where would you look?

Grammar Lesson

Possessive Nouns **Possessive nouns** show ownership. Possessives are formed in different ways for plural and singular nouns.

- **Singular noun:** add an apostrophe and *-s: player's.*
- **Plural noun that ends in** *-s:* add an apostrophe: *bees'.*
- **Plural noun not ending in** *-s:* add an apostrophe and *–s: children's.*

➤ **Examples:** *The bat of the player* becomes *the player's bat.*
The buzzing of the bees becomes *the bees' buzzing.*
The toys of the children becomes *the children's toys.*

Practice Rewrite each of the following using the possessive form.

1. the whistles of the coaches
2. the bathing suit of the swimmer
3. the career of the woman
4. the roles of the actors
5. the tails of the mice

MorePractice

For more practice with possessive nouns, see the Grammar Handbook, p. R31.

W͟G Prentice Hall Writing and Grammar Connection: Chapter 26, Section 5

Assessment Practice

Reading: Context Clues

Directions: *Read the selection. Then answer the questions.*

After her car accident, we visited my aunt in the hospital. She is a bit <u>verbose</u>, fond of using twenty words where two would do. Still, her <u>veracity</u> is admirable. She admitted that when it came down to a question of responsibility she was <u>culpable</u> because she did not notice the stop sign.

1. What does *verbose* mean in this selection?

 A angry

 B wordy

 C distant

 D cheerful

2. Which clue in the selection helped you determine the meaning of the word *verbose*?

 A fond of using twenty words

 B in the hospital

 C after her car accident

 D her veracity is admirable

3. In this selection, what does the word *veracity* mean?

 A truthfulness

 B strength

 C dishonesty

 D conversation

4. What does the word *culpable* mean in this selection?

 A sad

 B angry

 C guilty

 D worried

Timed Writing: Interpretation [Analyzing]

Review the excerpt from *An American Childhood* or "The Luckiest Time of All." Recall the chase from either story and the narrator's feelings at the end of the chase. Then, write an interpretation of why the narrator feels as she does. **(20 minutes)**

 ## Writing Workshop: *Work in Progress*

Descriptive Essay

Revise the details of places and events from your writing portfolio. Look at the words you used to describe sensory images. If you wrote "the place smells bad," change *bad* to a more descriptive word or phrase, such as *sickening, musty,* or *sour.*

Fiction and Nonfiction

Fiction is prose writing that tells about imaginary characters and events. Novels, novellas, and short stories are types of fiction. **Nonfiction** is prose writing that presents and explains ideas or that tells about real people, places, objects, or events. News articles, essays, and historical accounts are types of nonfiction.

Comparing Fiction and Nonfiction

While one is fiction and the other nonfiction, the selections here are both examples of **narrative writing.** They each tell a story with the following elements:

- a *narrator* who tells the story
- *characters,* or people living the story
- *dialogue,* or the conversations that the characters have
- story *events* that make up the action

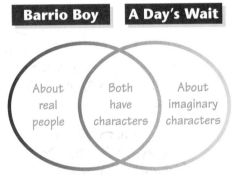

However, these selections are not completely alike. The excerpt from *Barrio Boy* tells about an important real event in the writer's life. In contrast, "A Day's Wait" is the story of an imagined boy on a single day. As you read, use a chart like the one shown to note ways in which the works are similar and different.

Vocabulary Builder

from Barrio Boy

- **reassuring** (rē´ ə shoor´ iŋ) *adj.* having the effect of restoring confidence (p. 70) *The sound of applause was reassuring to the nervous performer.*

- **contraption** (kən trap´ shən) *n.* device or machine regarded as strange (p. 70) *I don't think that it is safe to drive that rickety contraption.*

- **formidable** (fôr´ mə də bəl) *adj.* impressive (p. 71) *The titles on the long summer reading list were formidable.*

A Day's Wait

- **epidemic** (ep´ ə dem´ ik) *n.* outbreak of a contagious disease (p. 76) *The flu epidemic caused school to close.*

- **flushed** (flusht) *v.* drove from hiding (p. 77) *The dogs flushed birds out of the bushes.*

- **evidently** (ev´ ə dent´ lē) *adv.* clearly; obviously (p. 77) *The dark clouds evidently promised rain.*

Build Understanding

Connecting to the Literature

Reading/Writing Connection In this excerpt from *Barrio Boy,* Ernesto Galarza describes the experience of attending a new school. Think of a time when you had a new experience, such as moving to a new neighborhood or joining a sports league. Write a description of your thoughts and feelings both before and during the experience. Use at least three of the following words: *comprehend, focus, interpret, respond, distort.*

Meet the Authors

Ernesto **Galarza** (1905–1984)

When he was seven years old, Ernesto Galarza moved from Mexico to California. There, his family harvested crops in the fields of Sacramento and struggled to make ends meet. Galarza learned English quickly and won a scholarship for college.

Helping Farm Workers From 1936 to 1947, Galarza served as chief of the Division of Labor and Social Information for the Pan-American Union, dealing with education and labor in Latin America. When he returned to California, he worked to gain rights for farm workers.

Ernest **Hemingway** (1899–1961)

A true adventurer, Ernest Hemingway based much of his writing on his own experiences. He served as an ambulance driver in World War I, worked as a journalist, traveled the world, and enjoyed outdoor sports.

Writing About the Familiar Hemingway's fiction celebrates his spirit of adventure. The story "A Day's Wait" captures the quiet bravery of many of his characters.

Go **Online**
Author Link

For: More information about the authors
Visit: www.PHSchool.com
Web Code: eme-9106

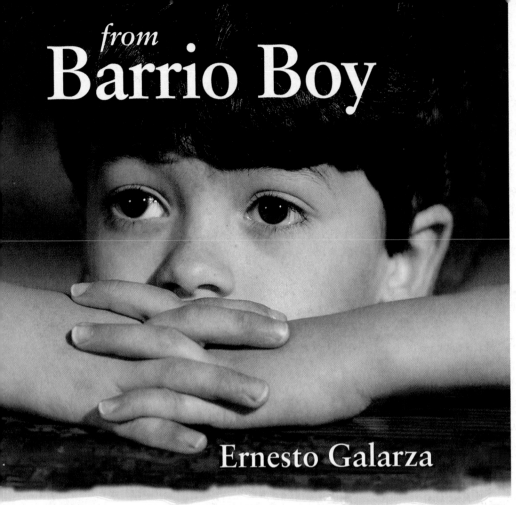

from Barrio Boy

Ernesto Galarza

My mother and I walked south on Fifth Street one morning to the corner of Q Street and turned right. Half of the block was occupied by the Lincoln School. It was a three-story wooden building, with two wings that gave it the shape of a double-T connected by a central hall. It was a new building, painted yellow, with a shingled roof that was not like the red tile of the school in Mazatlán. I noticed other differences, none of them very <u>reassuring</u>. We walked up the wide staircase hand in hand and through the door, which closed by itself. A mechanical <u>contraption</u> screwed to the top shut it behind us quietly.

Up to this point the adventure of enrolling me in the school had been carefully rehearsed. Mrs. Dodson had told us how to find it and we had circled it several times on our walks. Friends in the barrio[1] explained that the director was called a principal, and that it was a lady and not a man. They assured

Vocabulary Builder
reassuring (rē ə sho͞or´ iŋ) *adj.* having the effect of restoring confidence

contraption (kən trap´ shən) *n.* device or machine regarded as strange

---

1. barrio (bär´ ē ō) *n.* part of a town or city where most of the people are Hispanic.

us that there was always a person at the school who could speak Spanish.

Exactly as we had been told, there was a sign on the door in both Spanish and English: "Principal." We crossed the hall and entered the office of Miss Nettie Hopley.

Miss Hopley was at a roll-top desk to one side, sitting in a swivel chair that moved on wheels. There was a sofa against the opposite wall, flanked by two windows and a door that opened on a small balcony. Chairs were set around a table and framed pictures hung on the walls of a man with long white hair and another with a sad face and a black beard.

The principal half turned in the swivel chair to look at us over the pinch glasses crossed on the ridge of her nose. To do this she had to duck her head slightly as if she were about to step through a low doorway.

What Miss Hopley said to us we did not know but we saw in her eyes a warm welcome and when she took off her glasses and straightened up she smiled wholeheartedly, like Mrs. Dodson. We were, of course, saying nothing, only catching the friendliness of her voice and the sparkle in her eyes while she said words we did not understand. She signaled us to the table. Almost tiptoeing across the office, I maneuvered myself to keep my mother between me and the gringo lady. In a matter of seconds I had to decide whether she was a possible friend or a menace.[2] We sat down.

Then Miss Hopley did a <u>formidable</u> thing. She stood up. Had she been standing when we entered she would have seemed tall. But rising from her chair she soared. And what she carried up and up with her was a buxom superstructure,[3] firm shoulders, a straight sharp nose, full cheeks slightly molded by a curved line along the nostrils, thin lips that moved like steel springs, and a high forehead topped by hair gathered in a bun. Miss Hopley was not a giant in body but when she mobilized[4] it to a standing position she seemed a match for giants. I decided I liked her.

She strode to a door in the far corner of the office, opened it and called a name. A boy of about ten years appeared in the doorway. He sat down at one end of the table. He was brown like us, a plump kid with shiny black hair combed straight back, neat, cool, and faintly obnoxious.

---

2. **menace** (men´ əs) *n.* danger; threat.
3. **buxom superstructure** full figure.
4. **mobilized** (mō´ bə līzd´) *v.* put into motion.

Literary Analysis
Nonfiction Who is the narrator of this work? How can you tell?

Vocabulary Builder
formidable (fôr´ mə də bəl) *adj.* impressive

**Reading Check**

Where do the narrator and his mother go?

▲ Critical Viewing
How does the
classroom in this
photograph compare
with the narrator's
impressions of
school? [Compare
and Contrast]

Miss Hopley joined us with a large book and some papers in her hand. She, too, sat down and the questions and answers began by way of our interpreter. My name was Ernesto. My mother's name was Henriqueta. My birth certificate was in San Blas. Here was my last report card from the Escuela Municipal Numero 3 para Varones of Mazatlán,[5] and so forth. Miss Hopley put things down in the book and my mother signed a card.

As long as the questions continued, Doña[6] Henriqueta could stay and I was secure. Now that they were over, Miss Hopley saw her to the door, dismissed our interpreter and without further ado took me by the hand and strode down the hall to Miss Ryan's first grade. Miss Ryan took me to a seat at the front of the room, into which I shrank—the better to survey her. She was, to skinny, somewhat runty me, of a withering height when she patrolled the class. And when I least

---

5. Escuela Municipal Numero 3 para Varones of Mazatlán (es kwä lä mōō nē sē päl′ nōō′ me rō trās pä′ rä bä rō′ nes mä sät län′) Municipal School Number 3 for Boys of Mazatlán.
6. Doña (dō′ nyä) Spanish title of respect meaning "lady" or "madam."

expected it, there she was, crouching by my desk, her blond radiant face level with mine, her voice patiently maneuvering me over the awful idiocies of the English language.

During the next few weeks Miss Ryan overcame my fears of tall, energetic teachers as she bent over my desk to help me with a word in the pre-primer. Step by step, she loosened me and my classmates from the safe anchorage of the desks for recitations at the blackboard and consultations at her desk. Frequently she burst into happy announcements to the whole class. "Ito can read a sentence," and small Japanese Ito, squint-eyed and shy, slowly read aloud while the class listened in wonder: "Come, Skipper, come. Come and run." The Korean, Portuguese, Italian, and Polish first graders had similar moments of glory, no less shining than mine the day I conquered "butterfly," which I had been persistently pronouncing in standard Spanish as boo-ter-flee. "Children," Miss Ryan called for attention. "Ernesto has learned how to pronounce *butterfly*!" And I proved it with a perfect imitation of Miss Ryan. From that celebrated success, I was soon able to match Ito's progress as a sentence reader with "Come, butterfly, come fly with me."

Like Ito and several other first graders who did not know English, I received private lessons from Miss Ryan in the closet, a narrow hall off the classroom with a door at each end. Next to one of these doors Miss Ryan placed a large chair for herself and a small one for me. Keeping an eye on the class through the open door she read with me about sheep in the meadow and a frightened chicken going to see the king, coaching me out of my phonetic ruts in words like *pasture, bow-wow-wow, hay,* and *pretty,* which to my Mexican ear and eye had so many unnecessary sounds and letters. She made me watch her lips and then close my eyes as she repeated words I found hard to read. When we came to know each other better, I tried interrupting to tell Miss Ryan how we said it in Spanish. It didn't work. She only said "oh" and went on with *pasture, bow-wow-wow,* and *pretty.* It was as if in that closet we were both discovering together the secrets of the English language and grieving together over the tragedies of Bo-Peep. The main reason I was graduated with honors from the first grade was that I had fallen in love with Miss Ryan. Her radiant, no-nonsense character made us either afraid not to love her or love her so we would not be afraid, I am not sure

Literary Analysis
Nonfiction What details in this section help you appreciate the importance of the author's actual experience?

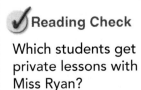

Reading Check

Which students get private lessons with Miss Ryan?

which. It was not only that we sensed she was with it, but also that she was with us. Like the first grade, the rest of the Lincoln School was a sampling of the lower part of town where many races made their home. My pals in the second grade were Kazushi, whose parents spoke only Japanese; Matti, a skinny Italian boy; and Manuel, a fat Portuguese who would never get into a fight but wrestled you to the ground and just sat on you. Our assortment of nationalities included Koreans, Yugoslavs, Poles, Irish, and home-grown Americans.

At Lincoln, making us into Americans did not mean scrubbing away what made us originally foreign. The teachers called us as our parents did, or as close as they could pronounce our names in Spanish or Japanese. No one was ever scolded or punished for speaking in his native tongue on the playground. Matti told the class about his mother's down quilt, which she had made in Italy with the fine feathers of a thousand geese. Encarnación acted out how boys learned to fish in the Philippines. I astounded the third grade with the story of my travels on a stagecoach, which nobody else in the class had seen except in the museum at Sutter's Fort. After a visit to the Crocker Art Gallery and its collection of heroic paintings of the golden age of California, someone showed a silk scroll with a Chinese painting. Miss Hopley herself had a way of expressing wonder over these matters before a class, her eyes wide open until they popped slightly. It was easy for me to feel that becoming a proud American, as she said we should, did not mean feeling ashamed of being a Mexican.

Literary Analysis
Nonfiction What type of details in this paragraph tell about each character in the narrative?

Thinking About the Selection

1. **Respond:** What could you do to help a newcomer feel welcome and secure at your school?

2. **(a) Recall:** Why is Galarza afraid of Miss Ryan at first? **(b) Interpret:** What does Galarza mean when he says Miss Ryan "was with it" and "with us"?

3. **(a) Recall:** In what ways does Miss Ryan help Galarza overcome his fears of his new teacher and class? **(b) Speculate:** In what ways were the seeds of Galarza's success planted in the first grade?

4. **Analyze:** What experiences in Lincoln School help Galarza realize his dream of "becoming a proud American"?

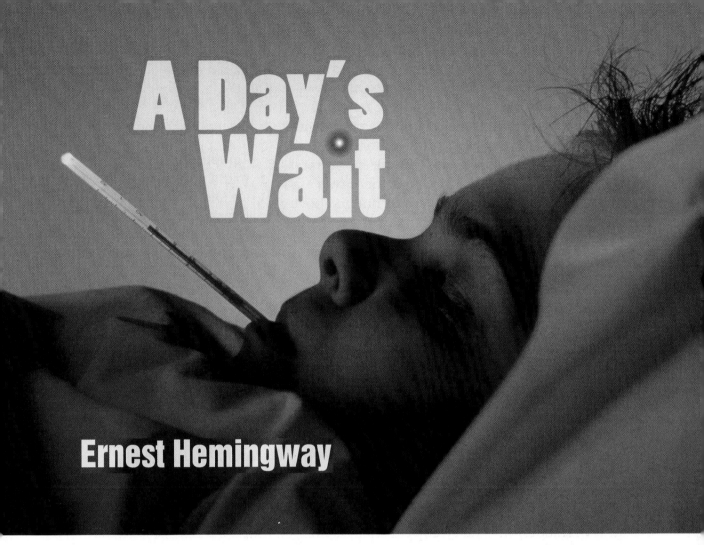

A Day's Wait

Ernest Hemingway

He came into the room to shut the windows while we were still in bed and I saw he looked ill. He was shivering, his face was white, and he walked slowly as though it ached to move.

"What's the matter, Schatz[1]?"

"I've got a headache."

"You better go back to bed."

"No. I'm all right."

"You go to bed. I'll see you when I'm dressed."

But when I came downstairs he was dressed, sitting by the fire, looking a very sick and miserable boy of nine years. When I put my hand on his forehead I knew he had a fever.

"You go up to bed," I said, "you're sick."

"I'm all right," he said.

When the doctor came he took the boy's temperature.

"What is it?" I asked him.

"One hundred and two."

---

1. **Schatz** (shäts) German term of affection, used here as a loving nickname.

▲ Critical Viewing
Describe how you think the boy in this picture might feel. [Connect]

Downstairs, the doctor left three different medicines in different colored capsules with instructions for giving them. One was to bring down the fever, another a purgative, the third to overcome an acid condition. The germs of influenza can only exist in an acid condition, he explained. He seemed to know all about influenza and said there was nothing to worry about if the fever did not go above one hundred and four degrees. This was a light <u>epidemic</u> of flu and there was no danger if you avoided pneumonia.

Back in the room I wrote the boy's temperature down and made a note of the time to give the various capsules.

"Do you want me to read to you?"

"All right. If you want to," said the boy. His face was very white and there were dark areas under his eyes. He lay still in the bed and seemed very detached from what was going on.

I read aloud from Howard Pyle's *Book of Pirates*; but I could see he was not following what I was reading.

"How do you feel, Schatz?" I asked him.

"Just the same, so far," he said.

I sat at the foot of the bed and read to myself while I waited for it to be time to give another capsule. It would have been natural for him to go to sleep, but when I looked up he was looking at the foot of the bed, looking very strangely.

"Why don't you try to go to sleep? I'll wake you up for the medicine."

"I'd rather stay awake."

After a while he said to me, "You don't have to stay in here with me, Papa, if it bothers you."

"It doesn't bother me."

"No. I mean you don't have to stay if it's going to bother you."

I thought perhaps he was a little light-headed and after giving him the prescribed capsules at eleven o'clock I went out for a while. It was a bright, cold day, the ground covered with a sleet that had frozen so that it seemed as if all the bare trees, the bushes, the

Vocabulary Builder
epidemic (ep′ ə dem′ ik) *n.* outbreak of a contagious disease

cut brush and all the grass and the bare ground had been varnished with ice. I took the young Irish setter for a little walk up the road and along a frozen creek, but it was difficult to stand or walk on the glassy surface and the red dog slipped and slithered and I fell twice, hard, once dropping my gun and having it slide away over the ice.

We <u>flushed</u> a covey of quail under a high clay bank with overhanging brush and I killed two as they went out of sight over the top of the bank. Some of the covey lit in trees but most of them scattered into brush piles and it was necessary to jump on the ice-coated mounds of brush several times before they would flush. Coming out while you were poised unsteadily on the icy, springy brush they made difficult shooting, and I killed two, missed five, and started back pleased to have found a covey close to the house and happy there were so many left to find on another day.

At the house they said the boy had refused to let anyone come into the room.

"You can't come in," he said. "You mustn't get what I have."

I went up to him and found him in exactly the position I had left him, white-faced, but with the tops of his cheeks flushed by the fever, staring still, as he had stared at the foot of the bed.

I took his temperature.

"What is it?"

"Something like a hundred," I said. It was one hundred and two and four tenths.

"It was a hundred and two," he said.

"Who said so?"

"The doctor."

"Your temperature is all right," I said. "It's nothing to worry about."

"I don't worry," he said, "but I can't keep from thinking."

"Don't think," I said. "Just take it easy."

"I'm taking it easy," he said and looked straight ahead. He was <u>evidently</u> holding tight on to himself about something.

"Take this with water."

"Do you think it will do any good?"

"Of course it will."

I sat down and opened the *Pirate* book and commenced to read, but I could see he was not following, so I stopped.

"About what time do you think I'm going to die?" he asked.

"What?"

Vocabulary Builder
flushed (flusht) *v.* drove from hiding

Literary Analysis
Fiction Who is the narrator of this work? How do you know?

Vocabulary Builder
evidently (ev´ ə dent´ lē) *adv.* clearly; obviously

**Reading Check**

How does the boy know his temperature?

"About how long will it be before I die?"

"You aren't going to die. What's the matter with you?"

"Oh, yes, I am. I heard him say a hundred and two."

"People don't die with a fever of one hundred and two. That's a silly way to talk."

"I know they do. At school in France the boys told me you can't live with forty-four degrees. I've got a hundred and two."

He had been waiting to die all day, ever since nine o'clock in the morning.

"You poor Schatz," I said. "Poor old Schatz. It's like miles and kilometers. You aren't going to die. That's a different thermometer. On that thermometer thirty-seven is normal. On this kind it's ninety-eight."

"Are you sure?"

"Absolutely," I said. "It's like miles and kilometers. You know, like how many kilometers we make when we do seventy miles in the car?"

"Oh," he said.

But his gaze at the foot of the bed relaxed slowly. The hold over himself relaxed too, finally, and the next day it was very slack and he cried very easily at little things that were of no importance.

Literary Analysis
Fiction What does the boy's question reveal about his behavior throughout the story?

Thinking About the Selection

1. **Respond:** Do you find the boy's actions brave, touching, or silly? Explain your answer.

2. **(a) Recall:** Why does the boy tell his father to leave the sick-room? **(b) Infer:** What does this reveal about the boy?

3. **(a) Recall:** Why does the boy think he will die? **(b) Interpret:** What is the meaning of the story's title?

4. **(a) Analyze:** Which of the boy's words and actions give clues that he believes something terrible is wrong? **(b) Evaluate:** Do you think the story is about the boy's bravery or about the boy's fear? Explain. **(c) Speculate:** What do you think would have happened if the boy had shared his fears with his father earlier in the day?

Apply the Skills

from *Barrio Boy* • *A Day's Wait*

Comparing Fiction and Nonfiction

1. **(a)** For each selection, tell whether the narrator and events are real or imagined. **(b)** Based on your answer, what rules about truth and accuracy did each writer follow for writing these selections?

2. Complete a chart like the one shown to help you analyze one character in each story.

Character	Detail	Fiction or Nonfiction?
The boy in "A Day's Wait"		
Miss Ryan in *Barrio Boy*		

3. **(a)** How might "A Day's Wait" be different if it were nonfiction? **(b)** How might *Barrio Boy* change if it were fiction?

Writing to Compare Literary Works

Compare and contrast the narrators of *Barrio Boy* and "A Day's Wait." In a brief essay, discuss how the fictional narrator and the nonfiction author present the events in each work. Use these questions to get started:

- Which work includes more personal details about the narrator?
- How is dialogue used in each work?
- Do the narrator's thoughts and actions build toward a specific theme or insight?
- Which story features a narrator who is central to the narrative's action?

Vocabulary Builder

For each item below, write a sentence that correctly uses the word groups indicated.

1. flushed; bats from a cave
2. contraption; Grandfather
3. formidable; athlete
4. epidemic; community
5. reassuring; panic
6. evidently; cancelled

QuickReview

Fiction: writing that tells about imaginary characters and events

Nonfiction: writing that presents and explains ideas or that tells about real people, places, objects, or events

Go Online
Assessment
For: Self-test
Visit: www.PHSchool.com
Web Code: ema-6107

Reading

Directions: *Questions 1–5 are based on the following selection.*

In 1922, an Egyptologist named Howard Carter discovered a buried staircase that led to a <u>sealed</u> tomb. When the tomb was opened, Carter found fantastic treasures—items made of gold, alabaster, ebony, and precious stones. The <u>mummified</u> body of King Tutankhamen, the 18-year-old Egyptian boy king, had been buried with jewelry and other items that <u>indicated</u> his importance. He had clearly been of <u>noble</u> birth.

1. **In the context of this selection, the word *sealed* means**
   A open.
   B missing.
   C tightly closed.
   D damp.

2. **What context clue helps you clarify the meaning of *sealed?***
   A a buried staircase
   B When the tomb was opened
   C Howard Carter discovered a buried staircase
   D Carter found fantastic treasures

3. **In the selection, which word does not have context clues to reveal its meaning?**
   A fantastic
   B mummified
   C tomb
   D sealed

4. **In the selection, the word *indicated* means**
   A minimized.
   B diminished.
   C buried.
   D pointed out.

5. **In the selection, which word does not help you understand the significance of *alabaster?***
   A gold
   B treasures
   C precious
   D opened

6. **Which phrase in the selection identifies King Tutankhamen?**
   A in 1992
   B an Egyptologist
   C found fantastic treasures
   D Egyptian boy king

Vocabulary

Directions: *Choose the word that best completes each of the following sentences.*

7. Before we allow you to vote, we will have to_____your name and address.
   A   verify
   B   significance
   C   context
   D   clarify

8. What is the_____ of lighting a candle in the window?
   A   verify
   B   significance
   C   context
   D   reveal

9. The man took off his mask to_____his true identity.
   A   verify
   B   clarify
   C   context
   D   reveal

10. Please,_____your answer by giving specific examples.
    A   verify
    B   clarify
    C   context
    D   reveal

11. Looking at the_____will help you define that word.
    A   verify
    B   clarify
    C   context
    D   reveal

Directions: *Based on your knowledge of word origins, choose the most likely meaning for each word.*

12. **verifiable**
    A   able to be proven
    B   dependable
    C   false
    D   unbelievable

13. **revelation**
    A   belief
    B   question
    C   realization
    D   institution

14. **verity**
    A   exactly as said
    B   conforming to the truth
    C   acting with someone
    D   displaying signs of distrust

15. **significant**
    A   something that is important
    B   something that is conveyed
    C   something that is in writing
    D   something that is displayed

Description: Descriptive Essay

Descriptive language engages your attention by creating vivid images that help you "see" the action as it unfolds. **A descriptive essay** creates a picture of a person, place, thing, or event. Follow the steps outlined in this workshop to write your own descriptive essay.

Assignment Write a descriptive essay about a place or an event that is meaningful to you.

What to Include Your descriptive essay should feature the following elements:
- vivid sensory details to appeal to the five senses
- a main impression supported by each detail
- clear, consistent organization
- links between details and the feelings or thoughts they inspire
- effective transitions
- error-free writing, including correct spelling of plural nouns

To preview the criteria on which your descriptive essay may be judged, see the rubric on page 86.

Prewriting

Choosing Your Topic

Make a timeline. To choose a place or event that has special meaning for you, make a timeline of the important happenings in your life. Jot down ideas about a few of these experiences. Then, choose an event or a place associated with it as the topic of your description.

Gathering Details

Cubing to gather details. Follow these steps to "cube" your subject and uncover information that will bring your description to life:

1. **Describe it.** Explain how it looks, sounds, feels, tastes, or smells.
2. **Associate it.** List feelings or stories it calls to mind.
3. **Apply it.** Show how your topic can be used.
4. **Analyze it.** Divide it into parts.
5. **Compare and contrast it.** Compare it with a related subject.
6. **Argue for or against it.** Show its good and bad points.

Using the Form

You may use description in almost any form of writing, including
- short stories
- poems
- journals
- travel brochures

Work in Progress

Review the work you did on pages 15, 19, 45, and 67.

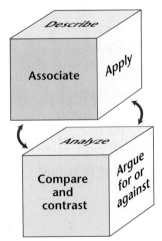

Drafting

Shaping Your Writing

Organize your ideas. Present your details in a pattern that will make sense to readers. Use a chart like the one shown to select a general organizational plan for your essay. You may use elements of more than one plan as you write. For example, you may use chronological order as your *overall*

Spatial Order	If you are writing about a place or object, use a form of spatial order, such as near to far, left to right, front to back, or bottom to top.
Chronological Order	If you are describing an event, present details in the order they happen.
Order of Importance	If you are describing to show the significance of your subject, begin with your least important details and build up to the most important.

organizational plan to describe an event. However, you may use elements of spatial order to describe the setting.

Providing Elaboration

Elaborate to create a main impression. Set a mood or use an idea to unify your essay. For example, you might create a feeling of suspense, a calm atmosphere, or a flurry of activity. Focus on including sensory details that strengthen this overall impression.

Revising

Revising for organization and transition. Review your draft to find places to clarify the organization of your composition. Add transition words and phrases to show the connection between details and ideas.

To read the complete student model, see page 85.

Student Model: Revising for Organization and Transition

During the rest of the season, if

~~If~~ you continue to walk, you will experience new additions to

the spring line-up. ~~You'll~~ start to smell the earth. As the

Not long after you've heard the peepers, you'll

ground warms up, it gives off a soft, distinct "spring-like"

smell.

> These additions reinforce the links between sentences.

Revise word choice. Highlight vague or empty adjectives like *nice* and *good*, which do not add information to your description. Replace them with precise words that tell how or why your subject is *nice* or *good*.

> **Vague Adjective:** A *bad* wind blew.
> **Precise Adjective:** A *ferocious* wind blew.

Integrating Grammar Skills

Revising Incorrect Forms of Plural Nouns

The plural form of a noun indicates that more than one person, place, or thing is being named. Plural forms are either regular or irregular.

Identifying Incorrect Forms of Plural Nouns To identify and fix incorrect forms of plural nouns you must first know how to create plural nouns. Regular nouns form their plurals by adding -s or -es.

Prentice Hall Writing and Grammar Connection: Chapter 24, Section 1

Regular Plural Nouns

Singular:	bus	monkey	radio
Plural:	bus**es**	monkey**s**	radio**s**

Sometimes the singular and plural forms of a noun are the same.

Irregular Plural Nouns

Singular: ox	goose	woman	mouse	deer	clothes
Plural: oxen	geese	women	mice	deer	clothes

Fixing Incorrect Forms of Plural Nouns To fix an incorrect form of a plural noun, verify the correct spelling using one of these methods:

1. **Review the rules for forming regular plural nouns.** First, write the singular form of the noun and circle the last two letters. Then, find the corresponding rule in the chart.

Forming Regular Plural Nouns	
Word Ending	**Rule**
-o or -y preceded by a vowel -ff	Add -s
-s, -ss, -x, -z, -zz, -sh, -ch -o preceded by a consonant	Add -es (exceptions: solo and other musical terms)
-y preceded by a consonant	Change y to i and add -es
-fe	Change f to v and add -es
-f	Add s OR Change f to v and add -es

2. **Use a dictionary to look up correct spelling.**

Apply It to Your Editing

Choose two paragraphs in your draft and circle each plural noun. If the spelling is faulty, fix it using one of the methods described.

Student Model: Charity Jackson, Fort Wayne, IN

Spring Into Spring

Spring is the perfect time to get outdoors and get active. The spring season brings the freshness of a new beginning. If you've been cooped up all winter, the perfect start to spring is a brisk walk. If you walk during the day, you will feel the sunshine warming up the pavement; a breeze may ruffle your hair; you'll hear the songs of birds that you'd almost forgotten about over the winter. If you walk in the early evening, in the purple-gray dusk, you may even hear the "spring peepers," little frogs that become suddenly vocal around April. You might mistake them for crickets, because they have that same high-pitched monotonous chirping sound, but peepers are more shrill and persistent. Any one of these sensations by itself is enough to raise a little hope that winter is over. If you're lucky enough to experience them all at once on your first spring walk, you'll feel uplifted and energized by the knowledge that soon that stuffy old winter coat can be put in storage for many months.

During the rest of the season, if you continue to walk, you will experience new additions to the spring line-up. Not long after you've heard the peepers, you'll start to smell the earth. As the ground warms up, it gives off a soft, distinct "spring-like" smell. The scent of warm earth says "spring" the way the scent of pine says "winter." Because the ground is warming up, the smell of flowers can't be far behind! The first flowers of spring, though, are more a treat for the eyes than the nose. The brilliant yellow forsythia don't have much of an aroma, but they're so bright, they don't really need one to announce their arrival! The shy hyacinth, which blooms shortly after, is not as easily spotted, but your nose will tell you that the strong perfume in the air means a hyacinth is hiding somewhere nearby. Neighbors working their gardens—some of whom you may not have seen all winter—will call a friendly hello. Everyone seems friendlier at the beginning of spring.

Later in the season, when you begin to hear the growl and grumble of lawnmowers around the neighborhood, you'll know that spring has done its work. When the grass grows tall enough to need mowing, it's time to start thinking about those summer sensations!

Sensory details about sunshine, breezes, birdsongs, and the colors of dusk appeal to the senses of touch, hearing, and sight.

Charity reinforces the overall impression of lightness and energy to contrast with the stuffy winter coat.

The description is organized in time order—new details are introduced in the order in which they appear as spring progresses.

Here, and at various points in the essay, Charity includes her feelings and reactions to what is being described.

Transitions that indicate time help readers follow the chronological organization of the description.

Editing and Proofreading

Proofread your essay to eliminate errors in grammar, spelling, or punctuation.

Focus on Spelling: Use a dictionary to confirm the spelling of troublesome words in your essay. If you used a word-processor to draft, use the spell-check function to search for errors. Then, review each word because spell-check will not catch homophones such as *there* and *their*—words that are spelled correctly but have several correct spellings and meanings.

Publishing and Presenting

Consider one of the following ways to share your writing:

Tape-record your essay. Read your description aloud on tape. Add sound effects or background music that reinforces the main impression of your description. Play the tape for a group of classmates.

Post your composition. Put your description on a class bulletin board or post it on a school Web site. Add photos or art if possible.

Reflecting on Your Writing

Writer's Journal Jot down your thoughts about what you learned from writing a descriptive essay. Begin by answering these questions:

- Which strategy did you find most useful for creating vivid details? Explain.
- As you described your subject, what associations did you find surprising?

Prentice Hall Writing and Grammar Connection: Chapter 6

Rubric for Self-Assessment

To assess your descriptive essay, use the following rubric:

Criteria	Rating Scale *not very* *very*
Focus: How clear is the main impression?	1 2 3 4 5
Organization: How clear and consistent is the organization?	1 2 3 4 5
Support/Elaboration: How effectively do you use sensory details in your description?	1 2 3 4 5
Style: How effective are your transitions?	1 2 3 4 5
Conventions: How correct is your grammar, especially your use of plural nouns?	1 2 3 4 5

Unit 1
Part 2
Author's Purpose

Skills You Will Learn

Reading Skill: *Recognize Details That Indicate Author's Purpose*
Literary Analysis: *Setting*

Reading Skill: *Use Background Information to Recognize Author's Purpose*
Literary Analysis: *Historical Context*

Reading Skill: *Identify Purpose of a Web Site*

Literary Analysis: *Comparing Authors' Purposes*

Literature You Will Read

Reading: Author's Purpose

▶ An **author's purpose** is his or her main reason for writing.

Skills and Strategies You Will Learn in Part 2
In Part 2 you will learn
- to **recognize details that indicate the author's purpose.** (p. 90)
- to **use background information to determine the author's purpose.** (p. 116)
- to **identify the purpose** of a Web site. (p. 138)

Using the Skills and Strategies in Part 2
In this part you will learn to recognize the **author's purpose** or reason for writing. The author's purpose influences what the author says and how he or she says it. You will practice using text clues and background knowledge to determine the author's reasons for writing.

The chart gives you some examples of clues that help to determine the author's purpose.

Author's Purpose	Clues
To persuade	Strong language, favors one side of an issue
To entertain	Silly, humorous, suspenseful, exciting details
To inform	Facts and details
To reflect on an experience	Descriptions, comments by the writer

Academic Vocabulary: Words for Discussing Author's Purpose

The following words will help you write and talk about author's purpose as you read the selections in this unit.

Word	Definition	Example Sentence
previous *adj.*	occurring before in time or order	The author's *previous* works were more persuasive.
recall *v.*	to call back; remember	Can you *recall* the story details?
background *n.*	a person's experience or knowledge	The author's *background* influences the setting of the story.
establish *v.*	determine; make sure of	Knowing the author's background helped *establish* the author's purpose.
prior *adj.*	coming before in time; earlier	*Prior* to reading the story, we learned about the author.

Vocabulary Skills: Prefixes

> A **prefix** is a syllable or group of syllables joined to the beginning of a word to change its meaning or to make a new word.

In Part 2 you will learn

- the prefix *re-* (p. 114)
- the prefix *pre-* (p. 136)

Once you learn to recognize a prefix, you can use its meaning to help you understand and remember the meanings of words that begin with the prefix.

Prefix	Meanings of Prefix	Example
pre-	before, in front, prior to	previous
re-	again, back, undo, answer	recall

Activity Use a dictionary to find two more words with each prefix. Explain how one of the meanings of the prefix can help you understand and remember the meaning of the words you choose.

These skills will help you become a better reader. Practice them with either "All Summer in a Day" (p. 92) or "Suzy and Leah" (p. 103).

Reading Skill

Fiction writers may write for a variety of **purposes.** They may wish to entertain, to teach, to call to action, or to reflect on experiences. **Recognizing details that indicate the author's purpose** can give you a rich understanding of a text. As you read, use a chart like the one shown to note details from the story that fit the different possible purposes of the author.

Entertain
Funny details or details that create interest

Teach
Explanations

Reflect
Details that create a mood

Literary Analysis

The **setting** of a story is the time and place of the action. In this example, the details in italics help establish the story's setting:

As *night fell,* the hungry raccoons roamed the *forest* for food.

- In some stories, setting is just a backdrop. The same story events could take place in a completely different setting.
- In other stories, setting is very important. It develops a specific atmosphere or mood in the story. The setting may even relate directly to the story's central conflict or problem.

Vocabulary Builder

All Summer in a Day

- **slackening** (slak´ ən iŋ) *v.* easing; becoming less active (p. 94) *The dying man's strength was slackening.*
- **vital** (vīt´´l) *adj.* extremely important or necessary (p. 96) *Food and water are vital for survival.*
- **tumultuously** (tōō mul´ chōō əs lē) *adv.* noisily and violently (p. 97) *The angry crowd protested tumultuously.*
- **resilient** (ri zil´ yənt) *adj.* springing back into shape (p. 97) *Rubber is a resilient material.*

Suzy and Leah

- **refugee** (ref yōō jē´) *n.* person who flees home or country to seek shelter from war or cruelty (p. 103) *The refugee crossed the border into safety.*
- **porridge** (pôr´ ij) *n.* soft food made of cereal boiled in water or milk (p. 104) *The porridge that we ate for breakfast was hot and filling.*
- **permanent** (pʉr´ mə nənt) *adj.* lasting for all time (p. 108) *His accident left a permanent scar.*

Build Understanding • *All Summer in a Day*

Background

Venus "All Summer in a Day" is set on Venus, the second planet from the sun. Today, we know that Venus has a surface temperature of almost 900° Fahrenheit. In 1950, when Ray Bradbury wrote this story, some scientists believed that the clouds of Venus concealed a watery world. That information may have led Bradbury to create a setting of soggy jungles and constant rain.

Connecting to the Literature

Reading/Writing Connection In "All Summer in a Day," rain has fallen for seven years straight. Give three reasons to explain whether or not you could live in such a climate. Use at least three of the following words: *benefit, survive, require, adjust.*

Meet the Author

Ray **Bradbury** (b. 1920)

As a boy, Ray Bradbury loved magicians, circuses, and science-fiction stories. He began writing his own imaginative tales and by age seventeen had his first story published in a magazine called *Imagination!*

A Science-Fiction Wonder In 1950, Bradbury won fame for his book of science-fiction stories called *The Martian Chronicles.* One story describes how a group of Earthlings struggle on the rainy world of Venus. Bradbury began to wonder how a child might react to the sun's brief appearance on Venus. Four years later, he answered his own question by writing "All Summer in a Day."

Fast Facts

▶ Many of Bradbury's stories have been adapted for the television series *The Twilight Zone.*

▶ He has served as a consultant to the Disney Company, the New York World's Fair, and a number of architects.

Go **Online**
Author Link

For: More about the author
Visit: www.PHSchool.com
Web Code: eme-9108

All Summer in a Day

Ray Bradbury

Nonfiction

Ready?"

"Ready."

"Now?"

"Soon."

"Do the scientists really know? Will it happen today, will it?"

"Look, look; see for yourself!"

The children pressed to each other like so many roses, so many weeds, intermixed, peering out for a look at the hidden sun.

It rained.

It had been raining for seven years; thousands upon thousands of days compounded and filled from one end to the other with rain, with the drum and gush of water, with the sweet crystal fall of showers and the concussion of storms so heavy they were tidal waves come over the islands. A thousand forests had been crushed under the rain and grown up a thousand times to be crushed again. And this was the way life was forever on the planet Venus and this was the schoolroom of the children of the rocket men and women who had come to a raining world to set up civilization and live out their lives.

"It's stopping, it's stopping!"

"Yes, yes!"

Margot stood apart from them, from these children who could never remember a time when there wasn't rain and rain and rain. They were all nine years old, and if there had been a day, seven years ago, when the sun came out for an hour and showed its face to the stunned world, they could not recall. Sometimes, at night, she heard them stir, in remembrance, and she knew they were dreaming and remembering gold or a yellow crayon or a coin large enough to buy the world with. She knew they thought they remembered a warmness, like a blushing in the face, in the body, in the arms and legs and trembling hands. But then they always awoke to the tatting drum, the endless shaking down of clear bead necklaces upon the roof, the walk, the gardens, the forests, and their dreams were gone.

All day yesterday they had read in class about the sun. About how like a lemon it was, and how hot. And they had written small stories or essays or poems about it:

I think the sun is a flower,

That blooms for just one hour.

◀ **Critical Viewing**
Based on the emotion this image conveys, do you expect this story to be happy or sad? **[Predict]**

Reading Skill
Author's Purpose
List three details Bradbury provides to describe conditions on the Venus that he imagines.

Literary Analysis
Setting How have seven years of constant rain affected the children?

Reading Check

What do the children hope will happen today?

That was Margot's poem, read in a quiet voice in the still classroom while the rain was falling outside.

"Aw, you didn't write that!" protested one of the boys.

"I did," said Margot. "I did."

"William!" said the teacher.

But that was yesterday. Now the rain was <u>slackening</u>, and the children were crushed in the great thick windows.

"Where's teacher?"

"She'll be back."

"She'd better hurry, we'll miss it!"

They turned on themselves, like a feverish wheel, all fumbling spokes.

Margot stood alone. She was a very frail girl who looked as if she had been lost in the rain for years and the rain had washed out the blue from her eyes and the red from her mouth and the yellow from her hair. She was an old photograph dusted from an album, whitened away, and if she spoke at all her voice would be a ghost. Now she stood, separate, staring at the rain and the loud wet world beyond the huge glass.

"What're you looking at?" said William.

Margot said nothing.

"Speak when you're spoken to." He gave her a shove. But she did not move; rather she let herself be moved only by him and nothing else.

▲ Critical Viewing
What aspects of the story's setting do you see in this picture? [Connect]

Vocabulary Builder
slackening (slak´ ən iŋ) v. easing; becoming less active

They edged away from her, they would not look at her. She felt them go away. And this was because she would play no games with them in the echoing tunnels of the underground city. If they tagged her and ran, she stood blinking after them and did not follow. When the class sang songs about happiness and life and games her lips barely moved. Only when they sang about the sun and the summer did her lips move as she watched the drenched windows.

And then, of course, the biggest crime of all was that she had come here only five years ago from Earth, and she remembered the sun and the way the sun was and the sky was when she was four in Ohio. And they, they had been on Venus all their lives, and they had been only two years old when last the sun came out and had long since forgotten the color and heat of it and the way it really was. But Margot remembered.

"It's like a penny," she said once, eyes closed.

"No, it's not!" the children cried.

"It's like a fire," she said, "in the stove."

"You're lying, you don't remember!" cried the children.

But she remembered and stood quietly apart from all of them and watched the patterning windows. And once, a month ago, she had refused to shower in the school shower rooms, had clutched her hands to her ears and over her head, screaming the water mustn't touch her head. So after that,

Literary Analysis
Setting How was Margot's former home on Earth different from her home on Venus?

Reading Check

What is the difference between Margot and the other children?

dimly, dimly, she sensed it, she was different and they knew her difference and kept away.

There was talk that her father and mother were taking her back to Earth next year; it seemed <u>vital</u> to her that they do so, though it would mean the loss of thousands of dollars to her family. And so, the children hated her for all these reasons of big and little consequence. They hated her pale snow face, her waiting silence, her thinness, and her possible future.

"Get away!" The boy gave her another push. "What're you waiting for?"

Then, for the first time, she turned and looked at him. And what she was waiting for was in her eyes.

"Well, don't wait around here!" cried the boy savagely. "You won't see nothing!"

Her lips moved.

"Nothing!" he cried. "It was all a joke, wasn't it?" He turned to the other children. "Nothing's happening today. Is it?"

They all blinked at him and then, understanding, laughed and shook their heads. "Nothing, nothing!"

"Oh, but," Margot whispered, her eyes helpless. "But this is the day, the scientists predict, they say, they know, the sun . . ."

"All a joke!" said the boy, and seized her roughly. "Hey, everyone, let's put her in a closet before teacher comes!"

"No," said Margot, falling back.

They surged[1] about her, caught her up and bore her, protesting, and then pleading, and then crying, back into a tunnel, a room, a closet, where they slammed and locked the door. They stood looking at the door and saw it tremble from her beating and throwing herself against it. They heard her muffled cries. Then, smiling, they turned and went out and back down the tunnel, just as the teacher arrived.

"Ready, children?" She glanced at her watch.

---

1. surged (sʉrjd) *v.* moved in a violent swelling motion.

"Yes!" said everyone.

"Are we all here?"

"Yes!"

The rain slackened still more.

They crowded to the huge door.

The rain stopped.

It was as if, in the midst of a film concerning an avalanche, a tornado, a hurricane, a volcanic eruption, something had, first, gone wrong with the sound apparatus, thus muffling and finally cutting off all noise, all of the blasts and repercussions and thunders, and then, second, ripped the film from the projector and inserted in its place a peaceful tropical slide which did not move or tremor. The world ground to a standstill. The silence was so immense and unbelievable that you felt your ears had been stuffed or you had lost your hearing altogether. The children put their hands to their ears. They stood apart. The door slid back and the smell of the silent, waiting world came in to them.

The sun came out.

It was the color of flaming bronze and it was very large. And the sky around it was a blazing blue tile color. And the jungle burned with sunlight as the children, released from their spell, rushed out, yelling, into the springtime.

"Now, don't go too far," called the teacher after them. "You've only two hours, you know. You wouldn't want to get caught out!"

But they were running and turning their faces up to the sky and feeling the sun on their cheeks like a warm iron; they were taking off their jackets and letting the sun burn their arms.

"Oh, it's better than the sun lamps, isn't it?"

"Much, much better!"

They stopped running and stood in the great jungle that covered Venus, that grew and never stopped growing, tumultuously, even as you watched it. It was a nest of octopi, clustering up great arms of fleshlike weed, wavering, flowering in this brief spring. It was the color of rubber and ash, this jungle, from the many years without sun. It was the color of stones and white cheeses and ink, and it was the color of the moon.

The children lay out, laughing, on the jungle mattress, and heard it sigh and squeak under them, resilient and alive. They

Reading Skill
Author's Purpose
How do the details in this paragraph affect your response to the story?

Vocabulary Builder
tumultuously (too mul′choo əs lē) *adv.* noisily and violently

resilient (ri zil′yənt) *adj.* springing back into shape

Reading Check

Why are the children excited about the sunshine?

ran among the trees, they slipped and fell, they pushed each other, they played hide-and-seek and tag, but most of all they squinted at the sun until tears ran down their faces, they put their hands up to that yellowness and that amazing blueness and they breathed of the fresh, fresh air and listened and listened to the silence which suspended them in a blessed sea of no sound and no motion. They looked at everything and savored everything. Then, wildly, like animals escaped from their caves, they ran and ran in shouting circles. They ran for an hour and did not stop running.

And then—

In the midst of their running one of the girls wailed.

Everyone stopped.

The girl, standing in the open, held out her hand.

"Oh, look, look," she said, trembling.

They came slowly to look at her opened palm.

In the center of it, cupped and huge, was a single raindrop.

She began to cry, looking at it.

▲ **Critical Viewing**
Do you think this picture illustrates emotions that the children felt while playing outside? Why or why not?
[Connect]

They glanced quietly at the sky.

"Oh, Oh."

A few cold drops fell on their noses and their cheeks and their mouths. The sun faded behind a stir of mist. A wind blew cool around them. They turned and started to walk back toward the underground house, their hands at their sides, their smiles vanishing away.

A boom of thunder startled them and like leaves before a new hurricane, they tumbled upon each other and ran. Lightning struck ten miles away, five miles away, a mile, a half mile. The sky darkened into midnight in a flash.

They stood in the doorway of the underground for a moment until it was raining hard. Then they closed the door and heard the gigantic sound of the rain falling in tons and avalanches, everywhere and forever.

"Will it be seven more years?"

"Yes. Seven."

Then one of them gave a little cry.

"Margot!"

"What?"

"She's still in the closet where we locked her."

"Margot."

They stood as if someone had driven them, like so many stakes, into the floor. They looked at each other and then looked away. They glanced out at the world that was raining now and raining and raining steadily. They could not meet each other's glances. Their faces were solemn and pale. They looked at their hands and feet, their faces down.

"Margot."

One of the girls said, "Well . . .?"

No one moved.

"Go on," whispered the girl.

They walked slowly down the hall in the sound of cold rain. They turned through the doorway to the room in the sound of the storm and thunder, lightning on their faces, blue and terrible. They walked over to the closet door slowly and stood by it.

Behind the closet door was only silence.

They unlocked the door, even more slowly, and let Margot out.

Literary Analysis
Setting How does the change in the weather affect the children's mood?

Reading Skill
Author's Purpose What details here help to reveal the author's purpose? Explain.

Apply the Skills

All Summer in a Day

Thinking About the Selection

1. **Respond:** What is your reaction to the way the other children treat Margot? Why?
2. **(a) Recall:** How does Margot know what the sun is like?
   (b) Infer: Why do the children reject her description of it?
3. **(a) Recall:** Why do the children want the teacher to hurry back to the classroom at the beginning of the story?
   (b) Infer: Who is the "leader" of the class when the teacher is out of the room? **(c) Draw Conclusions:** Why do the children go along with the prank that is played on Margot?
4. **(a) Recall:** How do the children react when they realize that Margot missed the sun because of their prank? **(b) Draw Conclusions:** Why do you think they react as they do?
   (c) Generalize: What do the children learn from their experiences?
5. **(a) Speculate:** How do you think Margot will respond to the children after the incident? **(b) Support:** Why do you think so? **(c) Discuss:** In a small group, discuss your responses. As a group, choose one answer to share with the class.

Reading Skill

6. What are two things the author might have wished to teach his audience?
7. **(a)** Did the author mean to entertain his audience?
   (b) Which details support your answer? Explain.
8. In your own words, what was the author's main **purpose** in writing this story?

Literary Analysis

9. How does the **setting** of this story affect the events that occur?
10. Using a chart like the one shown, give two examples from the story to show how setting affects a character's mood.

Setting	Character's Mood

QuickReview

Who's Who in the Story

Margot: a girl who once lived on Earth

William: a boy who has always lived on Venus

Go Online
Assessment
For: Self-test
Visit: www.PHSchool.com
Web Code: ema-6108

Author's Purpose: an author's reason for writing

Setting: the time and place of the action

Vocabulary Builder

Practice **Analogies** show relationships between word pairs. Use a word from the "All Summer in a Day" vocabulary list on page 90 to complete each analogy. Your choice should create a word pair whose relationship matches the relationship between the first two words given.

1. *Quickly* is to *rapidly* as *noisily* is to _____.
2. *More* is to *increasing* as *less* is to _____.
3. *Steel* is to *unbreakable* as *rubber* is to _____.
4. *Singing* is to *optional* as *breathing* is to _____.

Writing

Write a **news report** that tells about the day when the sun appeared on Venus. The report should answer the questions *who, what, when, where, why,* and *how.*

- First, list questions that your news report will answer. For example: *When did the sun make its appearance?*
- Answer each question. Use story details to help you.
- Write your report, based on your answers. Present the most important information in your opening paragraph.

For *Grammar, Vocabulary,* and *Assessment,*
see **Build Language Skills,** pages 114–115.

Extend Your Learning

Listening and Speaking In a small group, hold a **discussion** about the message of the story. Use these questions to guide you:
- At the end of the story, did you feel more sorry for Margot or her classmates?
- What did the story teach you?
As a group, identify two lessons readers might learn from the story.

Research and Technology With a group, make an **annotated bibliography** for a report about the planet Venus. Use the Internet or the library to find possible resources. Compile a list of resources, using the MLA format for bibliographies, which you will find on page R25. Then, write a short description of each resource.

Short Story

Background

War Refugee Board "Suzy and Leah" is based on actual events. The United States established the War Refugee Board in January 1944 with the goal of rescuing victims of Nazi persecution from death in German-occupied Europe. In one rescue effort, 982 people from eighteen countries were brought to a refugee camp in Oswego, New York.

Connecting to the Literature

Reading/Writing Connection In "Suzy and Leah," Leah is a European war refugee who has recently come to America. Make a list of three hardships or challenges that you imagine a young person in a new country might face. Use at least three of the following words: *adapt, interpret, participate, communicate*. Making your list will help you appreciate Leah's difficulties in adjusting.

Review

For **Reading Skill, Literary Analysis,** and **Vocabulary Builder,** see page 90.

Meet the Author

Jane **Yolen** (b. 1939)

Jane Yolen's storytelling career began in first grade, when she wrote a class musical about vegetables. Since then, she has written more than two hundred books. "I am a person in love with story and with words," says Yolen. "I wake up, and I have to write."

Finding Inspiration Yolen is never at a loss for ideas. Whenever an idea strikes her, she jots it down and places it in an "idea file" that she keeps. Then, when searching for a new story to write, she simply consults the file. "I don't care whether the story is real or fantastical," she explains. "I tell the story that needs to be told."

A Personal Interest Although Yolen is known primarily for her fantasy stories, her Jewish heritage inspired her to write "Suzy and Leah," the story of a Holocaust survivor. Yolen wrote about the Holocaust so that her own children could understand and remember what happened to Jews in Europe during World War II.

Go **Online**
Author Link

For: More about the author
Visit: www.PHSchool.com
Web Code: eme-9109

Suzy and Leah

Jane Yolen

August 5, 1944

Dear Diary,

Today I walked past that place, the one that was in the newspaper, the one all the kids have been talking about. Gosh, is it ugly! A line of rickety wooden buildings just like in the army. And a fence lots higher than my head. With barbed wire[1] on top. How can anyone—even a <u>refugee</u>—live there?

I took two candy bars along, just like everyone said I should. When I held them up, all those kids just swarmed over to the fence, grabbing. Like in a zoo. Except for this one girl, with two dark braids and bangs nearly covering her eyes. She was just standing to one side, staring at me. It was so creepy. After a minute I looked away. When I looked back, she was gone. I mean gone. Disappeared as if she'd never been.

Suzy

August 5, 1944

My dear Mutti,[2]

I have but a single piece of paper to write on. And a broken pencil. But I will write small so I can tell all. I address it to you, Mutti, though you are gone from me forever. I write in English, to learn better, because I want to make myself be understood.

Today another girl came. With more sweets. A girl with yellow hair and a false smile. Yonni and Zipporah and Ruth, my friends, all grabbed for the sweets. Like wild animals. Like . . .

---

1. barbed wire twisted wire with sharp points all along it, used for fences and barriers.
2. Mutti (moo´ tē) German equivalent of "Mommy."

like prisoners. But we are not wild animals. And we are no longer prisoners. Even though we are still penned in.

I stared at the yellow-haired girl until she was forced to look down. Then I walked away. When I turned to look back, she was gone. Disappeared. As if she had never been.

Leah

September 2, 1944

Dear Diary,

I brought the refugee kids oranges today. Can you believe it—they didn't know you're supposed to peel oranges first. One boy tried to eat one like an apple. He made an awful face, but then he ate it anyway. I showed them how to peel oranges with the second one. After I stopped laughing.

Mom says they are going to be coming to school. Of course they'll have to be cleaned up first. Ugh. My hand still feels itchy from where one little boy grabbed it in his. I wonder if he had bugs.

Suzy

September 2, 1944

My dear Mutti,

Today we got cereal in a box. At first I did not know what it was. Before the war we ate such lovely <u>porridge</u> with milk straight from our cows. And eggs fresh from the hen's nest, though you know how I hated that nasty old chicken. How often she pecked me! In the German camp, it was potato soup—with onions when we were lucky, without either onion or potato when we were not. And after, when I was running from the Nazis, it was stale brown bread, if we could find any. But cereal in a box—that is something.

I will not take a sweet from that yellow-haired girl, though. She laughed at Yonni. I will not take another orange fruit.

Leah

September 5, 1944

Dear Diary,

So how are those refugee kids going to learn? Our teachers teach in English. This is America, after all.

Vocabulary Builder
porridge (pôr´ij) *n.* soft food made of cereal boiled in water or milk

Reading Skill
Author's Purpose
What purpose might the author have for including details about Leah's life before the war?

I wouldn't want to be one of them. Imagine going to school and not being able to speak English or understand anything that's going on. I can't imagine anything worse.

Suzy

▲ **Critical Viewing**
This photograph shows Jews fleeing their homes, as ordered by the Nazis. What do you find most upsetting about the picture? **[Respond]**

September 5, 1944

My dear Mutti,

The adults of the Americans say we are safe now. And so we must go to their school. But I say no place is safe for us. Did not the Germans say that we were safe in their camps? And there you and baby Natan were killed.

And how could we learn in this American school anyway? I have a little English. But Ruth and Zipporah and the others, though they speak Yiddish[3] and Russian and German, they have no English at all. None beyond *thank you* and *please* and *more sweets.* And then there is little Avi. How could he go to this school? He will speak nothing at all. He stopped speaking, they say, when he was hidden away in a cupboard by his grandmother who was taken by the Nazis after she swore there was no child in the house. And he was almost three days in that cupboard without food, without water, without words to comfort him. Is English a safer language than German?

There is barbed wire still between us and the world.

Leah

September 14, 1944

Dear Diary,

At least the refugee kids are wearing better clothes now. And they all have shoes. Some of them still had those stripy pajamas on when they arrived in America.

The girls all wore dresses to their first day at school, though. They even had hair bows, gifts from the teachers. Of

✓ **Reading Check**

What happened to Leah's mother?

---

3. Yiddish (yid'ish) *n.* language spoken by eastern European Jews and their descendants. It is written with Hebrew letters and contains words from Hebrew, German, Russian, and Polish.

course I recognized my old blue pinafore.[4] The girl with the dark braids had it on, and Mom hadn't even told me she was giving it away. I wouldn't have minded so much if she had only asked. It doesn't fit me anymore, anyway.

The girl in my old pinafore was the only one without a name tag, so all day long no one knew her name.

Suzy

September 14, 1944

My dear Mutti,

I put on the blue dress for our first day. It fit me well. The color reminded me of your eyes and the blue skies over our farm before the smoke from the burning darkened it. Zipporah braided my hair, but I had no mirror until we got to the school and they showed us the toilets. They call it a bathroom, but there is no bath in it at all, which is strange. I have never been in a school with boys before.

They have placed us all in low grades. Because of our English. I do not care. This way I do not have to see the girl with the yellow hair who smiles so falsely at me.

But they made us wear tags with our names printed on them. That made me afraid. What next? Yellow stars?[5] I tore mine off and threw it behind a bush before we went in.

Leah

Literary Analysis
Setting How did Leah's former home on the farm change during the war?

September 16, 1944

Dear Diary,

Mr. Forest has assigned each of us to a refugee to help them with their English. He gave me the girl with the dark braids, the one without the name tag, the one in my pinafore. Gee, she's as prickly as a porcupine. I asked if I could have a different kid. He said I was the best English student and she already spoke the best English. He wants her to learn as fast as possible so she can help the others. As if she would, Miss Porcupine.

Her name is Leah. I wish she would wear another dress.

Suzy

Reading Skill
Author's Purpose What purpose might the author have for describing Leah from Suzy's point of view?

---

4. **pinafore** (pin´ə fôr´) *n.* a sleeveless garment worn over a dress, often over a blouse.
5. **yellow stars** Jews were forced to wear fabric stars during the Holocaust to distinguish them from others.

September 16, 1944

My dear Mutti,

Now I have a real notebook and a pen. I am writing to you at school now. I cannot take the notebook back to the shelter. Someone there will surely borrow it. I will instead keep it here. In the little cupboard each one of us has been given.

I wish I had another dress. I wish I had a different student helping me and not the yellow-haired girl.

Leah

September 20, 1944

Dear Diary,

Can't she ever smile, that Leah? I've brought her candy bars and apples from home. I tried to give her a handkerchief with a yellow flower on it. She wouldn't take any of them.

Her whole name is Leah Shoshana Hershkowitz. At least, that's the way she writes it. When she says it, it sounds all different, low and growly. I laughed when I tried to say it, but she wouldn't laugh with me. What a grouch.

And yesterday, when I took her English paper to correct it, she shrank back against her chair as if I was going to hit her or something. Honestly!

Mom says I should invite her home for dinner soon. We'll have to get her a special pass for that. But I don't know if I want her to come. It's not like she's any fun at all. I wish Mr. Forest would let me trade.

Suzy

▼ **Critical Viewing**
What do the details in this photograph tell you about the lives and backgrounds of these children? **[Infer]**

September 20, 1944

My dear Mutti,

The girl with the yellow hair is called Suzy Ann McCarthy. It is a silly name. It means nothing. I asked her who she was named for, and she said, "For a book my mom liked." A book! I am named after my great-grandmother on my mother's side, who was an important woman in our village. I am proud to carry on her name.

This Suzy brings many sweets. But I must call them candies now. And a handkerchief. She expects me to be grateful.

✔ **Reading Check**

What do Suzy and Leah think of each other?

Suzy and Leah ■ 107

But how can I be grateful? She treats me like a pet, a pet she does not really like or trust. She wants to feed me like an animal behind bars.

If I write all this down, I will not hold so much anger. I have much anger. And terror besides. *Terror.* It is a new word for me, but an old feeling. One day soon this Suzy and her people will stop being nice to us. They will remember we are not just refugees but Jews, and they will turn on us. Just as the Germans did. Of this I am sure.

Leah

September 30, 1944

Dear Diary,

Leah's English is very good now. But she still never smiles. Especially she never smiles at me. It's like she has a <u>permanent</u> frown and permanent frown lines between her eyes. It makes her look much older than anyone in our class. Like a little old lady.

I wonder if she eats enough. She won't take the candy bars. And she saves the school lunch in her napkin, hiding it away in her pocket. She thinks no one sees her do it, but I do. Does she eat it later? I'm sure they get dinner at the shelter. Mom says they do. Mom also says we have to eat everything on our plates. Sometimes when we're having dinner I think of Leah Shoshana Hershkowitz.

Suzy

September 30, 1944

My dear Mutti,

Avi loves the food I bring home from school. What does he know? It is not even kosher.[6] Sometimes they serve ham. But

---

6. **kosher** (kō′shər) *adj.* fit to eat according to the Jewish laws of diet.

I do not tell Avi. He needs all the food he can get. He is a growing boy.

I, too, am growing fast. Soon I will not fit into the blue dress. I have no other.

Leah

October 9, 1944

Dear Diary,

They skipped Leah up to our grade, her English has gotten so good. Except for some words, like victory, which she pronounces "wick-toe-ree." I try not to laugh, but sometimes I just can't help it!

Leah knows a lot about the world and nothing about America. She thinks New York is right next to Chicago, for goodness sakes! She can't dance at all. She doesn't know the words to any of the top songs. And she's so stuck up, she only talks in class to answer questions. The other refugees aren't like that at all. Why is it only my refugee who's so mean?

Suzy

October 9, 1944

My dear Mutti,

I think of you all the time. I went to Suzy's house because Mr. Forest said they had gone to a great deal of trouble to get a pass for me. I did not want to go so much, my stomach hurt the whole time I was there.

Suzy's *Mutti* was nice, all pink and gold. She wore a dress with pink roses all over it and it reminded me of your dress, the blue one with the asters. You were wearing it when we were put on the train. And the last time I saw you at the camp with Natan. Oh, *Mutti.* I had to steel my heart against Suzy's mother. If I love her, I will forget you. And that I must never do.

I brought back food from her house, though, for Avi. I could not eat it myself. You would like the way Avi grows bigger and stronger. And he talks now, but only to me. He says, "More, Leah, please." And he says "light" for the sun. Sometimes when I am really lonely I call him Natan, but only at night after he has fallen asleep.

Leah

**Literary Analysis
Setting** How does being in Suzy's home affect Leah?

Reading Check

What does Leah do with her food at lunchtime?

October 10, 1944

Dear Diary,

Leah was not in school today. When I asked her friend Zipporah, she shrugged. "She is ill in her stomach," she said. "What did she eat at your house?"

I didn't answer "Nothing," though that would have been true. She hid it all in a handkerchief Mom gave her. Mom said, "She eats like a bird. How does she stay alive?"

Suzy

October 11, 1944

Dear Diary,

They've asked me to gather Leah's things from school and bring them to the hospital. She had to have her appendix out and nearly died. She almost didn't tell them she was sick until too late. Why did she do that? I would have been screaming my head off with the pain.

Mom says we have to visit, that I'm Leah's American best friend. Hah! We're going to bring several of my old dresses, but not my green one with the white trim. I don't want her to have it. Even if it doesn't fit me anymore.

Suzy

▲ **Critical Viewing** The girls pictured here are looking out of a ship's porthole as they prepare to go to America. Which girl has an expression you would expect to see on Leah's face? Explain. **[Connect]**

October 12, 1944

Dear Diary,

I did a terrible thing. I read Leah's diary. I'd kill anyone who did that to me!

At first it made no sense. Who were *Mutti* and Natan, and why were they killed? What were the yellow stars? What does kosher mean? And the way she talked about me made me furious. Who did she think she was, little Miss Porcupine? All I did was bring candy and fruit and try to make those poor refugee kids feel at home.

Then, when I asked Mom some questions, carefully, so she wouldn't guess I had read Leah's diary, she explained. She said the Nazis killed people, mothers and children as well as men. In places called concentration camps. And that all the Jews—people who weren't Christians like us—had to wear yellow stars on their clothes so they could be spotted blocks and blocks away. It was so awful I could hardly believe it, but Mom said it was true.

How was I supposed to know all that? How can Leah stand any of us? How could she live with all that pain?

Suzy

Reading Skill
Author's Purpose
What facts about World War II does the author teach in this entry?

October 12, 1944

My dear Mutti,

Suzy and her mother came to see me in the hospital. They brought me my notebook so now I can write again.

I was so frightened about being sick. I did not tell anyone for a long time, even though it hurt so much. In the German camp, if you were sick and could not do your work, they did not let you live.

But in the middle of the night, I had so much fever, a doctor was sent for. Little Avi found me. He ran to one of the guards. He spoke out loud for the first time. He said, "Please, for Leah. Do not let her go into the dark."

The doctor tells me I nearly died, but they saved me. They have given me much medicines and soon I will eat the food and they will be sure it is kosher, too. And I am alive. This I can hardly believe. *Alive!*

Then Suzy came with her *Mutti,* saying, "I am sorry. I am so sorry. I did not know. I did not understand." Suzy did a bad thing. She read my notebook. But it helped her understand. And then, instead of making an apology, she did a strange thing. She took a red book with a lock out of her pocket and gave it to me. "Read this," she said. "And when you are out of the hospital, I have a green dress with white trim I want you to have. It will be just perfect with your eyes."

I do not know what this trim may be. But I like the idea of a green dress. And I have a new word now, as well. It is this: *diary.*

A new word. A new land. And—it is just possible—a new friend.

Leah

Reading Skill
Author's Purpose
What purpose does the author achieve by telling a story through young characters?

Apply the Skills

Suzy and Leah

Thinking About the Selection

1. **Respond:** How do you think you would have reacted if you had tried to help Leah and she had rejected you? Explain.
2. **(a) Recall:** What kind of camp was Leah in before coming to the refugee camp? **(b) Interpret:** What does Leah mean by, "There is barbed wire still between us and the world"?
3. **(a) Recall:** How are Suzy and Leah forced to get to know each other? **(b) Analyze:** What do Suzy's early reactions to Leah tell you about Suzy? **(c) Analyze:** What do Leah's early reactions to Suzy tell you about Leah?
4. **(a) Recall:** What does Suzy learn about Leah when she reads her diary? **(b) Infer:** What is the "red book with a lock" that Suzy gives Leah to read? **(c) Draw Conclusions:** How have both girls changed by the end of the story?
5. **(a) Predict:** Do you think Suzy and Leah will become close friends in the future? **(b) Support:** What evidence from the story makes you feel this way? **(c) Discuss:** In a small group, share and discuss your responses. As a group, choose one answer to share with the class.

Reading Skill

6. What are two things the author might have wished to teach her audience?
7. **(a)** Did the author mean to entertain her audience? **(b)** Which details support your answer? Explain.
8. In your own words, what was the author's main **purpose** in writing this story?

Literary Analysis

9. How does the **setting** of this story affect the events that occur?
10. Using a chart like the one shown, give two examples from the story to show how setting affects a character's mood.

Setting	Character's Mood

QuickReview

Who's Who in the Story

Suzy: an American girl

Leah: a European war refugee

Mutti: Leah's mother

Go Online
Assessment
For: Self-test
Visit: www.PHSchool.com
Web Code: ema-6109

Author's Purpose: an author's reason for writing

Setting: the time and place of the action

Vocabulary Builder

Practice Explain your answer to each question.

1. Grape juice left a *permanent* stain on the carpet. Will the stain be easy to get out?

2. Would a *refugee* be able to go back home easily to get something he or she forgot?

3. Would a diet of only *porridge* be a healthy choice?

Writing

Write a **news report** that tells about the refugee camp where Leah is living. The report should answer the questions *who, what, when, where, why,* and *how.*

- First, list questions that your news report will answer. For example: *Why are the war refugees now living there?*
- Answer each question. Use story details to help you.
- Write your report, based on your answers. Present the most important information in your opening paragraph.

For *Grammar, Vocabulary,* and *Assessment,* see **Build Language Skills,** pages 114–115.

Extend Your Learning

Listening and Speaking In a small group, hold a **discussion** about how this story has affected your understanding of the Holocaust. Use these questions to guide you:
- What did you already know about the Holocaust?
- What did the story teach you?
- How did the character's ages change the way you felt about historic events?

Identify three questions you still have about the Holocaust.

Research and Technology With a group, make an **annotated bibliography** for a report about the Holocaust. Use the Internet or the library to find possible resources. Compile a list of resources, using the MLA format for bibliographies, which you can find on page R25. Then, write a short description of each resource.

Build Language Skills

All Summer in a Day • Suzy and Leah

Vocabulary Skill

Prefixes The word *recall* is made up of the word *call* with the prefix *re-* added. In this case, the prefix *re-* means "back." To recall is to "call something back" or "to remember."

The **prefix *re-*** has several meanings that can help you understand and remember words that begin with it.

Meanings	Words
Do action again or bring back an earlier state of affairs	review, recommend, research
Action to answer or undo a situation	revise, remove, respond
Backward action	return, recall, repel

Practice Answer each question in a complete sentence. Use the underlined word in your answer.

1. Why can't you <u>review</u> something you have not read yet?
2. How do you <u>respond</u> to funny stories?
3. Why should you <u>revise</u> an essay before turning it in?
4. How can <u>research</u> help you learn more about an author?
5. What book would you <u>recommend</u> to someone else?

Grammar Lesson

Personal Pronouns A **personal pronoun** takes the place of a noun. Some personal pronouns take the place of the **subject**—the one doing the action. Other personal pronouns take the place of the **object**—the one receiving the action.

Subject Pronouns	Object Pronouns
I, we, you, he, she, it, they	me, us, you, him, her, it, them

Practice Write a sentence explaining why each pronoun is a subject or object pronoun.

1. Amy and Tina visited us.
2. Tina gave me a gift.
3. She made the gift with Amy.
4. Dad thanked them a lot.

MorePractice

For more practice with personal pronouns, see the Grammar Handbook, p. R31.

WG Prentice Hall Writing and Grammar Connection: Chapter 14, Section 2

Assessment Practice

Reading: Author's Purpose

Directions: *Read the selection. Then answer the questions.*

My dad loves to play April Fool's pranks. He started years ago by shaking our hands with a hidden buzzer that tickled us. My sisters and I loved that. Over time, the pranks got funnier and more creative. One April 1st, we awoke to find the furniture in our house rearranged! Mom's favorite joke was when Dad wrote her a big check and told her to cash it the next day. That's when she discovered it had been written with disappearing ink!

1. What is the author's purpose in this passage?
   - **A** to inform
   - **B** to persuade
   - **C** to entertain
   - **D** to teach

2. Which of these details does NOT indicate the author's purpose?
   - **A** Dad shook hands with a tickling buzzer.
   - **B** The family has furniture in their house.
   - **C** Dad rearranged the furniture.
   - **D** Mom got a check written with disappearing ink.

3. Which word best describes the details in the passage?
   - **A** serious
   - **B** urgent
   - **C** thoughtful
   - **D** amusing

4. Which of these details shows the author's feelings about her father?
   - **A** The buzzer tickles.
   - **B** She describes the pranks as "funnier and more creative."
   - **C** She describes her mother's favorite joke.
   - **D** The furniture was "rearranged."

Timed Writing: Description [Analyzing]

Review "All Summer in a Day" or "Suzy and Leah." Write a brief description of the story setting. Include details that describe how things look, feel, smell, taste, or sound. **(20 minutes)**

 ## Writing Workshop: *Work in Progress*

Autobiographical Narrative

Jot down a list of five people whom you know. They might be friends, family members, or teachers. Keep this list in your writing portfolio to refer to when you write your autobiographical narrative.

These skills will help you become a better reader.
Practice them with either "My First Free Summer"
(p. 118) or "My Furthest-Back Person" (p. 125).

Reading Skill

One way to determine the **author's purpose,**
or reason, for writing a nonfiction work is to
use background information that you already
know about the author and topic. For example, knowing that an
author was born outside the United States might help you determine
that he or she wrote an essay to inform readers about his or her
native country.

   As you read, use a chart like the one shown to help you determine
the author's purpose.

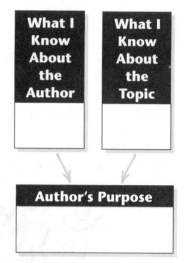

Literary Analysis

When a literary work is based on real events and real people, the
historical context can help you understand the action. **Historical
context**—the actual political and social events and trends of the
time—can explain why characters act and think the way they do.
As you read, look for factual details that link the text to a specific
place and time period.

Vocabulary Builder

My First Free Summer

- **vowed** (voud) *v.* promised solemnly
  (p. 118) *He vowed to tell the judge the whole
  truth.*

- **diplomats** (dip´ lə mats´) *n.* government
  representatives who work with other
  nations (p. 119) *The diplomats discussed a
  trade agreement that would benefit the gov-
  ernments of both countries.*

- **summoned** (sum´ ənd) *v.* called together
  (p. 120) *The coach summoned the team for a
  meeting.*

My Furthest-Back Person

- **intrigue** (in trēg´) *n.* curiosity and interest
  (p. 126) *The novel's intrigue and mystery
  make it exciting to read.*

- **uncanny** (un kan´ ē) *adj.* strange; eerie
  (p. 126) *The similarity between the two
  strangers was uncanny.*

- **eminent** (em´ ə nənt) *adj.* distinguished or
  outstanding (p. 127) *An eminent scholar
  spoke at the college in our town.*

- **destination** (des´ tə nā´ shən) *n.* place to
  which something is being sent (p. 133) *The
  letter arrived at its destination in London.*

Background

The Dominican Republic In 1930, Rafael L. Trujillo seized power in the Dominican Republic and controlled the country as dictator for thirty-one years. To protect his position, Trujillo placed family members in office, restricted basic human rights, and harmed his political opponents. Some Dominican citizens were forced to flee to the United States. The author of "My First Free Summer" moved to New York City with her family during this chaotic period.

Connecting to the Literature

Reading/Writing Connection Julia Alvarez is disappointed when political events interfere with her summer plans. Describe the way you might feel if events forced you to cancel your plans. Use at least three of the following words: *react, respond, restrict, adjust.*

Meet the Author

Julia **Alvarez** (b. 1950)

Shortly after her birth, Julia Alvarez moved from New York City to the Dominican Republic with her family. When Alvarez was ten, however, her family was forced to return to the United States because her father was involved in a rebellion against the country's dictator.

The Power of Words Alvarez had trouble adjusting to her new home. Turning inward, she began to read books and to write. Later, she said, "I fell in love with how words can make you feel complete in a way that I hadn't felt complete since leaving the island."

Fast Facts

▶ Alvarez writes poetry as well as fiction.
▶ Several years ago, Alvarez started a farm and school to help people in the Dominican Republic.

Go Online
Author Link

For: More about the author
Visit: www.PHSchool.com
Web Code: eme-9110

My First Free Summer

Julia Alvarez

I never had summer—I had summer school. First grade, summer school. Second grade, summer school. Thirdgradesummerschoolfourthgradesummerschool. In fifth grade, I <u>vowed</u> I would get interested in fractions, the presidents of the United States, Mesopotamia; I would learn my English.

That was the problem. English. My mother had decided to send her children to the American school so we could learn the language of the nation that would soon be liberating us. For thirty years, the Dominican Republic had endured a bloody and repressive dictatorship. From my father, who was involved in an underground plot, my mother knew that los américanos[1] had promised to help bring democracy to the island.

"You have to learn your English!" Mami kept scolding me.

"But why?" I'd ask. I didn't know about my father's activities. I didn't know the dictator was bad. All I knew was that my friends who were attending Dominican schools were often on holiday to honor the dictator's birthday, the dictator's saint day, the day the dictator became the dictator, the day the dictator's oldest son was born, and so on. They marched in parades and visited the palace and had their picture in the paper.

Vocabulary Builder
vowed (voud)
v. promised solemnly

Literary Analysis
Historical Context
How long has the dictator been in power?

---

1. **los americanos** (lōs ä me′ rĭ kä′ nōs) *n.* Spanish for "the Americans."

Meanwhile, I had to learn about the pilgrims with their funny witch hats, about the 50 states and where they were on the map, about Dick and Jane[2] and their tame little pets, Puff and Spot, about freedom and liberty and justice for all—while being imprisoned in a hot classroom with a picture of a man wearing a silly wig hanging above the blackboard. And all of this learning I had to do in that impossibly difficult, rocks-in-your-mouth language of English!

Somehow, I managed to scrape by. Every June, when my prospects looked iffy, Mami and I met with the principal. I squirmed in my seat while they arranged for my special summer lessons.

"She is going to work extra hard. Aren't you, young lady?" the principal would quiz me at the end of our session.

My mother's eye on me, I'd murmur, "Yeah."

"Yes, what?" Mami coached.

"Yes." I sighed. "Sir."

It's a wonder that I just wasn't thrown out, which was what I secretly hoped for. But there were extenuating circumstances, the grounds on which the American school stood had been donated by my grandfather. In fact, it had been my grandmother who had encouraged Carol Morgan to start her school. The bulk of the student body was made up of the sons and daughters of American diplomats and business people, but a few Dominicans—most of them friends or members of my family—were allowed to attend.

"You should be grateful!" Mami scolded on the way home from our meeting. "Not every girl is lucky enough to go to the Carol Morgan School!"

In fifth grade, I straightened out. "Yes, ma'am!" I learned to say brightly. "Yes, sir!" To wave my hand in sword-wielding swoops so I could get called on with the right answer. What had changed me? Gratitude? A realization of my luckiness? No, sir!

2. **Dick and Jane** characters in a reading book commonly used by students in the 1950s.

Vocabulary Builder
diplomats (dip′lə mats′) *n.* government representatives who work with other nations

◄ **Critical Viewing**
Rafael Trujillo was dictator of the Dominican Republic from 1930 to 1961. What details in the photograph make him look important? **[Analyze]**

✔ **Reading Check**
Why does Julia have to go to summer school?

The thought of a fun summer? Yes, ma'am! I wanted to run with the pack of cousins and friends in the common yard that connected all our properties. To play on the trampoline and go off to la playa[3] and get brown as a berry. I wanted to be free. Maybe American principles had finally sunk in!

The summer of 1960 began in bliss: I did not have to go to summer school! *Attitude much improved. Her English progressing nicely. Attentive and cooperative in classroom.* I grinned as Mami read off the note that accompanied my report card of Bs.

But the yard replete with cousins and friends that I had dreamed about all year was deserted. Family members were leaving for the United States, using whatever connections they could drum up. The plot had unraveled. Every day there were massive arrests. The United States had closed its embassy and was advising Americans to return home.

Literary Analysis
Historical Context
What daily events cause the U.S. government to advise Americans to return home?

My own parents were terrified. Every night black Volkswagens blocked our driveway and stayed there until morning. "Secret police," my older sister whispered.

"Why are they secret if they're the police?" I asked.

"Shut up!" my sister hissed. "Do you want to get us all killed?"

Day after day, I kicked a deflated beach ball around the empty yard, feeling as if I'd been tricked into good behavior by whomever God put in charge of the lives of 10-year-olds. I was bored. Even summer school would have been better than this!

One day toward the end of the summer, my mother <u>summoned</u> my sisters and me. She wore that too-bright smile she sometimes pasted on her terrified face.

Vocabulary Builder
summoned (sum´ ənd) *v.* called together

"Good news, girls! Our papers and tickets came! We're leaving for the United States!"

Our mouths dropped. We hadn't been told we were going on a trip anywhere, no less to some place so far away.

I was the first to speak up, "But why?"

My mother flashed me the same look she used to give me when I'd ask why I had to learn English.

I was about to tell her that I didn't want to go to the United States, where summer school had been invented and everyone spoke English. But my mother lifted a hand for silence. "We're leaving in a few hours. I want you all to go get ready! I'll be in to pack soon." The desperate look in her eyes did not allow for

Reading Skill
Author's Purpose
How does your background knowledge of Julia and her mother help you understand the look described here?

---

3. la playa (lä plä´ yä) *n.* the beach.

contradiction. We raced off, wondering how to fit the contents of our Dominican lives into four small suitcases.

Our flight was scheduled for that afternoon, but the airplane did not appear. The terminal lined with soldiers wielding machine guns, checking papers, escorting passengers into a small interrogation room. Not everyone returned.

"It's a trap," I heard my mother whisper to my father.

This had happened before, a cat-and-mouse game the dictator liked to play. Pretend that he was letting someone go, and then at the last minute, their family and friends conveniently gathered together—wham! The secret police would haul the whole clan away.

Of course, I didn't know that this was what my parents were dreading. But as the hours ticked away, and afternoon turned into evening and evening into night and night into midnight with no plane in sight, a light came on in my head. If the light could be translated into words, instead, they would say: Freedom and liberty and justice for all . . . I knew that ours was not a trip, but an escape. We had to get to the United States.

The rest of that night is a blur. It is one, then two the next morning. A plane lands, lights flashing. We are walking on the runway, climbing up the stairs into the cabin. An American lady wearing a cap welcomes us. We sit down, ready to depart. But suddenly, soldiers come on board. They go seat by seat, looking at our faces. Finally, they leave, the door closes, and with a powerful roar we lift off and I fall asleep.

Next morning, we are standing inside a large, echoing hall as a stern American official reviews our documents. What if he doesn't let us in? What if we have to go back? I am holding my breath. My parents' terror has become mine.

He checks our faces against the passport pictures. When he is done, he asks, "You girls ready for school?" I swear he is looking at me.

"Yes, sir!" I speak up.

The man laughs. He stamps our papers and hands them to my father. Then wonderfully, a smile spreads across his face. "Welcome to the United States," he says, waving us in.

▲ **Critical Viewing**
This is Julia's passport picture. Describe her based on this photo and what you have read. **[Infer]**

Reading Skill
Author's Purpose
How does this scene point to the author's main purpose for writing this story?

My First Free Summer ■ 121

Apply the Skills

My First Free Summer

Thinking About the Selection

1. **Respond:** Were you surprised by the Alvarez family's experience at the airport? Why or why not?

2. **(a) Recall:** Why does Julia Alvarez's mother send Julia to the American school? **(b) Compare and Contrast:** How does this school differ from other schools on the island?

3. **(a) Recall:** What is Alvarez's main reason for changing her behavior in fifth grade? **(b) Connect:** How is she successful?

4. **(a) Infer:** How do you think Alvarez feels when she learns that her family is leaving the country? **(b) Speculate:** Why does it take her so long to understand that her family is escaping?

5. **(a) Hypothesize:** What might Alvarez want readers to learn from this story? List each idea on a separate line in your notebook. **(b) Support:** What details in the story help to convey each idea you listed? Write the details next to your ideas. **(c) Discuss:** Share your responses with a partner; then, discuss how looking at someone else's responses did or did not change your ideas.

Reading Skill

6. What information from the Background on page 117 helps you understand that the **author's purpose** is to reflect on an experience?

7. **(a)** What other purposes for writing might Alvarez have had? **(b)** Which details in the essay support your response?

Literary Analysis

8. Using a chart like the one shown, give examples from the story that show how the **historical context** of the Dominican Republic affects Alvarez's actions in "My First Free Summer."

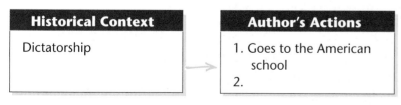

Historical Context	Author's Actions
Dictatorship	1. Goes to the American school 2.

9. List two details that help Alvarez finally realize that her family is making an escape from the island.

QuickReview

Essay at a Glance
The author describes events leading up to her family's escape from the Dominican Republic.

Go Online
Assessment
For: Self-test
Visit: www.PHSchool.com
Web Code: ema-6110

Author's Purpose: an author's main reason for writing

Historical Context: the political and social events and trends that serve as a backdrop to a literary work

Vocabulary Builder

Practice Explain your answer to each question.

1. If you *vowed* to keep a secret, would you tell anyone?

2. Would it be a problem if all *diplomats* were afraid to fly?

3. If you were *summoned* to an important meeting, what would you do?

Writing

Write a **letter** to young Julia Alvarez describing what it is like to go to school in the United States. Before you write, gather your ideas. First, write facts about your school day, such as the hours you attend, the subjects you study, and the amount of homework you are given. Next, write some of the things you like most and least about school. Remember to include the date, a greeting, a closing, and a signature. For a model business letter, see page R23.

For *Grammar, Vocabulary,* and *Assessment,* see **Build Language Skills,** pages 136–137.

Extend Your Learning

Listening and Speaking Conduct an **interview** with a friend, relative, or classmate who has moved to a new country or neighborhood, or who has attended a new school.

- Create a list of questions beforehand to guide the interview.
- During the interview, ask follow-up questions. For example, if your subject says his or her old school was more difficult, follow up with a question such as "How many hours a day did you attend?"

Present your findings to the class.

Research and Technology With a group of classmates, create a **timeline** of the major events in the recent history of the Dominican Republic. Begin with the dictatorship of Trujillo. Use the Internet and library resources to gather information. Make sure that you focus on major events and key people. In your timeline, present events in the order in which they occurred. Present your timeline to the class.

Autobiography

Background

Looking for Ancestors In "My Furthest-Back Person," Alex Haley traces his past. Many people are interested in learning about their ancestors. A person might use photographs, letters, newspaper clippings, or printed family histories. Government records such as birth certificates, marriage licenses, and death certificates may also provide information.

Connecting to the Literature

Reading/Writing Connection Alex Haley describes the experience of tracing his ancestors. Jot down your ideas about the value of learning about the past. Use at least three of the following words: *circumstance, acquire, identify, individual, survive.*

Review

For **Reading Skill**, **Literary Analysis**, and **Vocabulary Builder**, see page 116.

Meet the Author

Alex **Haley** (1921–1992)

As a boy, Alex Haley spent his summers on his grandmother's front porch in Henning, Tennessee, listening to stories of the family's history back through the days of slavery. The "furthest-back person" they spoke of was an ancestor they called "the African," who was kidnapped in his native country, shipped to Annapolis, Maryland, and sold into slavery.

A Writer's Roots After graduating from high school, Haley entered the U.S. Coast Guard. His life as a writer began at sea. He wrote short adventure stories. Twenty years later, Haley retired from the Coast Guard to become a full-time writer. Remembering the stories he had heard as a child, Haley began to research his past. This led to the publication of the book *Roots: Saga of an American Family.*

Fast Facts

▶ *Roots* was an immediate bestseller, selling more than 1.6 million copies in the first six months.
▶ The book led to a groundbreaking television mini-series, which set records for the number of viewers.

For: More about the author
Visit: www.PHSchool.com
Web Code: eme-9111

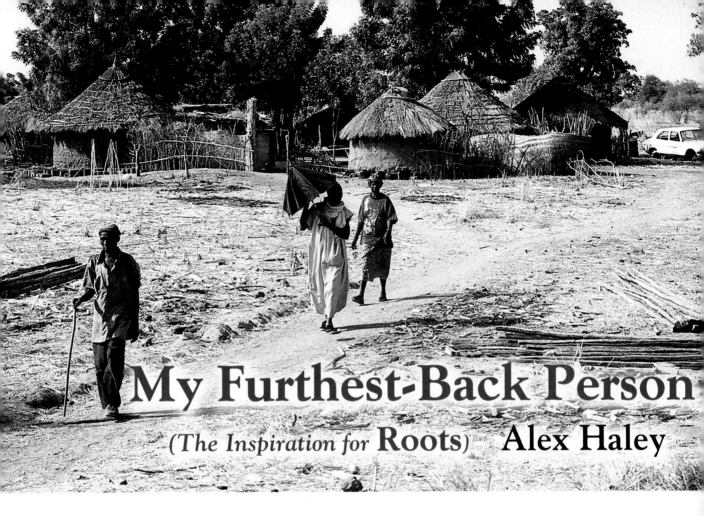

My Furthest-Back Person

(The Inspiration for Roots) Alex Haley

As a boy, Alex Haley spent his summers on his grandmother's front porch in Henning, Tennessee, listening to her and her sisters tell stories of the family's history back through the days of slavery. The "furthest-back person" they spoke of was an ancestor they called "The African," who was kidnapped in his native country, shipped to Annapolis, Maryland, and sold into slavery. These stories stayed with young Alex throughout his life.

One Saturday in 1965 I happened to be walking past the National Archives building in Washington. Across the interim years I had thought of Grandma's old stories—otherwise I can't think what diverted me up the Archives' steps. And when a main reading room desk attendant asked if he could help me, I wouldn't have dreamed of admitting to him some curiosity hanging on from boyhood about my slave forebears. I kind of bumbled that I was interested in census records of Alamance County, North Carolina, just after the Civil War.

▲ Critical Viewing
Does this photograph remind you of anywhere you have been? Explain. [Connect]

Reading Skill
Author's Purpose
What details here show that the author wants to describe a personal experience?

The microfilm rolls were delivered, and I turned them through the machine with a building sense of <u>intrigue</u>, viewing in different census takers' penmanship an endless parade of names. After about a dozen microfilmed rolls, I was beginning to tire, when in utter astonishment I looked upon the names of Grandma's parents: Tom Murray, Irene Murray . . . older sisters of Grandma's as well—every one of them a name that I'd heard countless times on her front porch.

It wasn't that I hadn't believed Grandma. You just *didn't* not believe my Grandma. It was simply so <u>uncanny</u> actually seeing those names in print and in official U.S. Government records.

During the next several months I was back in Washington whenever possible, in the Archives, the Library of Congress, the Daughters of the American Revolution Library. (Whenever black attendants understood the idea of my search, documents I requested reached me with miraculous speed.) In one source or another during 1966 I was able to document at least the highlights of the cherished[1] family story. I would have given anything to have told Grandma, but, sadly, in 1949 she had gone. So I went and told the only survivor of those Henning front-porch storytellers: Cousin Georgia Anderson, now in her 80's in Kansas City, Kan. Wrinkled, bent, not well herself, she was so overjoyed, repeating to me the old stories and sounds; they were like Henning echoes: "Yeah, boy, that African say his name was '*Kin-tay*'; he say the banjo was 'ko,' an' the river '*Kamby Bolong*,' an' he was off choppin' some wood to make his drum when they grabbed 'im!" Cousin Georgia grew so excited we had to stop her, calm her down, "You go 'head, boy! Your grandma an' all of 'em—they up there watching what you do!"

That week I flew to London on a magazine assignment. Since by now I was steeped in the old, in the past, scarcely a tour guide missed me—I was awed at so many historical places and treasures I'd heard of and read of. I came upon the Rosetta stone in the British Museum, marveling anew at how Jean Champollion, the French archaeologist, had miraculously deciphered its ancient demotic and hieroglyphic texts[2] . . .

---

1. **cherished** (cher´ isht) *v.* beloved; valued.
2. **demotic and hieroglyphic texts** (dē mät´ ik *and* hī´ ər ō´ glif´ ik) ancient Egyptian writing, using symbols and pictures to represent words.

Vocabulary Builder
intrigue (in´ trēg´) *n.* curiosity and interest

uncanny (un kan´ ē) *adj.* strange; eerie

Literary Analysis
Historical Context
According to Haley's cousin, what happened to the African called "Kintay"?

The thrill of that just kept hanging around in my head. I was on a jet returning to New York when a thought hit me. Those strange, unknown-tongue sounds, always part of our family's old story . . . they were obviously bits of our original African "*Kin-tay's*" native tongue. What specific tongue? Could I somehow find out?

Back in New York, I began making visits to the United Nations Headquarters lobby; it wasn't hard to spot Africans. I'd stop any I could, asking if my bits of phonetic sounds held any meaning for them. A couple of dozen Africans quickly looked at me, listened, and took off—understandably dubious about some Tennesseean's accent alleging "African" sounds.

My research assistant, George Sims (we grew up together in Henning), brought me some names of ranking scholars of African linguistics. One was particularly intriguing: a Belgian- and English-educated Dr. Jan Vansina; he had spent his early career living in West African villages, studying and tape-recording countless oral histories that were narrated by certain very old African men; he had written a standard textbook, "The Oral Tradition."

So I flew to the University of Wisconsin to see Dr. Vansina. In his living room I told him every bit of the family story in the fullest detail that I could remember it. Then, intensely, he queried[3] me about the story's relay across the generations, about the gibberish of "k" sounds Grandma had fiercely muttered to herself while doing her housework, with my brothers and me giggling beyond her hearing at what we had dubbed "Grandma's noises."

Dr. Vansina, his manner very serious, finally said, "These sounds your family has kept sound very probably of the tongue called 'Mandinka.'"

I'd never heard of any "Mandinka." Grandma just told of the African saying "*ko*" for banjo, or "*Kamby Bolong*" for a Virginia river.

Among Mandinka stringed instruments, Dr. Vansina said, one of the oldest was the "kora."

"*Bolong,*" he said, was clearly Mandinka for "river." Preceded by "*Kamby,*" it very likely meant "Gambia River."

Dr. Vansina telephoned an <u>eminent</u> Africanist colleague, Dr. Philip Curtin. He said that the phonetic "*Kin-tay*" was correctly spelled "*Kinte,*" a very old clan that had originated

---

3. **queried** (kwîr´ ēd) *v.* asked.

Reading Skill
Author's Purpose
What details in this paragraph show that the author wanted to include humor in his story?

Vocabulary Builder
eminent (em´ ə nənt)
adj. distinguished or outstanding

Reading Check

What does Haley learn about the strange sounds his Grandma used to make?

in Old Mali. The Kinte men traditionally were blacksmiths, and the women were potters and weavers.

I knew I must get to the Gambia River.

The first native Gambian I could locate in the U.S. was named Ebou Manga, then a junior attending Hamilton College in upstate Clinton, N.Y. He and I flew to Dakar, Senegal, then took a smaller plane to Yundum Airport, and rode in a van to Gambia's capital, Bathurst. Ebou and his father assembled eight Gambia government officials. I told them Grandma's stories, every detail I could remember, as they listened intently, then reacted. "'*Kamby Bolong*' of course is Gambia River!" I heard. "But more clue is your fore-father's saying his name was 'Kinte.'" Then they told me something I would never ever have fantasized—that in places in the back country lived very old men, commonly called *griots*, who could tell centuries of the histories of certain very old family clans. As for *Kintes*, they pointed out to me on a map some family villages, Kinte-Kundah, and Kinte-Kundah Janneh-Ya, for instance.

The Gambian officials said they would try to help me. I returned to New York dazed. It is embarrassing to me now, but despite Grandma's stories, I'd never been concerned much with Africa, and I had the routine images of African people living mostly in exotic jungles. But a compulsion now laid hold of me to learn all I could, and I began devouring books about Africa, especially about the slave trade. Then one Thursday's mail contained a letter from one of the Gambian officials, inviting me to return there.

Monday I was back in Bathurst. It galvanized me when the officials said that a *griot* had been located who told the *Kinte* clan history— his name was Kebba Kanga Fofana. To reach him, I discovered, required a modified safari: renting

Literature in Context

History Connection

The Gambia The Gambia, with a population of roughly 1.5 million, is the smallest independent country on the continent of Africa. A British colony since the nineteenth century, The Gambia regained its independence in February 1965. English is the official language of the country, although each of its nine ethnic groups speaks its own language. Its capital city, Banjul, formerly Bathurst, was founded in 1816 by the British as a trading post and a base for suppressing the slave trade, which was officially abolished in 1807.

Connect to the Literature

Why do you think Haley had to travel by boat to visit the *griot*?

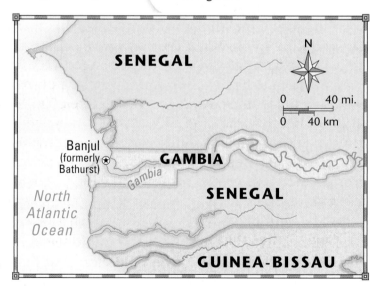

a launch to get upriver, two land vehicles to carry supplies by a roundabout land route, and employing finally 14 people, including three interpreters and four musicians, since a griot would not speak the revered clan histories without background music.

The boat Baddibu vibrated upriver, with me acutely tense: Were these Africans maybe viewing me as but another of the pith-helmets?[4] After about two hours, we put in at James Island, for me to see the ruins of the once British-operated James Fort. Here two centuries of slave ships had loaded thousands of cargoes of Gambian tribespeople. The crumbling stones, the deeply oxidized swivel cannon, even some remnant links of chain seemed all but impossible to believe. Then we continued upriver to the left-bank village of Albreda, and there put ashore to continue on foot to Juffure [joō′ foō rā], village of the *griot*. Once more we stopped, for me to see *toubob kolong*, the "white man's well," now almost filled in, in a swampy area with abundant, tall, saw-toothed grass. It was dug two centuries ago to "17 men's height deep" to insure survival drinking water for long-driven, famishing coffles[5] of slaves.

Walking on, I kept wishing that Grandma could hear how her stories had led me to the "*Kamby Bolong*." (Our surviving storyteller Cousin Georgia died in a Kansas City hospital during this same morning, I would learn later.) Finally, Juffure village's playing children, sighting us, flashed an alert. The 70-odd people came rushing from their circular, thatch-roofed, mud-walled huts, with goats bounding up and about, and parrots squawking from up in the palms. I sensed him in advance somehow, the small man amid them, wearing a pill-box cap and an off-white robe—the *griot*. Then the interpreters went to him, as the villagers thronged around me.

And it hit me like a gale wind: every one of them, the whole crowd, was *jet black*. An enormous sense of guilt swept me—a sense of being some kind of hybrid . . . a sense of being impure among the pure. It was an awful sensation.

The old *griot* stepped away from my interpreters and the crowd quickly swarmed around him—all of them buzzing. An interpreter named A.B.C. Salla came to me; he whispered: "Why they stare at you so, they have never seen here a black American." And that hit me: I was symbolizing for them

Literary Analysis
Historical Context
What do Haley's descriptions of crumbling stones, cannons, and chains tell you about the fort?

Reading Check

How does Haley find out what part of Africa is associated with his family?

---

4. **pith-helmets** *jargon* tourists or hunters on safari, who typically wore these hard hats.
5. **coffles** (kôf′ əlz) *n.* groups of animals or slaves chained or tied together in a line.

twenty-five millions of us they had never seen. What did they think of me—of us?

Then abruptly the old *griot* was briskly walking toward me. His eyes boring into mine, he spoke in Mandinka, as if instinctively I should understand—and A.B.C. Salla translated:

"Yes . . . we have been told by the forefathers . . . that many of us from this place are in exile . . . in that place called America . . . and in other places."

I suppose I physically wavered, and they thought it was the heat; rustling whispers went through the crowd, and a man brought me a low stool. Now the whispering hushed—the musicians had softly begun

▲ Critical Viewing This photograph comes from the television miniseries *Roots*. What do details in the photo suggest about the relationship between the characters? **[Analyze]**

playing *kora* and *balafon*, and a canvas sling lawn seat was taken by the *griot*, Kebba Kanga Fofana, aged 73 "rains" (one rainy season each year). He seemed to gather himself into a physical rigidity, and he began speaking the Kinte clan's ancestral oral history; it came rolling from his mouth across the next hours . . . 17th- and 18th-century *Kinte* lineage details, predominantly what men took wives; the children they "begot," in the order of their births; those children's mates and children.

Events frequently were dated by some proximate[6] singular physical occurrence. It was as if some ancient scroll were printed indelibly within the *griot's* brain. Each few sentences or so, he would pause for an interpreter's translation to me. I distill here the essence:

The *Kinte* clan began in Old Mali, the men generally blacksmiths ". . . who conquered fire," and the women potters and weavers. One large branch of the clan moved to

---

6. **proximate** (präk´sə mət) *adj.* near in time.

Mauretania from where one son of the clan, Kairaba Kunta Kinte, a Moslem Marabout holy man, entered Gambia. He lived first in the village of Pakali N'Ding; he moved next to Jiffarong village; ". . . and then he came here, into our own village of Juffure."

In Juffure, Kairaba Kunta Kinte took his first wife, ". . . a Mandinka maiden, whose name was Sireng. By her, he begot two sons, whose names were Janneh and Saloum. Then he got a second wife, Yaisa. By her, he begot a son, Omoro."

The three sons became men in Juffure. Janneh and Saloum went off and found a new village, Kinte-Kundah Janneh-Ya. "And then Omoro, the youngest son, when he had 30 rains, took as a wife a maiden, Binta Kebba."

"And by her, he begot four sons—Kunta, Lamin, Suwadu, and Madi . . ."

Sometimes, a "begotten," after his naming, would be accompanied by some later-occurring detail, perhaps as ". . . in time of big water (flood), he slew a water buffalo." Having named those four sons, now the griot stated such a detail.

"About the time the king's soldiers came, the eldest of these four sons, Kunta, when he had about 16 rains, went away from his village, to chop wood to make a drum . . . and he was never seen again . . ."

Goose-pimples the size of lemons seemed to pop all over me. In my knapsack were my cumulative notebooks, the first of them including how in my boyhood, my Grandma, Cousin Georgia and the others told of the African "*Kin-tay*" who always said he was kidnapped near his village—while chopping wood to make a drum . . .

I showed the interpreter, he showed and told the *griot*, who excitedly told the people; they grew very agitated. Abruptly then they formed a human ring, encircling me, dancing and chanting. Perhaps a dozen of the women carrying their infant babies rushed in toward me, thrusting the infants into my arms conveying, I would later learn, "the laying on of hands . . . through this flesh which is us, we are you, and you are us." The men hurried me into their mosque, their Arabic praying later being translated outside: "Thanks be to Allah for returning the long lost from among us." Direct descendants of Kunta Kinte's blood brothers were hastened, some of them from nearby villages, for a family portrait to be taken with me, surrounded by actual ancestral sixth cousins. More symbolic acts filled the remaining day.

Reading Skill
Author's Purpose
Why do you think Haley includes these incidents related by the *griot*?

Literary Analysis
Historical Context
What do the activities described here reveal about the traditions and values of the culture?

Reading Check

What happens after Haley shows his notebooks about his ancestor?

When they would let me leave, for some reason I wanted to go away over the African land. Dazed, silent in the bumping Land Rover, I heard the cutting staccato of talking drums. Then when we sighted the next village, its people came thronging to meet us. They were all—little naked ones to wizened elders—waving, beaming; amid a cacophony of crying out; and then my ears identified their words: *"Meester Kinte! Meester Kinte!"*

Let me tell you something: I am a man. But I remember the sob surging up from my feet, flinging up my hands before my face and bawling as I had not done since I was a baby . . . the jet-black Africans were jostling,[7] staring . . . I didn't care, with the feelings surging. If you really knew the odyssey of us millions of black Americans, if you really knew how we came in the seeds of our forefathers, captured, driven, beaten, inspected, bought, branded, chained in foul ships, if you really knew, you needed weeping . . .

Back home, I knew that what I must write, really, was our black saga, where any individual's past is the essence of the millions'. Now flat broke, I went to some editors I knew, describing the Gambian miracle, and my desire to pursue the research; Doubleday contracted to publish, and Reader's Digest to condense the projected book; then I had advances to travel further.

What ship brought Kinte to Grandma's "'Naplis" (Annapolis, Md., obviously)? The old *griot's* time reference to "king's soldiers" sent me flying to London. Feverish searching at last identified, in British Parliament records, "Colonel O'Hare's Forces," dispatched in mid-1767 to protect the then British-held James Fort whose ruins I'd visited. So Kunta Kinte was down in some ship probably sailing later that summer from the Gambia River to Annapolis.

Now I feel it was fated that I had taught myself to write in the U.S. Coast Guard. For the sea dramas I had concentrated on had given me years of experience searching among yellowing old U.S. maritime records. So now in English 18th Century marine records I finally tracked ships reporting themselves in and out to the Commandant of the Gambia River's James Fort. And then early one afternoon I found that a Lord Ligonier under a Captain Thomas Davies had sailed on the Sabbath of

Reading Skill
Author's Purpose
What do you learn about Haley's reason for writing this story? Why do you think he calls his experience a "miracle"?

---

7. jostling (jäs´ liŋ) *v.* bumping and pushing, as in a crowd.

The Purple Quilt (detail), 1986, Faith Ringgold, Courtesy of Bernice Steinbaum

July 5, 1767. Her cargo: 3,265 elephants' teeth, 3,700 pounds of beeswax, 800 pounds of cotton, 32 ounces of Gambian gold and 140 slaves; her <u>destination</u>: "Annapolis."

That night I recrossed the Atlantic. In the Library of Congress the Lord Ligonier's arrival was one brief line in "Shipping In The Port Of Annapolis—1748–1775." I located the author, Vaughan W. Brown, in his Baltimore brokerage office. He drove to Historic Annapolis, the city's historical society, and found me further documentation of her arrival on Sept. 29, 1767. (Exactly two centuries later, Sept. 29, 1967, standing, staring seaward from an Annapolis pier, again I knew tears.) More help came in the Maryland Hall of Records. Archivist Phebe Jacobsen found the Lord Ligonier's arriving customs declaration listing, "98 Negroes"—so in her 86-day crossing, 42 Gambians had died, one among the survivors being 16-year-old Kunta Kinte. Then the microfilmed Oct. 1, 1767, Maryland Gazette contained, on page two, an announcement to prospective buyers from the ship's agents, Daniel of St. Thos. Jenifer and John Ridout (the Governor's secretary): "from the River GAMBIA, in AFRICA . . . a cargo of choice, healthy SLAVES . . ."

▲ **Critical Viewing**
In what way does this quilt give a good representation of Haley's visit to Africa? **[Connect]**

Vocabulary Builder
destination (des′ tə nā′ shən) *n.* place to which something is being sent

Apply the Skills

My Furthest-Back Person

Thinking About the Selection

1. **Respond:** What questions would you like to ask Haley about his experience?
2. **(a) Recall:** What did Haley find in the National Archives in Washington? **(b) Infer:** Why was his discovery exciting?
3. **(a) Recall:** Describe Haley's reaction to the Rosetta stone. **(b) Compare and Contrast:** What is similar and different about the African sounds in Haley's family stories and the writing on the Rosetta stone?
4. **(a) Recall:** What does the griot tell Haley about his ancestor Kunta Kinte? **(b) Deduce:** Why does the griot know about Kunta Kinte? **(c) Connect:** In what way are the tales of the griot and the tales of Haley's family like two parts of the same puzzle?
5. **(a) Recall:** What is Haley's reaction when the villagers call out "Meester Kinte"? **(b) Infer:** Why is the moment such an emotional one? **(c) Discuss:** Share your responses with a partner; then, discuss how looking at someone else's responses did or did not change your interpretation.

Reading Skill

6. What information from the Background on page 124 helps you understand that the **author's purpose** is to reflect on an experience?
7. **(a)** What other purposes for writing might Haley have had? **(b)** Which details in the essay support your answer?

Literary Analysis

8. Using a chart like the one shown, give examples from the story that show how the **historical context** of the 1700s affects Haley's actions several centuries later.

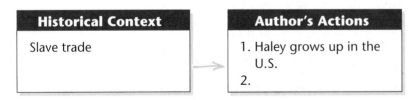

Historical Context	Author's Actions
Slave trade	1. Haley grows up in the U.S. 2.

9. List two details that give readers insight into how enslaved people were treated at James Fort.

QuickReview

Essay at a Glance
After years of intense research, the author traces one branch of his family tree back to a clan in an African village.

Go Online
—Assessment
For: Self-test
Visit: www.PHSchool.com
Web Code: ema-6111

Author's Purpose: his or her main reason for writing

Historical Context: the political and social events and trends that serve as a backdrop to a literary work

Vocabulary Builder

Practice Explain your answer to each question.

1. What makes a writer *eminent*?
2. Was Ghana Haley's *destination* in Africa?
3. If a story is filled with *intrigue,* is it boring?
4. Would seeing someone who looked just like you give you an *uncanny* feeling?

Writing

Alex Haley probably went to a book publisher and presented a proposal—an idea for a project that requires assistance or funding. Write a **letter of proposal** that Haley might have written to the publisher.

- Reread the essay and take notes on Haley's reason for writing the book, what he did before making the proposal, what remained to be done, and what he needed most from the publisher.

Use your notes to write a letter that covers all of the points listed. For a model business letter, see page R23.

For *Grammar, Vocabulary,* and *Assessment,* see **Build Language Skills,** pages 136–137.

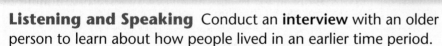

Extend Your Learning

Listening and Speaking Conduct an **interview** with an older person to learn about how people lived in an earlier time period.

- Create a list of questions beforehand to guide the interview.
- During the interview, ask follow-up questions. For example, if your subject says children had more family responsibility, follow up with a question such as "Which chores did you do?"

Present your findings to the class.

Research and Technology With a group of classmates, create a **timeline** of the key events in the American slave trade. Use the Internet and library resources to gather information. Make sure that you focus on major events and key people. In your timeline, present events in the order in which they occurred.

Build Language Skills

My First Free Summer • My Furthest-Back Person

Vocabulary Skill

Prefixes The word *previous* contains the **prefix *pre-,*** which means "before." *Previous* means "occurring before in time or order."

▶ **Example:** We had prepared during the *previous* week.

Words with the prefix *pre-*	Definition
predict	tell before
preview	look before

Practice Answer each question in a complete sentence. Use the underlined word in your answer.

1. Why can't you <u>predict</u> something that happened yesterday?
2. Why would you <u>preview</u> a book before buying it?
3. What is a <u>precaution</u> you should take when riding a bike?
4. What is something that <u>precedes</u> a storm?

MorePractice

For more practice with possessive pronouns, see the Grammar Handbook, p. R31.

Grammar Lesson

Possessive Pronouns A **possessive pronoun** is a pronoun that shows possession, or ownership. A possessive pronoun must agree in number and gender with the noun it refers to.

Pronouns	Possessive Pronouns	Example
I, we	my, mine, our, ours	I wore *my* hat. The hat is *mine.* We took *our* car.
you	your, yours	You ate *your* plum. The plum is *yours.*
he, she, it	his, her, hers, its	He wore *his* jersey. The gloves are *hers.*
they	their, theirs	They rode *their* horses. The horses are *theirs.*

Practice Identify the possessive pronouns in each sentence. Then rewrite each sentence, making the italicized word plural and adjusting the possessive pronoun as needed.

1. The *boy* took his football to the party.
2. When the *girl* left, she forgot her book.
3. The *man* said that the boat was his.
4. The *cat* sharpened its claws on the couch.
5. *I* forgot my assignment.

W̶G *Prentice Hall Writing and Grammar Connection: Chapter 14, Section 2, and Chapter 16, Section 1*

Assessment Practice

Reading: Author's Purpose

Directions: *Read the selection. Then, answer the questions.*

If you're in the market for a spectacular pair of running shoes, try our new Racer's Edge shoes. In last month's Lakeshore Run, three of the top five runners were wearing Racer's Edge shoes. What's so special about Racer's Edge shoes? Every Racer's Edge style is designed with both comfort and performance in mind. The soles of Racer's Edge shoes protect your feet as you run.

To see a demonstration of Racer's Edge shoes, come to the Runner's Best store in the High West Mall on Saturday, June 14th.

1. The author probably wrote this passage to
   A inform readers of the Lakeshore Run.
   B persuade readers to buy a pair of Racer's Edge shoes.
   C explain how to run on a rough surface.
   D describe a personal experience as a runner.

2. What word best supports the author's purpose?
   A market
   B spectacular
   C run
   D shoes

3. Why did the author include information about the demonstration at the Runner's Best store?
   A to convince readers to run often
   B to explain what the store sells
   C to encourage readers to come into the store
   D to inform readers about the location of the mall

4. Which phrase helps convince readers to buy a pair of Racer's Edge shoes?
   A *were wearing*
   B *last month's*
   C *comfort and performance*
   D *as you run*

Timed Writing: Explanation [Critical Stance]

Review "My First Free Summer" or "My Furthest-Back Person." Write a brief explanation of the ways in which the author was affected by historical events. Use examples from the essay to support your ideas. **(20 minutes)**

 ## Writing Workshop: *Work in Progress*

Refer to the list in your writing portfolio. Choose one or two people from this list, and create a timeline of a significant event you experienced with each one.

Reading Informational Materials

Web Sites

In Part 2, you are learning how to determine an author's purpose for writing by using your background knowledge and identifying details in the text. These skills can also help you determine the purpose of a Web site. If you read "My Furthest-Back Person" about Alex Haley's search for his ancestors, you will know that this Web site could have been helpful in Haley's search.

About Web Sites

A **Web site** is a specific location on the Internet. Web sites can be sponsored by news and entertainment media, encyclopedias, colleges and universities, or government institutions. Each Web site has its own unique Internet address, or URL (Uniform Resource Locator). Two pages from the Web site of the U.S. National Archives & Records Administration (NARA), a government organization, are shown here.

Web sites often include the following features:

- background information about the site and its creators
- an overview of the information contained on the site
- buttons that allow you to move among pages on the site
- contact information for those responsible for the site
- links to other Web sites with related information

Reading Skill

Like authors of text documents, the creators of Web sites usually have a specific **purpose** for what they write or present. Knowing who sponsors and maintains a Web site can help you determine that purpose. Often, the URL ending indicates the source of a site. The chart explains some common URL endings.

URL Ending	Description	Usual Intent
.edu or .gov	Site is maintained by an educational institution or government agency.	to provide reliable information
.org	Site is probably maintained by a nonprofit organization.	to provide information about an issue or cause
.com	Site is maintained commercially or personally.	to sell or promote something
.net	Site is maintained by a network.	varies

Click on this button to review a drop-down list of quick links to specific pages on the site, such as Frequently Asked Questions (FAQs).

http://www.archives.gov/index.html

Where Is...? / How Do I...?

NARA
U.S. NATIONAL ARCHIVES & RECORDS ADMINISTRATION

WELCOME
ABOUT US
RESEARCH ROOM
RECORDS MANAGEMENT
RECORDS CENTER PROGRAM
FEDERAL REGISTER
NHPRC & OTHER GRANTS
EXHIBIT HALL
DIGITAL CLASSROOM
RECORDS OF CONGRESS
PRESIDENTIAL LIBRARIES
SEARCH
SITE INDEX

NARA's NEW ERA BEGINS!
get the details & video ▶

celebrate the
Charters of Freedom
Declaration of Independence,
Constitution, & Bill of Rights
see the new exhibit ▶

"The ties that bind the lives of our people in one indissoluble union are perpetuated in the archives of our government."

The National Archives EXPERIENCE
ourdocuments
SUPPORT the National Archives
FIRSTGOV Your First Click to the U.S. Government

REGULATIONS.GOV

Contact NARA | Accessibility | FOIA | Privacy & Use

This list functions as a Table of Contents. It provides an overview of the other pages available on this site as well as links to those pages. Highlight a link for a brief description of its corresponding page. Click on a link to bring up the page.

These buttons provide links to related government Web sites.

Reading Informational Materials

> The Welcome page explains the purpose of NARA and what they hope to achieve with their Web site.

NARA   *...ready access to essential evidence...*

We the People

Welcome

Where Is...? / How Do I...?

September 27, 2004

- WELCOME
- ABOUT US
- RESEARCH ROOM
- RECORDS MANAGEMENT
- RECORDS CENTER PROGRAM

> Underlined words or phrases are links that take you to other pages on the Web site.

- PRESIDENTIAL LIBRARIES
- SEARCH
- SITE INDEX

The National Archives EXPERIENCE

ourdocuments

SUPPORT the National Archives

FIRSTGOV
Your First Click to the U.S. Government

Welcome to the
National Archives and Records Administration (NARA)

NARA, an independent Federal agency, is America's national recordkeeper.

Our mission is to ensure ready access to the essential evidence that documents the rights of American citizens, the actions of Federal officials, and the national experience.

We strive to make it easy for citizens to access these records anywhere at anytime, and we hope that by providing electronic public access to more and more of our records and services, we will better meet your records and information needs.

Among the treasures available to you here online are the cornerstone documents of our Government —

- the Declaration of Independence,
- the Constitution of the United States,
- and the Bill of Rights —

as well as many of our current and past exhibits. But the National Archives is more than famous documents. NARA is a public trust that safeguards the records upon which our democracy depends. We enable people to inspect for themselves the record of what government has done. We enable officials and agencies to review their actions, and we help citizens hold them accountable for those actions. Open, accessible records are essential for open, accessible government.

The records we hold belong to the citizens of the United States. They document our common heritage as Americans and the individual and collective experiences of our people and our great nation.

I hope you will take the time to explore the resources available here, such as the Archival Research Catalog (ARC) and the Digital Classroom, and to learn more about our new initiatives, such as the Electronic Records Archives and the National Archives Experience. You can also find out about changes we are making at NARA to improve customer service and implement our Strategic Plan.

Please let us know your comments and suggestions on how we can improve our services for you.

Thank you for visiting the National Archives and Records Administration.

JOHN W. CARLIN
Archivist of the United States

Biography of John W. Carlin

📄 PRINT-FRIENDLY VERSION

Privacy & Use | Accessibility | FAQs | Contact Us | Home

U.S. National Archives & Records Administration
700 Pennsylvania Avenue NW, Washington, DC 20408 • 1-86-NARA-NARA • 1-866-272-6272

> This is the physical address for NARA.

Reading: Author's Purpose

Directions: *Choose the letter of the best answer to each question.*

1. What is the main purpose of the Welcome Page of the NARA Web site?

   A to inform readers about the availability of public documents

   B to persuade readers to make use of the documents NARA provides

   C to entertain readers with historical anecdotes about the documents

   D to describe John W. Carlin's experiences with NARA

2. Which statement offers a clue about the purpose?

   A "NARA, an independent Federal Agency, is America's national recordkeeper."

   B "But the National Archives is more than famous documents."

   C "We strive to make it easy for citizens to access these records. . . ."

   D "Please let us know your comments and suggestions. . . ."

3. Based on the purpose of the site and the information presented, what is most likely the URL ending for the NARA Web site?

   A .edu

   B .gov

   C .org

   D .com

Reading: Comprehension and Interpretation

Directions: *Write your answers on a separate piece of paper.*

4. What is the purpose of the National Archives and Records Administration? **[Knowledge]**

5. How would you locate additional Web sites that contain similar information? **[Applying]**

6. What feature should you use if you want to learn more about NARA and its director? **[Analyzing]**

Timed Writing: Explanation [Critical Stance]

In a brief essay explain whether or not you feel it is necessary to have an organization such as NARA. Why does Carlin refer to the resources they provide as "cornerstone documents of our Government"? Do you think these documents are important? Why or why not? **(15 minutes)**

Author's Purpose

The **author's purpose** is his or her main reason for writing. For example, an author may want to entertain, inform, or persuade the reader. At other times, an author may be trying to teach a lesson or reflect on an experience. An author can convey his or her purpose through word choice, types of details, and kinds of support that develop the essay's central idea.

Comparing Authors' Purposes

Both essays presented here are autobiographical accounts of childhood experiences. However, each author has a different purpose for writing. You can determine the purpose of each essay by asking some of the following questions as you read:

	Melting Pot	Was Tarzan a Three-Bandage Man?
Subject		
Details		
Language		

Author's Purpose		

- **Content:** What is the writer's subject? Is the topic supported with facts or anecdotes, or a mix?

- **Language:** What kind of language does the author use? Is it playful or serious? Is it formal or informal?

As you read "Melting Pot" and "Was Tarzan a Three-Bandage Man?" compare the authors' purposes by completing a chart like the one shown.

Vocabulary Builder

Melting Pot

- **fluent** (flōō´ ənt) *adj.* able to write or speak easily and smoothly (p. 144) *Myra is fluent in three languages.*

- **bigots** (big´ əts) *n.* narrow-minded, prejudiced people (p. 144) *The immigrant family ignored the bigots and won the respect of their neighbors.*

Was Tarzan a Three-Bandage Man?

- **emulate** (em´ yōō lāt´) *v.* copy or be like someone (p. 147) *The child liked to emulate her sister by pretending to play the piano.*

- **dejectedly** (dē jek´ tid lē) *adv.* sadly; showing discouragement (p. 148) *After the loss, he returned dejectedly to his seat.*

Build Understanding

Connecting to the Literature

Reading/Writing Connection In "Melting Pot" and "Was Tarzan a Three-Bandage Man?" the authors describe memories from their youth. In a few sentences, explain why people enjoy sharing memories of childhood. Use at least three of these words: *impress, evoke, respond, transform, trigger.*

Meet the Authors

Anna **Quindlen** (b. 1953)

Anna Quindlen spent five years reporting for *The New York Times,* covering issues relating to her family and her neighborhood. "Melting Pot" originally appeared in "Life in the 30's," a popular column that Quindlen wrote for the *Times* from 1986 to 1988.

Building on Success In 1992 Quindlen's regular columns earned her a Pulitzer Prize. Later, she left the newspaper to write novels and has published several bestsellers, including *One True Thing, Black and Blue,* and *Blessings.*

Bill **Cosby** (b. 1937)

Even as a child, comedian Bill Cosby showed a talent for comedy. He was once described as a student who would rather "clown than study." After college, Cosby put his skill as a comedian to work. His performances have made him an easily recognized, much-loved actor and comic.

Changing Values Though Cosby idolized boxers in his youth, today he promotes achievement in education rather than in the boxing ring. He once said, "I think there's a lot to be said for fighting at the blackboard, with a piece of chalk as a weapon."

Go **Online**
Author Link

For: More about the authors
Visit: www.PHSchool.com
Web Code: eme-9106

Melting Pot
Anna Quindlen

"Sunday Afternoon," Ralph Fasanella

My children are upstairs in the house next door, having dinner with the Ecuadorian family that lives on the top floor. The father speaks some English, the mother less than that. The two daughters are <u>fluent</u> in both their native and their adopted languages, but the youngest child, a son, a close friend of my two boys, speaks almost no Spanish. His parents thought it would be better that way. This doesn't surprise me; it was the way my mother was raised, American among Italians. I always suspected, hearing my grandfather talk about the "No Irish Need Apply" signs outside factories, hearing my mother talk about the neighborhood kids, who called her greaseball, that the American fable of the melting pot was a myth. Here in our neighborhood it exists, but like so many other things, it exists only person-to-person.

The letters in the local weekly tabloid[1] suggest that everybody hates everybody else here, and on a macro level they do. The old-timers are angry because they think the new moneyed professionals are taking over their town. The professionals are tired of being blamed for the neighborhood's rising rents, particularly since they are the ones paying them. The old immigrants are suspicious of the new ones. The new ones think the old ones are <u>bigots</u>. Nevertheless, on a micro level most of us get along. We are friendly with the Ecuadorian family, with the Yugoslavs across the street, and with the Italians next door, mainly by virtue of our children's sidewalk friendships. It took awhile. Eight years ago we were the new people on the block, filling dumpsters with old plaster and lath, . . . (sitting) on the

---

1. tabloid (tab′ loid′) *n.* small newspaper.

stoop with our demolition masks hanging around our necks like goiters.[2] We thought we could feel people staring at us from behind the sheer curtains on their windows. We were right.

My first apartment in New York was in a gritty warehouse district, the kind of place that makes your parents wince. A lot of old Italians lived around me, which suited me just fine because I was the granddaughter of old Italians. Their own children and grandchildren had moved to Long Island and New Jersey. All they had was me. All I had was them.

I remember sitting on a corner with a group of half a dozen elderly men, men who had known one another since they were boys sitting together on this same corner, watching a glazier install a great spread of tiny glass panes to make one wall of a restaurant in the ground floor of an old building across the street. The men laid bets on how long the panes, and the restaurant, would last. Two years later two of the men were dead, one had moved in with his married daughter in the suburbs, and the three remaining sat and watched dolefully as people waited each night for a table in the restaurant. "Twenty-two dollars for a piece of veal!" one of them would say, apropos of nothing.[3] But when I ate in the restaurant they never blamed me. "You're not one of them," one of the men explained. "You're one of me." It's an argument familiar to members of almost any embattled race or class: I like you, therefore you aren't like the rest of your kind, whom I hate.

Change comes hard in America, but it comes constantly. The butcher whose old shop is now an antiques store sits day after day outside the pizzeria here like a lost child. The old people across the street cluster together and discuss what kind of money they might be offered if the person who bought their building wants to turn it into condominiums. The greengrocer stocks yellow peppers and fresh rosemary for the gourmands, plum tomatoes and broad-leaf parsley for the older Italians, mangoes for the Indians. He doesn't carry plantains, he says, because you can buy them in the bodega.[4]

Sometimes the baby slips out with the bath water. I wanted to throw confetti the day that a family of rough types who propped their speakers on their station wagon and played

Literary Analysis
Author's Purpose
What purpose might Quindlen have for including details about the neighborhood?

Reading Check

What attitude does Quindlen say most people have toward others who are new or different?

---

2. goiters (goit´ ərz) *n.* swellings in the lower front of the neck caused by an enlarged thyroid gland.

3. apropos (ap´ rə pō´) **of nothing** without connection.

4. bodega (bō dä´ gə) *n.* small Hispanic grocery store.

heavy metal music at 3:00 A.M. moved out. I stood and smiled as the seedy bar at the corner was transformed into a slick Mexican restaurant. But I liked some of the people who moved out at the same time the rough types did. And I'm not sure I have that much in common with the singles who have made the restaurant their second home.

Yet somehow now we seem to have reached a nice mix. About a third of the people in the neighborhood think of squid as calamari, about a third think of it as sushi, and about a third think of it as bait. Lots of the single people who have moved in during the last year or two are easygoing and good-tempered about all the kids. The old Italians have become philosophical about the new Hispanics, although they still think more of them should know English. The firebrand community organizer with the storefront on the block, the one who is always talking about people like us as though we stole our houses out of the open purse of a ninety-year-old blind widow, is pleasant to my boys.

Drawn in broad strokes, we live in a pressure cooker: oil and water, us and them. But if you come around at exactly the right time, you'll find members of all these groups gathered around complaining about the condition of the streets, on which everyone can agree. We melt together, then draw apart. I am the granddaughter of immigrants, a young professional—either an interloper[5] or a longtime resident, depending on your concept of time. I am one of them, and one of us.

---

5. **interloper** (in´ tər lō´ pər) *n.* one who intrudes on another.

Thinking About the Selection

1. **(a) Recall:** Identify the different groups in Quindlen's neighborhood. **(b) Connect:** What experiences do most of the residents share? **(c) Interpret:** How do these shared experiences both unite and divide the residents?

2. **Draw Conclusions:** What advice would Quindlen give on how people of different cultures can get along?

3. **(a) Analyze:** How is Quindlen both "one of them" and "one of us"? **(b) Make a Judgment:** Do you think it is possible to belong to both groups? **(c) Apply:** What does this essay suggest about the way people live in city neighborhoods in the United States?

Was Tarzan a Three-Bandage Man?

Bill Cosby

*I*n the days before athletes had learned how to incorporate[1] themselves, they were shining heroes to American kids. In fact, they were such heroes to me and my friends that we even imitated their walks. When Jackie Robinson, a pigeon-toed[2] walker, became famous, we walked pigeon-toed, a painful form of locomotion unless you were Robinson or a pigeon.

"Why you walkin' like that?" said my mother one day.

"This is Jackie *Robinson's* walk," I proudly replied.

"There's somethin' wrong with his shoes?"

"He's the fastest man in baseball."

"He'd be faster if he didn't walk like that. His mother should make him walk right."

A few months later, when football season began, I stopped imitating Robinson and began to walk bowlegged[3] like a player named Buddy Helm.

"Why you always tryin' to change the shape of your legs?" said my mother. "You keep doin' that an' they'll fall off—an' I'm not gettin' you new ones."

Although baseball and football stars inspired us, our real heroes were the famous prize fighters, and the way to <u>emulate</u> a fighter was to walk around with a Band-Aid over one eye. People with acne walked around that way too, but we hoped it was clear that we were worshipping good fists and not bad skin.

The first time my mother saw me being Sugar Ray, not Jackie Robinson, she said, "What's that bandage for?"

"Oh, nuthin'," I replied.

"Now that's a new kinda stupid answer. That bandage gotta be coverin' somethin'—besides your entire brain."

"Well, it's just for show. I wanna look like Sugar Ray Robinson."

Literary Analysis
Author's Purpose
Why might Cosby have chosen to include this dialogue in his essay?

Vocabulary Builder
emulate (em´ yoo lāt´) *v.* copy or be like someone

✔Reading Check
Who were the boys' biggest heroes?

---

1. **incorporate** (in kôr´ pə rāt´) *v.* form into a legal business.
2. **pigeon-toed** (pij´ ən tōd´) *adj.* having the feet turned in toward each other.
3. **bowlegged** (bō´ leg´ id) *adj.* having legs that are curved outward.

"The fastest man in baseball."

"No, that's a different one."

"You doin' Swiss Family Robinson[4] next?"

"Swiss Family Robinson? They live in the projects?"

"You'd know who they are if you read more books instead of makin' yourself look like an accident. Why can't you try to imitate someone like Booker T. Washington?"[5]

"Who does he play for?"

"Bill, let's put it this way: you take off that bandage right now or I'll have your father move you up to stitches."

The following morning on the street, I <u>dejectedly</u> told the boys, "My mother says I gotta stop wearin' a bandage. She wants my whole head to show."

"What's wrong with that woman?" said Fat Albert. "She won't let you do *nuthin'*."

"It's okay, Cos," said Junior, "'cause one bandage ain't enough anyway. My brother says the really tough guys wear two."

"One over each eye?" I asked him.

"Or one eye and one nose," he said.

"Man, I wouldn't want to mess with no two-bandage man," said Eddie.

And perhaps the toughest guys of all wore tourniquets around their necks. We were capable of such attire, for we were never more ridiculous than when we were trying to be tough and cool. Most ridiculous, of course, was that our hero worshipping was backwards: we should have been emulating the men who had caused the need for bandages.

---

4. **Swiss Family Robinson** fictional family stranded on a desert island.
5. **Booker T. Washington** (1856–1915) African American educator and author.

Literary Analysis
Author's Purpose
Which details create humor in this dialogue?

Vocabulary Builder
dejectedly (dē jek´ tid lē) *adv.* sadly; showing discouragement

Thinking About the Selection

1. **(a) Recall:** What does Cosby do to imitate his heroes?
   (b) Infer: Why does young Cosby admire them?

2. **(a) Infer:** How does Cosby believe people will view him if he acts like his heroes? **(b) Assess:** Does his plan work?

3. **(a) Interpret:** How does Cosby's attitude about "three-bandage men" change in the end? **(b) Infer:** What has Cosby realized? **(c) Interpret:** What does this story suggest about the ways that famous people influence others?

Apply the Skills

Melting Pot • Was Tarzan a Three-Bandage Man?

Comparing Authors' Purposes

1. What does Quindlen want readers to learn about her neighborhood?
2. Why does Cosby tell this story from his childhood?
3. How might Cosby's essay be different if his purpose in writing were to persuade the reader to agree with his point of view about athletes as role models?
4. How is the purpose of Quindlen's essay different from the purpose of Cosby's essay?

Writing to Compare Literary Works

Tone is the author's attitude toward his or her subject. It can be described in one word, such as *formal, humorous, friendly,* or *distant.* The author's purpose for writing affects the tone of the work. Use a chart like the one shown to compare and contrast the tones of "Melting Pot" and "Was Tarzan a Three-Bandage Man?"

	Melting Pot	Was Tarzan a Three-Bandage Man?
Author's Purpose		
Tone		
Words or ideas that help create the tone		

Use information from the chart to write a comparison of the authors' purposes and tones. Consider these questions:
- Which essay better communicates the writer's ideas?
- How is each writer's tone suited to each essay's purpose?

Vocabulary Builder

Practice For each item below, write a sentence that correctly uses the words given.

1. fluent; travel
2. bigots; respect
3. dejectedly; sold out
4. emulate; celebrity

QuickReview

Go Online
Assessment
For: Self-test
Visit: www.PHSchool.com
Web Code: ema-6112

Author's Purpose: the author's main reason for writing

Tone: the writer's attitude toward his or her audience and subject

Reading: Author's Purpose

Directions: *Questions 1–5 are based on the following selection.*

I believe that the only solution to the traffic on Main Street is to create a bypass. State traffic records show that more than 60 percent of the traffic on Main Street is simply passing through. These are drivers who are going somewhere else but have no choice except to drive on Main Street. These drivers would almost always use the bypass, thus reducing the traffic on Main Street. The county engineer says that Riverside Drive can be widened to serve as a bypass. This construction would cost relatively little and could be finished in less than a month. From my point of view, this is an obvious solution to the problem.

1. **What is the author's overall purpose?**
   A to inform
   B to entertain
   C to reflect
   D to teach

2. **Which sentence establishes the author's position?**
   A I believe that the only solution to the traffic on Main Street is to create a bypass.
   B These drivers would almost always use the bypass.
   C The construction would cost relatively little and could be finished in less than a month.
   D Riverside Drive can be widened to serve as a bypass.

3. **What background does the author provide?**
   A Information on traffic
   B Information on the town
   C Information on the condition of the road
   D Information on the people's opinions about the traffic

4. **If the author's purpose were to entertain, what details might you expect to find?**
   A many facts
   B funny stories
   C long descriptions
   D personal opinions

5. **How is the author's purpose supported?**
   A with examples
   B with facts
   C with personal opinion
   D with stories

Vocabulary

Directions: Choose the word that best completes each of the following sentences.

6. Knowing cultural and historical _____ helps you understand parts of literature.
   A prior
   B background
   C establishment
   D recollections

7. The _____ novel was more exciting than this one.
   A previous
   B established
   C recalled
   D background

8. Did the author write anything _____ to this?
   A prior
   B background
   C recalled
   D established

9. Can you _____ the character's name?
   A establish
   B recall
   C prior
   D previous

10. Once you _____ the author's purpose you can judge the effectiveness of the work.
    A establish
    B recall
    C prior
    D previous

11. We want to hire someone who has had _____ experience.
    A prepaid
    B previous
    C prearranged
    D preface

12. The parents want to _____ the movie before they let their children see it.
    A prefix
    B precede
    C preview
    D preheat

13. We could _____ how the movie would end.
    A revise
    B predict
    C review
    D predate

14. He cannot _____ the information he needs to answer the questions.
    A renew
    B rebuild
    C recall
    D recover

15. The rehearsal will _____ the performance.
    A recall
    B return
    C precede
    D review

Spelling Homophones

A **homophone** is a word that sounds exactly like another word but has a different spelling and meaning.

Two or Too? One of the most common "spelling" errors occurs when a writer uses the wrong homophone. Spell checker software will not find this kind of error, so proofread your work carefully. Use **mnemonic devices**, or memory aids, to help you remember which spelling to use. For example, to distinguish between *there* and *their,* notice that the word that means the opposite of *here* also contains the word *here.*

You are blocking our light!

Practice On your paper write the word from the Word List that matches each mnemonic clue. Use a different color pen or pencil to show the letters that the clue helps you remember.

1. If it is nice, you can **eat** outside.

2. The _____ is your **pal**.

3. **They** are in this word.

4. You get this number by putting one **with** one.

5. Decision words: **when**, _____ , **why**. (They all begin with the same two letters.)

6. This word contains its opposite. Not **here** but _____.

Word List
to
too
two
weather
whether
they're
their
there
principal
principle

A. Directions: *Write the letter of the sentence in which the homophone is used correctly.*

1. to
   A The puzzle had to many pieces.
   B She gave the puzzle to her brother.
   C Those to pieces look the same.
   D We tried that puzzle to.

2. whether
   A If the whether is nice, we will go to the park.
   B I don't know what the whether will be tomorrow.
   C We can't decide whether we should go to the park.
   D We will see if the whether is nice enough to go.

3. principle
   A Did the principle make the announcement?
   B That is the principle reason why I did not leave.
   C Mr. Stowe has two principle rules.
   D His main principle is to believe in his students.

4. too
   A She will help too.
   B She will help the too children.
   C She went to the store.
   D She paid her money too the clerk.

B. Directions: *Write the letter of the homophone that would be the correct spelling to fill in the blank.*

1. We have never been _____ before.
   A there
   B their
   C theyre
   D they're

2. Elizabeth has _____ brothers.
   A too
   B to
   C two
   D tow

3. The _____ was pleasant.
   A weather
   B wether
   C whether
   D wheather

4. _____ very young to be such good swimmers.
   A There
   B Their
   C Theyre
   D They're

5. Everyone met the new _____ on the first day of school.
   A principle
   B principel
   C princapel
   D principal

6. I saw _____ little sister at the movies.
   A there
   B their
   C theyre
   D they're

Narration: Autobiographical Narrative

Some of the best stories you may read are not made up—they tell of real events in the writer's life. Such stories are called **autobiographical narratives.** Follow the steps outlined in this workshop to write your own autobiographical narrative.

Assignment Write an autobiographical narrative about an event in your life that helped you grow or changed your outlook.

What to Include To succeed, your narrative should feature the following elements:

- a clear sequence of events involving you, the writer
- a problem or conflict, or a clear contrast between past and present viewpoints
- pacing that effectively builds the action
- specific details and quotations that help readers vividly imagine movement, gestures, and expressions
- error-free writing, including correct use of pronouns

To preview the criteria on which your autobiographical narrative may be judged, see the rubric on page 161.

Writing Workshop: *Work in Progress*

If you have completed the Work-in-Progress assignments, you already have in your portfolio ideas to use in your autobiographical narrative. Continue to develop these ideas, or you may choose to explore a new idea as you complete the Writing Workshop.

Using the Form

You may use elements of this form in these writing situations:

- letters
- reflective essays
- journals
- persuasive essays

Reading Writing
Connection

To get the feel for narrative nonfiction, read the selection from *An American Childhood* by Annie Dillard (p. 52).

Prewriting

Choosing Your Topic

To choose the right event from your life to narrate, use one of the following strategies:

- **Freewriting** Write for five minutes about whatever comes to mind on the following general topics: *funny times, sad times,* and *lessons I have learned.* When you are finished, review what you have written and circle any ideas that could make a good topic.

- **Listing** Make a chart with four columns, labeling the first column *People*, the second *Places*, the third *Things*, and the last *Events*. In each column, list names or descriptions of memorable people and things that you know from home, school, or travel. Next, review your chart to find connections between the items. For each connection you find, circle the two items and draw an arrow between them. Finally, review the connections you have found, and jot down ideas for stories that they suggest.

Narrowing Your Topic

Once you have a general idea of the story you will tell, get a better idea of its size and shape. For instance, if you have decided to write about a friend named Carlos, jot down notes on events involving him. Then, select just one event on which to focus your attention.

Gathering Details

Make a timeline. Once you have focused on a topic, begin to gather the details that you will use in your narrative. You might find it useful to fill out a timeline like the one shown.

Work in Progress
Review the work you did on pages 115 and 137.

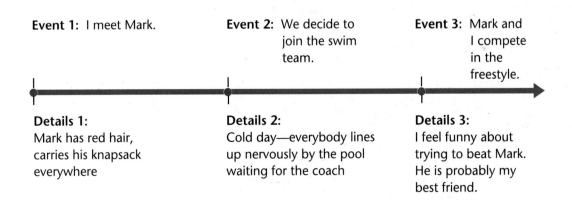

Event 1: I meet Mark.

Event 2: We decide to join the swim team.

Event 3: Mark and I compete in the freestyle.

Details 1:
Mark has red hair, carries his knapsack everywhere

Details 2:
Cold day—everybody lines up nervously by the pool waiting for the coach

Details 3:
I feel funny about trying to beat Mark. He is probably my best friend.

Drafting

Shaping Your Writing

Analyze your conflict. Review your prewriting notes and make a conflict chart like the one shown. In the center, write a brief description of the conflict. Fill in linked circles with specific narrative action related to the conflict. As you draft, refer to your chart to help connect details to your central conflict.

Make a story map. Using the conflict, map out the events of your story in sequence. Pace your story to build suspense. To decide what information a reader needs to follow your story, review your map and include additional details at appropriate points.

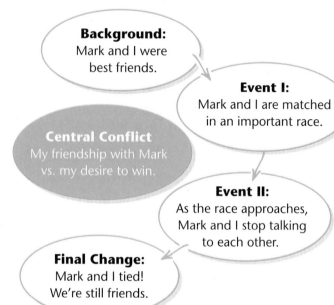

Background:
Mark and I were best friends.

Event I:
Mark and I are matched in an important race.

Central Conflict
My friendship with Mark vs. my desire to win.

Event II:
As the race approaches, Mark and I stop talking to each other.

Final Change:
Mark and I tied! We're still friends.

Providing Elaboration

Show, do not tell. As you write, show readers what happened, do not just tell them. Add life to your story with precise descriptions of places, people, and events.

Tells:	It was the first day of school. Ryan and I took our seats in our third-grade classroom.
Shows:	The first day of school was the first true day of autumn, with a rich blue sky and a nip in the air. When Ryan and I took our seats in the third-grade classroom, you could hear the noisy excitement of all the other students.

Use dialogue. Bring people to life by using dialogue, quoting what people said as they said it. Do not report everything a character says. Instead, choose the right conversations to vividly show the character's feelings, gestures, and expressions as they react to events.

Reading Writing Connection

To read the complete student model, see page 160.

Student Model: Using Dialogue to Elaborate

As we came around the corner of the bike path, I started picking up speed. By the time I realized what was happening, it was too late. "The hill!" I yelled to Erika.

"Your brakes! Use your brakes!" she shouted.

> This conversation builds interest and excitement.

Richard Peck
on Conflict in Fiction

Richard Peck

My novel *Fair Weather* is about a farm girl named Rosie Beckett who's never been anywhere until she and her family have the adventure of their lives. They visit the World's Columbian Exposition, the great Chicago world's fair of 1893. It's in the Women's Building at the fair where Rosie finds her future. But the story begins down on the farm because all fiction is based on contrast: young, old; male, female; country, city. . . .

"I wrote 'The Three-Century Woman' twelve times. . . ."
—————— **Richard Peck**

Professional Model:
from *Fair Weather*

It was the last day of our old lives and we didn't even know it.

 Strangely, this book was published on September 10, 2001.

I didn't. It looked like any old day to me, a sultry summer morning hot enough to ruffle the roofline. But then, any little thing could come as a surprise to us. We were just plain country people. I suppose we were poor, but we didn't know it. Poor but proud. There wasn't a ~~scrap~~ blister of paint in the house, but there were no hogs under the porch~~, and no rust on the implements~~.

 I decided to leave it with hogs. The detail about the rust wasn't necessary as further evidence of the family's pride.

I was sitting out in the old rope swing at the back of our place because the house was too full of Mama and my sister Lottie. I wasn't swinging. I thought I was pretty nearly too old to ~~be swinging~~ swing. In the fall I'd be fourteen, with only one more year of school to go.

 I wanted to suggest a conflict here between sister and mother, but to let the reader wonder what the problem is.

Revising

Revising Your Overall Structure

Check your pacing. A good story builds to a single most exciting moment, called the **climax**. The secret of building to a climax is **pacing**—the speed at which your story moves along. To improve the pacing of your story, use the following strategies:

- Cut details and events that do not build suspense or heighten reader interest.
- Revise or delete any paragraph not clearly connected to the central conflict.
- Make clear connections between other events to show readers how they relate to each other.

To read the complete student model, see page 160.

Student Model: Building to a Climax

It all started when I arrived at my grandparent's house

~~I made many friends in their neighborhood, but they spent most of their time riding bikes, and I didn't have one. Then, my~~

in Galesburg to spend the summer. ∧ My step-grandmother gave me

the almost new, metallic green bike that her grandson had

outgrown. I was overjoyed to have a bike. . .

> Adding these details introduces important information that helps move the story along: They show why success at bike-riding is so important to the writer.

Peer Review: Give your draft to one or two classmates to read. Ask them to highlight details that slow the story down or ideas that are unconnected to the central conflict. Use the feedback to eliminate any unnecessary details from your draft.

Revising Your Word Choice

Use specific, precise nouns. Look for nouns that are vague or general and might leave the reader wondering *what kind.* Replace general and vague nouns with specific and precise ones. Review your draft, circling any nouns that do not answer the questions *What exactly?* and *What kind?*. Replace these nouns with specific, precise nouns that convey a lively picture.

Vague	**Precise**
stuff ⟶	souvenirs

General	**Specific**
decorations ⟶	party streamers and balloons

Integrating Grammar Skills

Checking Pronoun–Antecedent Agreement

Incorrect pronoun–antecedent agreement occurs whenever a personal pronoun disagrees with its antecedent in person, number, and gender.

Identifying Incorrect Pronoun–Antecedent Agreement   An *antecedent* is the word or words for which a pronoun stands. A pronoun's antecedent may be a noun, a group of words acting as a noun, or another pronoun.

Prentice Hall Writing and Grammar Connection: Chapter 24, Section 2

	Antecedent		**Pronoun**
Example:	I told Alexis to bring a bathing suit with her.		

In this example, the pronoun *her* is third person and singular. It agrees with its feminine antecedent, *Alexis*, which is also third person (the person spoken about) and singular.

Fixing Agreement errors   To fix an incorrect pronoun–antecedent agreement, identify both the pronoun and the antecedent for which it stands. Then correct the agreement using one of the following methods.

1. **Identify the person of the antecedent** as first, second, or third, and choose a pronoun that matches the antecedent in person.

2. **Identify the number of the antecedent** as singular or plural, and choose a pronoun that matches the antecedent in number.

3. **Identify the gender of the antecedent** as masculine or feminine, and choose a pronoun that matches the antecedent in gender.

The Personal Pronouns		
	Singular	**Plural**
First Person	I, me, my, mine	we, us, our, ours
Second Person	you, your, yours	you, your, yours
Third Person	**Feminine:** she, her, hers **Masculine:** he, him, his **Neutral:** it, its	they, them, their, theirs

Apply It To Your Editing

Choose one or two paragraphs in your draft. Draw an arrow from each personal pronoun to its antecedent. If the pronoun–antecedent agreement is incorrect, fix it using one of the methods above.

Student Model: Alexander Baker
Palos Verdes, CA

Bicycle Braking Blues

Crash! Once again, I found myself flying off my bike and toward the grass. At age eight, crashes were an everyday occurrence, and I reminded myself that it was better to practice braking here by the lawn than to risk another episode like "The Club Hill Clobbering."

> With this hint, Alexander clearly connects his introduction to the central conflict of his story.

It all started when I arrived at my grandparents' house in Galesburg to spend the summer. I made many friends in their neighborhood, but they spent most of their time riding bikes, and I didn't have one. Then, my step-grandmother gave me the almost new, metallic green bike that her grandson had outgrown. I was overjoyed to have a bike. . . . I learned to ride it well enough—what I didn't learn was how to use the brakes. On the flat ground near my grandparents' house, I just let the bike slow down until I could put my feet down.

> Adding this detail helps move the story along—it shows why a bike is so important to Alexander.

One day my babysitter took me for lunch at the club grill. She rode my grandfather's golf cart while I rode my bike. When we had to climb the big hill leading up to the club, I walked my bike alongside the cart. After lunch, I mounted my bike while Erika drove Grandpa's golf cart. As we headed toward home, neither of us gave a thought to . . . the HILL.

> Alexander narrates events in clear sequence.

As we came around the corner of the bike path, I started picking up speed. By the time I realized what was happening, it was too late. "The hill!" I yelled to Erika. "Your brakes! Use your brakes!" she shouted. With the wind rushing in my ears, I could hardly hear her. Looking down the hill, I saw a golf cart was blocking the path. It seemed to be getting bigger and closer by the second. "Well," I thought to myself, "it's now or never." I steered my speeding bike toward the grass alongside the path and jumped off sideways. I leapt off and BAM! The world turned upside down and inside out. The next sound I heard was the grumbling of a golf cart engine. It sounded annoyed about the jumble of parts in its path. The next thing I saw was Erika's face. She was so scared that her face was stiff and pale. I stood up to show Erika that I was fine. The only damage I sustained was some dirt on my jeans, and the bike survived without too many scratches too. Also, my pride was hurt. How can you ride a bike if you can never go down hill? So every day, Erika took me to the hill and we'd go a little further up. That way, I learned to brake on a hill, little by little, rather than getting clobbered again!

> Using this precise noun helps vividly convey the scene to readers.

> Details like *stiff and pale* help readers vividly imagine Erika's expression.

Editing and Proofreading

Once you have completed your draft, read it over to correct for errors in spelling, grammar, and punctuation.

Focus on the Dialogue: As you proofread your story, pay close attention to the correct punctuation of **dialogue**—the actual words spoken by a character. All dialogue should be enclosed in quotation marks. For more information, see the section on quotation marks in the Grammar Handbook on page R31.

Publishing and Presenting

Consider one of the following ways to share your writing:

Present an oral narrative. Practice telling the story, using notes rather than reading from your draft, until you can deliver the story smoothly and naturally. Practice using gestures to emphasize key points. Tell your story to the class.

Make a poster. Arrange photos, artwork, or small souvenirs, along with a neat copy of your narrative, on posterboard to display in class.

Prentice Hall Writing and Grammar Connection: Chapter 4

Reflecting on Your Writing

Writer's Journal Jot down your thoughts about writing an autobiographical narrative. Begin by answering these questions:

- Which strategies in this chapter did you use for revising? How would you rate them?
- As you wrote, what new insights into your story did you have?

Rubric for Self-Assessment

To assess your autobiographical narrative, use the following rubric:

Criteria	Rating Scale
	not very very
Focus: How clearly does the narrative present the problem or conflict?	1 2 3 4 5
Organization: How clearly is the sequence of events presented?	1 2 3 4 5
Support/Elaboration: How vivid are details and quotations?	1 2 3 4 5
Style: How effectively is the action of the story paced?	1 2 3 4 5
Conventions: How correct is your grammar, especially your use of pronouns and antecedents?	1 2 3 4 5

Organizing and Delivering a Narrative Presentation

A **narrative presentation** is prepared and organized in much the same way as a written narrative. Unlike a written narrative, though, a narrative presentation can be enlivened by the way you use your voice and facial expressions. The following techniques and strategies will help you give an effective and interesting narrative presentation.

Organize Your Presentation

A narrative presentation tells story events in order, focusing on the central conflict, problem, or insight.

Make notes. Begin by writing your narrative, including dialogue and descriptive details. As you write, think about your audience. Choose words and a language style, such as serious or playful, that are appropriate for that audience.

Deliver Your Presentation

Rehearse your delivery. Whether or not you use a script, look up frequently. Use your facial expressions and voice to make the narrative interesting.

- **Vary the volume.** For example, speak loudly to express how a coach peps up her team or softly to describe how a baby falls asleep.

- **Switch the pitch.** For example, use a high voice to show excitement or panic, a low voice to show sternness or tiredness. Also, change the sound of your voice to indicate different speakers in dialogue.

Presentation Tips for Specific Audiences

Younger Audience	Older Audience
• Exaggerate reactions with dramatic facial expressions.	• Use more realistic voices and facial expressions.
• Use short sentences and simple vocabulary.	• Use varied sentences and sophisticated vocabulary level.
• Insert questions that invite audience participation. Make frequent eye contact.	• Maintain audience attention by changing your position and moving about as you speak. Make frequent eye contact.

As you rehearse, speak slowly and clearly. Remember to use a tone of voice and language style that are appropriate for your audience.

Activity ▶ *Prepare and Deliver a Speech* ▶ Choose a fictional story you would like to present. Determine who your audience is. Use the strategies in this workshop to organize and deliver your presentation. Ask a partner to give you feedback. Finally, deliver your presentation.

Farewell to Manzanar

Jeanne Wakatsuki Houston and James D. Houston

Bantam, 1973

Autobiography This autobiography traces Jeanne's coming of age in the 1940s when, as a Japanese American child, she and the rest of her family are interned after Pearl Harbor. Her account of coming to terms with internment-camp life—and then of adjusting to life outside after the war—is sometimes disquieting, sometimes humorous, and ultimately inspiring.

Letters from Rifka

Karen Hesse

Puffin, 1992

Novel While fleeing Russia to escape early twentieth-century anti-Semitism, young Rifka is separated from her family and forced to fend for herself until she can join them in America. The result is a popular, short coming-of-age novel told in a series of letters to a relative back in Russia.

Bearstone

Will Hobbs

Aladdin Paperbacks, 1989

Novel An orphaned Indian boy temporarily finds a home with an old prospector and rancher. Their attempts to understand each other, and their appreciation for the glorious mountain area of Colorado, lead them to mutual respect and affection.

Oliver Twist: A Pacemaker Classic

Charles Dickens

Globe Fearon, 1995

Novel Oliver Twist is abandoned at an early age and forced to live in a workhouse that is presided over by Mr. Bumble. The living conditions are so miserable that Oliver escapes to the streets of London, where he joins a group of young pickpockets—an underworld gang led by the crafty Fagin.

These titles are available in the Penguin/Prentice Hall Literature Library.
Consult your teacher before choosing one.

Think About It It is often said that "no two snowflakes are alike." The same thing can be said of people. The following selection is about a unique individual who made it his life's work to photograph snowflakes and chronicle the weather patterns of his Vermont town. Wilson A. Bentley was the first person to photograph the delicate artistry of snowflakes before they melted away.

A Special Gift
The Legacy of "Snowflake" Bentley

Barbara Eaglesham

Wilson Bentley received a gift on his 15th birthday that was to change his life—an old microscope his mother had once used in teaching. As birthday gifts go, it might not have seemed like much, but to this 1880s Vermont farm boy it was special indeed. "When the other boys of my age were playing with popguns and sling-shots, I was absorbed in studying things under this microscope," he later wrote.

And nothing fascinated him more than snowflakes. It would become a passion that would last a lifetime, earn him the nickname "Snowflake Bentley," and make him known around the world.

Focused on Beauty

If you have ever seen a snowflake design on a mug, or on jewelry, or maybe on a tote bag, chances are it was based on one of Bentley's more than 5,000 photomicrographs[1] of snow crystals (snow crystals are the building blocks of snowflakes).

At first, though, Bentley did not own a camera. He had only his eyes and his microscope, and no way to share his enjoyment of the delicate

---

1. **photomicrographs** photographs made through a microscope.

hexagons other than to draw them. As soon as the snow started to fly (and if his chores were done), he would collect some snow crystals on a board painted black. He'd spend hours inside his woodshed, where he had his microscope, picking up the most perfect ones on the end of a piece of straw from a broom and transferring them to a microscope slide. There, he would flatten them with a bird feather. Then, holding his breath, he would observe the crystal and hurry to draw what he saw before it evaporated into thin air. It was a frustrating business to try to capture all the details in a drawing while simultaneously being in a race against time.

Eventually, a few years later, Bentley noticed an advertisement for a microscope and camera that he knew was the answer to his dreams. The problem was, the equipment cost $100—equal to a whopping $2,000 today. His father, being a serious, hardworking farmer, felt that looking through a microscope was a waste of time. "Somehow my mother got him to spend the money." Bentley wrote, "but he never came to believe it had been worthwhile." That was probably a feeling shared by the locals of Jericho, who nicknamed him "Snowflake" Bentley.

Undeterred, he began his quest to photograph a snow crystal. Once he attached the microscope to the camera and rigged up a way to focus it without running back and forth (he couldn't reach the focus knob from behind the camera), he began experimenting with photography. In the 1880s, few people owned a camera, so Bentley had no one to ask for help. Time after frustrating time, his negatives appeared blank. Not until the following winter did he figure out that too much light was reaching the camera lens. His solution was to place a metal plate with a pinhole in the center beneath the stage of the microscope, to cut down the stray light and allow only the light waves carrying the image to reach the camera.

This was the key, and on January 15, 1885, at the age of 19, Bentley finally photographed a snowflake! Many hours over the next 45 years were spent in his tiny darkroom beneath the stairs developing negatives that he then carried, often by lantern-light, to the brook for washing. In all that time, he never saw two snow crystals that were exactly alike, although he realized that if he were able to collect two crystals side-by-side from the same cloud, there was a good chance that they might look the same. (Scientist Nancy Knight did just that in 1988, and indeed found two identical snow crystals!)

An artist as well as a scientist, Bentley wanted to find a way to make the shape of the crystal stand out more from the white background of the photo paper. He couldn't bring himself to alter his original glass plate negatives, so he began making copies of them and scraping the photographic emulsion away from the edges of the images with a knife, a time-consuming trick that allowed sunlight through, turning the background black when printed by sunlight.

Bentley's book, *Snow Crystals,* containing 2,453 of his photographs, was finally published and delivered to his house just weeks before his death in 1931. Bentley was pleased. He never made more than a few thousand dollars from his work, but it had been a labor of love and he was satisfied to know that he would finally be able to share the beauty of his snow crystals with the world.

He is remembered primarily for this accomplishment, but to his friends and family, he was kind, gentle, and funny "Willie." He was the man who would sometimes tie an insect to a blade of grass to photograph it covered with dew the next morning, and who always chewed every bite 36 times. He was a gifted pianist who also played the violin and clarinet. He was the bachelor farmer who lived in the same farm-

house all his life. To scientists, he was the untrained researcher who not only photographed snow crystals, but also kept a detailed daily log of local weather conditions throughout his life and developed a method to measure the size of raindrops. To the people of Jericho, he is remembered as the not-so-flaky-after-all "Snowflake" Bentley.

More to Explore

Odyssey: Adventures in Science is a magazine written for young science students. The magazine presents a science-related theme for each month and all the articles address that topic. This article—from the December 2002 issue—was written by Barbara Eaglesham, who is a frequent contributor to the magazine.

Readings in Science
Talk About It

Use the following questions to guide a discussion.

1. **(a)** What gift did Bentley receive for his fifteenth birthday? **(b)** How do you think this gift is different from the types of gifts that other boys his age were receiving?

2. **(a)** What problems did Bentley face when he attempted to draw the snowflakes he observed? **(b)** Why do you think Bentley's father agreed to buy the expensive equipment?

3. Bentley's work never made him rich, but the writer states that he was happy knowing he had shared his knowledge with others. In a small group, decide whether Bentley's work was useful to the world. Consider these questions:
   - Was Bentley's work beneficial to science?
   - What other benefits did Bentley's photographs have?
   - How do you think "Snowflake" would have felt if he had heard the news of Nancy Knight's discovery in 1988?

   Choose a point person to summarize your group's ideas.

Short Stories

Unit 2 Overview

Introduction
Exploring Short Stories

Part 1: Predicting

Part 2: Making
Inferences

Introduction:
Short Stories

Walter Dean Myers

From the Author's Desk

Walter Dean Myers
Talks About the Form

When I think of short stories I am reminded of my childhood in Harlem. My dad wasn't a writer but he liked to tell stories and I loved listening to them. Most of his stories were deliciously scary, always beginning in the dark of night, and always involving mysterious sounds that would send my imagination reeling. A few words into one of his stories I would know what kind of story it was going to be, and what problems would be encountered. Then I would just sit and hope that it wouldn't be too scary.

"Telling" Short Stories

My grandfather came to live with us when I was twelve and he, too, was a storyteller. His stories were almost always from the Bible and I was familiar with the **characters,** but I really liked the dramatic way my grandfather presented the stories. There would be different voices for each character and even different expressions on the old man's face. I also knew that the stories would never last longer than about ten minutes.

When I began to write I turned to the short story because it was a form that I had learned at home. My father and grandfather were "telling" short stories. I wrote my stories instead of telling them, but for me it had the same feel.

▲ Walter Dean Myers has written highly praised books about young adults coming of age and facing situations that test them as individuals.

▼ Critical Viewing The man in this illustration might be reading a short story. Based on what Walter Dean Myers says about stories, what qualities of the writing may have captured the man's attention? **[Connect]**

Setting up the Conflict Quickly

I learned to recognize the **short story** as a form in which I must set up the **conflict,** or struggle, quickly, establish believable characters, and work toward a logical conclusion.

I could usually write a story in one day (they were only three to four pages long), and I wrote dozens of them. I wanted to grip the reader, in the way that Stephen Vincent Benét suggests in his definition of a short story, shown here.

I was also reading short stories. It was my feeling that the short story, while handling only one aspect of the human experience, did so more intently than the novels I was reading. I still believe that to be the case in the best stories.

Something that can be read in an hour and remembered for a lifetime.

—Stephen Vincent Benét

In many ways I think, when I'm writing, that I'm doing the same thing that my father and grandfather did. I'm telling stories that I hope will be dramatic enough and rich enough to hold a reader's interest for a short while — and maybe stay in a reader's memory "for a lifetime."

More About the Author

Walter Dean **Myers** (b. 1937)

Walter Dean Myers grew up in the African American community of Harlem in New York City. Details from his background often appear in his stories — like Greg in "The Treasure of Lemon Brown," he loved playing basketball. When he writes, Myers begins with an outline, then cuts out pictures of his characters for a collage that hangs on the wall. He says, "When I walk into the room, I can see the characters, and I just get very close to them."

Fast Facts

▶ Having a severe speech difficulty when he was a child led Myers to communicate through writing.
▶ He conducted research for one of his novels by interviewing prison inmates in New York and New Jersey.

Learning About Short Stories

Elements of Short Stories

The possibilities for short stories are as endless as the bounds of a writer's imagination, so no two stories are ever alike. There are, however, some elements that all short stories share.

Characters are the people or animals who take part in a story's action. Characters are directed by **motivation**—the reason or reasons that explain why characters act as they do.

Characterization is the way a writer reveals a character's personality and qualities.

- In **direct characterization,** the writer describes the character.
- In **indirect characterization,** the writer reveals the character through speech and actions.

PEANUTS reprinted by permission of United Features Syndicate, Inc.

Theme is the central message expressed in a story. A **universal theme,** or a recurring theme, is a message about life that is expressed in different cultures and time periods. Some common universal themes are

- Hard work always pays off in the end.
- Youth can often see what adults cannot.

Themes such as the ones listed above will appear in stories across many societies despite great cultural differences.

Plot is the sequence of events in a short story. It is usually divided into five parts:

- **Exposition** introduces the **setting**—the time and place of the story, the characters, and the basic situation.
- **Rising action** introduces the **conflict,** or problem.
- **Climax** is the turning point of a story.
- **Falling action** is the part of a story when the conflict lessens.
- **Resolution** is the story's conclusion.

Literary Devices

Literary Devices are the tools writers often use to enhance their writing. Some common literary devices and narrative techniques you will come across while reading short stories are listed here.

- **Foreshadowing** is the use of clues early in a story to hint at events that are going to occur later.
- **Flashback** is the placement of a scene within a story that interrupts the sequence of events to reveal past occurrences.
- **Irony** is the general name given to literary techniques that involve surprising, interesting, or amusing contradictions. When a story includes irony, something unexpected happens.
- **Dialect** is the form of a language spoken by people in a particular region or group. The use of dialect gives a short story a more authentic feel and helps a character's words sound more realistic.

Check Your Understanding

Choose the letter of the short story element that best matches each item. Discuss your responses with a partner. Then, decide whether your answers have changed or your knowledge of the subject has grown based on your discussion.

1. a deserted beach at dawn
   a. setting   **b.** plot
2. a student struggles to pass an exam
   a. dialect   **b.** conflict
3. a wisecracking grandmother
   a. character   **b.** setting
4. an unlikely hero saves another person
   a. plot   **b.** flashback
5. an airplane bound for Hawaii
   a. conflict   **b.** setting

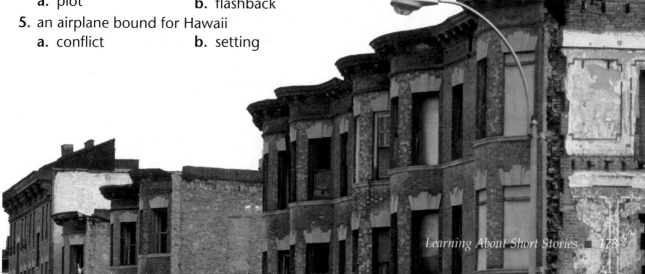

From the Author's Desk
Walter Dean Myers Introduces "The Treasure of Lemon Brown"

No one is "only" a writer. We all have complex, multi-faceted lives. In addition to being a writer, I'm an amateur musician, a sports nut, and a collector of historical items. My basement holds over ten thousand antique photographs, hundreds of documents, and many, many scrapbooks.

The items I collect represent stories to me. Scrapbooks in particular seem to be an effort by the persons putting them together to form a story. Sometimes the scrapbooks will cover one event, like a vacation trip or an important political event. Other scrapbooks will cover a longer event, such as a war.

Sources for the Story: A Scrapbook and an Incident

It intrigues me to pick up a scrapbook and see what someone has decided to save, to remember. It was while looking at such a scrapbook that the idea for "The Treasure of Lemon Brown" came to mind.

I combined this idea with an incident that happened when I was fourteen. I had a chance to play on a great basketball team and my father wouldn't give me the money for a uniform. I was furious with him. Later, as an adult, I knew my father wanted the best for me, but he couldn't afford everything that I wanted. Still, I included my youthful anger in the story.

A Flashback and a Foreshadowing

Many of the things I've done as a youngster (I was always in some kind of trouble) I've thought about as an adult. In "Lemon Brown" I am revisiting my life as a young ball player and my dad's concerns for me. That memory inspired a **flashback** near the start of the story, an argument between Greg and his father that occurred two nights before the story begins. I included this earlier dispute and the storm at the beginning of the story to **foreshadow** trouble to come.

The **Treasure** of Lemon Brown

WALTER DEAN MYERS

The dark sky, filled with angry, swirling clouds, reflected Greg Ridley's mood as he sat on the stoop of his building. His father's voice came to him again, first reading the letter the principal had sent to the house, then lecturing endlessly about his poor efforts in math.

"I had to leave school when I was thirteen," his father had said, "that's a year younger than you are now. If I'd had half the chances that you have, I'd . . ."

Greg had sat in the small, pale green kitchen listening, knowing the lecture would end with his father saying he couldn't play ball with the Scorpions. He had asked his father the week before, and his father had said it depended on his

▲ **Critical Viewing**
How do these colors compare with the story's mood? **[Compare]**

Walter Dean Myers
Author's Insight
I use the weather for establishing moods and in this case, as a reason to send Greg into the house with Lemon Brown.

next report card. It wasn't often the Scorpions took on new players, especially fourteen-year-olds, and this was a chance of a lifetime for Greg. He hadn't been allowed to play high school ball, which he had really wanted to do, but playing for the Community Center team was the next best thing. Report cards were due in a week,

Disequilibrium, 1987, Catherine Redmond, Courtesy of the artist

and Greg had been hoping for the best. But the principal had ended the suspense early when she sent that letter saying Greg would probably fail math if he didn't spend more time studying.

"And you want to play *basketball?*" His father's brows knitted over deep brown eyes. "That must be some kind of a joke. Now you just get into your room and hit those books."

That had been two nights before. His father's words, like the distant thunder that now echoed through the streets of Harlem, still rumbled softly in his ears.

It was beginning to cool. Gusts of wind made bits of paper dance between the parked cars. There was a flash of nearby lightning, and soon large drops of rain splashed onto his jeans. He stood to go upstairs, thought of the lecture that probably awaited him if he did anything except shut himself in his room with his math book, and started walking down the street instead. Down the block there was an old tenement[1] that had been abandoned for some months. Some of the guys had held an impromptu checker tournament there the week before, and Greg had noticed that the door, once boarded over, had been slightly ajar.

Pulling his collar up as high as he could, he checked for traffic and made a dash across the street. He reached the house just as another flash of lightning changed the night to day for

---

1. **tenement** (ten´ ə mənt) *n.* old, run-down apartment house.

an instant, then returned the graffiti-scarred building to the grim shadows. He vaulted over the outer stairs and pushed <u>tentatively</u> on the door. It was open, and he let himself in.

The inside of the building was dark except for the dim light that filtered through the dirty windows from the streetlamps. There was a room a few feet from the door, and from where he stood at the entrance, Greg could see a squarish patch of light on the floor. He entered the room, frowning at the musty smell. It was a large room that might have been someone's parlor at one time. Squinting, Greg could see an old table on its side against one wall, what looked like a pile of rags or a torn mattress in the corner, and a couch, with one side broken, in front of the window.

He went to the couch. The side that wasn't broken was comfortable enough, though a little creaky. From the spot he could see the blinking neon sign over the bodega[2] on the corner. He sat awhile, watching the sign blink first green then red, allowing his mind to drift to the Scorpions, then to his father. His father had been a postal worker for all Greg's life, and was proud of it, often telling Greg how hard he had worked to pass the test. Greg had heard the story too many times to be interested now.

For a moment Greg thought he heard something that sounded like a scraping against the wall. He listened carefully, but it was gone.

Outside the wind had picked up, sending the rain against the window with a force that shook the glass in its frame. A car passed, its tires hissing over the wet street and its red taillights glowing in the darkness.

Greg thought he heard the noise again. His stomach tightened as he held himself still and listened intently. There weren't any more scraping noises, but he was sure he had heard something in the darkness—something breathing!

He tried to figure out just where the breathing was coming from; he knew it was in the room with him. Slowly he stood, tensing. As he turned, a flash of lightning lit up the room, frightening him with its sudden brilliance. He saw nothing, just the overturned table, the pile of rags and an old newspaper on the floor. Could he have been imagining the sounds? He continued listening, but heard nothing and thought that it

---

2. **bodega** (bō dā´ gə) *n.* small grocery store serving a Latino neighborhood.

Vocabulary Builder
tentatively (ten´ tə tiv lē) *adv.* hesitantly; with uncertainty

Walter Dean Myers
Author's Insight
My dad always used sounds when he told stories. Sometimes he would hit the side of his foot against the leg of the chair he was sitting on.

Reading Check

Why does Greg prefer going to the tenement to going home?

might have just been rats. Still, he thought, as soon as the rain let up he would leave. He went to the window and was about to look when he heard a voice behind him.

"Don't try nothin' 'cause I got a razor here sharp enough to cut a week into nine days!"

Greg, except for an involuntary tremor[3] in his knees, stood stock still. The voice was high and brittle, like dry twigs being broken, surely not one he had ever heard before. There was a shuffling sound as the person who had been speaking moved a step closer. Greg turned, holding his breath, his eyes straining to see in the dark room.

The upper part of the figure before him was still in darkness. The lower half was in the dim rectangle of light that fell unevenly from the window. There were two feet, in cracked, dirty shoes from which rose legs that were wrapped in rags.

"Who are you?" Greg hardly recognized his own voice.

"I'm Lemon Brown," came the answer. "Who're you?"

"Greg Ridley."

"What you doing here?" The figure shuffled forward again, and Greg took a small step backward.

"It's raining," Greg said.

"I can see that," the figure said.

The person who called himself Lemon Brown peered forward, and Greg could see him clearly. He was an old man. His black, heavily wrinkled face was surrounded by a halo of crinkly white hair and whiskers that seemed to separate his head from the layers of dirty coats piled on his smallish frame. His pants were bagged to the knee, where they were met with rags that went down to the old shoes. The rags were held on with strings, and there was a rope around his middle. Greg relaxed. He had seen the man before, picking through the trash on the corner and pulling clothes out of a Salvation Army box. There was no sign of the razor that could "cut a week into nine days."

"What are you doing here?" Greg asked.

"This is where I'm staying," Lemon Brown said. "What you here for?"

"Told you it was raining out," Greg said, leaning against the back of the couch until he felt it give slightly.

"Ain't you got no home?"

Short Stories
Characterization
The way Lemon Brown speaks shows more about his background. His dialect also identifies and separates his voice from Greg's.

Walter Dean Myers
Author's Insight
I don't want the tension to be between Greg and Lemon Brown. I want Greg to learn from Lemon Brown, not fear him.

---

3. **involuntary** (in văl´ ən ter´ ē) **tremor** (trem´ ər) *n.* automatic trembling or shaking.

"I got a home," Greg answered.

"You ain't one of them bad boys looking for my treasure, is you?" Lemon Brown cocked his head to one side and squinted one eye. "Because I told you I got me a razor."

"I'm not looking for your treasure," Greg answered, smiling. "If you have one."

"What you mean, if I have one," Lemon Brown said. "Every man got a treasure. You don't know that, you must be a fool!"

"Sure," Greg said as he sat on the sofa and put one leg over the back. "What do you have, gold coins?"

"Don't worry none about what I got," Lemon Brown said. "You know who I am?"

"You told me your name was orange or lemon or something like that."

"Lemon Brown," the old man said, pulling back his shoulders as he did so, "they used to call me Sweet Lemon Brown."

"Sweet Lemon?" Greg asked.

"Yessir. Sweet Lemon Brown. They used to say I sung the blues so sweet that if I sang at a funeral, the dead would commence to rocking with the beat. Used to travel all over Mississippi and as far as Monroe, Louisiana, and east on over to Macon, Georgia. You mean you ain't never heard of Sweet Lemon Brown?"

"Afraid not," Greg said. "What . . . what happened to you?"

"Hard times, boy. Hard times always after a poor man. One day I got tired, sat down to rest a spell and felt a tap on my shoulder. Hard times caught up with me."

"Sorry about that."

"What you doing here? How come you didn't go on home when the rain come? Rain don't bother you young folks none."

"Just didn't." Greg looked away.

"I used to have a knotty-headed boy just like you." Lemon Brown had half walked, half shuffled back to the corner and sat down against the wall. "Had them big eyes like you got, I used to call them moon eyes. Look into them moon eyes and see anything you want."

"How come you gave up singing the blues?" Greg asked.

"Didn't give it up," Lemon Brown said. "You don't give up the blues; they give you up. After a while you do good for yourself, and it ain't nothing but foolishness singing about how hard you

Short Stories
Dialogue This conversation builds tension in the story.

Walter Dean Myers
Author's Insight The knotty-headed boy reference connects Greg with Lemon's son. This begins Lemon Brown's feeling for his son.

Reading Check

What changes in Lemon Brown and Greg's relationship have taken place so far?

The Treasure of Lemon Brown ■ 179

got it. Ain't that right?"

"I guess so."

"What's that noise?" Lemon Brown asked, suddenly sitting upright.

Greg listened, and he heard a noise outside. He looked at Lemon Brown and saw the old man pointing toward the window.

Greg went to the window and saw three men, neighborhood thugs, on the stoop. One was carrying a length of pipe. Greg looked back toward Lemon Brown, who moved quietly across the

room to the window. The old man looked out, then beckoned frantically for Greg to follow him. For a moment Greg couldn't move. Then he found himself following Lemon Brown into the hallway and up darkened stairs. Greg followed as closely as he could. They reached the top of the stairs, and Greg felt Lemon Brown's hand first lying on his shoulder, then probing down his arm until he finally took Greg's hand into his own as they crouched in the darkness.

"They's bad men," Lemon Brown whispered. His breath was warm against Greg's skin.

"Hey! Rag man!" A voice called. "We know you in here. What you got up under them rags? You got any money?"

Silence.

"We don't want to have to come in and hurt you, old man, but we don't mind if we have to."

Lemon Brown squeezed Greg's hand in his own hard, gnarled fist.

There was a banging downstairs and a light as the men entered. They banged around noisily, calling for the rag man.

"We heard you talking about your treasure." The voice was slurred. "We just want to see it, that's all."

"You sure he's here?" One voice seemed to come from the room with the sofa.

"Yeah, he stays here every night."

▲ **Critical Viewing**
What do the people in this picture have in common with Lemon Brown?
[Make Connections]

Walter Dean Myers
Author's Insight I'm hoping to make the reader want to know more about Lemon Brown's treasure. Is it real? Is Lemon just strange?

"There's another room over there; I'm going to take a look. You got that flashlight?"

"Yeah, here, take the pipe too."

Greg opened his mouth to quiet the sound of his breath as he sucked it in uneasily. A beam of light hit the wall a few feet opposite him, then went out.

"Ain't nobody in that room," a voice said. "You think he gone or something?"

"I don't know," came the answer. "All I know is that I heard him talking about some kind of treasure. You know they found that shopping bag lady with that money in her bags."

"Yeah. You think he's upstairs?"

"Hey, old man, are you up there?"

Silence.

"Watch my back, I'm going up."

There was a footstep on the stairs, and the beam from the flashlight danced crazily along the peeling wallpaper. Greg held his breath. There was another step and a loud crashing noise as the man banged the pipe against the wooden banister.[4] Greg could feel his temples throb as the man slowly neared them. Greg thought about the pipe, wondering what he would do when the man reached them—what he *could* do.

Then Lemon Brown released his hand and moved toward the top of the stairs. Greg looked around and saw stairs going up to the next floor. He tried waving to Lemon Brown, hoping the old man would see him in the dim light and follow him to the next floor. Maybe, Greg thought, the man wouldn't follow them up there. Suddenly, though, Lemon Brown stood at the top of the stairs, both arms raised high above his head.

"There he is!" A voice cried from below.

"Throw down your money, old man, so I won't have to bash your head in!"

Lemon Brown didn't move. Greg felt himself near panic. The steps came closer, and still Lemon Brown didn't move. He was an eerie sight, a bundle of rags standing at the top of the stairs, his shadow on the wall looming over him. Maybe, the thought came to Greg, the scene could be even eerier.

Greg wet his lips, put his hands to his mouth and tried to make a sound. Nothing came out. He swallowed hard, wet his lips once more and howled as evenly as he could.

---

4. **banister** (ban´ is tər) *n.* railing along a staircase.

Short Stories
Rising Action
Descriptions of light dancing "crazily," "loud crashing," and throbbing temples show that Greg's tension and the chance of conflict are increasing.

Reading Check

What is the difference between Greg's reaction to the thieves and Lemon Brown's reaction?

"What's that?"

As Greg howled, the light moved away from Lemon Brown, but not before Greg saw him hurl his body down the stairs at the men who had come to take his treasure. There was a crashing noise, and then footsteps. A rush of warm air came in as the downstairs door opened, then there was only an ominous silence.

Greg stood on the landing. He listened, and after a while there was another sound on the staircase.

"Mr. Brown?" he called.

"Yeah, it's me," came the answer. "I got their flashlight."

Greg exhaled in relief as Lemon Brown made his way slowly back up the stairs.

"You OK?"

"Few bumps and bruises," Lemon Brown said.

"I think I'd better be going," Greg said, his breath returning to normal. "You'd better leave, too, before they come back."

"They may hang around outside for a while," Lemon Brown said, "but they ain't getting their nerve up to come in here again. Not with crazy old rag men and howling spooks. Best you stay a while till the coast is clear. I'm heading out west tomorrow, out to East St. Louis."

"They were talking about treasures," Greg said. "You *really* have a treasure?"

"What I tell you? Didn't I tell you every man got a treasure?" Lemon Brown said. "You want to see mine?"

"If you want to show it to me," Greg shrugged.

"Let's look out the window first, see what them scoundrels be doing," Lemon Brown said.

They followed the oval beam of the flashlight into one of the rooms and looked out the window. They saw the men who had tried to take the treasure sitting on the curb near the corner. One of them had his pants leg up, looking at his knee.

"You sure you're not hurt?" Greg asked Lemon Brown.

"Nothing that ain't been hurt before," Lemon Brown said. "When you get as old as me all you say when something hurts is, 'Howdy, Mr. Pain, sees you back again.' Then when Mr. Pain see he can't worry you none, he go on mess with somebody else."

Short Stories
Falling Action
Greg's relief and Lemon Brown's words show the conflict's intensity has decreased.

Walter Dean Myers
Author's Insight
Greg has had a minor disappointment in his life in not being able to play basketball. Now he's interacting with a man who has had major disappointments. Hopefully, he will think about his father's having to leave school so early.

Greg smiled.

"Here, you hold this." Lemon Brown gave Greg the flashlight.

He sat on the floor near Greg and carefully untied the strings that held the rags on his right leg. When he took the rags away, Greg saw a piece of plastic. The old man carefully took off the plastic and unfolded it. He revealed some yellowed newspaper clippings and a battered harmonica.

"There it be," he said, nodding his head. "There it be."

Greg looked at the old man, saw the distant look in his eye, then turned to the clippings. They told of Sweet Lemon Brown, a blues singer and harmonica player who was appearing at different theaters in the South. One of the clippings said he had been the hit of the show, although not the headliner. All of the clippings were reviews of shows Lemon Brown had been in more than 50 years ago. Greg looked at the harmonica. It was dented badly on one side, with the reed holes on one end nearly closed.

"I used to travel around and make money for to feed my wife and Jesse—that's my boy's name. Used to feed them good, too. Then his mama died, and he stayed with his mama's sister. He growed up to be a man, and when the war come he saw fit to go off and fight in it. I didn't have nothing to give him except these things that told him who I was, and what he come from. If you know your pappy did something, you know you can do something too.

"Anyway, he went off to war, and I went off still playing and singing. 'Course by then I wasn't as much as I used to be, not without somebody to make it worth the while. You know what I mean?"

"Yeah," Greg nodded, not quite really knowing.

"I traveled around, and one time I come home, and there was this letter saying Jesse got killed in the war. Broke my heart, it truly did.

"They sent back what he had with him over there, and what it was is this old mouth fiddle and these clippings. Him carrying it around with him like that told me it meant something to him. That was my treasure, and when I give it to him he treated it just like that, a treasure. Ain't that something?"

"Yeah, I guess so," Greg said.

"You *guess* so?" Lemon Brown's voice rose an octave as he

Short Stories
Flashback Old newspaper stories reveal both Lemon Brown's success as a singer and his son's admiration for him. The scene fully explains the nature of the treasure.

Reading Check

What has happened to the men who were after Lemon Brown's treasure?

started to put his treasure back into the plastic. "Well, you got to guess 'cause you sure don't know nothing. Don't know enough to get home when it's raining."

"I guess . . . I mean, you're right."

"You OK for a youngster," the old man said as he tied the strings around his leg, "better than those scalawags[5] what come here looking for my treasure. That's for sure."

"You really think that treasure of yours was worth fighting for?" Greg asked. "Against a pipe?"

"What else a man got 'cepting what he can pass on to his son, or his daughter, if she be his oldest?" Lemon Brown said. "For a big-headed boy you sure do ask the foolishest questions."

Lemon Brown got up after patting his rags in place and looked out the window again.

"Looks like they're gone. You get on out of here and get yourself home. I'll be watching from the window so you'll be all right."

Lemon Brown went down the stairs behind Greg. When they reached the front door the old man looked out first, saw the street was clear and told Greg to scoot on home.

"You sure you'll be OK?" Greg asked.

"Now didn't I tell you I was going to East St. Louis in the morning?" Lemon Brown asked. "Don't that sound OK to you?"

"Sure it does," Greg said. "Sure it does. And you take care of that treasure of yours."

"That I'll do," Lemon said, the wrinkles about his eyes suggesting a smile. "That I'll do."

The night had warmed and the rain had stopped, leaving puddles at the curbs. Greg didn't even want to think how late it was. He thought ahead of what his father would say and wondered if he should tell him about Lemon Brown. He thought about it until he reached his stoop, and decided against it. Lemon Brown would be OK, Greg thought, with his memories and his treasure.

Greg pushed the button over the bell marked Ridley, thought of the lecture he knew his father would give him, and smiled.

Short Stories
Theme In this paragraph, Lemon Brown reveals the story's central message: a real treasure has value even though it may have no monetary worth.

Walter Dean Myers
Author's Insight
I started with the bad weather and signal the happy ending of the story with a change in the weather.

---

5. **scalawags** (skal′ ə wagz′) *n.* people who cause trouble; scoundrels.

Q. **What's the hardest thing about writing a short story?**

A. Knowing just where to start the story is always hard for me. The temptation is to provide background by including as many events prior to the main action of the story as possible. But the ideal place to begin is as close to the crucial actions as possible, using flashbacks or other clues to supply the background material.

Q. **How do you create your characters?**

A. I first find a photograph that fits what my characters look like in my mind. Then I do a timeline for the characters, noting the date of birth, when they started school, when they met their best friend, etc. I also note what was going on in the world during my characters' lifetime so I know what they have seen and experienced and what events might have influenced them.

Student Corner

Q. **Why does Greg want to play for the Scorpions so badly?**
    —Bryan Opremcak, Bernards Township, New Jersey

A. At fourteen I had a chance to play on a team—no, on THE team in my neighborhood. The team was called the Comanches. I didn't get to play for the team that year and by the next year I had dropped out of high school. Fast forward a whole bunch of years. I'm writing about a guy playing ball. I can make him as good as I want him to be, but memories of my own life keep creeping into the story. After all these years I'm still suffering and thinking about that team.

Writing Workshop: *Work in Progress*

Review of a Short Story

For a review you may be asked to write about short stories, ask yourself the following questions: What stories have I read that I enjoyed? What stories have I read that I did not enjoy? What stories contain characters who sparked a strong reaction in me? Jot down at least two answers to each question. Save this Story List in your writing portfolio.

Apply the Skills

Short Story

Thinking About the Selection

1. **Respond:** Do you agree with Greg Ridley's decision not to tell his father about Lemon Brown? Explain.

2. **(a) Recall:** List five facts you learn about Greg early in the story. **(b) Infer:** Why is Greg angry and upset? **(c) Analyze:** How does his mood set events in motion?

3. **(a) Recall:** In the first column of a chart, like the one shown here, identify Lemon Brown's treasures. **(b)** In the second column, explain what each treasure means to Brown. **(c)** With a partner, review your ideas. Together, complete the third column with information that explains why the treasures are an important part of the story.

Lemon Brown's Treasures

What It Says	What It Means	Why It Is Important

4. **(a) Analyze:** How does Greg's opinion of Lemon Brown change over the course of the story? **(b) Generalize:** What does Lemon Brown teach Greg? **(c) Speculate:** Why do you think Greg smiles at the end of the story?

Short Story Review

5. What realistic elements of **setting** appear in the fictional story "The Treasure of Lemon Brown"?

6. **(a)** What is the story's main **conflict**? **(b)** How is it resolved?

Using the Internet and print resources, create a **biographical timeline** of Walter Dean Myers's life.

- On the top half of your timeline, include important life dates, such as the year the author was born and the years he won awards.
- On the bottom half, include the title and publication dates of books Walter Dean Myers has written.

QuickReview

Story at a Glance
A homeless man shows a boy what treasures are worth.

Go Online
Assessment
For: Self-test
Visit: www.PHSchool.com
Web Code: ema-6201

Short Story: a brief work of fiction with characters, setting, and plot

Setting: the time and place of a story's action

Conflict: a problem or struggle

Skills You Will Learn

Reading Skill: *Use Prior Knowledge to Make Predictions*
Literary Analysis: *Plot*

Reading Skill: *Preview the Text to Make Predictions*

Reading Skill: *Reread or Read Ahead to Verify Predictions*
Literary Analysis: *Character*

Literary Analysis: *Comparing Characters*

Literature You Will Read

who says?
~SG

Reading: Make Predictions

> A **prediction** is an informed idea about what will happen based on details in the text and on your own experience.

Skills and Strategies You Will Learn in Part 1
In Part 1, you will learn
- to **use prior knowledge,** such as information, thoughts, or experiences you have before you begin reading, **to make predictions** (p. 190)
- to **read ahead to verify predictions,** or to **reread** to look for details (p. 222)
- to **preview the text** to make predictions (p. 218)

Using the Skills and Strategies in Part 1
Making predictions keeps you actively involved in a story. To anticipate what will happen next, you must keep track of plot events and consider details you have learned about the characters. You must also weigh what you have learned in the story against your own knowledge and experience. As you proceed through the story, you will check to see if your predictions are correct. If one of your predictions proves to be wrong, you can review the story to find details you might have overlooked.

This chart shows questions to ask as you make and verify predictions.

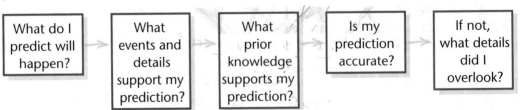

| What do I predict will happen? | → | What events and details support my prediction? | → | What prior knowledge supports my prediction? | → | Is my prediction accurate? | → | If not, what details did I overlook? |

As you read the literature in this part, you will learn to make predictions about what might happen in the story.

Academic Vocabulary: Words for Discussing Predictions

The following words will help you talk and write about making predictions as you read the selections in Part 1.

Word	Definition	Example sentence
predict *v.*	to say what is going to happen in the future	Because the team has practiced so hard, I *predict* they will win the game.
indicate *v.*	to point something out or point to something	All the clues in the mystery *indicate* that the butler is guilty of the crime.
verify *v.*	to check whether or not something is true	The scientists were called in to *verify* that the dinosaur bones were genuine.
anticipate *v.*	to consider something before it happens	As the leaves changed color, Jen began to *anticipate* the first snowfall.
plot *n.*	the sequence of events in a story	Mark outlined the *plot* before he began to write his story.

Vocabulary Skill: Roots

> A **root** is a word part that determines an important part of the meaning of a word.

Learning roots can help you learn the meanings of groups of words. For example, the words *dictionary* and *verdict* share the root *-dict-*, which means "to speak, talk, or say."

In Part 1, you will learn about the roots *-dict-* and *-ver-*.

Root	Meaning of Root	Examples
-dict-	to speak, talk, say	diction, dictionary, edict
-ver-	truth	aver, verdict

Activity Explain how the meaning of the root can help you understand the meaning of the words *diction*, *dictum*, and *verity*. Use what you know about the meaning of the roots to write a definition for each word.

These skills will help you become a better reader. Practice them with either "The Bear Boy" (p. 192) or "Rikki-tikki-tavi" (p. 199).

Reading Skill

Predicting means making an intelligent guess about what will happen next in a story based on details in the text. You can also **use prior knowledge to make predictions.** For example, if a character in a story sees dark clouds, you can predict that there will be a storm because you know from prior knowledge that dark clouds often mean stormy weather.

Making predictions while you read involves you in the story. As you read, use details from the story and your prior knowledge to make predictions about what characters will do.

Literary Analysis

Plot is the related sequence of events in a short story and other works of fiction. A plot has the following elements:

- **Exposition:** introduction of the setting, the characters, and the basic situation
- **Rising Action:** events that introduce a **conflict**, or struggle, and increase the tension
- **Climax:** the story's high point, at which the eventual outcome becomes clear
- **Falling Action:** events that follow the climax
- **Resolution:** the final outcome and tying up of loose ends

Vocabulary Builder

The Bear Boy

- **timid** (tim´ id) *adj.* showing shyness (p. 192) *The timid child was afraid of me.*

- **initiation** (i nish´ ē ā´ shən) *n.* process by which one becomes a member of a group (p. 192) *Jo looked forward to her initiation into the Honor Society.*

- **neglected** (ni glekt´ əd) *v.* failed to take care of (p. 193) *The cat neglected her kittens, so we raised them.*

Rikki-tikki-tavi

- **revived** (ri vīvd´) *v.* came back to consciousness (p. 199) *The rancher revived and looked for the horse that had thrown him.*

- **immensely** (i mens´ lē) *adv.* a great deal; very much (p. 200) *We enjoyed ourselves immensely at the circus.*

- **consolation** (kän´ sə lā´ shən) *n.* something that comforts a disappointed person (p. 209) *The sick boy got extra candy as consolation for missing the party.*

Build Understanding • *The Bear Boy*

Background

Animals in Native American Folk Tales In early times, Native Americans depended on animals for food, clothing, and shelter. As a result, Native Americans felt gratitude toward animals and included them as important characters in their oral stories. "The Bear Boy" is a Native American story that focuses on a mother bear and her cubs.

Connecting to the Literature

Reading/Writing Connection Usually, people think of themselves as teaching animals rather than as learning from them. However, many Native American groups believe animals have a lot to teach us. List the lessons that people might learn from animals. Use at least three of the following words: *appreciate, instinct, observe, survive.*

Meet the Author

Joseph **Bruchac** (b. 1942)

Joseph Bruchac was raised by his grandparents in the foothills of the Adirondack Mountains in New York State. There, his grandfather, who was of Abenaki Indian descent, taught Bruchac to appreciate the forest. From his grandmother, a law school graduate, Bruchac inherited a love of books and writing. Bruchac has written more than seventy books for children and has performed worldwide as a teller of Native American folk tales.

Respect for Tradition Bruchac respects the role that storytelling plays in Native American cultures. Like "The Bear Boy," many of his stories are based on traditional folk tales and on his ancestors' way of life. He has said, "I always go back to what I have heard, what I have seen, what I have experienced. And whatever I imagine or create new always comes out of that life experience."

Fast Facts

▶ The author lives today in the house where his grandparents lived in Greenfield Center, New York.

▶ Bruchac's younger sister and his two sons, James and Jesse, work for the preservation of Abenaki culture.

Go **Online**
Author Link
For: More about the author
Visit: www.PHSchool.com
Web Code: eme-9202

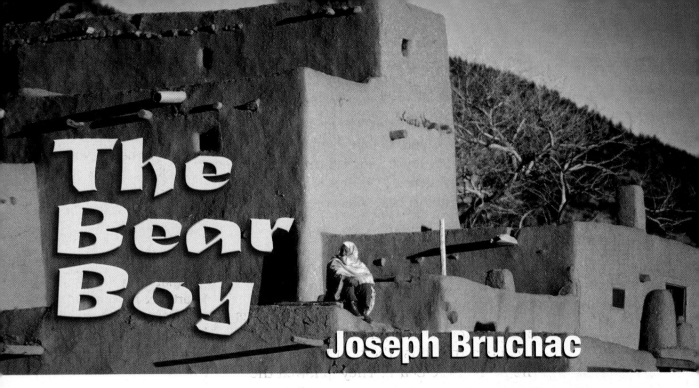

The Bear Boy

Joseph Bruchac

Long ago, in a Pueblo village, a boy named Kuo-Haya lived with his father. But his father did not treat him well. In his heart he still mourned the death of his wife, Kuo-Haya's mother, and did not enjoy doing things with his son. He did not teach his boy how to run. He did not show him how to wrestle. He was always too busy.

As a result, Kuo-Haya was a <u>timid</u> boy and walked about stooped over all of the time. When the other boys raced or wrestled, Kuo-Haya slipped away. He spent much of his time alone.

Time passed, and the boy reached the age when his father should have been helping him get ready for his <u>initiation</u> into manhood. Still Kuo-Haya's father paid no attention at all to his son.

One day Kuo-Haya was out walking far from the village, toward the cliffs where the bears lived. Now the people of the village always knew they must stay away from these cliffs, for the bear was a very powerful animal. It was said that if someone saw a bear's tracks and followed them, he might never come back. But Kuo-Haya had never been told about this. When he came upon the tracks of a bear, Kuo-Haya followed them along an arroyo, a small canyon[1] cut by a winding stream, up into the mesas.[2] The tracks led into a little box

---

1. canyon (kan´ yən) *n.* long narrow valley between high cliffs, often with a stream flowing through it.

2. mesas (mā´ səz) *n.* plateaus (or flat-topped hills) with steep sides.

▲ Critical Viewing
Based on this photograph, what do you think this story will be about? **[Predict]**

Vocabulary Builder
timid (tim´ id) *adj.* showing shyness

initiation (i nish´ ē ā´ shən) *n.* process by which one becomes a member of a group

Literary Analysis
Plot How does this paragraph build tension in the story?

canyon below some caves. There, he came upon some bear cubs.

When they saw Kuo-Haya, the little bears ran away. But Kuo-Haya sat down and called to them in a friendly voice.

"I will not hurt you," he said to the bear cubs. "Come and play with me." The bears walked back out of the bushes. Soon the boy and the bears were playing together. As they played, however, a shadow came over them. Kuo-Haya looked up and saw the mother bear standing above him.

"Where is Kuo-Haya?" the people asked his father.

"I do not know," the father said.

"Then you must find him!"

So the father and other people of the pueblo began to search for the missing boy. They went through the canyons calling his name. But they found no sign of the boy there. Finally, when they reached the cliffs, the best trackers found his footsteps and the path of the bears. They followed the tracks along the arroyo and up into the mesas to the box canyon. In front of a cave, they saw the boy playing with the bear cubs as the mother bear watched them approvingly, nudging Kuo-Haya now and then to encourage him.

The trackers crept close, hoping to grab the boy and run. But as soon as the mother bear caught their scent, she growled and pushed her cubs and the boy back into the cave.

"The boy is with the bears," the trackers said when they returned to the village.

"What shall we do?" the people asked.

"It is the responsibility of the boy's father," said the medicine man. Then he called Kuo-Haya's father to him.

"You have not done well," said the medicine man. "You are the one who must guide your boy to manhood, but you have <u>neglected</u> him. Now the mother bear is caring for your boy as you should have done all along. She is teaching him to be strong as a young man must be strong. If you love your son, only you can get him back."

Every one of the medicine man's words went into the father's heart like an arrow. He began to realize that he had been blind to his son's needs because of his own sorrow.

"You are right," he said. "I will go and bring back my son."

Kuo-Haya's father went along the arroyo and climbed the cliffs. When he came to the bears' cave, he found Kuo-Haya

Reading Skill
Predict Based on your knowledge of bears, what do you think will happen to Kuo-Haya?

▼ **Critical Viewing** What does this artifact show about the usual relationship between people and bears in Pueblo culture? **[Connect]**

Vocabulary Builder
neglected (ni gleckt′ əd) v. failed to take care of

✓ **Reading Check**
How does Kuo-Haya end up living with the bears?

The Bear Boy ■ 193

wrestling with the little bears. As the father watched, he saw that his son seemed more sure of himself than ever before.

"Kuo-Haya," he shouted. "Come to me."

The boy looked at him and then just walked into the cave. Although the father tried to follow, the big mother bear stood up on her hind legs and growled. She would not allow the father to come any closer.

So Kuo-Haya's father went back to his home. He was angry now. He began to gather together his weapons, and brought out his bow and his arrows and his lance.[3] But the medicine man came to his lodge and showed him the bear claw that he wore around his neck.

"Those bears are my relatives!" the medicine man said. "You must not harm them. They are teaching your boy how we should care for each other, so you must not be cruel to them. You must get your son back with love, not violence."

Kuo-Haya's father prayed for guidance. He went outside and sat on the ground. As he sat there, a bee flew up to him, right by his face. Then it flew away. The father stood up. Now he knew what to do!

"Thank you, Little Brother," he said. He began to make his preparations. The medicine man watched what he was doing and smiled.

Kuo-Haya's father went to the place where the bees had their hives. He made a fire and put green branches on it so that it made smoke. Then he blew the smoke into the tree where the bees were. The bees soon went to sleep.

Carefully Kuo-Haya's father took out some honey from their hive. When he was done, he placed pollen and some small pieces of turquoise[4] at the foot of the tree to thank the bees for their gift. The medicine man, who was watching all this, smiled again. Truly the father was beginning to learn.

Kuo-Haya's father traveled again to the cliffs where the bears lived. He hid behind a tree and saw how the mother bear treated Kuo-Haya and the cubs with love. He saw that Kuo-Haya was able to hold his own as he wrestled with the bears.

He came out from his hiding place, put the honey on the ground, and stepped back. "My friends," he said, "I have brought you something sweet."

▲ **Critical Viewing** How does this bear figurine compare with the description of the mother bear in the story? **[Compare and Contrast]**

Literary Analysis Plot What is the climax of the story? How do you know?

---

3. **lance** (lans) *n.* long spear.
4. **turquoise** (tur´ koiz´) *n.* greenish-blue gemstone.

The mother bear and her cubs came over and began to eat the honey. While they ate, Kuo-Haya's father went to the boy. He saw that his little boy was now a young man.

"Kuo-Haya," he said, putting his hands on his son's shoulders, "I have come to take you home. The bears have taught me a lesson. I shall treat you as a father should treat his son."

"I will go with you, Father," said the boy. "But I, too, have learned things from the bears. They have shown me how we must care for one another. I will come with you only if you promise you will always be friends with the bears." The father promised, and that promise was kept. Not only was he friends with the bears, but he showed his boy the love a son deserves. And he taught him all the things a son should be taught.

Everyone in the village soon saw that Kuo-Haya, the bear boy, was no longer the timid little boy he had been. Because of what the bears had taught him, he was the best wrestler among the boys. With his father's help, Kuo-Haya quickly became the greatest runner of all. To this day, his story is told to remind all parents that they must always show as much love for their children as there is in the heart of a bear.

Literary Analysis
Plot Is this scene part of the rising action? Explain your answer.

Literary Analysis
Plot Which details in this paragraph show how the story's conflict is resolved?

Literature in Context   Social Studies Connection

The Pueblo

The word "Pueblo" refers to the village-dwelling Native Americans of the southwestern U.S. Pueblo villages, like this one, are made of adobe and contain hundreds of rooms.

▶ Pueblo pottery is known for the beauty of its shape and decoration.

▶ This is the entrance to a *kiva*, or sacred ceremonial room.

Connect to the Literature   How was living in a village like the one shown an advantage to Kuo-Haya's father?

Apply the Skills

The Bear Boy

Thinking About the Selection

1. **Respond:** Do you think Kuo-Haya did the right thing by returning to live with his father? Why or why not?
2. **(a) Recall:** What kind of relationship does Kuo-Haya have with his father at the beginning of the story? **(b) Analyze Cause and Effect:** Describe the effect this relationship has on Kuo-Haya. **(c) Interpret:** Why does Kuo-Haya choose to spend so much time alone? **(d) Discuss:** Share your responses with a partner. Then, discuss how your partner's responses did or did not change your interpretation.
3. **(a) Recall:** What does Kuo-Haya do when he first sees the bear cubs? **(b) Compare and Contrast:** How is Kuo-Haya's life with the bears different from his life in the village?
4. **(a) Recall:** What advice does the medicine man offer the father? **(b) Connect:** How does seeing a bee help the father decide how to get his son back?
5. **(a) Analyze:** Native American folk tales often teach a lesson. What lesson does this folk tale teach? **(b) Evaluate:** Do you think the lesson applies to people of all cultures? Explain.

Reading Skill

6. What **prior knowledge** did you have from reading the Background for this story that helped you **predict** that Kuo-Haya would be accepted by the bears?
7. Think of another prediction based on prior knowledge that you made as you read this story. Use a graphic organizer like the one here to show how you made your prediction.

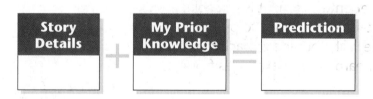

Literary Analysis

8. Identify two **plot** events that increase the tension of the story.
9. Identify two or three events that move the plot toward the **climax,** when Kuo-Haya's father asks his son to come home.

Vocabulary Builder

Practice Answer each question. Then, explain your answer.

1. Would a *timid* child look forward to making a speech in front of a crowd?

2. Does an *initiation* mark the beginning of a new phase in a person's life?

3. If you *neglected* a houseplant, what would happen to it?

Writing

Use details from the story to write an **informative article** on how a mother bear raises bear cubs. Write your article for third-grade students to read. Use easier vocabulary and simpler sentence structure than you would normally use.

An informative article usually contains these elements:
- an introduction, a body, and a conclusion
- details that tell *when, how much, how often,* or *to what extent*

For *Grammar, Vocabulary,* and *Assessment,* see **Build Language Skills,** pages 216–217.

Extend Your Learning

Listening and Speaking With a partner, engage in an **informal debate** on the training of wild animals. For example, consider whether animal training should be limited to purposes such as security or domestication, or whether entertainment is valuable, too. Each of you should pick an opposing viewpoint to present.

To convince your partner to agree with your ideas, back them up with information you have read or heard or with examples from your own experience.
- Remember to respect your partner's time to talk.
- Do not interrupt while he or she is speaking.

Research and Technology The bears in this story like honey. Use Internet and library resources to find out how bees make honey. Present your findings in a **diagram** with arrows to show how the bees move and communicate.

Build Understanding • *Rikki-tikki-tavi*

Background

Mongoose *vs.* Cobra In this story, a brave mongoose takes on a family of snakes known as Indian cobras. Cobras feed on small animals. The mongoose is a brown, furry animal about fifteen inches long—the perfect size for a cobra's meal. However, the fast, fierce mongoose usually wins a battle with a cobra.

Connecting to the Literature

Reading/Writing Connection Rudyard Kipling's story uses the character of a mongoose to show admirable qualities such as bravery. Write a few sentences about how a person might show bravery or courage. Use at least three of the following words: *demonstrate, exhibit, display, illustrate.*

Review

For **Reading Skill, Literary Analysis,** and **Vocabulary Builder,** see page 190.

Meet the Author

Rudyard **Kipling** (1865–1936)

Rudyard Kipling was born in Bombay, India, to English parents. Although he moved to England when he was five, Kipling remained strongly attached to the land of his birth. In 1882, he returned there as a journalist and began writing the stories that would make him famous.

International Popularity Published in England, Kipling's stories met immediate success, bringing the details of Indian life to an eager audience. Popularity in America soon followed. Kipling traveled a great deal and wrote several books of stories and poems, including *The Jungle Book* and *Captains Courageous.* In 1907, Kipling became the first English writer to win the Nobel Prize in Literature.

Fast Facts

▶ Organizations such as Boy Scouts and Girl Scouts grew out of ideas found in the original *Jungle Book.*
▶ The 1908 booklet "Scouting for Boys" included a short version of Kipling's novel *Kim.*

Go **Online**
Author Link

For: More about the author
Visit: www.PHSchool.com
Web Code: eme-9203

Rikki-tikki-tavi

Rudyard Kipling

This is the story of the great war that Rikki-tikki-tavi fought, single-handed, through the bathrooms of the big bungalow in Segowlee cantonment.[1] Darzee, the tailorbird bird, helped him, and Chuchundra (choo chun' drə) the muskrat, who never comes out into the middle of the floor, but always creeps round by the wall, gave him advice; but Rikki-tikki did the real fighting.

He was a mongoose, rather like a little cat in his fur and his tail, but quite like a weasel in his head and his habits. His eyes and the end of his restless nose were pink; he could scratch himself anywhere he pleased, with any leg, front or back, that he chose to use; he could fluff up his tail till it looked like a bottle brush, and his war cry as he scuttled through the long grass, was: "*Rikk-tikk-tikki-tikki-tchk!*"

One day, a high summer flood washed him out of the burrow where he lived with his father and mother, and carried him, kicking and clucking, down a roadside ditch. He found a little wisp of grass floating there, and clung to it till he lost his senses. When he <u>revived</u>, he was lying in the hot sun on the

---

1. Segowlee cantonment (sē gou' lē kan tän' mənt) *n.* living quarters for British troops in Segowlee, India.

Literary Analysis
Plot What important details about the mongoose are revealed in the exposition?

Vocabulary Builder
revived (ri vīvd')
v. came back to consciousness

middle of a garden path, very draggled[2] indeed, and a small boy was saying: "Here's a dead mongoose. Let's have a funeral."

"No," said his mother; "let's take him in and dry him. Perhaps he isn't really dead."

They took him into the house, and a big man picked him up between his finger and thumb and said he was not dead but half choked; so they wrapped him in cotton wool, and warmed him, and he opened his eyes and sneezed.

"Now," said the big man (he was an Englishman who had just moved into the bungalow); "don't frighten him, and we'll see what he'll do."

It is the hardest thing in the world to frighten a mongoose, because he is eaten up from nose to tail with curiosity. The motto of all the mongoose family is, "Run and find out"; and Rikki-tikki was a true mongoose. He looked at the cotton wool, decided that it was not good to eat, ran all round the table, sat up and put his fur in order, scratched himself, and jumped on the small boy's shoulder.

"Don't be frightened, Teddy," said his father. "That's his way of making friends."

"Ouch! He's tickling under my chin," said Teddy.

Rikki-tikki looked down between the boy's collar and neck, snuffed at his ear, and climbed down to the floor, where he sat rubbing his nose.

"Good gracious," said Teddy's mother, "and that's a wild creature! I suppose he's so tame because we've been kind to him."

"All mongooses are like that," said her husband. "If Teddy doesn't pick him up by the tail, or try to put him in a cage, he'll run in and out of the house all day long. Let's give him something to eat."

They gave him a little piece of raw meat. Rikki-tikki liked it immensely, and when it was finished he went out into the veranda and sat in the sunshine and fluffed up his fur to make it dry to the roots. Then he felt better.

"There are more things to find out about in this house," he said to himself, "than all my family could find out in all their lives. I shall certainly stay and find out."

He spent all that day roaming over the house. He nearly drowned himself in the bathtubs, put his nose into the ink on a writing table, and burned it on the end of the big man's cigar, for he climbed up in the big man's lap to see how

Reading Skill
Predict What might happen between Teddy and the mongoose, based on the father's statement and on earlier details?

Vocabulary Builder
immensely (i mens´ lē) *adv.* a great deal; very much

---

2. **draggled** (drag´ əld) *adj.* wet and dirty.

writing was done. At nightfall he ran into Teddy's nursery to watch how kerosene lamps were lighted, and when Teddy went to bed Rikki-tikki climbed up too; but he was a restless companion, because he had to get up and attend to every noise all through the night, and find out what made it. Teddy's mother and father came in, the last thing, to look at their boy, and Rikki-tikki was awake on the pillow. "I don't like that," said Teddy's mother; "he may bite the child." "He'll do no such thing," said the father. "Teddy's safer with that little beast than if he had a bloodhound to watch him. If a snake came into the nursery now—"

But Teddy's mother wouldn't think of anything so awful.

Early in the morning Rikki-tikki came to early breakfast in the veranda riding on Teddy's shoulder, and they gave him banana and some boiled egg; and he sat on all their laps one after the other, because every well-brought-up mongoose always hopes to be a house mongoose some day and have rooms to run about in, and Rikki-tikki's mother (she used to live in the General's house at Segowlee) had carefully told Rikki what to do if ever he came across Englishmen.

Then Rikki-tikki went out into the garden to see what was to be seen. It was a large garden, only half cultivated, with bushes as big as summer houses of Marshal Niel roses, lime and orange trees, clumps of bamboos, and thickets of high grass. Rikki-tikki licked his lips. "This is a splendid hunting ground," he said, and his tail grew bottlebrushy at the thought of it, and he scuttled up and down the garden, snuffing here and there till he heard very sorrowful voices in a thornbush.

It was Darzee, the tailorbird, and his wife. They had made a beautiful nest by pulling two big leaves together and stitching them up the edges with fibers, and had filled the hollow with cotton and downy fluff. The nest swayed to and fro, as they sat on the rim and cried.

"What is the matter?" asked Rikki-tikki.

"We are very miserable," said Darzee.

"One of our babies fell out of the nest yesterday and Nag ate him."

"H'm!" said Rikki-tikki, "that is very sad—but I am a stranger here. Who is Nag?"

Darzee and his wife only cowered down in the nest without answering, for from the thick grass at the foot of the bush there came a low hiss—a horrid cold sound that made

Reading Skill
Predict Based on the parents' thoughts about Rikki, what do you predict will happen in the story?

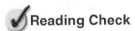

Reading Check

Who is Rikki-tikki-tavi, and how does he meet Teddy?

Rikki-tikki jump back two clear feet. Then inch by inch out of the grass rose up the head and spread hood of Nag, the big black cobra, and he was five feet long from tongue to tail. When he had lifted one third of himself clear of the ground, he stayed balancing to and fro exactly as a dandelion tuft balances in the wind, and he looked at Rikki-tikki with the wicked snake's eyes that never change their expression, whatever the snake may be thinking of.

"Who is Nag?" he said. "*I* am Nag. The great god Brahm[3] put his mark upon all our people when the first cobra spread his hood to keep the sun off Brahm . . . as he slept. Look, and be afraid!"

He spread out his hood more than ever, and Rikki-tikki saw the spectacle mark on the back of it that looks exactly like the eye part of a hook-and-eye fastening. He was afraid for the minute; but it is impossible for a mongoose to stay frightened for any length of time, and though Rikki-tikki had never met a live cobra before, his mother had fed him on dead ones, and he knew that all a grown mongoose's business in life was to fight and eat snakes. Nag knew that too, and at the bottom of his cold heart he was afraid.

"Well," said Rikki-tikki, and his tail began to fluff up again, "marks or no marks, do you think it is right for you to eat fledglings out of a nest?"

Nag was thinking to himself, and watching the least little movement in the grass behind Rikki-tikki. He knew that mongooses in the garden meant death sooner or later for him and his family; but he wanted to get Rikki-tikki off his guard. So he dropped his head a little, and put it on one side.

"Let us talk," he said. "You eat eggs. Why should not I eat birds?"

"Behind you! Look behind you!" sang Darzee.

Rikki-tikki knew better than to waste time in staring. He jumped up in the air as high as he could go, and just under him whizzed by the head of Nagaina (nə gī nə), Nag's wicked wife. She had crept up behind him as he was talking, to make an end of him; and he heard her savage hiss as the stroke missed. He came down almost across her back, and if he had been an old mongoose he would have known that then was the time to break her back with one bite; but he was afraid of the terrible lashing return

3. **Brahm** (bräm) short for *Brahma*, the name of the chief god in the Hindu religion.

▼ Critical Viewing
How might a mongoose like Rikki-tikki-tavi know that the cobra pictured here is ready to attack? [Interpret]

stroke of the cobra. He bit, indeed, but did not bite long enough, and he jumped clear of the whisking tail, leaving Nagaina torn and angry.

"Wicked, wicked Darzee!" said Nag, lashing up high as he could reach toward the nest in the thornbush; but Darzee had built it out of reach of snakes; and it only swayed to and fro.

Rikki-tikki felt his eyes growing red and hot (when a mongoose's eyes grow red, he is angry), and he sat back on his tail and hind legs like a little kangaroo, and looked all around him, and chattered with rage. But Nag and Nagaina had disappeared into the grass. When a snake misses its stroke, it never says anything or gives any sign of what it means to do next. Rikki-tikki did not care to follow them, for he did not feel sure that he could manage two snakes at once. So he trotted off to the gravel path near the house, and sat down to think. It was a serious matter for him.

If you read the old books of natural history, you will find they say that when the mongoose fights the snake and happens to get bitten, he runs off and eats some herb that cures him. That is not true. The victory is only a matter of quickness of eye and quickness of foot—snake's blow against mongoose's jump—and as no eye can follow the motion of a snake's head when it strikes, that makes things much more wonderful than any magic herb. Rikki-tikki knew he was a young mongoose, and it made him all the more pleased to think that he had managed to escape a blow from behind. It gave him confidence in himself, and when Teddy came running down the path, Rikki-tikki was ready to be petted.

But just as Teddy was stooping, something flinched a little in the dust, and a tiny voice said: "Be careful. I am death!" It was Karait (kə rīt′), the dusty brown snakeling that lies for choice on the dusty earth; and his bite is as dangerous as the

Literary Analysis
Plot What details intensify the conflict here?

Reading Skill
Predict What do you predict will be the outcome of the conflict? What prior knowledge helps you make that prediction?

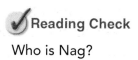Reading Check

Who is Nag?

cobra's. But he is so small that nobody thinks of him, and so he does the more harm to people.

Rikki-tikki's eyes grew red again, and he danced up to Karait with the peculiar rocking, swaying motion that he had inherited from his family. It looks very funny, but it is so perfectly balanced a gait that you can fly off from it at any angle you please; and in dealing with snakes this is an advantage. If Rikki-tikki had only known, he was doing a much more dangerous thing than fighting Nag, for Karait is so small, and can turn so quickly, that unless Rikki bit him close to the back of the head, he would get the return stroke in his eye or lip. But Rikki did not know: his eyes were all red, and he rocked back and forth, looking for a good place to hold. Karait struck out. Rikki jumped sideways and tried to run in, but the wicked little dusty gray head lashed within a fraction of his shoulder, and he had to jump over the body, and the head followed his heels close.

Teddy shouted to the house: "Oh, look here! Our mongoose is killing a snake"; and Rikki-tikki heard a scream from Teddy's mother. His father ran out with a stick, but by the time he came up, Karait had lunged out once too far, and Rikki-tikki had sprung, jumped on the snake's back, dropped his head far between his fore legs, bitten as high up the back as he could get hold, and rolled away. That bite paralyzed Karait, and Rikki-tikki was just going to eat him up from the tail, after the custom of his family at dinner, when he remembered that a full meal makes a slow mongoose, and if he wanted all his strength and quickness ready, he must keep himself thin.

He went away for a dust bath under the castor-oil bushes, while Teddy's father beat the dead Karait. "What is the use of that?" thought Rikki-tikki. "I have settled it all"; and then Teddy's mother picked him up from the dust and hugged him, crying that he had saved Teddy from death, and Teddy's father said that he was a providence,[4] and Teddy looked on with big scared eyes. Rikki-tikki was rather amused at all the fuss, which, of course, he did not understand. Teddy's mother might just as well have petted Teddy for playing in the dust. Rikki was thoroughly enjoying himself.

That night, at dinner, walking to and fro among the wine-glasses on the table, he could have stuffed himself three times

Literary Analysis
Plot What details in this paragraph increase the tension in the story?

---

4. **a providence** (präv´ ə dəns) n. a godsend; a valuable gift.

over with nice things; but he remembered Nag and Nagaina, and though it was very pleasant to be patted and petted by Teddy's mother, and to sit on Teddy's shoulder, his eyes would get red from time to time, and he would go off into his long war cry of "*Rikk-tikk-tikki-tikki-tchk!*"

Teddy carried him off to bed, and insisted on Rikki-tikki sleeping under his chin. Rikki-tikki was too well bred to bite or scratch, but as soon as Teddy was asleep he went off for his nightly walk round the house, and in the dark he ran up against Chuchundra the muskrat, creeping round by the wall. Chuchundra is a broken-hearted little beast. He whimpers and cheeps all the night, trying to make up his mind to run into the middle of the room, but he never gets there.

"Don't kill me," said Chuchundra, almost weeping. "Rikki-tikki don't kill me."

"Do you think a snake-killer kills muskrats?" said Rikki-tikki scornfully.

"Those who kill snakes get killed by snakes," said Chuchundra, more sorrowfully than ever. "And how am I to be sure that Nag won't mistake me for you some dark night?"

"There's not the least danger," said Rikki-tikki; "but Nag is in the garden, and I know you don't go there."

"My cousin Chua, the rat, told me—" said Chuchundra, and then he stopped.

"Told you what?"

"H'sh! Nag is everywhere, Rikki-tikki. You should have talked to Chua in the garden."

"I didn't—so you must tell me. Quick, Chuchundra, or I'll bite you!"

Chuchundra sat down and cried till the tears rolled off his whiskers. "I am a very poor man," he sobbed. "I never had spirit enough to run out into the middle of the room. H'sh! I mustn't tell you anything. Can't you *hear*, Rikki-tikki?"

Rikki-tikki listened. The house was as still as still, but he thought he could just catch the faintest scratch-scratch in the world—a noise as faint as that of a wasp walking on a window-pane—the dry scratch of a snake's scales on brickwork.

"That's Nag or Nagaina," he said to himself; "and he is crawling into the bathroom sluice.[5] You're right, Chuchundra; I should have talked to Chua."

He stole off to Teddy's bathroom, but there was nothing there, and then to Teddy's mother's bathroom. At the bottom of the smooth plaster wall there was a brick pulled out to make a sluice for the bath water, and as Rikki-tikki stole in by the masonry curb where the bath is put, he heard Nag and Nagaina whispering together outside in the moonlight.

"When the house is emptied of people," said Nagaina to her husband, "*he* will have to go away, and then the garden will be our own again. Go in quietly, and remember that the big man who killed Karait is the first one to bite. Then come out and tell me, and we will hunt for Rikki-tikki together."

"But are you sure that there is anything to be gained by killing the people?" said Nag.

"Everything. When there were no people in the bungalow, did we have any mongoose in the garden? So long as the bungalow is empty, we are king and queen of the garden; and remember that as soon as our eggs in the melon bed hatch (as they may tomorrow), our children will need room and quiet."

"I had not thought of that," said Nag. "I will go, but there is no need that we should hunt for Rikki-tikki afterward. I will kill the big man and his wife, and the child if I can, and come away quietly. Then the bungalow will be empty, and Rikki-tikki will go."

Rikki-tikki tingled all over with rage and hatred at this, and then Nag's head came through the sluice, and his five feet of cold body followed it. Angry as he was, Rikki-tikki was very frightened as he saw the size of the big cobra. Nag coiled himself up, raised his head, and looked into the bathroom in the dark, and Rikki could see his eyes glitter.

"Now, if I kill him here, Nagaina will know;—and if I fight him on the open floor, the odds are in his favor. What am I to do?" said Rikki-tikki-tavi.

Nag waved to and fro, and then Rikki-tikki-tikki heard him drinking from the biggest water jar that was used to fill the bath. "That is good," said the snake. "Now, when Karait was killed, the big man had a stick. He may have that stick still, but when he comes in to bathe in the morning he will

---

5. sluice (slōōs) *n.* drain.

Literary Analysis
Plot What details add to the conflict as Rikki overhears this conversation?

not have a stick. I shall wait here till he comes. Nagaina—do you hear me?—I shall wait here in the cool till daytime."

There was no answer from outside, so Rikki-tikki knew Nagaina had gone away. Nag coiled himself down, coil by coil, round the bulge at the bottom of the waterjar, and Rikki-tikki stayed still as death. After an hour he began to move, muscle by muscle, toward the jar. Nag was asleep, and Rikki-tikki looked at his big back, wondering which would be the best place for a good hold. "If I don't break his back at the first jump," said Rikki, "he can still fight; and if he fights—O Rikki!" He looked at the thickness of the neck below the hood, but that was too much for him; and a bite near the tail would only make Nag savage.

"It must be the head," he said at last; "the head above the hood; and, when I am once there, I must not let go."

Then he jumped. The head was lying a little clear of the water jar, under the curve of it; and, as his teeth met, Rikki braced his back against the bulge of the red earthenware to hold down the head. This gave him just one second's purchase,[6] and he made the most of it. Then he was battered to and fro as a rat is shaken by a dog—to and fro on the floor, up and down, and round in great circles: but his eyes were red, and he held on as the body cart-whipped over the floor, upsetting the tin dipper and the soap dish and the fleshbrush, and banged against the tin side of the bath. As he held he closed his jaws tighter and tighter, for he made sure he would be banged to death, and, for the honor of his family, he preferred to be found with his teeth locked. He was dizzy, aching, and felt shaken to pieces when something went off like a thunderclap just behind him; a hot wind knocked him senseless and red fire singed his fur. The big man had been wakened by the noise, and had fired both barrels of a shotgun into Nag just behind the hood.

Rikki-tikki held on with his eyes shut, for now he was quite sure he was dead; but the head did not move, and the big man picked him up and said: "It's the mongoose again, Alice; the little chap has saved our lives now." Then Teddy's mother came in with a very white face, and saw what was left of Nag, and Rikki-tikki dragged himself to Teddy's bedroom and spent half the rest of the night shaking himself tenderly to find out whether he really was broken into forty pieces, as he fancied.

---

6. **purchase** (pʉr′ chəs) *n.* firm hold.

Reading Skill
Predict What do you predict will be the outcome of this encounter between Rikki and Nag?

Reading Check

What does Rikki decide is the best way to attack Nag?

When morning came he was very stiff, but well pleased with his doings. "Now I have Nagaina to settle with, and she will be worse than five Nags, and there's no knowing when the eggs she spoke of will hatch. Goodness! I must go and see Darzee," he said.

Without waiting for breakfast, Rikki-tikki ran to the thornbush where Darzee was singing a song of triumph at the top of his voice. The news of Nag's death was all over the garden, for the sweeper had thrown the body on the rubbish heap.

"Oh, you stupid tuft of feathers!" said Rikki-tikki, angrily. "Is this the time to sing?"

"Nag is dead—is dead—is dead!" sang Darzee. "The valiant Rikki-tikki caught him by the head and held fast. The big man brought the bang-stick and Nag fell in two pieces! He will never eat my babies again."

Literary Analysis
Plot Why is the death of Nag part of the rising action rather than the resolution?

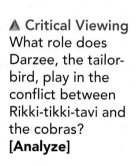

"All that's true enough; but where's Nagaina?" said Rikki-tikki, looking carefully round him.

"Nagaina came to the bathroom sluice and called for Nag," Darzee went on; "and Nag came out on the end of a stick—the sweeper picked him up on the end of a stick and threw him upon the rubbish heap. Let us sing about the great, the red-eyed Rikki-tikki!" and Darzee filled his throat and sang.

"If I could get up to your nest, I'd roll all your babies out!" said Rikki-tikki. "You don't know when to do the right thing at the right time. You're safe enough in your nest there, but it's war for me down here. Stop singing a minute, Darzee."

"For the great, the beautiful Rikki-tikki's sake, I will stop," said Darzee. "What is it, O Killer of the terrible Nag!"

"Where is Nagaina, for the third time?"

"On the rubbish heap by the stables, mourning for Nag. Great is Rikki-tikki with the white teeth."

"Bother my white teeth! Have you ever heard where she keeps her eggs?"

"In the melon bed, on the end nearest the wall, where the sun strikes nearly all day. She had them there weeks ago."

"And you never thought it worthwhile to tell me? The end nearest the wall, you said?"

▲ **Critical Viewing** What role does Darzee, the tailor-bird, play in the conflict between Rikki-tikki-tavi and the cobras? **[Analyze]**

"Rikki-tikki, you are not going to eat her eggs?"

"Not eat exactly; no. Darzee, if you have a grain of sense you will fly off to the stables and pretend that your wing is broken, and let Nagaina chase you away to this bush! I must get to the melon bed, and if I went there now she'd see me."

Darzee was a featherbrained little fellow who could never hold more than one idea at a time in his head; and just because he knew that Nagaina's children were born in eggs like his own, he didn't think at first that it was fair to kill them. But his wife was a sensible bird, and she knew that cobra's eggs meant young cobras later on; so she flew off from the nest, and left Darzee to keep the babies warm, and continue his song about the death of Nag. Darzee was very like a man in some ways.

She fluttered in front of Nagaina by the rubbish heap, and cried out, "Oh, my wing is broken! The boy in the house threw a stone at me and broke it." Then she fluttered more desperately than ever.

Nagaina lifted up her head and hissed, "You warned Rikki-tikki when I would have killed him. Indeed and truly, you've chosen a bad place to be lame in." And she moved toward Darzee's wife, slipping along over the dust.

"The boy broke it with a stone!" shrieked Darzee's wife.

"Well! It may be some <u>consolation</u> to you when you're dead to know that I shall settle accounts with the boy. My husband lies on the rubbish heap this morning, but before night the boy in the house will lie very still. What is the use of running away? I am sure to catch you. Little fool, look at me!"

Darzee's wife knew better than to do *that*, for a bird who looks at a snake's eyes gets so frightened that she cannot move. Darzee's wife fluttered on, piping sorrowfully, and never leaving the ground, and Nagaina quickened her pace.

Rikki-tikki heard them going up the path from the stables, and he raced for the end of the melon patch near the wall. There, in the warm litter about the melons, very cunningly[7] hidden, he found twenty-five eggs, about the size of a bantam's eggs,[8] but with whitish skin instead of shell.

"I was not a day too soon," he said; for he could see the baby cobras curled up inside the skin, and he knew that the

---

7. cunningly (kun´ iŋ lē) *adv.* cleverly.
8. bantam's (ban´ təmz) **eggs** *n.* eggs of a small chicken.

minute they were hatched they could each kill a man or a mongoose. He bit off the tops of the eggs as fast as he could, taking care to crush the young cobras, and turned over the litter from time to time to see whether he had missed any. At last there were only three eggs left, and Rikki-tikki began to chuckle to himself, when he heard Darzee's wife screaming:

"Rikki-tikki, I led Nagaina toward the house, and she has gone into the veranda, and—oh, come quickly—she means killing!"

Rikki-tikki smashed two eggs, and tumbled backward down the melon bed with the third egg in his mouth, and scuttled to the veranda as hard as he could put foot to the ground. Teddy and his mother and father were there at early breakfast; but Rikki-tikki saw that they were not eating anything. They sat stone-still, and their faces were white. Nagaina was coiled up on the matting by Teddy's chair, within easy striking distance of Teddy's bare leg, and she was swaying to and fro singing a song of triumph.

"Son of the big man that killed Nag," she hissed, "stay still. I am not ready yet. Wait a little. Keep very still, all you three. If you move I strike, and if you do not move I strike, Oh, foolish people, who killed my Nag!"

Teddy's eyes were fixed on his father, and all his father could do was to whisper, "Sit still, Teddy. You mustn't move. Teddy, keep still."

Then Rikki-tikki came up and cried: "Turn round, Nagaina; turn and fight!"

"All in good time," said she, without moving her eyes. "I will settle my account with *you* presently. Look at your friends,

Literary Analysis
Plot Do you think this scene is the climax or part of the rising action? Why?

▼ **Critical Viewing** Based on this photograph, which animal would you expect to win a match to the death— the cobra or the mongoose? **[Speculate]**

Rikki-tikki. They are still and white; they are afraid. They dare not move, and if you come a step nearer I strike."

"Look at your eggs," said Rikki-tikki, "in the melon bed near the wall. Go and look, Nagaina."

The big snake turned half round, and saw the egg on the veranda. "Ah-h! Give it to me," she said.

Rikki-tikki put his paws one on each side of the egg, and his eyes were blood-red. "What price for a snake's egg? For a young cobra? For a young king cobra? For the last—the very last of the brood? The ants are eating all the others down by the melon bed."

Nagaina spun clear round, forgetting everything for the sake of the one egg; and Rikki-tikki saw Teddy's father shoot out a big hand, catch Teddy by the shoulder, and drag him across the little table with the tea-cups, safe and out of reach of Nagaina.

"Tricked! Tricked! Tricked! *Rikk-tck-tck!*" chuckled Rikki-tikki. "The boy is safe, and it was I—I—I that caught Nag by the hood last night in the bathroom." Then he began to jump up and down, all four feet together, his head close to the floor. "He threw me to and fro, but he could not shake me off. He was dead before the big man blew him in two. I did it. *Rikki-tikki-tck-tck!* Come then, Nagaina. Come and fight with me. You shall not be a widow long."

Nagaina saw that she had lost her chance of killing Teddy, and the egg lay between Rikki-tikki's paws. "Give me the egg, Rikki-tikki. Give me the last of my eggs, and I will go away and never come back," she said, lowering her hood.

Literary Analysis
Plot What details increase the tension in the story at this point?

Reading Check

What does Rikki bring with him to the veranda?

"Yes, you will go away, and you will never come back; for you will go to the rubbish heap with Nag. Fight, widow! The big man has gone for his gun! Fight!"

Rikki-tikki was bounding all round Nagaina, keeping just out of reach of her stroke, his little eyes like hot coals. Nagaina gathered herself together, and flung out at him. Rikki-tikki jumped up and backward. Again and again and again she struck, and each time her head came with a whack on the matting of the veranda and she gathered herself together like a watchspring. Then Rikki-tikki danced in a circle to get behind her, and Nagaina spun round to keep her head to his head, so that the rustle of her tail on the matting sounded like dry leaves blown along by the wind.

He had forgotten the egg. It still lay on the veranda, and Nagaina came nearer and nearer to it, till at last, while Rikki-tikki was drawing breath, she caught it in her mouth, turned to the veranda steps, and flew like an arrow down the path, with Rikki-tikki behind her. When the cobra runs for her life, she goes like a whiplash flicked across a horse's neck.

Rikki-tikki knew that he must catch her, or all the trouble would begin again. She headed straight for the long grass by the thornbush, and as he was running Rikki-tikki heard Darzee still singing his foolish little song of triumph. But Darzee's wife was wiser. She flew off her nest as Nagaina came along, and flapped her wings about Nagaina's head. If Darzee had helped they might have turned her; but Nagaina only lowered her hood and went on. Still, the instant's delay brought Rikki-tikki up to her, and as she plunged into the rat hole where she and Nag used to live, his little white teeth were clenched on her tail, and he went down with her—and very few mongooses, however wise and old they may be, care to follow a cobra into its hole. It was dark in the hole; and Rikki-tikki never knew when it might open out and give Nagaina room to turn and strike at him. He held on savagely, and struck out his feet to act as brakes on the dark slope of the hot, moist earth.

Then the grass by the mouth of the hole stopped waving, and Darzee said: "It is all over with Rikki-tikki! We must sing his death song. Valiant Rikki-tikki is dead! For Nagaina will surely kill him underground."

So he sang a very mournful song that he made up all on the spur of the minute, and just as he got to the most touching

Reading Skill
Predict Based on events in the story, what do you predict will be the outcome of Rikki-tikki's fight with Nagaina? Explain.

Literary Analysis
Plot How does Darzee's comment add to the tension?

part the grass quivered again, and Rikki-tikki, covered with dirt, dragged himself out of the hole leg by leg, licking his whiskers. Darzee stopped with a little shout. Rikki-tikki shook some of the dust out of his fur and sneezed. "It is all over," he said. "The widow will never come out again." And the red ants that live between the grass stems heard him, and began to troop down one after another to see if he had spoken the truth.

Rikki-tikki curled himself up in the grass and slept where he was—slept and slept till it was late in the afternoon, for he had done a hard day's work.

"Now," he said, when he awoke, "I will go back to the house. Tell the Coppersmith, Darzee, and he will tell the garden that Nagaina is dead."

The Coppersmith is a bird who makes a noise exactly like the beating of a little hammer on a copper pot; and the reason he is always making it is because he is the town crier to every Indian garden, and tells all the news to everybody who cares to listen. As Rikki-tikki went up the path, he heard his "attention" notes like a tiny dinner gong; and then the steady "*Ding-dong-tock!* Nag is dead—*dong!* Nagaina is dead! *Ding-dong-tock!*" That set all the birds in the garden singing, and the frogs croaking; for Nag and Nagaina used to eat frogs as well as little birds.

When Rikki got to the house, Teddy and Teddy's mother and Teddy's father came out and almost cried over him; and that night he ate all that was given him till he could eat no more, and went to bed on Teddy's shoulder, where Teddy's mother saw him when she came to look late at night.

"He saved our lives and Teddy's life," she said to her husband. "Just think, he saved all our lives."

Rikki-tikki woke up with a jump, for all the mongooses are light sleepers.

"Oh, it's you," said he. "What are you bothering for? All the cobras are dead; and if they weren't, I'm here."

Rikki-tikki had a right to be proud of himself; but he did not grow too proud, and he kept that garden as a mongoose should keep it, with tooth and jump and spring and bite, till never a cobra dared show its head inside the walls.

Literary Analysis
What part of the plot does Rikki's comment illustrate?

Literary Analysis
Plot How has Rikki changed, based on the events of the story?

Apply the Skills

Rikki-tikki-tavi

Thinking About the Selection

1. **Respond:** Did you find the story suspenseful? Explain.
2. **(a) Recall:** How does Rikki feel about the cobras? How do they feel about Rikki? **(b) Compare:** Compare Rikki's and the cobras' personalities.
3. **(a) Recall:** What is the relationship between Nag and Nagaina? **(b) Analyze:** What does Nagaina do to make matters worse for Nag and herself? **(c) Draw Conclusions:** Why does this plan make her a villain?
4. **(a) Analyze:** What role does Darzee play in the story? **(b) Compare and Contrast:** Whose approach to life, Darzee's or Rikki's, do you think is more effective? Why?
5. **(a) Analyze:** "Rikki-tikki-tavi" is among the most widely read short stories ever written. How do you explain the story's enduring popularity? **(b) Evaluate:** Do you think the story deserves this standing? Explain. **(c) Discuss:** Share your responses with a partner. Then, discuss how looking at someone else's responses did or did not change your evaluation.

Reading Skill

6. What **prior knowledge** did you have from reading the Background for this story that helped you **predict** that Rikki-tikki-tavi would be able to defeat the cobras?
7. Think of another prediction based on prior knowledge that you made as you read this story. Use a graphic organizer like the one here to show how you made your prediction.

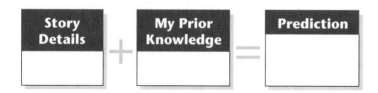

Literary Analysis

8. What are two **plot** events that increase the tension between Rikki and Nag?
9. Identify two or three events that move the plot toward the **climax,** when Rikki and Nagaina battle.

Vocabulary Builder

Practice In your notebook, answer each question. Then, explain your answer.

1. Would someone who has just been *revived* be ready to run a race?

2. If you like a person *immensely*, how do you feel about him or her?

3. Is missing dinner *consolation* for getting home late?

Writing

Use details from the story to write an **informative article** on mongooses. Write your article for third-grade students to read. Use easier vocabulary and simpler sentence structure than you would normally use. An informative article usually contains these elements:

- an introduction, a body, and a conclusion
- details that tell readers *when, how much, how often,* or *to what extent*

For *Grammar, Vocabulary,* and *Assessment,* see **Build Language Skills,** pages 216–217.

Extend Your Learning

Listening and Speaking With a partner, engage in an **informal debate.** One of you will defend the mongoose, and the other will defend the cobra. Explain why your animal is the more interesting of the two.

To persuade your partner to agree with your ideas, back them up with information you have read or heard.

- Remember to respect your partner's time to talk.
- Do not interrupt while he or she is speaking.

Research and Technology Using the Internet and library resources, find out where in the world cobras live. Present your findings in a **diagram** showing the places you would expect to find cobras.

Build Language Skills

The Bear Boy • Rikki-tikki-tavi

Vocabulary Skill

Roots The **root** *-dict-,* means "speak." Words that contain this root have meanings related to *saying* or *speaking.*

Practice Answer each question in a complete sentence that includes the italicized word. Then explain how the meaning "speak or say" contributes to the meaning of each italicized word. For example, to *predict* is to say what you think will happen.

1. What do you *predict* will happen to a plant if no one waters it?
2. What kind of ruler is a *dictator*?
3. How do you *indicate* you are present when the teacher calls your name?
4. What does a judge want when she requests a *verdict*?
5. Is clear *diction* important for actors? Why or why not?

Grammar Lesson

Verbs are words that express an action (action verbs) or a state of being (linking verbs). Linking verbs join the subject of a sentence with a word or phrase that describes or renames the subject.

➤ **Action Verbs:** Jake *rode* his bike.
Let's *skate* in the park.
➤ **Linking Verbs:** Jake *seems* happy.
James *is* a member of the club.
Her voice *sounds* beautiful.

Practice Identify the action verbs and linking verbs in the following sentences.

1. Thomas seems happy about his team's record.
2. Jen is always eager for a field trip.
3. Mr. Tan teaches history and science.
4. Gran waved at the children by the fence.
5. Sam joined the club and was a good member.

MorePractice

For more practice with verbs, see Grammar Hand-book, p. R32.

WG Prentice Hall Writing and Grammar Connection: Chapter 15, Sections 1 and 2

Assessment Practice

Reading: Make Predictions

Directions: *Read the selection. Then answer the questions.*

Julie put the finishing touches on her report. Giving her dog, Fluffy, a pat on the head, Julie slipped the report in her backpack, along with her lunch bag. She kissed her Mom and little brother goodbye as they headed out the door and ran upstairs to get ready for school. She returned minutes later, and her backpack was empty. Julie looked high and low for the valuable contents. They were nowhere in the house. Then she searched through the backyard, but the only thing she saw was Fluffy, resting in his doghouse.

1. Which would best help you make predictions from this selection?
   A Reports are long term assignments.
   B Children can be careless.
   C Dogs take food.
   D Julia was extremely careful.

2. What piece of information helps you predict the identity of the thief?
   A Julie kissed her mom and little brother goodbye.
   B Julie put her report into the backpack along with her lunch bag.
   C Julie ran upstairs to get dressed for school.
   D Julie put the finishing touches on her report.

3. Where do you think Julia will find her report?
   A in the bottom of her backpack
   B on the kitchen table
   C in her mother's briefcase
   D in the doghouse

4. What do you predict Julie will do when she gets home from school?
   A prepare another copy of her report
   B persuade her mother to punish her brother
   C give Fluffy a bath
   D help her mother and father make dinner

Timed Writing: Summary [Cognition]

Review "The Bear Boy" or "Rikki-tikki-tavi." Retell the plot of one of the stories, giving details of the rising and falling action and the climax. Then, explain the resolution of the story. **(20 minutes)**

 ## Writing Workshop: *Work in Progress*

Review of a Short Story
Refer to the list of stories in your writing portfolio. Choose three stories and make a note of the setting and main characters in each. Briefly summarize each story and explain what you like about it.

Reading Informational Materials

Magazine Articles

In Part 1, you are learning how to make predictions. When you flip through a magazine, the titles, pictures, and subheads may help you predict what an article will be about. If you read "Rikki-tikki-tavi," you may be interested in this magazine article, which gives information about mongooses.

About Magazine Articles

A magazine is a form of print media that is published at regular intervals, such as weekly, monthly, or even quarterly (four times a year). Magazines usually contain photographs, advertisements, and a variety of articles by different writers. Some magazines provide information on current issues and events that are of interest to a wide audience. Other magazines are organized with a very specific audience in mind, such as runners, artists, or animal-lovers.

Reading Skill

Before you begin reading a magazine article, you should **preview the text** for clues that can help you make predictions about what the article is about and whether it is useful or interesting. To preview, look over the article but do not read every word. Look at the following elements that can give you a sense of the article.

- title
- subheads
- charts and graphs
- photos
- captions
- quotations

Before you read "Mongoose on the Loose," use a graphic organizer like the one shown to predict what the article is about.

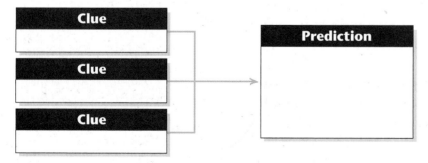

Mongoose on the Loose

Larry Luxner

The title and photo help you predict what the article will be about.

In 1872 a Jamaican sugar planter imported nine furry little mongooses from India to eat the rats which were devouring his crops. They did such a good job, the planter started breeding his exotic animals and selling them to eager farmers on neighboring islands.

Population Explodes

Boldface subtitles break up the text for easier reading.

With no natural predators—like wolves, coyotes, or poisonous snakes—the mongoose population exploded, and within a few years, they were killing not just rats but pigs, lambs, chickens, puppies, and kittens. Dr. G. Roy Horst, a U.S. expert on mongooses, says that today mongooses live on seventeen Caribbean islands as well as Hawaii and Fiji, where they have attacked small animals, threatened endangered species, and have even spread minor rabies epidemics.

In Puerto Rico there are from 800,000 to one million of them. That is about one mongoose for every four humans. In St. Croix, there are 100,000 mongooses, about twice as many as the human population. "It's impossible to eliminate the mongoose population, short of nuclear war," says Horst. "You can't poison them, because cats, dogs, and chickens get poisoned, too. I'm not a prophet crying in the wilderness, but the potential for real trouble is there," says Horst.

According to Horst, great efforts have been made to rid the islands of mongooses, which have killed off a number of species including the Amevia lizard on St. Croix, presumed extinct for several decades. On Hawaii, the combination of mongooses and sports hunting has reduced the Hawaiian goose, or nene, to less than two dozen individuals.

Scientist Studies Problem

The fifty-nine-year-old biology professor, who teaches at Potsdam College in upstate New York, recently finished his third season at the 500-acre Cabo Rojo National Wildlife Refuge in southwestern Puerto Rico, using microchips to study the life cycle and reproductive habits of the Caribbean mongoose. (He is also doing similar work at the Sandy Point Fish and Wildlife Refuge on St. Croix in the U.S. Virgin Islands.) "I want to know what happens when you take a small animal and put him in an area with no competition. This is a model that doesn't exist anywhere else in the world."

Horst's five-year, $60,000 study is being sponsored by Earthwatch Incorporated, a non-profit group that has funded some 1,300 research projects in eighty-seven countries. Volunteers pay $1,500 each (not including airfare) to come to Puerto Rico for ten days and help Horst set out mongoose traps, study the animals, and keep records. Often he and his volunteers spend a sweaty day walking about ten miles while setting out mongoose traps in the wilderness. Later, they perform surgery on their unwilling subjects to implant the electronic devices that will allow them to track the animal's habits.

Horst has tagged more than 400 mongooses with PITs (permanently implanted transponders), a new microchip technology, which he says has changed his work dramatically. "You couldn't do this with ear tags. It was very hard to permanently mark these animals until this technology came along," he said.

Horst has caught thousands of mongooses and has reached some interesting conclusions. Among them: mongooses have a life expectancy of six to ten years, much longer than the previously accepted figure of three years. Horst says his research will provide local and federal health officials with extremely valuable information if they ever decide to launch a campaign against rabies in Puerto Rico or the U.S. Virgin Islands.

> This is a model that doesn't exist anywhere else in the world.

This quotation highlights an idea presented in the article.

Pictures and captions give additional information about the content of the article.

A mongoose gets tagged.

Reading: Making Predictions

Directions: *Choose the letter of the best answer to each question about "Mongoose on the Loose."*

1. Which of the following clues does **not** help you predict what this article is about?
   A photos and captions
   B article subheads
   C charts and graphs
   D article title

2. Which of the following clues helps you identify where you will find information about changes in the number of mongooses?
   A the title "Mongoose on the Loose"
   B the subhead "Population Explodes"
   C the subhead "Scientist Studies Problem"
   D the caption "A mongoose gets tagged."

3. Which of the following clues hints at the work being done by volunteers to help Horst conduct his research in Puerto Rico?
   A the title "Mongoose on the Loose"
   B the subhead "Population Explodes"
   C the subhead "Scientist Studies Problem"
   D the caption "A mongoose gets tagged."

Reading: Comprehension and Interpretation

Directions: *Write your answers on a separate piece of paper.*

4. How were mongooses first introduced to the islands?

5. Explain how Horst manages to track mongooses in order to learn about their habits.

6. Describe one way the mongoose population could be controlled. Support your answer with details from the text.

Timed Writing: Description

Describe a mongoose. Include specific details from the magazine article that describe its appearance and behavior. Include vivid words and phrases that create strong images for readers. **(15 minutes)**

These skills will help you become a better reader. Practice them with either the excerpt from *Letters from Rifka* (p. 224) or "Two Kinds" from *The Joy Luck Club* (p. 231).

Reading Skill

A **prediction** is an informed guess about what will happen. Use details in the text to make predictions as you read. Then, **read ahead to verify predictions**—to check whether your predictions are correct.

- As you read, ask yourself whether new details support your predictions. If they do not, revise your predictions based on the new information.
- If the predictions you make turn out to be wrong, **reread to look for details** you might have missed.

Use a graphic organizer like the one shown to record and verify predictions as you read the story.

Prediction	Details
Revised or Confirmed Prediction	New details
Actual Outcome	Details from rereading (if necessary)

Literary Analysis

A **character** is a person or animal who takes part in the action of a literary work.

- A **character's motives** are the emotions or goals that drive him or her to act one way or another.
- **Character traits** are the individual qualities that make each character unique.

Characters' motives and traits influence what characters do and how they interact with others. As you read, think about what the characters are like and why they do what they do.

Vocabulary Builder

from **Letters from Rifka**

- **distract** (di strakt´) *v.* draw attention away in another direction (p. 225) *A toy will* distract *the crying child.*

- **emerged** (ē mʉrjd´) *v.* came into view; became visible (p. 225) *The sun* emerged *from behind the clouds.*

- **huddled** (hud´ 'ld) *v.* crowded or nestled close together (p. 227) *Cows* huddled *under a tree in the rain.*

Two Kinds

- **reproach** (ri prōch´) *n.* disgrace; blame (p. 232) *She was so nearly perfect, she was beyond* reproach.

- **conspired** (kən spīrd´) *v.* planned together secretly (p. 238) *The girls* conspired *to surprise their mother.*

- **devastated** (dev´ ə stā´ tid) *v.* destroyed; completely upset (p. 240) *The fire* devastated *the city.*

Build Understanding • from *Letters from Rifka*

Background

Jews in Russia For most of the nineteenth and early twentieth centuries, the Jews of Russia faced prejudice and unfair treatment. This caused thousands of Jews to leave the country, many fleeing to the United States. In this excerpt from *Letters from Rifka*, a Jewish family begins their escape from Russia after the turmoil of World War I.

Connecting to the Literature

Reading/Writing Connection In *Letters from Rifka*, the main character describes some of her difficulties in escaping from Russia. Jot down a few conveniences you use every day. Then, describe one that you think you could live without and one that you would have trouble giving up. Use at least three of the following words: *adjust, adapt, deprive, dispose*. As you read, compare your choices with the kinds of choices the characters make.

Meet the Author

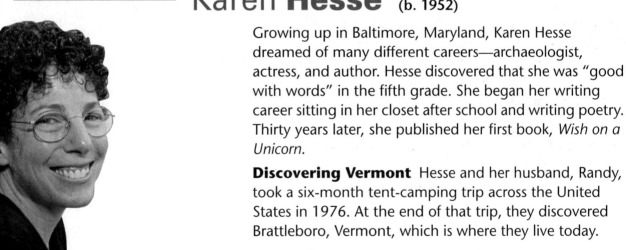

Karen **Hesse** (b. 1952)

Growing up in Baltimore, Maryland, Karen Hesse dreamed of many different careers—archaeologist, actress, and author. Hesse discovered that she was "good with words" in the fifth grade. She began her writing career sitting in her closet after school and writing poetry. Thirty years later, she published her first book, *Wish on a Unicorn*.

Discovering Vermont Hesse and her husband, Randy, took a six-month tent-camping trip across the United States in 1976. At the end of that trip, they discovered Brattleboro, Vermont, which is where they live today.

Fast Facts

▶ Hesse started writing *Letters from Rifka* about twenty times, until she was happy with the "voice" of the main character.

▶ As a child, Hesse often went to the local public library and "devoured every book" the librarian gave her. Her early love of reading led to her interest in writing.

Go Online
Author Link

For: More about the author
Visit: www.PHSchool.com
Web Code: eme-9204

from *Letters from Rifka* ■ 223

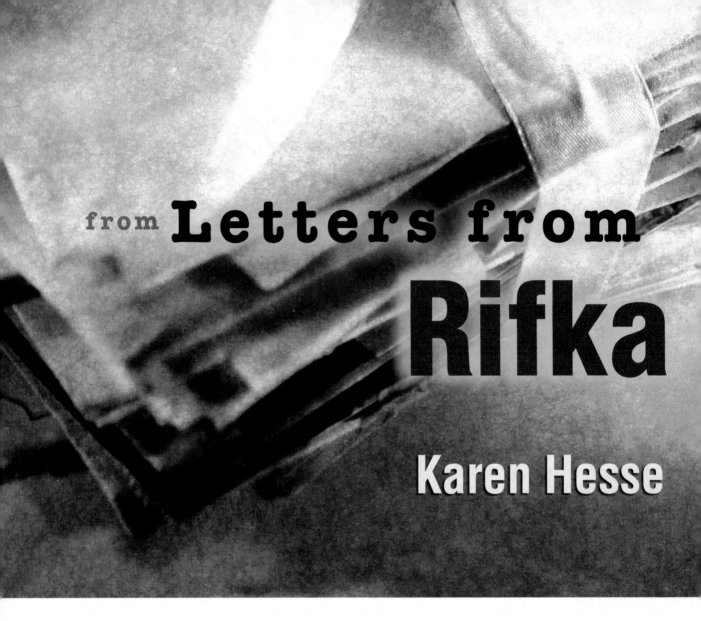

from **Letters from Rifka**

Karen Hesse

My Dear Cousin Tovah,

We made it! If it had not been for your father, though, I think my family would all be dead now: Mama, Papa, Nathan, Saul, and me. At the very best we would be in that filthy prison in Berdichev,[1] not rolling west through Ukraine on a freight train bound for Poland.

I am sure you and Cousin Hannah were glad to see Uncle Avrum come home today. How worried his daughters must have been after the locked doors and whisperings of last night.

Reading Skill
Predict Based on the first paragraph, what do you think this story will be about?

---

1. **Berdichev** (byir dĕ´ chif) *n.* a city in Russia, now Ukraine.

Soon Bubbe Ruth, my dear little grandmother, will hear of our escape. I hope she gives a big pot of Frusileh's cream to Uncle Avrum. How better could she thank him?

When the sun rose above the trees at the train station in Berdichev this morning, I stood alone outside a boxcar, my heart knocking against my ribs.

I stood there, trying to look older than my twelve years. Wrapped in the new shawl Cousin Hannah gave to me, still I trembled.

"Wear this in health," Hannah had whispered in my ear as she draped the shawl over my shoulders early this morning, before we slipped from your house into the dark.

"Come," Papa said, leading us through the woods to the train station.

I looked back to the flickering lights of your house, Tovah.

"Quickly, Rifka," Papa whispered. "The boys, and Mama, and I must hide before light."

"You can <u>distract</u> the guards, can't you, little sister?" Nathan said, putting an arm around me. In the darkness, I could not see his eyes, but I felt them studying me.

"Yes," I answered, not wanting to disappoint him.

At the train station, Papa and Mama hid behind bales of hay in boxcars to my right. My two giant brothers, Nathan and Saul, crouched in separate cars to my left. Papa said that we should hide in different cars. If the guards discovered only one of us, perhaps the others might still escape.

Behind me, in the dusty corner of a boxcar, sat my own rucksack. It waited for me, holding what little I own in this world. I had packed Mama's candlesticks, wrapped in my two heavy dresses, at the bottom of the sack.

Your gift to me, the book of Pushkin, I did not pack. I kept it out, holding it in my hands.

I would have liked to fly away, to race back up the road, stopping at every door to say good-bye, to say that we were going to America.

But I could not. Papa said we must tell no one we were leaving, not even Bubbe Ruth. Only you and Hannah and Uncle Avrum knew. I'm so glad at least you knew, Tovah.

As Papa expected, not long after he and Mama and the boys had hidden themselves, two guards <u>emerged</u> from a wooden shelter. They thundered down the platform in their heavy boots climbing in and out of the cars, making their search.

Literary Analysis
Character What do Rifka's remarks about her grandmother and Uncle Avrum reveal about her character?

Vocabulary Builder
distract (di strakt´) *v.* draw attention away in another direction

Vocabulary Builder
emerged (ē mʉrjd´) *v.* came into view; became visible

Reading Check

Where is Rifka as she writes this letter?

They did not notice me at first. Saul says I am too little for anyone to notice, but you know Saul. He never has a nice word to say to me. And I am small for a girl of twelve. Still, my size did not keep the guards from noticing me. I think the guards missed seeing me at first because they were so busy in their search of the train. They were searching for Nathan.

You know as well as I, Tovah, that when a Jewish boy deserts the Russian Army, the army tries hard to find him. They bring him back and kill him in front of his regiment[2] as a warning to the others. Those who have helped him, they also die.

Late last night, when Nathan slipped away from his regiment and appeared at our door, joy filled my heart at seeing my favorite brother again. Yet a troubled look worried Nathan's face. He hugged me only for a moment. His dimpled smile vanished as quickly as it came.

"I've come," he said, "to warn Saul. The soldiers will soon follow. They will take him into the army."

I am ashamed, Tovah, to admit that at first hearing

▲ **Critical Viewing** Based on this image and the details in the text, how would you describe Rifka's journey? **[Synthesize]**

---

2. regiment (rej´ ə mənt) *n.* a military unit consisting of a large number of persons.

Nathan's news made me glad. I wanted Saul gone. He drives me crazy. From his big ears to his big feet, I cannot stand the sight of him. Good riddance, I thought.

How foolish I was not to understand what Nathan's news really meant to our family.

"You should not have come," Mama said to Nathan. "They will shoot you when you return."

Papa said, "Nathan isn't going to return. Hurry! We must pack!"

We all stared at him.

"Quickly," Papa said, clapping his hands. "Rifka, run and fill your rucksack[3] with all of your belongings." I do not know what Papa thought I owned.

Mama said, "Rifka, do you have room in your bag for my candlesticks?"

"The candlesticks, Mama?" I asked.

"We either take them, Rifka, or leave them to the greedy peasants. Soon enough they will swoop down like vultures to pick our house bare," Mama said.

Papa said, "Your brothers in America have sent for us, Rifka. It is time to leave Russia and we are not coming back. Ever."

"Don't we need papers?" I asked.

Papa looked from Nathan to Saul. "There is no time for papers," he said.

Then I began to understand.

We <u>huddled</u> in your cellar through the black night, planning our escape. Uncle Avrum only shut you out to protect you, Tovah.

Hearing the guards speak this morning, I understand his precaution. It was dangerous enough for you to know we were leaving. We could not risk telling you the details of our escape in case the soldiers came to question you.

The guards were talking about Nathan. They were saying what they would do to him once they found him, and what they would do to anyone who had helped him.

Nathan hid under a stack of burlap bags, one boxcar away from me. I knew, no matter how frightened I was, I must not let them find Nathan.

▼ **Critical Viewing**
Why might Rifka want to take family items like candlesticks with her? **[Infer]**

Vocabulary Builder
huddled (hud´ 'ld) *v.* crowded or nestled close together

---

3. rucksack (ruk´ sak´) *n.* a kind of knapsack or backpack worn over the shoulders.

Apply the Skills

from *Letters from Rifka*

Thinking About the Selection

1. **(a) Respond:** Which of Rifka's qualities do you most admire? Explain. **(b) Discuss:** In a small group, share your responses. As a group, choose one response to share with the class.
2. **(a) Support:** What details in the story reveal Rifka's age? **(b) Analyze:** How do you think Rifka's age affects the way she feels about the story's events?
3. **(a) Recall:** What risks did Nathan take by escaping from the Russian army? **(b) Speculate:** How do you think he felt as he appeared at his family's door? Explain.
4. **(a) Analyze:** Why was Rifka not allowed to say goodbye to her friends and neighbors? **(b) Make a Judgment:** Do you think she was wise to have left silently? Why?
5. **(a) Speculate:** Why might the author have chosen to write this book as a series of letters? **(b) Evaluate:** Do you think the technique is effective? Why or why not?

Reading Skill

6. **(a)** Did you **predict** that the guards would discover Rifka? **(b)** Did reading ahead cause you to change your prediction? Explain.
7. **(a)** At what point in the story were you able to predict the family's reason for leaving Russia? **(b)** Did your prediction change from what you thought when you first started reading? Explain.

Literary Analysis

8. Using a diagram like the one shown, identify Rifka's **character traits**. Support your answers with details from the story.

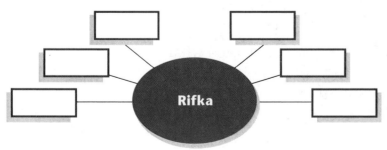

9. What are Nathan's **motives** for leaving the Russian Army?

QuickReview

Who's Who in the Story

Rifka: a young girl

Mama and Papa: Rifka's parents

Nathan and Saul: Rifka's brothers

Go **O**nline
——Assessment
For: Self-test
Visit: www.PHSchool.com
Web Code: ema-6204

Prediction: an informed guess about what will happen next

Character: person or animal who takes part in the action of a literary work

Character traits: qualities that a character possesses

Character motives: emotions or goals that drive a character

Vocabulary Builder

Practice Make up an answer to each question. Use a complete sentence that includes the italicized word.

1. How can they *distract* the children?
2. What *emerged* from the egg?
3. What animals *huddled* under the bushes?

Writing

Rifka wrote letters to her cousin Tovah throughout her journey from Berdichev. These letters tell her story, much as a journal might. Reread the passage from *Letters from Rifka,* and then write a **journal entry** as if you were one of the other family members—Nathan, Saul, Mama, or Papa.

- Jot down words that reflect feelings about the escape.
- Include details about the situation from the family member's point of view.

For *Grammar, Vocabulary,* and *Assessment,* see **Build Language Skills,** pages 246–247.

Extend Your Learning

Listening and Speaking With a partner, hold a **discussion** about whether Nathan should have left the Russian army and appeared at his family's door. Discuss his motives and the risks he took. Before your discussion, identify points that support your position. Listen carefully to your partner's points. Write down the points that you and your partner make. Identify the strongest point each of you makes and share these ideas with the class.

Research and Technology Go to the library or use Internet resources to learn more about the persecution of Jews in Russia in the early twentieth century. First, locate background information about the times. Then, summarize your findings in an **outline.** State briefly in your own words the main points and key details of what you learned.

Build Understanding • *Two Kinds*

Background

China In 1949, the Communist party seized control of China, following years of civil war. Like the mother in "Two Kinds," a number of Chinese who feared Communists fled to the United States. Many of them lost everything except their hopes for a better future. They placed these hopes on the shoulders of the children born in the new land. As you read, note how the daughter in "Two Kinds" deals with her mother's expectations.

Connecting to the Literature

Reading/Writing Connection In "Two Kinds," the narrator's mother has dreams of greatness for her daughter. Jot down three daydreams of success you have for yourself. Use at least three of the following words: *achieve, attain, promote, pursue.*

Review

For **Reading Skill, Literary Analysis,** and **Vocabulary Builder,** see page 222.

Meet the Author

Amy **Tan** (b. 1952)

If Amy Tan's mother had gotten her way, Amy would have two professions—doctor and concert pianist. Although Tan showed early promise in music, at thirty-seven she became a successful fiction writer instead. Tan's first novel, *The Joy Luck Club*, drew on her troubled relationship with her mother, who was born in China.

The Writing Life Tan has written many books—most for adults, some for children. Writing is sometimes tough, says Tan, but she keeps this in mind: "A story should be a gift." That thought propels Tan to keep creating memorable characters and events.

Fast Facts

▶ Tan's favorite writing schedule is 9 A.M. to 7 P.M.
▶ Many of her stories are about difficult mother-daughter relationships.
▶ Tan sometimes performs in a rock group with fellow writer Stephen King to raise money for charity.

Go **Online**
Author Link

For: More about the author
Visit: www.PHSchool.com
Web Code: eme-9205

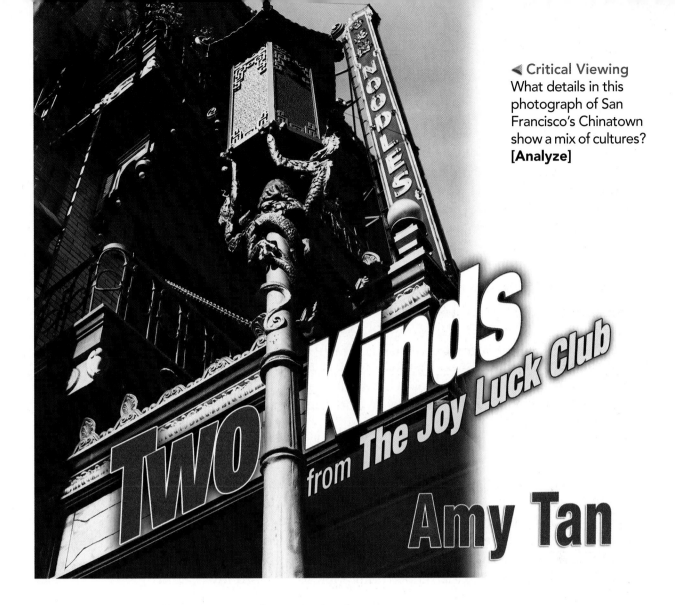

◀ **Critical Viewing**
What details in this photograph of San Francisco's Chinatown show a mix of cultures? **[Analyze]**

Two Kinds
from *The Joy Luck Club*
Amy Tan

My mother believed you could be anything you wanted to be in America. You could open a restaurant. You could work for the government and get good retirement. You could buy a house with almost no money down. You could become rich. You could become instantly famous.

"Of course you can be prodigy[1], too," my mother told me when I was nine. "You can be best anything. What does Auntie Lindo know? Her daughter, she is only best tricky."

America was where all my mother's hopes lay. She had come here in 1949 after losing everything in China: her mother and father, her family home, her first husband, and two daughters, twin baby girls. But she never looked back with regret. There were so many ways for things to get better.

Literary Analysis
Character In what ways might the details in this paragraph contribute to the mother's motives?

---

1. **prodigy** (präd´ ə jē) *n.* child of unusually high talent.

We didn't immediately pick the right kind of prodigy. At first my mother thought I could be a Chinese Shirley Temple.[2] We'd watch Shirley's old movies on TV as though they were training films. My mother would poke my arm and say, "Ni kan" [nē kän]—You watch. And I would see Shirley tapping her feet, or singing a sailor song, or pursing her lips into a very round O while saying, "Oh my goodness."

"*Ni kan*," said my mother as Shirley's eyes flooded with tears. "You already know how. Don't need talent for crying!"

Soon after my mother got this idea about Shirley Temple, she took me to a beauty training school in the Mission district and put me in the hands of a student who could barely hold the scissors without shaking. Instead of getting big fat curls, I emerged with an uneven mass of crinkly black fuzz. My mother dragged me off to the bathroom and tried to wet down my hair.

"You look like Negro Chinese," she lamented, as if I had done this on purpose.

The instructor of the beauty training school had to lop off these soggy clumps to make my hair even again. "Peter Pan is very popular these days," the instructor assured my mother. I now had hair the length of a boy's, with straight-across bangs that hung at a slant two inches above my eyebrows. I liked the haircut and it made me actually look forward to my future fame.

In fact, in the beginning, I was just as excited as my mother, maybe even more so. I pictured this prodigy part of me as many different images, trying each one on for size. I was a dainty ballerina girl standing by the curtains, waiting to hear the right music that would send me floating on my tiptoes. I was like the Christ child lifted out of the straw manger, crying with holy indignity. I was Cinderella stepping from her pumpkin carriage with sparkly cartoon music filling the air.

In all of my imaginings, I was filled with a sense that I would soon become *perfect*. My mother and father would adore me. I would be beyond <u>reproach</u>. I would never feel the need to sulk for anything.

Literary Analysis
Character What are the mother's motives for taking her daughter to beauty training school?

Vocabulary Builder
reproach (ri prōch´) *n.* disgrace; blame

---

2. Shirley Temple American child star of the 1930s. She starred in her first movie at age three and won an Academy Award at age six.

But sometimes the prodigy in me became impatient. "If you don't hurry up and get me out of here, I'm disappearing for good," it warned. "And then you'll always be nothing."

Every night after dinner, my mother and I would sit at the Formica kitchen table. She would present new tests, taking her examples from stories of amazing children she had read in *Ripley's Believe It or Not,* or *Good Housekeeping, Reader's Digest,* and a dozen other magazines she kept in a pile in our bathroom. My mother got these magazines from people whose houses she cleaned. And since she cleaned many houses each week, we had a great assortment. She would look through them all, searching for stories about remarkable children.

The first night she brought out a story about a three-year-old boy who knew the capitals of all the states and even most of the European countries. A teacher was quoted as saying the little boy could also pronounce the names of the foreign cities correctly.

"What's the capital of Finland?" my mother asked me, looking at the magazine story.

All I knew was the capital of California, because Sacramento was the name of the street we lived on in Chinatown. "Nairobi!"[3] I guessed, saying the most foreign word I could think of. She checked to see if that was possibly one way to pronounce "Helsinki" [hel siŋ´ kē] before showing me the answer.

The tests got harder—multiplying numbers in my head, finding the queen of hearts in a deck of cards, trying to stand on my head without using my hands, predicting the daily temperatures in Los Angeles, New York, and London.

One night I had to look at a page from the Bible for three minutes and then report everything I could remember. "Now Jehoshaphat had riches and honor in abundance and . . . that's all I remember, Ma," I said.

And after seeing my mother's disappointed face once again, something inside of me began to die. I hated the tests, the raised hopes and failed expectations. Before going to bed that night, I looked in the mirror above the bathroom sink and when I saw only my face staring back—and that it would always be this ordinary face—I began to cry. Such a

Literary Analysis
Character Why is the mother interested in stories about remarkable children?

Reading Skill
Predict How do you think the narrator will do on the harder tests? Read on to verify your prediction.

Reading Check

Whom does the narrator's mother want her to be like?

---

3. **Nairobi** (nī rō´ bē) *n.* capital of Kenya, a country in east central Africa.

sad, ugly girl! I made high-pitched noises like a crazed animal, trying to scratch out the face in the mirror.

And then I saw what seemed to be the prodigy side of me—because I had never seen that face before. I looked at my reflection, blinking so I could see more clearly. The girl staring back at me was angry, powerful. This girl and I were the same. I had new thoughts, willful thoughts, or rather thoughts filled with lots of won'ts. I won't let her change me, I promised myself. I won't be what I'm not.

So now on nights when my mother presented her tests, I performed listlessly, my head propped on one arm. I pretended to be bored. And I was. I got so bored I started counting the bellows of the foghorns out on the bay while my mother drilled me in other areas. The sound was comforting and reminded me of the cow jumping over the moon. And the next day, I played a game with myself, seeing if my mother would give up on me before eight bellows. After a while I usually counted only one, maybe two bellows at most. At last she was beginning to give up hope.

Two or three months had gone by without any mention of my being a prodigy again. And then one day my mother was watching *The Ed Sullivan Show*[4] on TV. The TV was old and the sound kept shorting out. Every time my mother got halfway up from the sofa to adjust the set, the sound would go back on and Ed would be talking. As soon as she sat down, Ed would go silent again. She got up, the TV broke into loud piano music. She sat down. Silence. Up and down, back and forth, quiet and loud. It was like a stiff embraceless dance between her and the TV set. Finally she stood by the set with her hand on the sound dial.

She seemed entranced by the music, a little frenzied piano piece with this mesmerizing[5] quality, sort of quick passages and then teasing lilting ones before it returned to the quick playful parts.

"*Ni kan*," my mother said, calling me over with hurried hand gestures. "Look here."

I could see why my mother was fascinated by the music. It was being pounded out by a little Chinese girl, about nine years old, with a Peter Pan haircut. The girl had the sauciness[6] of a

Reading Skill
Predict What is your prediction about the mother's reaction when the girl performs poorly on the tests? Why?

▼ **Critical Viewing** How does this photograph of the author compare with your own image of the story's narrator? **[Compare and Contrast]**

---

4. *The Ed Sullivan Show* popular variety show, hosted by Ed Sullivan, that ran from 1948 to 1971.
5. mesmerizing (mez´ mər īz´ iŋ) *adj.* hypnotizing.
6. sauciness (sô´ sē nes) *n.* liveliness; boldness; spirit.

Shirley Temple. She was proudly modest like a proper Chinese child. And she also did this fancy sweep of a curtsy, so that the fluffy skirt of her white dress cascaded slowly to the floor like the petals of a large carnation.

In spite of these warning signs, I wasn't worried. Our family had no piano and we couldn't afford to buy one, let alone reams of sheet music and piano lessons. So I could be generous in my comments when my mother bad-mouthed the little girl on TV.

"Play note right, but doesn't sound good! No singing sound," complained my mother.

"What are you picking on her for?" I said carelessly. "She's pretty good. Maybe she's not the best, but she's trying hard." I knew almost immediately I would be sorry I said that.

"Just like you," she said. "Not the best. Because you not trying." She gave a little huff as she let go of the sound dial and sat down on the sofa.

The little Chinese girl sat down also to play an encore of "Anitra's Dance" by Grieg.[7] I remember the song, because later on I had to learn how to play it.

Three days after watching *The Ed Sullivan Show,* my mother told me what my schedule would be for piano lessons and piano practice. She had talked to Mr. Chong, who lived on the first floor of our apartment building. Mr. Chong was a retired piano teacher and my mother had traded house cleaning services for weekly lessons and a piano for me to practice on every day, two hours a day, from four until six.

When my mother told me this, I felt as though I had been sent to hell. I whined and then kicked my foot a little when I couldn't stand it anymore.

"Why don't you like me the way I am? I'm not a genius! I can't play the piano. And even if I could, I wouldn't go on TV if you paid me a million dollars!" I cried.

My mother slapped me. "Who ask you be genius?" she shouted. "Only ask you be your best. For you sake. You think I want you be genius? Hnnh! What for! Who ask you!"

"So ungrateful," I heard her mutter in Chinese. "If she had as much talent as she has temper, she would be famous now."

Mr. Chong, whom I secretly nicknamed Old Chong, was very strange, always tapping his fingers to the silent music of an invisible orchestra. He looked ancient in my eyes. He had lost

---

Literary Analysis

Character What does this conversation indicate about the difference between the mother's and daughter's traits and motives?

Reading Check

Why does the mother decide that the narrator should play the piano?

---

7. Grieg (grēg) *n.* Edvard Grieg (1843–1907), Norwegian composer.

most of the hair on top of his head and he wore thick glasses and had eyes that always looked tired and sleepy. But he must have been younger than I thought, since he lived with his mother and was not yet married.

I met Old Lady Chong once and that was enough. She had this peculiar smell like a baby that had done something in its pants. And her fingers felt like a dead person's, like an old peach I once found in the back of the refrigerator; the skin just slid off the meat when I picked it up.

I soon found out why Old Chong had retired from teaching piano. He was deaf. "Like Beethoven!"[8] he shouted to me. "We're both listening only in our head!" And he would start to conduct his frantic silent sonatas.

Our lessons went like this. He would open the book and point to different things, explaining their purpose: "Key! Treble! Bass! No sharps or flats! So this is C major! Listen now and play after me!"

And then he would play the C scale a few times, a simple chord, and then, as if inspired by an old, unreachable itch, he gradually added more notes and running trills and a pounding bass until the music was really something quite grand.

I would play after him, the simple scale, the simple chord, and then I just played some nonsense that sounded like a cat running up and down on top of garbage cans. Old Chong smiled and applauded and then said, "Very good! But now you must learn to keep time!"

So that's how I discovered that Old Chong's eyes were too slow to keep up with the wrong notes I was playing. He went through the motions in half-time. To help me keep rhythm, he stood behind me, pushing down on my right shoulder for every beat. He balanced pennies on top of my wrists so I would keep them still as I slowly played scales and arpeggios.[9]

Reading Skill
Predict How do you think the narrator will react to Old Chong's piano lessons? Read on to verify your prediction.

---

8. Beethoven (bā′ tō′ vən) *n.* Ludwig van Beethoven (1770–1827), German composer who began to lose his hearing in 1801. Some of his greatest pieces were written when he was completely deaf.
9. arpeggios (är pej′ ē ōz) *n.* notes in a chord played in quick succession.

He had me curve my hand around an apple and keep that shape when playing chords. He marched stiffly to show me how to make each finger dance up and down, staccato[10] like an obedient little soldier.

He taught me all these things, and that was how I also learned I could be lazy and get away with mistakes, lots of mistakes. If I hit the wrong notes because I hadn't practiced enough, I never corrected myself. I just kept playing in rhythm. And Old Chong kept conducting his own private reverie.

So maybe I never really gave myself a fair chance. I did pick up the basics pretty quickly, and I might have become a good pianist at that young age. But I was so determined not to try, not to be anybody different that I learned to play only the most ear-splitting preludes, the most discordant hymns.

Literary Analysis
Character What motivates the daughter to play piano badly?

Over the next year, I practiced like this, dutifully in my own way. And then one day I heard my mother and her friend Lindo Jong both talking in a loud bragging tone of voice so others could hear. It was after church, and I was leaning against the brick wall wearing a dress with stiff white petticoats. Auntie Lindo's daughter, Waverly, who was about my age, was standing farther down the wall about five feet away. We had grown up together and shared all the closeness of two sisters squabbling over crayons and dolls. In other words, for the most part, we hated each other. I thought she was snotty. Waverly Jong had gained a certain amount of fame as "Chinatown's Littlest Chinese Chess Champion."

"She bring home too many trophy," lamented Auntie Lindo that Sunday. "All day she play chess. All day I have no time do nothing but dust off her winnings." She threw a scolding look at Waverly, who pretended not to see her.

"You lucky you don't have this problem," said Auntie Lindo with a sigh to my mother.

And my mother squared her shoulders and bragged: "Our problem worser than yours. If we ask Jing-mei wash dish, she hear nothing but music. It's like you can't stop this natural talent."

And right then, I was determined to put a stop to her foolish pride.

✔ **Reading Check**

What useful information does the narrator learn about her piano teacher?

---

10. staccato (stə kät´ ō) *adv.* played crisply, with distinct breaks between notes.

Chinese Girl Under Lantern, Pamela Chin Lee, Courtesy of the artist

A few weeks later, Old Chong and my mother <u>conspired</u> to have me play in a talent show which would be held in the church hall. By then, my parents had saved up enough to buy me a secondhand piano, a black Wurlitzer spinet with a scarred bench. It was the showpiece of our living room.

For the talent show, I was to play a piece called "Pleading Child" from Schumann's[11] *Scenes from Childhood*. It was a simple, moody piece that sounded more difficult than it was. I was supposed to memorize the whole thing, playing the repeat parts twice to make the piece sound longer. But I dawdled over it, playing a few bars and then cheating, looking up to see what notes followed. I never really listened to what I was playing. I daydreamed about being somewhere else, about being someone else.

The part I liked to practice best was the fancy curtsy: right foot out, touch the rose on the carpet with a pointed foot, sweep to the side, left leg bends, look up and smile.

A Critical Viewing
How does the contrast between the modern and the traditional in this painting reflect the title of the story? **[Connect]**

Vocabulary Builder
conspired (kən spīrd′) *v.* planned together secretly

---

11. Schumann (shōō′ män) *n.* Robert Alexander Schumann (1810–1856), German composer.

My parents invited all the couples from the Joy Luck Club[12] to witness my debut. Auntie Lindo and Uncle Tin were there. Waverly and her two older brothers had also come. The first two rows were filled with children both younger and older than I was. The littlest ones got to go first. They recited simple nursery rhymes, squawked out tunes on miniature violins, twirled Hula Hoops, pranced in pink ballet tutus, and when they bowed or curtsied, the audience would sigh in unison, "Awww," and then clap enthusiastically.

When my turn came, I was very confident. I remember my childish excitement. It was as if I knew, without a doubt, that the prodigy side of me really did exist. I had no fear whatsoever, no nervousness. I remember thinking to myself, This is it! This is it! I looked out over the audience, at my mother's blank face, my father's yawn, Auntie Lindo's stiff-lipped smile, Waverly's sulky expression. I had on a white dress layered with sheets of lace, and a pink bow in my Peter Pan haircut. As I sat down I envisioned people jumping to their feet and Ed Sullivan rushing up to introduce me to everyone on TV.

And I started to play. It was so beautiful. I was so caught up in how lovely I looked that at first I didn't worry how I would sound. So it was a surprise to me when I hit the first wrong note and I realized something didn't sound quite right. And then I hit another and another followed that. A chill started at the top of my head and began to trickle down. Yet I couldn't stop playing, as though my hands were bewitched. I kept thinking my fingers would adjust themselves back, like a train switching to the right track. I played this strange jumble through two repeats, the sour notes staying with me all the way to the end.

When I stood up, I discovered my legs were shaking. Maybe I had just been nervous and the audience, like Old Chong, had seen me go through the right motions and had not heard anything wrong at all. I swept my right foot out, went down on my knee, looked up and smiled. The room was quiet, except for Old Chong, who was beaming and shouting, "Bravo! Bravo! Well done!" But then I saw my mother's face, her stricken face. The audience clapped weakly, and as I walked back to my chair, with my whole face quivering as I tried not to cry, I heard a little boy whisper loudly to his mother, "That was awful," and the mother whispered back, "Well, she certainly tried."

Reading Skill
Predict How do you predict the mother will react to her daughter's poor piano playing?

Reading Check

What happens at the talent show?

---

12. **Joy Luck Club** four Chinese women who have been meeting for years to socialize.

And now I realized how many people were in the audience, the whole world it seemed. I was aware of eyes burning into my back. I felt the shame of my mother and father as they sat stiffly throughout the rest of the show.

We could have escaped during intermission. Pride and some strange sense of honor must have anchored my parents to their chairs. And so we watched it all: the eighteen-year-old boy with a fake mustache who did a magic show and juggled flaming hoops while riding a unicycle. The breasted girl with white makeup who sang from *Madama Butterfly* and got honorable mention. And the eleven-year-old boy who won first prize playing a tricky violin song that sounded like a busy bee.

After the show, the Hsus, the Jongs, and the St. Clairs from the Joy Luck Club came up to my mother and father.

"Lots of talented kids," Auntie Lindo said vaguely, smiling broadly.

"That was somethin' else," said my father, and I wondered if he was referring to me in a humorous way, or whether he even remembered what I had done.

Waverly looked at me and shrugged her shoulders. "You aren't a genius like me," she said matter-of-factly. And if I hadn't felt so bad, I would have pulled her braids and punched her stomach.

But my mother's expression was what <u>devastated</u> me: a quiet, blank look that said she had lost everything. I felt the same way, and it seemed as if everybody were now coming up, like gawkers at the scene of an accident, to see what parts were actually missing. When we got on the bus to go home, my father was humming the busy-bee tune and my mother was silent. I kept thinking she wanted to wait until we got home before shouting at me. But when my father unlocked the door to our apartment, my mother walked in and then went to the back, into the bedroom. No accusations. No blame. And in a way, I felt disappointed. I had been waiting for her to start shouting, so I could shout back and cry and blame her for all my misery.

I assumed my talent-show fiasco meant I never had to play the piano again. But two days later, after school, my mother came out of the kitchen and saw me watching TV.

"Four clock," she reminded me as if it were any other day. I was stunned, as though she were asking me to go through the talent-show torture again. I wedged myself more tightly in front of the TV.

"Turn off TV," she called from the kitchen five minutes later.

I didn't budge. And then I decided. I didn't have to do what my mother said anymore. I wasn't her slave. This wasn't China. I had listened to her before and look what happened. She was the stupid one.

She came out from the kitchen and stood in the arched entryway of the living room. "Four clock," she said once again, louder.

"I'm not going to play anymore," I said nonchalantly. "Why should I? I'm not a genius."

She walked over and stood in front of the TV. I saw her chest was heaving up and down in an angry way.

"No!" I said, and I now felt stronger, as if my true self had finally emerged. So this was what had been inside me all along.

"No! I won't!" I screamed.

She yanked me by the arm, pulled me off the floor, snapped off the TV. She was frighteningly strong, half pulling, half carrying me toward the piano as I kicked the throw rugs under my feet. She lifted me up and onto the hard bench. I was sobbing by now, looking at her bitterly. Her chest was heaving even more and her mouth was open, smiling crazily as if she were pleased I was crying.

"You want me to be someone that I'm not!" I sobbed. "I'll never be the kind of daughter you want me to be!"

"Only two kinds of daughters," she shouted in Chinese. "Those who are obedient and those who follow their own mind! Only one kind of daughter can live in this house. Obedient daughter!"

"Then I wish I wasn't your daughter. I wish you weren't my mother," I shouted. As I said these things I got scared. It felt like worms and toads and slimy things crawling out of my chest, but it also felt good, as if this awful side of me had surfaced, at last.

"Too late change this," said my mother shrilly.

And I could sense her anger rising to its breaking point. I wanted to see it spill over. And that's when I remembered the babies she had lost in China, the ones we never talked

Literary Analysis
Character What motivates the narrator to ignore her mother's demands?

Literary Analysis
Character What character traits contribute to the daughter's outburst?

Reading Check

How does the narrator feel about her performance at the talent show?

about. "Then I wish I'd never been born!" I shouted. "I wish I were dead! Like them."

It was as if I had said the magic words. Alakazam!—and her face went blank, her mouth closed, her arms went slack, and she backed out of the room, stunned, as if she were blowing away like a small brown leaf, thin, brittle, lifeless.

It was not the only disappointment my mother felt in me. In the years that followed, I failed her so many times, each time asserting my own will, my right to fall short of expectations. I didn't get straight A's. I didn't become class president. I didn't get into Stanford. I dropped out of college.

For unlike my mother, I did not believe I could be anything I wanted to be. I could only be me.

And for all those years, we never talked about the disaster at the recital or my terrible accusations afterward at the piano bench. All that remained unchecked, like a betrayal that was now unspeakable. So I never found a way to ask her why she had hoped for something so large that failure was inevitable.

And even worse, I never asked her what frightened me the most: Why had she given up hope?

For after our struggle at the piano, she never mentioned my playing again. The lessons stopped. The lid to the piano was closed, shutting out the dust, my misery, and her dreams.

So she surprised me. A few years ago, she offered to give me the piano, for my thirtieth birthday. I had not played in all those years. I saw the offer as a sign of forgiveness, a tremendous burden removed.

"Are you sure?" I asked shyly. "I mean, won't you and Dad miss it?"

"No, this your piano," she said firmly. "Always your piano. You only one can play."

"Well, I probably can't play anymore," I said. "It's been years."

Untitled Portrait, Pamela Chin Lee, Courtesy of the artist

▲ **Critical Viewing**
Do you think this image accurately portrays the "two kinds" of daughters the mother describes? **[Evaluate]**

Reading Skill
Predict How do you predict the narrator will respond to the gift of the piano?

"You pick up fast," said my mother, as if she knew this was certain. "You have natural talent. You could been genius if you want to."

"No I couldn't."

"You just not trying," said my mother. And she was neither angry nor sad. She said it as if to announce a fact that could never be disproved. "Take it," she said.

But I didn't at first. It was enough that she had offered it to me. And after that, every time I saw it in my parents' living room, standing in front of the bay windows, it made me feel proud, as if it were a shiny trophy I had won back.

Reading Skill
Predict What details here help you test the prediction you made on page 242?

Last week I sent a tuner over to my parents' apartment and had the piano reconditioned, for purely sentimental reasons. My mother had died a few months before and I had been getting things in order for my father, a little bit at a time. I put the jewelry in special silk pouches. The sweaters she had knitted in yellow, pink, bright orange—all the colors I hated—I put those in moth-proof boxes. I found some old Chinese silk dresses, the kind with little slits up the sides. I rubbed the old silk against my skin, then wrapped them in tissue and decided to take them home with me.

After I had the piano tuned, I opened the lid and touched the keys. It sounded even richer than I remembered. Really, it was a very good piano. Inside the bench were the same exercise notes with handwritten scales, the same secondhand music books with their covers held together with yellow tape.

I opened up the Schumann book to the dark little piece I had played at the recital. It was on the left-hand side of the page, "Pleading Child." It looked more difficult than I remembered. I played a few bars, surprised at how easily the notes came back to me.

And for the first time, or so it seemed, I noticed the piece on the right-hand side. It was called "Perfectly Contented." I tried to play this one as well. It had a lighter melody but the same flowing rhythm and turned out to be quite easy. "Pleading Child" was shorter but slower; "Perfectly Contented" was longer, but faster. And after I played them both a few times, I realized they were two halves of the same song.

Reading Skill
Predict What do you think the narrator will do now that the piano has been tuned after all these years?

Apply the Skills

Two Kinds

Thinking About the Selection

1. **(a) Respond:** What advice would you give the mother and daughter? **(b) Discuss:** In a small group, share your responses. As a group, choose one response to share with the class.
2. **(a) Recall:** In what ways does the mother pressure her daughter for change? **(b) Draw Conclusions:** How does the difference in their attitudes create problems?
3. **(a) Recall:** What were the titles of the two pieces in the Schumann books that the daughter thinks about at the end of the story? **(b) Connect:** In what ways do the titles and pieces reflect the daughter's feelings about herself?
4. **(a) Evaluate:** Do you agree that people can be anything they want to be? Why or why not? **(b) Make a Judgment:** Should the narrator's mother have pushed the daughter as she did? Explain.

Reading Skill

5. **(a)** What **prediction** did you make about how the narrator would perform at the piano recital? **(b)** Did reading ahead cause you to change your prediction? Explain.
6. **(a)** At what point in the story were you able to predict that the daughter would refuse to play the piano? **(b)** Did your prediction change from what you thought when you first started reading? Explain.

Literary Analysis

7. Using a diagram like the one shown, identify the daughter's **character traits.** Support your answers with story details.

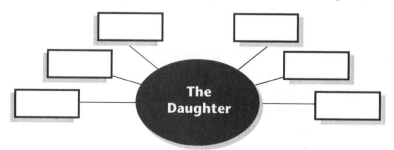

8. What **motives** does the daughter have to rebel against her mother finally?

QuickReview

Story at a Glance
A strong-willed daughter rebels against her mother's attempts to make her a prodigy.

For: Self-test
Visit: www.PHSchool.com
Web Code: ema-6205

Prediction: an informed guess about what will happen

Character: person or animal who takes part in the action of a literary work

Character traits: qualities that a character possesses

Character motives: emotions or goals that drive a character

Vocabulary Builder

Practice Make up an answer to each question. Use a complete sentence that includes the italicized word.

1. Who *conspired* to make the party a surprise?

2. Why did the *reproach* bother him?

3. What kind of weather *devastated* the crops?

Writing

Write a **journal entry** that the narrator might have made on the night after the piano recital.

- Write as if you were the narrator—using the word *I.*
- Include the narrator's thoughts and feelings at the end of the day.
- Use details from the story to justify the ideas you include.

For *Grammar, Vocabulary,* and *Assessment,* see **Build Language Skills,** pages 246–247.

Extend Your Learning

Listening and Speaking With a partner, hold a **discussion** about the following quotation by Henri Frédéric Amiel, a Swiss philosopher: *Doing easily what others find difficult is talent; doing what is impossible for talent is genius.*

- Determine whether "Two Kinds" proves or disproves Amiel's ideas.
- Identify questions you might ask to challenge the statement.
- Use your prior knowledge or experience to support your position on the quotation.

Research and Technology Use encyclopedias, books on China, and the Internet to research traditional Chinese beliefs and customs about the relationship between parents and children. Then, summarize your findings in an **outline.** State briefly in your own words the main points and key details of what you learned. Share your findings to help other students understand why the mother in the story insists on obedience.

Build Language Skills

from *Letters from Rifka* • *Two Kinds*

Vocabulary Skill

Roots The root -*ver*- means *truth*. Words that contain this root have meanings related to truth. For example, to *verify* something is to confirm or prove that it is true.

-*ver*-	aver, verify, verity, verdict, verification, verifiable, very, verisimilar

Practice Use a dictionary to find the meaning of each word on the chart. Explain how each word is related to the meaning of the root. Use each word in a sentence.

Grammar Lesson

Regular and Irregular Verbs **Regular verbs** form their tenses in a predictable way.

Irregular verbs do not follow a predictable pattern.

▶ **Example:** I *am* cold. I *was* cold yesterday, too. I have *been* cold before.

There are four main forms for every verb, called the principal parts. Each indicates when something happened. The principal parts are **present, present participle, past,** and **past participle.**

MorePractice

For more practice with verbs, see Grammar Handbook, p. R38.

	Present	**Present Participle**	**Past**	**Past Participle**
Regular	Today I **talk.**	I am **talking** now.	Yesterday we **talked.**	We have **talked** often.
Irregular	He **sits** down.	He is **sitting** down.	Yesterday he **sat** down.	He has often **sat** there.

Practice Rewrite each sentence, using a different principal part. Explain how this changes the meaning of the sentence.

1. We **walked** three miles to the gas station.
2. They **are going** on vacation in the fall.
3. The Johnsons **have moved** to a new neighborhood.
4. Sean **sings** all the high notes.
5. The woman **supported** herself through college.

WG Prentice Hall Writing and Grammar Connection: Chapter 22, Section 1

Assessment Practice

Reading: Making Predictions

Directions: *Read the selection. Then answer the questions.*

Thomas decided to help his mother by doing the laundry. First, he gathered all the clothing from the hamper. Then, he put it all in the washing machine. He had to push very hard to get it all in. There was a lot of laundry, so Thomas poured in half a bottle of detergent. He turned the machine on and went out to play baseball while the washing machine did its work.

1. Based on the first sentence, which of the following is most likely to happen?
   A Thomas will be punished.
   B Thomas will do the laundry.
   C The clothing will be ruined.
   D Thomas will not do the laundry.

2. Which prediction is probably incorrect?
   A The washing machine will overflow.
   B Thomas's mother will be unhappy.
   C Thomas's mother will have to clean up a mess.
   D Thomas will fold the clothes after the game.

3. What prediction is best supported by the passage?
   A Thomas will run out of detergent.
   B Bubbles will spill out of the machine.
   C Thomas will open his own laundry business.
   D The laundry will not be clean.

4. Which new information would most likely change the outcome of the story?
   A Thomas plays first base.
   B The game goes into extra innings.
   C Thomas leaves his mom a note.
   D Thomas decides to stay home.

Timed Writing: Explanation [Connections]

Review the excerpt from *Letters from Rifka* or "Two Kinds." Choose an event in the story. Explain the connection between this event and a lesson the main character learns or a way the character changes. **(20 minutes)**

 ## Writing Workshop: *Work in Progress*

Review of a Short Story
Use your Work-in-Progress assignment. For each story you describe, create a two-column chart with the labels "What I Liked" and "What I Disliked." In the corresponding columns, note specific scenes, characters, images, or actions in the story that support your judgment.

Character

A **character** is a person or animal who takes part in the action of a literary work. In literature, you will find characters with a range of personalities and attitudes. For example, a character might be dependable and smart but also stubborn. The qualities that make each character unique are called **character traits**.

Writers use the process of **characterization** to create and develop characters. There are two types of characterization:

- **Direct characterization:** The writer directly states or describes the character's traits.
- **Indirect characterization:** The writer reveals a character's personality through his or her words and actions, and through the thoughts, words, and actions of others.

Comparing Characters

Both "Seventh Grade" and "Stolen Day" feature school-aged boys. As you read, look for character traits that show each boy's qualities, attitudes, and values. In addition, notice how the writers develop each character. Use these questions to help you fill out a chart like the one shown.

- What words does the author use to directly describe the character?
- What does the character do and say?
- What do other characters say about him or her?

	Seventh Grade	Stolen Day
Main Character		
Direct Descriptions		
Words and Actions		
What other characters say about him		

Vocabulary Builder

Seventh Grade

- **elective** (ē lek´ tiv) *n.* optional course (p. 250) *Lauren chose studio art as her elective.*
- **scowl** (skoul) *v.* make an unpleasant expression by contracting the eyebrows and lowering the corners of the mouth (p. 251) *When the man scowled at the children, he looked very angry.*
- **conviction** (kən vik´ shən) *n.* belief (p. 251) *It is her conviction that school is important.*

Stolen Day

- **solemn** (säl´ əm) *adj.* serious; somber (p. 257) *The solemn child never smiled.*
- **affects** (a fekts´) *v.* produces an effect on; causes a change (p. 257) *Hot weather affects the plants in my garden.*

Build Understanding

Connecting to the Literature

Reading/Writing Connection The characters in "Seventh Grade" and "Stolen Day" attempt to catch the attention of someone else through their actions. Think of something you have done to catch the attention of a person or a group of people. Write a few sentences describing this experience. Use at least three of the following words: *demonstrate, display, emphasize, exhibit, impress.*

Meet the Authors

Gary **Soto** (b. 1952)

Like the characters in many of his works, Gary Soto grew up in Fresno and once harvested crops in the fields of California.

A Sense of Belonging Soto began writing while in college. In the fiction and poetry he has written since, he reaches back to the sense of belonging he felt in Fresno. He often writes for young adults, who he knows are also searching for their own community and their own place. When he is not writing, Soto enjoys basketball, karate, and Aztec dance.

Sherwood **Anderson** (1876–1941)

As a teenager, Sherwood Anderson worked as a newsboy, housepainter, and stable groom. Later, he fought in Cuba in the Spanish-American War. Even though Anderson did not begin to write until he was forty years old, he is considered an important writer of the twentieth century.

A Powerful Influence Anderson's novel *Winesburg, Ohio* was published in 1919. In it, Anderson used simple, everyday language to capture the sense of loneliness and lost hope of characters living in a small town. The book was different from anything that had been published before in literature.

Go Online
Author Link

For: More about the authors
Visit: www.PHSchool.com
Web Code: eme-9206

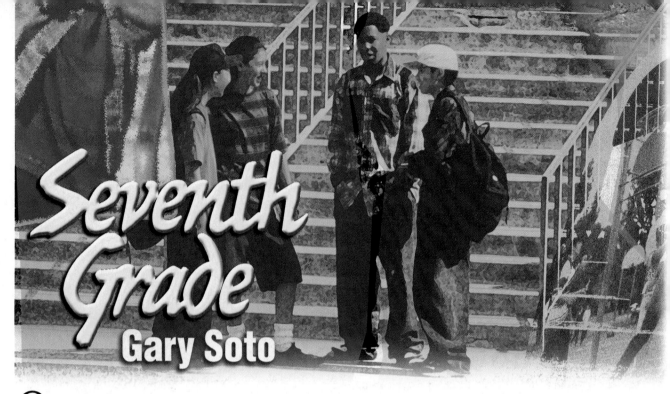

Seventh Grade
Gary Soto

On the first day of school, Victor stood in line half an hour before he came to a wobbly card table. He was handed a packet of papers and a computer card on which he listed his one <u>elective</u>, French. He already spoke Spanish and English, but he thought some day he might travel to France, where it was cool; not like Fresno, where summer days reached 110 degrees in the shade. There were rivers in France and huge churches, and fair-skinned people everywhere, the way there were brown people all around Victor.

Besides, Teresa, a girl he had liked since they were in catechism classes at Saint Theresa's, was taking French, too. With any luck they would be in the same class. Teresa is going to be my girl this year, he promised himself as he left the gym full of students in their new fall clothes. She was cute. And good in math, too, Victor thought as he walked down the hall to his homeroom. He ran into his friend, Michael Torres, by the water fountain that never turned off.

They shook hands, *raza*-style, and jerked their heads at one another in a *saludo de vato.*[1] "How come you're making a face?" asked Victor.

"I ain't making a face, *ese.*[2] This is my face." Michael said his face had changed during the summer. He had read a *GQ*

Vocabulary Builder
elective (ē lek′ tiv)
n. optional course

Literary Analysis
Character What can you tell about Victor based on his thoughts in this paragraph?

---

1. *raza*-style . . . *saludo de vato* (sä loo′ dō dā bä′ tō) Spanish gestures of greeting between friends.
2. *ese* (es′ ā) *n.* Spanish word for "man."

magazine that his older brother had borrowed from the Book Mobile and noticed that the male models all had the same look on their faces. They would stand, one arm around a beautiful woman, and _scowl_. They would sit at a pool, their rippled stomachs dark with shadow, and _scowl_. They would sit at dinner tables, cool drinks in their hands, and _scowl_.

"I think it works," Michael said. He scowled and let his upper lip quiver. His teeth showed along with the ferocity of his soul. "Belinda Reyes walked by a while ago and looked at me," he said.

Victor didn't say anything, though he thought his friend looked pretty strange. They talked about recent movies, baseball, their parents, and the horrors of picking grapes in order to buy their fall clothes. Picking grapes was like living in Siberia,[3] except hot and more boring.

"What classes are you taking?" Michael said, scowling.

"French. How 'bout you?"

"Spanish. I ain't so good at it, even if I'm Mexican."

"I'm not either, but I'm better at it than math, that's for sure."

A tinny, three-beat bell propelled students to their home-rooms. The two friends socked each other in the arm and went their ways, Victor thinking, man, that's weird. Michael thinks making a face makes him handsome.

On the way to his homeroom, Victor tried a scowl. He felt foolish, until out of the corner of his eye he saw a girl looking at him. Umm, he thought, maybe it does work. He scowled with greater conviction.

In homeroom, roll was taken, emergency cards were passed out, and they were given a bulletin to take home to their parents. The principal, Mr. Belton, spoke over the crackling loud-speaker, welcoming the students to a new year, new experiences, and new friendships. The students squirmed in their chairs and ignored him. They were anxious to go to first period. Victor sat calmly, thinking of Teresa, who sat two rows away, reading a paperback novel. This would be his lucky year. She was in his homeroom, and would probably be in his English and math classes. And, of course, French.

The bell rang for first period, and the students herded nois-ily through the door. Only Teresa lingered, talking with the homeroom teacher.

---

3. **Siberia** (sī bir′ ē ə) _n._ region in northern Asia known for its harsh winters.

Vocabulary Builder
scowl (skoul) _v._ make an unpleasant expression by contracting the eyebrows and lowering the corners of the mouth

Vocabulary Builder
conviction (kən vik′ shən) _n._ belief

Reading Check

Why does Victor choose to study French?

"So you think I should talk to Mrs. Gaines?" she asked the teacher. "She would know about ballet?"

"She would be a good bet," the teacher said. Then added, "Or the gym teacher, Mrs. Garza."

Victor lingered, keeping his head down and staring at his desk. He wanted to leave when she did so he could bump into her and say something clever.

He watched her on the sly. As she turned to leave, he stood up and hurried to the door, where he managed to catch her eye. She smiled and said, "Hi, Victor."

He smiled back and said, "Yeah, that's me." His brown face blushed. Why hadn't he said, "Hi, Teresa," or "How was your summer?" or something nice?

As Teresa walked down the hall, Victor walked the other way, looking back, admiring how gracefully she walked, one foot in front of the other. So much for being in the same class, he thought. As he trudged to English, he practiced scowling.

In English they reviewed the parts of speech. Mr. Lucas, a portly man, waddled down the aisle, asking, "What is a noun?"

"A person, place, or thing," said the class in unison.

"Yes, now somebody give me an example of a person—you, Victor Rodriguez."

"Teresa," Victor said automatically. Some of the girls giggled. They knew he had a crush on Teresa. He felt himself blushing again.

"Correct," Mr. Lucas said. "Now provide me with a place."

Mr. Lucas called on a freckled kid who answered, "Teresa's house with a kitchen full of big brothers."

After English, Victor had math, his weakest subject. He sat in the back by the window, hoping that he would not be called on. Victor understood most of the problems, but some of the stuff looked like the teacher made it up as she went along. It was confusing, like the inside of a watch.

Literary Analysis
Character What does Victor's blush say about him?

Literary Analysis
Character How does Victor deal with subjects that are difficult for him?

◄ **Critical Viewing** How do the expressions of these girls compare with the descriptions of the moods of the students in the story? **[Compare and Contrast]**

After math he had a fifteen-minute break, then social studies, and, finally, lunch. He bought a tuna casserole with buttered rolls, some fruit cocktail, and milk. He sat with Michael, who practiced scowling between bites.

Girls walked by and looked at him.

"See what I mean, Vic?" Michael scowled. "They love it."

"Yeah, I guess so."

They ate slowly, Victor scanning the horizon for a glimpse of Teresa. He didn't see her. She must have brought lunch, he thought, and is eating outside. Victor scraped his plate and left Michael, who was busy scowling at a girl two tables away.

The small, triangle-shaped campus bustled with students talking about their new classes. Everyone was in a sunny mood. Victor hurried to the bag lunch area, where he sat down and opened his math book. He moved his lips as if he were reading, but his mind was somewhere else. He raised his eyes slowly and looked around. No Teresa.

He lowered his eyes, pretending to study, then looked slowly to the left. No Teresa. He turned a page in the book and stared at some math problems that scared him because he knew he would have to do them eventually. He looked to the right. Still no sign of her. He stretched out lazily in an attempt to disguise his snooping.

Then he saw her. She was sitting with a girlfriend under a plum tree. Victor moved to a table near her and daydreamed about taking her to a movie. When the bell sounded, Teresa looked up, and their eyes met. She smiled sweetly and gathered her books. Her next class was French, same as Victor's.

They were among the last students to arrive in class, so all the good desks in the back had already been taken. Victor was forced to sit near the front, a few desks away from Teresa, while Mr. Bueller wrote French words on the chalkboard. The bell rang, and Mr. Bueller wiped his hands, turned to the class, and said, "*Bonjour.*"[4]

"*Bonjour,*" braved a few students.

"*Bonjour,*" Victor whispered. He wondered if Teresa heard him. Mr. Bueller said that if the students studied hard, at the end of the year they could go to France and be understood by the populace.

One kid raised his hand and asked, "What's 'populace'?"

"The people, the people of France."

---

4. **Bonjour** (bōn zhōōr´) French for "Hello"; "Good day."

Literary Analysis
Character Describe Victor's actions here in one or two words.

Reading Check

Who or what is Victor thinking of during lunch?

Mr. Bueller asked if anyone knew French. Victor raised his hand, wanting to impress Teresa. The teacher beamed and said, "*Très bien. Parlez-vous français?*"[5]

Victor didn't know what to say. The teacher wet his lips and asked something else in French. The room grew silent. Victor felt all eyes staring at him. He tried to bluff his way out by making noises that sounded French.

"La me vave me con le grandma," he said uncertainly.

Mr. Bueller, wrinkling his face in curiosity, asked him to speak up.

Great rosebushes of red bloomed on Victor's cheeks. A river of nervous sweat ran down his palms. He felt awful. Teresa sat a few desks away, no doubt thinking he was a fool. Without looking at Mr. Bueller, Victor mumbled, "Frenchie oh wewe gee in September."

Mr. Bueller asked Victor to repeat what he had said.

"Frenchie oh wewe gee in September," Victor repeated.

Mr. Bueller understood that the boy didn't know French and turned away. He walked to the blackboard and pointed to the words on the board with his steel-edged ruler.

"*Le bateau,*" he sang.

"*Le bateau,*" the students repeated.

"*Le bateau est sur l'eau,*"[6] he sang.

"*Le bateau est sur l'eau.*"

Victor was too weak from failure to join the class. He stared at the board and wished he had taken Spanish, not French. Better yet, he wished he could start his life over. He had never been so embarrassed. He bit his thumb until he tore off a sliver of skin.

The bell sounded for fifth period, and Victor shot out of the room, avoiding the stares of the other kids, but had to return for his math book. He looked sheepishly at the teacher, who was erasing the board, then widened his eyes in terror at

Literature in Context

Vocabulary Connection

New English Words At the beginning of the story, Victor and Michael shake hands *raza*-style and give each other a *saludo de vato*. These Spanish terms may be unfamiliar to many English speakers. However, the following words originated in Spanish and are now very familiar in English.

tortilla: a thin, flat, round cake made of cornmeal or flour and cooked on a griddle

fiesta: a celebration or holiday

siesta: a brief nap or rest taken after the noon meal

Connect to the Literature

How does Soto use Spanish to help him develop characters in the story?

---

5. **Très bien. Parlez-vous français?** (trā byan pär lā vōō′ frän sā′) French for "Very well. Do you speak French?"
6. *Le bateau est sur l'eau* (lə bä tō′ ā sŏor lō) French for "The boat is on the water."

Teresa who stood in front of him. "I didn't know you knew French," she said. "That was good."

Mr. Bueller looked at Victor, and Victor looked back. Oh please, don't say anything, Victor pleaded with his eyes. I'll wash your car, mow your lawn, walk your dog—anything! I'll be your best student and I'll clean your erasers after school.

Mr. Bueller shuffled through the papers on his desk. He smiled and hummed as he sat down to work. He remembered his college years when he dated a girlfriend in borrowed cars. She thought he was rich because each time he picked her up he had a different car. It was fun until he had spent all his money on her and had to write home to his parents because he was broke.

Victor couldn't stand to look at Teresa. He was sweaty with shame. "Yeah, well, I picked up a few things from movies and books and stuff like that." They left the class together. Teresa asked him if he would help her with her French.

"Sure, anytime," Victor said.

"I won't be bothering you, will I?"

"Oh no, I like being bothered."

"*Bonjour,*" Teresa said, leaving him outside her next class. She smiled and pushed wisps of hair from her face.

"Yeah, right, *bonjour,*" Victor said. He turned and headed to his class. The rose-bushes of shame on his face became bouquets of love. Teresa is a great girl, he thought. And Mr. Bueller is a good guy.

He raced to metal shop. After metal shop there was biology, and after biology a long sprint to the public library, where he checked out three French textbooks.

He was going to like seventh grade.

Literary Analysis
Character Based on his actions in this paragraph, describe one of Mr. Bueller's character traits.

Thinking About the Selection

1. **Respond:** What advice would you give Victor about the way he tries to impress Teresa?

2. **(a) Recall:** Why does Michael scowl?
   (b) Compare and Contrast: What is similar about Michael's scowling and Victor's pretending to speak French?

3. **(a) Infer:** How does Victor view Teresa? **(b) Support:** What examples from the story indicate his feelings?

4. **(a) Analyze:** What does Victor probably learn from his experiences? **(b) Apply:** How can you apply this lesson to your own life?

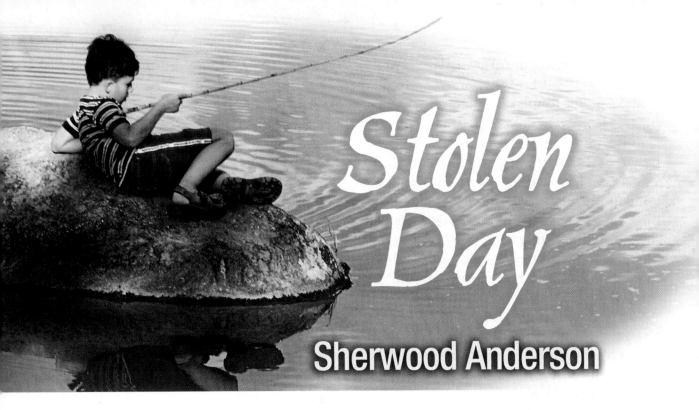

Stolen Day

Sherwood Anderson

It must be that all children are actors. The whole thing started with a boy on our street named Walter, who had inflammatory rheumatism.[1] That's what they called it. He didn't have to go to school.

Still he could walk about. He could go fishing in the creek or the waterworks pond. There was a place up at the pond where in the spring the water came tumbling over the dam and formed a deep pool. It was a good place. Sometimes you could get some big ones there.

I went down that way on my way to school one spring morning. It was out of my way but I wanted to see if Walter was there.

He was, inflammatory rheumatism and all. There he was, sitting with a fish pole in his hand. He had been able to walk down there all right.

It was then that my own legs began to hurt. My back too. I went on to school but, at the recess time, I began to cry. I did it when the teacher, Sarah Suggett, had come out into the schoolhouse yard.

She came right over to me.

"I ache all over," I said. I did, too.

▲ **Critical Viewing**
Based on the title and the picture, what do you think this story is about? **[Preview]**

Literary Analysis
Character What can you tell about the narrator based on the pain he experiences?

---

1. inflammatory rheumatism (in flam′ ə tôr′ ē roo′ mə tiz′ əm) *n.* a disease in which the joints swell painfully and gradually break down.

I kept on crying and it worked all right.

"You'd better go on home," she said.

So I went. I limped painfully away. I kept on limping until I got out of the schoolhouse street.

Then I felt better. I still had inflammatory rheumatism pretty bad but I could get along better.

I must have done some thinking on the way home.

"I'd better not say I have inflammatory rheumatism," I decided. "Maybe if you've got that you swell up."

I thought I'd better go around to where Walter was and ask him about that, so I did—but he wasn't there.

"They must not be biting today," I thought.

I had a feeling that, if I said I had inflammatory rheumatism, Mother or my brothers and my sister Stella might laugh. They did laugh at me pretty often and I didn't like it at all.

"Just the same," I said to myself, "I have got it." I began to hurt and ache again.

I went home and sat on the front steps of our house. I sat there a long time. There wasn't anyone at home but Mother and the two little ones. Ray would have been four or five then and Earl might have been three.

It was Earl who saw me there. I had got tired sitting and was lying on the porch. Earl was always a quiet, <u>solemn</u> little fellow.

He must have said something to Mother for presently she came.

"What's the matter with you? Why aren't you in school?" she asked.

I came pretty near telling her right out that I had inflammatory rheumatism but I thought I'd better not. Mother and Father had been speaking of Walter's case at the table just the day before. "It <u>affects</u> the heart," Father had said. That frightened me when I thought of it. "I might die," I thought. "I might just suddenly die right here; my heart might stop beating."

On the day before I had been running a race with my brother Irve. We were up at the fairgrounds after school and there was a half-mile track.

"I'll bet you can't run a half-mile," he said. "I bet you I could beat you running clear around the track."

And so we did it and I beat him, but afterwards my heart did seem to beat pretty hard. I remembered that lying there on

Literary Analysis
Character Why does the narrator's pain suddenly disappear?

Vocabulary Builder
solemn (säl´ əm) *adj.* serious; somber

affects (ə fekts´) *v.* produces an effect upon; causes a change

Reading Check

What does Father say about Walter's inflammatory rheumatism?

the porch. "It's a wonder, with my inflammatory rheumatism and all, I didn't just drop down dead," I thought. The thought frightened me a lot. I ached worse than ever.

"I ache, Ma," I said. "I just ache."

She made me go in the house and upstairs and get into bed.

It wasn't so good. It was spring. I was up there for perhaps an hour, maybe two, and then I felt better.

I got up and went downstairs. "I feel better, Ma," I said.

Mother said she was glad. She was pretty busy that day and hadn't paid much attention to me. She had made me get into bed upstairs and then hadn't even come up to see how I was.

I didn't think much of that when I was up there but when I got downstairs where she was, and when, after I had said I felt better and she only said she was glad and went right on with her work, I began to ache again.

I thought, "I'll bet I die of it. I bet I do."

I went out to the front porch and sat down. I was pretty sore at Mother.

"If she really knew the truth, that I have the inflammatory rheumatism and I may just drop down dead any time, I'll bet she wouldn't care about that either," I thought.

I was getting more and more angry the more thinking I did.

"I know what I'm going to do," I thought; "I'm going to go fishing."

I thought that, feeling the way I did, I might be sitting on the high bank just above the deep pool where the water went over the dam, and suddenly my heart would stop beating.

And then, of course, I'd pitch forward, over the bank into the pool and, if I wasn't dead when I hit the water, I'd drown sure.

They would all come home to supper and they'd miss me.

"But where is he?"

Then Mother would remember that I'd come home from school aching.

She'd go upstairs and I wouldn't be there. One day during the year before, there was a child got drowned in a spring. It was one of the Wyatt children.

Right down at the end of the street there was a spring under a birch tree and there had been a barrel sunk in the ground.

Everyone had always been saying the spring ought to be kept covered, but it wasn't.

So the Wyatt child went down there, played around alone, and fell in and got drowned.

Mother was the one who had found the drowned child. She had gone to get a pail of water and there the child was, drowned and dead.

This had been in the evening when we were all at home, and Mother had come running up the street with the dead, dripping child in her arms. She was making for the Wyatt house as hard as she could run, and she was pale.

She had a terrible look on her face, I remembered then.

"So," I thought, "they'll miss me and there'll be a search made. Very likely there'll be someone who has seen me sitting by the pond fishing, and there'll be a big alarm and all the town will turn out and they'll drag the pond."

I was having a grand time, having died. Maybe, after they found me and had got me out of the deep pool, Mother would grab me up in her arms and run home with me as she had run with the Wyatt child.

I got up from the porch and went around the house. I got my fishing pole and lit out for the pool below the dam. Mother was busy—she always was—and didn't see me go. When I got there I thought I'd better not sit too near the edge of the high bank.

By this time I didn't ache hardly at all, but I thought.

"With inflammatory rheumatism you can't tell," I thought.

"It probably comes and goes," I thought.

"Walter has it and he goes fishing," I thought.

I had got my line into the pool and suddenly I got a bite. It was a regular whopper. I knew that. I'd never had a bite like that.

I knew what it was. It was one of Mr. Fenn's big carp.

Mr. Fenn was a man who had a big pond of his own. He sold ice in the summer and the pond was to make the ice. He had bought some big carp and put them into his pond and then, earlier in the spring when there was a freshet,[2] his dam had gone out.

So the carp had got into our creek and one or two big ones had been caught—but none of them by a boy like me.

The carp was pulling and I was pulling and I was afraid he'd break my line, so I just tumbled down the high bank holding onto the line and got right into the pool. We had it out, there

---

2. **freshet** (fresh´ it) a great rise or overflowing of a stream caused by heavy rains or melted snow.

Literary Analysis

Character Based on this imaginary scene, how would you describe the narrator in a word or two?

Reading Check

What happened to the Wyatt child?

Stolen Day ■ 259

in the pool. We struggled. We wrestled. Then I got a hand under his gills and got him out.

He was a big one all right. He was nearly half as big as I was myself. I had him on the bank and I kept one hand under his gills and I ran.

I never ran so hard in my life. He was slippery, and now and then he wriggled out of my arms; once I stumbled and fell on him, but I got him home.

So there it was. I was a big hero that day. Mother got a washtub and filled it with water. She put the fish in it and all the neighbors came to look. I got into dry clothes and went down to supper—and then I made a break that spoiled my day.

There we were, all of us, at the table, and suddenly Father asked what had been the matter with me at school. He had met the teacher, Sarah Suggett, on the street and she had told him how I had become ill.

"What was the matter with you?" Father asked, and before I thought what I was saying I let it out.

"I had the inflammatory rheumatism," I said—and a shout went up. It made me sick to hear them, the way they all laughed.

It brought back all the aching again, and like a fool I began to cry.

"Well, I *have* got it—I *have*, I *have*," I cried, and I got up from the table and ran upstairs.

I stayed there until Mother came up. I knew it would be a long time before I heard the last of the inflammatory rheumatism. I was sick all right, but the aching I now had wasn't in my legs or in my back.

Literary Analysis
Character What do the narrator's actions with the carp reveal about his physical condition?

Thinking About the Selection

1. **(a) Recall:** What inspires the narrator to think he has inflammatory rheumatism? **(b) Infer:** Why does the narrator think this would be an appealing disease to have? **(c) Evaluate:** What do you think of his idea? Explain.

2. **(a) Recall:** What does the narrator do after he gets home? **(b) Infer:** Why does his mother pay him little attention?

3. **(a) Recall:** How does his family respond when the narrator says he has inflammatory rheumatism? **(b) Defend:** Do you think the narrator's family should have been more understanding? Why or why not?

Apply the Skills

Seventh Grade • Stolen Day

Comparing Characters

1. Identify one example of **direct characterization** and one example of **indirect characterization** for the boy in each story.

2. **(a)** What does Victor pretend to be able to do in "Seventh Grade"? **(b)** Why does he do this?

3. **(a)** What does the narrator of "Stolen Day" do that causes his teacher to send him home? **(b)** Why does he do this?

4. Complete a Venn diagram to show how Victor and the narrator of "Stolen Day" are alike and how they are different.

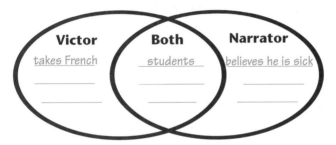

Victor — takes French

Both — students

Narrator — believes he is sick

Writing to Compare Literary Works

In an essay, compare and contrast Victor in "Seventh Grade" with the narrator of "Stolen Day." First, discuss each character's traits and the problem each one faces. Then, explain whether you feel that the events of the stories will help each boy grow or change. Support your answer with details from the story. Use these suggestions to get started:

- Identify a few traits of each character.
- Consider how much responsibility each boy has in creating his own problem.
- Decide which character will probably learn the most.

Vocabulary Builder

Practice For each item below, write a sentence that correctly uses the words given.

1. solemn; expression
2. conviction; important
3. elective; course
4. scowl; face
5. affects; weather

QuickReview

Character: person or animal who takes part in the action of a literary work

Characterization: the process a writer uses to create and develop a character, including methods of *direct* and *indirect characterization*

Character traits: qualities, attitudes, and values of a character

Go Online
Assessment
For: Self-test
Visit: www.PHSchool.com
Web Code: ema-6206

Reading

Directions: *Read the selection. Then answer the questions.*

"We interrupt this program to warn of a serious thunderstorm in our area." Outdoors, Jenna and her little brother Tim noticed dark clouds building on the horizon. They decided to go indoors. Jenna had taken a weather safety course, and she knew that there was danger from lightning, even if a storm seemed far away.

Earlier, Mom had called to say she would be a little late getting home. Tim suggested to Jenna that they get dinner started. The two were cutting up vegetables when a loud crack of thunder shook the house. Startled, Jenna went to see the news on television. Just then, there was a flash of lightning and the house lost power. Jenna then grabbed Tim by the hand and led him to a hall in the center of the house. Then, the lights came on, and she heard the sound of a car pulling into the driveway.

1. **From information in the first paragraph, you can predict that Jenna and Tim**
   A will be unaware that the brewing storm is serious.
   B will do well in the soccer tryouts.
   C will watch television when they go indoors.
   D will try to escape from the storm.

2. **What detail helps you predict that Jenna will know what to do when the lights go out?**
   A She is Tim's older sister.
   B She has taken a weather safety course.
   C She wants to check the news.
   D She sees dark clouds on the horizon.

3. **What prediction is supported by the lights coming on?**
   A The storm will become stronger.
   B The worst part of the storm is over.
   C The storm will continue.
   D There is still a lot of lightning.

4. **Based on details in the story, who do you predict is in the car?**
   A Jenna and Tim's mother
   B a neighbor checking on the children
   C the soccer coach from school
   D a television reporter

5. **Based on your prior knowledge and details in the story, what do you predict will happen when Mom gets home?**
   A Jenna and Tim will go back to playing soccer.
   B Everyone will go right to bed.
   C Mom and the children will finish preparing dinner.
   D The children will act as if nothing has happened.

Vocabulary

Directions: *Choose the word that best completes each of the following sentences.*

6. Use a check mark to _____ the lunch selection you prefer.
   - A predict
   - B indicate
   - C dictate
   - D contradict

7. The city council members handed down the final _____ on the issue.
   - A diction
   - B veracity
   - C dictionary
   - D verdict

8. It is impossible to _____ which team will win the game on Friday.
   - A predict
   - B indicate
   - C dictate
   - D contradict

9. The television reporter's perfect _____ helped her get the job of her dreams.
   - A diction
   - B veracity
   - C dictionary
   - D verdict

10. Our teacher posted a list of rules, and they _____ how we behave in class.
    - A predict
    - B indicate
    - C dictate
    - D contradict

Directions: *Based on your knowledge of word roots, choose the most likely meaning for each word.*

11. veritable
    - A real
    - B contained
    - C complete
    - D misleading

12. edict
    - A entertainment
    - B honesty
    - C announcement
    - D delight

13. verity
    - A something that is planned
    - B something that is said
    - C something that is decided
    - D something that is true

14. contradiction
    - A harmony
    - B disagreement
    - C union
    - D regularity

15. diction
    - A knowledge
    - B direction
    - C position
    - D wording

Response to Literature: Review of a Short Story

Discussing what you like and do not like about a work of literature can help you understand how and why it affects you. Writing that discusses such topics is called **a response to literature**. Follow the steps outlined in this workshop to write a response to literature.

Assignment Choose a short story you feel strongly about and write about what it means to you.

What to Include Your review should feature the following elements:
- a strong, interesting focus on an aspect of the short story
- an organization that focuses on several clear ideas or images
- a summary of important features of the work
- a judgment about the value of the work
- support to defend your ideas
- error-free writing, including correct verb tenses

To preview the criteria on which your review may be judged, see the rubric on page 268.

Prewriting

Choosing Your Topic

Find Connections After you have decided on a story, read or review the selection carefully to find a topic for your essay. Then, complete a chart like the one shown. Fill in each column by answering the corresponding question. Look over what you have written and highlight details that connect in ways that interest you. To create a focused topic, sum up your highlighted details in a sentence.

Characters	Settings	Actions	Motivations
Who did the action?	When or where was it done?	What was done?	Why was it done?

Gathering Details

To give your readers a feeling for the story, and to support your judgments about it, gather details about the story and the topic you have chosen. Before you write to prove a point, look for the supporting details that will show readers why you believe in your ideas.

Using the Form
You may use elements of this form in these types of writing:
- letters to authors
- book reviews
- movie reviews

Work in Progress
Review the work you did on pages 185, 217, and 247.

Drafting

Shaping Your Writing

Define and develop your focus. Review your prewriting notes to find a main idea or focus for your response. The focus statement sums up your reaction to one aspect of the story. Answer questions like the ones shown. Then, write one good sentence that states the focus and references a literary element. Include this sentence in your introduction, and elaborate on it in the body of your review.

> **1. My Response**
> What is my main response to my topic?
>
> *I thoroughly enjoyed the story.*

> **2. What Causes It**
> What features of the story cause my reaction?
>
> • *the suspense*
> • *the believability of the characters*

> **3. My Focus**
> What conclusion can I draw about the story's features?
>
> *The author creates suspense and believable characters, producing a realistic story.*

Providing Elaboration

Use examples to provide support. Rely on examples from the story to support your main ideas. Refer to specific scenes, characters, images, and actions. Justify your interpretations with direct quotations from the text.

Revising

Revising Your Overall Structure

Revise to organize around your strongest idea. Review your draft to find places to support your main point. Follow these steps:

1. Circle your strongest point—your most profound insight or the quotation that pulls your response together. Consider moving this point to the end.

2. If you move your strongest point to the end, revise your last paragraph to add a transition sentence clearly explaining the connection between this point and your other ideas.

3. Go back to other paragraphs to link each paragraph to your concluding point. For example, *Another example that shows the story's humor is when . . .*

Integrating Grammar Skills

Revising for Correct Verb Tense

Verbs indicate action or a state of being. Verbs have tenses, or different forms, that tell when something happens or exists.

Identifying Verb Tense In English, verbs have six tenses: present, past, future, present perfect, past perfect, and future perfect.

Present indicates an action that happens regularly or states a general truth: *I walk my dog Squeegee every morning.*

Past indicates an action that has already happened: *We walked earlier than usual yesterday.*

Future indicates an action that will happen: *We will walk on the beach this summer.*

Present perfect indicates an action that happened at some indefinite time in the past or an action that happened in the past and is still happening now: *We have walked here almost every day for two years.*

Past perfect indicates an action that was completed before another action in the past: *We had walked around the corner when Squeegee started to bark.*

Future perfect indicates an action that will have been completed before another: *We will have walked two hundred miles before I need new shoes.*

Fixing Incorrect Verb Tense To fix an incorrect form of a verb, first identify any questionable verbs in your review. Then verify the correct form using one of the following methods.

1. **Review the basic forms of the six tenses.** First, identify the time—present, past, or future—in which the action occurs. Then, review the examples provided above to determine which form corresponds with that time.

2. **Rewrite the sentence.** Consider which verb tense will make your idea as precise as possible. Revise using that tense.

Apply It to Your Editing

Choose a paragraph in your draft. Underline the verb in each sentence of the paragraph. If the tense for any verb is faulty, fix it using one of the methods described here.

> *Prentice Hall Writing and Grammar Connection: Chapter 22, Section 2*

Student Model: Tyler Blair
Somerset, KY

The Lesson of "Rikki-tikki-tavi"

The short story "Rikki-tikki-tavi" is a well-known short story written by Rudyard Kipling, who wrote many other novels, such as *Kim* and *Captains Courageous*. "Rikki-tikki-tavi" is a story about two natural enemies: a mongoose and a cobra. The message of the story is that although you may be small, you can still overcome major enemies. This story is enjoyable because it can teach you helpful morals while keeping you entertained at the same time.

> Tyler focuses on the message, or theme, of the story.

The beginning of this story is heavyhearted and dramatic. A small boy named Teddy thinks that the mongoose is dead following a bout with its first enemy—a flood that swept him away from his burrow. The mood of the story changes when the boy realizes that the mongoose is still alive, but weak. He decides to keep it, and takes care of it much like a pet, feeding it and naming it Rikki-tikki-tavi.

When Rikki-tikki goes outside into the little boy's garden to explore his surroundings, he comes upon a bird, which he confronts. The story switches back to a gloomy mood when the mongoose discovers that Nag, a cobra, ate one of the bird's eggs. When Rikki-tikki hears this, Nag comes out of the tall grass behind him.

This is when the story gets scary because Rikki faces another enemy. Nag quickly spreads his hood to intimidate the small mongoose. Then, Nagaina, Nag's wife, pulls a surprise attack on Rikki-tikki and nearly eats him. Because Rikki-tikki is young and dodges the cobra's blow from behind, he gains plenty of confidence. Readers wonder whether the mongoose will stay safe.

As the story progresses, Rikki meets Karait, another snake and this builds excitement and tension. This snake isn't after the mongoose, although he is after the family. When Teddy runs out to pet Rikki-tikki, the snake strikes at the boy, but Rikki-tikki lunges at the snake and paralyzes it by biting it before it can bite Teddy.

> Tyler summarizes the most important plot events in the story in the order in which they occur.

Later, after Rikki-tikki discovers that the cobras are going to go after his owners, he is filled with rage and he takes on the challenge. The moment the reader is waiting for arrives. The mongoose and the cobra fight to kill. At one point Rikki-tikki has his teeth in Nag as Nag flings himself about. Readers may think that Rikki-tikki will surely die from the beating that he is taking, but he holds on and, thankfully, Teddy's dad hears the fighting and shoots Nag behind the hood with a shotgun, easily ending the brutal battle which leaves Nag dead and Rikki-tikki dizzy, but alive.

> Tyler supports his ideas about the story by giving examples of how Rikki-tikki fights several enemies even though he is small.

This story is exciting and thought provoking. It ends, leaving me and other readers to think about its real meaning. Most people can relate to a time when they have faced a challenge in their life, but have felt that they were unable to overcome it. However, when they kept trying and put their minds to it, they eventually ended with success, as Rikki-tikki did.

> Tyler explains what message readers can take away from the story.

Editing and Proofreading

Review your draft to eliminate errors in grammar, spelling, and punctuation.

Focus on Quotations: A response to a literary work will probably include a number of quotations from the work. Pay careful attention to the punctuation, indentation, and capitalization of quotations. Use quotation marks to set off short quotations. Longer ones of four or more lines should be indented.

Publishing and Presenting

Consider these ideas to share your writing with a larger audience:
Share your review. Discuss your response with a group of classmates. Invite classmates to respond with their opinions and reactions.
Build a collection. Work with your classmates to assemble your responses to literature in a book for your school or local library. Include a rating system and rate each work to which you have responded.

Reflecting on Your Writing

Writer's Journal Jot down your thoughts on the experience of writing a review of a short story. Begin by answering these questions:
- Which prewriting activity did you find most useful? How did it help you?
- How did writing about the work help you understand it? Why might it be useful to keep a reader's journal?

> *Prentice Hall Writing and Grammar Connection: Chapter 12*

Rubric for Self-Assessment

To assess your short story review, use the following rubric:

Criteria	Rating Scale				
	not very				*very*
Focus: How well does your response present a strong, interesting aspect of the work?	1	2	3	4	5
Organization: How logical and consistent is your organization?	1	2	3	4	5
Support/Elaboration: How convincing are your supporting examples?	1	2	3	4	5
Style: How clearly do you express your judgment about the work?	1	2	3	4	5
Conventions: How correct is your grammar, especially your use of verb tense?	1	2	3	4	5

Skills You Will Learn

Reading Skill: *Recognize Details to Make Inferences*
Literary Analysis: *Conflict and Resolution*

Reading Skill: *Make Generalizations*

Reading Skill: *Read Between the Lines by Asking Questions*
Literary Analysis: *Theme*

Literary Analysis: *Comparing Irony*

Literature You Will Read

Reading: Make Inferences

Inferences are logical assumptions about information or ideas that are not directly stated.

Skills and Strategies you will learn in Part 2

In Part 2, you will learn

- to **recognize details** in the story in order to make **inferences** (p. 272)
- to **make inferences and generalizations** based on details in nonfiction texts (p. 296)
- to **read between the lines by asking questions** (p. 300)

Using the Skills and Strategies in Part 2

In Part 2, you will learn to use details in fiction and nonfiction to make inferences and generalizations. By recognizing details and asking questions, you will understand information and ideas not directly stated by the writer.

The chart shows how you can apply the skills and strategies in Part 2.

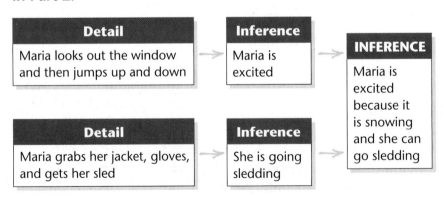

Detail	**Inference**	**INFERENCE**
Maria looks out the window and then jumps up and down	Maria is excited	Maria is excited because it is snowing and she can go sledding
Detail	**Inference**	
Maria grabs her jacket, gloves, and gets her sled	She is going sledding	

Academic Vocabulary Words for Discussing Inferences

The following words will help you talk and write about the inferences you make as you read the selections in this unit.

Word	Definition	Example sentence
conclude *v.*	to form an opinion or make a judgment, based on evidence presented	From the details of the setting I can *conclude* that the story takes place during a war.
subject *n.*	the main idea or topic	The *subject* of this book is the early life of Aesop.
object *n.*	a thing that can be seen or touched	The *objects* in the room led me to infer that these people were wealthy.
credible *adj.*	easy to believe	An inference is *credible* if it is based on logic.
perspective *n.*	an assessment of a situation, especially from one person's point of view	The main character's *perspective* was formed by his background.

Vocabulary Skill: Prefixes

> A **prefix** is a syllable or group of syllables joined to the beginning of a word to change its meaning or to make a new word.

In Part 2, you will learn
- the prefix *con-* (p. 320)
- the prefix *sub-* (p. 320)
- the prefix *ob-* (p. 294)

Remembering the meaning of *sub-*, *con-*, and *ob-* will help you remember the words that begin with those prefixes.

Prefix	Meaning of Prefix	Example
con-	with; together	concert
sub-	under; below	subcontract
ob-	against	obstruction

Activity Use a dictionary to find two more examples of words that begin with each prefix. Add the new words to the chart. Make sure the words you choose actually begin with the prefix, not just the same letters. Explain how the meaning of each word from the chart incorporates the meaning of the prefix.

These skills will help you become a better reader. Practice them with either "The Third Wish" (p. 274) or "Amigo Brothers" (p. 283).

Reading Skill

Short story writers do not directly tell you every-thing there is to know about the characters, setting, and events. Instead, they leave it to you to **make inferences,** or logical guesses, about unstated information.

- To form inferences, you must **recognize details** in the story and consider their importance.
- As you read, use a chart like the one shown to record details that can help you make inferences.

Details
Jake laughs a lot while watching the movie.
Jake says he wants to see it again.

Inference
Jake likes the movie.

Literary Analysis

Most fictional stories center on a **conflict**—a struggle between opposing forces. There are two kinds of conflict:

- When there is an **external conflict,** a character struggles with an outside force such as another character or nature.
- When there is an **internal conflict,** a character struggles with himself or herself to overcome opposing feelings, beliefs, needs, or desires. The **resolution,** or outcome of the conflict, often comes toward the end of the story, when the problem is settled in some way.

A story can have smaller conflicts that build the main conflict.

Vocabulary Builder

The Third Wish

- **presumptuous** (prē zump´ choo əs) *adj.* overconfident; arrogant (p. 275) *Only a presumptuous person brags a lot.*

- **rash** (rash) *adj.* thoughtless; reckless (p. 276) *It is rash to marry the first person you date.*

- **remote** (ri mōt´) *adj.* far away from every-thing else (p. 276) *Living on a remote farm can be lonely.*

- **malicious** (mə lish´ əs) *adj.* spiteful; hateful (p. 279) *Her malicious expression showed she disliked him.*

Amigo Brothers

- **devastating** (dev´ ə stāt´ iŋ) *adj.* destructive; overwhelming (p. 284) *A devastating storm destroyed the town.*

- **perpetual** (pər pech´ oo əl) *adj.* constant; unending (p. 287) *Toddlers are in perpetual motion, never standing still.*

- **dispelled** (di speld´) *adj.* driven away; made to disappear (p. 289) *My worries were dispelled by the good news.*

- **evading** (ē vād´ iŋ) *adj.* avoiding (p. 290) *We hid behind the fence, evading the bullies.*

Build Understanding • *The Third Wish*

Background

Traditional Tales "The Third Wish" is, as the title suggests, a story about three wishes. Almost every culture in the world has a traditional fairy tale or folk tale about a character who is granted three wishes, uses two unwisely, and then needs the third to undo one or both of the first two wishes.

Connecting to the Literature

Reading/Writing Connection In the following story, a man is granted three wishes. Make a list of three wishes that you think any person would be wise to request. Use at least three of the following words: *maximize, minimize, grant, obtain.*

Meet the Author

Joan **Aiken** (1924–2004)

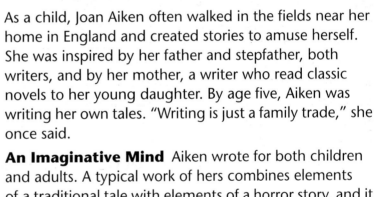

As a child, Joan Aiken often walked in the fields near her home in England and created stories to amuse herself. She was inspired by her father and stepfather, both writers, and by her mother, a writer who read classic novels to her young daughter. By age five, Aiken was writing her own tales. "Writing is just a family trade," she once said.

An Imaginative Mind Aiken wrote for both children and adults. A typical work of hers combines elements of a traditional tale with elements of a horror story, and it usually deals with fantastic or mysterious events. "The Third Wish" comes from a collection with a title that sums up much of Aiken's writing—*Not What You Expected.*

Fast Facts

▶ Five-year-old Aiken began taking notes and composing on a pad that she had bought with her birthday money.

▶ Aiken produced ninety-two novels in her lifetime, as well as many plays, poems, and short stories.

Go **O**nline
Author Link

For: More about the author
Visit: www.PHSchool.com
Web Code: eme-9208

The Third Wish

Joan Aiken

Once there was a man who was driving in his car at dusk
on a spring evening through part of the forest of Savernake.
His name was Mr. Peters. The primroses were just beginning
but the trees were still bare, and it was cold; the birds had
stopped singing an hour ago.

As Mr. Peters entered a straight, empty stretch of road he
seemed to hear a faint crying, and a struggling and thrashing,
as if somebody was in trouble far away in the trees. He left his
car and climbed the mossy bank beside the road. Beyond the
bank was an open slope of beech trees leading down to thorn
bushes through which he saw the gleam of water. He stood a
moment waiting to try and discover where the noise was coming from, and presently heard a rustling and some strange
cries in a voice which was almost human—and yet there was
something too hoarse about it at one time and too clear and
sweet at another. Mr. Peters ran down the hill and as he
neared the bushes he saw something white among them
which was trying to extricate[1] itself; coming closer he found

Critical Viewing In
this story, a swan has
magical powers.
What details of the
photograph make
this swan look
powerful? [Relate]

---

1. **extricate** (eks´ tri kāt´) *v.* set free.

that it was a swan that had become entangled in the thorns growing on the bank of the canal.

The bird struggled all the more frantically as he approached, looking at him with hate in its yellow eyes, and when he took hold of it to free it, it hissed at him, pecked him, and thrashed dangerously with its wings which were powerful enough to break his arm. Nevertheless he managed to release it from the thorns, and carrying it tightly with one arm, holding the snaky head well away with the other hand (for he did not wish his eyes pecked out), he took it to the verge of the canal and dropped it in.

The swan instantly assumed great dignity and sailed out to the middle of the water, where it put itself to rights with much dabbling and preening, smoothing its feathers with little showers of drops. Mr. Peters waited, to make sure that it was all right and had suffered no damage in its struggles. Presently the swan, when it was satisfied with its appearance, floated in to the bank once more, and in a moment, instead of the great white bird, there was a little man all in green with a golden crown and long beard, standing by the water. He had fierce glittering eyes and looked by no means friendly.

"Well, Sir," he said threateningly, "I see you are <u>presumptuous</u> enough to know some of the laws of magic. You think that because you have rescued—by pure good fortune—the King of the Forest from a difficulty, you should have some fabulous reward."

"I expect three wishes, no more and no less," answered Mr. Peters, looking at him steadily and with composure.[2]

"Three wishes, he wants, the clever man! Well, I have yet to hear of the human being who made any good use of his three wishes—they mostly end up worse off than they started. Take your three wishes then"—he flung three dead leaves in the air—"don't blame me if you spend the last wish in undoing the work of the other two."

Mr. Peters caught the leaves and put two of them carefully in his briefcase. When he looked up, the swan was sailing about in the middle of the water again, flicking the drops angrily down its long neck.

Mr. Peters stood for some minutes reflecting on how he should use his reward. He knew very well that the gift of three magic wishes was one which brought trouble more often than

---

2. composure (kəm pō´ zhər) *n.* calmness of mind.

Literary Analysis
Conflict and Resolution What external conflict does Mr. Peters face after he finds the swan?

Vocabulary Builder
presumptuous (prē zump´ chōō əs) *adj.* overconfident; arrogant

Reading Check

What does the King of the Forest give Mr. Peters?

not, and he had no intention of being like the forester who first wished by mistake for a sausage, and then in a rage wished it on the end of his wife's nose, and then had to use his last wish in getting it off again. Mr. Peters had most of the things which he wanted and was very content with his life. The only thing that troubled him was that he was a little lonely, and had no companion for his old age. He decided to use his first wish and to keep the other two in case of an emergency. Taking a thorn he pricked his tongue with it, to remind himself not to utter <u>rash</u> wishes aloud. Then holding the third leaf and gazing round him at the dusky under-growth, the primroses, great beeches and the blue-green water of the canal, he said:

"I wish I had a wife as beautiful as the forest."

A tremendous quacking and splashing broke out on the surface of the water. He thought that it was the swan laughing at him. Taking no notice he made his way through the dark-ening woods to his car, wrapped himself up in the rug and went to sleep.

When he awoke it was morning and the birds were begin-ning to call. Coming along the track towards him was the most beautiful creature he had ever seen, with eyes as blue-green as the canal, hair as dusky as the bushes, and skin as white as the feathers of swans.

"Are you the wife that I wished for?" asked Mr. Peters.

"Yes, I am," she replied. "My name is Leita."

She stepped into the car beside him and they drove off to the church on the outskirts of the forest, where they were married. Then he took her to his house in a <u>remote</u> and lovely valley and showed her all his treasures—the bees in their white hives, the Jersey cows, the hyacinths, the silver candle-sticks, the blue cups and the luster bowl for putting prim-roses in. She admired everything, but what pleased her most was the river which ran by the foot of his garden.

"Do swans come up there?" she asked.

Literary Analysis
Conflict and Resolution What inner conflict is resolved for Mr. Peters when he gets a wife?

"Yes, I have often seen swans there on the river," he told her, and she smiled.

Leita made him a good wife. But as time went by Mr. Peters began to feel that she was not happy. She seemed restless, wandered much in the garden, and sometimes when he came back from the fields he would find the house empty and she would return after half an hour or so with no explanation of where she had been. On these occasions she was always especially tender and would put out his slippers to warm and cook his favorite dish—Welsh rarebit[3] with wild strawberries—for supper.

One evening he was returning home along the river path when he saw Leita in front of him, down by the water. A swan had sailed up to the verge and she had her arms round its neck and the swan's head rested against her cheek. She was weeping, and as he came nearer he saw that tears were rolling, too, from the swan's eyes.

"Leita, what is it?" he asked, very troubled.

"This is my sister," she answered. "I can't bear being separated from her."

Now he understood that Leita was really a swan from the forest, and this made him very sad because when a human being marries a bird it always leads to sorrow.

"I could use my second wish to give your sister human shape, so that she could be a companion to you," he suggested.

"No, no," she cried, "I couldn't ask that of her."

"Is it so very hard to be a human being?" asked Mr. Peters sadly.

"Very, very hard," she answered.

"Don't you love me at all, Leita?"

"Yes, I do, I do love you," she said, and there were tears in her eyes again. "But I missed the old life in the forest, the cool grass and the mist rising off the river at sunrise and the feel of the water sliding over my feathers as my sister and I drifted along the stream."

"Then shall I use my second wish to turn you back into a swan again?" he asked, and his tongue pricked to remind him of the old King's words, and his heart swelled with grief inside him.

"Who will take care of you?"

---

3. **Welsh rarebit** a dish of melted cheese served on crackers or toast.

Reading Skill
Make Inferences
What inferences can you make about Leita based on the detail that she and a swan are crying?

 **Reading Check**

What happens after Mr. Peters makes his first wish?

"I'd do it myself as I did before I married you," he said, trying to sound cheerful.

She shook her head. "No, I could not be as unkind to you as that. I am partly a swan, but I am also partly a human being now. I will stay with you."

Poor Mr. Peters was very distressed on his wife's account and did his best to make her life happier, taking her for drives in the car, finding beautiful music for her to listen to on the radio, buying clothes for her and even suggesting a trip round the world. But she said no to that; she would prefer to stay in their own house near the river.

He noticed that she spent more and more time baking wonderful cakes—jam puffs, petits fours, eclairs and meringues. One day he saw her take a basketful down to the river and he guessed that she was giving them to her sister.

He built a seat for her by the river, and the two sisters spent hours together there, communicating in some wordless manner. For a time he thought that all would be well, but then he saw how thin and pale she was growing.

One night when he had been late doing the account he came up to bed and found her weeping in her sleep and calling:

"Rhea! Rhea! I can't understand what you say! Oh, wait for me, take me with you!"

Then he knew that it was hopeless and she would never be happy as a human. He stooped down and kissed her goodbye, then took another leaf from his notecase, blew it out of the window, and used up his second wish.

Next moment instead of Leita there was a sleeping swan lying across the bed with its head under its wing. He carried it out of the house and down to the brink of the river, and then he said, "Leita! Leita!" to waken her, and gently put her into the water. She gazed round her in astonishment for a moment, and then came up to him and rested her head lightly against his hand; next instant she was flying away over the trees towards the heart of the forest.

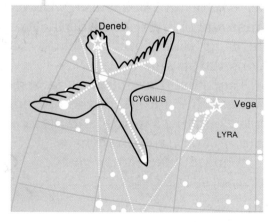

He heard a harsh laugh behind him, and turning round saw the old King looking at him with a <u>malicious</u> expression.

"Well, my friend! You don't seem to have managed so wonderfully with your first two wishes, do you? What will you do with the last? Turn yourself into a swan? Or turn Leita back into a girl?"

"I shall do neither," said Mr. Peters calmly. "Human beings and swans are better in their own shapes."

Vocabulary Builder
malicious (mə lish´ əs) *adj.* spiteful; hateful

But for all that he looked sadly over towards the forest where Leita had flown, and walked slowly back to his house.

Next day he saw two swans swimming at the bottom of the garden, and one of them wore the gold chain he had given Leita after their marriage; she came up and rubbed her head against his hand.

Mr. Peters and his two swans came to be well known in that part of the country; people used to say that he talked to swans and they understood him as well as his neighbors. Many people were a little frightened of him. There was a story that once when thieves tried to break into his house they were set upon by two huge white birds which carried them off bodily and dropped them into the river.

As Mr. Peters grew old everyone wondered at his contentment. Even when he was bent with rheumatism[4] he would not think of moving to a drier spot, but went slowly about his work, with the two swans always somewhere close at hand.

Sometimes people who knew his story would say to him:

"Mr. Peters, why don't you wish for another wife?"

"Not likely," he would answer serenely. "Two wishes were enough for me, I reckon. I've learned that even if your wishes are granted they don't always better you. I'll stay faithful to Leita."

One autumn night, passers-by along the road heard the mournful sound of two swans singing. All night the song went on, sweet and harsh, sharp and clear. In the morning Mr. Peters was found peacefully dead in his bed with a smile of great happiness on his face. In his hands, which lay clasped on his breast, were a withered leaf and a white feather.

⊿ Critical Viewing
What experiences pictured here might Leita miss as a human? **[Analyze]**

Reading Skill
Make Inferences
What inferences can you make from knowing what Mr. Peters held in his hands when he died?

---

4. **rheumatism** (roo´ mə tiz´ əm) *n.* pain and stiffness of the joints and muscles.

Apply the Skills

The Third Wish

Thinking About the Selection

1. **Respond:** What advice would you have given Mr. Peters on how to use his third wish? Explain your answer. In a small group, share your responses. As a group, choose one answer to share with the class.
2. **(a) Recall:** How does Mr. Peters get the opportunity to ask for three wishes? **(b) Predict:** How did you think Mr. Peters's wishing would turn out? Was your prediction correct?
3. **(a) Recall:** How does Mr. Peters use his first wish? **(b) Speculate:** Why do you think he does not wish for riches?
4. **(a) Make a Judgment:** Do you think Mr. Peters used his wishes wisely? **(b) Support:** What evidence from the story makes you feel that way?
5. **Apply:** Many cultures have traditional tales about wishes that do not work out. Why do you think this kind of story is so common?

Reading Skill

6. List two details in the story that support the **inference** that Mr. Peters loves Leita more than he loves himself.
7. List two details in the story that support the inference that Leita still loves Mr. Peters even after changing back to a swan.
8. List two details that suggest that Mr. Peters is not afraid to die.

Literary Analysis

9. **(a)** What **conflict** does Mr. Peters's first wish introduce? **(b)** What **resolution** does Mr. Peters find for the conflict?
10. On a chart like the one shown, identify two smaller conflicts that build toward Mr. Peters's main conflict, and tell how each is resolved.

Smaller Conflict	Resolution

Main Conflict

QuickReview

Who's Who in the Story

Mr. Peters: a man who is granted three wishes

Leita: his wife, who was originally a swan

Rhea: Leita's sister, a swan

Go Online
—Assessment
For: Self-test
Visit: www.PHSchool.com
Web Code: ema-6207

Inference: intelligent guesses about a story, based on details included in text

Conflict: a struggle between opposing forces

Resolution: the outcome of a conflict

Vocabulary Builder

Practice Use your knowledge of the italicized words to answer each question. Explain your responses.

1. To people in the Americas, does Australia seem *remote*?
2. If you think things over carefully, are you making a *rash* choice?
3. What would you do if you faced a *malicious* person?
4. Is it *presumptuous* of a host to invite guests to a party?

Writing

Write an **anecdote,** or brief story, using the three-wishes pattern that Aiken's story follows.

- First, think of a problem that could result from a wish.
- Then, think of ways that the character could try to solve the problem.
- Next, decide on one resolution to the conflict.

Using these ideas, write an anecdote. At the end of the anecdote, include a sentence that states the lesson that your character learns.

For *Grammar, Vocabulary,* and *Assessment,* see **Build Language Skills,** pages 294–295.

Extend Your Learning

Listening and Speaking Write a **news story** that announces the death of Mr. Peters and hails him as a local hero. Use details from "The Third Wish" to give examples of Mr. Peters's good deeds and good nature. Organize your story to present your details in the most effective order. For instance, you might present your examples from weakest to strongest. Practice reading your news story aloud before presenting it to the class.

Research and Technology Use library search resources, such as subject listings in the card catalog or an electronic catalog, to find another tale about wishes. Read the tale you locate, then prepare a **comparison-and-contrast chart** of "The Three Wishes" and the other story. Use a Venn diagram to show how the tales are alike and how they are different.

Build Understanding • *Amigo Brothers*

Background

Amateur Boxing In "Amigo Brothers," two teenage boys want to compete in the annual Golden Gloves tournament. In this competition—probably the most famous amateur boxing event in the United States—local and regional elimination bouts lead to final championship matches.

Connecting to the Literature

Reading/Writing Connection The characters in "Amigo Brothers" are friends, yet they are forced to compete against each other in a boxing match. Write three reasons why facing a rivalry with a friend might be more difficult than the physical challenge of the sport. Use at least three of these words: *accomplish, benefit, involve, isolate.*

Review

For **Reading Skill, Literary Analysis,** and **Vocabulary Builder,** see p. 272.

Meet the Author

Piri **Thomas** (b. 1928)

Growing up on the streets of New York City's Spanish Harlem, Piri Thomas faced many challenges—poverty, gangs, and racism among them. He later related those struggles in his best-selling autobiographical novel, *Down These Mean Streets.* The book introduced many non-Hispanics to the world of *el barrio*—"the neighborhood."

An Avid Reader As a youth, Thomas sought to avoid the difficult world around him by surrounding himself with books. "My one island of refuge in *el barrio* was the public library," Thomas has recalled. "I gorged myself on books. . . . Reading helped me to realize that there was a world out there far vaster than the narrow confines of *el barrio.*"

Fast Facts

▶ Thomas has written many magazine articles reflecting on ways for people everywhere to achieve peace and justice.
▶ He has often spoken to audiences, both young and old, on the theme "Unity Among Us."

Go Online
Author Link

For: More about the author
Visit: www.PHSchool.com
Web Code: eme-9209

Amigo Brothers

Piri Thomas

Antonio Cruz and Felix Vargas were both seventeen years old. They were so together in friendship that they felt themselves to be brothers. They had known each other since childhood, growing up on the lower east side of Manhattan in the same tenement building on Fifth Street between Avenue A and Avenue B.

Antonio was fair, lean, and lanky, while Felix was dark, short, and husky. Antonio's hair was always falling over his eyes, while Felix wore his black hair in a natural Afro style.

Each youngster had a dream of someday becoming lightweight champion of the world. Every chance they had the boys worked out, sometimes at the Boys Club on 10th Street and Avenue A and sometimes at the pro's gym on 14th Street. Early morning sunrises would find them running along the East River Drive, wrapped in sweat shirts, short towels around their necks, and handkerchiefs Apache style around their foreheads.

While some youngsters were into street negatives, Antonio and Felix slept, ate, rapped, and dreamt positive. Between them, they had a collection of *Fight* magazines second to none, plus a scrapbook filled with torn tickets to every boxing match they had ever attended, and some clippings of their own. If asked a question about any given fighter, they would immediately zip out from their memory banks divisions, weights, records of fights, knock-outs, technical knock-outs, and draws or losses.

Each had fought many bouts representing their community and had won two gold-plated medals plus a silver and bronze medallion. The difference was in their style. Antonio's lean form and long reach made him the better boxer, while Felix's short and muscular frame made him the better slugger. Whenever they had met in the ring for sparring sessions, it had always been hot and heavy.

Now, after a series of elimination bouts, they had been informed that they were to meet each other in

Reading Skill
Make Inferences
What can you infer about the boys based on their dedication to boxing?

✔ **Reading Check**

What dream do Antonio and Felix share?

▷ **Critical Viewing** What does the protective gear in this photograph tell you about boxing? **[Analyze Cause and Effect]**

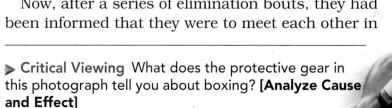

the division finals that were scheduled for the seventh of August, two weeks away—the winner to represent the Boys Club in the Golden Gloves Championship Tournament.

The two boys continued to run together along the East River Drive. But even when joking with each other, they both sensed a wall rising between them.

One morning less than a week before their bout, they met as usual for their daily work-out. They fooled around with a few jabs at the air, slapped skin, and then took off, running lightly along the dirty East River's edge.

Antonio glanced at Felix who kept his eyes purposely straight ahead, pausing from time to time to do some fancy leg work while throwing one-twos followed by upper cuts to an imaginary jaw. Antonio then beat the air with a barrage of body blows and short <u>devastating</u> lefts with an overhand jaw-breaking right. After a mile or so, Felix puffed and said, "Let's stop a while, bro. I think we both got something to say to each other." Antonio nodded. It was not natural to be acting as though nothing unusual was happening when two ace-boon buddies were going to be blasting each other within a few short days.

They rested their elbows on the railing separating them from the river. Antonio wiped his face with his short towel. The sunrise was now creating day.

Felix leaned heavily on the river's railing and stared across to the shores of Brooklyn. Finally, he broke the silence.

"Man, I don't know how to come out with it."

Antonio helped. "It's about our fight, right?"

"Yeah, right." Felix's eyes squinted at the rising orange sun.

"I've been thinking about it too, *panín*. In fact, since we found out it was going to be me and you, I've been awake at night, pulling punches on you, trying not to hurt you."

"Same here. It ain't natural not to think about the fight. I mean, we both are *cheverote* fighters and we both want to win. But only one of us can win. There ain't no draws in the eliminations."

Felix tapped Antonio gently on the shoulder. "I don't mean to sound like I'm bragging, bro. But I wanna win, fair and square."

Antonio nodded quietly. "Yeah. We both know that in the ring the better man wins. Friend or no friend, brother or no . . ."

Felix finished it for him. "Brother. Tony, let's promise something right here. Okay?"

Literary Analysis
Conflict and Resolution What external conflict is introduced in this part of the story?

Vocabulary Builder
devastating (dev´ ə stāt´ iŋ) *adj.* destructive; overwhelming

Reading Skill
Make Inferences What do the details in this conversation suggest about the boys' relationship?

"If it's fair, *hermano*, I'm for it." Antonio admired the courage of a tugboat pulling a barge five times its welterweight size.

"It's fair, Tony. When we get into the ring, it's gotta be like we never met. We gotta be like two heavy strangers that want the same thing and only one can have it. You understand, don'tcha?"

"*Sí*, I know." Tony smiled. "No pulling punches. We go all the way."

"Yeah, that's right. Listen, Tony. Don't you think it's a good idea if we don't see each other until the day of the fight? I'm going to stay with my Aunt Lucy in the Bronx. I can use Gleason's Gym for working out. My manager says he got some sparring partners with more or less your style."

Tony scratched his nose pensively. "Yeah, it would be better for our heads." He held out his hand, palm upward. "Deal?"

"Deal." Felix lightly slapped open skin.

"Ready for some more running?" Tony asked lamely.

"Naw, bro. Let's cut it here. You go on. I kinda like to get things together in my head."

"You ain't worried, are you?" Tony asked.

"No way, man." Felix laughed out loud. "I got too much smarts for that. I just think it's cooler if we split right here. After the fight, we can get it together again like nothing ever happened."

The amigo brothers were not ashamed to hug each other tightly.

"Guess you're right. Watch yourself, Felix. I hear there's some pretty heavy dudes up in the Bronx. *Suavecito*, okay?"

"Okay. You watch yourself too, *sabe?*"

Tony jogged away. Felix watched his friend disappear from view, throwing rights and lefts. Both fighters had a lot of psyching up to do before the big fight.

The days in training passed much too slowly. Although they kept out of each other's way, they were aware of each other's progress via the ghetto grapevine.

The evening before the big fight, Tony made his way to the roof of his tenement. In the quiet early dark, he peered over the ledge. Six stories below the lights of the city blinked and the sounds of cars mingled with the curses and the laughter of children in the street. He tried not to think of Felix, feeling he had succeeded in psyching his mind. But only in the ring would he really know. To spare Felix hurt, he would have to knock him out, early and quick.

Literary Analysis
Conflict and Resolution What internal conflict do Tony and Felix each face before the fight?

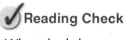

Reading Check

What deal do Antonio and Felix reach about their training period before the fight?

Up in the South Bronx, Felix decided to take in a movie in an effort to keep Antonio's face away from his fists. The flick was *The Champion* with Kirk Douglas, the third time Felix was seeing it.

The champion was getting hit hard. He was saved only by the sound of the bell.

Felix became the champ and Tony the challenger.

The movie audience was going out of its head. The challenger, confident that he had the championship in the bag, threw a left. The champ countered with a dynamite right.

Felix's right arm felt the shock. Antonio's face, superimposed[1] on the screen, was hit by the awesome blow. Felix saw himself in the ring, blasting Antonio against the ropes. The champ had to be forcibly restrained. The challenger was allowed to crumble slowly to the canvas.

When Felix finally left the theatre, he had figured out how to psyche himself for tomorrow's fight. It was Felix the Champion vs. Antonio the Challenger.

He walked up some dark streets, deserted except for small pockets of wary-looking kids wearing gang colors. Despite the fact that he was Puerto Rican like them, they eyed him as a stranger to their turf. Felix did a fast shuffle, bobbing and weaving, while letting loose a torrent of blows that would demolish whatever got in its way. It seemed to impress the brothers, who went about their own business.

Finding no takers, Felix decided to split to his aunt's. Walking the streets had not relaxed him, neither had the fight flick. All it had done was to stir him up. He let himself quietly into his Aunt Lucy's apartment and went straight to bed, falling into a fitful sleep with sounds of the gong for Round One.

Antonio was passing some heavy time on his rooftop. How would the fight tomorrow affect his relationship with Felix? After all, fighting was like any other profession. Friendship had nothing to do with it. A gnawing doubt crept in. He cut negative thinking real quick by doing some speedy fancy dance steps, bobbing and weaving like mercury.[2]

---

1. superimposed (sōō′ pər im pōzd′) *adj.* put or stacked on top of something else.
2. mercury (mʉr′ kyōōr ē) *n.* the element mercury, also known as quicksilver because it is so quick and fluid.

The night air was blurred with <u>perpetual</u> motions of left hooks and right crosses. Felix, his *amigo* brother, was not going to be Felix at all in the ring. Just an opponent with another face. Antonio went to sleep, hearing the opening bell for the first round. Like his friend in the South Bronx, he prayed for victory, via a quick clean knock-out in the first round.

Large posters plastered all over the walls of local shops announced the fight between Antonio Cruz and Felix Vargas as the main bout.

The fight had created great interest in the neighborhood. Antonio and Felix were well liked and respected. Each had his own loyal following. Antonio's fans counted on his boxing skills. On the other side, Felix's admirers trusted in his dynamite-packed fists.

Felix had returned to his apartment early in the morning of August 7th and stayed there, hoping to avoid seeing Antonio. He turned the radio on to *salsa* music sounds and then tried to read while waiting for word from his manager.

The fight was scheduled to take place in Tompkins Square Park. It had been decided that the gymnasium of the Boys Club was not large enough to hold all the people who were sure to attend. In Tompkins Square Park, everyone who wanted could view the fight, whether from ringside or window fire escapes or tenement rooftops.

The morning of the fight Tompkins Square was a beehive of activity with numerous workers setting up the ring, the seats, and the guest speakers' stand. The scheduled bouts began shortly after noon and the park had begun filling up even earlier.

The local junior high school across from Tompkins Square Park served as the dressing room for all the fighters. Each was given a separate classroom with desk tops, covered with mats, serving as resting tables. Antonio thought he caught a glimpse of Felix waving to him from a room at the far end of the corridor. He waved back just in case it had been him.

The fighters changed from their street clothes into fighting gear. Antonio wore white trunks, black socks, and black shoes. Felix wore sky blue trunks, red socks, and white boxing shoes. Each had dressing gowns to match their fighting trunks with their names neatly stitched on the back.

The loudspeakers blared into the open windows of the school. There were speeches by dignitaries, community leaders, and great boxers of yesteryear. Some were well prepared, some improvised on the spot. They all carried the same

Vocabulary Builder
perpetual (pər pech′ o͞o əl) *adj.* constant; unending

Reading Skill
Make Inferences
What does Antonio's wave from the dressing room suggest about his feelings for Felix?

Reading Check

Why are so many people in the neighborhood interested in watching the fight?

message of great pleasure and honor at being part of such a historic event. This great day was in the tradition of champions emerging from the streets of the lower east side.

Interwoven with the speeches were the sounds of the other boxing events. After the sixth bout, Felix was much relieved when his trainer Charlie said, "Time change. Quick knockout. This is it. We're on."

Waiting time was over. Felix was escorted from the classroom by a dozen fans in white T-shirts with the word FELIX across their fronts.

Antonio was escorted down a different stairwell and guided through a roped-off path.

As the two climbed into the ring, the crowd exploded with a roar. Antonio and Felix both bowed gracefully and then raised their arms in acknowledgment.

Antonio tried to be cool, but even as the roar was in its first birth, he turned slowly to meet Felix's eyes looking directly into his. Felix nodded his head and Antonio responded. And both as one, just as quickly, turned away to face his own corner.

Bong—bong—bong. The roar turned to stillness.

"Ladies and Gentlemen. *Señores y Señoras.*"

The announcer spoke slowly, pleased at his bilingual efforts.

"Now the moment we have all been waiting for—the main event between two fine young Puerto Rican fighters, products of our lower east side. In this corner, weighing 134 pounds, Felix Vargas. And in this corner, weighing 133 pounds, Antonio Cruz. The winner will represent the Boys Club in the tournament of champions, the Golden Gloves. There will be no draw. May the best man win."

The cheering of the crowd shook the window panes of the old buildings surrounding Tompkins Square Park. At the center of the ring, the referee was giving instructions to the youngsters.

"Keep your punches up. No low blows. No punching on the back of the head. Keep your heads up. Understand. Let's have a clean fight. Now shake hands and come out fighting."

Both youngsters touched gloves and nodded. They turned and danced quickly to their corners. Their head towels and dressing gowns were lifted neatly from their shoulders by their trainers' nimble fingers. Antonio crossed himself. Felix did the same.

▼ **Critical Viewing**
How do you think this boxer feels as he waits for the bell to start the match? **[Connect]**

BONG! BONG! ROUND ONE. Felix and Antonio turned and faced each other squarely in a fighting pose. Felix wasted no time. He came in fast, head low, half hunched toward his right shoulder, and lashed out with a straight left. He missed a right cross as Antonio slipped the punch and countered with one-two-three lefts that snapped Felix's head back, sending a mild shock coursing through him. If Felix had any small doubt about their friendship affecting their fight, it was being neatly <u>dispelled</u>.

Antonio danced, a joy to behold. His left hand was like a piston pumping jabs one right after another with seeming ease. Felix bobbed and weaved and never stopped boring in. He knew that at long range he was at a disadvantage. Antonio had too much reach on him. Only by coming in close could Felix hope to achieve the dreamed-of knockout.

Antonio knew the dynamite that was stored in his *amigo* brother's fist. He ducked a short right and missed a left hook. Felix trapped him against the ropes just long enough to pour some punishing rights and lefts to Antonio's hard midsection. Antonio slipped away from Felix, crashing two lefts to his head, which set Felix's right ear to ringing.

Bong! Both *amigos* froze a punch well on its way, sending up a roar of approval for good sportsmanship.

Felix walked briskly back to his corner. His right ear had not stopped ringing. Antonio gracefully danced his way toward his stool none the worse, except for glowing glove burns, showing angry red against the whiteness of his midribs.

"Watch that right, Tony." His trainer talked into his ear. "Remember Felix always goes to the body. He'll want you to drop your hands for his overhand left or right. Got it?"

Antonio nodded, spraying water out between his teeth. He felt better as his sore midsection was being firmly rubbed.

Felix's corner was also busy.

"You gotta get in there, fella." Felix's trainer poured water over his curly Afro locks. "Get in there or he's gonna chop you up from way back."

Bong! Bong! Round two. Felix was off his stool and rushed Antonio like a bull, sending a hard right to his head. Beads of water exploded from Antonio's long hair.

Antonio, hurt, sent back a blurring barrage of lefts and rights that only meant pain to Felix, who returned with a short left to the head followed by a looping right to the body.

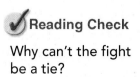

Reading Check

Why can't the fight be a tie?

Antonio countered with his own flurry, forcing Felix to give ground. But not for long.

Felix bobbed and weaved, bobbed and weaved, occasionally punching his two gloves together.

Antonio waited for the rush that was sure to come. Felix closed in and feinted[3] with his left shoulder and threw his right instead. Lights suddenly exploded inside Felix's head as Antonio slipped the blow and hit him with a pistonlike left catching him flush on the point of his chin.

Bedlam[4] broke loose as Felix's legs momentarily buckled. He fought off a series of rights and lefts and came back with a strong right that taught Antonio respect.

Antonio danced in carefully. He knew Felix had the habit of playing possum when hurt, to sucker an opponent within reach of the powerful bombs he carried in each fist.

A right to the head slowed Antonio's pretty dancing. He answered with his own left at Felix's right eye that began puffing up within three seconds.

Antonio, a bit too eager, moved in too close and Felix had him entangled into a rip-roaring, punching toe-to-toe slugfest that brought the whole Tompkins Square Park screaming to its feet.

Rights to the body. Lefts to the head. Neither fighter was giving an inch. Suddenly a short right caught Antonio squarely on the chin. His long legs turned to jelly and his arms flailed out desperately. Felix, grunting like a bull, threw wild punches from every direction. Antonio, groggy, bobbed and weaved, evading most of the blows. Suddenly his head cleared. His left flashed out hard and straight catching Felix on the bridge of his nose.

Felix lashed back with a haymaker,[5] right off the ghetto streets. At the same instant, his eye caught another left hook from Antonio. Felix swung out trying to clear the pain. Only the frenzied screaming of those along ringside let him know that he had dropped Antonio. Fighting off the growing haze, Antonio struggled to his feet, got up, ducked, and threw a smashing right that dropped Felix flat on his back.

Felix got up as fast as he could in his own corner, groggy but still game. He didn't even hear the count. In a fog, he heard the roaring of the crowd, who seemed to have gone insane. His head cleared to hear the bell sound at the end of the round. He was very glad. His trainer sat him down on the stool.

3. **feinted** (fānt´ əd) v. pretended to make a blow.
4. **Bedlam** (bed´ ləm) n. condition of noise and confusion.
5. **haymaker** punch thrown with full force.

Literary Analysis
Conflict and Resolution How does the author increase the external conflict in this paragraph?

Vocabulary Builder
evading (ē vād´ iŋ) v. avoiding

Reading Skill
Make Inferences What can you infer from the fact that Felix is groggy and glad to sit down?

In his corner, Antonio was doing what all fighters do when they are hurt. They sit and smile at everyone.

The referee signaled the ring doctor to check the fighters out. He did so and then gave his okay. The cold water sponges brought clarity to both *amigo* brothers. They were rubbed until their circulation ran free.

Bong! Round three—the final round. Up to now it had been tic-tac-toe, pretty much even. But everyone knew there could be no draw and this round would decide the winner.

This time, to Felix's surprise, it was Antonio who came out fast, charging across the ring. Felix braced himself but couldn't ward off the barrage of punches. Antonio drove Felix hard against the ropes.

The crowd ate it up. Thus far the two had fought with *mucho corazón.* Felix tapped his gloves and commenced his attack anew. Antonio, throwing boxer's caution to the winds, jumped in to meet him.

Both pounded away. Neither gave an inch and neither fell to the canvas. Felix's left eye was tightly closed. Claret red blood poured from Antonio's nose. They fought toe-to-toe.

The sounds of their blows were loud in contrast to the silence of a crowd gone completely mute. The referee was stunned by their savagery.

Bong! Bong! Bong! The bell sounded over and over again. Felix and Antonio were past hearing. Their blows continued to pound on each other like hailstones.

Finally the referee and the two trainers pried Felix and Antonio apart. Cold water was poured over them to bring them back to their senses.

They looked around and then rushed toward each other. A cry of alarm surged through Tompkins Square Park. Was this a fight to the death instead of a boxing match?

The fear soon gave way to wave upon wave of cheering as the two *amigos* embraced.

No matter what the decision, they knew they would always be champions to each other.

BONG! BONG! BONG! "Ladies and Gentlemen. *Señores* and *Señoras.* The winner and representative to the Golden Gloves Tournament of Champions is . . ."

The announcer turned to point to the winner and found himself alone. Arm in arm the champions had already left the ring.

▼ **Critical Viewing**
Why do you think that competitors in boxing matches wear contrasting colors such as the blue in this picture and the red in the picture on page 288?
[Hypothesize]

Apply the Skills

Amigo Brothers

Thinking About the Selection

1. **Respond:** How do you feel about the author's decision not to tell you which of the two boys won the fight?
2. **(a) Recall:** What is the boys' plan for training before they face each other in the ring? **(b) Evaluate:** What are the advantages and disadvantages of their plan? **(c) Discuss:** Do you think the plan is mostly good or mostly bad? Explain your answer. In a small group, share your responses. As a group, choose one response to share with the class.
3. **(a) Analyze:** In what ways does the boys' friendship both help them and hurt them during the fight? **(b) Apply:** Why is it harder for each of them to compete against a friend than a stranger?
4. **Speculate:** Do you think the boys will be willing to box against each other in the future? Explain your response.

Reading Skill

5. List two details that support the **inference** that the boys care for each other more than they care for themselves.
6. List two details in the story that support the inference that the boys have few other friends besides each other.
7. List two details that suggest that neither boy is the type to give up easily.

Literary Analysis

8. **(a)** What **conflict** does the boys' dream introduce? **(b)** What **resolution** do the boys find for their conflict?
9. On a chart like the one shown, identify two smaller conflicts that build toward the main conflict, and tell how each is resolved.

Smaller Conflict	Resolution

↓

Main Conflict

QuickReview

Who's Who in the Story

Antonio and Felix: two 17-year-old boxers who are friends

Go **O**nline
—**Assessment**
For: Self-test
Visit: www.PHSchool.com
Web Code: ema-6208

Inference: intelligent guesses about a story, based on details included in text

Conflict: a struggle between opposing forces

Resolution: the outcome of a conflict

Vocabulary Builder

Practice Use your knowledge of the italicized words to answer each question. Explain your responses.

1. How do most people respond to *devastating* news?
2. What would you do if a friend's lateness were *perpetual*?
3. If someone has *dispelled* a rumor, would you believe it?
4. What type of answer would you give if you were *evading* a question?

Writing

Write an **anecdote,** or brief story, that tells what might have happened if Antonio or Felix had been knocked out during the fight.
- First, jot down details about the fight.
- Then, make notes on how each boy feels about the knockout.
- Next, decide how both boys get beyond the knockout and resume—or do not resume—their friendship.

Using these ideas, write your anecdote. At the end of the anecdote, include a sentence that states the lesson that the characters learned.

For *Grammar, Vocabulary,* and *Assessment,*
see **Build Language Skills,** pages 294–295.

Extend Your Learning

Listening and Speaking Present a **news story** that describes the fight between Antonio and Felix. Use details from "Amigo Brothers" to tell what happened both during and after the match. Include quotations from both boxers. Practice reading your news story aloud before presenting it to the class.

Research and Technology Use library search resources, such as subject listings in the card catalog or an electronic catalog, to locate sources that explain amateur boxing and professional boxing. Read the sources you locate, and then prepare a **comparison-and-contrast chart** for the two sports. Use a Venn diagram to show how the two sports are alike and how they are different.

Build Language Skills

The Third Wish • Amigo Brothers

Vocabulary Skill

Prefixes The **prefix** *-ob-* generally means "against" or "blocking." An *object*, which is a thing that can be seen or touched, would block you from moving forward if it were placed in your way. With a different pronunciation, *object* is a verb that means "speak out against." Other words that begin with the prefix *-ob-* have meanings related to being blocked, or "not able to continue."

Practice Rewrite each sentence replacing a word or words with one of the words that begins with the prefix *-ob-*. Your new sentence should have the same meaning as the original sentence.

obstruction   *obstructed*   *obstacle*   *objected*   *objection*

1. The mudslide blocked the road.
2. The mayor expressed his feelings against the newspaper's claim that he was biased.
3. The boulders in the path were a block that kept us from moving forward.
4. The students had no reason to speak against a longer vacation.
5. In gym class we ran a course that had something intended to block us and make it more challenging to move forward.

MorePractice

For more practice with adjectives, see Grammar Handbook, p. R32.

Grammar Lesson

Adjectives An **adjective** modifies or describes a noun or pronoun. An adjective may answer the questions *what kind? how many? which one?* or *whose?*

Practice Identify the adjective in each sentence. Then, tell which question the adjective answers. Use each adjective in a sentence of your own.

1. You have a beautiful house.
2. It has six rooms in all.
3. There is a small patio in back.

What kind?	Dan bought a red jacket.
How many?	We sold fifty tickets.
Which one?	Please hand me that one.
Whose?	We saw Kathy's play.

4. Would you like to see David's room?
5. We see many squirrels in the yard.

W͟G Writing and Grammar Connection: Chapter 16, Section 1

Assessment Practice

Reading: Make Inferences

Directions: *Read the selection. Then, answer the questions.*

Mr. Jenkins began to speak at the business meeting. His hands shook so badly that he could barely read his note cards. Beads of sweat formed on his forehead. He paused and took a sip of water. "I can do this," Mr. Jenkins thought to himself. He took a deep breath and continued his presentation. In time, smiles appeared on faces in the audience. When he finished his speech, Mr. Jenkins received enthusiastic applause.

1. Based on the passage, what can you infer about Mr. Jenkins at the start of his speech?
   A He is confident.
   B He is tired.
   C He is nervous.
   D He is confused.

2. What detail suggests that Mr. Jenkins had prepared for his speech?
   A He has note cards.
   B He drinks water.
   C He is at a business meeting.
   D He takes a deep breath.

3. What detail suggests that Mr. Jenkins is determined to succeed?
   A He speaks in a loud voice.
   B His audience smiles.
   C He tells himself, "I can do this."
   D His hands shake badly.

4. What can you infer from the audience's looks and applause?
   A They are glad the speech is over.
   B They felt nervous themselves.
   C The speaker ended early.
   D The speech improved greatly.

Timed Writing: Literary Interpretation [Interpretation]

Review "The Third Wish" or "Amigo Brothers." State the main conflict of either story. Then, explain how the personality and beliefs of the character or characters helped them resolve the conflict. Support your interpretation with details from the story. **(30 minutes)**

 ## Writing Workshop: *Work in Progress*

Short Story

For a short story you may write, briefly describe four conflicts that you have experienced, witnessed, or seen in the news. These conflicts may have occurred in school, at home, in your community, or in a distant location. Put this conflict list in your writing portfolio.

Reading Informational Materials

Government Publications

In Part 2, you are learning about making inferences while reading literature. Making inferences can also help you understand and use the information in government publications. If you read "Amigo Brothers," you met two characters who would agree with the topic of this government publication—exercise is good for you.

About Government Publications

The United States government issues publications on a wide variety of topics. Some publications are just a few pages long, while others run well over 100 pages. All are available free of charge or for a small fee. Chances are good that, no matter what topic interests you, there is at least one **government publication** on that topic.

Examples of government publications include

- Explanations of new or proposed legislation (laws)
- Details of budgets and spending
- Minutes from a city council meeting
- Instructions for evaluating drinking water
- Guidelines for choosing a doctor

The government publication shown here is published by the President's Council on Physical Fitness and Sports.

Reading Skill

An **inference** is a logical guess about information that is not directly stated, based on details in the text and your own knowledge and experience. When you apply an inference in a general way, you are making a generalization. A **generalization** is a broad statement that applies to many examples and is supported by evidence. For example, a person with several well-behaved dogs might make the generalization that dogs are loyal, friendly pets. As you read the government publication, use a chart like the one shown to record evidence that supports a generalization about walking.

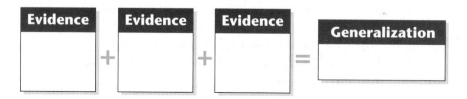

Walking for Exercise and Pleasure

The President's Council on Physical Fitness and Sports

Walking: An Exercise for All Ages

Walking is easily the most popular form of exercise. Other activities generate more conversation and media coverage, but none of them approaches walking in number of participants. Approximately half of the 165 million American adults (18 years of age and older) claim they exercise regularly, and the number who walk for exercise is increasing every year.

Walking is the only exercise in which the rate of participation does not decline in the middle and later years. In a national survey, the highest percentage of regular walkers (39.4%) for any group was found among men 65 years of age and older.

Unlike tennis, running, skiing, and other activities that have gained great popularity fairly recently, walking has been widely practiced as a recreational and fitness activity throughout recorded history.

Classical and early English literature seems to have been written largely by men who were prodigious walkers, and Emerson and Thoreau helped carry on the tradition in America. Among American presidents, the most famous walkers included Jefferson, Lincoln, and Truman.

Walking: The Slower, Surer Way to Fitness

People walk for many reasons: for pleasure . . . to rid themselves of tensions . . . to find solitude . . . or to get from one place to another. Nearly everyone who walks regularly does so at least in part because of a conviction that it is good exercise.

Often dismissed in the past as being "too easy" to be taken seriously, walking recently has gained new respect as a means of improving physical fitness. Studies show that, when done briskly on a regular schedule, it can improve the body's ability to consume oxygen during exertion, lower the resting heart rate, reduce blood pressure, and increase the efficiency of the heart and

> Headings within the document divide the information into sections and give you a clue as to what each section is about.

> Government publications often include statistics telling you how many Americans are affected by the topic.

> This line tells you which office of the government published the document.

Reading Informational Materials

lungs. It also helps burn excess calories.

Walking burns approximately the same amount of calories per mile as does running, a fact particularly appealing to those who find it difficult to sustain the jarring effects of long distance jogging. Briskly walking one mile in 15 minutes burns just about the same number of calories as jogging an equal distance in 8 1/2 minutes. In weight-bearing activities like walking, heavier individuals will burn more calories than lighter persons. For example, studies show that a 110-pound person burns about half as many calories as a 216-pound person walking at the same pace for the same distance.

In addition to the qualities it has in common with other activities, walking has several unique advantages. Some of these are:

Almost everyone can do it.
You don't have to take lessons to learn how to walk. Probably all you need to do to become a serious walker is step up your pace and distance and walk more often.

You can do it almost anywhere.
All you have to do to find a place to walk is step outside your door. Almost any sidewalk, street, road, trail, park, field, or shopping mall

will do. The variety of settings available is one of the things that makes walking such a practical and pleasurable activity.

You can do it almost anytime.
You don't have to find a partner or get a team together to walk, so you can set your own schedule. Weather doesn't pose the same problems and uncertainties that it does in many sports. Walking is not a seasonal activity, and you can do it in extreme temperatures that would rule out other activities.

It doesn't cost anything.
You don't have to pay fees or join a private club to become a walker. The only equipment required is a sturdy, comfortable pair of shoes.

Listen to Your Body

Listen to your body when you walk. If you develop dizziness, pain, nausea, or any other unusual symptom, slow down or stop. If the problem persists, see your physician before walking again.

The most important thing is simply to set aside part of each day and walk. No matter what your age or condition, it's a practice that can make you healthier and happier.

> These advantages may be reasons why walking is a popular exercise.

> When giving instructions, government publications use short paragraphs and clear, direct language.

Reading: Making Generalizations

Directions: *Choose the letter of the best answer to each question.*

1. Which of the following is the main generalization in this publication?
   A Americans are walking incorrectly.
   B Older people like to walk.
   C Walking is good for you.
   D Americans have poor exercise habits.

2. Choose the detail that best supports this generalization: "People should make time to walk."
   A Almost everyone can do it, almost anywhere, at no cost.
   B Walking has been widely practiced as a recreational activity throughout recorded history.
   C Classical and early English literature seems to have been written largely by writers who were prodigious walkers.
   D Walking is the most popular form of exercise.

3. What generalization can you make based on this passage: *"Walking burns approximately the same amount of calories per mile as does running, a fact particularly appealing to those who find it difficult to sustain the jarring effects of long distance jogging"?*
   A Runners should switch to walking.
   B Americans should not jog long distances.
   C Walkers are healthier than runners.
   D Running is hard on your body.

Reading: Comprehension and Interpretation
Directions: *Write your answers on a separate sheet of paper.*

4. Describe the physical benefits of walking.
5. Compare and contrast the physical effects of running and walking.

Timed Writing: Persuasion

Write an open letter to your neighbors inviting them to start a walking group in your neighborhood. Use persuasive language to convince them of the importance of this goal. Include facts and details that support your arguments. **(10 minutes)**

These skills will help you become a better reader. Practice them with either "Zoo" (p. 302) or "Ribbons" (p. 307).

Reading Skill

An **inference** is an intelligent guess, based on what the text tells you, about things *not* stated directly in the text. For example, suppose a story opens with a man running down a dark alley while looking over his shoulder. You can infer from these details that the man is trying to get away from someone or something.

- One way to make inferences is to **read between the lines by asking questions** such as "Why does the writer include these details?" and "Why does the writer leave out certain information?"
- As you read, jot down questions and answers in a chart like the one shown.

Why Does the Writer...	Answer (inference)
Show the man looking over his shoulder?	To tell readers someone or something is chasing the man
Place the man in a dark alley?	To create an atmosphere of fear
Not start by naming the chaser?	To emphasize the man who looks back

Literary Analysis

A story's **theme** is its central idea, message, or insight into life. Occasionally, the author states the theme directly. More often, however, the theme is implied.

As you read, look at what the characters say and do, where the story takes place, and objects that seem important to help you determine the theme—what the author wants to teach you about life.

Vocabulary Builder

Zoo

- **interplanetary** (in´ tər plan´ ə ter´ ē) *adj.* between planets (p. 302) *The interplanetary tour went from Venus to Mars.*

- **awe** (ô) *n.* mixed feelings of fear and wonder (p. 302) *His eyes grew wide in awe at the sight of a large elephant.*

- **expense** (ek spens´) *n.* financial cost (p. 302) *Paying for college is a huge expense.*

Ribbons

- **sensitive** (sen´ sə tiv) *adj.* easily hurt (p. 308) *Susan is sensitive and cries often.*

- **meek** (mēk) *adj.* timid; not showing anger (p. 308) *The meek man allowed the bully to cut in front of him in line.*

- **coax** (kōks) *v.* use gentle persuasion (p. 309) *Sal used a dog biscuit to coax the puppy into its box.*

- **laborious** (lə bôr´ ē əs) *adj.* taking much work or effort (p. 309) *Moving the piano was a laborious task.*

- **exertion** (eg zʉr´ shən) *n.* physical work (p. 310) *The exertion of rowing the boat exhausted Larry.*

Build Understanding • *Zoo*

Background

Zoos Since early times, people have studied wild animals. In fact, experts believe that the first zoos were developed as far back as 4500 B.C. Until modern times, animals in zoos lived mostly in cages. However, many of today's zoos house animals in natural habitats, filled with native plants and other animals. In this story, you will read about a zoo that is unlike any other.

Connecting to the Literature

Reading/Writing Connection In your notebook, jot down sentences that describe a zoo you have visited or seen in pictures. Write from the perspective, or point of view, of an animal that lives there. Use at least three of the following words in your sentences: *benefit, establish, emphasize, minimize.*

Meet the Author

Edward D. **Hoch** (b. 1930)

When he writes mystery stories, Edward Hoch does not attempt to create fast-paced scenes with lots of suspense and action. Instead, he prefers to create tension by making his readers guess what will happen next. Hoch creates stories that have unusual plots and carefully selected clues for readers to follow.

Magazine Writer Hoch's first mystery story appeared in 1955 in the magazine *Famous Detective Stories*. A few years later, he began writing for *Ellery Queen's Mystery Magazine,* the longest-running magazine in existence for mystery fiction. Since then, Hoch has published more than 450 stories for the magazine.

Fast Facts

▶ Many of Hoch's stories feature the same characters. A character named Captain Leopold appears in more than one hundred Hoch stories.

▶ Before becoming a full-time writer, Hoch worked as a researcher in a library.

For: More about the author
Visit: www.PHSchool.com
Web Code: eme-9210

ZOO

Edward D. Hoch

The children were always good during the month of August, especially when it began to get near the twenty-third. It was on this day that the great silver spaceship carrying Professor Hugo's Interplanetary Zoo settled down for its annual six-hour visit to the Chicago area.

Before daybreak the crowds would form, long lines of children and adults both, each one clutching his or her dollar and waiting with wonderment[1] to see what race of strange creatures the Professor had brought this year.

In the past they had sometimes been treated to three-legged creatures from Venus, or tall, thin men from Mars, or even snakelike horrors from somewhere more distant. This year, as the great round ship settled slowly to earth in the huge tri-city parking area just outside of Chicago, they watched with awe as the sides slowly slid up to reveal the familiar barred cages. In them were some wild breed of nightmare—small, horse-like animals that moved with quick, jerking motions and constantly chattered in a high-pitched tongue. The citizens of Earth clustered around as Professor Hugo's crew quickly collected the waiting dollars, and soon the good Professor himself made an appearance, wearing his many-colored rainbow cape and top hat. "Peoples of Earth," he called into his microphone. The crowd's noise died down and he continued. "Peoples of Earth, this year you see a real treat for your single dollar—the little-known horse-spider people of Kaan—brought to you across a million miles of space at great expense. Gather around, see them, study them, listen to them, tell your friends about them. But hurry! My ship can remain here only six hours!"

And the crowds slowly filed by, at once horrified and fascinated by these strange creatures that looked like horses but ran up the walls of their cages like spiders. "This is certainly worth a dollar," one man remarked, hurrying away. "I'm going home to get the wife."

All day long it went like that, until ten thousand people had filed by the barred cages set into the side of the spaceship.

---

1. **wonderment** (wun´ dər mənt) *n.* astonishment.

Vocabulary Builder
interplanetary (in´ tər plan´ ə ter´ ē) *adj.* between planets

awe (ô) *n.* mixed feelings of fear and wonder

Literary Analysis
Theme Why are the people so eager to see the horse-like animals?

Vocabulary Builder
expense (ek spens´) *n.* financial cost

Then, as the six-hour limit ran out, Professor Hugo once more took the microphone in hand. "We must go now, but we will return next year on this date. And if you enjoyed our zoo this year, telephone your friends in other cities about it. We will land in New York tomorrow, and next week on to London, Paris, Rome, Hong Kong, and Tokyo. Then on to other worlds!"

He waved farewell to them, and as the ship rose from the ground, the Earth peoples agreed that this had been the very best Zoo yet. . . .

Some two months and three planets later, the silver ship of Professor Hugo settled at last onto the familiar jagged rocks of Kaan, and the odd horse-spider creatures filed quickly out of their cages. Professor Hugo was there to say a few parting words, and then they scurried away in a hundred different directions, seeking their homes among the rocks.

In one house, the she-creature was happy to see the return of her mate and offspring. She babbled a greeting in the strange tongue and hurried to embrace them. "It was a long time you were gone. Was it good?"

And the he-creature nodded. "The little one enjoyed it especially. We visited eight worlds and saw many things."

The little one ran up the wall of the cave. "On the place called Earth it was the best. The creatures there wear garments over their skins, and they walk on two legs."

"But isn't it dangerous?" asked the she-creature.

"No," her mate answered. "There are bars to protect us from them. We remain right in the ship. Next time you must come with us. It is well worth the nineteen commocs it costs."

And the little one nodded. "It was the very best Zoo ever. . . ."

Reading Skill
Make Inferences
Based on the details in this paragraph, what can you infer about Professor Hugo's life?

▼ Critical Viewing
Describe the Earth people's reactions to seeing the horse spiders. **[Analyze]**

Apply the Skills

Zoo

Thinking About the Selection

1. **Respond:** Would you choose to visit Hoch's Interplanetary Zoo? Why or why not?
2. **(a) Recall:** Describe the creatures that Professor Hugo brings to Earth. **(b) Interpret:** Why does the crowd view the creatures as "some wild breed of nightmare"? **(c) Draw Conclusions:** What does this label say about how humans view things that look different from them?
3. **(a) Recall:** How do humans on Earth react to people from Kaan? **(b) Recall:** How do Kaan people react to Earth people? **(c) Compare and Contrast:** In a small group, discuss your answers. Together, decide what the similarities and differences tell you.
4. **(a) Recall:** Why did the horse spiders feel safe on their trip? **(b) Analyze:** How do you think Hoch wants readers to react to the end of the story? **(c) Evaluate:** Do you think the ending was successful? Explain your answer.

Reading Skill

5. What **inference** can you make from the first two sentences of the story?
6. **(a)** What details does the author include about Professor Hugo's clothing? **(b)** What inference can you make about Professor Hugo from these details?
7. What inference did you make when you read that the professor charges one dollar to view the creatures? Explain.

Literary Analysis

What **theme** does the story convey about people and their differences? In a graphic organizer like this one, give details about the setting and characters that support the theme.

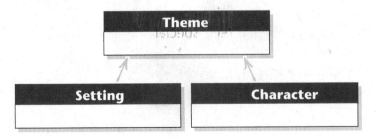

QuickReview

Who's Who in the Story

Professor Hugo: person in charge of the Interplanetary Zoo

Zoo visitors: citizens of Chicago

Horse-spider creatures: creatures from the planet Kaan

Go **Online**
—Assessment

For: Self-test
Visit: www.PHSchool.com
Web Code: ema-6209

Inference: intelligent guess about a story, based on details included in text

Theme: a story's central idea, message, or insight into life

Vocabulary Builder

Practice Follow the directions in each item. Then, explain your answers.

1. Name two items—one that would be a huge *expense* and another that would be a small expense.

2. Give one reason to explain why *interplanetary* travel is rare.

3. Name a person, event, or achievement that you look at with *awe*.

Writing

Use your response to "Zoo" as the springboard for a **letter to the editor** of a local newspaper. In your letter, take a position about whether zoo animals should live in natural habitats instead of cages.

- First, list at least one reason in support of each position. Then, choose which side to take.
- As you draft, state your opinion and include the reasons and details that will convince readers to take your side.

For *Grammar, Vocabulary,* and *Assessment,* see
Build Language Skills, pages 320–321.

Extend Your Learning

Listening and Speaking In "Zoo," some characters say the trip to Earth was worth the expense, while others worry about the safety of travel. Choose a faraway location you would like to visit. Prepare and present a **short speech** to describe the challenges and benefits of traveling to the place you have chosen.

Research and Technology Use the Internet and library or community resources to learn about a zoo in your town, city, or state. Create a **poster** that provides zoo hours, admission fees, special exhibits, and the animals you would recommend others visit. Display your poster with those of your classmates, and compare and contrast the presentation of information.

Build Understanding • *Ribbons*

Background

Cultural Differences The way people show respect for one another often depends on their cultural background. For example, many people in the United States shake hands upon meeting and look directly into other peoples' eyes. In some other cultures, this behavior is considered rude. In "Ribbons," a young American girl faces the problem of reaching across cultures to get to know her Chinese grandmother.

Connecting to the Literature

Reading/Writing Connection Write three sentences of advice that you might give to two people from different cultures who are meeting for the first time. Use at least three of these words: *maximize, minimize, rely, research, ignore.*

Review

For **Reading Skill, Literary Analysis,** and **Vocabulary Builder,** see page 300.

Meet the Author

Laurence **Yep** (b. 1948)

Laurence Yep was born in San Francisco. He grew up in an apartment above his family's grocery store in an African American neighborhood. During his elementary and middle school years, Yep rode a bus to a bilingual school in Chinatown. He feels that these experiences with different cultures led him to write science fiction and fantasy stories in which characters face new worlds and learn new languages and customs.

Adults' Influence When a high school teacher encouraged him to send out his stories for publication, Yep decided to become a professional writer. He is the author of more than forty books, including the Newbery Honor Book *Dragonwings.*

Fast Facts

▶ Yep writes realistic fiction, science fiction, and fantasy for children and teens.

▶ When Yep was 18, he sold his first story to a science-fiction magazine for a penny a word.

Go Online
Author Link

For: More about the author
Visit: www.PHSchool.com
Web Code: eme-9211

Ribbons

Laurence Yep

The sunlight swept over the broad grassy square, across the street, and onto our living-room rug. In that bright, warm rectangle of light, I practiced my ballet. Ian, my little brother, giggled and dodged around me while I did my exercises.

A car stopped outside, and Ian rushed to the window. "She's here! She's here!" he shouted excitedly. "Paw-paw's here!" *Paw-paw* is Chinese for grandmother—for "mother's mother."

I squeezed in beside Ian so I could look out the window, too. Dad's head was just disappearing as he leaned into the trunk of the car. A pile of luggage and cardboard boxes wrapped in rope sat by the curb. "Is that all Grandmother's?" I said. I didn't see how it would fit into my old bedroom.

Mom laughed behind me. "We're lucky she had to leave her furniture behind in Hong Kong." Mom had been trying to get her mother to come to San Francisco for years. Grandmother had finally agreed, but only because the British were going to return the city to the Chinese Communists in 1997. Because Grandmother's airfare and legal expenses had been so high, there wasn't room in the family budget for Madame Oblomov's ballet school. I'd had to stop my daily lessons.

The rear car door opened, and a pair of carved black canes poked out like six-shooters. "Wait, Paw-paw," Dad said, and slammed the trunk shut. He looked sweaty and harassed.

Grandmother, however, was already using her canes to get to her feet. "I'm not helpless," she insisted to Dad.

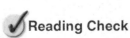

✓ Reading Check

Why does the narrator have to stop her daily ballet lessons?

▲ **Critical Viewing** What do you think this story will be about, based on the picture and the title? **[Predict]**

Ian was relieved. "She speaks English," he said.

"She worked for a British family for years," Mom explained.

Turning, Ian ran toward the stairs. "I've got the door," he cried. Mom and I caught up with him at the front door and made him wait on the porch. "You don't want to knock her over," I said. For weeks, Mom had been rehearsing us for just this moment. Ian was supposed to wait, but in his excitement he began bowing to Grandmother as she struggled up the outside staircase.

Grandmother was a small woman in a padded silk jacket and black slacks. Her hair was pulled back into a bun behind her head. On her small feet she wore a pair of quilted cotton slippers shaped like boots, with furred tops that hid her ankles.

"What's wrong with her feet?" I whispered to Mom.

"They've always been that way. And don't mention it," she said. "She's <u>sensitive</u> about them."

I was instantly curious. "But what happened to them?"

"Wise grandchildren wouldn't ask," Mom warned.

Mom bowed formally as Grandmother reached the porch. "I'm so glad you're here," she said.

Grandmother gazed past us to the stairway leading up to our second-floor apartment. "Why do you have to have so many steps?" she said.

Mom sounded as <u>meek</u> as a child. "I'm sorry, Mother," she said.

Dad tried to change the subject. "That's Stacy, and this little monster is Ian."

"*Joe sun, Paw-paw*," I said. "Good morning, Grandmother." It was afternoon, but that was the only Chinese I knew, and I had been practicing it.

Mother had coached us on a proper Chinese greeting for the last two months, but I thought Grandmother also deserved an American-style bear hug. However, when I tried to put my arms around her and kiss her, she stiffened in surprise. "Nice children don't drool on people," she snapped at me.

To Ian, anything worth doing was worth repeating, so he bowed again. "*Joe sun, Paw-paw*."

Grandmother brightened in an instant. "He has your eyes," she said to Mom.

Mom bent and hefted Ian into her arms. "Let me show you our apartment. You'll be in Stacy's room."

Vocabulary Builder
sensitive (sen´ sə tiv) *adj.* easily hurt

meek (mēk) *adj.* timid; not showing anger

Reading Skill
Make Inferences
Why might Grandmother complain about "so many steps"?

Three Studies of a Dancer in Fourth Position, © 1879/80, Edgar Degas, Art Institute of Chicago

Grandmother didn't even thank me. Instead, she stumped up the stairs after Mom, trying to <u>coax</u> a smile from Ian, who was staring at her over Mom's shoulder.

Grandmother's climb was long, slow, <u>laborious</u>. *Thump, thump, thump.* Her canes struck the boards as she slowly mounted the steps. It sounded like the slow, steady beat of a mechanical heart.

Mom had told us her mother's story often enough. When Mom's father died, Grandmother had strapped my mother to her back and walked across China to Hong Kong to escape the Communists who had taken over her country. I had always thought her trek was heroic, but it seemed even braver when I realized how wobbly she was on her feet.

I was going to follow Grandmother, but Dad waved me down to the sidewalk. "I need you to watch your grandmother's

Vocabulary Builder

coax (kōks) *v.* use gentle persuasion

laborious (lə bôr´ ē əs) *adj.* taking much work or effort

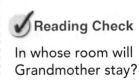Reading Check

In whose room will Grandmother stay?

things until I finish bringing them up," he said. He took a suitcase in either hand and set off, catching up with Grandmother at the foot of the first staircase.

While I waited for him to come back, I inspected Grandmother's pile of belongings. The boxes, webbed with tight cords, were covered with words in Chinese and English. I could almost smell their exotic scent, and in my imagination I pictured sunlit waters lapping at picturesque docks. Hong Kong was probably as exotic to me as America was to Grandmother. Almost without thinking, I began to dance.

Dad came back out, his face red from <u>exertion</u>. "I wish I had half your energy," he said. Crouching, he used the cords to lift a box in each hand.

I pirouetted,[1] and the world spun round and round. "Madame Oblomov said I should still practice every day." I had waited for this day not only for Grandmother's sake but for my own. "Now that Grandmother's here, can I begin my ballet lessons again?" I asked.

Dad turned toward the house. "We'll see, hon."

Disappointment made me protest. "But you said I had to give up the lessons so we could bring her from Hong Kong," I said. "Well, she's here."

Dad hesitated and then set the boxes down. "Try to understand, hon. We've got to set your grandmother up in her own apartment. That's going to take even more money. Don't you want your room back?"

Poor Dad. He looked tired and worried. I should have shut up, but I loved ballet almost as much as I loved him. "Madame put me in the fifth division even though I'm only eleven. If I'm absent much longer, she might make me start over again with the beginners."

"It'll be soon. I promise." He looked guilty as he picked up the boxes and struggled toward the stairs.

Dad had taken away the one hope that had kept me going during my exile[2] from Madame. Suddenly I felt lost, and the following weeks only made me more confused. Mom started laying down all sorts of new rules. First, we couldn't run around or make noise because Grandmother had to rest.

Vocabulary Builder
exertion (eg zʉr´ shən)
n. physical work

Reading Skill
Make Inferences
What can you infer about Stacy from her dancing and her talk with Dad?

---

1. pirouetted (pir´ ōō et´ əd) *v.* whirled around on one foot.
2. exile (eg´ zīl) *n.* a forced absence.

Then we couldn't watch our favorite TV shows because Grandmother couldn't understand them. Instead, we had to watch Westerns on one of the cable stations because it was easier for her to figure out who was the good guy and who was the bad one.

Worst of all, Ian got all of her attention—and her candy and anything else she could bribe him with. It finally got to me on a warm Sunday afternoon a month after she had arrived. I'd just returned home from a long walk in the park with some friends. I was looking forward to something cool and sweet, when I found her giving Ian an ice cream bar I'd bought for myself. "But that was my ice cream bar," I complained as he gulped it down.

"Big sisters need to share with little brothers," Grandmother said, and she patted him on the head to encourage him to go on eating.

When I complained to Mom about how Grandmother was spoiling Ian, she only sighed. "He's a boy, Stacy. Back in China, boys are everything."

It wasn't until I saw Grandmother and Ian together the next day that I thought I really understood why she treated him so much better. She was sitting on a kitchen chair with her head bent over next to his. She had taught Ian enough Chinese so that they could hold short, simple conversations. With their faces so close, I could see how much alike they were.

Ian and I both have the same brown eyes, but his hair is black, while mine is brown, like Dad's. In fact, everything about Ian looks more Chinese. Except for the shape of my eyes, I look as Caucasian as Dad. And yet people sometimes stare at me as if I were a freak. I've always told myself that it's because they're ignorant and never learned manners, but it was really hard to have my own grandmother make me feel that way.

Even so, I kept telling myself: Grandmother is a hero. She saved my mother. She'll like me just as much as she likes Ian once she gets to know me. And, I thought in a flash, the best way to know a person is to know what she loves. For me, that was the ballet.

Ever since Grandmother had arrived, I'd been practicing my ballet privately in the room I now shared with Ian. Now I got out the special box that held my satin toe shoes. I had been so

Reading Skill
Make Inferences
Read between the lines about candy and ice cream to infer Stacy's feelings about living with her Grandmother.

Literary Analysis
Theme What does this passage tell you about the treatment of boys in China? What message about life do these details suggest?

Reading Check

How do things change when Grandmother moves into the house?

proud when Madame said I was ready to use them. I was the youngest girl on pointe[3] at Madame's school. As I lifted them out, the satin ribbons fluttered down around my wrists as if in a welcoming caress. I slipped one of the shoes onto my foot, but when I tried to tie the ribbons around my ankles, the ribbons came off in my hands.

I could have asked Mom to help me reattach them, but then I remembered that at one time Grandmother had supported her family by being a seamstress.

Grandmother was sitting in the big recliner in the living room. She stared uneasily out the window as if she were gazing not upon the broad, green lawn of the square but upon a Martian desert.

"Paw-paw," I said, "can you help me?"

Grandmother gave a start when she turned around and saw the ribbons dangling from my hand. Then she looked down at my bare feet, which were callused from three years of daily lessons. When she looked back at the satin ribbons, it was with a hate and disgust that I had never seen before. "Give those to me." She held out her hand.

I clutched the ribbons tightly against my stomach. "Why?"

"They'll ruin your feet." She lunged toward me and tried to snatch them away.

Angry and bewildered, I retreated a few steps and showed her the shoe. "No, they're for dancing!"

All Grandmother could see, though, was the ribbons. She managed to totter to her feet without the canes and almost fell forward on her face. Somehow, she regained her balance. Arms reaching out, she stumbled clumsily after me. "Lies!" she said.

"It's the truth!" I backed up so fast that I bumped into Mom as she came running from the kitchen.

Mom immediately assumed it was my fault. "Stop yelling at your grandmother!" she said.

By this point, I was in tears. "She's taken everything else. Now she wants my toe-shoe ribbons."

Grandmother panted as she leaned on Mom. "How could you do that to your own daughter?"

"It's not like you think," Mom tried to explain.

However, Grandmother was too upset to listen. "Take them away!"

Reading Skill
Make Inferences
What can you infer about Grandmother based on her reaction to the ribbons?

---

3. **on pointe** (pwant) dancing on the tip of the toe (of the ballet shoe).

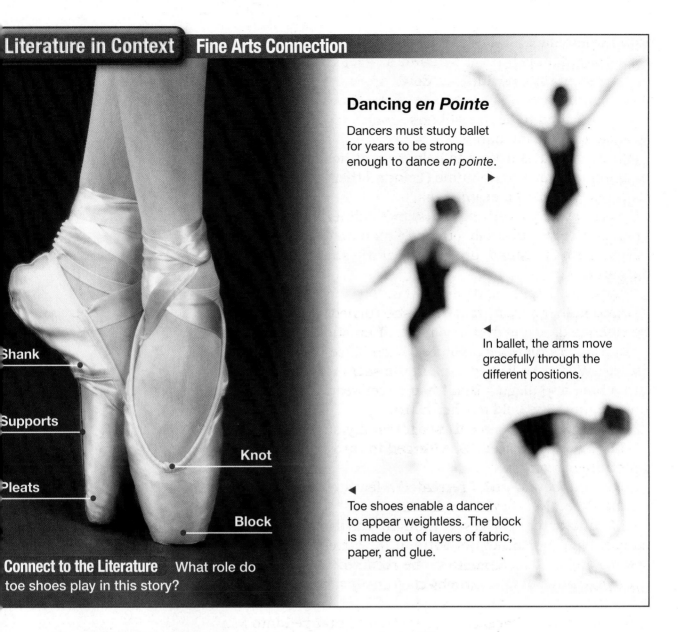

Shank

Supports

Pleats

Knot

Block

Dancing *en Pointe*

Dancers must study ballet for years to be strong enough to dance *en pointe*. ▶

◀ In ballet, the arms move gracefully through the different positions.

◀ Toe shoes enable a dancer to appear weightless. The block is made out of layers of fabric, paper, and glue.

Connect to the Literature What role do toe shoes play in this story?

Mom helped Grandmother back to her easy chair. "You don't understand," Mom said.

All Grandmother did was stare at the ribbons as she sat back down in the chair. "Take them away. Burn them. Bury them."

Mom sighed. "Yes, Mother."

As Mom came over to me, I stared at her in amazement. "Aren't you going to stand up for me?"

But she acted as if she wanted to break any ties between us. "Can't you see how worked up Paw-paw is?" she whispered. "She won't listen to reason. Give her some time. Let her cool off." She

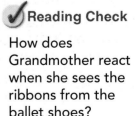

Reading Check

How does Grandmother react when she sees the ribbons from the ballet shoes?

worked the ribbons away from my stunned fingers. Then she also took the shoe.

For the rest of the day, Grandmother just turned away every time Mom and I tried to raise the subject. It was as if she didn't want to even think about satin ribbons.

That evening, after the dozenth attempt, I finally said to Mom, "She's so weird. What's so bad about satin ribbons?"

"She associates them with something awful that happened to her," Mom said.

That puzzled me even more. "What was that?"

She shook her head. "I'm sorry. She made me promise never to talk about it to anyone."

The next morning, I decided that if Grandmother was going to be mean to me, then I would be mean to her. I began to ignore her. When she entered a room I was in, I would deliberately turn around and leave.

For the rest of the day, things got more and more tense. Then I happened to go into the bathroom early that evening. The door wasn't locked, so I thought it was unoccupied, but Grandmother was sitting fully clothed on the edge of the bathtub. Her slacks were rolled up to her knees and she had her feet soaking in a pan of water.

"Don't you know how to knock?" she snapped, and dropped a towel over her feet.

However, she wasn't quick enough, because I saw her bare feet for the first time. Her feet were like taffy that someone

Madame X, 1993, Hung Liu, Courtesy Steinbaum Krauss Gallery, New York, New York

▲ **Critical Viewing** Based on this painting and on Grandmother's actions, what do you conclude about her experiences with ribbons? **[Draw Conclusions]**

had stretched out and twisted. Each foot bent downward in a way that feet were not meant to, and her toes stuck out at odd angles, more like lumps than toes. I didn't think she had all ten of them, either.

"What happened to your feet?" I whispered in shock.

Looking ashamed, Grandmother flapped a hand in the air for me to go. "None of your business. Now get out."

She must have said something to Mom, though, because that night Mom came in and sat on my bed. Ian was outside playing with Grandmother. "Your grandmother's very upset, Stacy," Mom said.

"I didn't mean to look," I said. "It was horrible." Even when I closed my eyes, I could see her mangled feet.

I opened my eyes when I felt Mom's hand on my shoulder. "She was so ashamed of them that she didn't like even me to see them," she said.

"What happened to them?" I wondered.

Mom's forehead furrowed as if she wasn't sure how to explain things. "There was a time back in China when people thought women's feet had to be shaped a certain way to look beautiful. When a girl was about five, her mother would gradually bend her toes under the sole of her foot."

"Ugh." Just thinking about it made my own feet ache. "Her own mother did that to her?"

Mom smiled apologetically. "Her mother and father thought it would make their little girl attractive so she could marry a rich man. They were still doing it in some of the back areas of China long after it was outlawed in the rest of the country."

I shook my head. "There's nothing lovely about those feet."

"I know. But they were usually bound up in silk ribbons." Mom brushed some of the hair from my eyes. "Because they were a symbol of the old days, Paw-paw undid the ribbons as soon as we were free in Hong Kong—even though they kept back the pain."

I was even more puzzled now. "How did the ribbons do that?"

Mom began to brush my hair with quick, light strokes. "The ribbons kept the blood from circulating freely and bringing more feeling to her feet. Once the ribbons were gone, her feet ached. They probably still do."

I rubbed my own foot in sympathy. "But she doesn't complain."

Literary Analysis

Theme Which details here about Chinese customs in the past help you see the message of this story?

Reading Check

What happened to Grandmother's feet when she was a child?

"That's how tough she is," Mom said.

Finally the truth dawned on me. "And she mistook my toe-shoe ribbons for her old ones."

Mom lowered the brush and nodded solemnly. "And she didn't want you to go through the same pain she had."

I guess Grandmother loved me in her own way. When she came into the bedroom with Ian later that evening, I didn't leave. However, she tried to ignore me—as if I had become tainted by her secret.

When Ian demanded a story, I sighed. "All right. But only one."

Naturally, Ian chose the fattest story he could, which was my old collection of fairy tales by Hans Christian Andersen. Years of reading had cracked the spine so that the book fell open automatically in his hands to the story that had been my favorite when I was small. It was the original story of "The Little Mermaid"—not the cartoon. The picture illustrating the tale showed the mermaid posed like a ballerina in the middle of the throne room.

"This one," Ian said, and pointed to the picture of the Little Mermaid.

When Grandmother and Ian sat down on my bed, I began to read. However, when I got to the part where the Little Mermaid could walk on land, I stopped.

Ian was impatient. "Come on, read," he ordered, patting the page.

"After that," I went on, "each step hurt her as if she were walking on a knife." I couldn't help looking up at Grandmother.

This time she was the one to pat the page. "Go on. Tell me more about the mermaid."

So I went on reading to the very end, where the Little Mermaid changes into sea foam. "That's a dumb ending," Ian said. "Who wants to be pollution?"

"Sea foam isn't pollution. It's just bubbles," I explained. "The important thing was that she wanted to walk even though it hurt."

▲ Critical Viewing
How would it feel to wear toe shoes?
[Connect]

"I would rather have gone on swimming," Ian insisted.

"But maybe she wanted to see new places and people by going on the land," Grandmother said softly. "If she had kept her tail, the land people would have thought she was odd. They might even have made fun of her."

When she glanced at her own feet, I thought she might be talking about herself—so I seized my chance. "My satin ribbons aren't like your old silk ones. I use them to tie my toe shoes on when I dance." Setting the book down, I got out my other shoe. "Look."

Grandmother fingered the dangling ribbons and then pointed at my bare feet. "But you already have calluses there."

I began to dance before Grandmother could stop me. After a minute, I struck a pose on half-toe. "See? I can move fine."

She took my hand and patted it clumsily. I think it was the first time she had showed me any sign of affection. "When I saw those ribbons, I didn't want you feeling pain like I do."

I covered her hands with mine. "I just wanted to show you what I love best—dancing."

"And I love my children," she said. I could hear the ache in her voice. "And my grandchildren. I don't want anything bad to happen to you."

Suddenly I felt as if there were an invisible ribbon binding us, tougher than silk and satin, stronger even than steel; and it joined her to Mom and Mom to me.

I wanted to hug her so badly that I just did. Though she was stiff at first, she gradually softened in my arms.

"'Let me have my ribbons and my shoes," I said in a low voice. "Let me dance."

"Yes, yes," she whispered fiercely.

I felt something on my cheek and realized she was crying, and then I began crying, too.

"So much to learn," she said, and began hugging me back. "So much to learn."

Literary Analysis
Theme What details in this paragraph support a theme of understanding cultural differences?

Reading Skill
Make Inferences Why do you think the narrator and her grandmother are crying?

Apply the Skills

Ribbons

Thinking About the Selection

1. **Respond:** What do you think is the hardest part of Stacy's experiences with her grandmother? Explain.
2. **(a) Recall:** Identify two examples that show how life changes in Stacy's house when Grandmother arrives. **(b) Analyze Cause and Effect:** For each, tell how you would expect Stacy to feel about these changes. **(c) Evaluate:** Discuss with a partner whether or not you sympathize with Stacy. Then discuss how hearing your partner's responses did or did not change your view.
3. **(a) Recall:** How does Stacy learn the secret of Grandmother's feet? **(b) Connect:** How does Stacy's attitude change after her mother explains older Chinese customs?
4. **(a) Recall:** Why does Grandmother react so violently to Stacy's ribbons? **(b) Deduce:** How do Stacy and her grandmother eventually come to appreciate each other?

Reading Skill

5. The author describes Grandmother's arrival by saying, "The rear car door opened, and a pair of carved black canes poked out like six-shooters." Why do you think he includes those details instead of simply introducing the characters by name?
6. Grandmother carried her daughter on her back to Hong Kong to escape her enemy. What questions might you ask to help you make an **inference** about Grandmother's life?

Literary Analysis

7. What **theme** does the story convey about understanding between grandparents and grandchildren? In a graphic organizer like this one, give details about the setting and the characters that support the theme.

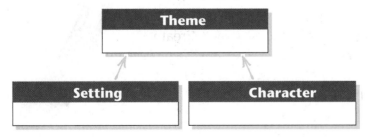

QuickReview

Story at a Glance

When a Chinese grandmother comes to live with her American family, the granddaughter learns an important lesson.

Go Online
——Assessment
For: Self-test
Visit: www.PHSchool.com
Web Code: ema-6210

Inference: intelligent guess about a story, based on details included in text

Theme: a story's central idea, message, or insight into life

Vocabulary Builder

Practice Using a vocabulary word from the "Ribbons" vocabulary list on page 300, rewrite each of the following sentences to convey the same basic meaning.

1. Moving the furniture out of the room was a difficult task.
2. After the strain of the long swim, we took a rest.
3. How can we persuade her to sit in the dentist's chair?
4. That big dog is as timid and shy as a little lamb.
5. My younger sister is fun to tease because she is very easily irritated.

Writing

Use your response to "Ribbons" as the springboard for a **letter to the editor** of a local newspaper. In your letter, take a position about whether young people should participate in extra schooling by taking art classes or participating in sports.

- First, list at least one reason in support of each position. Then, choose which side to take.
- As you draft, state your opinion and include the reasons and details that will convince readers to take your side.

For *Grammar, Vocabulary,* and *Assessment,* see **Build Language Skills,** pages 320–321.

Extend Your Learning

Listening and Speaking At the end of "Ribbons," Stacy has learned to accept and better understand her grandmother. Prepare and present a **short speech** that Stacy might give to her classmates to explain the challenges and benefits of her experiences.

Research and Technology Use the Internet and library resources to conduct research on Stacy's passion—ballet. Create a **poster** that provides information about the basic arm and foot positions and the benefits of learning ballet. Display your poster with those of your classmates, and compare and contrast your presentation of the information.

Build Language Skills

Zoo • Ribbons

Vocabulary Skill

Prefixes The word *conclude* begins with the **prefix con-,** which means "together" or "the same." One meaning of *conclude* is "pull together details to reach an opinion or an idea."

The **prefix sub-** means "under" or "below" and is the prefix in the word "subject." One meaning of *subject* is "a topic under study or discussion."

Practice Write a possible meaning for each word based on the meaning of the prefix and the context of the sentence. Check the meanings in a dictionary. Explain any differences in the meaning you suggested and the actual meaning. Then, use each word in a sentence.

1. The king's *subjects* obeyed his commands.
2. We reached a *conclusion* based on the clues.
3. The children were *subjected* to a stern lecture.
4. Our plans are *subject* to change based on the weather.
5. The ceremony *concluded* with a song.

Grammar Lesson

Adverbs An **adverb** is a word that modifies or describes a verb, an adjective, or another adverb. Adverbs provide information by answering the question *how? when? where? how often?* or *to what extent?* Many adverbs end in the suffix *-ly.* The chart shows examples:

MorePractice

For more practice with adverbs, see R32.

How?	When?	Where?	How often?	To what extent?
She paced *nervously.*	I will finish it *later.*	The robins flew *away.*	Linda *always* laughs.	Luke moved *slightly.*

Practice Identify each adverb and the word it modifies. Tell what question it answers.

1. He proudly held the team's trophy.
2. I have the magazine here.
3. Dave filled the jar completely.
4. Juan never runs in a race.
5. I will visit my aunt tomorrow.

W͟G Prentice Hall Writing and Grammar Connection: Chapter 16, Section 2

Reading: Make Inferences

Directions: *Read the passage. Then, answer the questions.*

Ella absentmindedly pushed a damp strand of hair away from her brow as she walked up the stairs to the library. "I'd love a nice, cool drink of lemonade right about now," she thought.

Ms. Lincoln had already assigned her English class a report. Ella had decided to write about her favorite subject, pets.

Ella sat down at the table and began looking through the books she had gathered from the shelves. An hour later, Ella stacked the books she wanted to take home from the library. "I'll type my notes up when I get home," she thought. "And I'll have a cool drink while I work."

1. What inference can you make about the weather?
   A It is hot.
   B It is very cold.
   C It is cloudy and rainy.
   D It is a cool and breezy.

2. You can infer that Ms. Lincoln is
   A the librarian.
   B Ella's mother.
   C Ella's English teacher.
   D Ella's aunt.

3. The books Ella gathers are
   A cookbooks that tell how to make lemonade.
   B picture books for children.
   C books about libraries.
   D books about taking care of pets.

4. Which word best describes Ella?
   A brave
   B responsible
   C unhappy
   D cautious

Timed Writing: Literary Interpretation [Interpretation]

Review "Zoo" or "Ribbons." In a brief essay, identify and discuss the theme of the story. Support your interpretation with examples from the text. **(30 minutes)**

 Writing Workshop: *Work in Progress*

Short Story

Choose two conflicts from the list in your portfolio. For each conflict, jot down two or three ideas about how it might be resolved.

Irony

Irony involves a contradiction or contrast of some kind.

- In **situational irony**, something takes place that a character or reader does not expect to happen. For example, people note the irony when a fire station burns down.
- In **verbal irony,** a writer, speaker, or character says something that deliberately contradicts what he or she actually means. A jealous runner-up who says to an arch rival, "You deserved the medal" may be speaking ironically if the runner-up means, "You deserved the *second-place* medal."

Comparing Irony

As you read "After Twenty Years" and "He—y, Come on Ou—t!" look for examples of situational irony. Ask yourself questions like these to help understand the author's use of irony:

- What details lead you to expect a certain outcome?
- What happens instead of the outcome you expect?
- What details may have been clues to the outcome?

Use a graphic organizer like this to record your observations.

	Story
Problem	
Expected Outcome	
Details Supporting This Idea	
Actual Ending	
Clues in Story	

Vocabulary Builder

After Twenty Years

- **spectators** (spek´ tāt´ erz) *n.* onlookers (p. 324) *The spectators watched the burning house in horror.*

- **intricate** (in´ tri kit) *adj.* complex; detailed (p. 324) *The oil painting had an intricate frame.*

- **destiny** (des´ tə nē) *n.* fate; pre-planned course of events (p. 325) *I hope my destiny is to live a long time.*

- **simultaneously** (sī´ məl tā´ nē əs lē) *adv.* at the same time (p. 327) *The racers start simultaneously, but only one can win.*

He—y, Come on Ou—t!

- **apparent** (ə par´ ənt) *adj.* seeming (p. 330) *Her eyes, still red from crying, undercut her apparent cheer.*

- **plausible** (plô´ zə bəl) *adj.* seemingly true; acceptable (p. 330) *His excuse was plausible, so I did not question it.*

- **proposal** (prə pōz´ əl) *n.* plan; offer (p. 330) *Everyone welcomed Mom's proposal that she drive us to the movies.*

Build Understanding

Connecting to the Literature

Reading/Writing Connection The stories "After Twenty Years" and "He—y, Come on Ou—t!" involve surprises. Think about a time when you were surprised by a person or an event. Write a few sentences telling about this experience. Use at least three of the following words: *affect, anticipate, react, reveal.*

Meet the Authors

O. **Henry** (1862–1910)

O. Henry is the pen name of William Sydney Porter. He is known for his warm, witty short stories featuring ordinary people. Porter held many jobs, including working on a sheep ranch, in a bank, in a newspaper office, and as the publisher of a humor magazine. Later, Porter was sentenced to prison for stealing bank funds, a crime he may not have committed.

Finding a New Identity While serving time, Porter wrote short stories. On his release, he moved to New York City and started a career as a writer, using the name O. Henry to shield his identity. Many of his 300 stories are inspired by his time in prison, where he gained an understanding of people on both sides of the law.

Shinichi **Hoshi** (1926–1997)

Shinichi Hoshi, a Japanese writer, is known for his "short-short stories," in which he makes observations about human nature and society. Hoshi wrote more than a thousand short-short stories as well as longer fantasy stories, detective stories, biographies, and travel articles. In addition, he was one of the first Japanese science-fiction writers. Hoshi's stories have been translated into many languages, and devoted readers enjoy their unexpected plot turns.

Go Online
Author Link
For: More about the authors
Visit: www.PHSchool.com
Web Code: eme-9212

After Twenty Years

O. Henry

The policeman on the beat moved up the avenue impressively. The impressiveness was habitual and not for show, for <u>spectators</u> were few. The time was barely 10 o'clock at night, but chilly gusts of wind with a taste of rain in them had well nigh[1] depeopled the streets.

Trying doors as he went, twirling his club with many <u>intricate</u> and artful movements, turning now and then to cast his watchful eye down the pacific thoroughfare,[2] the officer, with his stalwart form and slight swagger, made a fine picture of a guardian of the peace. The vicinity was one that kept early hours. Now and then you might see the lights of a cigar store or of an all-night lunch counter; but the majority of the doors belonged to business places that had long since been closed.

When about midway of a certain block the policeman suddenly slowed his walk. In the doorway of a darkened hardware store a man leaned, with an unlighted cigar in his mouth. As the policeman walked up to him the man spoke up quickly.

"It's all right, officer," he said, reassuringly. "I'm just waiting for a friend. It's an appointment made twenty years ago. Sounds a little funny to you, doesn't it? Well, I'll explain if you'd like to make certain it's all straight. About that long ago there used to be a restaurant where this store stands—'Big Joe' Brady's restaurant."

"Until five years ago," said the policeman. "It was torn down then."

The man in the doorway struck a match and lit his cigar. The light showed a pale, square-jawed face with keen eyes, and a little white scar near his right eyebrow. His scarfpin was a large diamond, oddly set.

"Twenty years ago tonight," said the man, "I dined here at 'Big Joe' Brady's with Jimmy Wells, my best chum, and the finest chap in the world. He and I were raised here in New York, just like two brothers, together. I was eighteen and

---

1. well nigh (nī) very nearly.
2. pacific thoroughfare calm street.

Vocabulary Builder

spectators (spek′ tāt′ erz) *n.* onlookers

intricate (in′ tri kit) *adj.* complex; detailed

Nighthawks, Edward Hopper, The Art Institute of Chicago

Jimmy was twenty. The next morning I was to start for the West to make my fortune. You couldn't have dragged Jimmy out of New York; he thought it was the only place on earth. Well, we agreed that night that we would meet here again exactly twenty years from that date and time, no matter what our conditions might be or from what distance we might have to come. We figured that in twenty years each of us ought to have our <u>destiny</u> worked out and our fortunes made, whatever they were going to be."

"It sounds pretty interesting," said the policeman. "Rather a long time between meets, though, it seems to me. Haven't you heard from your friend since you left?"

"Well, yes, for a time we corresponded," said the other. "But after a year or two we lost track of each other. You see, the West is a pretty big proposition, and I kept hustling around over it pretty lively. But I know Jimmy will meet me here if he's alive, for he always was the truest, stanchest old chap in the world. He'll never forget. I came a thousand miles to stand in this door tonight, and it's worth it if my old partner turns up."

The waiting man pulled out a handsome watch, the lids of it set with small diamonds.

"Three minutes to ten," he announced. "It was exactly ten o'clock when we parted here at the restaurant door."

"Did pretty well out West, didn't you?" asked the policeman.

▲ **Critical Viewing**
What details in this painting match the setting of the story? **[Connect]**

Vocabulary Builder
destiny (des´ tə nē) *n.* fate; preplanned course of events

✓ **Reading Check**

What is the officer doing?

"You bet! I hope Jimmy has done half as well. He was a kind of plodder, though, good fellow as he was. I've had to compete with some of the sharpest wits going to get my pile. A man gets in a groove in New York. It takes the West to put a razor-edge on him."

The policeman twirled his club and took a step or two.

"I'll be on my way. Hope your friend comes around all right. Going to call time on him sharp?"

"I should say not!" said the other. "I'll give him half an hour at least. If Jimmy is alive on earth he'll be here by that time. So long, officer."

"Good-night, sir," said the policeman, passing on along his beat, trying doors as he went.

There was now a fine, cold drizzle falling, and the wind had risen from its uncertain puffs into a steady blow. The few foot passengers astir in that quarter hurried dismally and silently along with coat collars turned high and pocketed hands. And in the door of the hardware store the man who had come a thousand miles to fill an appointment, uncertain almost to absurdity,[3] with the friend of his youth, smoked his cigar and waited.

About twenty minutes he waited, and then a tall man in a long overcoat, with collar turned up to his ears, hurried across from the opposite side of the street. He went directly to the waiting man.

"Is that you, Bob?" he asked, doubtfully.

"Is that you, Jimmy Wells?" cried the man in the door.

"Bless my heart!" exclaimed the new arrival, grasping both the other's hands with his own. "It's Bob, sure as fate. I was certain I'd find you here if you were still in existence. Well, well, well!—twenty years is a long time. The old restaurant's gone, Bob; I wish it had lasted, so we could have had another dinner there. How has the West treated you, old man?"

"Bully;[4] it has given me everything I asked it for. You've changed lots, Jimmy. I never thought you were so tall by two or three inches."

"Oh, I grew a bit after I was twenty."

"Doing well in New York, Jimmy?"

"Moderately. I have a position in one of the city departments. Come on, Bob; we'll go around to a place I know of, and have a good long talk about old times."

Literary Analysis
Irony Based on the story so far, do you expect the old friends to reunite? Explain your answer.

Literary Analysis
Irony Did you expect Jimmy to show up for the meeting? Why or why not?

---

3. **absurdity** (ab sur′də tē) nonsense.
4. **Bully** interj. very good.

The two men started up the street, arm in arm. The man from the West, his egotism enlarged by success, was beginning to outline the history of his career. The other, submerged in his overcoat, listened with interest.

At the corner stood a drug store, brilliant with electric lights. When they came into this glare each of them turned <u>simultaneously</u> to gaze upon the other's face.

The man from the West stopped suddenly and released his arm.

"You're not Jimmy Wells," he snapped. "Twenty years is a long time, but not long enough to change a man's nose from a Roman to a pug."[5]

"It sometimes changes a good man into a bad one," said the tall man. "You've been under arrest for ten minutes, 'Silky' Bob. Chicago thinks you may have dropped over our way and wires us she wants to have a chat with you. Going quietly are you? That's sensible. Now, before we go to the station here's a note I was asked to hand to you. You may read it here at the window. It's from Patrolman Wells."

The man from the West unfolded the little piece of paper handed him. His hand was steady when he began to read, but it trembled a little by the time he had finished. The note was rather short.

Bob: I was at the appointed place on time. When you struck the match to light your cigar I saw it was the face of the man wanted in Chicago. Somehow I couldn't do it myself, so I went around and got a plain clothes man to do the job. Jimmy.

---

5. **change a man's nose from a Roman to a pug** A Roman nose has a high, prominent bridge, but a pug nose is short, thick, and turned up at the end.

Literary Analysis
Irony Which of the two men seems to have had more success in the twenty years since they last met?

Vocabulary Builder
simultaneously (sī məl tā′ nē əs lē) *adv.* at the same time

Literary Analysis
Irony How does the patrolman's name indicate the irony of the conversation with the policeman at the beginning of this story?

Thinking About the Selection

1. **(a) Recall:** Where is the story set? **(b) Analyze:** Describe the atmosphere, or mood, using two details from the story.

2. **(a) Recall:** How does Bob describe Jimmy—both his strengths and weaknesses? **(b) Infer:** How did Bob spend his time away from his hometown?

3. **(a) Support:** What evidence shows that both Bob and Jimmy are proud of their accomplishments? **(b) Make a Judgment:** Who has been more successful, Bob or Jimmy? Explain your answer.

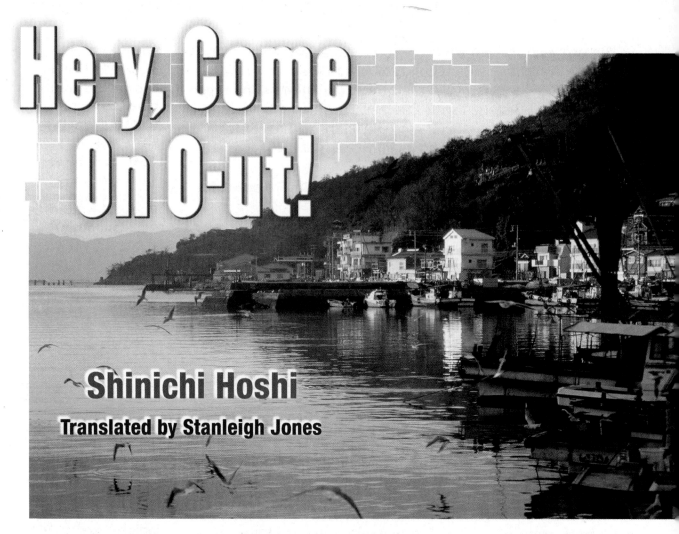

He-y, Come On O-ut!

Shinichi Hoshi

Translated by Stanleigh Jones

The typhoon had passed and the sky was a gorgeous blue. Even a certain village not far from the city had suffered damage. A little distance from the village and near the mountains, a small shrine had been swept away by a landslide.

"I wonder how long that shrine's been here."

"Well, in any case, it must have been here since an awfully long time ago."

"We've got to rebuild it right away."

While the villagers exchanged views, several more of their number came over.

"It sure was wrecked."

"I think it used to be right here."

"No, looks like it was a little more over there."

Just then one of them raised his voice. "Hey, what in the world is this hole?"

Where they had all gathered there was a hole about a meter in diameter. They peered in, but it was so dark nothing could

▲ Critical Viewing
In what ways do people who live in towns like the one shown have to depend on their environment?
[Analyze]

be seen. However, it gave one the feeling that it was so deep it went clear through to the center of the earth.

There was even one person who said, "I wonder if it's a fox's hole."

"He—y, come on ou—t!" shouted a young man into the hole. There was no echo from the bottom. Next he picked up a pebble and was about to throw it in.

"You might bring down a curse on us. Lay off," warned an old man, but the younger one energetically threw the pebble in. As before, however, there was no answering response from the bottom. The villagers cut down some trees, tied them with rope and made a fence which they put around the hole. Then they repaired to the village.

"What do you suppose we ought to do?"

"Shouldn't we build the shrine up just as it was over the hole?"

A day passed with no agreement. The news traveled fast, and a car from the newspaper company rushed over. In no time a scientist came out, and with an all-knowing expression on his face he went over to the hole. Next, a bunch of gawking curiosity seekers showed up; one could also pick out here and there men of shifty glances who appeared to be concessionaires.[1] Concerned that someone might fall into the hole, a policeman from the local substation kept a careful watch.

One newspaper reporter tied a weight to the end of a long cord and lowered it into the hole. A long way down it went. The cord ran out, however, and he tried to pull it out, but it would not come back up. Two or three people helped out, but when they all pulled too hard, the cord parted at the edge of the hole. Another reporter, a camera in hand, who had been watching all of this, quietly untied a stout rope that had been wound around his waist.

The scientist contacted people at his laboratory and had them bring out a high-powered bull horn, with which he was going to check out the echo from the hole's bottom. He tried switching through various sounds, but there was no echo. The scientist was puzzled, but he could not very well give up with everyone watching him so intently. He put the bull horn right up to the hole, turned it to its highest volume, and let it sound continuously for a long time. It was a noise that would

Literary Analysis
Irony What expectations does the author create in the reader's mind about the hole?

Reading Check

What is unusual about the hole where the shrine used to be?

---

1. **concessionaires** (kən sesh′ ə nerz′) *n.* business people.

have carried several dozen kilometers above ground. But the hole just calmly swallowed up the sound.

In his own mind the scientist was at a loss, but with a look of <u>apparent</u> composure he cut off the sound and, in a manner suggesting that the whole thing had a perfectly <u>plausible</u> explanation, said simply, "Fill it in."

Safer to get rid of something one didn't understand.

The onlookers, disappointed that this was all that was going to happen, prepared to disperse. Just then one of the concessionaires, having broken through the throng and come forward, made a <u>proposal</u>.

"Let me have that hole. I'll fill it in for you."

"We'd be grateful to you for filling it in," replied the mayor of the village, "but we can't very well give you the hole. We have to build a shrine there."

"If it's a shrine you want, I'll build you a fine one later. Shall I make it with an attached meeting hall?"

Before the mayor could answer, the people of the village all shouted out.

"Really? Well, in that case, we ought to have it closer to the village."

"It's just an old hole. We'll give it to you!"

So it was settled. And the mayor, of course, had no objection.

The concessionaire was true to his promise. It was small, but closer to the village he did build for them a shrine with an attached meeting hall.

About the time the autumn festival was held at the new shrine, the hole-filling company established by the concessionaire hung out its small shingle at a shack near the hole.

The concessionaire had his cohorts mount a loud campaign in the city. "We've got a fabulously deep hole! Scientists say it's at least five thousand meters deep! Perfect for the disposal of such things as waste from nuclear reactors."

Government authorities granted permission. Nuclear power plants fought for contracts. The people of the village were a bit worried about this, but they consented when it was explained that there would be absolutely no above-ground contamination[2] for several thousand years and that they would share in the profits. Into the bargain, very shortly a magnificent road was built from the city to the village.

---

2. **contamination** (kən tam´ ə nā´ shən) *n.* pollution by poison or other dangerous substances.

Trucks rolled in over the road, transporting lead boxes. Above the hole the lids were opened, and the wastes from nuclear reactors tumbled away into the hole.

From the Foreign Ministry and the Defense Agency boxes of unnecessary classified documents were brought for disposal. Officials who came to supervise the disposal held discussions on golf. The lesser functionaries, as they threw in the papers, chatted about pinball.

The hole showed no signs of filling up. It was awfully deep, thought some; or else it might be very spacious at the bottom. Little by little the hole-filling company expanded its business.

Bodies of animals used in contagious disease experiments at the universities were brought out, and to these were added the unclaimed corpses of vagrants. Better than dumping all of its garbage in the ocean, went the thinking in the city, and plans were made for a long pipe to carry it to the hole.

The hole gave peace of mind to the dwellers of the city. They concentrated solely on producing one thing after another. Everyone disliked thinking about the eventual consequences. People wanted only to work for production companies and sales corporations; they had no interest in becoming junk

▲ Critical Viewing
What feelings do you think people would have after visiting a shrine like the one shown? [Connect]

Literary Analysis
Irony Does this use of the hole seem like a good idea? Why or why not?

✓ Reading Check
In what ways has the concessionaire used the hole to his advantage?

dealers. But, it was thought, these problems too would gradually be resolved by the hole.

Young girls whose betrothals[3] had been arranged discarded old diaries in the hole. There were also those who were inaugurating new love affairs and threw into the hole old photographs of themselves taken with former sweethearts. The police felt comforted as they used the hole to get rid of accumulations of expertly done counterfeit bills. Criminals breathed easier after throwing material evidence into the hole.

Whatever one wished to discard, the hole accepted it all. The hole cleansed the city of its filth; the sea and sky seemed to have become a bit clearer than before.

Aiming at the heavens, new buildings went on being constructed one after the other.

One day, atop the high steel frame of a new building under construction, a workman was taking a break. Above his head he heard a voice shout:

"He—y, come on ou—t!"

But, in the sky to which he lifted his gaze there was nothing at all. A clear blue sky merely spread over all. He thought it must be his imagination. Then, as he resumed his former position, from the direction where the voice had come, a small pebble skimmed by him and fell on past.

The man, however, was gazing in idle reverie[4] at the city's skyline growing ever more beautiful, and he failed to notice.

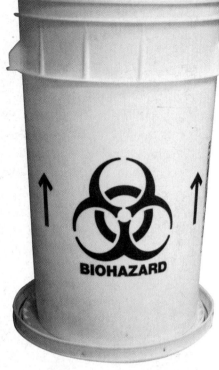

▲ **Critical Viewing**
What does the labeling on the container tell you about its contents? **[Hypothesize]**

---

3. betrothals (bē trōth´ əlz) *n.* promises of marriage.
4. idle reverie (rev´ ə rē) *n.* daydreaming.

Thinking About the Selection

1. **(a) Recall:** What had stood before the hole appeared, and for how long? **(b) Infer:** What is the author suggesting about the site?

2. **(a) Recall:** What does the concessionaire offer to do with the hole? **(b) Analyze Causes and Effects:** What is the result of the concessionaire's action?

3. **(a) Synthesize:** What comment do you think the author may be making about people and the environment? **(b) Generalize:** What message does the author suggest when a voice and a pebble apparently come out of the hole?

Apply the Skills

Comparing Irony

1. Ironic endings can entertain or shock. Did the end of O. Henry's story entertain or shock you? Explain.

2. Ironic endings can make a point about a social issue. Did the ending of "He—y, Come on Ou—t!" change your mind or confirm your thinking about something? Explain.

3. Create a chart to compare the irony in these stories. **(a)** In the first column, identify the irony you found. **(b)** In the second column, explain what the irony tells you about the characters. **(c)** In the third column, explain what message the author makes through the use of irony.

	What It Says	What It Means	Why It Is Important
After Twenty Years			
He—y, Come on Ou—t!			

Writing to Compare Literary Works

In an essay, compare your reactions to "After Twenty Years" and "He—y, Come on Ou—t!" based on the authors' use of irony. Use these questions to get started:

- Which story did you find more believable?
- Is believability important to you when you respond to ironic stories?
- Which story's ironic message did you understand more easily? Why?

Vocabulary Builder

Practice Use each word pair correctly in a sentence.

1. proposal; business
2. apparent; mistake
3. simultaneously; laugh
4. spectators; concert
5. intricate; pattern
6. plausible; court
7. destiny; life

QuickReview

Irony: a contradiction between what is expected and what happens, including *situational irony* and *verbal irony*.

Go Online
—Assessment
For: Self-test
Visit: www.PHSchool.com
Web Code: ema-6211

Reading

Directions: *Read the selection. Then, answer the questions.*

Tina skipped down the boardwalk and onto the sand. The morning sun glistened on the waves, and a warm breeze stirred the dune grasses. Humming quietly to herself, Tina walked along, picking up interesting shells as she went. She was assembling a collection for her grandmother, who liked to use them in craft projects. Later, Tina would wrap the shells carefully to prevent them from breaking. Then she would put them in a box and mail them off to her grandmother. In the meantime, she would enjoy her beautiful surroundings, because tomorrow her family would head back home. She would be glad to see her friends after a two-week absence, but Tina really hated to think of leaving.

1. **From details in the first two sentences, you can infer that the story is set**
   A   in a park.
   B   at the beach.
   C   near the mountains.
   D   on an island.

2. **What can you infer about shells from the detail about sending the shells to Tina's grandmother?**
   A   Shells are delicate.
   B   Shells are hard to find.
   C   Shells come in many colors.
   D   Shells are popular keepsakes.

3. **Which two details help you infer that Tina is on vacation?**
   A   She is in a place with warm breezes, and she hums to herself.
   B   She skips down the boardwalk, and she picks up shells.
   C   She is on the sand, and she mails a package to her grandmother.
   D   She will go home tomorrow, and she has been away for two weeks.

4. **Based on details, which word best describes how Tina feels at the beginning of the story?**
   A   contented
   B   nervous
   C   overjoyed
   D   bored

5. **Based on details in the last sentence, what can you infer about Tina?**
   A   She has enjoyed her vacation.
   B   She does not like her home.
   C   She is good at making friends.
   D   She has a supportive family.

Vocabulary

Directions: *Choose the word that best completes each of the following sentences.*

6. An informative article should be written by an expert to be _____.
   A subjective
   B exemplary
   C credible
   D argumentative

7. From all of the evidence the jury _____ that the defendant was guilty.
   A subjected
   B objected
   C concluded
   D required

8. The adult's _____ on the snowstorm was different from the child's view.
   A objective
   B perspective
   C inference
   D obligation

9. My favorite _____ is history; I like to study events of the past.
   A subject
   B object
   C conclusion
   D prediction

10. The _____ of all the attention was a small, brown puppy.
    A subject
    B object
    C conclusion
    D reason

Directions: *Choose the most likely meaning for each word.*

11. subterranean
    A on the surface of the Earth
    B beneath the Earth's surface
    C above the Earth's surface
    D near the Earth's surface

12. consensus
    A an agreement arrived at by a group
    B an argument
    C something without sense
    D an action against an individual

13. constellation
    A the light that shines from a star
    B the motion of stars
    C a group of stars that form a pattern
    D everything that exists under the stars

14. subdivision
    A a tract of land divided into small lots for sale
    B several parcels of land purchased together
    C public opinion against development
    D a single lot with a house built on it

15. obstruct
    A to contain
    B to block
    C to regard
    D to build

Tricky Syllables

▶ A **syllable** is a part of a word that has a single vowel sound.

See the Letters. The syllables in some words are barely heard, and because of this letters are often left out in spelling. Look at the Word List. Say each word as you look at it. Notice the unstressed syllables or syllables where two or more letters combine to spell a single sound.

Write the Syllables. Look up each word in a dictionary. Notice how the word is broken into syllables. Say the word aloud while you look at it and exaggerate your pronunciation of the sounds and syllables.

Word List
different
temperature
extraordinary
practically
average
restaurant
family
schedule
sincerely
laboratory

Practice Write the word from the Word List that matches each clue. Then write the word with syllable breaks. Circle any letters that combine to make a single sound. Finally use each word in a sentence.

▶ **Example:** extraordinary   ex•traor•di•nar•y
      We saw some *extraordinary* gems at the museum.

1. word used in the closing of a letter
2. great and unusual
3. something to keep you on time
4. place where experiments are done
5. opposite of *same*

6. how hot or cold something is
7. place to eat a meal
8. almost
9. neither too good nor too bad
10. mother, father, sisters, brothers

Assessment Practice

A. Directions: *Choose the sentence in which the underlined word is spelled correctly.*

1. **A** Jack just wants an <u>avrage</u> meal.
    B He isn't looking for anything <u>extrordinary</u>.
    C He should try that <u>resterant</u>.
    D He can get <u>practically</u> anything he wants there.

2. **A** Tina is the smartest one in our <u>famly</u>.
    B She recently got her new school <u>skedule</u>.
    C She works in the science <u>laboratory</u>.
    D She records the <u>temperture</u> of animals.

3. **A** I <u>sincerley</u> hope you are not angry.
    B Everyone has a <u>diffrent</u> idea about how to do this project.
    C The <u>scheduel</u> is difficult.
    D It would be <u>extraordinary</u> if we all could agree.

4. **A** Neither of my brothers likes that <u>restaurant</u>.
    B They say that the <u>temprature</u> of the food is always wrong.
    C They would like <u>diferent</u> choices.
    D The <u>averige</u> price of dinners is high.

B. Directions: *Choose the letter of the correctly spelled word.*

5. This old couch is _____ useless.
    A practicly
    B practicaly
    C practiclly
    D practically

6. She signed the letter "_____ yours."
    A Sincerely
    B Sincerly
    C Sincerley
    D Sinserely

7. A new _____ has moved in next door.
    A famly
    B fambly
    C family
    D famley

8. Travis's dad has a job in a _____.
    A labortory
    B laboratory
    C labratory
    D labritory

9. The _____ of this water is lukewarm.
    A temperture
    B temprature
    C temprachure
    D temperature

10. The _____ score on that test was 88.
    A avrage
    B avrige
    C average
    D averige

Narration: Short Story

Sometimes a work of literature transports you to a place you have never been and introduces you to a whole new world of engaging characters. One type of writing that can accomplish this is the short story. A **short story** is a brief creative, fictional narrative. Follow the steps outlined in this workshop to write your own short story.

Assignment Write a short story about an interesting or original situation that will capture readers' attention.

What to Include Your short story should feature the following elements:

- one or more well-developed characters
- a conflict that keeps the reader asking, "What will happen next?"
- a clear story line or sequence told from a consistent point of view
- effective pacing
- narrative that develops dialogue, suspense, and other literary elements and devices
- a title that catches the reader's attention
- precise vocabulary and effective word choice
- error-free writing, including correct use of comparatives

To preview the criteria on which your short story may be judged, see the rubric on page 345.

Using the Form

You may use elements of this form in these types of writing:

- autobiographical essays
- drama
- feature articles
- biographies

Writing Workshop: *Work in Progress*

If you have completed the Work-in-Progress assignments, you already have a wealth of ideas to use in your short story. Work with these ideas, or explore a new idea as you complete the Writing Workshop.

To get the feel for a short story, review "The Third Wish" by Joan Aiken, p. 274, or "Amigo Brothers" by Piri Thomas, p. 283.

Prewriting

Choosing Your Topic

Use one of these strategies to get ready to write a short story:

- **Magazine Flip-Through** Review magazines, looking for photographs, articles, or ads that spark your interest. Use sticky notes to mark your finds. Later, review the flagged pages, and take notes on the most promising ideas for your story.

- **What If?** Try using a "What If?" strategy to get you started. Fill in the blanks of a sentence such as the one shown here. Try a number of situations and choose the one that interests you the most.

  What if _____ (describe a person) suddenly _____ (describe a problem)?

Work in Progress
Review the work you did on pages 295 and 321.

Narrowing Your Topic

Identify the conflict. A conflict is a struggle between two opposing forces. A character's conflict may be *external,* as when a sheriff has a conflict with an outlaw, or *internal,* as when that outlaw struggles with his conscience. By identifying the conflict inside your story idea, you can focus your topic and get your story moving. To identify the conflict, answer these questions:

- Who is the main character of my story?
- What does the main character want?
- What is preventing him or her from getting it?

Gathering Details

Use listing and itemizing. Your next step is to gather details to include in your story. Follow these steps:

1. Quickly jot down a list of everything that comes to mind about a general idea.

2. Circle the most interesting item on the list.

3. Itemize that detail—create another list of everything that comes to mind about it.

4. After you have generated several lists in this way, look for connections among all the circled items on your lists. These connections will help you decide which details to include in your story.

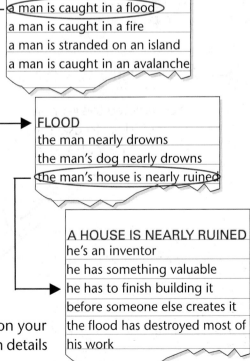

a man is caught in a flood
a man is caught in a fire
a man is stranded on an island
a man is caught in an avalanche

FLOOD
the man nearly drowns
the man's dog nearly drowns
the man's house is nearly ruined

A HOUSE IS NEARLY RUINED
he's an inventor
he has something valuable
he has to finish building it
before someone else creates it
the flood has destroyed most of
his work

Drafting

Shaping Your Writing

Create a plot. Begin by mapping out your plot. A **plot** is the arrangement of actions in the story. In most stories, the plot follows this pattern:

- The **exposition** introduces the main characters and their basic situation, including the central conflict or problem.
- The **conflict** intensifies during the rising action.
- The **climax** is the high point of interest.
- The story's falling action leads to the **resolution**, in which the conflict is resolved in some way.

Climax

Falling Action

Rising Action

Conflict Introduced

Exposition

Resolution

As you write, be sure to set the right pace so that your story does not drag or move too quickly.

Use literary elements and devices. A good story builds to a single exciting moment. To achieve this, writers rely on literary elements and devices. For example, **foreshadowing** is the use of clues hinting at future plot events. This creates **suspense**, a technique that makes the reader wonder what will happen next.

Providing Elaboration

Use details to define character and setting. As you draft your story, add details that reveal what your characters look like, how they act, what they think, and how others react to them. Make sure readers know when and where the action is taking place.

Show, do not tell. Although it can be useful to tell readers something directly, usually you should show them rather than tell them. As you draft, choose words that show your characters' thoughts, feelings, actions, and reactions.

Reading Writing Connection

To read the complete student model, see page 344.

Student Model: Show, Do Not Tell

~~gripped my father's pendant for reassurance, clenching the jade~~

~~cross and~~

I ~~reassured myself~~, willing myself to be strong.

> The writer chooses words that show rather than tell the character's feelings.

From the Author's Desk

Walter Dean Myers

Walter Dean Myers

On Revising to Heighten Tension

As a child listening to the stories from the Old Testament, I formed images in my mind of what exactly was going on. At first I only sympathized with the character Joseph, but as I grew older I wondered how his eldest brother, Reuben, must have felt. So, I explored Reuben's feelings in a short story entitled "Reuben and Joseph." This section from my draft of the story shows how I revise to heighten tension.

> *"Often the minor characters interest me the most."*
>
> ——Walter Dean Myers

Professional Model:

from "Reuben and Joseph"

~~Joseph lives~~. My brother lives. Like a man risen from the dead, he has appeared from the ashes of memory. ~~We are bid~~ He tells us that we are to go home tomorrow and tell our father the good news. But ~~those glad tidings~~ that good news, the joyous celebration he envisions, ~~will also speak of my disgrace~~ is filled with danger and disgrace for the messengers. Grief and fear sit in the pit of my stomach like two huge rocks. If I could scream silently, I would do so. If my tears could speak, I would let them.

~~Tonight I spent hours waiting for sleep and then, when sleep finally came, I awoke with a start, my heart pounding.~~ I have been tossing and turning all night. Sleep comes now and again, but then I quickly wake, my heart pounding. The room is too warm, and I hear the breathing of my brothers who lie on mats around me. . . .

It was more important to establish that he is talking about his brother than to give his brother's name. I want the reader to wonder, Why does he worry that his brother lives?

Okay, so I'm into what I imagine to be the jargon of the day, but I need to get on with my story.

Saying that there is danger here immediately heightens the tension. "Also speak of my disgrace" is too stiff.

"I have been tossing and turning all night" is more direct than the sentence I crossed out and creates more drama.

Revising

Revising Your Paragraphs

Improve Your Characterization. Cut a five-pointed star out of construction paper and label the points *dialogue, movement, gestures, feelings,* and *expressions.* Slide the star down your draft as you look for places where you can add details that reveal more about your characters. When you find a place to include information, make notes in the margin and start over.

> **Dialogue:** Write conversations that show how the character speaks, using the words and phrasing he or she might use.
>
> **Movement:** Describe a character's movements using words like *rushed, timid,* or *excited.*
>
> **Gestures:** Include information to show whether characters use their hands when they talk, whether they stand tall or slouched, and insert other details that show how characters look and act.
>
> **Feelings:** Consider the way events will make your characters feel, and include words and details to reveal these emotions.
>
> **Expressions:** Tell your readers about the facial expressions your characters make to convey their ideas and feelings without words.

Peer Review: Give your draft to one or two classmates to read. Ask them to highlight places where you can include details that help develop stronger characters.

Revising Your Word Choice

Use vivid verbs. Review your draft to find places where you can add details that will bring your ideas to life. Look for vague verbs that you can replace with precise, vivid action verbs.

To read the complete student model, see page 344.

Model: Revising to Use Vivid Verbs

The waves ~~pushed~~ *crashed against* my boat like hail pounding on a window. I was ~~moved~~ *violently thrown* back and forth in my boat!

The wave ~~threw me~~ *sent me hurtling* toward the rock! I ~~hit~~ *slammed into* the rock with full force!

> The writer replaces vague verbs with vivid verbs.

Integrating Grammar Skills

Comparison of Adjectives and Adverbs

Most adjectives and adverbs have three degrees of comparison: the *positive,* the *comparative,* and the *superlative.*

Identifying Degrees of Adjectives and Adverbs The positive is used when no comparison is made. The comparative is used when two things are being compared. The superlative is used when three or more things are being compared.

> *Prentice Hall Writing and Grammar Connection: Chapter 25, Section 1*

Positive: Hannah is a *fast* runner.
Comparative: Eva is a *faster* runner than Hannah.
Superlative: Emmy is the *fastest* runner on the team.

Forming Comparative and Superlative Degrees	
Use *-er* or *more* to form the comparative degree.	faster, taller, narrower, sunnier, more narrow, more sunny, more quickly
Use *-est* or *most* to form the superlative degree.	fastest, tallest, narrowest, sunniest, most narrow, most sunny, most quickly
Use *more* and *most* with modifiers of three or more syllables.	more popular, more intelligently, most popular, most intelligently

Fixing Incorrect Use of Comparative and Superlative Degrees To fix the incorrect use of comparative and superlative degrees of adjectives and adverbs, use one or more of the following methods:

1. **Identify the number of things being compared.** Review the rules for comparison, and use the correct word or word-ending.

2. **Identify the number of syllables in the modifier.** Review the rules for modifiers with a specific number of syllables, and use the correct word or word-ending.

3. **Read the words aloud.** If the words sound awkward, combine the modifier with a different word or word-ending.

Apply It to Your Editing

Choose two paragraphs in your draft. Underline every sentence that compares two or more things. If the use of a comparative or superlative degree of any adjective or adverb is faulty, fix it.

Student Model: KC Marker
Portland, OR

The Leaky Boat

It was a cold September evening. My linen cuffs flapped uncontrollably in a biting wind baring its white teeth of snow. The sun had long since set, and all was quiet on the sea. A cool mist had settled around the bay, sending a sharp chill down my spine. I continued to row; I had seen worse. I could still hear the voice ringing through my head:

"This is it, son. Either you're ready or you're not."

I was ready. The fire in my lantern flickered as another wind blew across the bay, carrying more frightening sounds from the distance. I gripped my father's pendant for reassurance, clenching the jade cross and willing myself to be strong. I was ready.

No one dared go out on such a night. Tonight was Friday—the 13th. I was the only one traveling the waters, or so I thought. Ever since the coast guard had shown us out, no one dared go fishin' even if it was for a big fish; I mean a *big* fish, a legend, and a monster! But it wasn't a fish any one in my family could bring themselves to kill. It was ancient, and it had, in a distant time, saved one of my ancestors from being swallowed by the sea.

Now, I had survived many a boating trip before, but what happened next would become a remarkable memory for the rest of my life.

As I shifted in my seat I could feel it. Something was wrong. I shifted once more and that's when I heard it. The wind blew hard against my face, the cold stinging my eyes. Rushing water all around me—a storm! It had come slowly at first. I had not thought much of it, but now it was at its nastiest, and I was in the middle of it! The waves crashed against my boat like hail pounding on a window. I was violently thrown back and forth in my boat! I turned to the side. How close was I to the rocky shore?

Another wave hit, revealing a large rock off the starboard side. A wave came from the opposite side drenching me with water, but that was not all. The wave sent me hurtling toward the rock! I slammed into the rock with full force! I was swept aside by another, smaller wave as water poured into my boat! What was I to do? Thunder roared overhead.

As I struggled to keep upright, a massive wave came up from behind, plunging me into the water. I swam with all my strength to the surface, taking in a big breath of air, and holding tight to my father's pendant.

The water churned around me fiercely, tossing to and fro. The foam swirled around me, and the salt stung my eyes as it hit me. I was plunged under again. I swam up for air with my strength rapidly leaving me. Disaster struck! I felt a wave come. I could not see it. I felt the necklace being ripped from my neck, leaving the sanctuary of my head, and spiraling down to the murky depths. I looked down for it, squinting to open my burning eyes; I saw an eye and a long slender body, and then all went dark.

I awoke the next morning on an unfamiliar shore, not knowing where I was. I felt something cold against my neck—the pendant! How had it been retrieved? How had I survived? The fish. The family fish had saved my family again. I still don't know how I obtained the pendant or where I had to go, for that is another story.

KC uses descriptive language to set the scene for the story.

The story is told from a first-person point of view. Readers learn about the narrator from what he thinks and experiences.

KC develops suspense by foreshadowing something dangerous.

The varied sentence structure and length make the pacing of the story's conflict suspenseful.

Vivid details and tension make the reader want to know what is going to happen next.

Editing and Proofreading

Choose a strong title for your story. Then, review your draft to eliminate errors in grammar, spelling, and punctuation.

Focus on Dialogue: Enclose a character's exact words in quotation marks. If dialogue comes *before* the words announcing speech, use a comma, question mark, or exclamation point at the end of the quotation—not a period. If dialogue comes *after* the words announcing speech, use a comma before the quotation.

"I heard the siren," Benjamin said.

Sally jumped and shouted, "So did I, but it still surprised me!"

Publishing and Presenting

Share your writing with a wider audience:

Submit your story. Submit your story to a school literary magazine, a national publication, an online journal, or a contest.

Give a reading. Read your story aloud to your class or to a group of friends. Prepare posters announcing your reading, and distribute signed copies of your story at the event.

Reflecting on Your Writing

Writer's Journal Jot down your thoughts on the experience of writing a short story. Begin by answering these questions:

- What drafting advice would you give another student?
- How has your experience changed the way you read short stories?

> *Prentice Hall Writing and Grammar Connection: Chapter 5.*

Rubric for Self-Assessment

To assess your short story, use the following rubric:

Criteria	Rating Scale
	not very → very
Focus: How well-developed are your characters?	1 2 3 4 5
Organization: How clearly organized is the story line or sequence of events?	1 2 3 4 5
Support/Elaboration: How well do the dialogue and suspense support the plot?	1 2 3 4 5
Style: How precise is your word choice?	1 2 3 4 5
Conventions: How correct is your grammar, especially your use of comparative adjectives and adverbs?	1 2 3 4 5

Communications Workshop

Organizing and Delivering an Oral Summary

An **oral summary** shares many of the characteristics of a written summary. The guidelines below will help you plan what you want to say and help you say it with confidence.

Organizing Content
Like its written counterpart, an oral summary should briefly state the main idea of a work, with only as many details as needed to give a complete, but concise, picture of the work.

Note the main idea and significant details. Write the "big idea"—the overall statement of the work's content—on a note card. If you want to include a direct quotation, write it word for word and remember to tell your audience it is a quotation by saying, "I quote."

Show a comprehensive understanding. Do not just string together fact after fact. Ask yourself, "What does all this mean?" Try to convey a genuine understanding of what you have seen or read, not just the surface details.

Planning Your Delivery
Plan and practice your delivery so that you do not wander from the main points when presenting. Do not go over the time that you have been given for your summary.

Use your voice well. Be lively and energetic, but speak clearly and precisely. Speak slowly enough for your listeners to catch everything you say.

Vary your sentence structure. To add interest to your summary, vary your sentence structure just as you do when you write. Listen to your words and monitor yourself for errors in grammar.

Use visual aids. A flip chart or poster that outlines the main points will help your audience follow your summary. As you indicate relationships between events and ideas, underline key words and phrases.

Big Idea
Giant pandas have become rare because hunters kill them.

Facts: There are only about 1000 living in the wild. There are only 15 in zoos.

Conclusion
If we can support the efforts to save pandas, maybe there will be more pandas in the world of our children and grandchildren.

Activity **Deliver an Oral Summary** Choose and summarize a news article from a current newspaper or magazine. Be sure that your planned summary answers all important questions about the article. Then, deliver your summary in front of your classmates, using the speaking techniques outlined in this workshop.

The Jungle Book: A Pacemaker Classic

Rudyard Kipling

Pearson Education, Inc., 1967

Novel Many of Kipling's celebrated Mowgli stories are retold and gathered together in this book. Mowgli is a wild child who lives in the jungle in India with the Wolf Pack. He spends his time with Bagheera, a black panther, and Baloo, a brown bear, trying to avoid the tiger Shere Khan and Kaa the rock snake, and to learn the Law of the Jungle.

The Devil's Arithmetic

Jane Yolen

Puffin Books, 1990

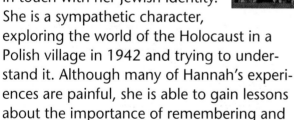

Novel Students will relate to Hannah as she experiences a magical time-travel process that puts her in touch with her Jewish identity. She is a sympathetic character, exploring the world of the Holocaust in a Polish village in 1942 and trying to understand it. Although many of Hannah's experiences are painful, she is able to gain lessons about the importance of remembering and learning from historical events.

Miracle's Boys

Jacqueline Woodson

Puffin Books, 2000

Novel This novel tells the story of Ty'ree, Charlie, and Lafayette, three brothers who must put their lives back together after losing their father in a drowning accident and their mother to diabetes. Each boy deals with his grief in his own way. Ty'ree has given up his dreams of college to work full time to support the others. Charlie has slipped into a life of crime and is just back from two years at a correctional facility. Lafayette, the youngest, has retreated inward, avoiding his friends and blaming himself for his mother's death. Struggling against great odds, the brothers learn that "brother to brother to brother" they can survive.

Child of the Owl

Laurence Yep

Pearson Prentice Hall, 2000

Novel After her father is hospitalized, twelve-year-old Casey is sent to live with her grandmother in San Francisco's Chinatown. Casey feels lost in Chinatown. However, in her new home, Casey begins to discover aspects of her family history and Chinese heritage she never knew before. In this novel, a grandmother's wisdom helps change a tough, independent girl with no real sense of home into a young woman with a new awareness of who she is and where she belongs.

These titles are available in the Penguin/Prentice Hall Literature Library.
Consult your teacher before choosing one.

Think About It People put a lot of thought into names—whether they are naming children or pets, or giving a friend a new nickname. Names often follow a person throughout life and can have positive and negative associations. The following poems talk about the care that is given to names. The poems also provide insight into how names affect their owners.

from

Locomotion

Jacqueline
Woodson

How I Got My Name

Whenever that song came on that goes
Come on, baby, do the Locomotion, Mama
would make us dance with her.
We'd do this dance called the Locomotion

when we'd bend our elbows and move
our arms in circles at our sides.
Like our arms were train wheels.
I can see us doing it now—in slow motion.

Mama grinning and singing along
Saying all proud "My kids got rhythm!"
Sometimes Lili got behind me and we'd
do the Locomotion around our little living room. Till

the song ended.
And we fell out on the couch
Laughing. Mama would say
You see why I love that song so much, Lonnie?

See why I had to make it your name?
Lonnie Collins Motion, Mama would say.
Lo Co Motion
Yeah.

Hey Dog

Hey Dog!
That's how you call your boys.
Hey Dog. You want to hoop?
Then you and your dogs are throwing
the ball around and talking about
girls and ballplayers and stuff
you're gonna have one day
A red car
some slamming kicks
a shearling coat
a pocket full of money
a pretty girl
a satellite dish *and* cable
on and on you and your dogs
two college degrees, straight A straight up
a phat deal with the Lakers
no, the Knicks
no, the Nets
Nah—the Nets ain't nothing.
What you talking about, Dog? The Nets got game.
Yeah, a game of checkers!!
Game of tag, maybe.
Game of pin the tail on the donkey!
Just grinning and talking junk
shooting hoops
not even knowing where
or when people started calling the people
they like to be around *Dog*
but liking it and feeling good when
your dog slaps your hand, gives you a quick hug, says
What's up, Dog?

Rodney

He comes in the door and sets a big duffel bag down,
lifts Miss Edna up like she weighs two pounds
and she's laughing
and punching
his shoulders and crying all at the same time.
Then he lifts me up, says *Look at Little Brother Lonnie*
all growed up
You almost a man now, aren't you.

Little brother.
Little brother Lonnie.
My big brother Rodney.
Imagine that!

There's roast beef and ribs and potato salad.
There's rice and peas and corn bread and greens.
There's sweet potatoes and macaroni and cheese and
even some fried okra
There's three kinds of pie and two kinds of cake
and we eat
and we eat and we eat till the thought of eating
another bite makes us feel like crying.
All the while Rodney's telling us how he's come on home,
gonna get himself a job here. Says
Ain't nothing for me upstate anymore.

He has Miss Edna's dark skin and straight
  teeth. They
even laugh the same.
He's tall and his shoulders are wide
  like somebody
who could

get a pro football contract if they wanted to.
I lift my own skinny shoulders, wishing they'd spread
out like Rodney's do.

Little Brother, he called me.

The kitchen is warm.
Miss Edna can't stop grinning.
Rodney's voice sounds like it should always be
in this house.

Little Brother, he called me.
Little Brother Lonnie.

Meet the Author

Jacqueline Woodson lives in Brooklyn, New York, and writes full time. Before her writing career was well established, she was a drama therapist for underprivileged children. Woodson works with emerging writers and encourages young people to write every day.

Readings in Contemporary Poetry
Talk About It

Use these questions to guide a discussion.

1. **(a)** How do you picture the dance called the "Locomotion," described in the poem "How I Got My Name"? **(b)** Why do you think the speaker's mother names him after this particular song?

2. Do you have nicknames for people you know? How did you come up with their names?

3. With a small group, talk about the positive and negative effects of nicknames. Consider the following ideas:

   • How do people choose or get nicknames?

   • When are nicknames best used? When are more formal names better suited?

   • What kind of nicknames stand the test of time?

   Choose a point-person to share your ideas with the class.

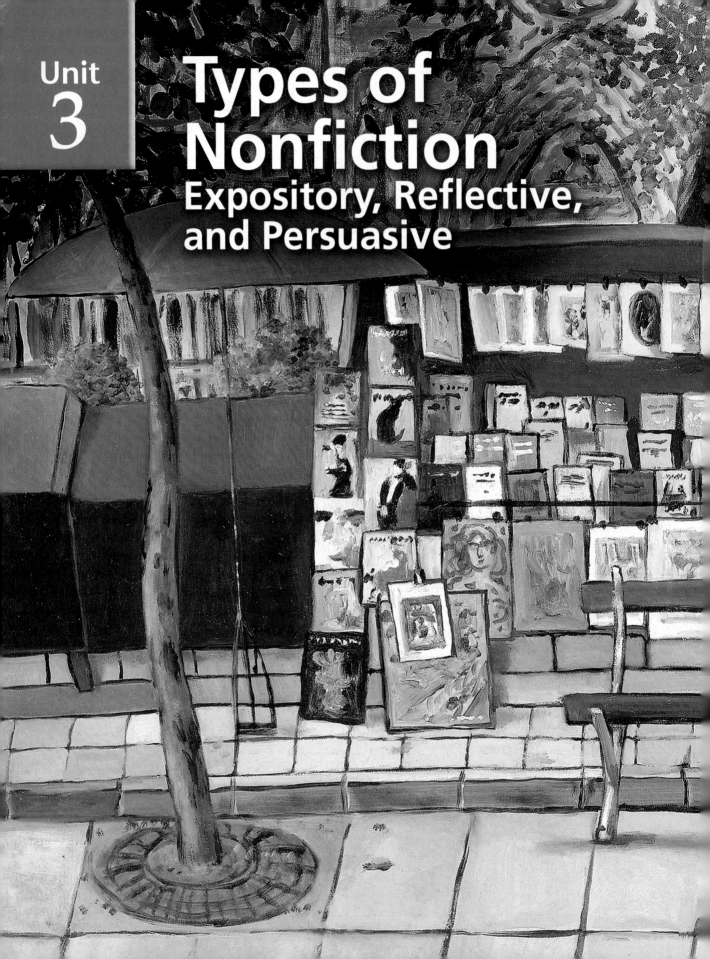

Types of Nonfiction
Expository, Reflective, and Persuasive

Unit 3 Overview

Introduction
Exploring Types of Nonfiction

Part 1: Main Idea

Part 2: Fact and Opinion

Introduction:
Types of Nonfiction

From the Author's Desk

Richard Mühlberger
Talks About the Forms

Richard
Mühlberger

Essays and articles, two types of nonfiction, are like "classrooms in print." They are "places" we go to learn things. An **essay** is a medium-sized prose discussion of a topic that sometimes tells you as much about the writer as it does about the topic. An **article** is a brief prose composition that focuses in on the facts of a subject.

▲ Richard Mühlberger has written a number of books that introduce young readers to the work of great artists.

Different Audiences, Different Purposes

As the definitions suggest, these print classrooms serve different **audiences** and have different **purposes.** Essays, which can be found in some well-known magazines and in essay collections, tend to attract readers looking for inspiration as well as for information. Articles, which appear in newspapers, journals, and encyclopedias, attract readers looking for facts.

The best way I can give you the flavor of these two types of nonfiction is to tell you how I have experienced them in my own chosen field, the history of art.

As a youngster, I loved paintings. Through study in college, I learned more about art, and my first job was in a museum. I read the articles about art that arrived at the museum every month in magazine-like publications. I also became very familiar with articles in dictionaries and encyclopedias of art that helped me understand what I was reading about in the periodicals.

◀ Critical Viewing Using Richard Mühlberger's distinction between an article and an informal essay, explain which form the author in this picture is probably writing. **[Apply]**

My Career: Articles and, Someday, an Essay

In time, my personal interest focused on seventeenth-century Dutch art. And I have written articles about "my" Dutch painters. I collect facts through research, and then set them into the narrative of each artist's life as I can reconstruct it. Then, I collect my articles and publish them in slim books.

Someday, I would like to write an essay about Dutch art. I said earlier that an essay is like a classroom. It is, but the personal essay I would like to write would be a classroom for one student. This essay would speak directly to a single reader just as Phillip Lopate describes in the passage shown here.

The hallmark of the personal essay is its intimacy. The writer seems to be speaking directly into your ear, confiding everything from gossip to wisdom.

from "Introduction" to *The Art of the Personal Essay*
—Phillip Lopate

In an essay, I could share with the reader my passion for Dutch art and not just my knowledge of it. Essays would be a new kind of writing for me. Articles can express the author's **bias,** or slant on a topic, but they don't usually allow much leeway for the author's personal feelings. Essays go deeper, coming close, at their best, to being poetry.

More About the Author

Richard **Mühlberger** (b. 1938)

For much of his career, Richard Mühlberger has been interested in teaching people about the arts. As an author and an educator working in museums, he used words to help people get beyond words as they looked at paintings. He wanted people to *experience* pictures that communicate — wordlessly — through color, shape, and line. Today, he teaches art at Western New England College.

Fast Facts

▶ When writing about Rembrandt's use of shadow, Mühlberger remembered a scene from his boyhood: his grandmother huddling over the radio in a dark house.
▶ While researching a biography of Vincent Van Gogh, Mühlberger met the artist's nephew.

Learning About Types of Nonfiction

Common Forms of Nonfiction Writing

Nonfiction writing is about real people, places, ideas, and experiences. Here are some common forms of nonfiction writing:

Letters and **journals** contain personal thoughts and reflections.

Biographies and **autobiographies** are life stories.

- A **biography** is the life story of someone that is written by another person.
- An **autobiography** is a writer's account of his or her own life.

Media accounts are nonfiction works written for newspapers, magazines, television, or radio.

PEANUTS reprinted by permission of United Feature Syndicate, Inc.

Essays and **articles** are short nonfiction works about a particular subject. Both may follow the format of these types of writing:

- **Expository writing** presents facts, discusses ideas, or explains a process.
- **Persuasive writing** is meant to convince the reader to adopt a particular point of view or to take a particular course of action.
- **Reflective writing** addresses an event or experience and includes the writer's insights about the event's importance.
- **Humorous writing** is meant to entertain and evoke laughter. However, humor can also be used to present serious themes.
- **Narrative writing** tells about real-life experiences.
- **Descriptive writing** appeals to the five senses.
- **Analytical writing** breaks a large idea into parts to help the reader see how they work together as a whole.

Elements of Nonfiction Writing

Organization Well-written essays and articles are organized in a way that presents information clearly and logically.

- **Chronological organization** presents details in time order, from first to last—or sometimes from last to first.
- **Comparison-and-contrast organization** shows the ways in which two or more subjects are similar and different.
- **Cause-and-effect organization** shows the relationship among events.
- **Problem-and-solution organization** identifies a problem and then proposes a solution.

Author's Purpose The information presented in essays and articles is related to the author's reason for writing. Writers often produce nonfiction to explain, to entertain, to inform, or to persuade.

Check Your Understanding

1. Which method of organization would you expect each of these works of nonfiction to follow? Explain your answers.
   a. Television Is Better Than Movies
   b. Keeping Your Room Clean

2. Identify the type of essay each title suggests. Explain your answers.
   a. My Life As a Chef
   b. How a Bill Becomes a Law

From the Author's Desk
Richard Mühlberger Introduces His Article

For most of my career, I worked in education departments of museums, finding ways to get our visitors to pause and look hard at art.

The Analytical Article: Facts and Opinions

So as you read my **analytical article** on Rembrandt's famous painting *The Night Watch,* imagine I'm a guide standing next to you in a museum. Be sure to check what I tell you against the painting itself—it's on the page, if not on the wall—to see if my **facts** are correct. For example, if I say that there is a dog in the painting, find it.

Also, distinguish the facts I provide from my **opinions.** My statement that all "that honors the citizen soldiers and their work is illuminated" is an opinion. Look at the painting carefully and decide whether you agree.

My Purpose: Getting You to Experience the Painting

My **purpose** in analyzing the painting is getting you to experience it. That's why I tried to select words that place you in front of the painting and that make the painting enter your mind.

I chose this purpose because viewing *The Night Watch* has been one of the most wonderful experiences of *my* life. On trips to Holland, whenever I sat on one of the backless oak benches in Amsterdam's Rijksmuseum in front of *The Night Watch,* I was always impressed by its size. Imagine the illustration in your book blown up twenty-two times to match the imposing original.

Matching the Subjects' Strides

To experience this size when viewing a reproduction, I envision my own body in the poses of Captain Cocq and Lieutenant van Ruytenburgh and try to match the very big strides of the strapping volunteer soldiers. Even seated, I can feel my leg muscles stretch.

If my analysis of the painting gets you to experience it, we can walk with these lively men in our imagination.

What Makes a **Rembrandt** a *Rembrandt?*

Richard Mühlberger

Citizen Soldiers

A Dutch poet of Rembrandt's day wrote, "When the country is in danger, every citizen is a soldier." That was the idea behind the militia, or civic guard companies, which trained citizens how to fight and shoot in case their city was attacked. Each company drilled in archery, the crossbow, or the musket. By Rembrandt's time, militia companies were as much social clubs as military organizations.

Captain Frans Banning Cocq, out to impress everyone, chose Rembrandt to paint his militia company, with members of the company paying the artist to have their portraits included in the painting. The huge canvas was to be hung in the new hall of the militia headquarters, where it would be seen at receptions and celebrations along with other militia paintings.

By the mid-seventeenth century, there were more than one hundred big militia paintings hanging in public halls in the important cities of the Netherlands. In all of these group portraits, the men were evenly lined up so that each face got equal attention, just as they had been in traditional anatomy lesson paintings. Rembrandt did not like this way of presenting the scene. He had seen militia companies in action, and there were always people milling about who were not militiamen but who took part in their exercises and parades. To add realism to the piece, he decided to include some of these people, as well as a dog. There was room on the wall for a canvas about sixteen feet wide, large enough for Rembrandt to do what no other painter had ever done before. His idea was to show the exciting commotion before a parade began.

▲ **Critical Viewing**
What details in this image reflect a different century?
[Analyze]

Richard Mühlberger
Author's Insight
I researched many books in which *The Night Watch* was discussed to find out that the painting was more than a lively group portrait.

Two Handsome Officers

Everywhere in the painting, Rembrandt used sharp contrasts of dark and light. Everything that honors the citizen soldiers and their work is illuminated; everything else is in shadow. Captain Frans Banning Cocq is the man dressed in

Richard Mühlberger
Author's Insight
Figures coming out of darkness into light show a day-to-day event dramatically.

black with a red sash under his arm, striding forward in the center. Standing next to him is the most brightly lighted man in the painting, Lieutenant Willem van Ruytenburgh, attired in a glorious gold and yellow uniform, silk sash, soft leather cavalry boots, and a high hat with white ostrich plumes. His lancelike weapon, called a partisan, and the steel gorget[1] around his neck—a leftover from the days when soldiers wore full suits of armor—are the only hints that he is a military man. Rembrandt links him to Banning Cocq by contrasting the colors of their clothing and by painting the shadow of Banning Cocq's hand on the front of van Ruytenburgh's coat. The captain is giving orders to his lieutenant for the militia company to march off.

Banning Cocq is dressed in a black suit against a dark background, yet he does not disappear. Rembrandt made him the most important person in the composition. Van Ruytenburgh turns to listen to him, which shows his respect for his commander. Banning Cocq's face stands out above his bright red sash and white collar. How well Rembrandt knew that darkness makes faces shine! The captain's self-assured pace, the movement of the tassels at his knees, and the angle of his walking staff are proof of the energy and dignity of his stride.

Muskets and Mascots

On either side of these two handsome officers, broad paths lead back into the painting.

Rembrandt knew that when the huge group scene was placed above eye level on the wall of the militia headquarters, these empty areas would be the first to be seen. He wanted them to lead the eyes of viewers to figures in the painting who did not have the advantage of being placed in the foreground. In the middle of one of these paths is a man in red pouring gunpowder into the barrel of his musket. Behind the captain, only partially seen, another man shoots his gun into the air, and a third militiaman, to the right of van Ruytenburgh, blows on his

1. **gorget** (gôr´ jit) *n.* a piece of armor for the throat.

◄ **Critical Viewing** How has Rembrandt made the subject of this painting realistic? **[Distinguish]**

Richard Mühlberger Author's Insight I described the clothing of the leaders because I wanted to show that the Dutch value individuality. Except for Ruytenburgh's boots and gorget, nothing the militiamen wear resembles a uniform.

Nonfiction Supporting Paragraphs This paragraph develops the idea that Banning Cocq is a central figure in the painting.

✓ **Reading Check**

What technique did Rembrandt use to make the citizen soldiers stand out?

weapon to clean it. Loading, shooting, and cleaning were part of the standard drill for musketeers, and so they were included in the painting to demonstrate the men's mastery of their weapons.

Walking in a stream of bright light down the path on the left is a blond girl dressed in yellow with a dead chicken tied to her waist. She has a friend in blue behind her. In their public shows, the militia would choose two young girls to carry the emblems[2] of their company, here the claws of a bird. The yellow and blue of the girls' costumes are the militia's colors. In the parade that is being organized, these mascots will take a prominent place, the fair-haired girl holding aloft the chicken's claws.

Many of the background figures stand on stairs so that their faces can be seen. The man above the girl in yellow is Jan Corneliszoon Visscher, after Banning Cocq and van Ruytenburgh the highest-ranking person in the militia company. He waves a flag that combines the colors of the militia company with the three black crosses of Amsterdam. While Rembrandt did not pose him in bright light, he made him important by placing him high up on the stairs, by showing the sheen in his costume, and by giving him the large flag to unfurl.

▼▲ **Critical Viewing**
What do you notice about these portraits that you did not see on page 360?
[Respond]

A Red Ribbon and Fine Old Clothes

In spite of his partial appearance, the drummer on the right seems ready to come forward to lead a march with his staccato beat. The sound seems to bother the dusty dog below. Behind the drummer, two men appear to be figuring out their places in the formation. The one in the white collar and

2. emblems *n.* objects that stand for something else; symbols.

black hat outranks many of the others in the scene. His prestige is signaled in an unusual way: A red ribbon dangles over his head, tied to the lance of the man in armor behind van Ruytenburgh. Additional lances can be counted in the darkness, some leaning against the wall, others carried by militiamen. Their crisscross patterns add to the feeling of commotion that Rembrandt has captured everywhere on the huge canvas.

The costumes worn in this group portrait are much more ornate and colorful than what Dutchmen ordinarily wore every day. Some, like the breeches and helmet of the man shooting his musket behind Banning Cocq, go back a hundred years to the beginnings of the militia company. In the eyes of many Dutchmen, clothing associated with a glorious past brought special dignity to the company. What an opportunity for Rembrandt, perhaps the greatest lover of old clothes in Amsterdam!

Not a Night Watch

Night Watch is a mistaken title that was given to the painting over a hundred years after Rembrandt died, but it has stuck, and is what the painting is almost universally called. Although the exaggerated chiaroscuro[3] does give an impression of night time, there is daylight in the scene. It comes from the left, as the shadows under Banning Cocq's feet prove. And it is clear that no one in the painting is on watch, alert to the approach of an enemy. The official title of the painting is *Officers and Men of the Company of Captain Frans Banning Cocq and Lieutenant Willem van Ruytenburgh.*

Rembrandt completed the painting in 1642, when he was thirty-six years old. He probably had no idea that it would be the most famous Dutch painting of all time. In 1678, one of his former students wrote that it would "outlive all its rivals," and within another century the painting was considered one of the wonders of the world.

---

3. chiaroscuro (kē är′ ə skoor′ ō) *n.* a dramatic style of light and shade in a painting or drawing.

Nonfiction Writer's Style Mühlberger discusses the elaborate period costumes and adds his own enthusiasm for Rembrandt.

MODEL SELECTION

Nonfiction Organization The details in this paragraph are presented chronologically.

Techniques Rembrandt Used This annotated illustration appears in Mühlberger's book, *What Makes a Rembrandt a Rembrandt?* Rembrandt used *chiaroscuro* (kē ärə skoor´ō), the intense contrast of light and dark, to create dramatic effects.

▲ The Syndics of the Clothmakers' Guild

▲ The men are posed informally.

▲ The only bright color is red.

▲ The faces are portraits of individuals.

Connect to the Literature Which of these techniques that Rembrandt used can you see in *The Night Watch*?

Q. **Why are Rembrandt's paintings often so dark?**

A. My answer is just a guess. First, the interiors of houses were darker then. Second, Rembrandt was often more interested in the sitter's personality than in his features. He brings this out by contrasts of light and dark. Finally, by contrasting ordinary light colors with dark ones, Rembrandt causes the light ones to take on greater brightness.

Q. **What qualities make Rembrandt one of the most famous artists of all time?**

A. You can tell when Rembrandt thought one of his subjects was dull, boring, or, perhaps, dumb. These portraits are not inspiring. But when he found a spark in his subject, he made a glorious likeness that captures the sitter's inner life as well as his or her physical appearance. This is a rare quality in portraits, and it makes Rembrandt stand out from most other artists.

Student Corner

Q. **How was Rembrandt able to capture so much detail in the portraits?**

—**Karlesse Clayton, Pasadena, California**

A. Remember that a Rembrandt painting is far larger than the reproduction of it you see in the text. So he could include many details. Also, the page of a book is flat while Rembrandt's painted surfaces are full of textures. There are many flecks and small globs applied with brushes laden with paint. As you move away from them, they take on the appearance of familiar things—an eye, a mole, a button, or a glint of light, for instance.

 Writing Workshop: *Work in Progress*

How-to Essay

For a how-to essay you may write, make a list of five everyday tasks. These tasks can be anything you do, from brushing your teeth to opening your locker. Save this Everyday List in your writing portfolio.

Nonfiction

Thinking About the Selection

1. **Respond:** Now that you have read the essay, what new title would you give to Rembrandt's *The Night Watch*? Explain.

2. **(a) Recall:** Why was Rembrandt hired to paint Captain Banning Cocq's militia company? **(b) Generalize:** How did Rembrandt change the way military group portraits were painted?

3. **(a) Interpret:** How did Rembrandt use light and shadow to indicate rank? **(b) Support:** How did the painter make the background figures visible? **(c) Summarize:** What details reveal that a parade is being organized?

Nonfiction Review

4. **(a)** Use a chart like the one shown to analyze the types of writing Mühlberger uses in this essay. **(b)** With a partner, review your charts. Together discuss the **author's purpose** in using both kinds of writing. Share your ideas with the class.

Examples of Description	Examples of Exposition

Research the Author

Research the life and work of Richard Mühlberger and plan a **panel discussion** that you and three classmates will present to the class. Follow these steps:

- Appoint a chairperson of the panel and assign research topics to group members. Consider topics such as Mühlberger's background and education, books he has written about famous artists, and information about Mühlberger's career. Use online and print resources to research these topics.
- Once you have gathered information, share it in a presentation to the class. Set a time limit of two or three minutes for each presentation.
- Open the discussion to questions from the class to panel members.

QuickReview

Selection at a Glance

An art historian and author explains the meaning of Rembrandt's famous painting, *The Night Watch*.

Assessment
For: Self-test
Visit: www.PHSchool.com
Web Code: ema-6301

Essay: a short nonfiction work about a particular subject

Description: writing that appeals to the five senses (sight, hearing, taste, smell, and touch)

Exposition: writing that presents facts, discusses ideas, or explains a process

Author's Purpose: the author's reason for writing, often to explain, entertain, inform, or persuade

Skills You Will Learn

Reading Skill: *Adjust Your Reading Rate to Identify Main Ideas and Key Points*
Literary Analysis: *Expository Essay*

Reading Skill: *Make Connections Between Key Points and Supporting Details*
Literary Analysis: *Reflective Essay*

Reading Skill: *Outline*

Literary Analysis: *Comparing Biography and Autobiography*

Literature You Will Read

Reading: Main Idea

> **Main ideas** are the most important thoughts or points in a work.

Skills and Strategies You Will Learn in Part 1

In Part 1, you will learn

- to **adjust your reading rate to identify main ideas and key points.** (p. 370)
- to **make connections** between key points and supporting details to determine the **main idea.** (p. 388)
- to **outline** the **main ideas** of a problem-and-solution essay. (p. 406)

Using the Skills and Strategies in Part 1

In Part 1, you will learn to scan text for important, or key, details that support the main idea. You will also learn to make connections and see relationships among these key details. Recognizing these relationships will help you gain a clearer understanding of the work's meaning.

Scan to answer:
What words or phrases are repeated?
What idea stands out in each paragraph?
Which details are emphasized?
Make connections:
How are key details grouped or organized?
Which sentences pull relevant thoughts together?
Identify the main idea:
What is the point suggested or supported by these details?

Academic Vocabulary

The following words will help you write and talk about main ideas as you read the selections in this unit.

Word	Definition	Example Sentence
relevant *adj.*	having a logical connection with	This detail is *relevant* because it illustrates the author's point.
irrelevant *adj.*	not having a connection with	June could have left out many of those details because they were *irrelevant* to her argument.
significant *adj.*	having an important meaning	The antagonist's desire for revenge is *significant* to the plot development.
insignificant *adj.*	having little or no meaning	The detail is *insignificant* in your argument and should be left out of your essay.
identify *v.*	recognize something and be able to say what it is	Josh was able to *identify* the major points in the president's speech.

Vocabulary Skill: Prefixes

▶ A prefix is a word part that is added to the beginning of the word.

In Part 1, you will learn to use the

prefix *ir-* (p. 386)   prefix *in-* (p. 404)

Adding either of these prefixes usually creates an antonym of the original word. Look at the examples of words with these prefixes.

Original word	Prefix	Meaning of prefix	Examples
Responsible, resistible	*ir-*	without; not	irresponsible, irresistible
Sensitive, excusable	*in-*	without; not	insensitive, inexcusable

Activity Using a dictionary, find two words beginning with the prefix *ir-* and two beginning with the prefix *in-,* where each prefix has the meaning "not" or "without." Then, find the original word that is each word's antonym.

These skills will help you become a better reader.
Practice them with either "Life Without Gravity"
(p. 372) or "Conversational Ballgames" (p. 379).

Reading Skill

The **main idea** is the central point of a passage or text.
The main idea of a paragraph is usually stated in a
topic sentence that identifies the **key point**.
Supporting details give examples, explanations, or reasons.
   When reading nonfiction, **adjust your reading rate to recognize
main ideas and key points.**

- **Skim,** or look over the text quickly, to get a sense of the
  main idea before you begin reading.
- **Read closely** to learn what the main ideas are.
- **Scan,** or run your eyes over the text, to find answers to questions, to clarify, or to find supporting details.

   Refer to the chart shown as you look for main ideas.

Reading Rate	What to look for
Skimming before reading	organization, topic sentences, repeated words
Close reading	key points, supporting details
Scanning	particular word or idea

Literary Analysis

An **expository essay** is a short piece of nonfiction that explains,
defines, or interprets ideas, events, or processes. The organization
and presentation of information depends on the specific topic of
the essay.

Vocabulary Builder

Life Without Gravity

- **spines** (spīnz) *n.* backbones (p. 373) *Sitting
  up straight is good for our spines.*

- **feeble** (fē´ bəl) *adj.* weak; infirm (p. 374)
  The injured bird made a feeble attempt to fly.

- **blander** (bland´ ər) *adj.* more tasteless
  (p. 374) *The lack of spices in the chili made it
  even blander than the cornbread.*

Conversational Ballgames

- **elaboration** (ē lab´ ə rā´ shən) *n.* adding of
  more details (p. 380) *His elaboration of the
  main idea helped me grasp his point.*

- **murmuring** (mʉr´ mər iŋ) *v.* making low,
  indistinct, continuous sounds (p. 380) *My
  parents were murmuring in the hallway to
  each other.*

- **parallel** (par´ə lel´) *adv.* extending in the
  same direction and at the same distance
  apart (p. 381) *The train tracks ran parallel to
  the highway.*

- **indispensable** (in´ di spen´ sə bəl) *adj.*
  absolutely necessary (p. 383) *Sunscreen is
  indispensable in the strong summer sun.*

Background

Gravity and Weightlessness Here on Earth, gravity is the force that holds people and objects down and gives them weight. Beyond Earth's atmosphere, however, gravity is weaker. This causes people and things to weigh less. For astronauts in space, the weak gravity environment affects how they eat, drink, and move. It can even affect their bones and muscles, as "Life Without Gravity" points out.

Connecting to the Literature

Reading/Writing Connection In "Life Without Gravity," the author describes some difficult and strange experiences astronauts have as they adjust to being weightless. Write three sentences about how gravity affects your everyday life. Use at least three of these words: *enable, predict, react, require, transport.*

Robert **Zimmerman** (b. 1953)

As a boy, Robert Zimmerman became fascinated with science-fiction books. They appealed to him because "the time was the early 1960s, when the first humans were going into space, and these books had an optimistic and hopeful view of that endeavor, as well as the future."

Influence of TV Today, Zimmerman watches little television, but as a child, he remembers viewing the blastoff of Mercury, NASA's first manned spacecraft. He recalls thinking, "This is the United States. We can do anything if we put our minds to it!"

Fast Facts

▶ Zimmerman spent twenty years in the movie business as a screenwriter and producer, among other jobs.
▶ Exploring caves is one of Zimmerman's hobbies. He sees caving as similar to outer space exploration, because both are a hunt "for the unknown."

Go Online
Author Link
For: More about the author
Visit: www.PHSchool.com
Web Code: eme-9302

Life Without Gravity

Robert Zimmerman

Being weightless in space seems so exciting. Astronauts bounce about from wall to wall, flying! They float, they weave, they do somersaults and acrobatics without effort. Heavy objects can be lifted like feathers, and no one ever gets tired because nothing weighs anything. In fact, everything is fun, nothing is hard.

NOT! Since the first manned space missions in the 1960s, scientists have discovered that being weightless in space isn't just flying around like Superman. Zero gravity is alien stuff. As space tourist Dennis Tito said when he visited the international space station, "Living in space is like having a different life, living in a different world."

Worse, weightlessness can sometimes be downright unpleasant. Your body gets upset and confused. Your face puffs up, your nose gets stuffy, your back hurts, your stomach gets upset, and you throw up. If astronauts are to survive a one-year journey to Mars—the shortest possible trip to the Red Planet—they will have to learn how to deal with this weird environment.

Our bodies are adapted to Earth's gravity. Our muscles are strong in order to overcome gravity as we walk and run. Our inner ears[1] use gravity to keep us upright. And because gravity wants to pull all our blood down into our legs, our hearts are designed to pump hard to get blood up to our brains.

In space, the much weaker gravity makes the human body change in many unexpected ways. In microgravity,[2] your blood is rerouted, flowing from the legs, which become thin and sticklike, to the head, which swells up. The extra liquid in your head also makes you feel like you're hanging upside down or have a stuffed-up nose.

The lack of gravity causes astronauts to routinely "grow" between one and three inches taller. Their spines straighten out. The bones in the spine and the disks between them spread apart and relax.

But their bones also get thin and spongy. The body decides that if the muscles aren't going to push and pull on the bones, it doesn't need to lay down as much bone as it normally does. Astronauts who have been in space for several months can lose 10 percent or more of their bone tissue. If their bones got

◀ ▲ **Critical Viewing**
What is unusual about each of these photographs? Explain what is happening.
[Hypothesize]

Literary Analysis
Expository Essay
What information do you learn about the human body in these paragraphs?

Vocabulary Builder
spines (spīnz) *n.* backbones

Reading Check

What are some disadvantages of weightlessness?

---

1. **inner ears** (in′ ər irz) *n.* internal parts of the ears that give people a sense of balance.
2. **microgravity** (mī′ krō grav′ i tē) *n.* state of near-weightlessness that astronauts experience as their spacecraft orbits the earth.

much weaker, they would snap once the astronauts returned to Earth.

And their muscles get weak and flabby. Floating about in space is too easy. If astronauts don't force themselves to exercise, their muscles become so <u>feeble</u> that when they return to Earth they can't even walk.

Worst of all is how their stomachs feel. During the first few days in space, the inner ear—which gives people their sense of balance—gets confused. Many astronauts become nauseous. They lose their appetites. Many throw up. Many throw up a lot!

Weightlessness isn't all bad, however. After about a week people usually get used to it. Their stomachs settle down. Appetites return (though astronauts always say that food tastes <u>blander</u> in space). The heart and spine adjust.

Then, flying around like a bird becomes fun! Rooms suddenly seem much bigger. Look around you: The space above your head is pretty useless on Earth. You can't get up there to work, and anything you attach to the ceiling is simply something you'll bump your head on.

In space, however, that area is useful. In fact, equipment can be installed on every inch of every wall. In weightlessness you choose to move up or down and left or right simply by pointing your head. If you turn yourself upside down, the ceiling becomes the floor.

And you can't drop anything! As you work you can let your tools float around you. But you'd better be organized and neat. If you don't put things back where they belong when you are finished, tying them down securely, they will float away. Air currents will then blow them into nooks and crannies, and it might take you days to find them again.

In microgravity, you have to learn new ways to eat. Don't try pouring a bowl of cornflakes. Not only will the flakes float all over the place, the milk won't pour. Instead, big balls of milk will form. You can drink these by taking big bites out of them, but you'd better finish them before they slam into a wall, splattering apart and covering everything with little tiny milk globules.

Vocabulary Builder
feeble (fē´ bəl) *adj.*
weak; infirm

blander (bland´ ər)
adj. more tasteless

▲ **Critical Viewing**
How do you think water is able to act like it does in this photograph? **[Analyze]**

Reading Skill
Main Idea What is the main idea in this paragraph?

Some meals on the space station are eaten with forks and knives, but scooping food with a spoon doesn't work. If the food isn't gooey enough to stick to the spoon, it will float away.

Everyone in space drinks through a straw, since liquid simply refuses to stay in a glass. The straw has to have a clamp at one end, or else when you stop drinking, the liquid will continue to flow out, spilling everywhere.

To prevent their muscles and bones from becoming too weak for life on Earth, astronauts have to follow a boring two-hour exercise routine every single day. Imagine having to run on a treadmill for one hour in the morning and then ride an exercise bicycle another hour before dinner. As Russian astronaut Valeri Ryumin once said, "Ye-ech!"

Even after all this exercise, astronauts who spend more than two months in space are usually weak and uncomfortable when they get back to Earth. Jerry Linenger, who spent more than four months on the Russian space station, *Mir*[3] struggled to walk after he returned. "My body felt like a 500 pound barbell," he said. He even had trouble lifting and holding his fifteen-month-old son, John.

When Linenger went to bed that first night, his body felt like it was being smashed into the mattress. He was constantly afraid that if he moved too much, he would float away and out of control.

And yet, Linenger recovered quickly. In fact, almost two dozen astronauts have lived in space for more than six months, and four have stayed in orbit for more than a year. These men and women faced the discomforts of weightlessness and overcame them. And they all readapted to Earth gravity without problems, proving that voyages to Mars are possible . . . Even if it feels like you are hanging upside down the whole time!

---

3. *Mir* (mēr) *n.* Russian space station.

Literature in Context

Science Connection

Weighted Down Your weight in pounds is actually the measure of the downward force of gravity on you. How much force gravity puts on you depends on the size and mass of the planet on which you are standing.

Imagine that on Earth you weigh 100 pounds. Because the surface gravity of Jupiter is 2.64 times that of Earth, you would weigh 264 pounds on Jupiter without eating a forkful more. On the other hand, surface gravity on the moon is one-sixth of Earth's gravity. That means your moon weight would be just under 17 pounds, though you would look just the same.

Of course, when you are not on a planet or moon, you are out of gravity's pull, so you weigh nothing at all.

Connect to the Literature

Is weightlessness as described in "Life Without Gravity" something you would like to experience? Why or why not?

Apply the Skills

Life Without Gravity

Thinking About the Selection

1. **Respond:** What do you think is the most difficult thing about living in a weightless environment?
2. **(a) Recall:** List three unpleasant effects of weightlessness that are explained in the essay. **(b) Cause and Effect:** Describe the cause of each unpleasant effect.
3. **(a) Recall:** What are some of the fun aspects of weightlessness? **(b) Connect:** What new choices does living in a weightless environment give an astronaut?
4. **(a) Synthesize:** If the astronauts quoted in the article were offered another trip in space, what advice would you give them about the wisdom of taking the trip again? **(b) Discuss:** Talk about your advice in a small group. As a group, choose three important pieces of advice to share with the class.

Reading Skill

5. What ideas did you get about the article from **skimming** it before you read?
6. **(a)** What are three **key points** in the article? **(b)** What **supporting details** does the author provide for each point?
7. What is the **main idea** of the article?

Literary Analysis

8. Explain why "Life Without Gravity" is an **expository essay**. Give examples from the text to support your answer.
9. Fill out a chart like the one shown to organize the information provided in the essay.

What Is Weightlessness?	What Are Its Advantages?	What Are Its Disadvantages?	Author's Conclusions

QuickReview

Article at a Glance
The writer explores the way astronauts' bodies are affected by the lack of gravity in space.

Go Online
—**Assessment**
For: Self-test
Visit: www.PHSchool.com
Web Code: ema-6302

Main Idea: the most important point

Expository Essay: a short piece of nonfiction that explains, defines, or interprets ideas, events, or processes

Vocabulary Builder

Practice Rewrite each sentence so that it includes a word from the vocabulary list on page 370 and conveys the same basic meaning.

1. I could barely hear her weak voice over the noise of the radio.

2. My cold makes this food seem less tasty.

3. If we had no bones in our backs, we would not be able to stand.

Writing

Write a brief **problem-and-solution essay** in which you assess the difficulties of being an astronaut in space.
- Clearly state two problems astronauts face.
- Provide step-by-step solutions to the problems.
- Support each solution with examples from the article.

For *Grammar, Vocabulary,* and *Assessment,* see **Build Language Skills,** pages 386–387.

Extend Your Learning

Listening and Speaking In a small group, prepare and deliver an **oral summary** of Zimmerman's expository essay.
To prepare your summary:
- Outline the main ideas and important supporting details. Note specific quotations that you want to mention.
- Use visual aids such as photographs, illustrations, or charts.

To deliver your summary:
- Speak slowly and clearly.
- Show each visual aid as you talk about the point it illustrates.
- Conclude with a statement expressing the main message.

Research and Technology Using print and electronic sources, create a **bibliography** of resources about gravity and weightlessness. Working in a small group, divide the research topics and have each group create a list of resources. Then, put your lists together to make a master list. To list sources accurately, use the MLA format, which is located on page R25.

Expository Essay

Background

Cultural Diversity While people around the world have much in common, they also have cultural differences. For example, people express these differences in the foods they eat and the ways they dress. As you will learn in "Conversational Ballgames," a way of talking that may seem normal to you might be considered strange, or even rude, to a person from another culture.

Connecting to the Literature

Reading/Writing Connection In "Conversational Ballgames," the author describes her surprise when she realizes that the "rules" governing conversation in Japan are different from conversational rules in Western countries such as the United States. Write a few sentences to identify the customs or expressions that a newcomer to American culture might find confusing. Use at least three of these words: *comprehend, communicate, perceive, respond.*

Review

For **Reading Skill, Literary Analysis,** and **Vocabulary Builder,** see page 370.

Meet the Author

Nancy **Masterson Sakamoto** (b. 1931)

Nancy Masterson Sakamoto graduated from UCLA with an English degree. She married a Japanese artist and Buddhist priest, and the couple lived in Japan for twenty-four years. There, Sakamoto was a visiting professor at the University of Osaka, where she trained Japanese junior and senior high school English teachers.

Cultural Differences While living in Japan, Sakamoto was able to observe conversations from both the Japanese and American perspectives.

Fast Facts

▶ Sakamoto is now a professor of American Studies at Shitennoji Gakuen University in Hawaii.
▶ She is a speaker and seminar leader for many educational, business, and professional organizations.

For: More about the author
Visit: www.PHSchool.com
Web Code: eme-9303

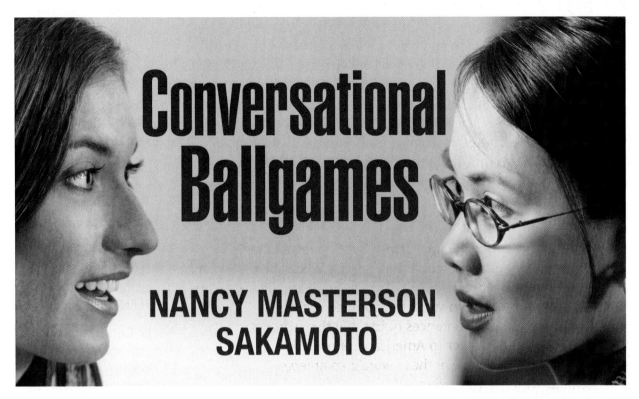

Conversational Ballgames

NANCY MASTERSON SAKAMOTO

After I was married and had lived in Japan for a while, my Japanese gradually improved to the point where I could take part in simple conversations with my husband and his friends and family. And I began to notice that often, when I joined in, the others would look startled, and the conversational topic would come to a halt. After this happened several times, it became clear to me that I was doing something wrong. But for a long time, I didn't know what it was.

Finally, after listening carefully to many Japanese conversations, I discovered what my problem was. Even though I was speaking Japanese, I was handling the conversation in a western[1] way.

Japanese-style conversations develop quite differently from western-style conversations. And the difference isn't only in the languages. I realized that just as I kept trying to hold western-style conversations even when I was speaking Japanese, so my English students kept trying to hold Japanese-style conversations even when they were speaking English. We were unconsciously playing entirely different conversational ballgames.

---

1. **western** *adj.* from the Western Hemisphere and Europe.

▲ **Critical Viewing**
Do these people appear to be having a meaningful conversation? Explain why or why not. **[Analyze]**

Literary Analysis
Expository Essay
What do you think the main topic of this essay might be?

**Reading Check**

What happens when the author tries to join Japanese conversations?

A western-style conversation between two people is like a game of tennis. If I introduce a topic, a conversational ball, I expect you to hit it back. If you agree with me, I don't expect you simply to agree and do nothing more. I expect you to add something—a reason for agreeing, another example, or an elaboration to carry the idea further. But I don't expect you always to agree. I am just as happy if you question me, or challenge me, or completely disagree with me. Whether you agree or disagree, your response will return the ball to me.

And then it is my turn again. I don't serve a new ball from my original starting line. I hit your ball back again from where it has bounced. I carry your idea further, or answer your questions or objections, or challenge or question you. And so the ball goes back and forth, with each of us doing our best to give it a new twist, an original spin, or a powerful smash.

And the more vigorous the action, the more interesting and exciting the game. Of course, if one of us gets angry, it spoils the conversation, just as it spoils a tennis game. But getting excited is not at all the same as getting angry. After all, we are not trying to hit each other. We are trying to hit the ball. So long as we attack only each other's opinions, and do not attack each other personally, we don't expect anyone to get hurt. A good conversation is supposed to be interesting and exciting.

If there are more than two people in the conversation, then it is like doubles in tennis, or like volleyball. There's no waiting in line. Whoever is nearest and quickest hits the ball, and if you step back, someone else will hit it. No one stops the game to give you a turn. You're responsible for taking your own turn.

But whether it's two players or a group, everyone does his best to keep the ball going, and no one person has the ball for very long.

A Japanese-style conversation, however, is not at all like tennis or volleyball. It's like bowling. You wait for your turn. And you always know your place in line. It depends on such things as whether you are older or younger, a close friend or a relative stranger to the previous speaker, in a senior or junior position, and so on.

When your turn comes, you step up to the starting line with your bowling ball, and carefully bowl it. Everyone else stands

Vocabulary Builder
elaboration (ē lab´ ə rā´ shən) *n.* adding of more details

Reading Skill
Main Idea What details in this paragraph support the idea that conversation is like tennis?

▶ **Critical Viewing** Do you agree that tennis is like a conversation? Explain. **[Relate]**

back and watches politely, <u>murmuring</u> encouragement. Everyone waits until the ball has reached the end of the alley, and watches to see if it knocks down all the pins, or only some of them, or none of them. There is a pause, while everyone registers your score.

Then, after everyone is sure that you have completely finished your turn, the next person in line steps up to the same starting line, with a different ball. He doesn't return your ball, and he does not begin from where your ball stopped. There is no back and forth at all. All the balls run <u>parallel</u>. And there is always a suitable pause between turns. There is no rush, no excitement, no scramble for the ball. No wonder everyone looked startled when I took part in Japanese conversations. I paid no attention to whose turn it was, and kept snatching the ball halfway down the alley and throwing it back at the bowler. Of course the conversation died. I was playing the wrong game.

This explains why it is almost impossible to get a western-style conversation or discussion going with English students

Vocabulary Builder

murmuring (mur´ mər iŋ) *v.* making low, indistinct, continuous sounds

parallel (par´ ə lel´) *adv.* extending in the same direction and at the same distance apart

 **Reading Check**

To what two sports does the author compare western-style conversation?

in Japan. I used to think that the problem was their lack of English language ability. But I finally came to realize that the biggest problem is that they, too, are playing the wrong game.

Whenever I serve a volleyball, everyone just stands back and watches it fall, with occasional murmurs of encouragement. No one hits it back. Everyone waits until I call on someone to take a turn. And when that person speaks, he doesn't hit my ball back. He serves a new ball. Again, everyone just watches it fall.

So I call on someone else. This person does not refer to what the previous speaker has said. He also serves a new ball. Nobody seems to have paid any attention to what anyone else has said. Everyone begins again from the same starting line, and all the balls run parallel. There is never any back and forth. Everyone is trying to bowl with a volleyball.

And if I try a simpler conversation, with only two of us, then the other person tries to bowl with my tennis ball. No wonder foreign English teachers in Japan get discouraged.

Now that you know about the difference in the conversational ball-games, you may think that all your troubles are over. But if you have been trained all your life to play one game, it is no simple matter to switch to another, even if you know the rules. Knowing the rules is not at all the same thing as playing the game.

Even now, during a conversation in Japanese I will notice a startled reaction, and belatedly realize that

▲ **Critical Viewing** Does this picture illustrate the author's ideas about Japanese conversation? Explain. **[Analyze]**

once again I have rudely interrupted by instinctively trying to hit back the other person's bowling ball. It is no easier for me to "just listen" during a conversation than it is for my Japanese students to "just relax" when speaking with foreigners. Now I can truly sympathize with how hard they must find it to try to carry on a western-style conversation.

If I have not yet learned to do conversational bowling in Japanese, at least I have figured out one thing that puzzled me for a long time. After his first trip to America, my husband complained that Americans asked him so many questions and made him talk so much at the dinner table that he never had a chance to eat. When I asked him why he couldn't talk and eat at the same time, he said that Japanese do not customarily think that dinner, especially on fairly formal occasions, is a suitable time for extended conversation.

Since westerners think that conversation is an <u>indispensable</u> part of dining, and indeed would consider it impolite not to converse with one's dinner partner, I found this Japanese custom rather strange. Still, I could accept it as a cultural difference even though I didn't really understand it. But when my husband added, in explanation, that Japanese consider it extremely rude to talk with one's mouth full, I got confused. Talking with one's mouth full is certainly not an American custom. We think it very rude, too. Yet we still manage to talk a lot and eat at the same time. How do we do it?

For a long time, I couldn't explain it, and it bothered me. But after I discovered the conversational ballgames, I finally found the answer. Of course! In a western-style conversation, you hit the ball, and while someone else is hitting it back, you take a bite, chew, and swallow. Then you hit the ball again, and then eat some more. The more people there are in the conversation, the more chances you have to eat. But even with only two of you talking, you still have plenty of chances to eat.

Maybe that's why polite conversation at the dinner table has never been a traditional part of Japanese etiquette.[2] Your turn to talk would last so long without interruption that you'd never get a chance to eat.

---

2. etiquette (et′ i kit) *n.* formal rules for polite behavior in society or in a particular group.

Apply the Skills

Conversational Ballgames

Thinking About the Selection

1. **Respond:** What is the most surprising thing you learned in this essay? Why is it surprising?
2. **(a) Recall:** What happened at first when the author joined in during conversations in Japan? **(b) Draw Conclusions:** What misunderstandings took place during those initial conversations?
3. **(a) Recall:** To what sports or games does the author compare Japanese-style and Western-style conversations?
   (b) Apply: What do the author and her family and friends need to understand about each other?
4. **(a) Recall:** How do the Japanese feel about conversing during dinner? **(b) Compare and Contrast:** How does this compare with Westerners' behavior during a meal?
5. **Evaluate:** When holding a conversation in another culture, who has the greater responsibility for playing by the culture's "conversational rules": the newcomer or the person already living there? Explain.

Reading Skill

6. What ideas did you get about the article from **skimming** it before you read?
7. What are three **key points** in the article? What **supporting details** does the author provide for each point?
8. What is the **main idea** of the article?

Literary Analysis

9. Explain why "Conversational Ballgames" is an **expository essay**. Give examples from the text to support your answer.
10. Fill out a chart like the one shown to organize the information provided in the essay.

Describe Polite Conversation in the United States	Describe Polite Conversation in Japan	Author's Conclusion

Vocabulary Builder

Practice Rewrite each sentence so that it includes a word from the vocabulary list on page 370 and conveys the same basic meaning.

1. The lines in the parking lot are side by side.

2. The low buzz of conversation went on for hours and hours.

3. Please, use many details when you write your descriptive essay.

4. A pencil sharpener is completely necessary in a classroom.

Writing

Write a brief **problem-and-solution essay** about the difficulties Japanese and Westerners have in conversing with each other.

- Clearly state one or more problems.
- Provide step-by-step solutions to the problems.
- Give evidence that supports your suggested solutions.

For *Grammar, Vocabulary,* and *Assessment,* see **Build Language Skills,** pages 386–387.

Extend Your Learning

Listening and Speaking In a small group, prepare and deliver an **oral summary** of Sakamoto's expository essay.

- Outline the main ideas and important supporting details. Note specific quotations that you want to mention.
- Use visual aids such as photographs, illustrations, or charts.
- Speak slowly and clearly.
- Show each visual aid as you talk about the point it illustrates.
- Conclude with a statement expressing the main message.

Research and Technology Use the Internet and library to prepare a **bibliography** of life in Japan today. Find books, videos, articles, and Web sites that depict life and work for children and adults in that country. To list sources accurately, use the MLA format, which is located on page R25.

Build Language Skills

Life Without Gravity • *Conversational Ballgames*

Vocabulary Skill

Prefixes The word **irrelevant** combines the prefix *ir-* and the word *relevant*. *Relevant* means "having a logical connection with the matter at hand." *Irrelevant* is an antonym of *relevant*. It means "having **no** logical connection with the matter at hand."

▶ **Example:** Marsha revised her essay to remove *irrelevant* details.

Practice Use your knowledge of prefixes to answer the following questions.

1. How might an *inaccurate* weather forecast affect your picnic plans?
2. Why might an *irregular* class schedule be confusing to students?
3. How might an *inactive* person spend his or her day?
4. Why do businesses try to avoid hiring *irresponsible* workers?
5. Why would an *indecisive* person make a poor judge?

Grammar Lesson

Conjunctions connect words or groups of words. **Coordinating conjunctions,** such as *but, and, nor, for, so, yet,* and *or,* connect words or groups of words that are similar in form. **Conjunctions** show the relationship between those two parts. In the following examples, the coordinating conjunctions are boldface. The words they connect are italicized.

MorePractice

For more practice with conjunctions, see the Grammar Handbook, p. R32.

▶ **Example: Nouns:** The *pen* **and** *paper* contained fingerprints.
   Verbs: Shall we *walk* **or** *ride* our bicycles?
   Groups of words: He *ran out the door,* **but** *the bus had already left.*

Practice Circle the coordinating conjunction in each sentence. Underline the words or groups of words connected by the conjunction. Then, write a sentence using a different conjunction.

1. There was a huge snowstorm, but they left the house anyway.
2. We invited the basketball team and the cheerleaders to the party.
3. Which do you prefer, biking or skating?
4. The fight was fierce yet fair.
5. After school and on weekends, Justin worked.

W͞G Prentice Hall Writing and Grammar Connection, Chapter 18, Section 1

■ *Types of Nonfiction*

Reading: Main Idea

Directions: *Read the selection. Then, answer the questions.*

For years, my home office was a mess. Papers were piled on my desktop in a disorganized way. It always took me a long time to find important forms and documents, if I found them at all.

I hired an office consultant and that changed my professional life. The consultant convinced me that everything must have a proper place. At her suggestion, I bought manila folders, labeled them by topic, and filed each paper in its appropriate folder. Then I organized the folders in a file drawer alphabetically. What an improvement! Working in an efficiently organized office has increased my productivity and saved me time. I can finally see the top of my desk!

1. What is the main idea of the passage?
   A Papers should be discarded.
   B The consultant gave the author bad advice.
   C A messy office is a creative office.
   D Keeping papers filed properly avoids clutter and saves time.

2. Which of these steps is part of the author's reorganization?
   A File papers in a different room.
   B Organize furniture and space.
   C Buy a new desk.
   D Label folders by topic.

3. What lesson did the author learn?
   A Blue folders are a boon to office work.
   B Every office needs a big file drawer.
   C Check your "To Do" list each morning.
   D It is more efficient to keep an organized office.

4. Choose the best title for this passage.
   A Clutter Is Better
   B My Office Is a Mess
   C How to Have an Efficient Office
   D Tomorrow Is Another Day

Timed Writing: Explanation [Cognition]

Review "Life Without Gravity" or "Conversational Ballgames." Recall some of the problems in the article and the solutions. Then, in your own words, explain one problem and the solution. Use examples from the article to support your work. **(20 minutes)**

 ## Writing Workshop: *Work in Progress*

How-to Essay

From the list in your portfolio, choose two activities that require four or more steps to perform, and briefly list the steps involved. Save your Steps List in your writing portfolio.

These skills will help you become a better reader. Practice them with either "I Am a Native of North America" (p. 390) or the excerpt from *In Search of Our Mothers' Gardens* (p. 397).

Reading Skill

The **main idea** is the most important thought or concept in a work or a passage of text. Sometimes the author directly states the main idea of a work and then provides key points that support it. These key points are supported in turn by details such as examples and descriptions. Other times the main idea is unstated. The author gives you *only* the key points or supporting details that add up to the main idea. To understand the main idea, **make connections between key points and supporting details.**

- Notice how the writer groups details.
- Look for sentences that pull details together.

Use a chart like the one shown to help you show the connections.

Literary Analysis

A **reflective essay** is a brief prose work that presents a writer's feelings and thoughts, or reflections, about an experience or idea. The purpose is to communicate these thoughts and feelings so that readers will respond with thoughts and feelings of their own. As you read a reflective essay, think about the ideas the writer is sharing.

Vocabulary Builder

I Am a Native of North America

- **distinct** (di stiŋkt´) *adj.* separate and different (p. 390) *Sparrows and owls are two <u>distinct</u> groups of birds.*

- **communal** (kə myo͞on´ əl) *adj.* shared by all (p. 390) *Campers of all ages ate together in a <u>communal</u> lunchroom.*

- **justifies** (jus´ tə fīz´) *v.* excuses (p. 391) *Nothing <u>justifies</u> the misuse of power.*

- **promote** (prə mōt´) *v.* encourage; contribute to the growth of (p. 393) *A doctor designed the menu to <u>promote</u> good eating habits.*

In Search of Our Mothers' Gardens

- **anonymous** (ə nän´ ə məs) *adj.* unacknowledged; by someone whose name is withheld or unknown (p. 398) *An <u>anonymous</u> phone call helped solve the mystery.*

- **profusely** (prō fyo͞os´ lē) *adv.* freely; plentifully (p. 399) *Sue thanked her aunt <u>profusely</u> for the generous gift.*

- **radiant** (rā´ dē ənt) *adj.* shining brightly (p. 400) *The boy flashed a <u>radiant</u> smile.*

- **hindered** (hin´ dərd) *adj.* held back (p. 400) *<u>Hindered</u> by an injury, I pitched poorly.*

Background

Vancouver Area Native Americans Chief Dan George was a member of the Coast Salish Indians in western Canada. His ancestors organized their lives according to a cycle of hunting, food gathering, and cultural activities. During winter, the people stayed in large villages near sheltered bays. In spring, they moved to the beaches, where they fished, hunted, and gathered berries. Then, in the fall, groups met along the rivers to fish. Their cycle of living connected them closely with the natural world.

Connecting to the Literature

Reading/Writing Connection Chief Dan George knew two cultures—the Native American culture and the Canadian culture in which he was raised. List ways that a person's cultural background can influence the person he or she becomes. Use at least three of the following words: *conserve, enrich, cooperate, evaluate.*

Meet the Author

Chief Dan **George** (1899–1981)

Chief Dan George, the son of a tribal chief, was named "Tes-wah-no" but was also known as Dan Slaholt. At age five, he was sent to a mission boarding school, where his last name was changed to George.

At seventeen, Dan George left school and began working. While working as a bus driver, he won the role of an aging Indian in a TV series.

Life as an Actor George was called one of the "finest natural actors anywhere." He won acting awards in Canada and earned parts in major motion pictures. With fame, George became a spokesman for Native Americans.

Fast Facts

▶ George was more than sixty years old when he became a movie actor.

▶ In 1970, George was nominated for an Academy Award for his role in *Little Big Man.*

Go Online
Author Link

For: More about the author
Visit: www.PHSchool.com
Web Code: eme-9304

I Am a Native of

In the course of my lifetime I have lived in two <u>distinct</u> cultures. I was born into a culture that lived in <u>communal</u> houses. My grandfather's house was eighty feet long. It was called a smoke house, and it stood down by the beach along the inlet.[1] All my grandfather's sons and their families lived in this large dwelling. Their sleeping apartments were separated by blankets made of bull rush reeds, but one open fire in the middle served the cooking needs of all. In houses like these, throughout the tribe, people learned to live with one another; learned to serve one another; learned to respect the rights of one another. And children shared the thoughts of the adult world and found themselves surrounded by aunts and uncles and cousins who loved them and did not threaten them. My father was born in such a house and learned from infancy how to love people and be at home with them.

And beyond this acceptance of one another there was a deep respect for everything in nature that surrounded them. My father loved the earth and all its creatures. The earth was his second mother. The earth and everything it contained was a gift from See-see-am[2] . . . and the way to thank this great spirit was to use his gifts with respect.

I remember, as a little boy, fishing with him up Indian River and I can still see him as the sun rose above the mountain top in the early morning . . . I can see him standing by the water's edge with his arms raised above his head while he softly

Vocabulary Builder
distinct (di stiŋkt')
adj. separate and
different

communal (kə myo͞on´
əl) *adj.* shared by all

Literary Analysis
Reflective Essay
What experience or
idea is the author
reflecting on here?

---

1. inlet (in´ let) *n.* narrow strip of water jutting into a body of land from a river, a lake, or an ocean.
2. See-see-am the name of the Great Spirit, or "The Chief Above," in the Salishan language of Chief George's people.

North America

Chief Dan George

moaned . . . "Thank you, thank you." It left a deep impression on my young mind.

And I shall never forget his disappointment when once he caught me gaffing for fish[3] "just for the fun of it." "My Son," he said, "the Great Spirit gave you those fish to be your brothers, to feed you when you are hungry. You must respect them. You must not kill them just for the fun of it."

This then was the culture I was born into and for some years the only one I really knew or tasted. This is why I find it hard to accept many of the things I see around me.

I see people living in smoke houses hundreds of times bigger than the one I knew. But the people in one apartment do not even know the people in the next and care less about them.

It is also difficult for me to understand the deep hate that exists among people. It is hard to understand a culture that <u>justifies</u> the killing of millions in past wars, and is at this very moment preparing bombs to kill even greater numbers. It is hard for me to understand a culture that spends more on wars and weapons to kill, than it does on education and welfare to help and develop.

It is hard for me to understand a culture that not only hates and fights its brothers but even attacks nature and abuses her. I see my white brother going about blotting out nature from his cities. I see him strip the hills bare, leaving ugly wounds on the face of mountains. I see him tearing things from the bosom of mother earth as though she were a monster, who refused to share her treasures with him. I see him

---

3. gaffing for fish using a barbed spear to catch river fish.

▲ Critical Viewing
What ideas expressed by Chief Dan George are connected to this photograph? **[Speculate]**

Vocabulary Builder
justifies (jus´ tə fīz´)
v. excuses; explains

**Reading Check**

In what two cultures has Chief Dan George lived?

Buffalo, 1992, Jaune Smith, Courtesy Steinbaum Krauss Gallery, NYC

▲ **Critical Viewing** Based on the points he makes, would Chief Dan George applaud or criticize this collage? Explain. **[Synthesize]**

throw poison in the waters, indifferent to the life he kills there; and he chokes the air with deadly fumes.

My white brother does many things well for he is more clever than my people but I wonder if he knows how to love well. I wonder if he has ever really learned to love at all. Perhaps he only loves the things that are his own but never learned to love the things that are outside and beyond him. And this is, of course, not love at all, for man must love all creation or he will love none of it. Man must love fully or he will become the lowest of the animals. It is the power to love that makes him the greatest of them all . . . for he alone of all animals is capable of love.

Love is something you and I must have. We must have it because our spirit feeds upon it. We must have it because without it we become weak and faint. Without love our self-esteem weakens. Without it our courage fails. Without love we can no longer look out confidently at the world. Instead we turn inwardly and begin to feed upon our own personalities and little by little we destroy ourselves.

Reading Skill
Main Idea What key words or sentences so far have helped you determine the essay's main idea?

You and I need the strength and joy that comes from knowing that we are loved. With it we are creative. With it we march tirelessly. With it, and with it alone, we are able to sacrifice for others.

There have been times when we all wanted so desperately to feel a reassuring hand upon us . . . there have been lonely times when we so wanted a strong arm around us . . . I cannot tell you how deeply I miss my wife's presence when I return from a trip. Her love was my greatest joy, my strength, my greatest blessing.

I am afraid my culture has little to offer yours. But my culture did prize friendship and companionship. It did not look on privacy as a thing to be clung to, for privacy builds up walls and walls <u>promote</u> distrust. My culture lived in big family communities, and from infancy people learned to live with others.

My culture did not prize the hoarding of private possessions; in fact, to hoard was a shameful thing to do among my people. The Indian looked on all things in nature as belonging to him and he expected to share them with others and to take only what he needed.

Everyone likes to give as well as receive. No one wishes only to receive all the time. We have taken much from your culture . . . I wish you had taken something from our culture . . . for there were some beautiful and good things in it.

Soon it will be too late to know my culture, for integration is upon us and soon we will have no values but yours. Already many of our young people have forgotten the old ways. And many have been shamed of their Indian ways by scorn and ridicule. My culture is like a wounded deer that has crawled away into the forest to bleed and die alone.

The only thing that can truly help us is genuine love. You must truly love us, be patient with us and share with us. And we must love you—with a genuine love that forgives and forgets . . . a love that forgives the terrible sufferings your culture brought ours when it swept over us like a wave crashing along a beach . . . with a love that forgets and lifts up its head and sees in your eyes an answering love of trust and acceptance.

This is brotherhood . . . anything less is not worthy of the name.

I have spoken.

Literary Analysis
Reflective Essay
What experiences does the author reflect on here?

Vocabulary Builder
promote (prə mōt′)
v. encourage; contribute to the growth of

Reading Skill
Main Idea What key word is repeated in this paragraph and throughout the essay? How does it help you determine the essay's main idea?

Apply the Skills

I Am a Native of North America

Thinking About the Selection

1. **Respond:** Do you agree that "the power to love" is the most important human quality? Why or why not?

2. **(a) Recall:** Name three things that people learn from growing up in communal homes. **(b) Compare and Contrast:** Identify several differences between the "two distinct cultures" in which Chief Dan George lived.

3. **(a) Recall:** What three things puzzle Chief Dan George about his "white brother"? **(b) Interpret:** When Chief Dan George says, "My white brother . . . is more clever than my people," what does he mean by *clever*?

4. **(a) Analyze:** What is the "brotherhood" that Chief Dan George talks about at the end of the essay? **(b) Evaluate:** Is this brotherhood important? Why or why not?

5. **Make a Judgment:** Can people maintain a sense of cultural identity while interacting with another group that does not have the same culture? Explain.

Reading Skill

6. **(a)** What details does Chief Dan George provide about his father's relationship with nature? **(b)** Give an example of a sentence from the work that pulls these details together.

7. What is the **main idea** of the essay?

Literary Analysis

8. Analyze the **reflective essay** in a chart like the one shown. In the first column, write George's reflections on three points, including the one provided. Then, write your response. Trade charts with a partner and discuss your responses. In the third column of your chart, explain whether your responses changed based on your discussion.

George's Reflections	My Responses	After Discussion
Father gives thanks on fishing trip		

Vocabulary Builder

Practice An **antonym** is a word that is opposite in meaning to another word. For the first word in each numbered item, find the answer choice that is its antonym. Explain your answers.

1. distinct: **(a)** similar **(b)** different **(c)** decided
2. communal: **(a)** busy **(b)** private **(c)** organized
3. justifies: **(a)** supports **(b)** opposes **(c)** excuses
4. promote: **(a)** encourage **(b)** advance **(c)** prevent

Writing

Make an **outline** of "I Am a Native of North America." Build your outline using this format:

- Use Roman numerals to identify each key point.
- Use capital letters to identify supporting details.

At the top of your outline, write a sentence stating the main idea of the essay in your own words.

For *Grammar, Vocabulary,* and *Assessment,* see **Build Language Skills,** pages 404–405.

Extend Your Learning

Listening and Speaking Present a **response** to the essay by stating whether you agree or disagree with the author's message. First, summarize the author's message. Then, give at least two reasons to explain why you agree or disagree. Use examples from the work in your response.

Research and Technology In a small group, prepare and deliver a brief **oral report** about one Native American group's traditional culture. Use text and photographs, maps, audio recordings, film clips, or other media. To begin, identify categories such as types of shelters or ways of gathering food. For information, use the Internet and the library. Make sure each member of the group plays an important role.

Build Understanding • *from In Search of Our Mothers' Gardens*

Background

Sharecroppers Alice Walker, the writer of this essay, was the daughter of sharecroppers. In exchange for housing, seed, and tools, sharecroppers worked long, hard hours and then gave the bulk of their crops to the landowners. This difficult lifestyle was common among African Americans who lived in the South at the time Walker was growing up.

Connecting to the Literature

Reading/Writing Connection In this essay, Alice Walker shares her memories of her mother. Write a few sentences about a person who has shaped your life in some way. Use at least three of these words: *appreciate, contribute, demonstrate, interact.*

Review

For **Reading Skill, Literary Analysis,** and **Vocabulary Builder,** see page 388.

Meet the Author

Alice **Walker** (b. 1944)

Alice Walker was born in Eatonville, Georgia, the child of Tallulah Grant Walker and Willie Lee Walker. Her sharecropper parents earned as little as $300 a year. All the Walker children had to help by working in the fields, milking cows, and doing other chores. Their mother stood at the center of the family and "made a way out of no way."

A Life Rich in Experiences Both of Walker's parents were gifted storytellers, and they recounted engaging folk tales as well as family stories. Tallulah Walker shared her spirit and her artistic creations—food, clothing, and flowers—with her family and community.

Despite her family's limited financial resources, Walker went to college. The artist in Walker blossomed, and she became a very popular writer. Her novel *The Color Purple* won the Pulitzer Prize.

Fast Facts

▶ Walker was the youngest of eight children.
▶ *The Color Purple* was made into a successful motion picture.

Go Online
Author Link

For: More about the author
Visit: www.PHSchool.com
Web Code: eme-9305

from

In Search of Our Mothers' Gardens

ALICE WALKER

My mother made all the clothes we wore, even my brothers' overalls. She made all the towels and sheets we used. She spent the summers canning vegetables and fruits. She spent the winter evenings making quilts enough to cover all our beds.

During the "working" day, she labored beside—not behind—my father in the fields. Her day began before sunup, and did not end until late at night. There was never a moment for her to sit down, undisturbed, to unravel her own private thoughts; never a time free from interruption—by work or the noisy inquiries of her many children. And yet, it is to my

Literary Analysis
Reflective Essay
What experience or idea do you think Walker will reflect on in this essay? Explain.

mother—and all our mothers who were not famous—that I went in search of the secret of what has fed that muzzled and often mutilated, but vibrant,[1] creative spirit that the black woman has inherited, and that pops out in wild and unlikely places to this day.

But when, you will ask, did my overworked mother have time to know or care about feeding the creative spirit?

The answer is so simple that many of us have spent years discovering it. We have constantly looked high, when we should have looked high—and low.

For example: in the Smithsonian Institution[2] in Washington, D.C., there hangs a quilt unlike any other in the world. In fanciful, inspired, and yet simple and identifiable figures, it portrays the story of the Crucifixion. It is considered rare, beyond price. Though it follows no known pattern of quilt-making, and though it is made of bits and pieces of worthless rags, it is obviously the work of a person of powerful imagination and deep spiritual feeling. Below this quilt I saw a note that says it was made by "an <u>anonymous</u> Black woman in Alabama, a hundred years ago."

If we could locate this "anonymous" black woman from Alabama, she would turn out to be one of our grandmothers—an artist who left her mark in the only materials she could afford, and in the only medium her position in society allowed her to use.

And so our mothers and grandmothers have, more often than not anonymously, handed on the creative spark, the seed of the flower they themselves never hoped to see: or like a sealed letter they could not plainly read.

And so it is, certainly, with my own mother. Unlike "Ma" Rainey's songs, which retained their creator's name even while blasting forth from Bessie Smith's mouth,[3] no song or poem will bear my mother's name. Yet so many of the stories that I write, that we all write, are my mother's stories. Only recently did I fully realize this: that through years of listening to my mother's stories of her life, I have absorbed not only the stories themselves, but something of the manner in which she spoke, something of the urgency that involves the knowledge

---

1. **mutilated, but vibrant** damaged, but still energetic and lively.
2. **Smithsonian Institution** museums with exhibits in the fields of science, art, and history.
3. **"Ma" Rainey's songs . . . Bessie Smith's mouth** Gertrude ("Ma") Rainey, one of America's first blues singers, lived during the early years of the twentieth century. Bessie Smith (1898?–1937) was a well-regarded blues singer who knew and learned from "Ma" Rainey.

that her stories—like her life—must be recorded. It is probably for this reason that so much of what I have written is about characters whose counterparts in real life are so much older than I am.

But the telling of these stories, which came from my mother's lips as naturally as breathing, was not the only way my mother showed herself as an artist. For stories, too, were subject to being distracted, to dying without conclusion. Dinners must be started, and cotton must be gathered before the big rains. The artist that was and is my mother showed itself to me only after many years. This is what I finally noticed:

Like Mem, a character in *The Third Life of Grange Copeland*,[4] my mother adorned with flowers whatever shabby house we were forced to live in. And not just your typical straggly country stand of zinnias, either. She planted ambitious gardens—and still does—with over fifty different varieties of plants that bloom <u>profusely</u> from early March until

Literary Analysis
Reflective Essay
What does Walker admire in her mother?

Vocabulary Builder
profusely (prō fyo͞os′ lē) *adv.* freely; plentifully

✔ **Reading Check**

What does Walker believe about the everyday work of women?

late November. Before she left home for the fields, she watered her flowers, chopped up the grass, and laid out new beds. When she returned from the fields she might divide clumps of bulbs, dig a cold pit,[5] uproot and replant roses, or prune branches from her taller bushes or trees—until night came and it was too dark to see.

Whatever she planted grew as if by magic, and her fame as a grower of flowers spread over three counties. Because of her creativity with her flowers, even my memories of poverty are seen through a screen of blooms—sunflowers, petunias, roses, dahlias, forsythia, spirea, delphiniums, verbena . . . and on and on.

And I remember people coming to my mother's yard to be given cuttings from her flowers; I hear again the praise showered on her because whatever rocky soil she landed on, she turned into a garden. A garden so brilliant with colors, so original in its design, so magnificent with life and creativity, that to this day people drive by our house in Georgia—perfect strangers and imperfect strangers—and ask to stand or walk among my mother's art.

I notice that it is only when my mother is working in her flowers that she is <u>radiant</u>, almost to the point of being invisible—except as Creator: hand and eye. She is involved in work her soul must have. Ordering the universe in the image of her personal conception of Beauty.

Her face, as she prepares the Art that is her gift, is a legacy[6] of respect she leaves to me, for all that illuminates and cherishes life. She has handed down respect for the possibilities—and the will to grasp them.

For her, so <u>hindered</u> and intruded upon in so many ways, being an artist has still been a daily part of her life. This ability to hold on, even in very simple ways, is work black women have done for a very long time.

This poem is not enough, but it is something, for the woman who literally covered the holes in our walls with sunflowers:

They were women then
My mama's generation
Husky of voice—Stout of

Reading Skill
Main Idea How do the details about flowers support the main idea of this essay?

Vocabulary Builder
radiant (rā′ dē ənt)
adj. shining brightly

Vocabulary Builder
hindered (hin′ dərd)
adj. held back

---

5. **cold pit** hole in which seedlings are planted at the beginning of spring.
6. **legacy** (leg′ ə sē) *n.* something handed down by a parent or an ancestor.

Step
With fists as well as
Hands
How they battered down
Doors
And ironed
Starched white
Shirts
How they led
Armies
Headragged[7] Generals
Across mined[8]
Fields
Booby-trapped
Kitchens
To discover books
Desks
A place for us
How they knew what we
Must know
Without knowing a page
Of it
Themselves.

▲ **Critical Viewing**
How is a garden like a work of art?
[Analyze]

Guided by my heritage of a love of beauty and a respect for strength—in search of my mother's garden, I found my own.

And perhaps in Africa over two hundred years ago, there was just such a mother; perhaps she painted vivid and daring decorations in oranges and yellows and greens on the walls of her hut; perhaps she sang—in a voice like Roberta Flack's[9] — sweetly over the compounds of her village; perhaps she wove the most stunning mats or told the most ingenious[10] stories of all the village storytellers. Perhaps she was herself a poet— though only her daughter's name is signed to the poems that we know.

Perhaps Phillis Wheatley's[11] mother was also an artist.

Perhaps in more than Phillis Wheatley's biological life is her mother's signature made clear.

Reading Skill
Main Idea Which details in this paragraph support the main idea?

---

7. **headragged** (hed´ ragd) *adj.* with head wrapped around by a rag or kerchief.
8. **mined** (mīnd) *adj.* filled with buried explosives that are set to go off when stepped on.
9. **Roberta Flack's** Roberta Flack, an African American singer, was very popular in the 1970s.
10. **ingenious** (in jēn´ yəs) *adj.* clever and inventive.
11. **Phillis Wheatley's** Phillis Wheatley (1753?–1784) was a poet, considered the first important black writer in America.

Apply the Skills

from *In Search of Our Mothers' Gardens*

Thinking About the Selection

1. **Respond:** Which of Walker's mother's personal qualities do you most admire? Why?
2. **(a) Recall:** Briefly describe the home and setting in which Walker grew up. **(b) Connect:** What does your description suggest about Walker's mother? **(c) Apply:** In what way does Walker's mother represent women in general?
3. **(a) Analyze:** Why does Walker call this essay "In Search of *Our* Mothers' Gardens" instead of "In Search of *My* Mother's Gardens"? **(b) Evaluate:** Explain why one title is more appropriate than the other.
4. **Make a Judgment:** Walker includes useful creations such as gardens and quilts in her definition of *art*. How does this compare with your definition of *art*? Explain.

Reading Skills

5. **(a)** What details does Walker provide about her mother's storytelling? **(b)** Give an example of a sentence from the work that pulls these details together.
6. What is the **main idea** of the essay?

Literary Analysis

7. Analyze the **reflective essay** in a chart like the one shown. In the first column, write Walker's reflections on three points, including the one provided. Then, write your response. Trade charts with a partner and discuss your responses. In the third column of your chart, explain whether your responses changed based on your discussion.

Walker's Reflections	My Responses	After Discussion
Mother worked from before sunup until late at night.		

QuickReview

Essay at a Glance
Alice Walker reflects on the ways ordinary women create art in their everyday lives.

Assessment
For: Self-test
Visit: www.PHSchool.com
Web Code: ema-6305

Main Idea: most important thought or concept

Reflective Essay: a brief work of prose that presents the writer's thoughts and feelings about an experience or idea

Vocabulary Builder

Practice An **antonym** is a word that is opposite in meaning to another word. For the first word in each numbered item, find the answer choice that is its antonym. Explain your answers.

1. anonymous: **(a)** mysterious **(b)** named **(c)** informed
2. profusely: **(a)** insufficiently **(b)** busily **(c)** freely
3. radiant: **(a)** healthy **(b)** sunny **(c)** dim
4. hindered: **(a)** helped **(b)** postponed **(c)** bothered

Writing

Make an **outline** that shows the flow of ideas in the excerpt from "In Search of Our Mothers' Gardens." Build your outline using this format:

- Use Roman numerals to identify each key point.
- Use capital letters to identify supporting details.

At the top of your outline, write a sentence stating the main idea of the essay in your own words.

For *Grammar, Vocabulary,* and *Assessment,* see **Build Language Skills,** pages 404–405.

Extend Your Learning

Listening and Speaking Present a **response** to the essay by stating whether you agree or disagree with the author's message. First, summarize the author's message. Then, give at least two reasons to explain why you agree or disagree. Use examples from the work in your response.

Research and Technology Throughout history, people have poured creative energy into making useful and necessary items. In a small group, prepare and deliver an **oral report** on one kind of creative output: quilts, clothing, food, or gardens. Include text and photographs, maps, audio recordings, film clips, or other media. Use the Internet and library resources to do research. Make sure each member of the group plays an important role.

Build Language Skills

Vocabulary Skill

Prefixes The word **insignificant** combines the prefix *in-* which means "without" or "not," and the word *significant*. The word *significant* means "having an important meaning." Adding the prefix creates an antonym that means "not having an important meaning."

▶ **Example:** An important detail is *significant*.
A detail that does not matter is *insignificant*.

Practice Add the prefix *in-* to create an antonym for each of the words listed. Then, write sentences that illustrate the meanings of the words.

1. complete
2. consistent
3. sensitive
4. sufficient
5. direct

Grammar Lesson

Prepositions and Prepositional Phrases A **preposition** relates a noun or pronoun that follows the preposition to another word in the sentence. In the sentence *The book is on the table,* the preposition *on* relates *table* to *book.* Common prepositions include *above, behind, below, beyond, for, into, near, of, on, outside, over, through, to, under,* and *with.* A **prepositional phrase** begins with a preposition and ends with the noun or pronoun that follows it. In *The book is on the table,* the prepositional phrase is *on the table.*

MorePractice

For more practice with prepositions and prepositional phrases, see the Grammar Handbook, p. R32.

Practice Write the prepositional phrase from each sentence. Then, substitute a different prepositional phrase into each sentence. Share your new sentences with a writing partner.

1. Marge hid her diary under the bed.
2. The field trip was canceled because of the bad weather.
3. Josh was sitting near the pond.
4. In the distance, we saw an auto accident.
5. Gran sends messages through the mail.

W̶G Prentice Hall Writing and Grammar Connection: Chapter 17, Sections 1 and 2

Reading: Main Idea

Directions: *Read the selection. Then, answer the questions.*

The man was gaining on us. He was a thin man, all action. . . .

He chased Mikey and me around the yellow house and up a backyard path we knew by heart: under a low tree, up a bank, through a hedge, down some snowy steps, and across the grocery store's delivery driveway.

. . .we ran across Edgerton to an alley and up our own sliding woodpile to the Halls' front yard; he kept coming. We ran up Lloyd Street and wound through mazy backyards. . . .

He chased us silently, block after block. . . .

from *An American Childhood*, Annie Dillard

1. Which two words are repeated and hint at the main idea?

   A knew and wound

   B snowy and scruffy

   C chased and entered

   D ran and chased

2. Which sums things up, hinting at the main idea?

   A He kept coming.

   B up Lloyd Street

   C We smashed through a gap.

   D He was a thin man, all action.

3. What is the main idea of this passage?

   A The narrator is chasing his friends.

   B The narrator is throwing snowballs.

   C The narrator is trying to escape from someone.

   D School has been canceled because of snow.

4. Where is the main idea stated?

   A in the first sentence

   B the first sentence of the 2nd paragraph

   C the first sentence of each paragraph

   D nowhere in the passage

Timed Writing: Persuasive [Connections]

Review "I Am a Native of North America" or "In Search of Our Mothers' Gardens." In a sentence or two, identify the author's message. Then, write a persuasive essay in which you present reasons that your audience should, or should not, agree with that message. **(25 minutes)**

Writing Workshop: *Work in Progress*

How-to Essay

Specific details tell readers exactly how a step should be performed. Review the steps listed for each process you described earlier. Consider what additional details would be useful to readers and add them to the appropriate steps.

Reading Informational Materials

Problem-and-Solution Essays

In Part 1, you are learning how to identify the main idea in literature. If you read "I Am a Native of North America," you learned some details about the life of a Native American who shows a deep respect for nature. Finding the main idea is also useful in reading a problem-and-solution essay. This article shows what can be done to reduce noise pollution in our society.

About Problem-and-Solution Essays

A **problem-and-solution essay** identifies and explains a problem and then presents one or more possible solutions to it. Look for the following characteristics in a problem-and-solution essay:

- a clearly stated problem and an explanation of the situation
- step-by-step solutions
- evidence that supports the suggested solution
- a consistent, logical organization

Reading Skill

An **outline** is a structure for recording the relationship between main ideas and supporting details. When reading informational materials, an outline helps you take notes on what you learn. It can also help you organize your notes before writing. Outlines may be formal or informal.

First, identify the **main ideas** in a piece of writing. Then, list subtopics for each main idea, and finally, list details. The example shows a formal outline structure you can use to take notes on "Keeping It Quiet."

I. First Main Idea

  A. First subtopic

    1. supporting detail

    2. supporting detail

  B. Second subtopic

    1. supporting detail

    2. supporting detail

II. Second Main Idea

  A. First subtopic

Keeping It Quiet

from *Prentice Hall Science Explorer*

A construction worker uses a jackhammer; a woman waits in a noisy airport; a spectator watches a car race. All three experience noise pollution. In the United States alone, 40 million people face danger to their health from noise pollution.

> The writer states the main idea or problem in the opening paragraph.

People start to feel pain at about 120 decibels. But noise that "doesn't hurt" can still damage your hearing. Exposure to 85 decibels (a kitchen blender) can slowly damage the hair cells in your cochlea. As many as 9 million Americans have hearing loss caused by noise. What can be done about noise pollution?

> Supporting facts and statistics explain specific dangers and identify the extent of the problem.

The Issues

What Can Individuals Do?

Some work conditions are noisier than others. Construction workers, airport employees, and truck drivers are all at risk. Workers in noisy environments can help themselves by using ear protectors, which can reduce noise levels by 35 decibels.

> Subheads break up the text for easier reading.

Many leisure activities also pose a risk. A listener at a rock concert or someone riding a motorbike can prevent damage by using ear protectors. People can also reduce noise at the source. They can buy quieter machines and avoid using lawnmowers or power tools at quiet times of the day. Simply turning down the volume on headphones for radios and CD players can help prevent hearing loss in young people.

> The writer outlines some solutions to the problem.

Reading Informational Materials

What Can Communities Do?

Transportation—planes, trains, trucks, and cars—is the largest source of noise pollution. About 15 million Americans live near airports or under airplane flight paths. Careful planning to locate airports away from dense populations can reduce noise. Cities can also prohibit late-night flights.

> This statistic supports the idea that the problem is widespread.

Many communities have laws against noise that exceeds a certain decibel level, but these laws are hard to enforce. In some cities, "noise police" can give fines to people who use noisy equipment.

What Can the Government Do?

A National Office of Noise Abatement and Control was set up in the 1970s. It required labels on power tools to tell how much noise they made. But in 1982, this office lost its funding. In 1997, lawmakers proposed The Quiet Communities Act to bring the office back and set limits to many types of noise. But critics say that national laws have little effect. They want the federal government to encourage—and pay for—research into making quieter vehicles and machines.

> The author outlines early attempts to solve the problem, as well as more recent solutions.

Reading: Identifying Main Ideas

Directions: *Choose the letter of the best answer to each question.*

1. What is the main idea of this essay?
   A There is too much noise pollution.
   B Noise pollution is the biggest problem in the United States.
   C Noise pollution is damaging the health of many Americans.
   D The government should limit noise pollution.

2. Which of the following details supports the main idea?
   A The Quiet Communities Act would limit noise pollution.
   B Ear protectors can reduce noise levels by 35 decibels.
   C Transportation is the largest source of noise pollution.
   D As many as nine million Americans have hearing loss caused by noise.

3. Which of the following ideas is <u>not</u> supported by details in this essay?
   A The National Office of Noise Abatement and Control should be fully funded.
   B Communities should have better laws against noise pollution.
   C Federal lawmakers cannot agree on an effective solution to noise pollution.
   D Individuals should make an effort to reduce their exposure to noise pollution.

Reading: Comprehension and Interpretation

Directions: *Write your answers on a separate piece of paper.*

4. Identify the largest source of noise pollution. Support your answer with details from the essay.

5. Explain why pain is not necessarily an indication of hearing damage.

6. Describe three ways you can reduce noise pollution in your own life.

Timed Writing: Summary

Write a brief summary of "Keeping It Quiet." Use your own words to briefly explain the problem and the solutions that are offered in the essay. Your summary should include only the main ideas and most important details. **(10 minutes)**

Biography and Autobiography

In an **autobiography,** a person tells his or her own life story. Writers may write about their own experiences to explain their actions, to provide insight into their choices, or to show the personal side of an event.

In contrast, in a **biography,** a writer tells the life story of another person. Writers of biographies often write to analyze a person's experiences and actions. Biographies often present their subject as an example from which readers can learn a lesson.

Some biographies and autobiographies are short essays that focus on a particular episode in the subject's life.

Comparing Biography and Autobiography

Both biography and autobiography focus on actual events and offer insight to explain a person's action or ideas. However, the forms have these important differences:

Biography
- More objective
- Based on research

Autobiography
- More personal
- Based on memory and emotion

Character Traits	

↑

Supporting Details	

As you read, notice the way the character and personality of each subject is presented. Use a chart like the one shown to record details that develop each subject's character.

Vocabulary Builder

Bernie Williams: Yankee Doodle Dandy

- **envisioned** (en vizh´ ənd) *v.* pictured in one's mind (p. 413) *While wearing braces, Lia envisioned straight teeth in her future.*

- **thrive** (thrīv) *v.* do well (p. 414) *With loving care, the flowers in my garden thrive.*

No Gumption

- **gumption** (gump´ shən) *n.* courage; enterprise (p. 416) *Not at all shy, Latoya had the gumption to run for class president.*

- **paupers** (pô´ pərz) *n.* people who are very poor (p. 417) *Twain wrote of a prince who lived with paupers and saw a life opposite his.*

- **crucial** (krōō´ shəl) *adj.* important; critical (p. 418) *Passing grades are crucial for graduation.*

- **aptitude** (ap´ tə tōōd) *n.* talent; ability (p. 420) *My aptitude for art got me into the art club.*

Build Understanding

Connecting to the Literature

Reading/Writing Connection "Bernie Williams: Yankee Doodle Dandy" is a word portrait of the baseball player Bernie Williams, and "No Gumption" is a written self-portrait of its author, Russell Baker. Write a few sentences about events that you would include in a portrait of yourself or a friend. Use three of the following words: *define, achieve, emphasize, participate, impress.*

Meet the Authors

Joel **Poiley** (b. 1957)

Joel Poiley grew up in Baltimore loving writing and playing sports of all kinds. As a sports writer, he enjoys interviewing athletes about what makes them successful. He also likes to ask them what they were like as kids and what they did to improve their athletic skills.

Personal Life Poiley writes for a variety of publications, including *Sports Illustrated for Kids* and *Boys' Life.* He lives in Tampa, Florida, with his family. His daughters like to play sports—particularly volleyball and tennis.

Russell **Baker** (b. 1925)

Newspaper columnist, author, and humorist Russell Baker grew up during the Great Depression, a period in the 1930s of poor business conditions and major unemployment. Baker's father, a stonemason, died when Baker was five years old. These facts provided the substance for much of Baker's later writing, which mixes humor with sadness.

Winning Honors Baker began his career as a journalist for the *Baltimore Sun* and *The New York Times.* He later won one Pulitzer Prize for his "Observer" column in the *Times* and another for his autobiography *Growing Up,* from which this essay comes.

Go **O**nline
Author Link

For: More about the authors
Visit: www.PHSchool.com
Web Code: eme-9306

BERNIE WILLIAMS:

Joel Poiley

New York Yankees center fielder[1] Bernie Williams understands the importance of being well-rounded.

By age 8, Williams could play Puerto Rican folk songs on the guitar. Later he was trained in classical guitar. At 17, he had excelled in baseball and was signed by the Yankees. He also enrolled in college and considered becoming a doctor.

"Probably all of it came from my parents' influence," Williams says. "My dad and my mom wanted me to stay off the streets and they enrolled me in a whole bunch of extracurricular activities.

"The good thing about it is that I developed a whole bunch of interests other than baseball."

Running for Fun

Williams won four gold medals at age 15 at an international track meet. He was one of the world's top 400-meter runners in his age group. "I could always run fast," Williams says. "When I was 8 or 9, I was better in track than baseball. All I could do was run. So my parents put me into a track club,

---

1. **center fielder** Of the nine players on a baseball team, six play in the infield and three play in the outfield. The middle player of the three outfielders is called the center fielder.

which was great, because it gave me a great base for my physical conditioning."

But Williams was determined to play baseball, and he practiced every day after school with his dad. Baseball ability ran in the family. One uncle played professional ball in the minor leagues in the 1950's, and another was a well-known amateur player in Puerto Rico.

Since Williams' high school specialized in music, it had no baseball team. He continued to learn about the game by playing in youth leagues and recreation ball. Williams played against future big-league all-stars Juan Gonzalez and Ivan Rodriguez in youth-league ball.

Hard to Leave Home

It wasn't easy for Williams to leave home and play pro ball. His mother, a teacher, encouraged him to continue his education.

"My dad was a merchant marine[2], a more aggressive-type person who encouraged me to play," Williams says. "The odds of making it aren't good. And back then, considering the type of player I was, I would have never <u>envisioned</u> this type of career."

Williams took college classes in biology during the off-seasons, but it reached a point where he had to make a decision between college and baseball.

The Long Climb

Williams showed the Yankees he had skills. But he was in high school and still learning the game when he signed. It took parts of seven years in the minor leagues before he made the majors for good in 1993.

He almost packed his bags and went home in 1990 after being sent back to the minors. His mother surprised him by encouraging him to keep at it.

"She said I had worked too hard to quit," Williams says. "I was not doing well in school because I didn't have the time to devote to it, and I wasn't developing as a player because my mind was on other stuff. So I made the decision to devote myself 100 percent to baseball."

By 1996, Bernie was a solid everyday player smashing home runs from either side of the plate. But his big national

Vocabulary Builder
envisioned (en vizh´ ənd) *v.* pictured in one's mind

Literary Analysis
Biography Describe the conflict at this point in Williams's life.

Reading Check

What was Williams's best sport when he was young?

---

2. **merchant marine** a sailor who works on a ship that transports freight.

splash occurred in the playoffs, when he helped the Yankees win their first world championship in 18 years.

No Hype Needed

With Williams getting stronger and more confident each season, the Yankees won three more world championships from 1998 to 2000. A five-time All-Star, Williams became known as a clutch player who delivered key hits with the game on the line.

Not bad for a guy who is so quiet in the locker room his teammates rarely know when he comes and goes.

"There's not too much flash to Bernie," former Yankees pitcher Andy Pettitte says. "The joke in the clubhouse is that we never know where Bernie is because he's so quiet."

Williams does his talking on the field with his bat and glove, which teammates and opponents respect.

"He's very laid back, but he's a very good player," says former Yankees right fielder Paul O'Neill, who retired before this season after playing next to Williams for eight years. "A lot of players can hit or they can throw or they can run, but Bernie can do a lot of things.

"The hype is unimportant to him. Some players need that to <u>thrive</u>, but Bernie doesn't."

A Relaxing Tune

Bernie unwinds by playing and listening to all types of music. He often entertains teammates with free concerts on his Fender Stratocaster electric guitar. He and O'Neill, who plays drums, have jammed together.

"He's very good," O'Neill says. "We've had a lot of fun playing together."

Opponents such as the Kansas City Royals' Roberto Hernandez enjoy playing against Williams because he doesn't show off or display emotion on the field.

"I'm happy to know him from our years in winter ball because he's a class individual," Hernandez says. "And he has not changed as he's become a star. He's the same person I knew when he started out.

"In Puerto Rico, everyone knows about players like Roberto Alomar and Juan Gonzalez. Bernie is definitely the quiet superstar because you never hear about him until the season starts. He just does his job."

Literary Analysis
Biography How do Williams's teammates describe him?

Vocabulary Builder
thrive (thrīv) *v.* do well

Bernie Williams isn't only a fan of music, he's a student. His schooling in Puerto Rico taught him to read, play and understand what makes rap different from rock and roll.

"In school they taught me a general appreciation of well-made music," Williams says. "It can be classical, rock, heavy metal; if it's well made, you notice.

"I like the blues. I like the freedom that jazz gives, as far as the improvisation (making it up as you go). I like classical because it's the pursuit of perfection. It can be a masterpiece that somebody wrote, and it's timed and specifically written for you to play it in a certain way and you can't deviate from that."

Williams once played on stage at The Bottom Line, a famous club in New York City. He also had his Fender Stratocaster electric guitar signed by "The Boss," rocker Bruce Springsteen.

"That was awesome," Williams says, smiling.

And what does he listen to before a game?

"It depends who's pitching," Williams says. "If it's a flamethrower I might listen to heavy metal to pump me up. Sometimes even new age. I like listening to jazz because it's challenging to figure out the harmonies and how the instruments come together."

▲ **Critical Viewing**
How does this photograph show that Bernie Williams is a well-rounded person? **[Connect]**

Literary Analysis
Biography How does the writer link Williams's interest in music and baseball?

Thinking About the Selection

1. **(a) Recall:** As a child, how did Williams spend his time when he was not in school? **(b) Analyze:** What role did Williams's parents play in his becoming a well-rounded adult?

2. **(a) Recall:** What advice did Williams's mother give him when he was deciding if he should leave his career in baseball? **(b) Infer:** What can you infer about Williams's mother from this advice?

3. **(a) Recall:** Why did Williams decide to devote himself "100 percent to baseball"? **(b) Generalize:** How would you describe his skills as a baseball player, based on his teammates' descriptions of him?

NO GUMPTION

Russell Baker

I began working in journalism when I was eight years old. It was my mother's idea. She wanted me to "make something" of myself and, after a level-headed appraisal[1] of my strengths, decided I had better start young if I was to have any chance of keeping up with the competition.

The flaw in my character which she had already spotted was lack of "<u>gumption</u>." My idea of a perfect afternoon was lying in front of the radio rereading my favorite Big Little Book,[2] *Dick Tracy Meets Stooge Viller.* My mother despised inactivity. Seeing me having a good time in repose, she was powerless to hide her disgust. "You've got no more gumption than a bump on a log," she said. "Get out in the kitchen and help Doris do those dirty dishes."

My sister Doris, though two years younger than I, had enough gumption for a dozen people. She positively enjoyed washing dishes, making beds, and cleaning the house. When she was only seven she could carry a piece of short-weighted cheese back to the A&P, threaten the manager with legal action, and come back triumphantly with the full quarter-pound we'd paid for and a few ounces extra thrown in for forgiveness. Doris could have made something of herself if she hadn't been a girl. Because of this

Vocabulary Builder
gumption (gumpˊ shən) *n.* courage; enterprise

THE SATURDAY EVENING POST

5c. the Copy

Fou... klin

728

November 27, 1937

WATER BUKIT

THIS PEACE IS A CHEAT—By JOHN GUNTHER

▲ Critical Viewing Judging by the clothing worn in this illustration, when does the story take place? [**Assess**]

---

1. **appraisal** (ə prāzˊ əl) *n.* judgment; evaluation.
2. **Big Little Book** a small, inexpensive picture book that often portrayed the adventures of comic-strip heroes like Dick Tracy.

defect, however, the best she could hope for was a career as a nurse or schoolteacher, the only work that capable females were considered up to in those days.

This must have saddened my mother, this twist of fate that had allocated all the gumption to the daughter and left her with a son who was content with Dick Tracy and Stooge Viller. If disappointed, though, she wasted no energy on self-pity. She would make me make something of myself whether I wanted to or not. "The Lord helps those who help themselves," she said. That was the way her mind worked.

She was realistic about the difficulty. Having sized up the material the Lord had given her to mold, she didn't overestimate what she could do with it. She didn't insist that I grow up to be President of the United States.

Fifty years ago parents still asked boys if they wanted to grow up to be President, and asked it not jokingly but seriously. Many parents who were hardly more than <u>paupers</u> still believed their sons could do it. Abraham Lincoln had done it. We were only sixty-five years from Lincoln. Many a grandfather who walked among us could remember Lincoln's time. Men of grandfatherly age were the worst for asking if you wanted to grow up to be President. A surprising number of little boys said yes and meant it.

I was asked many times myself. No, I would say, I didn't want to grow up to be President. My mother was present during one of these interrogations.[3] An elderly uncle, having posed the usual question and exposed my lack of interest in the Presidency, asked, "Well, what do you want to be when you grow up?"

I loved to pick through trash piles and collect empty bottles, tin cans with pretty labels, and discarded magazines. The most desirable job on earth sprang instantly to mind. "I want to be a garbage man," I said.

My uncle smiled, but my mother had seen the first distressing evidence of a bump budding on a log. "Have a little gumption, Russell," she said. Her calling me Russell was a signal of unhappiness. When she approved of me I was always "Buddy."

When I turned eight years old she decided that the job of starting me on the road toward making something of myself could no longer be safely delayed. "Buddy," she said one day,

Vocabulary Builder
paupers (pô´ pərz) *n.* people who are very poor

Literary Analysis
Autobiography
What does Baker reveal about himself with these details?

**Reading Check**

What is worrying Russell's mother?

---

3. **interrogations** (in ter ə´ gā´ shənz) *n.* situations in which a person is formally questioned.

"I want you to come home right after school this afternoon. Somebody's coming and I want you to meet him."

When I burst in that afternoon she was in conference in the parlor with an executive of the Curtis Publishing Company. She introduced me. He bent low from the waist and shook my hand. Was it true as my mother had told him, he asked, that I longed for the opportunity to conquer the world of business?

My mother replied that I was blessed with a rare determination to make something of myself.

"That's right," I whispered.

"But have you got the grit, the character, the never-say-quit spirit it takes to succeed in business?"

My mother said I certainly did.

"That's right," I said.

He eyed me silently for a long pause, as though weighing whether I could be trusted to keep his confidence, then spoke man-to-man. Before taking a <u>crucial</u> step, he said, he wanted to advise me that working for the Curtis Publishing Company placed enormous responsibility on a young man. It was one of the great companies of America. Perhaps the greatest publishing house in the world. I had heard, no doubt, of the *Saturday Evening Post*?

Heard of it? My mother said that everyone in our house had heard of the *Saturday Post* and that I, in fact, read it with religious devotion.

Then doubtless, he said, we were also familiar with those two monthly pillars of the magazine world, the *Ladies Home Journal* and the *Country Gentleman.*

Indeed we were familiar with them, said my mother.

Representing the *Saturday Evening Post* was one of the weightiest honors that could be bestowed in the world of business, he said. He was personally proud of being a part of that great corporation.

My mother said he had every right to be.

Again he studied me as though debating whether I was worthy of a knighthood. Finally: "Are you trustworthy?"

My mother said I was the soul of honesty.

"That's right," I said.

Vocabulary Builder
crucial (kroo′ shəl)
adj. important; critical

▼ **Critical Viewing**
How does your image of Russell Baker compare with this photograph of him with his sister? **[Compare and Contrast]**

The caller smiled for the first time. He told me I was a lucky young man. He admired my spunk. Too many young men thought life was all play. Those young men would not go far in this world. Only a young man willing to work and save and keep his face washed and his hair neatly combed could hope to come out on top in a world such as ours. Did I truly and sincerely believe that I was such a young man?

"He certainly does," said my mother.

"That's right," I said.

He said he had been so impressed by what he had seen of me that he was going to make me a representative of the Curtis Publishing Company. On the following Tuesday, he said, thirty freshly printed copies of the *Saturday Evening Post* would be delivered at our door. I would place these magazines, still damp with the ink of the presses, in a handsome canvas bag, sling it over my shoulder, and set forth through the streets to bring the best in journalism, fiction, and cartoons to the American public.

He had brought the canvas bag with him. He presented it with reverence fit for a chasuble.[4] He showed me how to drape the sling over my left shoulder and across the chest so that the pouch lay easily accessible[5] to my right hand, allowing the best in journalism, fiction, and cartoons to be swiftly extracted and sold to a citizenry whose happiness and security depended upon us soldiers of the free press.

The following Tuesday I raced home from school, put the canvas bag over my shoulder, dumped the magazines in, and, tilting to the left to balance their weight on my right hip, embarked on the highway of journalism.

We lived in Belleville, New Jersey, a commuter town at the northern fringe of Newark. It was 1932, the bleakest year of the Depression. My father had died two years before, leaving us with a few pieces of Sears, Roebuck furniture and not much else, and my mother had taken Doris and me to live with one of her younger brothers. This was my Uncle Allen. Uncle Allen had made something of himself by 1932. As salesman for a soft-drink bottler in Newark, he had an income of

▲ Critical Viewing
Does this picture fit your idea of Baker's mother? Explain. **[Connect]**

Literary Analysis
Autobiography
Does Russell have the same goals for himself that his mother has? Explain.

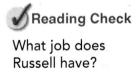
Reading Check

What job does Russell have?

---

4. **chasuble** (chaz′ ə bəl) *n.* sleeveless outer garment worn by priests.
5. **accessible** (ak ses′ ə bəl) *adj.* available.

$30 a week; wore pearl-gray spats,[6] detachable collars, and a three-piece suit; was happily married; and took in threadbare relatives.

With my load of magazines I headed toward Belleville Avenue. That's where the people were. There were two filling stations at the intersection with Union Avenue, as well as an A&P, a fruit stand, a bakery, a barber shop, Zuccarelli's drugstore, and a diner shaped like a railroad car. For several hours I made myself highly visible, shifting position now and then from corner to corner, from shop window to shop window, to make sure everyone could see the heavy black lettering on the canvas bag that said *The Saturday Evening Post*. When the angle of the light indicated it was suppertime, I walked back to the house.

"How many did you sell, Buddy?" my mother asked.

"None."

"Where did you go?"

"The corner of Belleville and Union Avenues."

"What did you do?"

"Stood on the corner waiting for somebody to buy a *Saturday Evening Post*."

"You just stood there?"

"Didn't sell a single one."

"For God's sake, Russell!"

Uncle Allen intervened. "I've been thinking about it for some time," he said, "and I've about decided to take the *Post* regularly. Put me down as a regular customer." I handed him a magazine and he paid me a nickel. It was the first nickel I earned.

Afterwards my mother instructed me in salesmanship. I would have to ring doorbells, address adults with charming self-confidence, and break down resistance with a sales talk pointing out that no one, no matter how poor, could afford to be without the *Saturday Evening Post* in the home.

I told my mother I'd changed my mind about wanting to succeed in the magazine business.

"If you think I'm going to raise a good-for-nothing," she replied, "you've got another think coming." She told me to hit the streets with the canvas bag and start ringing doorbells the instant school was out next day. When I objected that I didn't feel any <u>aptitude</u> for salesmanship, she asked how I'd like to

Literary Analysis
Autobiography Why do you think Baker includes this conversation between himself and his mother?

Vocabulary Builder
aptitude (ap′ tə to͞od) *n.* talent; ability

---

6. **spats** (spats) *n.* cloth or leather material that covers the upper part of a shoe or ankle.

lend her my leather belt so she could whack some sense into me. I bowed to superior will and entered journalism with a heavy heart.

My mother and I had fought this battle almost as long as I could remember. It probably started even before memory began, when I was a country child in northern Virginia and my mother, dissatisfied with my father's plain workman's life, determined that I would not grow up like him and his people, with calluses on their hands, overalls on their backs, and fourth-grade educations in their heads. She had fancier ideas of life's possibilities. Introducing me to the *Saturday Evening Post,* she was trying to wean me as early as possible from my father's world where men left with lunch pails at sunup, worked with their hands until the grime ate into the pores, and died with a few sticks of mail-order furniture as their legacy. In my mother's vision of the better life there were desks and white collars, well-pressed suits, evenings of reading and lively talk, and perhaps—if a man were very, very lucky and hit the jackpot, really made something important of himself—perhaps there might be a fantastic salary of $5,000 a year to support a big house and a Buick with a rumble seat[7] and a vacation in Atlantic City.

And so I set forth with my sack of magazines. I was afraid of the dogs that snarled behind the doors of potential buyers. I was timid about ringing the doorbells of strangers, relieved when no one came to the door, and scared when someone did. Despite my mother's instructions, I could not deliver an engaging sales pitch. When a door opened I simply asked, "Want to buy a *Saturday Evening Post?*" In Belleville few persons did. It was a town of 30,000 people, and most weeks I rang a fair majority of its doorbells. But I rarely sold my thirty copies. Some weeks I canvassed the entire town for six days and still had four or five unsold magazines on Monday evening; then I dreaded the

▼ **Critical Viewing** Based on this cover, do you think *The Saturday Evening Post* would be easy to sell? Why? **[Draw Conclusions]**

THE SATURDAY EVENING POST

5cts.

March 28, 1931

Myron C. Taylor—Alfred Noyes—Ida M. Evans—Clarence Budington Kelland
Isaac F. Marcosson—Struthers Burt—Bernard DeVoto—Ben Ames Williams

© The Curtis Publishing Company, Illustrator: Norman Rockwell

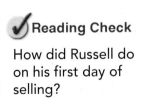

✓ **Reading Check**

How did Russell do on his first day of selling?

---

7. **rumble seat** in the rear of early automobiles, an open seat that could be folded shut.

coming of Tuesday morning, when a batch of thirty fresh *Saturday Evening Posts* was due at the front door.

"Better get out there and sell the rest of those magazines tonight," my mother would say.

I usually posted myself then at a busy intersection where a traffic light controlled commuter flow from Newark. When the light turned red I stood on the curb and shouted my sales pitch at the motorists.

"Want to buy a *Saturday Evening Post*?"

One rainy night when car windows were sealed against me I came back soaked and with not a single sale to report. My mother beckoned to Doris.

"Go back down there with Buddy and show him how to sell these magazines," she said.

Brimming with zest, Doris, who was then seven years old, returned with me to the corner. She took a magazine from the bag, and when the light turned red she strode to the nearest car and banged her small fist against the closed window. The driver, probably startled at what he took to be a midget assaulting his car, lowered the window to stare, and Doris thrust a *Saturday Evening Post* at him.

"You need this magazine," she piped, "and it only costs a nickel."

Her salesmanship was irresistible. Before the light changed half a dozen times she disposed of the entire batch. I didn't feel humiliated. To the contrary. I was so happy I decided to give her a treat. Leading her to the vegetable store on Belleville Avenue, I bought three apples, which cost a nickel, and gave her one.

"You shouldn't waste money," she said.

"Eat your apple." I bit into mine.

"You shouldn't eat before supper," she said. "It'll spoil your appetite."

Back at the house that evening, she dutifully reported me for wasting a nickel. Instead of a scolding, I was rewarded with a pat on the back for having the good sense to buy fruit instead of candy. My mother reached into her bottomless supply of maxims[8] and told Doris, "An apple a day keeps the doctor away."

By the time I was ten I had learned all my mother's maxims by heart. Asking to stay up past normal bedtime, I knew that

---

8. **maxims** (mak′ simz) *n.* wise sayings.

Literary Analysis
Autobiography
What do you learn about Russell based on his feelings about his sister's salesmanship?

▶ **Critical Viewing**
Which character in these illustrations seems most like Doris? Explain. **[Connect]**

a refusal would be explained with, "Early to bed and early to rise, makes a man healthy, wealthy, and wise." If I whimpered about having to get up early in the morning, I could depend on her to say, "The early bird gets the worm."

The one I most despised was, "If at first you don't succeed, try, try again." This was the battle cry with which she constantly sent me back into the hopeless struggle whenever I moaned that I had rung every doorbell in town and knew there wasn't a single potential buyer left in Belleville that week. After listening to my explanation, she handed me the canvas bag and said, "If at first you don't succeed . . ."

© The Curtis Publishing Company, Illustrator: Norman Rockwell

✓ **Reading Check**

What skill does Doris have that Russell does not?

Three years in that job, which I would gladly have quit after the first day except for her insistence, produced at least one valuable result. My mother finally concluded that I would never make something of myself by pursuing a life in business and started considering careers that demanded less competitive zeal.

One evening when I was eleven I brought home a short "composition" on my summer vacation which the teacher had graded with an A. Reading it with her own school-teacher's eye, my mother agreed that it was top-drawer seventh grade prose and complimented me. Nothing more was said about it immediately, but a new idea had taken life in her mind. Halfway through supper she suddenly interrupted the conversation.

"Buddy," she said, "maybe you could be a writer."

I clasped the idea to my heart. I had never met a writer, had shown no previous urge to write, and hadn't a notion how to become a writer, but I loved stories and thought that making up stories must surely be almost as much fun as reading them. Best of all, though, and what really gladdened my heart, was the ease of the writer's life. Writers did not have to trudge through the town peddling from canvas bags, defending themselves against angry dogs, being rejected by surly strangers. Writers did not have to ring doorbells. So far as I could make out, what writers did couldn't even be classified as work.

I was enchanted. Writers didn't have to have any gumption at all. I did not dare tell anybody for fear of being laughed at in the schoolyard, but secretly I decided that what I'd like to be when I grew up was a writer.

Literary Analysis
Autobiography How would a career in writing solve a problem that Baker had?

Thinking About the Selection

1. **(a) Recall:** Find two words or expressions that Baker uses to describe his traits as a young boy. **(b) Analyze:** How do those traits prevent Baker from being a good salesperson?

2. **(a) Recall:** Why does Baker's mother get him a job as a newsboy? **(b) Infer:** What goals does Baker's mother set for him as a child? **(c) Compare and Contrast:** Compare Baker's own aims in life as a child with the goals his mother sets for him.

3. **(a) Analyze:** Identify two examples that show Baker's sense of humor about his poor salesmanship. **(b) Connect:** What does Baker's sense of humor about his failures reveal about his personality?

Apply the Skills

Bernie Williams: Yankee Doodle Dandy • No Gumption

Comparing Biography and Autobiography

1. **(a)** In a chart like the one shown, list three details in "Yankee Doodle Dandy" that show the writer researched his subject. For each, indicate what source he may have used.

Details	Source

   (b) Are there occasions in a biography when readers get opinions directly from the subject? Explain.

2. **(a)** List two details in "No Gumption" that only Russell Baker could have known.
   (b) How would events in the narrative be told differently if Doris were telling the story?

QuickReview

Biography: nonfiction in which a writer tells the life story of another person

Autobiography: nonfiction in which a person tells his or her own life story

For: Self-test
Visit: www.PHSchool.com
Web Code: ema-6306

Writing to Compare Literary Works

In an essay, compare and contrast what you learned about Bernie Williams with what you learned about Russell Baker. As you write, consider how the rules of biography and autobiography helped you learn about these people. Use these questions as a guide.

- Which person do you think was most influenced by his parents?
- What is your overall impression of each person?
- What kind of information helped you form your impression?
- Which person do you feel you understand better?

Vocabulary Builder

Practice Write sentences correctly using the given word pairs.

1. paupers; charity
2. thrive; danger
3. crucial; step
4. envisioned; goal
5. aptitude; test
6. gumption; drive

Reading

Directions: *Questions 1–5 refer to the following selection.*

You can learn a lot about a bird by looking at its beak. Birds such as cardinals, sparrows, and finches have strong, thick, cone-shaped beaks. These beaks are perfect for cracking seeds. Bird lovers place feeders filled with seeds in their yards for songbirds. Woodpeckers, on the other hand, have long, chisel-shaped beaks. They use their beaks to peck holes in trees. Tiny hummingbirds have long, tubular bills that they use in much the same way that we use a straw.

Herons walk on long, slender legs. Herons have long, straight bills with sharp edges that keep a slippery fish from escaping. Other fish eaters, like the cormorant, have a hook on the end of the beak for holding a fish. Wading birds with long, narrow bills use their beaks to probe deep in the sand for tasty insects or worms.

1. **What is the unstated main idea of this selection?**
   A A bird's beak gives clues to what it eats.
   B Birds eat a wide variety of foods.
   C Fish eaters live near the shore.
   D Most birds' beaks are irrelevant.

2. **Which sentence does not directly support the main idea of paragraph 1?**
   A Birds . . . cone-shaped beaks.
   B Bird lovers . . . songbirds.
   C They use . . . in trees.
   D Tiny hummingbirds . . . straw.

3. **Which statement best describes the main idea of paragraph 2?**
   A The main idea is stated directly in the first sentence.
   B The main idea is unsupported by evidence in the paragraph.
   C The main idea is understood from details included in the paragraph.
   D The main idea of the paragraph does not contribute to the main idea of the passage.

4. **What is the main idea of paragraph 2?**
   A Herons are fish eaters.
   B You can guess a shore bird's diet by looking at its beak.
   C Most shore birds have long legs and are fish eaters.
   D Shore birds' beaks are different from those of birds that live in the woods.

5. **Which sentence in paragraph 2 does not directly support the main idea of the paragraph?**
   A Herons walk on long, slender legs.
   B Herons have long, straight bills with sharp edges that keep a slippery fish from escaping their grip.
   C Other fish eaters, like the cormorant, have a hook on the end of the beak for holding a fish.
   D Wading birds with long, narrow bills use their beaks to probe deep in the sand for tasty insects or worms.

Vocabulary Skill Review

Directions *Choose the word that best completes the following sentences.*

6. It is _____ to our history teacher that the national park contains historical sites.
   A irrelevant   C insignificant
   B significant   D factual

7. The _____ details did nothing to support the speaker's main point.
   A irrelevant   C significant
   B inactive   D irregular

8. The study of science is _____ to that profession.
   A factual   C identified
   B opinionated   D relevant

9. Even though he believes that novel is very meaningful, I think it is _____ compared with many other works.
   A factual   C insignificant
   B irreversible   D relevant

10. Our group quickly ____ the relevant details in this essay.
    A removed   C replaced
    B denounced   D identified

Directions *Choose the word that best completes each of the following sentences.*

11. Tim could not turn down the _____ chocolate cake.
    A irregular   C irrelevant
    B irresponsible   D irresistible

12. Heavy snows made the lodge above the mountain pass _____.
    A inactive   C inarguable
    B inaccessible   D inadequate

13. The players did not agree with the referee's call, but the decision was ____.
    A incontestable   C inconvenient
    B incomparable   D incompatible

14. The museum kept the _____ objects safely locked in a glass case.
    A irrelative   C irreformable
    B irreducible   D irreplaceable

15. The school dance was _____, so students dressed in school clothes instead of evening wear.
    A informal   C infeasible
    B infrequent   D inflexible

Exposition: How-to Essay

A **how-to essay** is a written, step-by-step explanation of how to do or make something. How-to essays can explain how to repair a bicycle, make brownies, or learn to juggle. Follow the steps outlined in this workshop to write your own how-to essay.

Assignment Write a how-to essay about a process that you know well enough to explain clearly.

What to Include Your how-to essay should feature these elements:
- a narrow, focused topic that can be fully explained in the essay
- a list of materials needed
- multi-step directions explained in sequential order
- optional relevant illustrations that help clarify the directions
- appropriate technical terms relating to your topic
- error-free writing, including use of conjunctions

To preview the criteria on which your how-to essay may be judged, see the rubric on page 432.

Prewriting

Choosing Your Topic

Brainstorm with a partner. With a classmate, list activities you know well. To get started, consider these categories: *Sports or other extra-curricular activities; items you know how to repair or maintain; foods you know how to cook or bake; or crafts.* Choose a topic from your list.

Gathering Details

List and itemize the details. You can gather most of the details from your own experience. Begin with a simple list of the materials or steps. Then, using the chart shown as a model, itemize each part of the list, adding specific details for each area.

Using the Form

You may use elements of this form in these types of writing:
- instruction booklets
- magazine articles
- technical directions
- explanations

Making Banana Bread

List	Itemize	
Preheat oven. Mix dry ingredients. Mix other ingredients. Prepare bananas. Ice the cake.	• 2 c. flour • 1 c. sugar	• 1 t. baking soda • 1 t. cinnamon
	Bananas should be ripe. Mash them with vanilla and yogurt.	

Work-in-Progress

Review the work you did on pages 365, 387, and 405.

Drafting

Shaping Your Writing

Organize directions in sequential order. Create a chain-of-events organizer using sticky notes or note cards so that you can arrange the steps in order and add steps as needed. As you draft, write the steps in your process in the order in which they occur.

Include relevant illustrations. To help readers follow your explanation, add illustrations to clarify one or more steps.

Providing Elaboration

Add details to make your essay more precise. Look for places to add details that show how much, how long, or how to complete a step.

Revising

Revising Your Sentences

Insert transitions. Time transitions are words that show sequential order. They include words such as *first, later, next,* and *finally,* as well as phrases such as *in about an hour* or *when the glue has dried.* Review your draft to add time transitions that clarify the order of events.

Student Model: Revising to Add Time Transitions

To start off,
1. Use a volleyball that is heavier than normal. It will be harder at the

beginning, but when you finally get your serve over. . .

Next is the toss, probably the most important part of the serve.
2. The most important part of the serve is the toss.

> Danielle added a few transitions to her how-to essay that show time order.

Revising Your Word Choice

Upgrade to technical vocabulary. When explaining a process, use appropriate technical terms associated with your topic. For example, an essay about baking would include the names of specific kitchen utensils. Review your draft, circling all general terms. Replace those words with precise words that help clarify the process.

General	Technical
scraping utensil $\longrightarrow$	spatula
mixing utensil $\longrightarrow$	whisk, eggbeater

Reading Writing Connection

To read the complete student model, see page 431.

Integrating Grammar Skills

Revising to Combine Sentences Using Conjunctions

Too many short sentences in a row can make your writing sound choppy. Using conjunctions to combine sentences will create a smoother, more varied writing style.

Identifying Sentences to Combine Combine sentences that express similar ideas by using words that clarify the relationship between the ideas. Here are two common ways to combine sentences:

Use a coordinating conjunction, such as *and* or *but*.

CHOPPY:	I really wanted to sleep. I had to walk my dogs.
COMBINED:	I really wanted to sleep, **but** I had to walk my dogs.

Add a subordinating conjunction, such as *after* or *until*.

CHOPPY:	You cannot read the book. I want a chance.
COMBINED:	You cannot read the book **until** I get a chance.

Fixing Choppy Sentences To fix choppy sentences, rewrite them using one of the following methods.

1. **Identify the relationship between sentences.** To create a smoother writing style, combine two short sentences that are equal in importance. By doing so, you are not simply linking two ideas: You are expressing a relationship between them.

2. **Combine the sentences using a conjunction.** See the conjunctions listed in the chart.

Coordinating Conjunctions	and, or, so, for, but, nor, yet
Common Subordinating Conjunctions	after, although, as, as if, as long as, because, before, even though, if, in order that, since, so that, than, though, unless, until, when, whenever, where, wherever, while

Apply It to Your Editing

Choose three paragraphs in your draft. Read them aloud, highlighting any passages that sound choppy. Then, revise by combining sentences using one of the methods described.

Prentice Hall Writing and Grammar Connection: Chapter 5, Section 4

Student Model: Danielle Spiess
LaPorte, IN

How to Serve Overhand in Volleyball

Volleyball is one of the most popular sports around. Knowing how to serve overhand will be useful if you ever decide to try out for a team. If you have ever seen anyone serve, it may look pretty easy, but it is not as easy as it looks. It takes a lot of practice!

To practice, you'll need a volleyball, a practice ball that is heavier than regulation balls, and a net.

1. To start off, use a volleyball that is heavier than normal. It will be more difficult at the beginning, but when you finally get your serve over, it will be a lot stronger. The regular volleyball is lighter, so you won't have to put as much force into your serve during games.

2. Next is the toss, probably the most important part of the serve. Throw the volleyball into the air. Try to get a high square toss. If your toss is too low or off to one side, the ball will not go over the net the way you want it to. It might also go too far in front of you or behind you. If this happens, catch the volleyball and start over.

   It will take you a while to get the perfect toss. So, you may need extra practice to make sure you can toss the ball well enough to set up a good serve. Work with a partner to get your toss in the right zone—straight up and not too low.

3. The final step is hitting it over. You can either use an open or a closed hand. Using an open hand is easier because when a closed hand is used, you sometimes hit the volleyball off your knuckles. After you toss the ball, wait until your toss reaches its peak, and then hit it. The volleyball may not go over the first time, but soon you will get it.

In volleyball, serving takes a lot of practice and a lot of effort, but it is a key skill for any serious player. As with any other athletic skill, set a goal for yourself. Then, just keep with it and don't give up!

Danielle focuses her essay on how to serve a volleyball.

This paragraph identifies the items necessary to complete the task.

Danielle explains why using a heavier ball is the best way to get started.

This paragraph clearly identifies the steps for tossing the ball.

Danielle explains all steps in sequential order.

Editing and Proofreading

Review your draft to eliminate errors in grammar, spelling, and punctuation.

Focus on Sentence Fragments. A sentence fragment is a group of words that is incorrectly punctuated as a sentence. A fragment is missing a subject, a predicate, or both. Therefore, it does not express a complete thought. Proofread your essay to make sure all of your sentences are complete.

Publishing and Presenting

Consider one of the following ways to share your writing:
Give a demonstration. Demonstrate your essay using props to show how to perform the process step by step.
Make a class anthology. With classmates, combine your essays into a how-to reference booklet. Display the book in your school or local library, where people can use it.

Reflecting on Your Writing

Writer's Journal Jot down your thoughts on the experience of writing a how-to essay. Begin by answering these questions:
- Which drafting strategy did you find most useful? Explain.
- What did you learn about your topic by writing to teach it?
- Do you think the process you explained would be difficult or easy to learn? Why?

> Prentice Hall Writing and Grammar Connection: Chapter 10

Rubric for Self-Assessment

To assess your how-to essay, use the following rubric.

Criteria	Rating Scale
	not very very
Focus: How well have you focused your topic?	1 2 3 4 5
Organization: How clearly organized are the list of materials and directions?	1 2 3 4 5
Support/Elaboration: How helpful are the illustrations?	1 2 3 4 5
Style: How appropriate are the technical terms?	1 2 3 4 5
Conventions: How correct is your grammar, especially your use of conjunctions?	1 2 3 4 5

Skills You Will Learn

Literature You Will Read

wwwReading: Fact and Opinion

> A **fact** is something that actually happened or that can be proved. An **opinion** is a person's belief or judgment and cannot be proved.

Skills and Strategies You Will Learn in Part 2

In Part 2, you will learn

- to **recognize clues** that indicate an **opinion.** (p. 436)
- to **use resources** to **check facts.** (p. 450)
- to **use manuals** as resources to distinguish **fact and opinion.** (p. 468)

Using the Skills and Strategies in Part 2

In Part 2, you will learn that separating facts from opinions helps you distinguish between statements that are proved true and statements that may be open to a different interpretation. Recognizing clue words that indicate an opinion and checking stated facts are methods of judging information.

The following shows the difference between a fact and an opinion.

Fact	Rivers such as the Tigris provide a source of water.
Opinion	The Tigris River has the most fascinating history of any river in the world.

As you read the literature in this part, you will practice evaluating statements and separating fact and opinion.

Academic Vocabulary

The following words will help you write and talk about facts and opinions as you read the selections in this unit.

Word	Definition	Example Sentence
check *v.*	confirm that something is true or accurate	Sal used an atlas to *check* the spelling of San Francisco.
almanac *n.*	a yearly publication with details of events	The *almanac* has the average temperature in the Raleigh-Durham area.
evaluate *v.*	examine something to make a judgment	Mark was wise to carefully *evaluate* the speaker's statement.
investigate *v.*	examine in order to gain information	Maria *investigated* the claim that the plays were written by Bacon.
valid *adj.*	justifiable, or logically correct	She had a *valid* argument for seeing the moonbow at Daniel Boone National Forest.

Vocabulary Skill: Borrowed and Foreign Words

In Part 2 you will learn some of the common words English has borrowed from other languages. The English language includes many **borrowed and foreign words.** Look at these examples.

Borrowed Word	Borrowed From
tea	Chinese
cookie	Dutch
dunk	German
yoga	Sanskrit
pajamas	Hindi
banjo	African languages

Borrowed Word	Borrowed From
hurricane	American Indian languages
balcony	Italian
giraffe	Arabic
garage	French
canyon	Spanish

Activity With two other classmates, list the words that you think may have been borrowed from other languages. Consider the foods you eat, the clothes you wear, and your activities. Check the origins of five of these words in a dictionary. Write a brief explanation of the origin of each borrowed word.

These skills will help you become a better reader.
Practice them with either "The Eternal Frontier"
(p. 438) or "All Together Now" (p. 443).

Reading Skill

When you read nonfiction, it is important to be able
to distinguish between fact and opinion.
- A **fact** is something that can be proved.
- An **opinion** is a person's judgment or belief. It may be supported by factual evidence, but it cannot be proved.

As you read, **recognize clues that indicate an opinion,** such as *I
believe* or *In my opinion.* Also look for words such as *always, never,
must, cannot, best, worst,* and *all,* which may be broad statements
that reveal a personal judgment. Emotional statements are also often
clues to opinion.

Literary Analysis

A **persuasive essay** is a piece of nonfiction that presents a series of
arguments to convince readers to believe or act in a certain way. The
chart shows some techniques that are often used in persuasive
essays. When you read persuasive essays, be alert for the use of these
techniques—you will need to decide whether they are powerful
enough to convince you to accept the author's ideas.

Persuasive Techniques
Appeals to authority
using opinions of experts and well-known people
Appeals to emotion
using words that convey strong feelings
Appeals to reason
using logical arguments backed by facts

Vocabulary Builder

The Eternal Frontier

- **frontier** (frun tir´) *n.* the developing, often
  uncivilized, region of a country; any new
  field of learning (p. 438) *Outer space is our
  frontier.*

- **preliminary** (prē lim´ə ner´ ē) *adj.* coming
  before or leading up to the main action
  (p. 438) *The doctor will do a preliminary
  exam before surgery.*

- **antidote** (an´ tə dōt´) *n.* remedy; cure
  (p. 438) *Laughter is the antidote for sadness.*

- **impetus** (im´ pə təs) *n.* driving force
  (p. 439) *A desire to succeed is her impetus to
  work hard.*

All Together Now

- **legislation** (lej´ is lā´ shən) *n.* law (p. 443)
  *The senators passed legislation to stop
  pollution.*

- **tolerant** (täl´ ər ənt) *adj.* accepting; free
  from bigotry or prejudice (p. 443) *A tolerant
  attitude can help resolve conflicts.*

- **fundamental** (fun´ də ment´ 'l) *adj.* basic;
  forming a foundation (p. 444) *The ability to
  read is a fundamental skill.*

- **optimist** (äp´ tə mist) *n.* someone who takes
  the most hopeful view of matters (p. 445)
  *An optimist always sees the positive side of
  things.*

Build Understanding • *The Eternal Frontier*

Persuasive Essay

Background

Space Exploration Not everyone agrees that exploring outer space is a good idea. Some people argue that space exploration has led to valuable inventions, such as scratch-resistant lenses and voice-controlled wheelchairs. Others, however, say that space exploration is too expensive. They argue that the money would be better spent dealing with issues here on Earth, such as improving schools and protecting the environment. In "The Eternal Frontier," Louis L'Amour expresses his opinions about the exploration of space.

Connecting to the Literature

Reading/Writing Connection In this essay, L'Amour takes a strong stand on space travel. Jot down four reasons why you do or do not support space exploration. Use at least three of these words: *contribute, invest, launch, obtain, undertake.*

Meet the Author

Louis **L'Amour** (1908–1988)

It is not surprising that Louis L'Amour became a writer of Western novels. He was born in North Dakota and often met cowboys as they traveled by railroad near the farm where he was raised. Two of L'Amour's uncles, who worked on his father's ranch, told the boy fascinating stories of frontier life.

What Makes a Good Story? L'Amour used the rules of all good fiction writing to write his Westerns. He has said, "A Western starts with a beginning and it goes to an end. It's a story about people, and that's the important thing to remember. Every story is about people—people against the canvas of their time."

Fast Facts

▶ L'Amour's first novel was not published until he was forty-two years old.

▶ At various times in his life, L'Amour worked as an elephant handler, a fruit picker, and a lumberjack.

Go **Online**
Author Link

For: More about the author
Visit: www.PHSchool.com
Web Code: eme-9308

The Eternal Frontier

Louis L'Amour

The question I am most often asked is, "Where is the frontier now?"

The answer should be obvious. Our frontier lies in outer space. The moon, the asteroids, the planets, these are mere stepping stones, where we will test ourselves, learn needful lessons, and grow in knowledge before we attempt those frontiers beyond our solar system. Outer space is a frontier without end, the eternal frontier, an everlasting challenge to explorers not [only] of other planets and other solar systems but also of the mind of man.

All that has gone before was preliminary. We have been preparing ourselves mentally for what lies ahead. Many problems remain, but if we can avoid a devastating war we shall move with a rapidity[1] scarcely to be believed. In the past seventy years we have developed the automobile, radio, television, transcontinental and transoceanic flight, and the electrification of the country, among a multitude of other such developments. In 1900 there were 144 miles of surfaced road in the United States. Now there are over 3,000,000. Paved roads and the development of the automobile have gone hand in hand, the automobile being civilized man's antidote to overpopulation.

What is needed now is leaders with perspective; we need leadership on a thousand fronts, but they must be men and women who can take the long view and help to shape the outlines of our future. There will always be the nay-sayers, those who cling to our lovely green planet as a baby clings to its mother, but there will be others like those who have taken us this far along the path to a limitless future.

> ▲ **Critical Viewing**
> Based on the pictures, what do you think is "The Eternal Frontier"? **[Draw Conclusions]**
>
> **Vocabulary Builder**
> **frontier** (frun tir´) *n.* the developing, often uncivilized, region of a country; any new field of learning
>
> **preliminary** (prē lim´ ə ner´ ē) *adj.* coming before or leading up to the main action
>
> **antidote** (an´ tə dōt´) *n.* remedy; cure
>
> **Reading Skill**
> **Fact and Opinion**
> Explain whether this paragraph states facts or opinions.

---

1. **rapidity** (rə pid´ ə tē) *n.* speed.

We are a people born to the frontier. It has been a part of our thinking, waking, and sleeping since men first landed on this continent. The frontier is the line that separates the known from the unknown wherever it may be, and we have a driving need to see what lies beyond . . .

A few years ago we moved into outer space. We landed men on the moon; we sent a vehicle beyond the limits of the solar system, a vehicle still moving farther and farther into that limitless distance. If our world were to die tomorrow, that tiny vehicle would go on and on forever, carrying its mighty message to the stars. Out there, someone, sometime, would know that once we existed, that we had the vision and we made the effort. Mankind is not bound by its atmospheric envelope or by its gravitational field, nor is the mind of man bound by any limits at all.

One might ask—why outer space, when so much remains to be done here? If that had been the spirit of man we would still be hunters and food gatherers, growling over the bones of carrion in a cave somewhere. It is our destiny to move out, to accept the challenge, to dare the unknown. It is our destiny to achieve.

Yet we must not forget that along the way to outer space whole industries are springing into being that did not exist before. The computer age has arisen in part from the space effort, which gave great <u>impetus</u> to the development of computing devices. Transistors, chips, integrated circuits, Teflon, new medicines, new ways of treating diseases, new ways of performing operations, all these and a multitude of other developments that enable man to live and to live better are linked to the space effort. Most of these developments have been so incorporated into our day-to-day life that they are taken for granted, their origin not considered.

If we are content to live in the past, we have no future. And today is the past.

Literary Analysis
Persuasive Essay To what emotions does L'Amour appeal in this paragraph? How?

Vocabulary Builder
impetus (im´ pə təs)
n. driving force

Apply the Skills

The Eternal Frontier

Thinking About the Selection

1. **Respond:** What questions would you like to ask L'Amour about the message in his essay?
2. **(a) Recall:** What does L'Amour refer to as "the eternal frontier"? **(b) Compare and Contrast:** How is the "eternal" frontier similar to and different from the Western frontier of L'Amour's novels?
3. **(a) Recall:** What kinds of leaders does L'Amour say we need now? **(b) Infer:** In which ways would those leaders support space travel?
4. **(a) Recall:** To what does L'Amour compare the "nay-sayers" who are opposed to space exploration? **(b) Make a Judgment:** Do you think that is a fair evaluation? Why or why not?
5. **(a) Draw Conclusions:** What message about space does the essay convey? **(b) Evaluate:** Does it present a positive message? Explain.

Reading Skill

6. List two examples of **facts** that L'Amour uses to support his argument.
7. In a chart like the one shown, record three **opinions** L'Amour expresses in the essay. Then, list the clues that helped you identify each opinion.

Opinion	Clues

Literary Analysis

8. Identify one appeal to emotion and one appeal to reason that L'Amour uses in this **persuasive essay**.
9. **(a)** What is the most convincing argument L'Amour makes in his persuasive essay? **(b)** Why is it convincing?

QuickReview

Essay at a Glance
The author strongly supports space exploration.

For: Self-test
Visit: www.PHSchool.com
Web Code: ema-6307

Fact: information that can be proved

Opinion: a person's judgment or belief

Persuasive essay: writing that tries to convince readers to believe or act a certain way

Vocabulary Builder

Practice Answer each question by writing a complete sentence that includes the italicized vocabulary word. Explain your answer.

1. Was the western United States ever a new *frontier*?
2. Are *preliminary* plans the last plans a person makes?
3. Is eating dessert an *antidote* to feeling full after a heavy meal?
4. Do some people need an *impetus* to start an assignment?

Writing

Imagine you are advising the government about space travel. Write a brief **persuasive letter** to address the following points:

- Explain whether you are for or against space travel. Clearly identify the goals you would set, such as landing on Mars or reaching another galaxy.
- Explain the compromises your priorities might cause you to make—for example, budget cuts in defense, education, or other programs.
- Defend the points you make in your letter.

For *Grammar, Vocabulary,* and *Assessment,* see **Build Language Skills,** pages 448–449.

Extend Your Learning

Listening and Speaking In a small group, plan a **public service announcement (PSA)** that encourages space travel.

- Use persuasive techniques in your writing.
- Apply cooperative techniques, such as giving everyone a turn and listening carefully when other members of the group are talking.
- Share your PSA with the class.

Research and Technology In a small group, use the Internet and other sources to research a twenty-year period in the history of space exploration. Present your information in a **timeline**. Topics you might research include early attempts at space travel, major successes and failures, development of spacecraft and equipment, or recent exploration and future plans.

Background

Rights for All Before the 1960s, some Americans faced racial discrimination at work, in schools, and on public transportation. Laws such as the Civil Rights Act of 1964 were passed to extend equal rights to all Americans. In "All Together Now," Barbara Jordan expresses support for these important laws, but also stresses her belief that people must work together to improve race relations.

Connecting to the Literature

Reading/Writing Connection Barbara Jordan describes the role of the civil rights movement in the 1960s. List things that people can do to ensure that everyone has equal rights. Use at least three of these words: *integrate, legislate, promote, resolve.*

Review

For **Reading Skill, Literary Analysis,** and **Vocabulary Builder,** see page 436.

Meet the Author

Barbara **Jordan** (1936–1996)

Barbara Jordan inherited her skill at public speaking from her father, a Baptist minister. As a high school student in Houston, Texas, Jordan participated in debates and won public speaking competitions.

Keynote Speaker Jordan was elected to the Texas Senate in 1966, and in 1972 she became a member of Congress. During the 1976 Democratic National Convention, she became the first African American to deliver the keynote speech at a major party's political convention. In her dynamic speech she said, ". . . there is something different about tonight. There is something special about tonight. What is different? What is special? I, Barbara Jordan, am a keynote speaker."

Fast Facts

▶ Jordan was the first African American woman to become a member of the Texas state senate.

▶ In 1990, the National Women's Hall of Fame voted her one of the most influential women of the twentieth century.

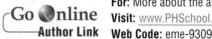

Go Online
Author Link

For: More about the author
Visit: www.PHSchool.com
Web Code: eme-9309

All Together Now
Barbara Jordan

When I look at race relations today I can see that some positive changes have come about. But much remains to be done, and the answer does not lie in more legislation. We *have* the legislation we need; we have the laws. Frankly, I don't believe that the task of bringing us all together can be accomplished by government. What we need now is soul force—the efforts of people working on a small scale to build a truly tolerant, harmonious society. And parents can do a great deal to create that tolerant society.

We all know that race relations in America have had a very rocky history. Think about the 1960s when Dr. Martin Luther King, Jr., was in his heyday and there were marches and

Vocabulary Builder
legislation (lej′ is lā′ shən) *n.* law

tolerant (täl′ ər ənt) *adj.* accepting; free from bigotry or prejudice

▼ **Critical Viewing**
What is happening in this photograph of Martin Luther King, Jr.? **[Analyze]**

protests against segregation[1] and discrimination. The movement culminated in 1963 with the March on Washington.

Following that event, race relations reached an all-time peak. President Lyndon B. Johnson pushed through the Civil Rights Act of 1964, which remains the <u>fundamental</u> piece of civil rights legislation in this century. The Voting Rights Act of 1965 ensured that everyone in our country could vote. At last, black people and white people seemed ready to live together in peace.

But that is not what happened. By the 1990's the good feelings had diminished. Today the nation seems to be suffering from compassion fatigue, and issues such as race relations and civil rights have never regained momentum.

Those issues, however, remain crucial. As our society becomes more diverse, people of all races and backgrounds will have to learn to live together. If we don't think this is important, all we have to do is look at the situation in Bosnia[2] today.

How do we create a harmonious society out of so many kinds of people? The key is tolerance—the one value that is indispensable in creating community.

If we are concerned about community, if it is important to us that people not feel excluded, then we have to do something. Each of us can decide to have one friend of a different race or background in our mix of friends. If we do this, we'll be working together to push things forward.

One thing is clear to me: We, as human beings, must be willing to accept people who are different from ourselves. I must be willing to accept people who don't look as I do and don't talk as I do. It is crucial that I am open to their feelings, their inner reality.

What can parents do? We can put our faith in young people as a positive force. I have yet to find a racist baby. Babies come into the world as blank as slates and, with their beautiful innocence, see others not as different but as enjoyable companions. Children learn ideas and attitudes from the adults who nurture them. I absolutely believe that children do not adopt prejudices unless they absorb them from their parents or teachers.

Vocabulary Builder
fundamental (fun′ də ment′ 'l) *adj.* basic; forming a foundation

Literary Analysis
Persuasive Essay
Which persuasive technique does Jordan use with this reference to Bosnia?

Reading Skill
Fact and Opinion
What clue words do you recognize here that show that the author is expressing an opinion?

---

1. segregation (seg′ rə gā′ shən) *n.* the practice of forcing racial groups to live apart from each other.
2. Bosnia (bäz′ nē ə) *n.* country, located on the Balkan Peninsula in Europe, that was the site of a bloody civil war between different ethnic and religious groups during the 1990s.

The best way to get this country faithful to the American dream of tolerance and equality is to start small. Parents can actively encourage their children to be in the company of people who are of other racial and ethnic backgrounds. If a child thinks, "Well, that person's color is not the same as mine, but she must be okay because she likes to play with the same things I like to play with," that child will grow up with a broader view of humanity.

I'm an incurable <u>optimist</u>. For the rest of the time that I have left on this planet I want to bring people together. You might think of this as a labor of love. Now, I know that love means different things to different people. But what I mean is this: I care about you because you are a fellow human being and I find it okay in my mind, in my heart, to simply say to you, I love you. And maybe that would encourage you to love me in return.

It is possible for all of us to work on this—at home, in our schools, at our jobs. It is possible to work on human relationships in every area of our lives.

Vocabulary Builder
optimist (äp´ tə mist)
n. someone who takes the most hopeful view of matters

▼ **Critical Viewing** Does this photograph reflect the attitude Jordan conveys in the essay? Explain. **[Assess]**

Apply the Skills

All Together Now

Thinking About the Selection

1. **Respond:** What questions would you ask Barbara Jordan about the message in her essay?
2. **(a) Recall:** How does Jordan summarize the history of race relations from the 1960s to the 1990s? **(b) Interpret:** In your own words, describe what Jordan means by "compassion fatigue."
3. **(a) Recall:** What "one value" is necessary to create "a harmonious society?" **(b) Analyze:** Why does Jordan suggest Americans "start small" to promote this value? **(c) Apply:** What types of behavior or activity might help reduce the problems Jordan describes?
4. **(a) Recall:** According to Jordan, how do children learn ideas and attitudes? **(b) Interpret:** What does Jordan mean when she says "I have yet to find a racist baby?"
5. **(a) Recall:** What does Jordan suggest parents do to foster a sense of community? **(b) Evaluate:** Do you think that Jordan's ideas could work to promote tolerance? Explain.

Reading Skill

6. List two **facts** Jordan uses to support her ideas.
7. In a chart like the one shown, record three **opinions** Jordan expresses in the essay. Then, list the clues that helped you identify each opinion.

Opinion	Clues

Literary Analysis

8. Identify one appeal to authority, one appeal to emotion, and one appeal to reason that Jordan uses in this **persuasive essay.**
9. **(a)** What is the most convincing argument Jordan makes in her persuasive essay? **(b)** Why is it convincing?

QuickReview

Speech at a Glance
Jordan discusses how people can make a difference in race relations.

Go Online
Assessment
For: Self-test
Visit: www.PHSchool.com
Web Code: ema-6308

Fact: information that can be proved

Opinion: a person's judgment or belief

Persuasive essay: writing that tries to convince readers to believe or act a certain way

Vocabulary Builder

Practice Using a word from the "All Together Now" vocabulary list on page 436, rewrite each of the following sentences so that it conveys the same basic meaning.

1. The family is the basic unit of social life.
2. The Congress passed new laws.
3. Joan takes a hopeful view of things.
4. Parents should teach their children to be free from bigotry.

Writing

Write a brief **persuasive letter** to a community leader advising him or her about how people in the community can promote tolerance. Address the following points:

- Clearly identify steps people can take at home.
- Explain the challenges that people might face in trying to achieve their goal of a tolerant society.
- Defend the points you make in your letter.

For *Grammar, Vocabulary,* and *Assessment,* see **Build Language Skills,** pages 448–449.

Extend Your Learning

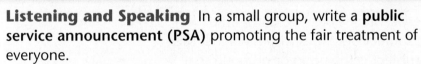

Listening and Speaking In a small group, write a **public service announcement (PSA)** promoting the fair treatment of everyone.

- Use persuasive techniques in your writing.
- Apply cooperative techniques, such as giving everyone a turn, and listen carefully when other members of your group are talking.
- Share your PSA with the class.

Research and Technology In a small group, use the Internet and other sources to research a twenty-year period in the history of the civil rights movement. Present your information in a **timeline**. Topics you might research include Dr. Martin Luther King, Jr., the March on Washington, the Civil Rights Act of 1964, and the Voting Rights Act of 1965.

Build Language Skills

The Eternal Frontier • All Together Now

Vocabulary Skill

Borrowed and Foreign Words When you read, you check statements to decide if they are facts or opinions. The word *check* is a word English speakers **borrowed** from Persian. This list shows examples of other words that were borrowed from foreign languages.

Word	Borrowed from	Meaning
taco	Spanish	a tortilla filled with meat and vegetables
denim	French	cotton fabric used for making jeans
sketch	Dutch	to draw quickly
piano	Italian	a large musical instrument
ski	Scandinavian	sliding on long boards over snow or water

Practice Write the borrowed word that completes each sentence. Then, write five sentences using other words from the list on page 435.

1. Carita stepped from her room onto the _____ to enjoy the view.
2. Amy could play a simple tune on the _____.
3. Jess walked to the bottom of the _____.
4. Mark protected his bicycle by keeping it in the _____.

Grammar Lesson

Subjects and Predicates Every sentence has two parts—the **subject** and the **predicate**. The **subject** describes whom or what the sentence is about. The **simple subject** is the noun or pronoun that states exactly whom or what the sentence is about.

The **predicate** is a verb that tells what the subject does, what is done to the subject, or what the condition of the subject is. The **simple predicate** is the verb or verb phrase that tells what the subject of the sentence does or is.

Practice Use each of these subjects in a sentence with one of the predicates listed.

Subjects: gorilla, state, the young child, music star
Predicates: decided, screeched, stared, ran

MorePractice

For more practice with subjects and predicates, see the Grammar Handbook, p. R32.

W̶G̶ Writing and Grammar Connection: Chapter 19, Section 1

Distinguishing Fact and Opinion

Directions: *Read the selection. Then, answer the questions.*

No student at my school should ever have a boring afternoon. There are after-school activities for every interest. Athletes can run track or play basketball. The Math Team challenges mathematicians to put their skills to work. They have a great time together. There are clubs for readers. There are also clubs for history buffs and cooks. The Chess Club is the best.

1. Which of these statements is an opinion expressed in the selection?
   A The Math Team and the mathematicians have a great time.
   B There are after-school activities.
   C Some students have boring afternoons.
   D Athletes stay trim by running track.

2. Which is a fact?
   A The best activity is the Chess Club.
   B Athletes can run track.
   C After-school activities.
   D Everyone should join the Cooking Club.

3. Which is an opinion?
   A There are clubs for readers.
   B Athletes can run track.
   C The Chess Club is the best.
   D There is a Math Team.

4. Which is a fact expressed in the selection?
   A There are no students in the after-school program.
   B There are clubs for history buffs.
   C The Chess Club sometimes challenges the Math Team to contests.
   D Dancers may join the athletes.

Timed Writing: Persuasive [Critical Stance]

Review the opinions in "The Eternal Frontier" or in "All Together Now." Write an explanation of whether you agree or disagree with the writer. Support your argument with evidence and quotes from the article. Organize your essay logically. **(20 minutes)**

 ## Writing Workshop: *Work in Progress*

Comparison-and-Contrast Essay For a comparison-and-contrast essay you may write, make a two-column chart of everyday decisions. In the left column, list six recent choices you have made. In the right column, jot down one alternative decision for each item. Keep this chart in your writing portfolio.

These skills will help you become a better reader.
Practice them with "The Real Story of a Cowboy's Life"
(p. 452) or "Rattlesnake Hunt" (p. 459).

Reading Skill

A **fact** is information you can prove. An **opinion** is a
judgment.
- **Fact:** The room is ten feet by twelve feet.
- **Opinion:** Green is the best color for the room.

Be aware that some writers present opinions or beliefs as facts. To
get to the truth, **use resources to check facts.** Using the resources
shown in this chart, you can confirm whether a statement is accurate.
As you read, identify information that the writer presents and indicate
which resource could help you check the facts.

Resources	Statement in Text
almanac	
atlas or map	
biographical dictionary	
dictionary	
encyclopedia	
reliable Web site	

Literary Analysis

A writer's **diction** is an important element of his or her writing. The
specific vocabulary a writer uses—his or her **word choice**—can make
writing seem difficult or easy, formal or informal. Diction includes not
only the writer's word choice but also the way the sentences are put
together. The answers to these questions shape a writer's diction:
- *What does the audience already know about the topic?* The
  writer may have to define terms or use simpler language.
- *What feeling will this work convey?* Word choice can make a
  work serious or funny, academic or personal. The length and
  style of the sentences can make a work seem simple or complex.

As you read, notice how the author's word choice and diction affects
the way you respond to a text.

Vocabulary Builder

The Real Story of a Cowboy's Life

- **gauge** (gāj) *v.* estimate or judge (p. 452)
  I can <u>gauge</u> your mood by your smile.

- **ultimate** (ul′ tə mit) *adj.* final (p. 453) *I will
  stop in Reno, but my <u>ultimate</u> destination is
  Tahoe.*

- **diversions** (də vʉr′ zhənz) *n.* amusements
  (p. 454) *The <u>diversions</u> of the sports report
  took my mind off work.*

Rattlesnake Hunt

- **desolate** (des′ ə lit) *adj.* lonely; solitary
  (p. 459) *In 1969, we explored <u>desolate</u> sites
  on the moon.*

- **arid** (ar′ id) *adj.* dry and barren (p. 460) *No
  plants grew in the <u>arid</u> land.*

- **mortality** (môr tal′ ə tē) *n.* the condition of
  being mortal, or having to die eventually
  (p. 461) *Every living thing faces <u>mortality</u>.*

Build Understanding • *The Real Story of a Cowboy's Life*

Background

Cowboys American cowboys were most active from the Civil War through the 1890s. The meat industry was growing, but transportation was lacking. To get cattle to market, cowboys drove them—that is, forced them to trudge—long distances. When people hear the word *cowboy,* they think of a life of daring, romance, and adventure. As this essay shows, that may not be an accurate image.

Connecting to the Literature

Reading/Writing Connection This essay describes life for nineteenth-century cowboys the way it really was. Before you read, imagine a day or night on a cattle drive. Write three sentences that express your ideas. Use at least three of the following words: *evoke, identify, presume, assume, association.*

Meet the Author

Geoffrey C. **Ward** (b. 1940)

Historian Geoffrey C. Ward strives to present an accurate portrayal of the past. He has written more than a dozen books about America and the people who played key roles in its growth. Ward's book *A First-Class Temperament,* about Franklin D. Roosevelt, won the 1989 National Critics Circle Award. Ward has written biographies of Mark Twain, Susan B. Anthony, Harry Truman, and Billy the Kid.

Screenwriter, Too In addition to his books, Ward has written or co-written more than a dozen screenplays for films, many of which have appeared on public television.

Fast Facts

▶ Ward teamed up with filmmaker Ken Burns to create the Emmy Award-winning PBS documentaries *The Civil War* and *Baseball.*

▶ He has been writing about the tigers and jungles of India for nearly fifteen years. With National Geographic photographer Michael Nichols, he created *The Year of the Tiger* in 1998.

Go **O**nline
Author Link

For: More about the author
Visit: www.PHSchool.com
Web Code: eme-9310

The Real Story of a Cowboy's Life

Geoffrey C. Ward

A drive's success depended on discipline and planning. According to Teddy Blue[1], most Texas herds numbered about 2,000 head with a trail boss and about a dozen men in charge—though herds as large as 15,000 were also driven north with far larger escorts. The most experienced men rode "point" and "swing," at the head and sides of the long herd; the least experienced brought up the rear, riding "drag" and eating dust. At the end of the day, Teddy Blue remembered, they "would go to the water barrel . . . and rinse their mouths and cough and spit up . . . black stuff. But you couldn't get it up out of your lungs."

They had to learn to work as a team, keeping the herd moving during the day, resting peacefully at night. Twelve to fifteen miles a day was a good pace. But such steady progress could be interrupted at any time. A cowboy had to know how to gauge the temperament of his cattle, how to chase down a stray without alarming the rest of the herd, how to lasso a steer using the horn of his saddle as a tying post. His saddle was his most prized possession; it served as his chair, his workbench, his pillow at night. Being dragged to death was the most common death for a cowboy, and so the most feared occurrence on the trail was the nighttime stampede. As Teddy Blue recalled, a sound, a smell, or simply the sudden movement of a jittery cow could set off a whole herd.

If . . . the cattle started running—you'd hear that low rumbling noise along the ground and the men on herd wouldn't need to come in and tell you, you'd know—then

---

1. Teddy Blue Edward C. Abbot; a cowboy who rode in a successful trail drive in the 1880s.

Reading Skill
Fact and Opinion
What resource could you use to check the size of Texas herds in the nineteenth century?

Vocabulary Builder
gauge (gāj) *v.*
estimate or judge

you'd jump for your horse and get out there in the lead, trying to head them and get them into a mill[2] before they scattered. It was riding at a dead run in the dark, with cut banks and prairie dog holes all around you, not knowing if the next jump would land you in a shallow grave.

Most cowboys had guns, but rarely used them on the trail. Some outfits made them keep their weapons in the chuck wagon to eliminate any chance of gunplay. Charles Goodnight[3] was still more emphatic: "Before starting on a trail drive, I made it a rule to draw up an article of agreement, setting forth what each man was to do. The main clause stipulated[4] that if one shot another he was to be tried by the outfit and hanged on the spot, if found guilty. I never had a man shot on the trail."

Regardless of its <u>ultimate</u> destination, every herd had to ford[5] a series of rivers—the Nueces, the Guadalupe, the Brazos, the Wichita, the Red.

A big herd of longhorns swimming across a river, Goodnight remembered, "looked like a million floating rocking chairs," and crossing those rivers one after another, a cowboy recalled, was like climbing the rungs of a long ladder reaching north.

"After you crossed the Red River and got out on the open plains," Teddy Blue remembered, "it was sure a pretty sight to see them strung out for almost a mile, the sun shining on their horns." Initially, the land immediately north of the Red

Vocabulary Builder
ultimate (ul′ tə mit)
adj. final

✓ **Reading Check**

What are two dangers cowboys face?

---

2. mill *n.* slow movement in a circle.
3. Charles Goodnight cowboy who rode successful trail drives beginning in the 1860s.
4. stipulated (stip′ yə lāt′ əd) *v.* stated as a rule.
5. ford (fôrd) *v.* cross a river at a shallow point.

River was Indian territory, and some tribes charged tolls for herds crossing their land—payable in money or beef. But Teddy Blue remembered that the homesteaders, now pouring onto the Plains by railroad, were far more nettlesome:

> There was no love lost between settlers and cowboys on the trail. Those jay-hawkers would take up a claim right where the herds watered and charge us for water. They would plant a crop alongside the trail and plow a furrow around it for a fence, and then when the cattle got into their wheat or their garden patch, they would come cussing and waving a shotgun and yelling for damages. And the cattle had been coming through there when they were still raising punkins in Illinois.

The settlers' hostility was entirely understandable. The big herds ruined their crops, and they carried with them a disease, spread by ticks and called "Texas fever," that devastated domestic livestock. Kansas and other territories along the route soon established quarantine lines[6], called "deadlines," at the western fringe of settlement, and insisted that trail drives not cross them. Each year, as settlers continued to move in, those deadlines moved farther west.

Sometimes, farmers tried to enforce their own, as John Rumans, one of Charles Goodnight's hands, recalled:

> Some men met us at the trail near Canyon City, and said we couldn't come in. There were fifteen or twenty of them, and they were not going to let us cross the Arkansas River. We didn't even stop. . . . Old man [Goodnight] had a shotgun loaded with buckshot and led the way, saying: "John, get over on that point with your Winchester and point these cattle in behind me." He slid his shotgun across the saddle in front of him and we did the same with our Winchesters. He rode right across, and as he rode up to them, he said: "I've monkeyed as long as I want to with you," and they fell back to the sides, and went home after we had passed.

There were few <u>diversions</u> on the trail. Most trail bosses banned liquor. Goodnight prohibited gambling, too. Even the songs for which cowboys became famous grew directly out of doing a job, remembered Teddy Blue:

Literary Analysis
Word Choice and Diction Compare Teddy Blue's diction with the narrator's.

Reading Skill
Fact and Opinion Where could you find information about "Texas fever"?

Vocabulary Builder
diversions (də vur′ zhənz) *n.* amusements

---

6. **quarantine** (kwôr′ ən tēn) **lines** *n.* boundaries created to prevent the spread of disease.

The singing was supposed to soothe [the cattle] and it did; I don't know why, unless it was that a sound they was used to would keep them from spooking at other noises. I know that if you wasn't singing, any little sound in the night—it might be just a horse shaking himself—could make them leave the country; but if you were singing, they wouldn't notice it.

The two men on guard would circle around with their horses on a walk, if it was a clear night and the cattle was bedded down and quiet, and one man would sing a verse of song, and his partner on the other side of the herd would sing another verse; and you'd go through a whole song that way. . . . "Bury Me Not on the Lone Prairie" was a great song for awhile, but . . . they sung it to death. It was a saying on the range that even the horses nickered it and the coyotes howled it; it got so they'd throw you in the creek if you sang it.

The number of cattle on the move was sometimes staggering: once, Teddy Blue rode to the top of a rise from which he could see seven herds strung out behind him; eight more up ahead; and the dust from an additional thirteen moving parallel to his. "All the cattle in the world," he remembered, "seemed to be coming up from Texas."

At last, the herds neared their destinations. After months in the saddle—often wearing the same clothes every day, eating nothing but biscuits and beef stew at the chuck wagon, drinking only water and coffee, his sole companions his fellow cowboys, his herd, and his horse—the cowboy was about to be paid for his work, and turned loose in town.

Literary Analysis
Word Choice and Diction To convey the same idea, what words could you use instead of "leave the country"?

▼ **Critical Viewing** Why do you think cowboys, like the one pictured, wear hats? **[Hypothesize]**

Apply the Skills

The Real Story of a Cowboy's Life

Thinking About the Selection

1. **Respond:** What surprised you in this essay? Explain.
2. **(a) Recall:** What details prove that Teddy Blue likes cattle drives? **(b) Evaluate:** What qualifies him as a reliable source of information?
3. **(a) Recall:** What challenges does the landscape present to cowboys? **(b) Analyze:** Did interactions between the cowboys and people living along the cattle routes reduce or add to those challenges? Explain.
4. **(a) Recall:** Identify two ways violence was kept down on the trail. **(b) Interpret:** Based on this information, what kind of person succeeded as a cowboy?
5. **(a) Recall:** Why do settlers object to cattle coming through? **(b) Infer:** Why do cowboys object to going around settled areas? **(c) Make a Judgment:** What solution or compromise would be most fair? Discuss your response with a few other students. Then, as a group, choose one idea to report to the class.

Reading Skill

6. Identify one **fact** and one **opinion** in the essay.
7. What resource would you use to check the distance between Canyon City and the Arkansas River?
8. How do both facts and opinions help the writer paint a full picture of his subject?

Literary Analysis

9. Review the author's **word choice** and **diction** by completing a chart like the one shown.

Technical Vocabulary	Formal Language	Informal Language

10. What feeling about cowboys do you think the author wanted to convey in this essay? Explain.

Vocabulary Builder

Practice For each item, write a single sentence using the words indicated.

1. diversion; long train ride
2. gauge; progress
3. ultimate; goal

Writing

For a new audience, write an **adaptation** of one of the incidents narrated in the essay. For example, tell the incident to a group of kindergarteners or a class of students learning English. Change the author's word choice as necessary for your audience.

- Choose an incident to retell and decide on an audience.
- Plan how to adapt the essay to reflect the needs and interests of your audience.
- Review your draft to find words or concepts that can be simplified. Revise to improve these sections.

For *Grammar, Vocabulary,* and *Assessment,* see **Build Language Skills,** pages 466–467.

Extend Your Learning

Listening and Speaking With a group, make a **plan for a multimedia presentation** about cowboys from 1860 to 1880. First, choose a focus or specific topic, such as famous cowboys or a day in the life of a cowboy. Then, decide on the best media—posters, slides, photographs, or recordings—to enliven the content. Describe your plan to the class.

Research and Technology Write a **help-wanted ad** for a modern job involving cattle or horses. Before you write, scan the help-wanted ads in your local newspaper or on an online career site. Notice the concise writing style of ads, and review what the ads cover, including job responsibilities, education, experience, skills, and personal traits the employer seeks.

Narrative Essay

Background

Snakes When people hear the word *snake,* they often react with fear, thinking of a dangerous and deadly creature. However, those who study and work with these sometimes poisonous reptiles have strategies for safety. In "Rattlesnake Hunt," you will see how professionals respect the potential danger of snakes while controlling their interactions with these reptiles.

Connecting to the Literature

Reading/Writing Connection In "Rattlesnake Hunt," the author overcomes a personal fear and gains a new understanding. In a few sentences, explain why facing something that scares you might be valuable. Use at least three of the following words: *benefit, process, respond, acquire.*

Review

For **Reading Skill, Literary Analysis,** and **Vocabulary,** see page 450.

Meet the Author

Marjorie Kinnan **Rawlings** (1896–1953)

After starting out as a journalist, Marjorie Kinnan Rawlings quit and moved to a farm she bought in northern Florida. There, her close exposure to nature inspired her to write several novels, including the 1939 Pulitzer Prize–winning book *The Yearling.* Her writing reflects an intimate understanding and appreciation of the outdoors.

A Disciplined Writer Rawlings devoted herself to writing but described it as "agony." She forced herself to type eight hours a day. Her daily goal was to produce at least six pages, although she would settle for three. She remained focused, refusing to let any outsiders interfere with her work. She felt that "living" with her characters was necessary in order to create a successful story.

Fast Facts

▶ When she worked on *The Yearling,* Rawlings prepared for key scenes by taking part in several bear hunts.

▶ She hunted for rattlesnakes in order to write this essay.

Go Online
Author Link

For: More about the author
Visit: www.PHSchool.com
Web Code: eme-9311

Rattlesnake Hunt

Marjorie Kinnan Rawlings

Ross Allen, a young Florida herpetologist,[1] invited me to join him on a hunt in the upper Everglades[2]—for rattlesnakes. Ross and I drove to Arcadia in his coupé[3] on a warm January day.

I said, "How will you bring back the rattlesnakes?"

"In the back of my car."

My courage was not adequate to inquire whether they were thrown in loose and might be expected to appear between our feet. Actually, a large portable box of heavy close-meshed wire made a safe cage. Ross wanted me to write an article about his work and on our way to the unhappy hunting grounds I took notes on a mass of data that he had accumulated in years of herpetological research. The scientific and dispassionate detachment of the material and the man made a desirable approach to rattlesnake territory. As I had discovered with the insects and varmints,[4] it is difficult to be afraid of anything about which enough is known, and Ross' facts were fresh from the laboratory.

The hunting ground was Big Prairie, south of Arcadia and west of the northern tip of Lake Okeechobee. Big Prairie is a <u>desolate</u> cattle country, half marsh, half pasture, with islands of palm trees and cypress and oaks. At that time of year the cattlemen and Indians were burning the country, on the theory that the young fresh wire grass that springs up from the roots after a fire is the best cattle forage.[5] Ross planned to hunt his rattlers in the forefront of the fires. They lived in winter, he said, in gopher holes, coming out in the midday warmth to forage, and would move ahead of the flames and be

---

▲ **Critical Viewing**
Would seeing a snake like this one frighten you? Why or why not? [**Connect**]

Vocabulary Builder
desolate (des´ ə lit)
adj. lonely; solitary

 **Reading Check**

Why is the narrator going on a rattlesnake hunt?

easily taken. We joined forces with a big man named Will, his snake-hunting companion of the territory, and set out in early morning, after a long rough drive over deep-rutted roads into the open wilds.

I hope never in my life to be so frightened as I was in those first few hours. I kept on Ross' footsteps, I moved when he moved, sometimes jolting into him when I thought he might leave me behind. He does not use the forked stick of conventional snake hunting, but a steel prong, shaped like an L, at the end of a long stout stick. He hunted casually, calling my attention to the varying vegetation, to hawks overhead, to a pair of the rare whooping cranes that flapped over us. In mid-morning he stopped short, dropped his stick, and brought up a five-foot rattlesnake draped limply over the steel L. It seemed to me that I should drop in my tracks.

"They're not active at this season," he said quietly. "A snake takes on the temperature of its surroundings. They can't stand too much heat for that reason, and when the weather is cool, as now, they're sluggish."

Reading Skill
Fact and Opinion
What reference source could confirm this fact about a snake's temperature?

The sun was bright overhead, the sky a translucent blue, and it seemed to me that it was warm enough for any snake to do as it willed. The sweat poured down my back. Ross dropped the rattler in a crocus sack and Will carried it. By noon, he had caught four. I felt faint and ill. We stopped by a pond and went swimming. The region was flat, the horizon limitless, and as I came out of the cool blue water I expected to find myself surrounded by a ring of rattlers. There were only Ross and Will, opening the lunch basket. I could not eat. Will went back and drove his truck closer, for Ross expected the hunting to be better in the afternoon. The hunting was much better. When we went back to the truck to deposit two more rattlers in the wire cage, there was a rattlesnake lying under the truck.

Ross said, "Whenever I leave my car or truck with snakes already in it, other rattlers always appear. I don't know whether this is because they scent or sense the presence of other snakes, or whether in this <u>arid</u> area they come to the car for shade in the heat of the day."

The problem was scientific, but I had no interest.

That night Ross and Will and I camped out in the vast spaces of the Everglades prairies. We got water from an abandoned well and cooked supper under buttonwood bushes by a flowing stream. The camp fire blazed cheerfully under the

Vocabulary Builder
arid (ar´ id) *adj.* dry and barren

stars and a new moon lifted in the sky. Will told tall tales of the cattlemen and the Indians and we were at peace.

Ross said, "We couldn't have a better night for catching water snakes."

After the rattlers, water snakes seemed innocuous[6] enough. We worked along the edge of the stream and here Ross did not use his L-shaped steel. He reached under rocks and along the edge of the water and brought out harmless reptiles with his hands. I had said nothing to him of my fears, but he understood them. He brought a small dark snake from under a willow root.

"Wouldn't you like to hold it?" he asked. "People think snakes are cold and clammy, but they aren't. Take it in your hands. You'll see that it is warm."

Again, because I was ashamed, I took the snake in my hands. It was not cold, it was not clammy, and it lay trustingly in my hands, a thing that lived and breathed and had <u>mortality</u> like the rest of us. I felt an upsurgence of spirit.

The next day was magnificent. The air was crystal, the sky was aquamarine, and the far horizon of palms and oaks lay against the sky. I felt a new boldness and followed Ross bravely. He was making the rounds of the gopher holes. The rattlers came out in the mid-morning warmth and were never far away. He could tell by their trails whether one had come out or was still in the hole. Sometimes the two men dug the snake out. At times it was down so long and winding a tunnel that the digging was hopeless. Then they blocked the entrance and went on to other holes. In an hour or so they made the original rounds, unblocking the holes. The rattler in every case came out hurriedly, as though anything were preferable to being shut in. All the time Ross talked to me, telling me the scientific facts he had discovered about the habits of the rattlers.

"They pay no attention to a man standing perfectly still," he said, and proved it by letting Will unblock a hole while he stood at the entrance as the snake came out. It was exciting to watch the snake crawl slowly beside and past the man's legs. When it was at a safe distance he walked within its range of vision, which he had proved to be no higher than a man's knee, and the snake whirled and drew back in an attitude[7] of

---

6. **innocuous** (in näk´ yōō əs) *adj.* harmless.
7. **attitude** (at´ ə tōōd´) *n.* a position or posture of the body.

▲ Critical Viewing
What makes the snake in this photograph appear dangerous? **[Analyze]**

Vocabulary Builder
mortality (môr tal´ ə tē) *n.* the condition of being mortal, or having to die eventually

Reading Check

How are the narrator's feelings changing?

fighting defense. The rattler strikes only for paralyzing and killing its food, and for defense.

"It is a slow and heavy snake," Ross said. "It lies in wait on a small game trail and strikes the rat or rabbit passing by. It waits a few minutes, then follows along the trail, coming to the small animal, now dead or dying. It noses it from all sides, making sure that it is its own kill, and that it is dead and ready for swallowing."

A rattler will lie quietly without revealing itself if a man passes by and it thinks it is not seen. It slips away without fighting if given the chance. Only Ross' sharp eyes sometimes picked out the gray and yellow diamond pattern, camouflaged among the grasses. In the cool of the morning, chilled by the January air, the snakes showed no fight. They could be looped up limply over the steel L and dropped in a sack or up into the wire cage on the back of Will's truck. As the sun mounted in the sky and warmed the moist Everglades earth, the snakes were warmed too, and Ross warned that it was time to go more cautiously. Yet having learned that it was we who were the aggressors; that immobility meant complete safety; that the snakes, for all their lightning flash in striking, were inaccurate in their aim, with limited vision; having watched again and again the liquid grace of movement, the beauty of pattern, suddenly I understood that I was drinking in freely the magnificent sweep of the horizon, with no fear of what might be at the moment under my feet. I went off hunting by myself, and though I found no snakes, I should have known what to do.

The sun was dropping low in the west. Masses of white cloud hung above the flat marshy plain and seemed to be tangled in the tops of distant palms and cypresses. The sky turned orange, then saffron. I walked leisurely back toward the truck. In the distance I could see Ross and Will making their way in too. The season was more advanced than at the Creek, two hundred miles to the north, and I noticed that spring flowers were blooming among the lumpy hummocks. I leaned over to pick a white violet. There was a rattlesnake under the violet.

If this had happened the week before, if it had happened the day before, I think I should have lain down and died on top of the rattlesnake, with no need of being struck and poisoned. The snake did not coil, but lifted its head and whirred its rattles lightly. I stepped back slowly and put the violet in a buttonhole. I reached forward and laid the steel L across the

Reading Skill
Fact and Opinion Is Ross stating fact or opinion in this paragraph? How do you know?

Literary Analysis
Word Choice and Diction How would you rephrase "drinking in freely the magnificent sweep of the horizon" in less formal language?

snake's neck, just back of the blunt head. I called to Ross:

"I've got one."

He strolled toward me.

"Well, pick it up," he said.

I released it and slipped the L under the middle of the thick body.

"Go put it in the box."

He went ahead of me and lifted the top of the wire cage. I made the truck with the rattler, but when I reached up the six feet to drop it in the cage, it slipped off the stick and dropped on Ross' feet. It made no effort to strike.

"Pick it up again," he said. "If you'll pin it down lightly and reach just back of its head with your hand, as you've seen me do, you can drop it in more easily."

I pinned it and leaned over.

"I'm awfully sorry," I said, "but you're pushing me a little too fast."

He grinned. I lifted it on the stick and again as I had it at head height, it slipped off, down Ross' boots and on top of his feet. He stood as still as a stump. I dropped the snake on his feet for the third time. It seemed to me that the most patient of rattlers might in time resent being hauled up and down, and for all the man's quiet certainty that in standing motionless there was no danger, would strike at whatever was nearest, and that would be Ross.

I said, "I'm just not man enough to keep this up any longer," and he laughed and reached down with his smooth quickness and lifted the snake back of the head and dropped it in the cage. It slid in among its mates and settled in a corner. The hunt was over and we drove back over the uneven trail to Will's village and left him and went on to Arcadia and home. Our catch for the two days was thirty-two rattlers.

I said to Ross, "I believe that tomorrow I could have picked up that snake."

Back at the Creek, I felt a new lightness. I had done battle with a great fear, and the victory was mine.

Literature in Context

Language Connection

Scientific Words From Greek Origins Ross Allen studies herpetology. The word *herpetology* comes from the Greek words *herpein,* meaning "to creep," and *logo,* meaning "word." Other scientific words derived from Greek and ending with the suffix *-ology* (meaning "science or theory of") include *biology,* the study of animals and plants; *anthropology,* the study of humans; *ichthyology,* the study of fish; and *paleontology,* the study of life forms from the past, especially fossils.

Connect to the Literature

How does the origin of the word *herpetology* explain why herpetologists study snakes?

Literary Analysis
Word Choice and Diction On this page, find an example of an informal expression that is used by the author.

Apply the Skills

Rattlesnake Hunt

Thinking About the Selection

1. **Respond:** Would you like to go on a rattlesnake hunt? Explain.
2. **(a) Recall:** Why does Rawlings go on the hunt? **(b) Infer:** Why do Rawlings's feelings about snakes change when she holds one?
3. **(a) Recall:** What does Rawlings learn about rattlesnakes? **(b) Speculate:** How does this knowledge contribute to her feeling of "boldness" on the second day?
4. **(a) Recall:** Note two ways in which Rawlings shows that she has partly overcome her fears. **(b) Infer:** Why does the author announce at the end of the hunt that she has won a "victory"?
5. **(a) Analyze:** In what ways does the hunt change how Rawlings thinks about nature and herself? **(b) Generalize:** What general truth does this essay suggest? In a small group, share your response, and defend it. As a group, choose one idea to share with the class.

Reading Skill

6. Identify one **fact** in the essay and one **opinion**.
7. What resource would you use to check the facts about a rattlesnake's vision?
8. How do both facts and opinions help the writer explain her experience with snakes?

Literary Analysis

9. Review the author's **word choice** and **diction** by completing a chart like the one shown.

Technical Vocabulary	Formal Language	Informal Language

10. What feeling about snakes and her own experience do you think the author wanted to convey in this essay? Explain.

QuickReview

Who's Who in the Essay

Ross Allen: a snake expert on a hunt

Will: another man on the hunt

Narrator: Marjorie Kinnan Rawlings on her first snake hunt

Assessment
For: Self-test
Visit: www.PHSchool.com
Web Code: ema-6310

Fact: a statement that can be proved

Opinion: a statement of judgment or belief

Word Choice: the specific words a writer uses

Diction: a writer's word choice and sentence structure

Vocabulary Builder

Practice For each item, write a single sentence using the words indicated.

1. arid; farmer
2. mortality; medicine
3. desolate; midnight

Writing

For a new audience, write an **adaptation** of one of the incidents narrated in the essay. For example, tell the incident to a group of kindergarteners or a class of students learning English. Change the author's word choice as necessary for your audience.

- Choose an incident to retell and decide on an audience.
- Plan how to adapt the essay to reflect the needs and interests of your audience.
- Review your draft to find words or concepts that could be simplified. Revise to improve these sections.

For *Grammar, Vocabulary,* and *Assessment,*
see **Build Language Skills,** pages 466–467.

Extend Your Learning

Listening and Speaking With a group, make a **plan for a multimedia presentation** about the life of a rattlesnake. First, choose a specific topic, such as a snake's life stages, its natural enemies, or its natural habitat. Then, decide on the best media—posters, slides, photographs, or musical recordings—to enliven the content. Describe your plan to the class.

Research and Technology Write a **help-wanted ad** for a person to work with Ross Allen. Before you write, scan the help-wanted ads in your local newspaper or on an online career site. Notice the concise writing style of ads, and review what the ads cover, including job responsibilities, education, experience, skills, and personal traits the employer seeks.

Build Language Skills

Vocabulary Skill

Borrowed and Foreign Words If you say, "Take the car out of the garage; we are going to the ranch in the canyon," you have used words borrowed from both French and Spanish. The list below shows examples of other commonly used words that have been borrowed from foreign languages.

Words relating to—	Foods	Animals	Clothing
Borrowed words	ketchup noodle spaghetti	gorilla coyote gazelle	jeans dungaree moccasin
Borrowed from—	Chinese German Italian	African languages Spanish Arabic	French Hindi American Indian languages

Practice Choose one of the categories above and write a paragraph which includes borrowed words. You may add other borrowed words if you choose.

Grammar Lesson

Compound Subjects and Predicates A **compound subject** contains two or more subjects that share the same verb. A **compound predicate** contains two or more verbs that share the same subject. Both compound subjects and compound predicates are joined by conjunctions such as *and* and *or*.

Compound subject: *Bob* and *I* entertained at the talent show.

Compound predicate: We *clapped* and *laughed*.

Practice Identify the compound subjects and compound predicates in the following items. Then replace them with other nouns or verbs. Explain how the substitution changes the sentence.

1. Cats and lions belong to the same family.
2. Many people live or work in our town.
3. He and I laughed and danced.
4. The fish sizzled and crackled.
5. Rain, snow, or sleet will fall today.

MorePractice

For more practice with compound subjects and predicates, see the Grammar Handbook, p. R32.

W̶G̶ Writing and Grammar Connection: Chapter 19, Section 3

Reading: Fact and Opinion

Directions: *Read the selection. Then, answer the questions.*

   Professional baseball is a more exciting game today than it was fifty years ago. Today, there are more major league teams than there were decades ago. New rules have made the game more interesting. We now have allowances, such as the designated hitter, that did not exist fifty years ago. The playing season has more games than seasons of decades past. Naturally, more games create more drama and suspense in the race for the pennant.

1. Which of the following best describes the first sentence of the paragraph?
   A a fact
   B an opinion
   C both a fact and an opinion
   D neither a fact nor an opinion

2. Which of these statements is an opinion?
   A There are more teams now than there were decades ago.
   B The designated hitter did not exist fifty years ago.
   C The season now has more games than in the past.
   D More games create more drama and suspense.

3. Which of these statements is a fact?
   A There are more major league teams now than before.
   B New rules have made the game more interesting.
   C Pro ball is more exciting today than it was fifty years ago.
   D More games create more drama and intrigue.

4. Which resource would be most useful for checking the information in the passage?
   A an atlas
   B a dictionary
   C a book on baseball
   D a newspaper

Timed Writing: Summary [Cognition]

Review "The Real Story of a Cowboy's Life" or "Rattlesnake Hunt." Write a summary of the work. In your summary, distinguish between the facts and opinions the author expresses. **(20 minutes)**

Writing Workshop: *Work in Progress*

Comparison-and-Contrast Essay

Choose three sets of items from the chart in your writing portfolio. For each set, answer the following question: What do these two items have in common? Save this work in your writing portfolio.

Reading Informational Materials

Manuals

In Part 2, you are learning to distinguish between fact and opinion in a literary work. This skill can also help you understand and use the information found in a manual. Reference materials, such as manuals, often present facts objectively, without including the author's opinions. If you read "Rattlesnake Hunt," you learned facts that also apply to this manual on venomous snakes.

About Manuals

A **manual** is a book of facts or instructions that offers guidance or information on a particular topic. Manuals focus on topics such as writing term papers, photography, do-it-yourself repairs, driving, or health. This first-aid manual explains how people in North America can identify common types of venomous snakes. It also outlines the steps for treating a snake bite.

Many manuals include the following features:

- clearly labeled illustrations or diagrams
- safety warnings that describe "do's" and "don'ts"
- a bulleted or numbered list of steps to follow

Reading Skill

You can **check facts by using reference sources.** Manuals are one source. Other sources include dictionaries, encyclopedias, reliable Web sites, or unbiased experts. Determine which details in the following statements are facts and which are opinions. Use the manual to verify facts.

Statement	The most striking of the pit vipers is the copperhead, with its diamond-shaped markings.	Pit vipers are the most frightening snakes. They puncture their victims with fangs.	Coral snakes have beautiful colors: red, black, and yellow.
Which details can be verified as fact?			
Which details are opinion?			

How to Recognize Venomous Snakes in North America

Most snakes in North America are not venomous. The two types of poisonous snakes you should be aware of, pit vipers and coral snakes, are described in this chart.

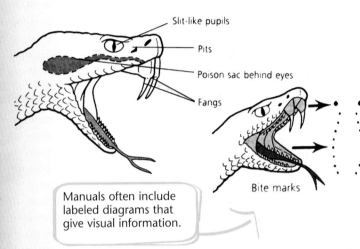

- Slit-like pupils
- Pits
- Poison sac behind eyes
- Fangs
- Bite marks

> Manuals often include labeled diagrams that give visual information.

Rattlesnakes, copperheads, and cottonmouths are all *pit vipers.* You can recognize a pit viper by its triangular head, fangs, narrow, vertical pupils, and the pits between its nostrils and its eyes. The coral snake has round pupils and is not a pit viper; it does have fangs, but they may or may not be visible. Nonvenomous snakes have round pupils and no fangs, pits, or rattles.

Rattlers grow up to 8 feet long. There are about 30 species of rattlesnake in the U.S., but any rattler can be recognized by the rattles at the end of its tail.

Copperheads grow up to 4 feet long and have diamond-shaped markings down their backs. They vibrate their tails when angry, but have no rattles.

The cottonmouth, also known as the water moccasin, grows up to 4 feet long. When alarmed, it opens its mouth, revealing the white lining for which it is named.

Coral snakes grow up to 3 feet long and have distinctive red, black, and yellow or white rings and a black nose. Other snakes have similar colors, but only the coral snake has red bands bordered by white or yellow.

> Color photographs help the reader identify each type of snake.

Reading Informational Materials

First Aid for a Snake Bite

- **Call EMS.**
- **Try to identify the type of snake.** If it can be done quickly and without danger to you, kill the snake and have it identified. (Be aware that venomous snakes can bite reflexively even after they die.)
- **Call ahead to the emergency department** so the correct antivenin can be prepared.

> **DO NOT** cut into a snake bite.
>
> **DO NOT** apply cold compresses to a snake bite.
>
> **DO NOT** apply a tourniquet.
>
> **DO NOT** raise the site of the bite above the level of the victim's heart.
>
> **DO NOT** give the victim aspirin, stimulants, or pain medication unless a physician says to.
>
> **DO NOT** allow the victim to exercise. If necessary, carry him or her to safety.

> This list describes actions that can worsen the victim's reaction to the bite.

1. Check the victim's ABCs. Open the airway; check breathing and circulation. If necessary, begin rescue breathing, CPR, or bleeding control. (See the Emergency Action Guides on pages 199–210.)

2. If the victim is having breathing problems, keep his or her airway open. A conscious victim will naturally get into the position in which it is easiest to breathe.

3. Calm and reassure the victim. Anxiety aggravates all reactions.

4. Wash the bite with soap and water.

5. Remove any rings or constricting items, since the bitten area may swell.

> Numbered steps help readers follow the instructions for helping a snakebite victim.

6. Take steps to slow the rate at which the venom spreads in the victim's body. Have the victim lie still. Place the injured site below the level of the victim's heart and immobilize it in a comfortable position.

7. Look for signs of shock, such as decreased alertness or increased paleness If shock develops, lay the victim flat, raise his or her feet 8 to 12 inches, and cover the victim with a coat or blanket. *Do not* elevate the bitten area, and *do not* place the victim in this position if you suspect any head, neck, back, or leg injury or if the position makes the victim uncomfortable. (See **Shock** on page 172.)

8. Stay with the victim until you get medical help.

Reading: Distinguishing Between Fact and Opinion

Directions: *Use the information in the manual to choose the best answer to each question.*

1. Which of the following statements is a fact?
   A The sound of a rattler's vibrating tail is paralyzing.
   B Venomous snakes can bite reflexively even after they die.
   C It is best to avoid hiking in areas where snakes can be found.
   D Hysteria is a natural response to a snake bite.

2. Which of the following statements is an opinion?
   A More Americans should learn basic first aid.
   B Decreased alertness and increased paleness are signs of shock.
   C It usually takes several hours for snake venom to kill.
   D Antivenin can save a victim's life if administered properly.

3. What other reference source can you use to check a statement about pit vipers?
   A an editorial
   B a movie critic
   C an encyclopedia
   D a short story

Reading: Comprehension and Interpretation

Directions: *Write your answers on a separate sheet of paper.*

4. Identify three things you should *not* do when someone has been bitten by a poisonous snake.

5. Why is it important to keep a bite victim calm?

6. Compare and contrast the physical characteristics of venomous and nonvenomous snakes.

Timed Writing: Explanation

In an essay explain the most effective way to care for a snake-bite victim until help arrives. **(10 minutes)**

Humorous Essays

Humorous essays are works of nonfiction meant to amuse readers. To entertain, authors may use one or more of these comic techniques:

- present an illogical, inappropriate, improper, or unusual situation
- contrast reality with characters' mistaken views
- exaggerate the truth, or exaggerate the feelings, ideas, and actions of characters

While most humorists want to entertain the reader, many also write to convey a serious message.

Comparing Humorous Essays

Writers of humorous essays often develop humor through the characters they present. In fact, in "Alligator" and "The Night the Bed Fell," the writers make humorous characters central to their essays. As you read these essays, use a cluster diagram like the one shown to note comic details in the descriptions and actions of Aunt Belle in "Alligator" and Briggs in "The Night the Bed Fell."

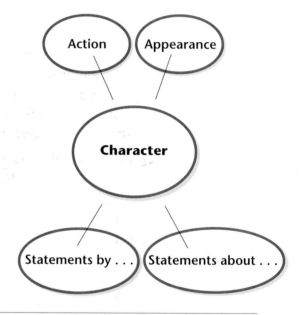

Vocabulary Builder

Alligator

- **cattails** (kat´ tālz) *n.* tall reeds with furry, brown spikes, found in marshes and swamps (p. 474) *A frog dozed by the cattails.*

- **exultant** (eg zult´ 'nt) *adj.* expressing great joy or triumph (p. 474) *I was exultant when I finished the race.*

- **bellow** (bel´ ō) *v.* roar deeply (p. 474) *My father will bellow when his team loses a big game.*

The Night the Bed Fell

- **ominous** (äm´ ə nəs) *adj.* threatening (p. 477) *We ran when we heard the ominous siren.*

- **perilous** (per´ ə ləs) *adj.* dangerous (p. 479) *During a storm, the highways become perilous.*

- **deluge** (del´ yōōj´) *n.* a great flood (p. 481) *I cannot deal with the deluge of phone calls.*

- **pungent** (pun´ jənt) *adj.* sharp-smelling (p. 481) *The pungent odor of burning tires was disgusting.*

- **culprit** (kul´ prit) *n.* guilty person (p. 482) *When we found the culprit, we turned her over to the principal.*

Build Understanding

Connecting to the Literature

Reading/Writing A situation that makes one person laugh may not seem humorous to another person. Think of the kinds of people and events that have made you laugh out loud. Write a few sentences describing your ideas about what makes something funny. Use at least three of the following words: *react, focus, rely, analyze, demonstrate.*

Meet the Authors

Bailey **White** (b. 1950)

Bailey White reads her humorous essays on *All Things Considered,* a radio program. She describes people and situations she encounters in and around Thomasville, Georgia, where she was born and lives today.

Juggling Two Careers White began writing when she was a teen. On graduation from Florida State University, she returned to Thomasville to teach first grade. During the twenty years she taught, she wrote in her spare time. Today, White pursues her writing career full-time.

James **Thurber** (1894–1961)

According to James Thurber, if you had lived in his Columbus, Ohio, home, you would have observed absurd events. He wrote of such events—but always showed his care and affection for his quirky relatives.

Understanding Humor To Thurber, humor results from the contrast between the confusion of a moment and the insight gained later. In "The Night the Bed Fell," Thurber calmly recounts and makes sense of one instance of total confusion—and the result is laughter. Thurber's literary home was *The New Yorker* magazine, where he wrote essays that gently poked fun at the world. He often did line drawings for his essays, even when his sight began to fail him.

Go **O**nline
Author Link

For: More about the authors
Visit: www.PHSchool.com
Web Code: eme-9312

ALLIGATOR
Bailey White

I remember as a little child watching my Aunt Belle's wide rump disappear into the <u>cattails</u> and marsh grass at the edge of a pond as she crawled on her hands and knees to meet a giant alligator face to face. She was taming him, she said. We children would wait high up on the bank with our eyes and mouths wide open, hoping that the alligator wouldn't eat her up, but not wanting to miss it if he did.

Finally Aunt Belle would get as close to him as she wanted, and they would stare at each other for some minutes. Then my aunt would jump up, wave her arms in the air, and shout, "Whoo!" With a tremendous leap and flop the alligator would throw himself into the water. The little drops from that splash would reach all the way to where we were standing, and my aunt would come up the bank drenched and <u>exultant</u>. "I have to show him who's boss," she would tell us.

Later, Aunt Belle taught that alligator to <u>bellow</u> on command. She would drive the truck down to the edge of the pond

Vocabulary Builder
cattails (kat′ tālz) *n.*
tall reeds with furry brown spikes, found in marshes and swamps

exultant (eg zult′ ′nt)
adj. expressing great joy or triumph

bellow (bel′ ō) *v.* roar deeply

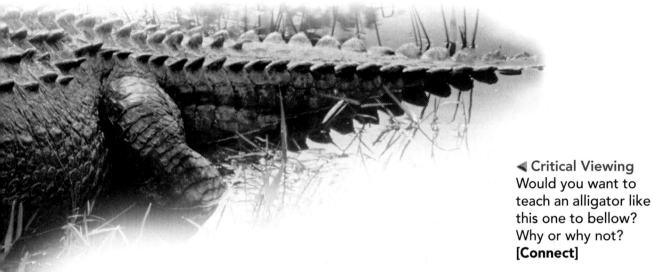

◀ **Critical Viewing**
Would you want to teach an alligator like this one to bellow? Why or why not? **[Connect]**

and gun the engine. We would sit in the back, craning our necks to see him coming. He would come fast across the pond, raising two diagonal waves behind him as he came. He would haul himself into the shallow water and get situated just right. His back was broad and black. His head was as wide as a single bed. His tail would disappear into the dark pond water. He was the biggest alligator anyone had ever seen.

Literary Analysis
Humorous Essay
Which details make this paragraph funny?

Then my aunt would turn off the engine. We would all stop breathing. The alligator would swell up. He would lift his head, arch his tail, and bellow. The sound would come from deep inside. It was not loud, but it had a carrying quality. It was like a roar, but with more authority than a lion's roar. It was a sound you hear in your bones. If we were lucky, he would bellow ten times. Then Aunt Belle would throw him a dead chicken.

The day came when she could just walk down to the pond and look out across the water. The alligator would come surging up to the bank, crawl out, and bellow.

By this time he was very old. My aunt got old, too. Her children had all grown up. She got to where she was spending a lot of time down at the pond. She'd go down there and just sit on the bank. When the alligator saw her, he'd swim over and climb out. He never bellowed anymore. They would just sit

✓**Reading Check**

How does the alligator respond when Aunt Belle goes down to the pond?

and look at each other. After a while my aunt would walk back to the house. The alligator would swim out to where the water was deep and black, and float for a minute; then he'd just disappear, without even a ripple. That's how he did.

But one day he didn't come when Aunt Belle went to the pond. He didn't come the next day, or the day after. All that summer, Aunt Belle walked around and around the pond looking, listening, and sniffing. "Something as big as that, you'd know if he was dead, this hot weather," she'd say. Finally, she stopped going down to the pond.

But sometimes, on the nights of the full moon in springtime, I can hear an alligator bellow. It comes rolling up through the night. It's not loud, but it makes me sit up in bed and hold my breath. Sometimes I hear it ten times. It's a peaceful sound.

◀ Critical Viewing
This alligator appears to be smiling. Describe how its smile makes you feel. [Connect]

Literary Analysis
Humorous Essay
Which details in this paragraph are probably exaggerated? Explain.

Thinking About the Selection

1. **Respond:** What might have been Aunt Belle's reason for taming the alligator in the first place?

2. **(a) Recall:** According to the second paragraph, what were some early interactions between Aunt Belle and the alligator?
   (b) Infer: What does Aunt Belle mean when she says she has to "show him who's boss"?

3. **(a) Recall:** What words and phrase does White use to describe the bellowing of the alligator? **(b) Speculate:** How would the story have been different if White had used a more realistic style to describe the scene?

4. **(a) Compare and Contrast:** How are the alligator and Aunt Belle similar at the end of the essay? **(b) Analyze:** How does the relationship between the alligator and Aunt Belle change over the years? **(c) Draw Conclusions:** What serious message might this humorous essay convey?

The Night the Bed Fell

James Thurber

I suppose that the high-water mark of my youth in Columbus, Ohio, was the night the bed fell on my father. It makes a better recitation (unless, as some friends of mine have said, one has heard it five or six times) than it does a piece of writing, for it is almost necessary to throw furniture around, shake doors, and bark like a dog, to lend the proper atmosphere and verisimilitude[1] to what is admittedly a somewhat incredible tale. Still, it did take place.

It happened, then, that my father had decided to sleep in the attic one night, to be away where he could think. My mother opposed the notion strongly because, she said, the old wooden bed up there was unsafe: it was wobbly and the heavy headboard would crash down on father's head in case the bed fell, and kill him. There was no dissuading him, however, and at a quarter past ten he closed the attic door behind him and went up the narrow twisting stairs. We later heard <u>ominous</u> creakings as he crawled into bed. Grandfather, who usually slept in the attic bed when he was with us, had disappeared some days before. On these occasions he was usually gone six or eight days and returned growling and out of temper, with

Vocabulary Builder
ominous (äm´ ə nəs)
adj. threatening

 **Reading Check**

What kind of a story does the narrator say he is going to tell?

---

1. **verisimilitude** (ver´ ə si mil´ ə t o͞od) *n.* appearance of truth or reality.

the news that the Federal Union[2] was run by a passel of blockheads and that the Army of the Potomac[3] didn't have a chance.

We had visiting us at this time a nervous first cousin of mine named Briggs Beall, who believed that he was likely to cease breathing when he was asleep. It was his feeling that if he were not awakened every hour during the night, he might die of suffocation. He had been accustomed to setting an alarm clock to ring at intervals until morning, but I persuaded him to abandon this. He slept in my room and I told him that I was such a light sleeper that if anybody quit breathing in the same room with me, I would wake instantly. He tested me the first night—which I had suspected he would—by holding his breath after my regular breathing had convinced him I was asleep. I was not asleep, however, and called to him. This seemed to allay his fears a little, but he took the precaution of putting a glass of spirits of camphor[4] on a little table at the head of his bed. In case I didn't arouse him until he was almost gone, he said, he would sniff the camphor, a powerful reviver. Briggs was not the only member of his family who had his crotchets.[5] Old Aunt Melissa Beall (who could whistle like a man, with two fingers in her mouth) suffered under the premonition that she was destined to die on South High Street, because she had been born on South High Street and married on South High Street. Then there was Aunt Sarah Shoaf, who never went to bed at night without the fear that a burglar was going to get in and blow chloroform[6] under her door through a tube. To avert this calamity—for she was in greater dread of anesthetics than of losing her household goods—she always piled her money, silverware, and other valuables in a neat stack just outside her bedroom, with a note reading: "This is all I have. Please take it and do not use your chloroform, as this is all I have." Aunt Gracie Shoaf also had a burglar phobia, but she met it with more fortitude. She was confident that burglars had been getting into her house every night for forty years. The fact that she never missed any thing was to her no proof to the contrary. She always claimed that she scared

---

2. **Federal Union** northern side during the Civil War of the 1860s. He is under the illusion that the Civil War has not yet ended.
3. **Army of the Potomac** one of the northern armies during the Civil War.
4. **spirits of camphor** liquid with a powerful odor.
5. **crotchets** (kräch´ its) *n.* peculiar ideas.
6. **chloroform** (klôr´ ə fôrm´) *n.* substance used at one time as an anesthetic.

them off before they could take anything, by throwing shoes down the hallway. When she went to bed she piled, where she could get at them handily, all the shoes there were about her house. Five minutes after she had turned off the light, she would sit up in bed and say "Hark!" Her husband, who had learned to ignore the whole situation as long ago as 1903, would either be sound asleep or pretend to be sound asleep. In either case he would not respond to her tugging and pulling, so that presently she would arise, tiptoe to the door, open it slightly and heave a shoe down the hall in one direction, and its mate down the hall in the other direction. Some nights she threw them all, some nights only a couple of pair.

But I am straying from the remarkable incidents that took place during the night that the bed fell on father. By midnight we were all in bed. The layout of the rooms and the disposition[7] of their occupants is important to an understanding of what later occurred. In the front room upstairs (just under father's attic bedroom) were my mother and my brother Herman, who sometimes sang in his sleep, usually "Marching Through Georgia" or "Onward, Christian Soldiers." Briggs Beall and myself were in a room adjoining this one. My brother Roy was in a room across the hall from ours. Our bull terrier, Rex, slept in the hall.

My bed was an army cot, one of those affairs which are made wide enough to sleep on comfortably only by putting up, flat with the middle section, the two sides which ordinarily hang down like the sideboards of a drop-leaf table. When these sides are up, it is <u>perilous</u> to roll too far toward the edge, for then the cot is likely to tip completely over, bringing the whole bed down on top of one, with a tremendous banging crash. This, in fact, is precisely what happened about two o'clock in the morning. (It was my mother who, in recalling the scene later, first referred to it as "the night the bed fell on your father.")

"Aunt Gracie Shoaf Throwing Shoes" by James Thurber

▲ **Critical Viewing** How would Gracie Shoaf defend the actions shown in this drawing? **[Analyze]**

Vocabulary Builder
perilous (per´ ə ləs) *adj.* dangerous

 **Reading Check**

What does Briggs fear will happen to him?

---

7. **disposition** (dis´ pə zish´ ən) *n.* arrangement.

"*Briggs Suffocating*" by James Thurber

Always a deep sleeper, slow to arouse (I had lied to Briggs), I was at first unconscious of what had happened when the iron cot rolled me onto the floor and toppled over on me. It left me still warmly bundled up and unhurt, for the bed rested above me like a canopy. Hence I did not wake up, only reached the edge of consciousness and went back. The racket, however, instantly awakened my mother, in the next room, who came to the immediate conclusion that her worst dread was realized: the big wooden bed upstairs had fallen on father. She therefore screamed, "Let's go to your poor father!" It was this shout, rather than the noise of my cot falling, that awakened Herman, in the same room with her. He thought that mother had become, for no apparent reason, hysterical. "You're all right, Mamma!" he shouted, trying to calm her. They exchanged shout for shout for perhaps ten seconds: "Let's go

Literary Analysis
Humorous Essay
What misunderstanding makes this situation humorous?

to your poor father!" and "You're all right!" That woke up Briggs. By this time I was conscious of what was going on, in a vague way, but did not yet realize that I was under my bed instead of on it. Briggs, awakening in the midst of loud shouts of fear and apprehension, came to the quick conclusion that he was suffocating and that we were all trying to "bring him out." With a low moan, he grasped the glass of camphor at the head of his bed and instead of sniffing it poured it over himself. The room reeked of camphor. "Ugf, ahfg," choked Briggs, like a drowning man, for he had almost succeeded in stopping his breath under the <u>deluge</u> of <u>pungent</u> spirits. He leaped out of bed and groped toward the open window, but he came up against one that was closed. With his hand, he beat out the glass, and I could hear it crash and tinkle on the alleyway below. It was at this juncture that I, in trying to get up, had the uncanny sensation of feeling my bed above me! Foggy with sleep, I now suspected, in my turn, that the whole uproar was being made in a frantic endeavor to extricate me from what must be an unheard-of and perilous situation. "Get me out of this!" I bawled. "Get me out!" I think I had the nightmarish belief that I was entombed in a mine. "Gugh," gasped Briggs, floundering in his camphor.

By this time my mother, still shouting, pursued by Herman, still shouting, was trying to open the door to the attic, in order to go up and get my father's body out of the wreckage. The door was stuck, however, and wouldn't yield. Her frantic pulls on it only added to the general banging and confusion. Roy and the dog were now up, the one shouting questions, the other barking.

Father, farthest away and soundest sleeper of all, had by this time been awakened by the battering on the attic door. He

Vocabulary Builder
deluge (del′ yōōj′) *n.* a great flood

pungent (pun′ jənt) *adj.* sharp-smelling

Reading Check

Whose bed falls?

"Briggs and Rex" by James Thurber

◄ Critical Viewing How does the action in this drawing capture the mood of the story? **[Analyze]**

decided that the house was on fire. "I'm coming, I'm coming!" he wailed in a slow, sleepy voice—it took him many minutes to regain full consciousness. My mother, still believing he was caught under the bed, detected in his "I'm coming!" the mournful, resigned note of one who is preparing to meet his Maker. "He's dying!" she shouted.

"I'm all right!" Briggs yelled to reassure her. "I'm all right!" He still believed that it was his own closeness to death that was worrying mother. I found at last the light switch in my room, unlocked the door, and Briggs and I joined the others at the attic door. The dog, who never did like Briggs, jumped for him—assuming that he was the <u>culprit</u> in whatever was going on—and Roy had to throw Rex and hold him. We could hear father crawling out of bed upstairs. Roy pulled the attic door open, with a mighty jerk, and father came down the stairs, sleepy and irritable but safe and sound. My mother began to weep when she saw him. Rex began to howl. "What in the name of heaven is going on here?" asked father.

The situation was finally put together like a gigantic jigsaw puzzle. Father caught a cold from prowling around in his bare feet but there were no other bad results. "I'm glad," said mother, who always looked on the bright side of things, "that your grandfather wasn't here."

Literary Analysis
Humorous Essay
What characteristics make Mother amusing?

Vocabulary Builder
culprit (kul′ prit) *n.* guilty person

Thinking About the Selection

1. **(a) Recall:** Who is in the house on the night described? **(b) Compare:** What quality or qualities do these characters share? **(c) Support:** What examples illustrate the shared qualities?

2. **(a) Recall:** Describe the layout of the rooms. **(b) Analyze:** Why is the placement of the rooms in the house important to the story?

3. **(a) Recall:** What do Briggs, Aunt Sarah Shoaf, and Aunt Gracie Shoaf do before going to bed? **(b) Infer:** What do you suppose the author, looking back, thinks of this behavior? **(c) Make a Judgment:** Do you think the author treats his relatives fairly in the essay? Why or why not?

4. **Evaluate:** Do you think Thurber's essay is funny? Why or why not?

Apply the Skills

Alligator • The Night the Bed Fell

Comparing Humorous Essays

1. Complete a chart like the one shown to analyze the techniques each author uses to create humor.

	Humorous Scene	Details	Humorous Techniques
"Alligator"			
"The Night the Bed Fell"			

Writing to Compare Literary Works

In your opinion, which essay is more humorous—"Alligator" or "The Night the Bed Fell"? In an essay, provide details to support your answer. Use these questions to start thinking about both works:

- What events and characters from the essays made you laugh?
- Whom did you find funnier: Aunt Belle in "Alligator" or a character in "The Night the Bed Fell"? Who was more touching? Why?
- What purpose might the authors have had beyond amusing you?
- Which author would you choose to read again? Why?

Vocabulary Builder

Review the words on the vocabulary lists on page 472. Then, identify the word in each of the following groups that does not belong. Explain your answers.

1. perilous, protected, dangerous
2. offender, culprit, hero
3. drizzle, deluge, hurricane
4. pungent, sharp, bland
5. exultant, angry, animated
6. sinister, soothing, ominous
7. cattails, palms, platters
8. whisper, murmur, bellow

QuickReview

Humorous essays: works of nonfiction meant to amuse readers

Go Online
Assessment

For: Self-test
Visit: www.PHSchool.com
Web Code: ema-6311

Reading

Directions: *Questions 1–4 are based on the following selection.*

Georgia O'Keeffe is the greatest American artist. She was born in Sun Prairie, Wisconsin, in 1887. O'Keeffe loved experimenting with art as a child. Later, she studied art in college. For a while, she supported herself as a commercial artist. I don't believe this work suited her, though. After a while, she turned her attention to art education. She taught in schools around the country, winding up in the high plains of Texas.

O'Keeffe's move to the Southwest was wonderful for her. Many think it marked a turning point in her life as an artist. She said that the stark beauty of the land appealed to her. She began painting actively to capture her surroundings on canvas. She painted pictures of flowers, bleached animal bones, rolling hills, and clouds. I believe she did her best work during this period. Many of these paintings are included in museum collections around the world.

1. **Which statement can be proved?**
   A Georgia O'Keeffe is the greatest American artist.
   B O'Keeffe loved experimenting with art as a child.
   C For a while, she supported herself as a commercial artist.
   D I don't believe this work suited her.

2. **Which statement is an opinion?**
   A She was born in Sun Prairie, Wisconsin, in 1887.
   B Later, she studied art in college.
   C For a while, she supported herself as a commercial artist.
   D I don't believe this work suited her, though.

3. **Which detail can be supported but not proved?**
   A Georgia O'Keeffe is the greatest American artist.
   B She was born in Sun Prairie, Wisconsin, in 1887.
   C She studied art in college.
   D She supported herself as a commercial artist.

4. **Which statement is an opinion?**
   A She said that the stark beauty of the land appealed to her.
   B She began painting actively to capture her surroundings on canvas.
   C She painted pictures of flowers, bleached animal bones, rolling hills, and clouds.
   D I believe she did her best work during this period.

Vocabulary

Directions *Write the letter of the word which does NOT fit into the sentence.*

5. Would you _____ the claims of that advertisement?

   A check   C investigate
   B evaluate   D valid

6. The detectives _____ the evidence carefully.

   A repudiated   C investigated
   B evaluated   D checked

7. An _____ is a good reference tool for general statistics.

   A encyclopedia   C novel
   B almanac   D database

8. The students will _____ the use of technology in their school.

   A sketch   C evaluate
   B investigate   D check

Directions *Choose the borrowed word that best answers the following questions.*

9. What might you order to eat in a traditional Mexican restaurant?

   A noodles
   B tacos
   C cookies
   D spaghetti

10. Which word borrowed from Dutch means "to draw quickly"?

    A ski
    B chess
    C dunk
    D sketch

11. Which word borrowed from Sanskrit is used to describe a type of exercise?

    A yoga
    B banjo
    C soy
    D moccasin

12. What word borrowed from French describes the fabric used to make jeans?

    A pajamas
    B denim
    C moccasin
    D ski

13. Which word comes from the Arabic language?

    A horse
    B giraffe
    C dog
    D whale

Tools for Checking Spelling

It can be hard to figure out whether you have spelled certain words correctly. Fortunately, there are reference tools that can help you.

Computer Spell-Checkers Most word-processing programs contain a spell-checking feature. After you type a word incorrectly, the program will mark it. Here are a few things you should remember about spell-checking programs, though:

- They cannot tell you if you used the wrong homophone.
- They cannot tell you if you typed the wrong word by mistake—for example, *is* instead of *in*.

I told you spell check can't tell the difference between hat and bat

Dictionaries Use a dictionary for spelling by following these steps:

- **Check the first letter of a word.** If you wrote *rench* and it looks wrong, think of other spellings of that "r" sound.
- **Check the other letters.** Once you spell the first sound right, sound out the rest of the word.

Sound	Some Ways to Spell It	Sound	Some Ways to Spell It
"k"	**k**ennel, **c**arrot, **ch**aracter	"s"	**s**even, **c**enter, **sc**ene
"j"	**j**ump, **g**emstone, le**dge**	"f"	**f**orget, **ph**rase, tou**gh**
"g"	**g**o, **g**uest, **gh**ost	"n"	**n**ever, **kn**ife, **gn**aw

Practice Match the phonetic spelling with the word list.

1. rīt   **2.** nōō   **3.** nät   **4.** rēth   **5.** nōt   **6.** rông

Word List

knew

new

note

knot

not

write

right

wrong

wreath

real

Directions: *There are ten errors in the following paragraph. Some are misspellings. Others are problems with homophones or other incorrect words used by mistake. On a separate piece of paper, write the number of each sentence. Then, write the spelling corrections it needs. If a sentence has no errors, write "none." Use the chart if you need help.*

(1) Every year I dread the first day of school because of one class. (2) That class is sience. (3) I know I will have too do experiments, and I know I will do something wrong. (4) Last year I made a gastly error with my very first experiment. (5) I had to mix two liquids is a container. (6) As usual, I was in too much of a hurry. (7) I did not take enouf time to get the materials ready. (8) Instead of lining up the pear of liquids in the center of my work table, I left them on the ege. (9) Then I heard a loud noise and turned around suddenly, banging into the table. (10) You can ghess what happened: liquid and broken glass went flying everywear. (11) It's quite clear to me that I should never plan to be a kemist.

There are five errors in the following paragraph. Identify the errors and explain why they are errors. Then correct the sentences.

(1) This particuler work is not Thomas' best. (2) One finds that you are constantly attempting to understand another symbol, another image, another simily. (3) It is wearisome work. (4) Thomas' first poetic efforts effected the reading public because of its simplicity. (5) Its a shame that the latter work is so difficult.

Exposition: Comparison-and-Contrast Essay

A **comparison-and-contrast essay** analyzes the similarities and differences between two or more related subjects. It can help you to decide which shoes to wear or which bicycle to buy. A good comparison-and-contrast essay can even change your perspective— as when a reviewer compares the latest hit song with an old album, letting you hear the startling similarities. Follow the steps outlined in this workshop to write your own comparison-and-contrast essay.

Assignment Write a comparison-and-contrast essay that helps readers make a decision or see old things in a fresh way.

What to Include Your essay should feature these elements:
- a topic involving two or more things that are neither nearly identical nor extremely different
- details illustrating both similarities and differences
- clear organization that highlights the points of comparison
- an introduction that grabs a reader's interest, and a strong, memorable conclusion
- error-free writing, including correct use of adjectives and adverbs

To preview the criteria on which your comparison-and-contrast essay may be judged, see the rubric on page 495.

Writing Workshop: *Work in Progress*

If you have completed the Work-in-Progress assignments, you already have a wealth of ideas to use in your comparison-and-contrast essay. Develop these ideas, or explore a new idea to complete the Writing Workshop.

Using the Form

You may use elements of this form in these types of writing:
- persuasive essays
- advertisements
- reviews
- journals

Reading Writing Connection

To get the feel for comparison-and-contrast writing, read "Conversational Ballgames" by Nancy Masterson Sakamoto on page 379.

Prewriting

Choosing Your Topic

To choose topics for your essay, use one of these strategies:

- **Quicklist** Fold a piece of paper in thirds lengthwise. In the first column, list recent choices you have made—for instance, products you have bought or activities you have completed. In the second column, next to each choice, write a descriptive phrase. In the third column, give an alternative to your choice.

▶ **Example:** polka dot sweatshirt / playful, silly / team jacket

Review your list, and choose the most interesting pairing to compare and contrast:

- **BUT Chart** Write the word BUT down the center of a piece of paper. On the left, list items with something in common. List differences among them on the right. Choose your topic from this list.

Things That Are Similar	B U T	Differences Between Them
My bike and Kara's bike: blue frame and two wheels		Kara's has thick, heavy tread tires. My bike has thin, smooth tires. My bike has curved handlebars. Kara's bike has upright handlebars.

Work in Progress
Review the work you did on pages 449 and 467.

Narrowing Your Topic

You may find that your topic is too broad to cover in a brief essay. Use these strategies to jot notes that can help narrow your topic.
- **Describe it** to someone who is not familiar with it.
- **Apply it,** explaining what you can do with it, on it, or to it.
- **Analyze it** by breaking it into parts.
- **Argue for or against it,** explaining good and bad points.

Circle details from your notes to create a focused topic.

Gathering Details

Focus on gathering details that show similarities and differences between your subjects. Use a Venn diagram to organize your details. Draw two large circles that overlap in the middle. Fill in details about one subject on the left side of the diagram and details about the other on the right side. Use the middle for common features.

Drafting

Shaping Your Writing

Organize the body of your draft. Your essay should be easy for readers to follow and understand. There are two main ways to organize a comparison-and-contrast essay. Choose the one that is most appropriate to your topic and purpose.

- **Block Method** Present all the details about one of your subjects, then all the details about your next subject. This method works well if you are writing about more than two subjects or if your topic is complex.

- **Point-by-Point Method** Discuss one aspect of both subjects, then another aspect of both subjects, and so on.

Providing Elaboration

Layer ideas using SEE. Often, the most interesting parts of an essay are the details you offer to support your main ideas. Use the SEE method to develop strong elaboration.

- *State* your main idea in every paragraph to help you stay on topic.
- *Extend* the idea with an example that proves the main idea.
- *Elaborate* by offering further details to describe your example.

Methods of Organization

Block Method

A. Theater
    1. amount of variety
    2. intensity
    3. realism
B. Television
    1. amount of variety
    2. intensity
    3. realism

Point-by-Point Comparison

A. Amount of Variety
    1. Theater
    2. Television
B. Intensity
    1. Theater
    2. Television
C. Realism
    1. Theater
    2. Television

Student Model: Using the SEE Method

Statement: In live theater, every show is different.

Extension: When you watch a rerun on television, it's the exact same thing every time. With theater, you get a different experience every night.

Elaboration: You can go see the same show with a different cast or director, and the performance will be totally different. . . .

> The SEE method creates a strong paragraph in which each sentence connects with the others.

Clarify relationships. Use words and phrases that clearly state the relationship between features. Transitions that show comparisons include *also, just as, like,* and *similarly.* Transitions that show contrasts include *although, but, however, on the other hand, whereas,* and *while.*

Reading Writing Connection

To read the complete student model, see page 494.

From the Author's Desk

Richard Mühlberger

On Getting Readers Involved

Richard Mühlberger

Whether you are writing compare-and-contrast or another form of exposition, you need to keep the reader's interest and attention. Everyone involved in producing my book about Monet, the French Impressionist painter, knew before it was printed that it would be a success. Monet was the number one artist in popularity among adults. But the book was for middle-school students. My job was to get them involved in exploring Monet's art.

"I write with my audience in mind."

— Richard Mühlberger

Professional Model:

from *What Makes a Monet a Monet?*

Oscar-Claude Monet was born in Paris, France, on November 14, 1840. When he was five years old, his family moved to the seaside city of Le Havre. He went to school there, but he was not much of a student. He liked to draw irreverent caricatures of his teachers, who tried in vain to get him to concentrate on other subjects. Monet later confessed that he did not learn much in school except some spelling. "It seemed like a prison, and I could never bear to stay there, even for four hours a day, especially when the sunshine beckoned and the sea was smooth," he said.

Monet's favorite activity was wandering along the beaches, making caricatures of tourists. He usually pictured a person with a very small body and a very large head, exaggerating the nose or some other part of the face. He sold his caricatures for ten to twenty francs, more than what his teachers earned in a day!

I wanted to establish right away that Monet had only one interest in life—making art.

The word *sunshine* summarizes the essence of many of his paintings. Alone, that word may not compel a young person to read on. So I placed it in a context that makes the young artist sound like a maverick who might interest young readers.

My book does not contain a caricature by Monet so I had to come up with a description that would draw a picture in the reader's mind.

Revising

Revising Your Overall Structure

Heighten interest. Check your essay to make sure it grabs and holds your reader's attention. Use one or more of the following strategies.

- Sharpen your introduction to intrigue readers, encouraging them to read further and find out more. Consider including a strong image, a surprising comparison, or a thought provoking question.
- Add details that are surprising, colorful, and important.
- Add language to emphasize similarities or differences.
- Rework your conclusion to add impact or leave readers with a lingering question. Be sure your conclusion makes the value of the comparison and contrast clear.

To read the complete student model, see page 494.

Student Model: Revising to Heighten Interest

On television, everything has to be perfect or they do a
~~You never see television actors miss a line or trip over their feet.~~
retake. Since there is no second chance in theater, everything
is more spontaneous.

> Strong language and interesting details point out a key difference.

Revising Your Sentences

Avoid repetition. Check your writing for unnecessary repetition. Sometimes writers will repeat a point but add something slightly different the second time. If this is the case, consider combining the two sentences to preserve your additional material while avoiding repetition.

Repetitive: Lastly, the best thing about theater is it's real. What I mean is you see when people make mistakes. You see people being human by making mistakes every so often.

Combined: Lastly, the best thing about theater is it's human and real. What I mean is you see when people make mistakes.

Peer Review: Read your revised draft to a classmate. Ask your partner whether you repeated information. Together, look for ways to make the writing clearer and less repetitive.

Integrating Grammar Skills

Revising Errors in Adjective and Adverb Usage

The common modifiers *just* and *only* often cause problems in both speaking and writing.

Identifying Errors in Adjective and Adverb Usage Usage problems with adjectives and adverbs typically occur when these words are placed incorrectly in a sentence or are confused because of similar meanings. When used as an adverb, **just** often means "no more than." When *just* has this meaning, place it right before the word it logically modifies.

Prentice Hall Writing and Grammar Connection: Chapter 25, Section 2

Incorrect: Do you *just* want one brownie for dessert?
Correct: Do you want *just* one brownie for dessert?

The position of **only** can affect the entire meaning of a sentence.

Only he ate the cake. (Nobody else ate it.)
He *only* ate the cake. (He did nothing else with the cake.)
He ate *only* the cake. (He ate nothing else.)

Fixing Errors in Adjective and Adverb Usage To fix a usage problem with adjectives and adverbs, use one of the following methods.

1. **For *only*:** If the word is intended as an adverb meaning "no more than," place it right before the word it logically modifies.

2. **For *just*:** First, identify the intended meaning of the sentence. Then, position *just* in the sentence so that the meaning is clear.

3. **For other common problems:** See the chart or use a dictionary.

Commonly Confused Modifiers	
bad: (adjective) He was a *bad* skater.	**badly:** (adverb) I played *badly* at the recital.
fewer: answers "How many?" He had *fewer* questions.	**less:** answers "How much?" He drank *less* water today.

Apply It to Your Editing

Choose two paragraphs in your draft. Underline every sentence that contains one of the modifiers discussed, or another modifier you think you may have used incorrectly. Fix any usage problems.

Student Model: Mackenzie Ames
Daytona Beach, FL

Stage vs. Set

Theater or television? If you are under eighteen, you more than likely said "television." Have you ever stopped to consider what the magical world of theater has to offer?

Anyone who has been to the theater can tell you that there is nothing like the feeling of sitting and watching people perform. Actors get something special out of theater, too. Knowing that hundreds of people are watching your every move creates a special kind of excitement.

There's also variety. In live theater, every show is different. When you watch a rerun on television, it's the exact same thing every time. With theater, you get a different experience every night. You can go to see the same show with a different cast or director and the performance will be totally different. Even if you go to a show with the same cast and director, it will be different. An actor might forget a line and improvise or suddenly decide to change the way he or she is playing a character in a scene. The audience never knows exactly what will happen.

Theater is also larger than the drama you see on television. I don't care how big a screen your television has, theater will always be BIGGER—the emotion more passionate, the voices louder, and the effect more profound. In theater, you have to project your voice and movements so that they carry to the back rows of the audience. In television, actors just need to be seen and heard by the cameras and microphones.

Lastly, the best thing about theater is it's human and real. You see when people make mistakes. On television, everything has to be perfect or they do a retake. You never see television actors miss a line or trip over their feet. Since there is no second chance in theater, everything is more spontaneous. When a performance takes an unexpected turn, the audience gets to see the professionalism of the actors as they respond to something new.

Next time you're channel surfing and there's nothing good on, why not take some time to check out what's playing in your community playhouse? Who knows? Maybe you'll discover a rising talent. Even better, maybe you'll decide you want to become an actor or actress after you see how thrilling a live production really is.

In the first paragraph, Mackenzie introduces the comparison in a way that grabs the reader's attention. She compares things that are alike, yet different.

The author develops her argument by including examples and explanations, using the point-by-point method of organization.

In the final paragraph, Mackenzie offers a strong conclusion that challenges the reader to accept her point of view.

Editing and Proofreading

Review your draft to eliminate errors.

Focus on Empty Language: Review your work to delete words that do not add value or meaning. Consider cutting words such as *very* and *really* and clauses such as *I think, as I said,* and *you know.*

Publishing and Presenting

Consider one of the following ways to share your writing:
Be a consumer watchdog. If your essay contains information useful to consumers, form a Consumer Information Panel with classmates. Read your essays to the class, using visual aids to enhance your presentation.
Submit it to a magazine. Submit your essay to a magazine that specializes in the subject you have chosen. You can find publishing information and an address in a recent edition of the magazine.

Reflecting on Your Writing

Writer's Journal Jot down your thoughts about writing a comparison-and-contrast essay. Begin by answering these questions:
- What was the most important improvement you made when revising?
- Did the writing process lead you to new ideas about your topic? Explain.

> *Prentice Hall Writing and Grammar Connection: Chapter 8*

Rubric for Self-Assessment

To assess your comparison-and-contrast essay, use this rubric:

Criteria	Rating Scale				
	not very				*very*
Focus: How clearly does the essay address two or more related subjects?	1	2	3	4	5
Organization: How effectively are points of comparison organized?	1	2	3	4	5
Support/Elaboration: How well do you use details to describe similarities and differences?	1	2	3	4	5
Style: How well have you used language that grabs the reader's interest?	1	2	3	4	5
Conventions: How correct is your grammar, especially your use of adjectives and adverbs?	1	2	3	4	5

Communications Workshop

Evaluating a Persuasive Presentation

A **persuasive presentation** is similar to a persuasive composition. Its purpose is to persuade the listener to do, or buy, or believe something. The following strategies will help you assess the strengths and weaknesses of the presenter's statements.

Evaluating Content

Like its written counterpart, effective persuasive presentations include clear statements of position and relevant supporting evidence. Listen to every word and be thinking about these ways to evaluate:

Determine the speaker's attitude. Determine how the speaker feels about his or her subject. Look for appeals to emotion or to reason. Watch the speaker's body language.

Listen for a logical organization. Follow the argument from point to point. Listen for the connections between ideas. Listen for a convincing introduction and conclusion.

Listen for strong evidence. Be aware of the anecdotes, descriptions, facts and statistics, and specific examples that support the speaker's position. Is the support convincing? Why or why not?

Responding Constructively

As a listener, it is your job to respond politely and constructively to a persuasive presentation.

Ask questions. Never be afraid to ask questions. You will find out how thoroughly the speaker has researched the topic by probing deeply.

Challenge. If you disagree with something the presenter has said, do not hesitate to express your opinion. If you suspect a piece of evidence is wrong, challenge it by asking for its source.

Offer Affirmations. If you agree with something the presenter has said, it is appropriate to let him or her know. You might share a personal anecdote or observation that affirms the speaker's position and can support future presentations.

Activity ⟩ *Evaluate a Persuasive Message* ⟩ With a partner, observe and listen to a persuasive sales pitch, either live or on videotape or television. Use the feedback form shown to evaluate what you see. Compare and discuss your evaluations.

> **Feedback Form Persuasive**
>
> **Content** Rate 1 – 5
>
> 1. Clear position
> 2. Clear attitude
> 3. Logical organization
> 4. Strong evidence
>
> **Impression**
>
> 1. What impact did the presentation have on you?
> 2. What questions does the presentation raise for you?
> 3. On what point would you challenge the speaker?
> 4. How can you confirm the speaker's points?

The Red Pony

John Steinbeck

Penguin Books, 1965

Novel *The Red Pony* is made up of four interrelated stories about the coming-of-age of a boy named Jody. Raised on a ranch in northern California, Jody is used to hard work. He is used to the way of horses, too. His father gives him a pony called Gabilan. Under ranch hand Billy Buck's guidance, Jody learns to care for and train his pony. Along the way, Jody also learns about the ways of nature and the ways of people.

Black Beauty

Anna Sewell

Signet Classic, 1986

Novel *Black Beauty* is a handsome, well-bred colt with a strong spirit. However, when his owners are forced to sell him, his fortunes change from a life of comfort and kindness to one of hard labor and cruelty. Black Beauty soon learns how unpredictable life can be. Told in the first person from the horse's point of view, the novel is the story of Black Beauty's long and varied life, from a carefree colt in a pleasant meadow to an elegant carriage horse for a gentleman to a painfully overworked cab horse.

Nonfiction Readings Across the Curriculum

Pearson Prentice Hall, 2000

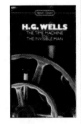

Anthology These selections on a variety of subjects—literature, science, social studies, math, sports, and the arts—will help the reader to gain a better understanding of the world. Many different types of nonfiction are included in the anthology: biographies, autobiographies, descriptive essays, how-to essays, informational essays, magazine articles, and diary entries.

The Time Machine: A Pacemaker Classic

H. G. Wells

Prentice Hall, 1985

Novel In 1895, an inventor builds a time machine in which he travels into the far distant future. It is a frightening world in which the Eloi and the Morlocks live and dispute. As the story goes on, the time traveler tries to convince his co-workers that he has just returned from exploring London in the year 802,701. *The Time Machine* transports the time traveler's readers into the far distant future and an extraordinary world.

These titles are available in the Penguin/Prentice Hall Literature Library.
Consult your teacher before choosing one.

Think About It Yao Ming is a basketball player from China who was launched into the American spotlight after being the number one draft pick for the NBA in 2002. His fame has spanned the globe and he has become a hero in both China and the United States. Read more about the start of Ming's amazing career and what effects it has had and will have on the economy of his native country.

Yao Ming:
NBA Giant Is Big in U.S., Bigger in China
Brian Handwerk

On the court and off, Houston Rockets basketball star Yao Ming is a true giant. During his rookie year, the Chinese sensation created a stir in the NBA and across the globe. Battling both Shaq and the skeptics, the seven-foot-five-inch (226-centimeter) center displayed skills that silenced the critics and earned him a trip to the All-Star game.

While Yao could quickly become one of the league's dominant players, his off-court impact is already colossal. At 22, he is a marketing megastar. Like Madonna or Elvis, Yao needs a first name-only reference—as sure a sign of superstardom as any. He's come to symbolize the aspirations of a rapidly changing China—while undergoing some serious life changes of his own.

The business that is the NBA is global, both on and off the court. This spring NBA teams included 65 international players from 34 countries and territories. The diverse product on the court helps attract new audiences around the world.

And perhaps the most important foreign player to suit up is the Rockets' Yao. To understand why, one only need look to China's 1.3 billion residents—and potential basketball fans.

Two other members of the Chinese National Team play in the NBA. Wang Zhizhi plays for the Los Angeles Clippers, while Mengke Bateers suits up for the San Antonio Spurs. But Yao is in a class all his own. The National Team star is a towering hero in China and elsewhere in Asia.

Yao has made the NBA a hot proposition in the emerging markets of the Far East. That means major league business opportunities. And Yao may be the ultimate marketing tool for the rapidly growing Chinese market. As China's economy continues to grow larger and more global, multinational companies continue to compete for pieces of the country's enormous consumer market.

Within China, Yao appears ever present, a marketing icon ready to connect China with global markets.

"The Little Giant"

Yao was the first number one NBA draft pick to come from an international basketball league. In the 2002–2003 season, "the Little Giant" proved he was up to the competition, ranking among the league's top 20 players for rebounds and blocked shots.

While those are very solid numbers for a rookie, Yao posts even more impressive stats. "When Yao plays basketball, 300 million people watch him," said Lisa Ling, the *Ultimate Explorer* television host who recently profiled Yao. "That's more than the population of the United States and only a fraction of the population of China. You can imagine what that means in terms of marketing dollars."

It also means a tremendous amount of pressure on the basketball star. But with the weight of a nation on his shoulders, not to mention that of his team and the NBA, Yao handles the pressure and responsibility with aplomb.

"All of the Chinese people, the Asian people say, 'Oh Yao Ming, you are all the Chinese, all of Asia's hopes,'" Yao told *Ultimate Explorer*. "That's a lot of pressure," he said. "I'm just a basketball player."

But to many, Yao is more than that. He's a symbol of China's emergence on the international stage, a commercial powerhouse with the second largest economy in the world.

Same Planet, Different Worlds

Yao is also a source of unabashed pride. "For China, he encompasses everything that [people] want to be," Ling said. "He's larger than life, strong, intelligent, an international star, a family man, and a team player. He embodies much of what China is becoming," she said.

Lost in the hype is the fact that Yao is a 22-year-old experiencing a dramatic lifestyle change. Both of Yao's parents played for China's national teams. From a young age, he lived and played basketball at state-run facilities for elite athletes.

That prestigious but insular world could not have prepared him

National Geographic Explorer host Lisa Ling with Houston Rocket Yao Ming in Texas

for the culture shock of superstardom that followed the Chinese government's decision to allow him to jump to the NBA. (The Chinese government collects half of his U.S. $18 million dollar annual salary, and Yao remains obligated to play on China's national team.)

Now in the U.S., Yao lives inside a media crucible few others experience. "He's probably one of the most swamped people in the world," said Ling. "The press follows him everywhere. I've been out with Brittany Spears and other huge celebrities, but no one has gotten the kind of attention that Yao has. It's incredible. He can't exactly put on a hat and glasses and sort of blend into the crowd."

While Yao's career in the NBA is just beginning, his stardom is already realized on two continents. It's a lot to ask, but this 22-year-old basketball player might just become a symbol of how the two worlds can grow together.

More to Explore

This article appeared in the **National Geographic Society** Web site. The National Geographic Society was founded in 1888 with the goal of increasing geographic knowledge. It is a good resource for students of all ages.

Readings in Sports
Talk About It

Use these questions to guide a discussion.

1. **(a)** How does the author compare Yao Ming to Madonna and Elvis? **(b)** What does this comparison say about Yao's celebrity?

2. **(a)** Why is Yao's career exciting for the NBA and its fans? **(b)** Why is his career important to the Chinese and U.S. economies?

3. Like Yao Ming, many athletes who compete in sports throughout the world have high expectations placed on them. In a small group, consider these questions:
   - Why are competitive sports popular throughout the world?
   - What kind of prestige does a country receive when one of its athletes wins an international competition?
   - Why are sports profitable for countries around the world?
   Choose a point-person to share your group's ideas with the class.

Poetry

Unit 4 Overview

Introduction
Exploring Poetry

Part 1: Drawing Conclusions

Part 2: Paraphrasing

Introduction:
Poetry

Pat
Mora

Pat Mora
Talks About the Form

▲ **Pat Mora** stresses the importance of family and cultural heritage in her work.

"How do you make a poem?" asked a brown-eyed, curious student. *Make* is a good, concrete verb, isn't it? We *make* cookies, paper airplanes, music. In part, I'm a writer because I love words, their sounds, meanings, histories. The etymology or origin of the word *poet* actually means *maker*. I like that little detail. So what do poets make or compose?

Poetry: Stories and Words

All of us experience strong feelings. A friend gossips about us, and we feel really angry. An aunt has a stroke, and we feel sad. Someone screams in a movie, and we feel scared. Some people dance those feelings, some paint those feelings, and some sing those feelings that rise up inside us almost like a wave in the ocean.

Orally and on the page, poets create **poetry** to explore their feelings and the stories they want to share. Poets listen to words and play with them the way a musician listens to notes and melodies, re-writing, improving the sound and impact. Poetry's "tools" include forms or patterns, **rhythm, rhyme, repetition.** Poetry sings.

▶ Critical Viewing In what ways does this image suggest what poets do when they compose a poem? **[Interpret]**

How Poetry Began

Long before poetry was a written form, it was recited and sung from memory. All over the world in thousands of languages, humans created poems that were hero stories or praise songs or verses of sorrow. The creator of the piece repeated and improved what he or she enjoyed saying and hearing, and sometimes others added new parts or memorized what the first person had created or made.

Today we can still write group poems or collaborative pieces. Most often, though, the writer sits with a blank page and begins to listen to the inside voice and play. But as a great Chilean poet says in the quotation shown here, the poet's solitary effort can benefit everyone.

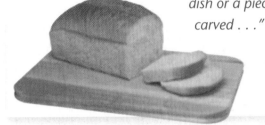

"I have always maintained that the writer's task has nothing to do with mystery or magic, and that the poet's . . . must be a personal effort for the benefit of all. The closest thing to poetry is a loaf of bread or a ceramic dish or a piece of wood lovingly carved . . ."

from *Memoirs*
—*Pablo Neruda*

When I graduated from eighth grade, my parents gave me a gray typewriter. Alone, I put my fingers on the keys and wrote poems. I enjoy writing nonfiction and prose stories too, but there's something special about poetry for me. Maybe the challenge and tension of using fewer words and having less room to communicate gives me energy. I need to weigh each word and sound. What a zing when a poem works!

More About the Author

Pat **Mora** (b. 1942)

When she was in grade school, Pat Mora read comics, mysteries, magazines, and library books. "I was soaking up language," she says. The setting of her works is chiefly the American Southwest, where she was born. Mora often deals with the theme of identity in her writing. Discovering her Mexican heritage as a subject, she realized that she had "a vein of gold."

Fast Facts

▶ Mora has worked to have April 30th named as a national day to celebrate children, books, and culture.
▶ She reads her poems out loud when she revises them.

Learning About Poetry

Characteristics of Poetry

Poems are usually divided into lines and then grouped into **stanzas,** or verses.

Figurative Language is writing or speech not meant to be taken literally. Poets use figures of speech to state ideas in new ways.

- **Metaphors** describe one thing as if it were something else. *The house was a zoo this morning!*

- **Personification** gives human qualities to something that is not human. *The cars growled in the traffic.*

- **Similes** use *like* or *as* to compare two apparently unlike things. *He stormed into the meeting like a tornado.*

- A **symbol** is anything that represents something else. For example, a dove is a common symbol for peace.

CALVIN AND HOBBES © 1992 Watterson. Reprinted with permission of UNIVERSAL PRESS SYNDICATE. All rights reserved.

Sound Devices enhance a poem's mood and meaning.

- **Alliteration** is the repetition of consonant sounds in the beginning of words, as in *slippery slope.*

- **Repetition** is the use of any element of language—a sound, word, phrase, clause, or sentence—more than once.

- **Assonance** is the repetition of vowel sounds followed by different consonants in stressed syllables, as in *blade* and *maze.*

- **Consonance** is the repetition of similar consonant sounds at the ends of accented syllables, as in *wind* and *sand.*

- **Onomatopoeia** is the use of words that imitate sounds. *Crash, bang,* and *hiss* are all examples of onomatopoeia.

- **Rhyme** is the repetition of sounds at the ends of words, as in *speech* and *teach.*

- **Meter** is the rhythmical pattern in a poem.

Forms of Poetry

Narrative poetry tells a story in verse. Narrative poems often have elements similar to those in short stories, such as plot and characters.

Haiku is a three-line Japanese verse form. The first and third lines each have five syllables and the second line has seven.

Free Verse poetry is defined by its lack of strict structure. It has no regular meter, rhyme, fixed line length, or specific stanza pattern.

Lyric poetry expresses the thoughts and feelings of a single speaker, often in highly musical verse.

Ballads are songlike poems that tell a story, often dealing with adventure and romance.

Concrete poems are shaped to look like their subjects. The poet arranges the lines to create a picture on the page.

Limericks are humorous, rhyming, five-line poems with a specific rhythm pattern and rhyme scheme.

Rhyming couplets are pairs of rhyming lines, usually of the same meter and length.

Check Your Understanding

For each item below, identify the correct literary term for the underlined portion.

1. <u>Fire flamed ferociously</u> throughout the <u>farmer's field.</u>
2. The plane <u>whizzed</u> by on its way to the airport.
3. <u>Spring arrived</u> in the garden and <u>awoke all of the sleeping flowers.</u>

From the Author's Desk
Pat Mora Introduces Her Poetry

Everyone is full of stories—growing-up stories, family stories. I like to listen to people's stories for writing ideas. One day when I was a university administrator in my native border city of El Paso, Texas, I chatted with a professor in the music department whose name was Abraham Chávez. He was also the conductor of the local symphony orchestra.

The Inspiration for "Maestro"

"How did you become interested in music?" I asked. He smiled and told me about when he was a little boy in the neighboring city of Juárez (hwä´ res´), Mexico, across the Rio Grande. I decided to write "Maestro" to try to create what he described, but also to show how the little boy was still inside the professor who now directed the orchestra.

"The Desert Is My Mother": Bilingual Poetry

Because I have the good fortune to be bilingual, I write poetry in both English and Spanish. I can choose *master musician* or *maestro*. Sometimes, my poems not only include words in Spanish but are published in both languages, such as the **lyric poem** "The Desert Is My Mother/El desierto es mi madre."

El Paso is a city in the Chihuahua (chi wä´ wä) desert. I love deserts and have written poems and stories and children's books about the desert's plants, animals, and sounds. In this poem, the desert is protective, like a mother who takes care of my needs. People who don't know the desert may find it bare and frightening. I wanted to show how the desert comforts me.

"Bailando": Sensory Language Helps You See

My aunt in "Bailando" comforted me too. I used **sensory language** to describe her when she was young, giving you a picture of her "long, black hair free in the wind." I also enjoyed sharing her humor with you, like her remark that her tottering walk as an elder is also a dance!

Maestro
Pat Mora

He hears her
when he bows.
Rows of hands clap
again and again he bows
5   to stage lights and upturned faces
but he hears only his mother's voice

years ago in their small home
singing Mexican songs
one phrase at a time
10 while his father strummed the guitar
or picked the melody with quick fingertips.
Both cast their music in the air
for him to snare with his strings,
songs of lunas[1] and amor[2]
15 learned bit by bit.
She'd nod, smile, as his bow slid
note to note, then the trio
     voz,[3] guitarra,[4] violín[5]
would blend again and again
20 to the last pure note
sweet on the tongue.

---

1. **lunas** (lōō´näs) *n.* Spanish for "moons."
2. **amor** (ä´ môr´) *n.* Spanish for "love."
3. **voz** (vōs) *n.* Spanish for "voice."
4. **guitarra** (gē tär´rä) *n.* Spanish for "guitar."
5. **violín** (vē ō lēn´) *n.* Spanish for "violin."

▲ **Critical Viewing**
How does this violinist compare with the one described in the poem? **[Connect]**

Pat Mora
Author's Insight
Notice the first line of the poem. I want you to be curious: Who is "he" and whom does he hear?

Vocabulary Builder
maestro (mīs´ trō) *n.*
great musician

The Desert Is My Mother

Pat Mora

"I say feed me.
She serves red prickly pear[1] on a spiked cactus.

I say tease me.
She sprinkles raindrops in my face on a sunny day.

5   I say frighten me.
She shouts thunder, flashes lightning.

I say hold me. She whispers, "Lie in my arms."

I say heal me.
She gives me chamomile, oregano, peppermint.

10   I say caress me.
She strokes my skin with her warm breath.

I say make me beautiful.
She offers turquoise for my fingers,
a pink blossom for my hair.

15   I say sing to me.
She chants her windy songs.

I say teach me.
She blooms in the sun's glare,
the snow's silence,
20   the driest sand.

The desert is my mother.
El desierto es mi madre.
The desert is my strong mother.

Pat Mora
Author's Insight
Substitute "fruit" for "prickly pear" and read the line out loud. Do you hear the difference when I'm more specific?

Poetry
Personification Here, the desert speaks with a woman's voice.

---

1. **prickly pear** *n.* a species of cactus with sharp spines and an edible fruit.

El desierto es mi madre
Pat Mora

Le digo, dame de comer.
Me sirve rojas tunas en nopal espinoso.

Le digo, juguetea conmigo.
Me salpica la cara con gotitas de lluvia en día asoleado.

5   Le digo, asústame.
Me grita con truenos y me tira relámpagos.

Le digo, abrázame.
Me susurra, "Acuéstate aquí."

Le digo, cúrame.
10 Me da manzanilla, orégano, yerbabuena.

Le digo, acaríciame.
Me roza la cara con su cálido aliento.

Le digo, hazme bella.
Me ofrece turquesa para mis dedos,
15 una flor rosada para mi cabello.

Le digo, cántame.
Me arrulla con sus canciones de viento.

Le digo, enséñame.
Y florece en el brillo del sol,
20 en el silencio de la nieve,
en las arenas más secas.

El desierto es mi madre.
El desierto es mi madre poderosa.

Poetry
Repetition The repetition of "I say" in the English and "Le digo" in the Spanish adds rhythm to the poems.

Bailando[1]

PAT MORA

I will remember you dancing,
spinning round and round
a young girl in Mexico,
your long, black hair free in the wind,
5 spinning round and round
a young woman at village dances
your long, blue dress swaying
to the beat of La Varsoviana,[2]
smiling into the eyes of your partners,
10 years later smiling into my eyes
when I'd reach up to dance with you,
my dear aunt. who years later
danced with my children,
you, white-haired but still young
15 waltzing on your ninetieth birthday,
more beautiful than the orchid
pinned on your shoulder,
tottering now when you walk
but saying to me, "Estoy[3] bailando,"
20 and laughing.

Pat Mora
Author's Insight
When I repeat these "spinning" lines (lines 2 and 5), I want you to feel the movement my aunt felt and to feel the poem's movement.

Poetry
Sound Devices The word "smiling" in lines 9 and 10 adds musical quality to the poem.

◀ Critical Viewing
What word in the poem best suits this picture? [Connect]

1. **Bailando** (bī län′ dō) v. Spanish for "dancing."
2. **La Varsoviana** (lä bär′ sō byä′ nä) n. a lively folk dance.
3. **Estoy** (es toī′) Spanish for "I am."

Q. Is it different to write poems in Spanish and in English?

A. Although I have always been bilingual, I usually write in English first because I was taught in English at school. I enjoy braiding the two languages I know and choosing when a word in Spanish will add special music to a poem.

Q. Which of these poems did you revise the most?

A. In a way, trying to recall how a poem or book was written is like looking at a photo album and trying to remember the details of a moment or day. I might have revised "Maestro" most since it was about someone else. I needed to use my imagination more to imagine Abraham Chávez as a young boy.

Q. Have your poems ever been set to music and sung?

A. When people ask me this question, I smile. It means they hear the music in the poems. A composer in Australia has set some of my poems for adults to music.

Student Corner

Q. Did you enjoy poetry when you were young?
—Tara Sou, Clackamas, Oregon

A. Definitely! When I was a young reader, I enjoyed reading nursery rhymes and rhyming poems to myself. In elementary school, my teachers asked us to memorize many poems. When I was in eighth grade, my teacher handed out a poem on Monday, and we were expected to recite and write it by Friday. Guess what? After all these years, I still remember some of those poems.

 Writing Workshop: *Work in Progress*

Writing for Assessment

Timed writing requires quick development of the idea you will address in an essay. One method is to use the language of the question in your thesis statement: You can add "I think that . . .," or "I disagree that . . ."; or you can recast the question as a statement. Write a thesis statement to answer this timed-writing question: *Is sound an important element in poetry? Explain.*

Apply the Skills

Poetry

Thinking About the Selections

1. **Respond:** Which poem do you think would sound best when read aloud? Why?

2. **(a) Recall:** What words or lines in "Maestro" show that the musician is a professional? **(b) Infer:** Is the audience or his family a more important influence on him as a musician? Explain. **(c) Interpret:** Why do you think the musician remembers his childhood during his performance?

3. **(a) Recall:** In the poem "Bailando," who remembers the dancing? **(b) Analyze:** Besides dancing, what is the subject of this poem? **(c) Generalize:** What emotion does this poem convey? Support your answer with details from the writing.

Poetry Review

4. Find one example of **repetition** in each poem.

5. **(a)** Find examples of **personification** in "The Desert Is My Mother." In a chart like the one shown compare and contrast the language used to describe the desert. **(b)** Share your answers with a classmate. How has your understanding of the poem grown or changed?

Words that show that the desert is . . .

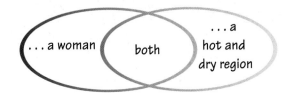

. . . a woman | both | . . . a hot and dry region

Research the Author

Consult library sources for information about Pat Mora. Follow these steps to create an **author booklet** to display in your class-room.

- Open with a brief biography of the author.
- Include a list of awards Mora has won.
- Choose one or two poems to include in your booklet. Add photos and illustrations.

QuickReview

Poems at a Glance

In **"Maestro,"** a musician thinks about his family as he performs. **"Bailando"** describes how a beloved aunt dances. **"The Desert Is My Mother"** compares the desert to a human.

Go **Online**
—Assessment
For: Self-test
Visit: www.PHSchool.com
Web Code: ema-6401

Personification: figurative language that gives human qualities to nonhuman objects or concepts

Repetition: the use of a sound, word, phrase, clause, or sentence more than once in a poem to add a musical quality

Skills You Will Learn

Literature You Will Read

Reading: Draw Conclusions

> A **conclusion** is a logical decision or opinion you reach by pulling together several facts or details.

Skills and Strategies You Will Learn in Part 1

In Part 1, you will learn

- to **ask questions** to identify important details that build to **conclusions**. (p. 518)
- to **connect details** to **form conclusions**. (p. 534)
- to **recognize propaganda techniques** and **faulty reasoning**. (p. 552)

Using the Skills and Strategies in Part 1

In Part 1, you will learn to ask questions that help you identify important details in a work. You will practice connecting details to determine the relationship among them. Finally, you will also apply these connections between important details to draw logical conclusions. Drawing conclusions helps you recognize ideas that are not directly stated in a text.

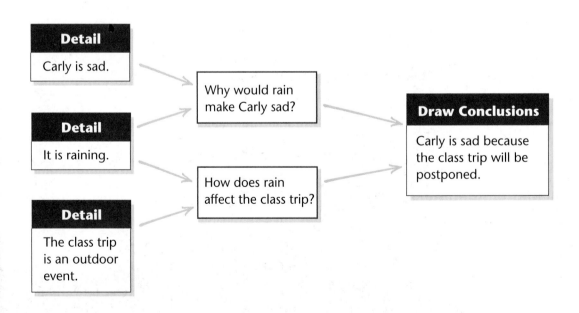

Detail
Carly is sad.

Detail
It is raining.

Detail
The class trip is an outdoor event.

Why would rain make Carly sad?

How does rain affect the class trip?

Draw Conclusions
Carly is sad because the class trip will be postponed.

Academic Vocabulary: Words for Discussing Drawing Conclusions

The following words will help you state and support conclusions about the selections in this unit.

Word	Definition	Example Sentence
infer *v.*	make a logical assumption based on evidence or reasoning	The character is mean so I *infer* that he is not the hero.
refer *v.*	1. consult a source to find information 2. mention a source of information	Andy had to *refer* to last week's lesson before he could finish his assignment.
transform *v.*	change the shape or structure of	The author *transforms* the character from a criminal to a kind, caring person.
detect *v.*	notice or discover something	I *detect* some sarcasm in the character's comments.
conclude *v.*	form an opinion based on evidence	Ms. Lopez *concluded* that her students had mastered the skill.

Vocabulary Skill: Word Analysis

▶ **Word analysis** means breaking words into their parts to study them.

In Part 1, you will study these word parts
- the word root *-fer-*
- the prefix *trans-*

In Part 1, you will learn to use word parts to understand and remember the meanings of whole words. In addition, you will learn to recognize relationships among words based on parts such as roots and prefixes.

Activity Sort the list into two groups—words that contain the word root *-fer-* and words that contain the prefix *trans-*. Use a dictionary to confirm the meaning of each word. Then, briefly explain how the meanings of the words in each group are related.

- infer
- transcribe
- offer
- transport
- transit
- refer

You can apply the skills on this page to these poems.

Poetry Collection 1
The Rider, p. 520
Seal, p. 522
Haiku, p. 523

Poetry Collection 2
Winter, p. 527
Forsythia, p. 528
Haiku, p. 529

Reading Skill

Drawing conclusions means arriving at an overall judgment or idea by pulling together several details. By drawing conclusions, you recognize meanings that are not directly stated. **Asking questions** like the following can help you identify details and make connections that lead to a conclusion.

- What details does the writer include and emphasize?
- How are the details related?
- What do the details mean all together?

Use a chart like the one shown to record details from the poems and draw conclusions from the details.

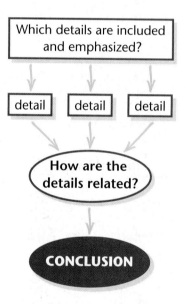

Literary Analysis

There are many different **forms of poetry**. A poet will follow different rules depending on the structure of a poem.

- A **lyric poem** expresses the poet's thoughts and feelings about a single image or idea in vivid, musical language.
- In a **concrete poem**, the poet arranges the letters and lines to create a visual image that suggests the poem's subject.
- **Haiku** is a traditional form of Japanese poetry that is often about nature. The first line always has five syllables, the second line has seven syllables, and the third line has five syllables.

Vocabulary Builder

Poetry Collection 1

- **luminous** (lōō′ mə nəs) *adj.* giving off light (p. 521) *The luminous moon stood out in the dark sky.*

- **swerve** (swɜrv) *n.* curving motion (p. 522) *With a swerve, the skater avoided hitting me.*

- **utter** (ut′ ər) *v.* speak (p. 522) *The shy boy refused to utter a word.*

- **weasel** (wē′ səl) *n.* small mammal that eats rats, mice, birds, and eggs (p. 523) *The weasel chased the rabbit but failed to catch it.*

Poetry Collection 2

- **burrow** (bɜr′ ō) *v.* dig a hole for shelter (p. 527) *Some animals burrow under tree roots to make dens.*

Build Understanding • *Poetry Collection 1*

Connecting to the Literature

Reading/Writing Connection Each of these poems expresses a poet's observations or feelings in a creative way. Think about what you know about the way poems look and sound. Then, in a brief paragraph, explain the reasons writers might choose to put their thoughts in a poem rather than in prose or drama. Use at least three of the following words: *elaborate, communicate, generate, reinforce.*

Meet the Authors

Naomi Shihab **Nye** (b. 1952)
The Rider (pages 520–521)
    As a teenager, Naomi Shihab Nye probably felt the loneliness she describes in this poem. When Nye was fourteen, her family moved from Missouri to the Middle East. Though she now values learning about her Arab heritage, the move was not easy. Nye has published volumes of poetry as well as books for children.

William Jay **Smith** (b. 1918)
Seal (page 522)
    Smith was born in Winnfield, Louisiana. He has taught college students, written poetry and essays, translated Russian and French poetry, and even served in the Vermont State Legislature for two years. Like "Seal," many of Smith's poems show that poetry can be pure and simple—and fun.

Buson (1716–1784)
Haiku (page 523)
    Japanese poet Buson was not only a skilled writer of haiku but also a talented painter. His love of color and interest in the visual world are reflected in much of his poetry. At age thirty-six, Buson became the "master" at the haiku school in Kyoto, Japan. When a student asked him to reveal the secret of haiku, Buson responded, "Use the commonplace to escape the commonplace."

Go Online
Author Link
For: More about these poets
Visit: www.PHSchool.com
Web Code: eme-9402

The Rider

Naomi Shihab Nye

A boy told me
if he rollerskated fast enough
his loneliness couldn't catch up to him,

the best reason I ever heard
5   for trying to be a champion.

What I wonder tonight
pedaling hard down King William Street
is if it translates to bicycles.

A victory! To leave your loneliness
10 panting behind you on some street corner
while you float free into a cloud of sudden azaleas,
luminous pink petals that have
        never felt loneliness,
no matter how slowly they fell.

Literary Analysis
Forms of Poetry
Whose feelings does
the poem express—
"a boy's" or the
speaker's? Explain.

Vocabulary Builder
luminous (lōō′mə nəs)
adj. giving off light

◀ **Critical Viewing** What details of this photograph convey the feelings the poem describes? **[Analyze]**

Seal

WILLIAM JAY SMITH

See how he dives
   From the rocks with a zoom!
  See how he darts
    Through his watery room
5 Past crabs and eels
    And green seaweed,
   Past fluffs of sandy
   Minnow feed![1]
    See how he swims
10 With a <u>swerve</u> and a twist,
   A flip of the flipper,
   A flick of the wrist!
   Quicksilver-quick,
   Softer than spray,
15 Down he plunges
   And sweeps away;
   Before you can think,
  Before you can <u>utter</u>
 Words like "Dill pickle"
20 Or "Apple butter,"
 Back up he swims
 Past Sting Ray and Shark,
 Out with a zoom,
 A whoop, a bark;
25 Before you can say
   Whatever you wish,
    He plops at your side
     With a mouthful of fish!

Literary Analysis
Forms of Poetry
Why might the poet have arranged the lines of the poem this way?

Vocabulary Builder
swerve (swʉrv) *n.* curving motion

utter (utʹ ər) *v.* speak

---

1. feed (fēd) *n.* tiny particles that minnows feed on.

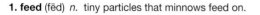

▶ **Critical Viewing** What details in this photograph remind you of the poem? **[Analyze]**

HAIKU
BUSON

O foolish ducklings,
you know my old green pond is
watched by a <u>weasel</u>!

Vocabulary Builder
weasel (wē′ zəl) *n.* a
small mammal that
eats rats, mice, birds,
and eggs

Deep in a windless
wood, not one leaf dares to move. . . .
Something is afraid.

Reading Skill
Draw Conclusions
What is the speaker
in the first haiku
worried about?

After the moon sets,
slow through the forest, shadows
drift and disappear.

Apply the Skills

Poetry Collection 1

Thinking About the Selections

1. **Respond:** Which of these poems do you like best? Why?
2. **(a) Recall:** What two sports are discussed in "The Rider"?
   (b) Compare: What do the two sports have in common?
3. **(a) Recall:** Identify six words that describe the movement of the seal in "Seal." **(b) Infer:** How would you describe the mood or feeling that these words create?
4. **(a) Recall:** In the first haiku, what does the speaker warn the ducklings about? **(b) Analyze:** How would you describe the speaker's attitude toward the ducks?
5. **(a) Make a Judgment:** Do you think these poems are meaningful for people your age? Explain in writing why you answered as you did. **(b) Discuss:** Share your responses with a partner. Then, discuss how looking at someone else's responses did or did not change your judgment.

Reading Skill

6. For each poem, identify a question that helps you **draw the conclusion** given.
   (a) The speaker in "The Rider" values speed.
   (b) The seal in "Seal" zooms around quickly.
   (c) The speaker in the haiku values nature.

Literary Analysis

7. On a chart like the one shown, place a checkmark under each characteristic of the **poetic form** that classifies each poem.

Poem	Characteristics of Poem				
	Musical language	Single image or idea	Thoughts of one speaker	Lines shaped like subject	Three lines; 17 syllables
The Rider (lyric)					
Seal (concrete)					
Haiku (haiku)					

QuickReview

Poems at a Glance

The Rider: a lyric poem

Seal: a concrete poem

Haiku: three-line Japanese verses

Go Online
Assessment
For: Self-test
Visit: www.PHSchool.com
Web Code: ema-6402

Draw Conclusions: arrive at an overall opinion or idea by pulling together details

Poetic Form: the physical structure of a poem. Three common forms of poetry are *lyric, concrete,* and *haiku.*

Vocabulary Builder

Practice Rewrite the following sentences so that each includes a vocabulary word from the Collection 1 vocabulary list on page 518 and conveys the same basic meaning.

1. The rabbits raced for cover when they spotted the small brown mammal watching them.
2. The shining face of the clock was the only thing visible in the dark.
3. The sled made a movement to turn at the bottom of the hill.
4. Frozen by stage fright, the actor could not speak a word.

Writing

Write a **lyric poem, concrete poem,** or **haiku** to share your thoughts in new, creative ways.

- Pick a subject that interests you. Put the subject in the center of a piece of paper, and create a cluster diagram around it.
- Brainstorm for details—vivid descriptions, action words, thoughts, and feelings—to put into the cluster diagram.
- Review the characteristics of each poetic form. Then, use your notes to draft your poem.
- Choose a creative title for your poem.

For *Grammar, Vocabulary,* and *Assessment,* see **Build Language Skills,** pages 532–533.

Extend Your Learning

Listening and Speaking In the library or online, find a recording of a poet reading his or her own lyric poems. Then, in a small group, listen to one or more of the poems. Finally, in a brief **presentation** to your group, tell what you like about the poet's reading and give reasons for your opinion.

Research and Technology Use one or more computer programs, such as a word-processing or drawing program, to write, format, and **publish a poem.** If you wrote a poem for the writing assignment, you can format that one.

Build Understanding • *Poetry Collection 2*

Connecting to the Literature

Reading/Writing Connection Each of the poems in this collection expresses the poet's observations or feelings about nature. In a brief paragraph, discuss something in nature that might inspire you to write a poem. Use at least three of the following words: *capture, concentrate, emphasize, display.*

Review

For **Reading Skill, Literary Analysis,** and **Vocabulary Builder,** see page 518.

Meet the Authors

Nikki **Giovanni** (b. 1943)
Winter (p. 527)

Nikki Giovanni's poems highlight the major events in her life. In "Winter," however, she writes about a universal subject: the changing of the seasons. In addition to being a poet, Giovanni is a college professor who teaches both English literature and African American studies.

Mary Ellen **Solt** (b. 1920)
Forsythia (p. 528)

Mary Ellen Solt was born in Iowa in 1920. As a writer, she has devoted much of her energy to studying and creating concrete poetry. In the introduction to her book, *Concrete Poetry—A World View,* Solt wrote, "[The reader] must now perceive the poem as an object and participate in the poet's act of creating it, for the concrete poem communicates first and foremost its structure."

Matsuo **Bashō** (1644–1694)
Haiku (p. 529)

Matsuo Bashō was born near Kyoto, Japan. He began studying poetry at an early age and became one of Japan's most famous poets. Along with writing poetry, Bashō taught poetry, served as a noble in the court, and entered a monastery.

Go Online
Author Link
For: More about the poets
Visit: www.PHSchool.com
Web Code: eme-9403

WINTER
NIKKI GIOVANNI

Frogs <u>burrow</u> the mud
snails bury themselves
and I air my quilts
preparing for the cold

5   Dogs grow more hair
   mothers make oatmeal
   and little boys and girls
   take Father John's Medicine[1]

   Bears store fat
10 chipmunks gather nuts
   and I collect books
   For the coming winter

▲ **Critical Viewing**
What do you think
this chipmunk is
doing? **[Speculate]**

Vocabulary Builder
burrow (bʉrʹ ō) v. dig
a hole for shelter

Reading Skill
Draw Conclusions
Why are all the
activities described in
the poem necessary?

---

1. **Father John's Medicine** old-fashioned cough syrup.

Forsythia

MARY ELLEN SOLT

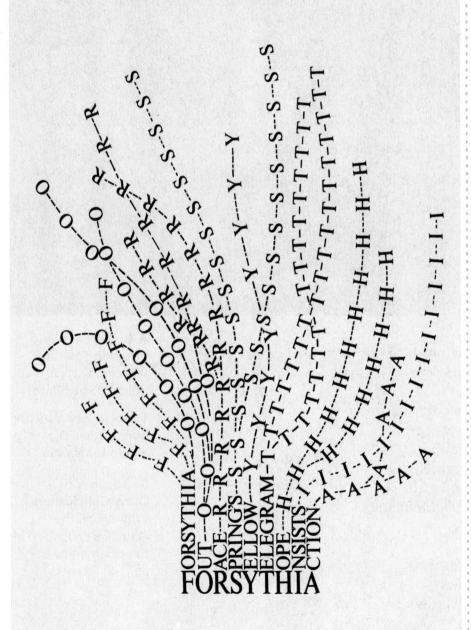

Literary Analysis
Forms of Poetry
Why might the poet have arranged the words and letters on the page in this way?

HAIKU

BASHŌ

On sweet plum blossoms
The sun rises suddenly.
Look, a mountain path!

Has spring come indeed?
On that nameless mountain lie
Thin layers of mist.

Temple bells die out.
The fragrant blossoms remain.
A perfect evening!

Literary Analysis
Forms of Poetry
How are these three
poems similar?

Apply the Skills

Thinking About the Selections

1. **Respond:** Which of these poems do you like best? Why?
2. **(a) Recall:** What are the animals, mothers, and "little boys and girls" doing in "Winter"? **(b) Connect:** How do these actions connect with winter in your experience?
3. **(a) Infer:** What does the bottom line of "Forsythia" say? List the words that grow out of that bottom line. **(b) Interpret:** Tell the meaning of these lines.
4. **(a) Recall:** Name one important element of nature in each of the three haiku. **(b) Analyze:** How would you describe Bashō's attitude toward nature in these three poems?
5. **(a) Make a Judgment:** Do you think these poems are meaningful for people your age? Explain in writing why you answered as you did. **(b) Discuss:** Share your responses with a partner. Then, discuss how looking at someone else's responses did or did not change your judgment.

Reading Skill

6. For each poem, identify a question that helps you **draw the conclusion** given.
   (a) The speaker in "Winter" accepts the changing seasons as part of the natural cycle of life.
   (b) Forsythia grows in a tangled, wild way.
   (c) The speaker in the three haiku values nature.

Literary Analysis

7. On a chart like the one shown, place a checkmark under each characteristic of the **poetic form** that classifies each poem.

Poem	Characteristics of Poem				
	Musical language	Single image or idea	Thoughts of one speaker	Lines shaped like subject	Three lines; 17 syllables
Winter (lyric)					
Forsythia (concrete)					
Haiku (haiku)					

QuickReview

Poems at a Glance
Winter: a lyric poem
Forsythia: a concrete poem
Haiku: three-line Japanese verses

Go Online
—Assessment
For: Self-test
Visit: www.PHSchool.com
Web Code: ema-6403

Draw Conclusions: arrive at an overall opinion or idea by pulling together details

Poetic Form: the physical structure of a poem. Three common forms of poetry are *lyric, concrete,* and *haiku.*

Vocabulary Builder

Practice Use the vocabulary word *burrow* in a sentence that illustrates its meaning as a noun. Then, write another sentence using *burrow* as a verb. Next, use a thesaurus to find *synonyms*, words that have almost the same meaning, for *burrow*. Determine which words work as synonyms for the noun, and which are synonyms for the verb. Rewrite each sentence using one of the synonyms you found.

Writing

Write a **lyric poem, concrete poem**, or **haiku** to share your thoughts in new, creative ways.

- Pick a subject that interests you. Put the subject in the center of a piece of paper, and create a cluster diagram around it.
- Brainstorm for details—vivid descriptions, action words, thoughts and feelings—to put into the cluster diagram
- Review the characteristics of each poetic form. Then, use your notes to draft your poem in the form you have chosen.
- Choose a creative title for your poem.

For *Grammar, Vocabulary,* and *Assessment,* see **Build Language Skills,** pages 532–533.

Extend Your Learning

Listening and Speaking In the library or online, find a recording of a poet reading his or her own lyric poems. Then, in a small group, listen to one or more of the poems. Finally, in a brief **presentation** to your group, tell what you like about the poet's reading and give reasons for your opinion.

Research and Technology Use one or more computer programs, such as a word-processing or drawing program, to write, format, and **publish a poem.** If you completed the writing assignment on this page, you can format the poem you wrote.

Build Language Skills

Poetry Collection 1 • Poetry Collection 2

Vocabulary Skill

Word Analysis The word *transform* contains the **prefix *trans-*,** which means "across" or "through." Good readers *transform* words into ideas or pictures in their mind. Words that contain the prefix *trans-* will have something to do with *across* or *through*.

▶ **Example:** His acting *transformed* a flat character into a fascinating part of the play.

Practice Use your knowledge of the prefix *trans-* to predict the meaning of each of the following words. Then, check the word's definition in a dictionary. Explain how the meaning you predicted compares to the actual definition.

1. transmit   **3.** transition   **5.** translate

2. transfer   **4.** transient

Grammar Lesson

Infinitives and Infinitive Phrases An **infinitive** is a verb form that acts as a noun, an adjective, or an adverb. An infinitive usually begins with the word *to*. The examples show infinitives.

MorePractice

For more practice with infinitives, see the Grammar Handbook, p. R31.

▶ **Examples:** *To learn* is her goal. (noun)
She is the one *to see*. (adjective)
Everyone waited *to hear*. (adverb)

An **infinitive phrase** is an infinitive plus its own modifiers or complements. The examples show infinitive phrases acting as different parts of speech.

▶ **Examples:** <u>*To read Spanish fluently*</u> is my goal. (noun)
She is the one <u>*to see*</u> *for advice.* (adjective)
Everyone waited <u>*to hear*</u> *the news.* (adverb)

Practice Write the infinitive phrase from each sentence. Underline the infinitive. Then use each infinitive phrase in a new sentence.

1. To run on the slippery trail is dangerous.

2. The winter seemed to drag on.

3. The athletes tried to do what the coach asked of them.

4. The campers had no choice but to sleep on the ground.

5. The young girl's dream was to become a famous scientist.

W̶G Prentice Hall Writing and Grammar Connection: Chapter 20, Section 1

Reading: Draw Conclusions

Directions: *Read the selection. Then, answer the questions.*

Each Native American group who lived in what is now Texas had a distinct lifestyle. The Caddo people in the eastern woodlands built sturdy homes. The rich soil provided beans, squash, and corn, while hunters found plenty of deer and other game in the forests. The Jumanos lived near the Rio Grande in homes of adobe bricks. Thick adobe kept the homes cool in the summer. Farmers hauled river water to keep crops growing. In the plains, Comanches followed migrating buffalo. They used the buffalo for food, clothing and the skins for tepees. These dwellings could be easily taken down and put up when the Comanches moved.

1. Which conclusion about the Caddo people is best supported by the paragraph?
   A They did not move frequently.
   B They moved from place to place.
   C They built their homes from the skins of deer.
   D They struggled to find food.

2. What can you conclude about the Comanches?
   A did not build sturdy houses.
   B needed to move on a regular basis.
   C did not include meat in their diet.
   D lived in an area with a cold climate.

3. You can conclude that the Jumanos
   A were skilled hunters and gatherers.
   B had a special respect for builders.
   C lived in a hot and dry area.
   D were similar to the Caddos.

4. Which conclusion about Texas is supported by the passage?
   A People from a variety of backgrounds live there today.
   B It has many types of climates.
   C There are more rural areas than urban areas.
   D Beans, corn, and squash are popular foods there.

Timed Writing: Description [Cognition]

Review the haiku by either Buson or Bashō. Then, describe a haiku using the poem to provide examples that illustrate your points. In your description, include details about the structure and the typical subject matter. **(20 minutes)**

 ## Writing Workshop: *Work in Progress*

Assessment Writing
Assessment writing requires you support your ideas quickly, but clearly. List three ideas that could support the main idea that school should begin later in the morning. Put this work in your portfolio.

You can apply the skills on this page to these poems.

Poetry Collection 1
Life, p. 536
The Courage That My Mother Had, p. 537
Loo-Wit, p. 538

Poetry Collection 2
Mother to Son, p. 543
The Village Blacksmith, p. 544
Fog, p. 547

Reading Skill

A **conclusion** is a decision or opinion that you reach after considering the details in a literary work. **Connecting the details** can help you draw conclusions as you read. For example, if the speaker in a poem describes beautiful flowers, bright sunshine, and happy children playing, you might conclude that he or she has a positive outlook. As you read, identify important details. Then, look at the details together and draw a conclusion about the poem or the speaker.

Literary Analysis

Figurative language is language that is not meant to be taken literally. Writers use figures of speech to express ideas in vivid and imaginative ways. Common figures of speech include the following:

- A **simile** compares two unlike things using *like* or *as.*
- A **metaphor** compares two unlike things by stating one thing is another.
- **Personification** gives human characteristics to a nonhuman subject.
- A **symbol** is an object, person, animal, place, or image that represents something other than itself.

Simile
My love is like a red, red rose.

Metaphor
Life is a bowl of cherries.

Personification
The stars were dancing heel to toe.

Symbol
dove = peace, harmony heart = love, romance

Vocabulary Builder

Poetry Collection 1

- **crouches** (krouch´ iz) *v.* stoops or bends low (p. 539) *Rachel crouches to pick up a flower.*
- **unravel** (un rav´ əl) *v.* become untangled or separated (p. 539) *The kitten began to unravel the ball of yarn.*
- **dislodge** (dis läj´) *v.* force from a position or place (p. 539) *We struggled to dislodge the boulder.*

Poetry Collection 2

- **sinewy** (sin´ yoo ē) *adj.* tough and strong (p. 544) *He carved the stone with sinewy hands.*
- **brawny** (brôn´ ē) *adj.* strong and muscular (p. 544) *The piano mover had brawny arms.*
- **haunches** (hônch´ iz) *n.* upper legs and hips of an animal (p. 547) *The hamster sat on its haunches.*

Connecting to the Literature

Reading/Writing Connection In "Loo-Wit," poet Wendy Rose describes a volcano in an unusual way. Write several sentences of your own that describe a volcano. Use at least three of these words in your writing: *consist, occur, indicate, considerable, expel, impress.*

Meet the Authors

Naomi Long **Madgett** (b. 1923)
Life (page 536)

Naomi Long Madgett first discovered poetry at the age of seven or eight, while reading in her father's study. She was most inspired by poets Alfred, Lord Tennyson and Langston Hughes, though their styles are quite different. Madgett once said, "I would rather be a good poet than anything else." Her ambition to write good poetry has led to more than seven collections of poems.

Edna St. Vincent **Millay** (1892–1950)
The Courage That My Mother Had (page 537)

Edna St. Vincent Millay's mother was a hard-working nurse who instilled in her daughters a sense of independence and a love for reading. Millay's mother had a powerful influence on young Edna, who grew up to be a widely published writer and political activist. Born in Rockland, Maine, Millay published her first poem at the age of fourteen. She was the first woman to win the Pulitzer Prize for poetry.

Wendy **Rose** (b. 1948)
Loo-Wit (page 538)

Wendy Rose was born in Oakland, California, to a Hopi father and a Scots-Irish-Miwok mother. Rose is also an anthropologist who has worked to protect Native American burial sites from developers, and a painter who illustrated some of her own books. "Loo-Wit" is based on legends of the Cowlitz people of Washington State.

Go Online
Author Link
For: More about the poets
Visit: www.PHSchool.com
Web Code: eme-9404

Life

NAOMI LONG MADGETT

Life is but a toy that swings on a bright gold chain
Ticking for a little while
To amuse a fascinated infant,
Until the keeper, a very old man,
5   Becomes tired of the game
And lets the watch run down.

Literary Analysis
Figurative Language
What type of figurative language does the poet use to describe life?

The Courage That My Mother Had

Edna St. Vincent Millay

▲ **Critical Viewing**
Why might someone treasure an item—like this pin—that once belonged to a close relative?
[Connect]

The courage that my mother had
Went with her, and is with her still:
Rock from New England quarried;[1]
Now granite in a granite hill.

5   The golden brooch[2] my mother wore
She left behind for me to wear;
I have no thing I treasure more:
Yet, it is something I could spare.

Oh, if instead she'd left to me
10 The thing she took into the grave!—
That courage like a rock, which she
Has no more need of, and I have.

Reading Skill
Draw Conclusions
What detail in the third stanza shows how the speaker feels about her mother?

---

1. quarried (kwôr′ ēd) *adj.* carved out of the ground
2. brooch (brōch) *n.* large ornamental pin.

Loo-Wit

Wendy Rose

The way they do
this old woman
no longer cares
what others think
5   but spits her black tobacco
any which way
stretching full length
from her bumpy bed.
Finally up
10   she sprinkles ashes
on the snow,
cold buttes²
promise nothing
but the walk
15   of winter.
Centuries of cedar
have bound her
to earth,
huckleberry ropes
20   lay prickly
on her neck.
Around her
machinery growls,
snarls and plows
25   great patches
of her skin.

---

1. Loo-Wit name given by the Cowlitz people to Mount St. Helens, an active
volcano in Washington State. It means "lady of fire."
2. buttes (byo͞ots) *n.* steep hills standing alone in flat land.

▶ **Critical Viewing** Which lines of the poem best
capture the action of this photograph? **[Assess]**

She crouches
in the north,
her trembling
30 the source
of dawn.
Light appears
with the shudder
of her slopes,
35 the movement
of her arm.
Blackberries unravel,
stones dislodge;
it's not as if
40 they weren't warned.
She was sleeping
but she heard the boot scrape,
the creaking floor,
felt the pull of the blanket
45 from her thin
   shoulder.
With one free hand
she finds her weapons
and raises them high;
clearing the twigs from her
   throat
50 she sings, she
   sings,
shaking the sky
like a blanket about her
Loo-wit sings and sings and
   sings!

Vocabulary Builder
crouches (krouch´ iz)
v. stoops or bends
low

unravel (un rav´ əl) *v.*
become untangled or
separated

dislodge (dis läj´) *v.*
force from a position
or place

Literary Analysis
Figurative Language
Which details does
the writer use to
compare the volcano
to an old woman?

Apply the Skills

Poetry Collection 1

Thinking About the Selections

1. **Respond:** Which poem contains the most vivid images? Explain your answer by giving examples.
2. **(a) Recall:** In "Life," what image does Madgett use to describe life? **(b) Interpret:** What does this image suggest about life? **(c) Evaluate:** Is it a good image for life? Explain.
3. **(a) Recall:** What physical item did the mother leave behind for the speaker in "The Courage That My Mother Had"? **(b) Interpret:** Why would the speaker rather have her mother's character than the item her mother left her? **(c) Discuss:** Share your response with a partner. Then, discuss how looking at someone else's responses did or did not change your interpretation.
4. **(a) Recall:** What details describe the eruption of the volcano in "Loo-Wit"? **(b) Analyze Causes and Effects:** According to the poem, what causes the eruption?

Reading Skill

5. Use a graphic organizer like this one to connect details from the poem "Life" to reach the **conclusion** that is given.

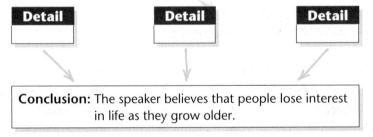

Detail	Detail	Detail

Conclusion: The speaker believes that people lose interest in life as they grow older.

6. Which details from "Loo-Wit" support the conclusion that people are disturbing the mountain?

Literary Analysis

7. **(a)** What is a symbol for strength in "The Courage That My Mother Had"? **(b)** How do you know?
8. **(a)** To what is life compared in "Life"? **(b)** Which type of **figurative language** does Madgett use to make this comparison?
9. Give three examples of personification in "Loo-Wit."

Vocabulary Builder

Practice Rewrite each sentence so that it includes a word from Collection 1 on page 534 and conveys the same meaning.

1. The rushing water will knock the rocks out of the wall.
2. Can you untangle the yarn?
3. Notice how the cat bends low before pouncing.

Writing

Write a **metaphor** about life. Begin by comparing life to something else, such as an object, an idea, or an animal. Then, extend the metaphor by making several connected comparisons. Use vivid images and descriptive language.

For *Grammar, Vocabulary,* and *Assessment,* see **Build Language Skills,** pages 550–551.

Extend Your Learning

Listening and Speaking Work with a group of classmates to present a **poetry reading** of other poems by one of the poets in this collection. First, select a poet. Then, choose the poems that you will read aloud.

- Rehearse your readings alone and with the group.
- Practice reading slowly and with expression.
- Speak clearly, and make eye contact with your audience.

After you have finished rehearsing, hold a reading for the class.

Research and Technology Working with two other students, use library resources to find out more about volcanic eruptions. Topics may include how volcanoes form, warning signals of an eruption, where and why volcanoes typically erupt, or famous volcanic eruptions of the past.

Present your findings in the form of a **scientific explanation**. Use diagrams, illustrations, photographs, maps, or other visuals in your explanation. Make sure you put information from your research into your own words.

Build Understanding • *Poetry Collection 2*

Connecting to the Literature

Reading/Writing Connection The speakers in the poems "Mother to Son" and "The Village Blacksmith" pay tribute to people they admire. In your notebook, describe a person you admire. Use at least three of the following words: *appreciate, aspire, display, survive.*

Review

For **Reading Skill, Literary Analysis,** and **Vocabulary Builder,** see page 534.

Meet the Authors

Langston **Hughes** (1902–1967)
Mother to Son (page 543)

Langston Hughes published his first work just a year after his high school graduation. Though he wrote in many genres, Hughes is best known for his poetry. He was one of the main figures in the Harlem Renaissance, a creative movement among African Americans that took place in the 1920s in New York City.

Henry Wadsworth **Longfellow** (1807–1882)
The Village Blacksmith (pages 544–546)

Although his father wanted him to become a lawyer, Henry Wadsworth Longfellow preferred to become a poet and college professor. Longfellow was part of a group of poets called the Fireside poets, so named because families often gathered around their fireplaces, reading aloud poems such as "The Village Blacksmith."

Carl **Sandburg** (1878–1967)
Fog (page 547)

The son of Swedish immigrants, Carl Sandburg was born in Illinois. Although he won the Pulitzer Prize in both poetry and history, he was not a typical scholar. By the time his first book appeared, he had been a farm worker, a stagehand, a railroad worker, a soldier, and a cook, among other things.

Go Online
Author Link

For: More about the poets
Visit: www.PHSchool.com
Web Code: eme-9405

Mother to Son

LANGSTON HUGHES

Well, son, I'll tell you:
Life for me ain't been no crystal stair.
It's had tacks in it,
And splinters,
5 And boards torn up,
And places with no carpet on the floor—
Bare.
But all the time
I'se been a-climbin' on,
10 And reachin' landin's,
And turnin' corners,
And sometimes goin' in the dark
Where there ain't been no light.
So boy, don't you turn back.
15 Don't you set down on the steps
'Cause you finds it's kinder hard.
Don't you fall now—
For I'se still goin', honey,
I'se still climbin',
20 And life for me ain't been no crystal stair.

Literary Analysis
Figurative Language
What does the staircase symbolize?

Reading Skill
Draw Conclusions
What details in the poem support the conclusion that life has not been easy for the mother?

The Village Blacksmith

Henry Wadsworth Longfellow

Under a spreading chestnut tree
    The village smithy[1] stands;
The smith, a mighty man is he,
    With large and <u>sinewy</u> hands;
5   And the muscles of his <u>brawny</u> arms
Are strong as iron bands.

His hair is crisp,[2] and black, and long,
    His face is like the tan;
His brow is wet with honest sweat,
10   He earns whate'er he can,
And looks the whole world in the face,
    For he owes not any man.

Week in, week out, from morn till night,
    You can hear his bellows[3] blow;
15 You can hear him swing his heavy sledge,[4]
    With measured beat and slow,
Like a sexton[5] ringing the village bell,
    When the evening sun is low.

1. **smithy** (smith´ ē) *n.* workshop of a blacksmith.
2. **crisp** (krisp) *adj.* closely curled and wiry.
3. **bellows** (bel´ ōz) *n.* device for quickening the fire by blowing air in it.
4. **sledge** (slej) *n.* sledgehammer; a long, heavy hammer, usually held with both hands.
5. **sexton** (seks´ tən) *n.* person who cares for church property and rings church bells.

Vocabulary Builder
sinewy (sin´ yo͞o wē)
adj. tough and strong

brawny (brôn´ ē) *adj.*
strong and muscular

▲ **Critical Viewing**
Describe what it might feel like to work in a place like the smithy in this painting. **[Connect]**

And children coming home from school
20   Look in at the open door;
They love to see the flaming forge,
      And hear the bellows roar,
And catch the burning sparks that fly
      Like chaff from a threshing floor.

25 He goes on Sunday to the church,
      And sits among his boys;
He hears the parson pray and preach,
      He hears his daughter's voice,
Singing in the village choir,
30   And it makes his heart rejoice.
It sounds to him like her mother's voice,
      Singing in Paradise!
He needs must think of her once more,
      How in the grave she lies;
35 And with his hard, rough hand he wipes
      A tear out of his eyes.

Literary Analysis
Figurative Language
Find an example of a simile in this stanza.

Reading Skill
Draw Conclusions
What conclusion can you draw about the blacksmith's wife from the details in lines 25–36?

✓ **Reading Check**

What kind of hours does the village blacksmith keep?

Toiling—rejoicing—sorrowing,
　　Onward through life he goes;
Each morning sees some task begin,
40　　Each evening sees it close;
Something attempted, something done,
　　Has earned a night's repose.

Thanks, thanks to thee, my worthy friend,
　　For the lesson thou hast taught!
45 Thus at the flaming forge of life
　　Our fortunes must be wrought;
Thus on its sounding anvil shaped
　　Each burning deed and thought.

▲ Critical Viewing
What is the blacksmith
probably doing for this
horse? [Use Prior
Knowledge]

Fog

CARL SANDBURG

The fog comes
on little cat feet.

It sits looking
over harbor and city
5   on silent <u>haunches</u>
and then moves on.

▼ **Critical Viewing**
Based on the poem, what would the poet see in this photograph? **[Connect]**

Vocabulary Builder
haunches (hônch´iz) *n.* upper legs and hips of an animal

Apply the Skills

Poetry Collection 2

Thinking About the Selections

1. **Respond:** Which poem did you like the best? Explain why.
2. **(a) Recall:** Identify three details in "The Village Blacksmith" that show how hard the blacksmith works. **(b) Distinguish:** Does the poet present hard work as a positive or a negative thing? Support your answer. **(c) Discuss:** Decide whether you agree with the poet's ideas about work. Share your response with a partner. Then, discuss how looking at someone else's responses did or did not change your interpretation.
3. **(a) Recall:** What three things does the fog do in "Fog"? **(b) Connect:** What qualities of fog make it a good subject for a poem?
4. **(a) Analyze:** What qualities does the mother in "Mother to Son" demonstrate through her words and actions? **(b) Synthesize:** Why does she need these qualities?

Mother to Son: A mother tells her son that life is not easy.

The Village Blacksmith: The speaker describes the life of a strong, hardworking blacksmith.

Fog: The speaker shares a clever description of fog.

Reading Skill

5. Use a graphic organizer like this one to connect details from "Mother to Son" to reach the **conclusion** that is given.

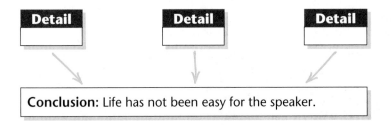

Conclusion: Life has not been easy for the speaker.

6. Which details from "The Village Blacksmith" support the conclusion that the blacksmith sets an example for his family?

Literary Analysis

7. Which type of **figurative language** can you identify in the following lines from "The Village Blacksmith"?

> You can hear him swing his heavy sledge,
> With measured beat and slow,
> Like a sexton ringing the village bell,
> When the evening sun is low.

8. In "Mother to Son," identify several symbols of hardship.

Vocabulary Builder

Practice Answer each question. Then, explain your answer.

1. Would a dog sit on its *haunches* if it were running?
2. Would you expect a weight lifter to be *brawny*?
3. Who would you expect to have *sinewy* hands?

Writing

Write a **metaphor** about a quality or an idea, such as love or loyalty or death. Begin by comparing your subject to something else, such as an object, an idea, or an animal. Then, extend the metaphor by making several connected comparisons. Use vivid images and descriptive language.

For *Grammar, Vocabulary,* and *Assessment,* see **Build Language Skills,** pages 550–551.

Extend Your Learning

Listening and Speaking Work with a group of classmates to present a **poetry reading** of other poems by one of the poets in this collection. First, select a poet. Then, choose the poems that you will read aloud.

- Rehearse your readings alone and with the group.
- Practice reading slowly and with expression.
- Speak clearly, and make eye contact with your audience.

After you have finished rehearsing, hold a reading for the class.

Research and Technology With a partner, write a **scientific explanation** that explains the difference between fog and smog. Use library resources to conduct your research. Take notes on the main points and significant details you find.

- Define each term.
- Describe one similarity and one difference.
- Identify two types of fog and smog.

Support your presentation with facts, details, and explanations. Use visuals such as a Venn diagram, a comparison chart, photos, and/or diagrams to clarify your findings.

Build Language Skills

Poetry Collection 1 • Poetry Collection 2

Vocabulary Skill

Word Analysis The word part *-fer-* comes from the Latin root *-ferre-*, which means "to bring or to carry." When you *infer,* you read between the lines and *bring into* literature meaning that is not directly stated.

The word *refer* comes from the word part *-fer-* and the prefix *re-*, which means "back." *Refer* means to consult or mention a source of information—to *bring* attention *back* to the source.

Practice Write the meaning of each word. Then, use each word in a sentence.

1. con (together) + fer = confer, means _____
2. trans + fer = transfer, means _____
3. re + fer + ral = referral, means _____

Grammar Lesson

Appositives and Appositive Phrases An **appositive** is a noun or pronoun placed after another noun or pronoun to identify, rename, or explain it.

An **appositive phrase** is a noun or pronoun with modifiers. It stands next to a noun or pronoun and adds information that identifies, names, or explains it.

Appositives	Appositive Phrases
Michelangelo, the painter, lived in Italy.	Louisa May Alcott, an American author, wrote *Little Women.*
Our cat, Midnight, likes to sleep on my bed.	Karina—a talented violinist—played a solo.

Practice Write the appositive or appositive phrase in each sentence. Then, write the word each one modifies.

1. Ryan, the pitcher, reached the mound.
2. Ryan's mother, a great influence in his life, taught him to work hard.
3. Edith Wharton, the novelist, often wrote her stories about society.
4. Bertha, my great aunt, wore purple tennis shoes.
5. The dictionary—a list of words and definitions—provides valuable information.

MorePractice

For more practice with appositives, see the Grammar Handbook, p. R31.

W̧G Prentice Hall Writing and Grammar Connection: Chapter 20, Section 1

Draw Conclusions

Directions: *Read the selection. Then, answer the questions.*

The Golden Gate bridge spans the San Francisco Bay, connecting northern California to the peninsula of San Francisco. The Golden Gate is a suspension bridge, with towers that hold up thick cables from which the bridge hangs. The floor of the bridge rises 220 feet above the water. A six-lane road on the bridge is bordered with sidewalks.

1. Which conclusion is best supported?
   - A The bridge enables many people to go from San Francisco to northern California.
   - B The bridge has the longest span of any other suspension bridge.
   - C Thick cables are best.
   - D The bridge is the most popular bridge in the Bay Area.

2. Which conclusion can you reach by connecting these details: The bridge is a suspension bridge. It is 220 feet above the water. It has towers.
   - A The bridge is not very big.
   - B The bridge will not stand for long.
   - C The bridge is visible from far away.
   - D The bridge is very unusual.

3. Which detail supports the conclusion that lots of traffic can move across the bridge?
   - A The bridge hangs from thick cables and is 220 feet above the water.
   - B The towers peek through the fog and are a symbol of San Francisco.
   - C The bridge spans San Francisco Bay and connects San Francisco to northern California.
   - D The bridge has six lanes for traffic and sidewalks for pedestrians.

4. Which conclusion is best supported?
   - A The writer likes other bridges better.
   - B The writer admires the Golden Gate Bridge.
   - C The writer likes bridges.
   - D The writer thinks the Golden Gate Bridge is the best.

Timed Writing: Interpretation [Critical Stance]

Review the poems in *Poetry Collection 1* or *Poetry Collection 2.* Interpret the theme or message of one poem. Support your interpretation by referring to specific words, phrases, and lines from the poem. **(25 minutes)**

 ## Writing Workshop: *Work in Progress*

Writing for Assessment
Using the list from your writing portfolio, number the supporting ideas. Use number 1 for the most important idea. Use that as the topic sentence of a paragraph. Write the paragraph in five minutes.

Reading Informational Materials

Advertisements

In Part 1, you are learning about drawing conclusions in literature. Drawing conclusions is also useful in reading advertisements. If you read the poem "Fog," you can connect the imagery of a cat's paws with comfortable feet in these advertisements.

About Advertisements

An **advertisement** is a paid message intended to attract customers for products or services. Advertisements appear on television, radio, and Web sites, and in newspapers and magazines. The language and artwork in advertisements may contain hidden messages and other persuasive techniques that are meant to convince consumers to purchase a product.

Reading Skill

To avoid drawing false conclusions about the benefits of a product or service, learn to **recognize propaganda techniques** and **faulty reasoning. Propaganda** is information that is one-sided or misleading. **Faulty reasoning** is an argument that does not follow the rules of logic: Points are supported with unrelated details or by suggesting connections that do not exist. The chart shows examples of these problems. Challenge advertisements that are based only on these types of claims.

Propaganda Technique	Explanation	Example
Broad generalizations	Sweeping claims that cannot be proved	"There's nothing like it in the world!"
Hidden messages	Pictures or words that convey an idea without stating it directly	A photo of an Olympic runner, suggesting you'll be a winner if you buy a certain brand of sneakers
Loaded language	Words that appeal to our emotions	"It's a miracle product!"
Bandwagon appeals	Implying that "everyone else" uses a certain product	"Thousands of allergy sufferers use Sneeze-Free."
Faulty reasoning	Using unrelated or unconnected details as support	More people have cats than dogs, so cats must be easier to take care of.

A Season of Fun for Everyone!

Jump into these sports shoes that let your feet enjoy life—and notice the difference they make in your day! No sissy footing here when there's hiking, picnicking or gardening to do. In many styles the Ball-Band scientific Arch-Gard* cradles your feet so leg muscles keep fresh when you're on the go.

And how those soles grip and help sure-footedness — how the rubber treads wear, and wear. Yes—for dad, mother, sister and brother—Ball-Band casual style and down-to-earth comfort is great for the outdoors when you want to forget your feet.

Naturally—Ball-Band for youngsters, too. These shoes give every active toe a chance for normal use and development. So make foot health the style—*your* family's style this summer. Nothing could be smarter to wear than Ball-Band. See the complete line at your favorite shoe store.

The hidden message in this picture is that wearing these shoes will provide family fun and recreation.

For every foot of the Family —Every step of the way

PREMIER . . . an Arch-Gard shoe in black or brown for father and son.

Broad generalizations claim that these shoes are good for everyone.

ARCADIA . . . in blue and red for sister and the toddlers.

CROWN . . . an Arch-Gard Oxford in blue or white for every member of the family.

ARCH-GARD*
GUARDS YOUR FEET AT ALL **3** VITAL POINTS

Cushions Metatarsal Arch

Cushions Long Arch

Cushions Heel Bone

The Ball-Band Arch-Gard firmly but gently supports foot muscles and bones in their most natural, comfortable position. It is scientifically "graded to size" in the last over which the shoes are made, so all three cushions are correctly placed for every member of the family.

The company makes scientific claims that are not proved.

Ball-Band
MISHAWAKA, INDIANA

Look for the Red Ball in the store and on the sole of the shoe.

TRADE MARK

Reg. U. S. Pat. Off. 1901

It's amazing what you can learn from a twelve-year-old!

The picture is meant to persuade readers that even twelve-year-olds know how comfortable this product is.

Our twelve-year-old likes to pick her own clothes and does it mighty well. She's the one who picked NEOLITE for her shoes.

"It'll save you money, Mummy!" she said. She was right.

NEOLITE Soles outlast any sole I ever saw. But they offer more than wear for my shoes—and for her father's, too.

This statement is a broad generalization that uses loaded language.

...ch further! Yes, easy-going ...twice the wear of leather! And ...g-in. They're flexible from the ...provide a firm platform for ...er how you look at it, NEOLITE ...for every type of shoe, every ...y!

INSIST ON GENUINE NEOLITE

The name is always plainly marked on the shank

NEOLITE SOLES

NEOLITE, AN ELASTOMER-RESIN BLEND. T.M.—THE GOODYEAR TIRE & RUBBER COMPANY, AKRON, OHIO

MAKE ANY SHOE A BETTER SHOE—ANY REPAIR JOB A BETTER JOB!

"Store-Window Beauty" lasts longer when soles are NEOLITE! So light, so firm—this wonder sole is a joy to designers of many famous-make shoes. NEOLITE makes possible a new daintiness at the instep, beauty of finish and lasting good looks! NEOLITE Soles are damp-proof, too—won't let wet weather twist your shoes out of shape.

Reading: Draw Conclusions

Directions: *Choose the letter of the best answer.*

1. Based on the Ball-Band ad, what can you conclude that these shoes will do for you?
   - **A** Heal all your foot problems.
   - **B** Allow you to have more fun with your family.
   - **C** Make you more popular.
   - **D** Make you run faster.

2. Which statement is a broad generalization that cannot be proved?
   - **A** Look for the Red Ball in the store.
   - **B** NEOLITE soles make any shoe a better shoe. . . .
   - **C** Premier . . . an Arch-Gard shoe in black or brown for father and son.
   - **D** She's the one who picked NEOLITE for her shoes.

3. Which statement is most accurate?
   - **A** Only the first ad uses propaganda techniques.
   - **B** Only the second ad uses propaganda techniques.
   - **C** Both ads use propaganda techniques.
   - **D** Neither ad uses propaganda techniques.

Reading: Comprehension and Interpretation

Directions: *Write your answers on a separate sheet of paper.*

4. Which words in the advertisements appeal to reader's emotions? Why do the writers use these words? **[Analysis]**

5. Explain how the aim of the Ball-Band ad differs from that of the Neolite ad. **[Organizing]**

6. Why do you think the price of the Ball-Band shoes or the Neolite soles is not stated in the advertisements? **[Generating]**

Timed Writing: Description [Connections]

Use the information in the Ball-Band ad to describe another product that the company might sell. Include the name of the product and its positive features. Describe one propaganda technique, including sample words or phrases, that the company may use in an advertisement for this product.
(15 minutes)

Narrative Poetry

Narrative poetry combines elements of fiction and poetry to tell a story.

- Like short stories, narrative poetry usually includes characters, setting, plot, conflict, and point of view.
- Like other poems, narrative poetry uses sound devices like rhythm and rhyme to bring out the musical qualities of language. It also uses figurative language to create memorable images or word pictures.

Narrative poetry is well suited to a wide range of stories. For example, narrative poems may tell about heroic deeds, amazing events, or larger-than-life characters. In contrast, the form may also be used to relate everyday stories about ordinary people.

Comparing Narrative Poems

The poems presented here blend elements of fiction and poetry in a memorable way. As you read the poems in this collection, look for ways in which they each demonstrate elements of narration and poetry. Note your ideas on a chart like this one.

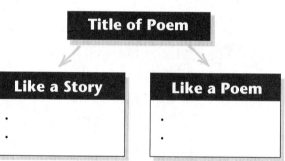

Vocabulary Builder

The Highwayman

- **torrent** (tôr´ ənt) *n.* flood (p. 558) *In the storm, a <u>torrent</u> washed the bridge away.*

- **bound** (bound) *v.* tied (p. 559) *To make the raft, we <u>bound</u> boards with rope.*

- **strive** (strīv) *v.* struggle (p. 560) *Jay will <u>strive</u> to finish the marathon.*

The Cremation of Sam McGee

- **whimper** (hwim´ pər) *v.* make low, crying sounds (p. 564) *I heard the hungry kitten <u>whimper</u> outside my door.*

- **loathed** (lōthd) *v.* hated (p. 565) *As a child, I <u>loathed</u> cleaning but liked my other family chores.*

How I Learned English

- **transfixed** (trans fikst´) *adj.* rooted to the spot (p. 568) *<u>Transfixed</u> by the headlights, the deer could not move.*

- **writhing** (rīth´ iŋ) *adj.* squirming, often in response to pain (p. 568) *<u>Writhing</u> after I twisted my ankle, I screamed for help.*

Build Understanding

Connecting to the Literature

Reading/Writing Connection "The Highwayman" and "The Cremation of Sam McGee" are narrative poems with rhythm and rhyme. Write a few sentences to explain what you think are the pros and cons of using rhythm and rhyme to tell a story. Use three of the following words: *benefit, establish, interpret, achieve, emphasize.*

Meet the Authors

Alfred **Noyes** (1880–1958)

The Englishman Alfred Noyes was a poet and a critic. Despite his great love for England's history and landscape, he moved to New Jersey to teach at Princeton University. There, he continued writing poems about legendary figures like Robin Hood.

Robert **Service** (1874–1958)

Born in England and raised in Scotland, Robert Service went to Canada at age twenty to work for a bank. In the Yukon Territory, he met fur trappers and gold prospectors. Leaving the bank, Service traveled in the Arctic, where he observed the people and recorded his adventures. "The Cremation of Sam McGee" grew out of these experiences.

Gregory **Djanikian** (b. 1949)

Born in Alexandria, Egypt, Gregory Djanikian moved to the U.S. at age eight with his family. Today he directs a creative writing program at the University of Pennsylvania and runs poetry workshops. Djanikian's experiences of immigrating and tackling a new language provided ideas for poems such as "How I Learned English."

Go **Online**
Author Link

For: More about the poets
Visit: www.PHSchool.com
Web Code: eme-9406

The Highwayman

Alfred Noyes

Background This poem takes place centuries ago, when highways were just dirt roads, and *highwayman* meant "robber." Travelers on horseback or in carriages stopped at inns to eat, sleep, and avoid the dangers of isolated highways in the dark of night. Although travelers feared outlaws, many—like Robin Hood, Pancho Villa, and Jesse James—became legendary.

Part One

The wind was a <u>torrent</u> of darkness among the gusty trees.
The moon was a ghostly galleon[1] tossed upon cloudy seas.
The road was a ribbon of moonlight over the purple moor,[2]
And the highwayman came riding—
5   Riding—riding—
The highwayman came riding, up to the old inn door.

He'd a French cocked-hat on his forehead, a bunch of
    lace at his chin,
A coat of the claret velvet, and breeches of brown doeskin.
They fitted with never a wrinkle. His boots were up to the
    thigh.
10 And he rode with a jeweled twinkle,
            His pistol butts a-twinkle,
His rapier hilt[3] a-twinkle, under the jeweled sky.

Over the cobbles he clattered and clashed in the dark
    innyard.
He tapped with his whip on the shutters, but all was
    locked and barred.
15 He whistled a tune to the window, and who should be
    waiting there
But the landlord's black-eyed daughter,

---

1. **galleon** (gal´ ē ən) *n.* large Spanish sailing ship.
2. **moor** (mŏŏr) *n.* open, rolling land with swamps.
3. **rapier** (rā´ pē ər) **hilt** large cup-shaped handle of a rapier, which is a type of sword.

Vocabulary Builder
torrent (tôr´ ənt) *n.*
flood

Literary Analysis
Narrative Poetry
What details of the setting are revealed here?

Bess, the landlord's daughter,
Plaiting a dark red love knot into her long black hair.

And dark in the dark old innyard a stable wicket creaked
20 Where Tim the ostler listened. His face was white and
peaked.
His eyes were hollows of madness, his hair like moldy hay,
But he loved the landlord's daughter,
The landlord's red-lipped daughter.
Dumb as a dog he listened, and he heard the robber say—
25 "One kiss, my bonny[4] sweetheart, I'm after a prize tonight,
But I shall be back with the yellow gold before the
morning light;
Yet, if they press me sharply, and harry me through the day,
Then look for me by moonlight,
Watch for me by moonlight,
30 I'll come to thee by moonlight, though hell should bar the
way."

He rose upright in the stirrups. He scarce could reach her
hand,
But she loosened her hair in the casement.[5] His face
burnt like a brand[6]
As the black cascade of perfume came tumbling over his
breast;
And he kissed its waves in the moonlight,
(O, sweet black waves in the moonlight!)
35 Then he tugged at his rein in the moonlight, and galloped
away to the west.

Part Two
He did not come in the dawning. He did not come at noon;
And out of the tawny sunset, before the rise of the moon,
When the road was a gypsy's ribbon, looping the purple moor,
40 A redcoat troop came marching—
Marching—marching—
King George's men[7] came marching, up to the old inn door.

They said no word to the landlord. They drank his ale instead
But they gagged his daughter, and <u>bound</u> her, to the foot of
her narrow bed.

---

4. **bonny** (bän´ ē) *adj.* Scottish for "pretty."
5. **casement** (kās´ mənt) *n.* window frame that opens on hinges.
6. **brand** (brand) *n.* piece of burning wood.
7. **King George's men** soldiers serving King George of England.

Literary Analysis
Narrative Poetry
What do you know so far about the main characters in this narrative poem?

Vocabulary Builder
bound (bound) *v.* tied

Reading Check

What did Tim overhear?

45 Two of them knelt at her casement, with muskets at their
    side!
There was death at every window;
            And hell at one dark window;
For Bess could see, through her casement, the road that
    he would ride.

They had tied her up to attention, with many a sniggering
    jest.[8]
50 They had bound a musket beside her, with the muzzle
    beneath her breast!
"Now, keep good watch!" and they kissed her. She heard
    the doomed man say—
Look for me by moonlight;
            Watch for me by moonlight;
I'll come to thee by moonlight, though hell should bar the
    way!

55 She twisted her hands behind her; but all the knots held
    good!
She writhed her hands till her fingers were wet with
    sweat or blood!
They stretched and strained in the darkness, and the
    hours crawled by like years,
Till, now, on the stroke of midnight,
            Cold, on the stroke of midnight,
60 The tip of one finger touched it! The trigger at least was
    hers!

The tip of one finger touched it. She strove no more for
    the rest.
Up, she stood up to attention, with the muzzle beneath
    her breast.
She would not risk their hearing; she would not <u>strive</u>
    again;
For the road lay bare in the moonlight;
65   Blank and bare in the moonlight;
And the blood of her veins, in the moonlight, throbbed to
    her love's refrain.

Tlot-tlot; tlot-tlot! Had they heard it? The horsehoofs
    ringing clear;

Literary Analysis
Narrative Poetry
What motivates the soldiers to mistreat Bess?

Literary Analysis
Narrative Poetry
How does line 60 build suspense in the narrative?

Vocabulary Builder
strive (strīv) *v.* struggle

---

8. sniggering (snig´ ər iŋ) **jest** sly joke.

Tlot-tlot, tlot-tlot, in the distance? Were they deaf that
   they did not hear?
Down the ribbon of moonlight, over the brow of the hill,
70 The highwayman came riding—
              Riding—riding—
The redcoats looked to their priming![9] She stood up,
   straight and still.

Tlot-tlot, in the frosty silence! Tlot-tlot, in the echoing night!
Nearer he came and nearer. Her face was like a light.
75 Her eyes grew wide for a moment; she drew one last deep
   breath,
Then her finger moved in the moonlight,
              Her musket shattered the moonlight,
Shattered her breast in the moonlight and warned him—
   with her death.

He turned. He spurred to the west; he did not know who
   stood
80 Bowed, with her head o'er the musket, drenched with her
   own blood!
Not till the dawn he heard it, and his face grew gray to hear
How Bess, the landlord's daughter,
              The landlord's black-eyed daughter,

9. **priming** (prī´ min) *n.* explosive used to set off the charge in a gun.

✓ Reading Check

How does Bess warn the highwayman?

Had watched for her love in the moonlight, and died in
    the darkness there.

85 Back, he spurred like a madman, shouting a curse to the
    sky,
With the white road smoking behind him and his rapier
    brandished[10] high.
Blood-red were his spurs in the golden noon; wine-red
    was his velvet coat;
When they shot him down on the highway,
          Down like a dog on the highway,
90 And he lay in his blood on the highway, with a bunch of
    lace at his throat.

And still of a winter's night, they say, when the wind is in
    the trees,
When the moon is a ghostly galleon tossed upon cloudy seas,
When the road is a ribbon of moonlight over the purple moor,
A highwayman comes riding—
95   *Riding—riding—*
A highwayman comes riding, up to the old inn door.

Over the cobbles he clatters and clangs in the dark innyard.
He taps with his whip on the shutters, but all is locked
    and barred.
He whistles a tune to the window, and who should be
    waiting there
100 *But the landlord's black-eyed daughter,*
          Bess, the landlord's daughter,
Plaiting a dark red love knot into her long black hair.

Literary Analysis
Narrative Poetry
What type of figurative language is used in this stanza?

---

10. brandished (bran´ dishd) *adj.* waved in a threatening way.

Thinking About the Selection

1. **(a) Recall:** At the beginning of the narrative, how does the highwayman tell Bess he has arrived? **(b) Infer:** What does this method of communication tell you about their relationship?

2. **(a) Recall:** Identify three details that make the highwayman appear a romantic figure. **(b) Compare and Contrast:** How do these details compare with the details about Tim the ostler, or stable worker?

3. **Draw Conclusions:** What do the last two stanzas suggest about the love between Bess and the highwayman?

The Cremation of Sam McGee

Robert Service

Background In this poem, two men prospect for gold in Canada's Yukon Territory. Located just east of Alaska, where the temperature can reach −60°F, the area long attracted fortune hunters who came for its mineral wealth. Gold was discovered in the Klondike River region in the 1890s, and many people, including poet Robert Service, came to look for it.

There are strange things done in the midnight sun
    By the men who moil[1] for gold;
The Arctic trails have their secret tales
    That would make your blood run cold;
5 The Northern Lights have seen queer sights,
    But the queerest they ever did see
Was that night on the marge[2] of Lake Lebarge
    I cremated Sam McGee.

Now Sam McGee was from Tennessee,
    where the cotton blooms and blows
10 Why he left his home in the South to roam
    'round the Pole, God only knows.
He was always cold, but the land of gold
    seemed to hold him like a spell;
Though he'd often say in his homely way
    that "he'd sooner live in hell."

On a Christmas Day we were mushing our way
    over the Dawson trail.
Talk of your cold! through the parka's fold
    it stabbed like a driven nail.

▲ **Critical Viewing**
Why do you think people in the Arctic, like the men in this poem, travel by dog sled as pictured here? **[Hypothesize]**

**Reading Check**

Why is Sam McGee in the Arctic?

---

1. moil (moil) *v.* toil and slave.
2. marge (märj) *n.* poetic word for the shore of the lake.

15 If our eyes we'd close, then the lashes froze
        til sometimes we couldn't see;
    It wasn't much fun, but the only one
        to <u>whimper</u> was Sam McGee.

    And that very night, as we lay packed tight
        in our robes beneath the snow,
    And the dogs were fed, and the stars o'erhead
        were dancing heel and toe,
    He turned to me, and "Cap," says he,
        "I'll cash in this trip, I guess;
20 And if I do, I'm asking that you
        won't refuse my last request."

    Well, he seemed so low that I couldn't say no;
        then he says with a sort of moan:
    "It's the cursed cold, and it's got right hold
        till I'm chilled clean through to the bone.
    Yet 'tain't being dead—it's my awful dread
        of the icy grave that pains;
    So I want you to swear that, foul or fair,
        you'll cremate my last remains."

25 A pal's last need is a thing to heed,
        so I swore I would not fail;
    And we started on at the streak of dawn;
        but God! he looked ghastly pale.
    He crouched on the sleigh, and he raved all day
        of his home in Tennessee;
    And before nightfall a corpse was all
        that was left of Sam McGee.

    There wasn't a breath in that land of death,
        and I hurried, horror-driven,
30 With a corpse half hid that I couldn't get rid,
        because of a promise given;
    It was lashed to the sleigh, and it seemed to say:
        "You may tax your brawn[3] and brains,
    But you promised true, and it's up to you
        to cremate those last remains."

---

3. **brawn** (brôn) *n.* physical strength.

Vocabulary Builder
whimper (hwim′ pər)
v. make low, crying
sounds

Literary Analysis
Narrative Poetry
Why does McGee
want to be cremated?

▲ **Critical Viewing**
How well does this
picture capture the
landscape described
in the poem?
[Evaluate]

Now a promise made is a debt unpaid,
    and the trail has its own stern code.
In the days to come, though my lips were dumb,
    in my heart how I cursed that load.
35 In the long, long night, by the lone firelight,
    while the huskies, round in a ring,
Howled out their woes to the homeless snows—
    O God! how I <u>loathed</u> the thing.
And every day that quiet clay
    seemed to heavy and heavier grow;
And on I went, though the dogs were spent
    and the grub was getting low;
The trail was bad, and I felt half mad,
    but I swore I would not give in;
40 And I'd often sing to the hateful thing,
    and it hearkened with a grin.

Till I came to the marge of Lake Lebarge,
    and a derelict[4] there lay;
It was jammed in the ice, but I saw in a trice
    it was called the "Alice May."
And I looked at it, and I thought a bit,
    and I looked at my frozen chum;
Then "Here," said I, with a sudden cry,
    "is my cre-ma-tor-eum."

45 Some planks I tore from the cabin floor,
    and I lit the boiler fire;
Some coal I found that was lying around,
    and I heaped the fuel higher;
The flames just soared, and the furnace roared—
    such a blaze you seldom see;
And I burrowed a hole in the glowing coal,
    and I stuffed in Sam McGee.

Then I made a hike, for I didn't like
    to hear him sizzle so;
50 And the heavens scowled, and the huskies howled,
    and the wind began to blow.

Vocabulary Builder
loathed (lōth͟d) *v.*
hated

Literary Analysis
Narrative Poetry
What problem, or conflict, does the speaker face?

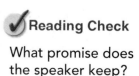

Reading Check

What promise does the speaker keep?

---

4. **derelict** (der´ ə likt´) *n.* abandoned ship.

It was icy cold, but the hot sweat rolled
    down my cheeks, and I don't know why;
And the greasy smoke in an inky cloak
    went streaking down the sky.

I do not know how long in the snow
    I wrestled with grisly fear;
But the stars came out and they danced about
    ere again I ventured near;
55 I was sick with dread, but I bravely said:
    "I'll just take a peep inside.
I guess he's cooked, and it's time I looked"; . . .
    then the door I opened wide.

And there sat Sam, looking cool and calm,
    in the heart of the furnace roar;
And he wore a smile you could see a mile,
    and he said: "Please close that door.
It's fine in here, but I greatly fear
    you'll let in the cold and storm—
60 Since I left Plumtree, down in Tennessee,
    it's the first time I've been warm."

There are strange things done in the midnight sun
    By the men who moil for gold;
The Arctic trails have their secret tales
    That would make your blood run cold;
65 *The Northern Lights have seen queer sights,*
    But the queerest they ever did see
Was that night on the marge of Lake Lebarge
    I cremated Sam McGee.

Literary Analysis
Narrative Poetry
What type of figurative language does the poet use in this stanza?

Thinking About the Selection

1. **(a) Recall:** What problem does Sam have with his surroundings? **(b) Deduce:** What prevents him from going home?

2. **(a) Recall:** Who is the speaker, and what does he promise Sam? **(b) Interpret:** Why is the speaker so determined to keep his promise?

3. **(a) Recall:** What does the speaker find when he opens the furnace door? **(b) Infer:** What reaction does the poet expect you to have to this unexpected occurrence?

How I Learned English

Gregory Djanikian

It was in an empty lot
Ringed by elms and fir and honeysuckle.
Bill Corson was pitching in his buckskin[1] jacket,
Chuck Keller, fat even as a boy, was on first,
His t-shirt riding up over his gut,
Ron O'Neill, Jim, Dennis, were talking it up
In the field, a blue sky above them
Tipped with cirrus.[2]
And there I was,
Just off the plane and plopped in the middle
Of Williamsport, Pa., and a neighborhood game,
Unnatural and without any moves,
My notions of baseball and America
Growing fuzzier each time I whiffed.[3]

So it was not impossible that I,
Banished to the outfield and daydreaming
Of water, or a hotel in the mountains,
Would suddenly find myself in the path

Literary Analysis
Narrative Poetry
Describe the setting of this poem in your own words.

1. **buckskin** *adj.* yellowish-gray leather made from the hide of a deer.
2. **cirrus** (sir′ əs) *n.* high, thin clouds.
3. **whiffed** (hwift) *v.* struck out.

▼ Critical Viewing
Does this boy look as if he might be the speaker or one of the other players on the team? Explain. **[Analyze]**

Of a ball stung[4] by Joe Barone.
20 I watched it closing in
Clean and untouched, <u>transfixed</u>
By its easy arc before it hit
My forehead with a thud.
                    I fell back.
25 Dazed, clutching my brow,
Groaning, "Oh my shin, oh my shin,"
And everybody peeled away from me
And dropped from laughter, and there we were,
All of us <u>writhing</u> on the ground for one reason
30 Or another.
                    Someone said "shin" again,
There was a wild stamping of hands on the ground,
A kicking of feet, and the fit
Of laughter overtook me too,
35 And that was important, as important
As Joe Barone asking me how I was
Through his tears, picking me up
And dusting me off with hands like swatters,
And though my head felt heavy,
40 I played on till dusk
Missing flies and pop-ups and grounders
And calling out in desperation things like
"Yours" and "take it," but doing all right,
Tugging at my cap in just the right way,
45 Crouching low, my feet set,
"Hum baby" sweetly on my lips.

---

4. stung *v.* hit hard.

Vocabulary Builder
transfixed (trans fikst´)
adj. rooted to the
spot

writhing (rīth´ iŋ) *adj.*
squirming, often in
response to pain

Literary Analysis
Narrative Poetry
What happens to the
speaker, and how
does he react?

Thinking About the Selection

1. **(a) Recall:** What details in lines 1–9 tell you a baseball game is underway? **(b) Infer:** Why does the speaker have trouble with the game?

2. **(a) Recall:** What does the speaker do when he is hit in the head with the baseball? **(b) Interpret:** Why do the others laugh?

3. **(a) Recall:** What help does Joe Barone offer the speaker?
   (b) Interpret: Why does the speaker choose to continue playing?

4. **Speculate:** Do you think the speaker learned English by playing baseball? Explain.

Apply the Skills

**The Highwayman • The Cremation of Sam McGee •
How I Learned English**

Comparing Narrative Poetry

1. Use a chart like this to find in each narrative poem at least one
   example of each element common in short stories.

Short Story Element	Poem	Poem	Poem
Setting			
Characters			
Conflict (problem to be solved)			
Outcome of conflict			

2. What sound devices or musical elements can you identify in
   each of the three narrative poems?

3. How would "The Cremation of Sam McGee" differ if it were
   told in free verse instead of in rhyme?

Writing to Compare Literary Works

In an essay, compare and contrast the ways stories are told in each of
the three narrative poems. Use these questions to get started:

- Who narrates each of the poems—someone in the story or
  someone outside the story?
- What kind of suspense, if any, does each poem present?
- How do poetic elements increase your interest or appreciation
  for the story?

Vocabulary Builder

Practice Use each word pair correctly in a sentence.

1. torrent; survivors
2. bound; released
3. strive; overcome
4. whimper; annoy
5. loathed; removed
6. transfixed; scenery
7. writhing; earthworm

QuickReview

Narrative poetry:
poetry that tells a
story, often with char-
acters, setting, plot,
conflict, and point of
view

Go Online
Assessment
For: Self-test
Visit: www.PHSchool.com
Web Code: ema-6406

Reading

Directions: *Questions 1–5 are based on the following selection.*

The auditorium was filled to capacity for the Autumn Band Concert, the biggest event of the fall in Cedar Corners. Jess nervously looked through his sheet music. Frowning and heaving a sigh, he placed the music on the stand. When the conductor lifted her baton, Jess began to play. The notes came out all wrong, though. The conductor gave him a startled look. She expected Jess to play well, since he was one of her best trumpet players. Finally, Jess gave up and just pretended to play.

After what seemed like an eternity to Jess, the concert ended. The large audience applauded generously. Later, the townspeople and band members gathered in the gym for refreshments. When friends, family members, and neighbors congratulated Jess on the band's performance, he quietly accepted their good wishes. Secretly, though, he just wanted to sneak out and go home.

1. **Based on details in the first paragraph, what can you conclude about Jess?**
   A He was not a very good musician.
   B He had not practiced for the concert.
   C He always enjoyed playing in the band.
   D He did not get along well with the conductor.

2. **Which conclusion about the townspeople is supported by details in the passage?**
   A The townspeople show up for all school events.
   B The townspeople enjoy the Autumn Band Concert.
   C The townspeople all have relatives or friends in the band.
   D The townspeople are fans of all kinds of music.

3. **What can you conclude about Jess at the end of the passage?**
   A He usually liked band performances.
   B He was glad to have the concert behind him.
   C He was annoyed at the conductor.
   D He didn't like the townspeople.

4. **Which two details can you connect in order to conclude that the audience enjoyed the music?**
   A The concert was a big event, and the auditorium was filled to capacity.
   B The conductor expected Jess to play well, and Jess pretended to play.
   C The audience applauded generously, and they congratulated Jess on the band's performance.
   D The auditorium was filled to capacity, and everyone gathered in the gym for refreshments.

Vocabulary

Directions: *Choose the word that best completes each of the following sentences.*

5. We _____ the paragraph into an essay by adding additional supporting details.
   A inferred   C transformed
   B concluded   D detected

6. Tina planned to _____ to her note cards as she gave a speech to the class.
   A infer   C detect
   B refer   D transform

7. After reading all the letters, the mayor had to _____ that the citizens did not want toll roads.
   A conclude   C transform
   B refer   D detect

8. The repairman could not _____ any serious problems with Amy's computer.
   A refer   C detect
   B infer   D conclude

9. One detail in the postcard note led Sal to _____ that his sister was homesick.
   A transform   C infer
   B detect   D refer

Directions: *Based on your knowledge of word parts, choose the best definition.*

10. transatlantic
    A between countries
    B across the Atlantic
    C above the Atlantic
    D under the Atlantic

11. confer
    A to bring together, usually to discuss
    B to look closely, usually at evidence
    C to carry information, usually from one person to another
    D to develop a case, usually in law

12. reference
    A to bring information
    B to find again
    C a large book with many subjects
    D to note

13. transcontinental
    A into the country
    B out of the country
    C across the continent
    D away from the continent

14. transfer
    A cut through
    B not move from one country to another
    C carry from one place to another
    D pass information

Writing for Assessment

You take essay tests and standardized writing tests that evaluate your writing skills. **Writing for assessment** often depends on specific instructions and limited time or space in which to write. Follow the steps in this workshop to practice writing for assessment.

Assignment Write an essay in response to the following prompt or to a prompt your teacher provides:
Choose two Americans, past or present, as role models for today's young people. In a brief essay, compare and contrast the achievements and leadership qualities of these two heroes.

What to Include Your essay should feature the following elements:

- a position that addresses the writing prompt
- clear, concise writing
- evidence supporting the main points of the essay, drawn from your reading or class discussion
- consistent organization
- error-free writing including correct use of verbals

To preview the criteria on which your essay may be judged, see the rubric on page 576.

Using the Form
You may use this form in these types of writing situations:

- unit or chapter tests
- final exams
- state exams
- application essays

Prewriting

Spend about one quarter of your time prewriting.

Identify Your Purpose

Analyze the Question Circle key words in the prompt to identify exactly what the question is asking. The chart shown here indicates what common verbs ask you to do.

Key Word	Writing Direction
Analyze	Examine how parts contribute to the whole.
Compare and Contrast	Explain similarities and differences.
Discuss	Support a generalization with facts and examples.
Explain	Clarify by providing reasons, causes, and effects.

Work in Progress
Review the work you did on pages 513, 533, and 551.

Gathering Details

List the right information for your answer. The information you prepare before you draft will help you write a strong essay. Based on the question, jot down key elements of your answers.

Drafting

Spend about half of your time drafting your essay.

Shaping Your Writing

Find a focus. Use the details you have gathered to formulate a sentence that states your thesis, or main idea. Prepare a quick list that identifies at least two main points you will use to support your thesis.

Providing Elaboration

Add details to strengthen your writing. As you draft, look for places where you can add a variety of supporting details. Consider adding facts, examples, or descriptions that you remember from your reading or class discussions.

Detail: students get together with classmates and friends

Focus: A school book club will encourage reading.

Detail: members recommend books they like

Detail: lively and interesting discussions

Revising

Spend about one quarter of your time revising.

Revising Your Overall Structure

Comparing the Question With the Answer Your essay will be judged mainly on how well you answer the test question. Check that you have followed the instructions in the question. Check the numbers and review the tasks.

Revising Your Word Choice

Identifying Main Ideas and Support Readers expect to find a clear main idea supported by relevant details. For each paragraph, identify the main idea. This is often stated in the topic sentence. If a paragraph does not have a topic sentence, add one for clarity. Next, check the details in each paragraph. Neatly cross out sentences that do not support the main idea. Consider replacing them with sentences offering more effective support.

To read the complete student model, see page 575.

Student Model: Revising to Identify Main Ideas and Support

I could interest future explorers to go on these quests and help discover things for the world. Exploring is beneficial for everybody. Without early explorers, the United States might not exist.

Without Lewis and Clark, we may never have known enough about the new land to interest settlers in moving there.

> Jason adds relevant details to support to his main idea.

Integrating Grammar Skills

Revising Sentences by Adding Verbals

A verbal is any verb that is used in a sentence not as a verb, but as another part of speech. Using verbals can help you avoid choppy sentences.

Identifying Verbals One type of verbal is a **participle**. A participle is often used as an adjective, modifying a noun or pronoun. It can stand alone or be part of a phrase.

- Present participles end in *-ing.*

Prentice Hall Writing and Grammar Connection: Chapter 20, Section 1

PRESENT PARTICIPLE   NOUN

Running, the mischievous boy snatched her purse.

- Past participles usually end in *-ed,* but may have an irregular ending, such as *-en* in *spoken.*

PAST PARTICIPLE   NOUN

She banged her fist against the closed window.

Fixing Choppy Passages by Using Verbals To fix a choppy passage, identify sentences that can be combined. Then rewrite the passage using one or more of the following methods:

1. **Combine sentences using a present participle.**

   ▶ **Example:** We arranged a tour. We would walk the grounds.
   We arranged a walking tour of the grounds.

2. **Combine sentences using a past participle.**

   ▶ **Example:** The food is cooked. It will not spoil.
   The cooked food will not spoil.

Apply It to Your Editing

Choose three paragraphs in your draft. Read the paragraphs aloud, highlighting any passages that sound choppy. Then, using one of the methods above, fix the choppy passages by combining sentences.

Student Model: Jason Allen, Meridian, ID

Writing Prompt: Write an essay in which you explain where or what you would like to explore. Be sure to clarify why this exploration is important to you or your community/world.

If I were an explorer, I would wish to explore the uncharted land of Antarctica. I believe we could be doing something with this land, other than throwing nuclear weapons at it for tests as we have in the past. If we could somehow learn to sustain life there, wouldn't that be something?

> Jason's introduction clearly identifies his focus.

It would be quite interesting to see the different things that people have been discovering in Antarctica, such as the meteorites from Mars that have landed in the region several times. The meteorites show possibility of primitive Martian life. Scientists have also built a seismic observatory eight kilometers from the South Pole because it is the quietest listening post on the planet. Two new species of dinosaur have been found in fossilized bone beneath the Arctic surface. These discoveries are only some of the hundreds that have been made in Antarctica. I know more discoveries can be made, and I would be happy to go and explore it to see what else we can do with the continent.

I believe it is adventure that drives explorers to keep exploring, and I believe I would find much of it in Antarctica. I believe I could do something useful there, and I have always wanted to be able to do that. I could look forward to the many nights I would spend on the beautiful continent. I love snow, and I would be sure to see that in Antarctica which is a yearlong winter wonderland. During my visit, I would hope to make a difference in the world for the better. Isn't that what all explorers want?

> Jason gives evidence to support his main point.

I would start my journey by sailing through the Weddell Sea until we hit Antarctic land. I would then travel to the center of Antarctica where many of the meteorite discoveries have taken place. I would love to get my hand on some of those meteorites and see what they are really like. I would bring drilling equipment and discover what is underneath the layers of snow and ice. I wonder if I could find fossils in the layers and discover ancient life we have never seen before.

Some manufacturing processes require cold temperatures, which is expensive to create in warmer climates. I would like to explore possible manufacturing processes that could be carried out more cost-effectively by using the naturally cold environment. While planning a trip there, I would plan for additional experiments I could do on my visit to further explore Antarctica.

> Here, Jason addresses the second part of the writing prompt by discussing the value of his exploration to the world.

I could interest future explorers to go on these quests and help discover things for the world. Exploring is beneficial for everybody. Without Lewis and Clark, we may never have known enough about the new land to interest settlers in moving there. Without early explorers, the United States might not exist. I can only hope that my exploration of Antarctica would be as dramatic, but I know I could make some impact on the world. And that's reason enough for me to explore.

> Jason concludes with a restatement of the importance of his exploration.

Editing and Proofreading

Review your draft to eliminate errors in grammar, spelling, or punctuation.

Focus on Complete Sentences: Look over each sentence in your draft. Read it by itself, starting at the beginning and ending at the period. Ask: *Does this sentence express a complete thought?* If not, correct the sentence by adding a subject or a verb, or by connecting it to another sentence.

Publishing and Presenting

Consider one of these ideas for sharing your work:
Organize a class discussion. In a small group, compare your essay with those of classmates. In your discussion, talk about how using rubrics can help you improve your work.
Prepare for future exams. As you get ready for a writing test, review your work to recall the strategies that worked for you with this assignment.

Reflecting on Your Writing

Writer's Journal Jot down your thoughts on the experience of writing for assessment. Begin by answering these questions:

- Which strategy presented might help you with your next essay test? Explain.
- What are your strengths and weaknesses as a test taker?

> *Prentice Hall Writing and Grammar Connection: Chapter 13*

Rubric for Self-Assessment

To assess your essay, use the following rubric:

Criteria	Rating Scale
	not very very
Focus: How well does your position address the prompt?	1 2 3 4 5
Organization: How consistent and logical is your organization?	1 2 3 4 5
Support/Elaboration: How well does the evidence support your main points?	1 2 3 4 5
Style: How clear and concise is your writing?	1 2 3 4 5
Conventions: How correct is your grammar, especially your use of participles?	1 2 3 4 5

Paraphrasing

Skills You Will Learn

Literature You Will Read

Reading: Paraphrasing

▶ **Paraphrasing** is restating, in your own words, something you have read.

Skills and Strategies You Will Learn in Part 2

In Part 2, you will learn

- to **read aloud** according to punctuation to identify complete thoughts in order to **paraphrase**. (p. 580)
- to **reread to clarify meaning** and to **paraphrase.** (p. 596)
- to **paraphrase**. (p. 614)

Using the Skills and Strategies in Part 2

In Part 2, you will practice using punctuation as you read aloud. Using punctuation will help you group words in long or difficult sentences before putting them into your own words. In addition, you will practice rereading to clarify the meaning of complex passages before paraphrasing them. Paraphrasing a text you have read is a good way to check whether you understand and remember the content of a text. It is also a good note-taking strategy.

Read aloud according to punctuation	Paraphrase by restating in your own words	Reread to make sure the meaning is clear
Keep reading when a line has no end punctuation.	Replace unfamiliar words with familiar synonyms.	Read the lines with the replacement words.
Pause at commas, dashes, and semicolons.	Do not add ideas of your own.	Check that the paraphrased lines make sense.
Stop at end marks.	Include main ideas.	Check content.

Academic Vocabulary: Words for Discussing Paraphrasing

The following words will help you write and talk about paraphrasing as you read the selections in this unit.

Word	Definition	Example Sentence
emphasize *v.*	stress the importance of something	Tran *emphasized* the most important words in the poem.
highlight *v.*	draw attention to something	Tamika used diagrams to *highlight* the important points in her talk.
paraphrase *v.*	restate something in your own words	When I *paraphrase* lines in a poem, it helps me understand their meaning.
restate *v.*	say something again; summarize	Mr. Hong asked Dora to *restate* what she had read in the news article.
passage *n.*	a section of writing	Tad had to read the *passage* several times before he understood it clearly.

Vocabulary Skill: Synonyms

▶ **Synonyms** are words with similar meanings.

In Part 2 you will learn to use synonyms, including
- synonyms for *emphasize*
- synonyms for *paraphrase*

Word	Synonyms	Sample Sentence
emphasize	stress, underline, highlight	Jay looked for new ways to _____ the important points in his paper.
paraphrase	reword, rephrase, restate	Rica was able to _____ the passage so that her little sister could understand it.

Activity Copy the sample sentences choosing one of the synonyms to fill in the blanks. Explain your choice.

You can apply the instruction on this page to these poems.

Poetry Collection 1
Sarah Cynthia Sylvia Stout,
p. 582
Weather, p. 584
One, p. 585

Poetry Collection 2
Full Fathom Five, p. 589
Onomatopoeia, p. 590
Train Tune, p. 591

Reading Skill

When you **paraphrase**, you restate something in your own words. To paraphrase a poem, you must first understand it. **Reading aloud according to punctuation** can help you identify complete thoughts in a poem. Observe the following rules when you read poetry:

- Keep reading when a line has no end punctuation.
- Pause at commas, dashes, and semicolons.
- Stop at periods, question marks, or exclamation points.

As you read, note the punctuation to help you paraphrase.

Literary Analysis

Sound devices create musical effects that appeal to the ear. Here are some common sound devices used in poetry:

- **Onomatopoeia** is the use of words whose sounds suggest their meanings.
- **Alliteration** is the repetition of sounds at the beginning of words.
- **Repetition** is the repeated use of words, phrases, or rhythms.

The chart gives examples of each type of sound device.

Examples
Onomatopoeia
The *shooshing* of skis in the fresh fallen snow;
Alliteration
*m*aggie and *m*illie and *m*olly and *m*ay Went down to the beach (to play one day)
Repetition
To the swinging and the ringing *Of the bells, bells, bells, Of the bells, bells, bells, bells*

Vocabulary Builder

Poetry Collection 1

- **withered** (wi*th*′ ərd) *adj.* dried up (p. 582) *The <u>withered</u> plants badly needed water.*

- **rancid** (ran′ sid) *adj.* spoiled and smelling bad (p. 583) *Food turned <u>rancid</u> in the broken refrigerator.*

- **stutter** (stut′ ər) *v.* to speak in a hesitant or faltering way (p. 585) *Some people <u>stutter</u> when they are nervous.*

Poetry Collection 2

- **spigot** (spig′ ət) *n.* faucet; spout (p. 590) *The dripping <u>spigot</u> made an annoying tapping sound.*

- **sputters** (sput′ ərz) *v.* makes hissing or spitting sounds (p. 590) *The car's engine <u>sputters</u> and dies on rainy days.*

- **groves** (grōvz) *n.* small groups of trees (p. 591) *The farmer planted apple <u>groves</u>.*

Build Understanding • *Poetry Collection 1*

Connecting to the Literature

Reading/Writing Connection Both James Berry and Shel Silverstein describe unique individuals in their poems. In a few sentences, describe the things that make you unique. Use at least three of the following words: *attitude, contribute, dedicate, embody, react.*

Meet the Authors

Shel **Silverstein** (1932–1999)
Sarah Cynthia Sylvia Stout Would Not Take the Garbage Out (p. 582)

    Shel Silverstein was a cartoonist, a composer, a folk singer, and a writer. He began writing poetry at an early age, before he had a chance to study any of the great poets. "I was so lucky that I didn't have anyone to copy," he has said. Silverstein is best known for two books of poetry, *Where the Sidewalk Ends* and *A Light in the Attic.* His poem *"The Unicorn Song"* was recorded by the Irish Rovers.

Eve **Merriam** (1916–1992)
Weather (p. 584)

    Eve Merriam was born and raised in Philadelphia, Pennsylvania. Although she also wrote fiction, nonfiction, and drama, Merriam had a lifelong love of poetry. "I do think poetry is great fun," she said. "That's what I'd like to stress more than anything else: the joy of the sounds of language."

James **Berry** (b. 1925)
One (p. 585)

    James Berry grew up in Jamaica, in a small village by the sea. He learned to read before he was four years old and began writing stories and poems when he got to school. In 1948, Berry moved to England, and soon after that, he began writing seriously. His poems include both English and Creole, the language he spoke growing up in Jamaica.

Go **Online**
Author Link

For: More about the poets
Visit: www.PHSchool.com
Web Code: eme-9409

Poetry

Sarah Cynthia Sylvia Stout Would Not Take the Garbage Out

Shel Silverstein

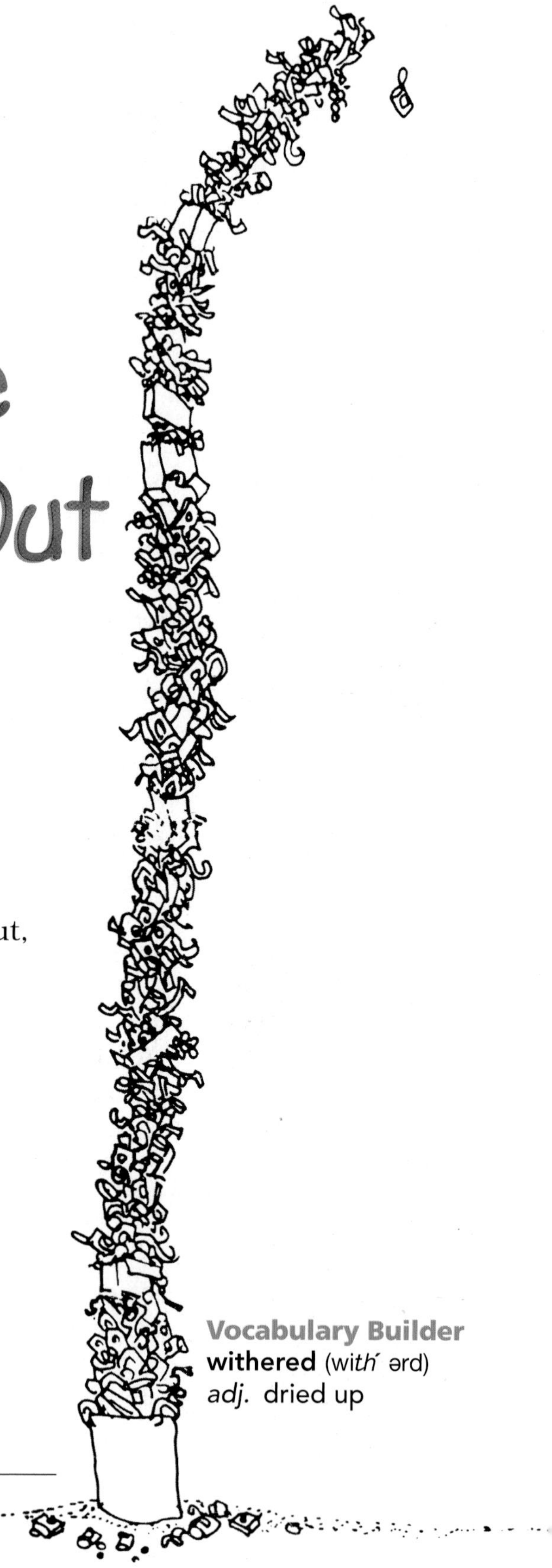

Sarah Cynthia Sylvia Stout
Would not take the garbage out!
She'd scour[1] the pots and scrape the pans,
Candy[2] the yams and spice the hams,
5 And though her daddy would scream and shout,
She simply would not take the garbage out.
And so it piled up to the ceilings:
Coffee grounds, potato peelings,
Brown bananas, rotten peas,
10 Chunks of sour cottage cheese.
It filled the can, it covered the floor,
It cracked the window and blocked the door
With bacon rinds[3] and chicken bones,
Drippy ends of ice cream cones,
15 Prune pits, peach pits, orange peel,
Gloppy glumps of cold oatmeal,
Pizza crusts and <u>withered</u> greens,
Soggy beans and tangerines,
Crusts of black burned buttered toast,

Vocabulary Builder
withered (with′ ərd)
adj. dried up

---

1. scour (skɔur) *v.* clean by rubbing vigorously.
2. candy (kan′ dē) *v.* coat with sugar.
3. rinds (rīndz) *n.* tough outer layers or skins.

20　Gristly bits of beefy roasts . . .
　　The garbage rolled on down the hall,
　　It raised the roof, it broke the wall . . .
　　Greasy napkins, cookie crumbs,
　　Globs of gooey bubblegum,
25　Cellophane from green baloney,
　　Rubbery blubbery macaroni,
　　Peanut butter, caked and dry,
　　Curdled milk and crusts of pie,
　　Moldy melons, dried up mustard,
30　Eggshells mixed with lemon custard,
　　Cold french fries and <u>rancid</u> meat,
　　Yellow lumps of Cream of Wheat.
　　At last the garbage reached so high
　　That finally it touched the sky.
35　And all the neighbors moved away,
　　And none of her friends would come to play.
　　And finally Sarah Cynthia Stout said,
　　"OK, I'll take the garbage out!"
　　But then, of course, it was too late
40　The garbage reached across the state,
　　From New York to the Golden Gate
　　And there, in the garbage she did hate
　　Poor Sarah met an awful fate,
　　That I cannot right now relate[4]
45　Because the hour is much too late.
　　But children, remember Sarah Stout
　　And always take the garbage out!

Literary Analysis
Sound Devices
Which sound device does the poet use in line 24? Explain.

Vocabulary Builder
rancid (ran´sid) *adj.*
spoiled and smelling bad

◀ **Critical Viewing**
The author drew the cartoons that accompany the poem. How does the art add to the humor of the poem?
[Assess]

---

4. relate (ri lāt´) *v.* tell.

Weather

Eve Merriam

Dot a dot dot   dot a dot dot
Spotting the windowpane.
Spack a spack speck   flick a flack fleck
Freckling the windowpane.

5   A spatter a scatter   a wet cat a clatter
A splatter a rumble outside.
Umbrella umbrella umbrella umbrella
Bumbershoot barrel of rain.

Slosh a galosh   slosh a galosh
10 Slither and slather and glide
A puddle a jump a puddle a jump
A puddle a jump puddle splosh
A juddle a pump a luddle a dump a
Puddmuddle jump in and slide!

Literary Analysis
Sound Devices
Which sound devices does the poet use in the last stanza? Explain.

One
James Berry

Only one of me
and nobody can get a second one
from a photocopy machine.

Nobody has the fingerprints I have.
5   Nobody can cry my tears, or laugh my laugh
or have my expectancy when I wait.

But anybody can mimic my dance with my dog.
Anybody can howl how I sing out of tune.
And mirrors can show me multiplied
10   many times, say, dressed up in red
or dressed up in grey.

Nobody can get into my clothes for me
or feel my fall for me, or do my running.
Nobody hears my music for me, either.

15   I am just this one.
Nobody else makes the words
I shape with sound, when I talk.

But anybody can act how I <u>stutter</u> in a rage.
Anybody can copy echoes I make.
20   And mirrors can show me multiplied
many times, say, dressed up in green
or dressed up in blue.

Reading Skill
Paraphrase How does the punctuation help you understand the meaning of lines 9–11?

Vocabulary Builder
stutter (stut´ər) v. speak in a hesitant or faltering way

Apply the Skills

Poetry Collection 1

Thinking About the Selections

1. **Respond:** Which of these poems has the most musical quality? Give examples from the poem to support your answer.
2. **(a) Infer:** What lesson might readers learn from "Sarah Cynthia . . ."? **(b) Analyze:** Do you think the poet intended to teach a lesson? Why or why not?
3. **(a) Recall:** Identify three made-up words in "Weather." **(b) Interpret:** What emotions or qualities do these words bring to the poem? **(c) Discuss:** Share your responses with a partner. Then, discuss how looking at someone else's responses did or did not change your answer.
4. **(a) Recall:** Identify three things that the speaker of "One" says are unique about him. **(b) Interpret:** How do you think the poet feels about the words *mimic* (line 7), *act* (line 18), and *copy* (line 19). Are these good or bad actions? **(c) Connect:** How do these words reinforce the central idea of his poem?

Reading Skill

5. In a chart like this, write an example from each poem in which you read according to punctuation rather than stopping at the end of a line. Then, **paraphrase** each example.

Poem	Example From Poem	Paraphrase
Sarah Cynthia . . .		
Weather		
One		

6. Does reading "One" according to the punctuation increase your understanding of it? Explain.

Literary Analysis

7. **(a)** Find two examples of **alliteration** in "Sarah Cynthia. . . ." **(b)** How does alliteration add to the humor of the poem?
8. **(a)** List two examples of **onomatopoeia** in "Weather" that imitate the sound of water. **(b)** List three words not used in the poem that also imitate the sound of water.
9. **(a)** Identify two examples of **repetition** in "One." **(b)** How does the repetition reinforce the poet's message?

QuickReview

Poems at a Glance
"Sarah Cynthia . . .": A young girl gets into trouble when she does not do her chores.

"Weather": The speaker describes the sounds of rain.

"One": The speaker describes the things that make him unique.

Go Online
Assessment
For: Self-test
Visit: www.PHSchool.com
Web Code: ema-6407

Paraphrase: restate in your own words

Sound Devices: techniques that create musical effects in poetry, such as *onomatopoeia, alliteration,* and *repetition*

Vocabulary Builder

Practice For each set of words, identify the word that does not belong and explain why.

1. shrunken withered swollen
2. rancid fresh stale
3. stutter recite swim

Writing

Write a **poem** called "Alliteration" that defines the term and gives examples of this sound device.

- First, review the definition of alliteration on page 580.
- Next, rewrite the definition in your own words. Then, look for places where you can expand your definition by adding examples of alliteration, such as "<u>S</u>ome <u>s</u>ay it <u>s</u>ounds funny."
- Share your finished poem with a partner.

For *Grammar, Vocabulary,* and *Assessment,* see **Build Language Skills,** on pages 594–595.

Extend Your Learning

Listening and Speaking Present a **poetry reading** of one of the poems from *Poetry Collection 1*. Practice several times, making sure that you are reading according to punctuation.
- read slowly
- read with expression in your voice
- speak clearly
- make eye contact periodically with your audience.

Research and Technology Create a **résumé** for Shel Silverstein, Eve Merriam, or James Berry. Research online to gather information about the poet's education, career, and published works. Do further research to find a standard résumé format. Use the information you have gathered to complete the poet's résumé.

Build Understanding • *Poetry Collection 2*

Connecting to the Literature

Reading/Writing Connection Each of these poems uses sound to create an image or to bring about a certain mood. Think about the effects of certain sounds—for example, birds singing, a creaking door hinge, or a clap of thunder. Identify some familiar sounds and explain how these sounds might change someone's mood. Use at least three of the following words: *affect, persist, contrast, generate.*

Review

For **Reading Skill, Literary Analysis,** and **Vocabulary Builder,** see page 580.

Meet the Authors

William **Shakespeare** (1564–1616)
Full Fathom Five (p. 589)

Many people regard William Shakespeare as the greatest writer in the English language. He wrote thirty-seven plays, many of which are still performed frequently today. They include *Romeo and Juliet, Hamlet,* and other classics. "Full Fathom Five" comes from *The Tempest,* one of Shakespeare's last plays.

Eve **Merriam** (1916–1992)
Onomatopoeia (p. 590)

Eve Merriam's fascination with words began at an early age. "I remember being enthralled by the sound of words," she said. This love, which led her to write poetry, fiction, nonfiction, and drama, is reflected in the poem "Onomatopoeia."

Louise **Bogan** (1897–1970)
Train Tune (p. 591)

Louise Bogan was born in Livermore Falls, Maine, and attended the Boston Girls' Latin School, where she developed an interest in poetry. During her writing career, Bogan became known for her compact use of language and for the traditional form of her poems. Because she was a very private person, Bogan struggled with her celebrity as a highly respected poet, critic, and lecturer.

Go **Online**
Author Link

For: More about the poets
Visit: www.PHSchool.com
Web Code: eme-9401

Full Fathom Five

William Shakespeare

Background "Full Fathom Five" is from Shakespeare's *The Tempest*. In the play, a spirit named Ariel sings these lines to Prince Ferdinand, whose father, King Alonso, is thought lost in a shipwreck. Ariel describes the king's death, though later it is revealed that the king is still alive.

> Full fathom[1] five thy father lies;
>   Of his bones are coral made;
> Those are pearls that were his eyes;
>   Nothing of him that doth fade
> 5   But doth suffer a sea change
> Into something rich and strange.
> Sea nymphs hourly ring his knell;[2]
>   Ding-dong.
> Hark! Now I hear them—ding-dong bell.

---

1. fathom (fa*th*´ əm) *n.* length of six feet used to measure water depth.
2. knell (nel) *n.* funeral bell.

Reading Skill
Paraphrase After which lines do you come to a complete stop when reading?

ONOMATOPOEIA
Eve Merriam

The rusty <u>spigot</u>
<u>sputters</u>,
utters
a splutter,
5   spatters a smattering of drops,
gashes wider;
slash,
splatters,
scatters,
10   spurts,
finally stops sputtering
and plash!
gushes rushes splashes
clear water dashes.

Vocabulary Builder
spigot (spig´ət) *n.*
faucet; spout

sputters (sput´ərz) *v.*
makes hissing or
spitting sounds

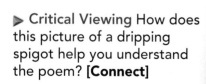

▶ **Critical Viewing** How does
this picture of a dripping
spigot help you understand
the poem? **[Connect]**

Train Tune
Louise Bogan

Back through clouds
Back through clearing
Back through distance
Back through silence

5 Back through groves
Back through garlands
Back by rivers
Back below mountains

Back through lightning
10 Back through cities
Back through stars
Back through hours

Back through plains
Back through flowers
15 Back through birds
Back through rain

Back through smoke
Back through noon
Back along love
20 Back through midnight

Vocabulary Builder
groves (grōvz) *n.*
small groups of trees

▼ **Critical Viewing**
How does the
movement of a steam
train relate to the
rhythm of this poem?
[Connect]

Apply the Skills

Thinking About the Selections

1. **Respond:** Which of these poems has the most musical quality? Give examples from the poem to support your answer.

2. **(a) Recall:** Name two changes that the speaker describes happening to the father in "Full Fathom Five." **(b) Interpret:** Why does the poet call these changes "rich and strange"?

3. **(a) Recall:** Describe the length of the lines in the poem "Onomatopoeia." **(b) Analyze:** How do the line lengths contribute to the effect of the poem on the reader?

4. **(a) Recall:** What emotion does the speaker mention in "Train Tune"? **(b) Speculate:** Why do you think the poet includes this detail? **(c) Discuss:** Share your responses with a partner. Then, discuss how looking at someone else's responses did or did not change your answer.

Reading Skill

5. In a chart like this one, write an example from each poem in which you read according to punctuation rather than stopping at the end of a line. Then, **paraphrase** each example.

Poem	Example From Poem	Paraphrase
Full Fathom Five		
Onomatopoeia		
Train Tune		

6. Why do you think the poet did not use any punctuation in "Train Tune"?

Literary Analysis

7. **(a)** What **sound device** is used in the title "Full Fathom Five"? **(b)** Find an example of another sound device in the poem.

8. **(a)** Identify three words from "Onomatopoeia" that sound like falling water. **(b)** List three words not used in the poem that also imitate the sound of water.

9. **(a)** Identify the **repetition** in "Train Tune." **(b)** What effect does this device have when you read the poem out loud?

QuickReview

Poems at a Glance

Full Fathom Five: The speaker describes an underwater landscape.

Onomatopoeia: The speaker describes the sounds of dripping water.

Train Tune: The speaker gives a rhythmic description of a train's journey.

Assessment
For: Self-test
Visit: www.PHSchool.com
Web Code: ema-6408

Paraphrase: restate in your own words

Sound Devices: techniques that create musical effects in poetry, such as *onomatopoeia, alliteration,* and *repetition*

Vocabulary Builder

Practice For each set of words, identify the word that does not belong and explain why.

1. spigot   faucet   closet
2. sputters   creaks   opens
3. prairies   groves   orchards

Writing

Write a **poem** called "Alliteration" that defines the term and gives examples of this sound device.

- First, review the definition of alliteration on page 580.
- Next, rewrite the definition in your own words. Then, look for places where you can expand your definition by adding examples of alliteration, such as "Some say it sounds funny."
- Share your finished poem with a partner.

For *Grammar, Vocabulary,* and *Assessment,* see **Build Language Skills,** on pages 594–595.

Extend Your Learning

Listening and Speaking Present a **poetry reading** of one of the poems from *Poetry Collection 2.* Practice several times, making sure that you are reading according to punctuation.
- read slowly
- read with expression in your voice
- speak clearly
- make eye contact periodically with your audience

Research and Technology Create a **résumé** for William Shakespeare, Eve Merriam, or Louise Bogan. Research online to gather information about the poet's education, career, and published works. Do further research to find a standard résumé format. Use the information you have gathered to complete the poet's résumé.

Build Language Skills

Vocabulary Skill

Synonyms The words *emphasize* and *highlight* are synonyms. Their meanings can be similar depending on the context of the sentence. In many cases, one of these words can replace the other in a sentence without changing the meaning of the sentence. There will be slight differences in the meaning of the sentence.

▶ **Example:** The writer used bold type to [*emphasize* or *highlight*] the main ideas in her essay.

Practice Write four sentences, each using a word from List A. Then, rewrite the sentence substituting the synonym from list B. Explain whether the meaning of the sentence changes.

A 1. stress   **2.** feature   **3.** underscore   **4.** emphasize

B 1. accent   **2.** showcase   **3.** underline   **4.** highlight

Grammar Lesson

Independent and Subordinate Clauses A **clause** is a group of words with its own subject and verb. The two major types of clauses are independent clauses and subordinate clauses.

An **independent clause** has a subject and a verb and can stand by itself as a complete sentence. A **subordinate clause** has a subject and a verb, but it is only part of a sentence.

Comparing Two Kinds of Clauses	
Independent	**Subordinate**
S V He arrived this morning.	S V *if* he arrived this morning
S V The mosque has a golden dome.	S V *since* the mosque has a dome

Practice Identify the independent and subordinate clauses. Then, rewrite each sentence, supplying a different subordinate clause.

1. We were all frightened when the lights went out.
2. After they won the game, the team went out for pizza.
3. Because she was a good swimmer, Mai got a job as a lifeguard.
4. Joey did not start the game until his friends had arrived.
5. When she was young, my mother lived on a ranch.

MorePractice

For more practice with independent and subordinate clauses, see the Grammar Handbook, p. R31.

W͟G͟ Prentice Hall Writing and Grammar Connection, Chapter 20, Section 2

Reading: Paraphrase

Directions: *Read the selection. Then, answer the questions.*

I have a little shadow that goes in and out with me,
And what can be the use of him is more than I can see.
He is very, very like me from the heels up to the head;
And I see him jump before me, when I jump into my bed.

—from "My Shadow" by Robert Louis Stevenson

1. Which is the best paraphrase of line 1?
   A My shadow goes everywhere I go.
   B I have a shadow, and it is very small.
   C It is hard to watch my shadow.
   D My shadow is always going some- where.

2. After which two lines would you come to a complete stop?
   A after lines 1 and 4
   B after lines 2 and 4
   C after lines 3 and 4
   D after lines 2 and 3

3. Which is the best paraphrase of line 3?
   A My shadow likes the way I look.
   B My shadow and I look very much alike.
   C My shadow is like me only in certain ways.
   D My shadow has heels and a head.

4. Which is the best paraphrase of line 2?
   A The more I see my shadow, the more useful he becomes.
   B My shadow has more uses than I ever knew.
   C I have no idea what my shadow is good for.
   D My shadow is useful only when I can see him.

Timed Writing: Explanation [Connections]

Write a letter to the editor of a local newspaper. In the letter explain how your school or community could better welcome new people. Use specific examples to support your ideas. **(20 minutes)**

 ## Writing Workshop: *Work in Progress*

Persuasive Writing

For a persuasive essay you might write, list three things that you would like to see changed in your school or community. Next to each item, jot down why you would like this changed. Put these notes in your writing folder.

You can apply the skills on this page to these poems.

Poetry Collection 1
Annabel Lee, p. 598
Martin Luther King, p. 600
I'm Nobody, p. 601

Poetry Collection 2
Jim, p. 605
Father William, p. 606
Stopping by Woods on a Snowy Evening, p. 608

Reading Skill

To **paraphrase** means to restate something in your own words to make the meaning clear to yourself. If you are unsure of a poem's meaning, **reread** the parts that are difficult.

- Look up unfamiliar words and replace them with words you know.
- Restate the line or passage using your own, everyday words.
- Reread the passage to make sure that your version makes sense.

As you read, use a chart like the one shown to help you paraphrase.

Literary Analysis

Rhythm and rhyme make poetry musical. **Rhythm** is a poem's pattern of stressed (´) and unstressed (˘) syllables.

Meter is a poem's rhythmical pattern. It is measured in *feet,* or single units of stressed and unstressed syllables.

Rhyme is the repetition of sounds at the ends of words. In the example, the words *sire* and *fire* create a rhyme.

Hálf / ĭn dreáms / hĕ sáw / hĭs síre /
Wíth / hĭs gréat / hănds fúll / ŏf fíre.

Original
Half in dreams, he saw his sire. With his great hands full of fire.
Unfamiliar Words
sire
Dictionary Definitions of Unfamiliar Words
sire = father
Paraphrase
Only half awake, he saw his father. His big hands were glowing with light.

Vocabulary Builder

Poetry Collection 1

- **coveted** (kuv´ it id) *v.* wanted; desired (p. 598) *The hockey team coveted the trophy.*

- **profound** (prō found´) *adj.* deeply or intensely felt (p. 600) *You have my profound sympathy.*

- **banish** (ban´ ish) *v.* send away; exile (p. 601) *The king will banish the troublemaker.*

Poetry Collection 2

- **incessantly** (in ses´ ənt lē) *adv.* without stopping (p. 607) *He played the drums incessantly.*

- **sage** (sāj) *n.* very wise person (p. 607) *The sage gave advice to all who approached him.*

- **supple** (sup´ əl) *adj.* able to bend easily; flexible (p. 607) *Rubber is a supple material.*

Build Understanding • *Poetry Collection 1*

Connecting to the Literature

Reading/Writing Connection The poems "Annabel Lee" and "Martin Luther King" each honor someone who is important to the speaker. Choose someone to whom you would like to pay tribute. Write three sentences that tell why that individual is special. Use at least three of these words: *affect, enrich, represent, promote, dedicate.*

Meet the Authors

Edgar Allan **Poe** (1809–1849)
Annabel Lee (p. 598)

Edgar Allan Poe won great literary success but suffered much personal loss in his life. His mother died when he was just two years old. He finished "Annabel Lee" about a year after the death of his beloved wife, Virginia. One Poe expert believes that the title character represents all the women Poe loved and lost in his life.

Raymond Richard **Patterson** (1929–2001)
Martin Luther King (p. 600)

Raymond Patterson's poetry appears in many anthologies. A native New Yorker, Patterson taught for many years at New York City College. His passion for sharing his knowledge of African American history was reflected in his newspaper column, "From Our Past," and in poems such as "Martin Luther King."

Emily **Dickinson** (1830–1886)
I'm Nobody (p. 601)

Emily Dickinson was born in Amherst, Massachusetts. In college, she grew so homesick that she returned home after just one year. After that, she rarely left her house. Quietly, however, she was writing the 1,775 poems that would make her famous after her death. In these brief works, she created a poetic self that flashes with humor and intelligence.

For: More about the poets
Visit: www.PHSchool.com
Author Link **Web Code:** eme-9411

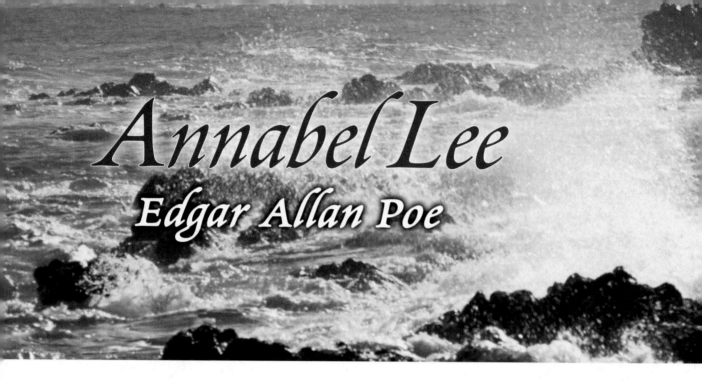

Annabel Lee
Edgar Allan Poe

It was many and many a year ago,
  In a kingdom by the sea.
That a maiden there lived whom you may know
  By the name of Annabel Lee;—
And this maiden she lived with no other thought
  Than to love and be loved by me.

She was a child and I was a child,
  In this kingdom by the sea.
5 But we loved with a love that was more than love—
  I and my Annabel Lee—
With a love that the wingèd seraphs[1] of Heaven
  <u>Coveted</u> her and me.

And this was the reason that, long ago,
  In this kingdom by the sea,
A wind blew out of a cloud by night
  Chilling my Annabel Lee;
So that her highborn kinsmen came
  And bore her away from me,
10 To shut her up in a sepulcher[2]
  In this kingdom by the sea.

---

1. **wingèd seraphs** (ser´ əfs) *n.* angels.
2. **sepulcher** (sep´əl kər) *n.* vault or chamber for burial; tomb.

The angels, not half so happy in Heaven,
    Went envying her and me:—
Yes! that was the reason (as all men know,
    In this kingdom by the sea)
That the wind came out of a cloud, chilling
    And killing my Annabel Lee.

But our love it was stronger by far than the love
    Of those who were older than we—
    Of many far wiser than we—
15 And neither the angels in Heaven above
    Nor the demons down under the sea,
Can ever dissever[3] my soul from the soul
    Of the beautiful Annabel Lee:—

For the moon never beams without bringing
    me dreams
Of the beautiful Annabel Lee;
And the stars never rise but I see the bright eyes
    Of the beautiful Annabel Lee;
20 And so, all the nighttide, I lie down by the side
Of my darling, my darling, my life and my bride,
    In her sepulcher there by the sea—
    In her tomb by the side of the sea.

▲ **Critical Viewing**
Compare the emotions this photograph sparks in you with those the speaker feels upon looking at the sea. **[Connect]**

Reading Skill
Paraphrase How would you paraphrase lines 15–18?

---

3. dissever (di sev´ər) *v.* separate; divide.

Martin Luther King

Raymond Patterson

Background Martin Luther King, Jr. (1929–1968) was a great civil rights leader. He used nonviolent methods to help end legal discrimination against African Americans in the United States. Tragically, in 1968, while fighting for justice and equality, he was assassinated at the age of 39.

He came upon an age
Beset[1] by grief, by rage—

His love so deep, so wide,
He could not turn aside.

5   His passion, so <u>profound</u>,
He would not turn around.

He taught a suffering earth
The measure of man's worth.

For this he was slain,
10   But he will come again.

---

1. Beset (bē set´) *adj.* attacked from all sides; harassed.

Vocabulary Builder
profound (prō fo͝und´)
adj. deeply or
intensely felt

◀ **Critical Viewing**
What characteristics of Martin Luther King, Jr., does this photograph show?
[Infer]

I'm Nobody

EMILY DICKINSON

I'm Nobody! Who are you?
Are you—Nobody—too?
Then there's a pair of us!
Don't tell! they'd <u>banish</u> us—you know!

5   How dreary—to be—Somebody!
How public—like a Frog—
To tell your name—the livelong June—
To an admiring Bog!

Vocabulary Builder
banish (ban´ish) v.
send away; exile

◀ **Critical Viewing**
Would you consider a frog like the one pictured a somebody or a nobody? Explain. **[Speculate]**

Apply the Skills

Poetry Collection 1

Thinking About the Selections

1. **Respond:** Which of the three poems do you think would make the best song? Support your answer.
2. **(a) Recall:** In "Annabel Lee," how does the speaker react to Annabel Lee's death? **(b) Infer:** What will prevent the separation of the speaker's soul from the soul of Annabel Lee?
3. **(a) Interpret:** In "Martin Luther King," what does the poet mean by King's "passion, so profound"? **(b) Synthesize:** Using ideas from the poem, name two qualities that are important in a leader. Explain your answer.
4. **(a) Recall:** In "I'm Nobody," what does the speaker say will happen if it is revealed that she is "nobody"? **(b) Infer:** How does the speaker feel about this consequence? **(c) Apply:** In what way does the poem suggest some of the difficulties celebrities face today?

Reading Skill

5. Reread the following lines, and then **paraphrase** them.
   (a) "Annabel Lee": lines 9–10
   (b) "Martin Luther King": lines 1–2
   (c) "I'm Nobody": lines 5–8
6. Identify two words in these poems that you might look up in a dictionary to help you paraphrase meaning.
7. Explain two ways in which a paraphrase differs from the actual text of a poem.

Literary Analysis

8. **(a)** Do all of the poems have a regular **rhythm**? Explain. **(b)** In your opinion, which poem has the most interesting rhythm? Why?
9. Use a chart like this to analyze the **rhyme** in each poem.

Poem	Rhyming Words
Annabel Lee	
Martin Luther King	
I'm Nobody	

QuickReview

Poems at a Glance

Annabel Lee: The speaker mourns his lost love.

Martin Luther King: The speaker praises Martin Luther King.

I'm Nobody: The speaker celebrates privacy and one's right to be different.

Paraphrase: restate in your own words

For: Self-test
Visit: www.PHSchool.com
Web Code: ema-6409

Rhythm: a poem's pattern of stressed and unstressed syllables

Meter: a poem's rhythmical pattern

Rhyme: the repetition of sounds at the ends of words

Vocabulary Builder

Practice **Analogies** show the relationships between pairs of words. Use a word from the vocabulary list on page 596 to complete each analogy. Your choice should make a word pair that matches the relationship between the first two words. Explain the relationship.

1. enter : exit : : _____ : welcome

2. ate : consumed : : _____ : wanted

3. excellent : great : : _____ : intense

Writing

Write a **paraphrase** of one of the poems in this collection.
- Read over each stanza of the original poem.
- Use a dictionary to define words you do not know. Replace these words with familiar synonyms, or words that have the same meaning.
- Restate the entire poem in your own language.
- Reread your paraphrase, making sure it has the same meaning as the original. Make revisions as necessary.

For *Grammar, Vocabulary,* and *Assessment,* see **Build Language Skills,** pages 612–613.

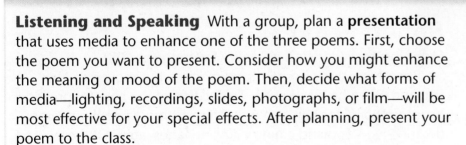

Extend Your Learning

Listening and Speaking With a group, plan a **presentation** that uses media to enhance one of the three poems. First, choose the poem you want to present. Consider how you might enhance the meaning or mood of the poem. Then, decide what forms of media—lighting, recordings, slides, photographs, or film—will be most effective for your special effects. After planning, present your poem to the class.

Research and Technology Conduct a **survey,** asking classmates to pick their favorite of the three poems in each of these categories: best character description; best overall use of language; and best rhythm, rhyme, and meter. Count the number of votes that each poem receives for each category.

Poetry

Connecting to the Literature

Reading/Writing Connection "Jim" and "Father William" both describe a character with special traits that make him memorable. What qualities do you think make someone memorable? Write three sentences that describe those traits. Use at least three of the following words: *affect, enrich, represent, promote, appreciate*.

Review

For **Reading Skill, Literary Analysis,** and **Vocabulary,** see page 596.

Meet the Authors

Gwendolyn **Brooks** (1917–2000)

Jim (p. 605)

Gwendolyn Brooks began writing at the age of seven and published her first poem, "Eventide," at the age of thirteen. As an adult, Brooks wrote hundreds of poems, many of which focus on the African American experience. In 1950, she became the first African American to win a Pulitzer Prize.

Lewis **Carroll** (1832–1898)

Father William (p. 606)

Lewis Carroll is the pen name of Charles Dodgson, a mathematics professor who was born in England. Under his pen name, Dodgson wrote *Alice's Adventures in Wonderland* and *Through the Looking Glass*. Like these classic novels, his poems are noted for their clever wordplay, nonsensical meanings, and delightfully zany worlds.

Robert **Frost** (1874–1963)

Stopping by Woods on a Snowy Evening (p. 608)

Robert Frost was born in San Francisco but moved to New England when he was eleven. This region of the country proved to be inspirational for him as a writer. Frost's most popular poems describe New England country life and landscapes. Of these, "Stopping by Woods on a Snowy Evening" is considered one of his best. Frost won the Pulitzer Prize four times—more than any other poet.

For: More about the poets
Visit: www.PHSchool.com
Web Code: eme-9412

Jim  Gwendolyn Brooks

There never was a nicer boy
Than Mrs. Jackson's Jim.
The sun should drop its greatest gold
On him.

5 Because, when Mother-dear was sick,
He brought her cocoa in.
And brought her broth, and brought her bread.
And brought her medicine.

And, tipping,[1] tidied up her room.
10 And would not let her see
He missed his game of baseball
Terribly.

1. **tipping** (tip´ in) *v.* tiptoeing.

Literary Analysis
Rhythm and Rhyme
Which syllables are
stressed in lines 5–6?

▼ **Critical Viewing**
Why might Jim leave
items like these out
instead of putting
them away?
[Speculate]

Father William

Lewis Carroll

▲ **Critical Viewing** Read the poem to identify which group of lines this drawing illustrates. **[Analyze]**

Background This poem, which comes from *Alice's Adventures in Wonderland,* is an amusing conversation between a father and son. Lewis Carroll wrote it as a humorous spoof on a serious poem by Robert Southey. In this version, Carroll pokes fun at the false ideas society often has about the way older people speak and behave.

"You are old, Father William," the young man said,
　　"And your hair has become very white;
And yet you <u>incessantly</u> stand on your head—
　　Do you think, at your age, it is right?"

5　"In my youth," Father William replied to his son,
　　"I feared it might injure the brain;
But, now that I'm perfectly sure I have none,
　　Why, I do it again and again."
"You are old," said the youth, "as I mentioned before.
10　And have grown most uncommonly[1] fat;
Yet you turned a back-somersault in at the door—
　　Pray, what is the reason of that?"

"In my youth," said the <u>sage</u>, as he shook his gray locks,
　　"I kept all my limbs very <u>supple</u>
15 By the use of this ointment—one shilling[2] the box—
　　Allow me to sell you a couple?"

"You are old," said the youth, "and your jaws are too weak
　　For anything tougher than suet;[3]
Yet you finished the goose, with the bones and the beak—
20　Pray, how did you manage to do it?"
"In my youth," said his father, "I took to the law,
　　And argued each case with my wife;
And the muscular strength, which it gave to my jaw
　　Has lasted the rest of my life."

25　"You are old," said the youth, "one would hardly suppose
　　That your eye was as steady as ever;
Yet you balanced an eel on the end of your nose—
　　What made you so awfully clever?"

"I have answered three questions, and that is enough,"
30　Said his father. "Don't give yourself airs!
Do you think I can listen all day to such stuff?
　　Be off, or I'll kick you downstairs!"

---

1. **uncommonly** (un käm´ən lē) *adv.* remarkably.
2. **shilling** (shil´iŋ) *n.* British coin.
3. **suet** (sōo´it) *n.* fat used in cooking.

Vocabulary Builder
incessantly (in ses´ənt lē) *adv.* without stopping

sage (sāj) *n.* very wise person

supple (sup´əl) *adj.* able to bend easily; flexible

Reading Skill
Paraphrase How would you paraphrase "Don't give yourself airs!"?

Stopping by Woods on a Snowy Evening

Robert Frost

Background A poem may contain several levels of meaning. In "Stopping by Woods on a Snowy Evening," the speaker is a traveler passing through the winter countryside. On one level, his journey may be regarded simply as a trip through the woods. As you read the poem, however, look for a deeper meaning that relates to a journey through life.

▲ Critical Viewing
Read the poem to identify what emotions a wintry scene like the one shown brings out in the speaker. **[Infer]**

Whose woods these are I think I know.
His house is in the village, though;
He will not see me stopping here
To watch his woods fill up with snow.

5   My little horse must think it queer
To stop without a farmhouse near
Between the woods and frozen lake
The darkest evening of the year.

He gives his harness bells a shake
10 To ask if there is some mistake.
The only other sound's the sweep
Of easy wind and downy flake.

The woods are lovely, dark, and deep,
But I have promises to keep,
15 And miles to go before I sleep,
And miles to go before I sleep.

Literary Analysis
Rhythm and Rhyme In lines 1–8, which lines end with rhyming words?

Reading Skill
Paraphrase How would you paraphrase lines 11–12?

Apply the Skills

Poetry Collection 2

Thinking About the Selections

1. **Respond:** Which of the three poems do you think would make the best song? Support your answer.
2. **(a) Recall:** In "Jim," what tasks does the boy perform for his mother? **(b) Infer:** What detail tells you that Jim is not selfish?
3. **(a) Recall:** In "Father William," what details from the poem describe Father William's appearance? **(b) Analyze:** How does his appearance make his actions seem especially surprising?
4. **(a) Recall:** In "Stopping by Woods on a Snowy Evening," why has the speaker stopped? **(b) Infer:** What about the place captures his attention?
5. **(a) Recall:** What words in Frost's poem describe sights and sounds? **(b) Apply:** What is the mood, or feeling, of the poem?

Reading Skill

6. Reread the following lines, and then **paraphrase** them.
   (a) lines 3–4 of "Jim"
   (b) lines 13–16 of "Father William"
   (c) lines 11–12 of "Stopping by Woods on a Snowy Evening"
7. Identify two words in these poems that you might look up in a dictionary to help you paraphrase meaning.
8. Explain two ways in which a paraphrase differs from the actual text of a poem.

Literary Analysis

9. **(a)** Do all of the poems have a regular **rhythm**? Explain. **(b)** In your opinion, which poem has the most interesting rhythm? Why?
10. Use a chart like this to analyze the **rhyme** in each poem.

Poem	Rhyming Words
Jim	
Father William	
Stopping by Woods …	

Vocabulary Builder

Practice Answer each question by writing a complete sentence that includes the underlined vocabulary word.

1. Is a car alarm that wails <u>incessantly</u> annoying?
2. What qualities does a person need to be considered a <u>sage</u>?
3. How can exercise help to give you a <u>supple</u> body?

Writing

Write a **paraphrase** of one of the poems in this collection.
- Read over each stanza of the original poem.
- Use a dictionary to define words you do not know. Replace these words with familiar synonyms, or words that have the same meaning.
- Restate the entire poem in your own language.
- Reread your paraphrase, making sure it has the same meaning as the original. Make revisions as necessary.

For *Grammar, Vocabulary,* and *Assessment,* see **Build Language Skills,** pages 612–613.

Extend Your Learning

Listening and Speaking With a group, plan a **presentation** that uses media to enhance one of the three poems. First, choose the poem you want to present. Consider how you might enhance the meaning or mood of the poem. Then, decide what forms of media—lighting, recordings, slides, photographs, or film—will be most effective for your special effects. After planning, present your poem to the class.

Research and Technology Conduct a **survey,** asking classmates to pick their favorite of the three poems in each of these categories: best character description; best overall use of language; and best rhythm, rhyme, and meter. Count the number of votes that each poem receives for each category.

Build Language Skills

Vocabulary Skill

Synonyms The words *paraphrase* and *restate* are synonyms. Their meanings are similar. Once you know the synonym for the base form of a word, you can apply your knowledge to use synonyms for other forms of the word.

Practice Supply a synonym for each word. Then, write another form of each word in the synonym pair. You may need to adjust your synonym choice.

▶ **Example:** know/understand
    knowledge/understanding

1. significant
2. notify

3. recognize
4. intend

Grammar Lesson

Sentence Structure A **simple sentence** is one *independent clause*—a group of words that has a subject and verb and can stand by itself as a complete thought. A **compound sentence** consists of two or more independent clauses linked by a word such as *and, but,* or *or*. A **complex sentence** contains one independent clause and one or more *subordinate clauses*—a group of words that has a subject and verb but is not a complete thought.

MorePractice

For more practice with types of sentences, see the Grammar Handbook, p. R31.

Simple sentence:	We planned a picnic.
	IND. CLAUSE IND. CLAUSE
Compound sentence:	We planned a picnic, but it rained.
	SUBORD. CLAUSE IND. CLAUSE
Complex sentence:	Because it rained, we ate indoors.

Practice Write a sentence for each numbered item. Then, identify the structure of each sentence you wrote.

1. to tell a friend what time it is
2. to tell a friend what time practice is on Friday
3. to tell a friend why the practice time was changed on Friday

4. to explain why you think your homework will take a long time
5. to state what kind of homework you have

W͞G Prentice Hall Writing and Grammar Connection: Chapter 20, Section 2

Reading: Paraphrase

Directions: *Read the selection. Then, answer the questions.*

Behold the monstrous blue whale!
Leviathan who rules majestically in the ocean blue,
With body the length of a football field,
Whose very presence causes sailors to quake;
The largest creature ever to inhabit the world,
Blue whale, rule on in your underwater domain!

1. Which of these lines best paraphrases line 1?
   A Let's hold the giant blue whale!
   B See the giant blue whale!
   C Look at the strange blue whale!
   D Hold on there, you dark blue whale!

2. Which phrase best replaces *Leviathan* in a paraphrase?
   A scary human being
   B busy servant
   C smart student
   D giant sea creature

3. Which of these lines best paraphrases line 4?
   A Whose body causes sailors to shake
   B Whose gifts make sailors move fast
   C Whose color causes sailors to be blinded
   D Whose eyes make sailors smile

4. Which phrase best replaces *underwater domain*?
   A thick skin
   B wet hiding place
   C ocean home
   D castle near the sea

Timed Writing: Persuasion [Connections]

Review the poems in *Collection 1* or *Collection 2*. Choose your favorite poem from the group. Write a **persuasive paragraph** that defends your choice. Support your opinion with details from the poem. **(20 minutes)**

 ## Writing Workshop: *Work in Progress*

Persuasive Writing
Choose one of the items on the list in your writing portfolio. Divide your paper in half lengthwise. Label the left column "For" and the right column, "Against." In the left column, list three points that support your view. In the right column, list three points that do not support your view. Put this paper in your writing portfolio.

Reading Informational Materials

Magazine Articles

In Part 2, you are learning about paraphrasing while reading literature. Paraphrasing is also useful in reading informational materials such as magazine articles. If you read "Stopping by Woods on a Snowy Evening," you recognized a certain rhythm to that poem. The magazine article that follows gives insight into how rhythmic phrases are achieved in poetry, traditional music, or rap.

About Magazine Articles

A **magazine article** is a form of print media that provides information and analysis about a topic. It appears in a magazine, which may be published weekly, monthly, or even quarterly (four times a year). Some magazines, and the articles in them, are organized with a specific audience in mind, such as parents or music-lovers. Other magazines provide information on current issues and events that appeal to a general audience. In either case, magazine articles can be used as a source of information and research.

Reading Skill

Paraphrasing, or restating something in your own words, is useful when you are reading a magazine article to gather information. When you paraphrase sentences or paragraphs, include all the details, but replace, combine, or rearrange words in a way that shows your understanding. Paraphrasing passages can help you make the meaning clear to yourself.

   As you read, identify words that can be replaced or combined. Use a chart like the one shown to help you paraphrase the article.

Sentence or Passage	Replacement Words	Paraphrase
Rap is about words, but rhythm makes them more powerful.	rhythm = beat more powerful = stronger but = although	Although words are the point of rap, its beat makes it stronger.

Photographs add visual interest to the page. They bring to life the concepts in the article.

The Rhythms of Rap

Kathiann M. Kowalski

Rap is about society; some songs get notoriety. But do your feet tap, when you hear rap?

Lots of rap tracks make you move along with them. Rap is about words, but rhythm makes them more powerful.

"Rhythm is the feeling of movement in time," explains Miami University (OH) music professor Chris Tanner. "Rhythm is the term we use in music for dividing time. Music can't exist without rhythm." In other words, one sound with no break is just noise. Play a sequence of notes for a certain time each, and you get music.

As music moves forward in time, your brain notes the duration of individual sounds and groups them together into bunches that let you perceive rhythm in the music. It could be the hammering lyrics of a rap artist. Or, it could be the beginning of Beethoven's *Fifth Symphony:* "Bum, bum, bum, bummm. Bum, bum, bum, bummm."

Knowing when the article was published tells you how up-to-date the information is. Jot down the magazine's name and issue date, in case you want to re-check information in an article.

Odyssey Magazine March, 2002

Saying Their Songs

Rap as a popular music style started in the late 1970s. But, notes music professor Adam Krims at the University of Alberta, "In some form or another, this kind of music has been around for about 250 years. It continues very old practices of rhyming and rhythm among African Americans."

This catchy title grabs readers' attention. It uses *alliteration,* the repetition of initial consonant sounds, to show that rap is poetic and musical.

Rap's style of rhythmic delivery sets it apart from talking or other styles of *declamatory* (words recited with music) delivery. "In rap, you're not just talking," notes Krims, "You're really foregrounding [bringing up front] the rhythmic aspects of what you're doing."

It's somewhat like the difference between reading a textbook and reading Dr. Seuss's *Green Eggs and Ham* aloud. However, stresses Krims, "Rap actually takes a lot of practice to do even slightly well." Effective rhythmic phrasing really draws listeners into the lyrics of an MC ("MC" is the same as "emcee" and stands for "master of ceremonies"—a name rap artists commonly use).

Often an MC works with words' natural

emphasis. Other times, the artist may deform words. "You purposely deliver them in a way that's a little perverse," explains Krims. So instead of "California," an MC might say "Californ-eye-ay."

In the Background

Sampling serves up yet more rhythms in rap. "Sampling is taking a little bit of music from another source," says Krims. Sampling may be the artist's own composition. It may be a segment from another popular song or even a classical piece.

> The text of a magazine article is often broken up with headings of a different size or color that provide hints about the main idea to follow.

The musician then makes a "loop" of the segment, which means that it's played over and over. Sampling adds background melody and harmony. Each bit of sampling also adds its own rhythms to a rap song.

The Beat Goes On

Underlying rap and almost all music is its pulse, or beat. "There are all kinds of rhythms going on in a *Sousa* march, but what do people march to?" says Tanner. It's not the rhythmic phrasing of the melody. Instead, he says, "They move their feet to the underlying pulse of the music."

Rap and other popular music forms often spell out the beat explicitly with drums. "Any popular music that we're used to usually has that characteristic," notes Tanner. "That's why it's fun to dance to. In fact, popular music is often designed for movement."

"Meter is simply organizing pulses into a regular cyclical pattern," adds Tanner. Instead of an endless series of beats, the musician may play cycles of "ONE, two, Three, four." This meter, known as "common time," stresses the first beat most. The third beat gets slight emphasis, too. Meter sets up a hierarchy, which the listener's brain can then remember and anticipate. That makes it possible for you to tap your foot or clap in time with the music.

Tempo is how fast a piece of music delivers its meter. Too slow, and a rap song sounds like a *dirge,* or funeral song. Too fast, and the brain can't perceive individual sounds. The music becomes one big blur.

Choose a tempo that's just quick enough, and listeners want to move with the music. Speed it up slightly or slow it down in places, and listeners respond to the music's different moods.

What Makes It Cool?

Hearing rhythm patterns in a song, listeners form expectations of what comes next. If music doesn't give enough for listeners to form those expectations, it sounds chaotic and grating. If music gets too predictable, however, it becomes boring.

Sophisticated rap music provides an innovative mix that satisfies and sometimes surprises listeners' expectations. With lyrics, an MC might stop in the middle of a line or give some offbeat accents. Sampling or the drum track may stress different notes than those that would usually be emphasized in the meter — a technique called *syncopation.*

Revel in the rhythms of your favorite music. Innovative rhythms not only move music forward in time, but they also make rap — and many other types of music — cool.

> The last paragraph often ties up the ideas in the article, giving closure to the piece.

Reading: Paraphrase

Directions: *Choose the letter of the best answer.*

1. Which is the best paraphrase of the first sentence in the article?

   A Rap reflects culture and some rap songs are unusual.

   B Rap is for parties and the notes are important.

   C Rap is about society and some rap songs get noticed.

   D Rap is songs about society.

2. Which sentence does not belong in a paraphrase of the section "Saying Their Songs"?

   A Rap became popular in the 1970s, but it has a longer history within African American music.

   B The 1970s was the first time anyone heard of rap music.

   C The way rap is spoken with a beat makes it different from just talking with music.

   D A rap artist might change the way a word is pronounced.

3. Which is the best paraphrase of the article's definition of *sampling*?

   A Sampling is a kind of rap song that the musician composes.

   B Sampling adds drumbeats to rap.

   C Sampling is a slice of music from another musical piece that is repeated to supply background.

   D Sampling means trying different rap songs with harmony.

Reading: Comprehension and Interpretation

Directions: *Write your answers on a separate sheet of paper.*

4. Why is the *tempo* important to a rap song? [**Applying**]

5. Explain the importance of the brain in appreciating music. [**Integrating**]

6. Paraphrase the section that explains how sampling is used. [**Generating**]

Timed Writing: Persuasion [Cognitive Stance]

Decide whether you think rap is a simple or sophisticated form of music. Then write a persuasive essay that expresses your position. Use information from the article to support your arguments. **(15 minutes)**

Imagery

In poetry, an **image** is a word or phrase that appeals to one or more of the five senses. Writers use **imagery** to bring poetry to life with descriptions of how their subjects look, sound, feel, taste, and smell.

Look at these examples:

- The phrase "the sweet, slippery mango slices" appeals to the senses of taste and touch.

- The phrase "glaring lights and wailing sirens" appeals to the senses of sight and hearing.

Comparing Imagery

Both "Miracles" and "in Just—" contain images that appeal to the senses. On a chart like the one shown, track the images in the two poems. Note the sense that an image appeals to and write the image in the appropriate box. Keep in mind that some images may appeal to more than one sense, so you may put an image into more than one box.

Sense	Images	
	"Miracles"	"in Just—"
Sight		
Hearing		
Touch/Movement		
Taste		
Smell		

Vocabulary Builder

Miracles

- **exquisite** (eks′ kwiz it) *adj.* beautiful in a delicate way (p. 621) *Hand-crafted, tiny petals make those silk flowers* <u>exquisite</u>.

- **distinct** (di stiŋkt′) *adj.* separate and different (p. 621) *Each twin has her own* <u>distinct</u> *tastes.*

Build Understanding

Connecting to the Literature

Reading/Writing Connection In "Miracles," Walt Whitman uses imagery to express his feeling that ordinary things can be miraculous. Write a short description of things that you find miraculous or wonderful in the world. Use at least three of these words: *appreciate, display, challenge, cooperate.*

Meet the Authors

Walt **Whitman** (1819–1892)

Walt Whitman grew up in Brooklyn, New York, and worked at many occupations during his life. He was a printer, carpenter, teacher, and newspaper reporter. During the Civil War, he nursed his wounded brother and other soldiers.

The Father of American Poetry In 1855, Whitman published the first edition of *Leaves of Grass*—twelve long poems that no established publisher would touch. In this book, Whitman abandoned regular rhyme and rhythm in favor of free verse, which followed no set pattern. Over the next twenty-six years, six new editions of *Leaves of Grass* were published. Eventually considered a masterpiece, the book led many critics to regard Whitman as the father of American poetry.

E. E. **Cummings** (1894 – 1962)

Edward Estlin Cummings first published a collection of poetry in the early 1920s. The work stood out, among other reasons, because of Cummings's original use of language and unusual punctuation, capitalization, and word spacing.

A Sense of Humor Cummings often wrote poems that were playful and humorous. These poems reflected his attitude that "the most wasted of all days is one without laughter." Although his style caused controversy among critics, he became one of America's most popular poets.

Go **O**nline
Author Link

For: More about the poets
Visit: www.PHSchool.com
Web Code: eme-9413

Miracles
Walt Whitman

Why, who makes much of a miracle?
As to me I know of nothing else but miracles,
Whether I walk the streets of Manhattan,
Or dart my sight over the roofs of houses toward the sky,
5   Or wade with naked feet along the beach just in the edge
        of the water,
Or stand under trees in the woods,
Or talk by day with any one I love . . .
Or sit at table at dinner with the rest.
Or look at strangers opposite me riding in the car,
10 Or watch honeybees busy around the hive of a summer
        forenoon
Or animals feeding in the fields,
Or birds, or the wonderfulness of insects in the air,
Or the wonderfulness of the sundown, or of stars shining
        so quiet and bright,
Or the <u>exquisite</u> delicate thin curve of the new moon in
        spring;
15 These with the rest, one and all, are to me miracles,
The whole referring, yet each <u>distinct</u> and in its place.

To me every hour of the light and dark is a miracle,
Every cubic inch of space is a miracle,
Every square yard of the surface of the earth is spread
        with the same,
20 Every foot of the interior swarms with the same.

To me the sea is a continual miracle,
The fishes that swim—the rocks—the motion of the
        waves—
the ships with men in them,
What stranger miracles are there?

◀ **Critical Viewing**
Identify a line in the poem that relates to this painting. Explain your choice.
[Connect]

Literary Analysis
Imagery Which image in the first seven lines appeals to the sense of touch?

Vocabulary Builder
exquisite (eks´ kwiz it) *adj.* beautiful in a delicate way

distinct (di stiŋkt´) *adj.* separate and different

Thinking About the Selection

1. **(a) Recall:** List five places mentioned in the poem. **(b) Infer:** Why is the sea a "continual miracle"?

2. **(a) Recall:** Name four events that Whitman calls miracles. **(b) Comparison and Contrast:** How does your definition of "miracle" compare with the speaker's definition?

in Just- E. E.Cummings

in Just—
spring   when the world is mud-
luscious the little
lame balloonman

5   whistles   far   and wee

and eddieandbill come
running from marbles and
piracies and it's
spring

10   when the world is puddle-wonderful

the queer
old balloonman whistles
far   and   wee
and bettyandisbel come dancing

15   from hop-scotch and jump-rope and

it's
spring
and
     the

20   goat-footed

balloonMan   whistles
far
and
wee

Literary Analysis
Imagery To what
sense does the term
"puddle-wonderful"
appeal?

Thinking About the Selection

1. (a) **Recall:** What scene does the poem describe?
   (b) **Interpret:** What might the speaker mean by
   "Just-spring" and by calling the world "mud-luscious"
   and "puddle-wonderful"?

Apply the Skills

Miracles • in Just—

Comparing Imagery

QuickReview

Image: word or phrase that appeals to one or more of the five senses

1. Give an example from each poem of an **image** that appeals to each of the following senses:

   (a) hearing

   (b) touch

2. (a) Using a chart like the one shown, identify and explain sight images in each poem. (b) Which poem has the most vivid sight images?

Go Online
—**Assessment**
For: Self-test
Visit: www.PHSchool.com
Web Code: ema-6411

Miracles	in Just—
Image: Effect:	Image: Effect:

3. Which of these poems uses imagery most successfully? Explain.

Writing to Compare Literary Works

Write an essay to recommend one of the two poems to someone your age. Choose the poem that you believe provides the best examples of imagery. Consider the following questions to get you started:

- What do you find fascinating or strange about the imagery in the poem you recommend?
- Which poem do you find the most musical?
- Which images are most meaningful to you?

Vocabulary Builder

Practice For each item, write a single sentence correctly using both words.

1. exquisite; artwork

2. distinct; communities

Paraphrase

Directions: *Questions 1–4 are based on the following excerpt.*

1   The Deer don't dine
When a Wolf's about,
And the Porcupine
Sticks his quill-points out.

5   The Minks won't tell
Where they hide or sleep,
And the Lynx looks well
Where he means to leap.

The Mice lie snug
10   When the Hoot Owls flit,
And the Lightning Bug
Keeps his tail-light lit.

—from **"Safety First,"** Arthur Guiterman

1. What is the best way to paraphrase lines 1 and 2?
  A   The deer and the wolf don't dine together.
  B   The deer don't stop to eat when wolves are nearby.
  C   The wolf is the enemy of the deer.
  D   Wolves and deer eat different kinds of food.

2. At the end of which line do you continue reading without a pause?
  A   line 2
  B   line 6
  C   line 7
  D   line 10

3. What is the best way to paraphrase lines 7 and 8?
  A   The lynx is nice to look at before it leaps.
  B   The lynx is mean when it leaps.
  C   The lynx looks carefully before it leaps.
  D   The lynx always leaps from one place to another.

4. To paraphrase line 10, what synonym might you use to replace *flit*?
  A   sleep
  B   fight
  C   cry
  D   fly

Synonyms

Directions: *Choose the word or words that best complete the sentence.*

5. Jody tried _____ the difficult passage in her chemistry book; _____ the information helped her understand it.
   - A emphasizing. . .highlighting
   - B rereading. . .featuring
   - C paraphrasing. . .restating
   - D underlining. . .eluding

6. We want to _____ that point by _____ it.
   - A invalidate. . .emphasizing
   - B emphasize. . .highlighting
   - C highlight. . .invalidating
   - D paraphrase. . .highlighting

7. The _____ was extremely difficult and needed to be _____ for the younger children.
   - A paraphrase. . .restated
   - B restated. . .paraphrased
   - C passage. . .restated
   - D passage. . .highlighted

8. The student _____ the idea in several ways before his friend understood the concept.
   - A emphasized
   - B highlighted
   - C stressed
   - D restated

9. We should _____ that the players must be here an hour before the game.
   - A emphasize
   - B summarize
   - C feature
   - D review

10. When he read the poem, he _____ the rhyme.
    - A paraphrased
    - B emphasized
    - C restated
    - D remembered

11. Be certain to _____ that point in your speech so your audience pays attention to the idea.
    - A paraphrase
    - B elude
    - C highlight
    - D add

12. Synonyms are helpful if you are trying to _____ a passage.
    - A paraphrase
    - B remember
    - C highlight
    - D add

13. The _____ was long and complex; it took Cassandra a long time to understand it.
    - A highlight
    - B passage
    - C stress
    - D drawing

14. Can we _____ that argument? It is too wordy.
    - A highlight
    - B emphasize
    - C restate
    - D retract

Words With Prefixes and Suffixes

Prefixes are added in front of a word, and the spelling of the base word does not change. When you add certain suffixes, the spelling of some base words changes.

Watch for Spelling Changes Prefixes should never cause you problems because they do not change the spelling of the base word. Suffixes can be a different story.

- When a one-syllable word ends in one vowel and one consonant, double the consonant before adding *ed* or *est*.
- When a word with more than one syllable ends in one vowel followed by one consonant, *and if the accent is on the last syllable,* double the consonant before adding *ed* or *est*.
- When a word ends in a consonant followed by a silent *e*, drop the *e* before adding *ing*.
- When a word ends in *y*, change *y* to *i* before adding *es* or *ed*.

The words with suffixes on the Word List change their base spelling before the suffix is added.

Word List
misspell
prearrange
reenlist
unnecessary
recognition
influential
suspension
muscular
ability
description

It's not that I doubt your ability William, but who is this Hamlet guy?

EDITOR

Practice Write the word from the Word List that is related to each word below. If the list word has a prefix, circle the prefix. If the list word has a suffix, circle the spelling change.

1. recognize
2. influence
3. enlist
4. describe
5. suspend
6. abilities
7. arrange
8. spell
9. necessary

A. Directions: *Write the letter of the sentence in which the underlined word is spelled correctly.*

1. **A** Marla Rimes is an <u>influencial</u> congresswoman.
   B She has received national <u>recognition</u> for her proposals.
   C She believes she has the <u>ableity</u> to change our country.
   D She does not look for fame because she thinks it is <u>unecessary</u>.

2. **A** Tony is a very <u>musclear</u> athlete.
   B He will <u>reenlist</u> to play basketball this season.
   C A typical newspaper <u>describshun</u> of him will focus on his strength.
   D Tony thinks he should also get <u>recognizion</u> for his speed.

3. **A** Liz will <u>prerrange</u> to have the documentary shown.
   B The film is about the building of a <u>suspencion</u> bridge.
   C Liz will made up an ad containing a <u>description</u> of the film.
   D Hopefully, she won't <u>mispell</u> any words in her ad.

4. **A** Some people have the <u>ability</u> to quickly memorize information.
   B For them, lengthy study periods are <u>unnecesary</u>.
   C Many <u>influenctial</u> Americans have this special skill.
   D If you like, I can <u>prearange</u> for you to meet a memory specialist.

B. Directions: *Write the letter of the word that would be the correct spelling to fill in the blank.*

1. Dave decided to _____ in the navy.
   A renlist
   B reenlist
   C reinlist
   D reinnlist

2. My father is tall and _____.
   A muscular
   B musclear
   C musclelar
   D musscular

3. She wanted _____ for her accomplishments.
   A recognizion
   B recogniztion
   C recognition
   D recognizhun

4. Please don't _____ my name on the program.
   A mispell
   B missppel
   C misspel
   D misspell

5. He was given a three-day _____.
   A suspension
   B suspendsion
   C suspenssion
   D suspencion

6. It is _____ to return this call.
   A unecessary
   B unnecesary
   C unnecessary
   D unneccesary

Persuasion: Persuasive Essay

When you use words to influence others, you are using persuasion. A **persuasive essay** is a brief work in which a writer presents the case for or against a particular position. Follow the steps outlined in this workshop to write your own persuasive essay.

Assignment Write a persuasive essay that influences readers to share your point of view on an issue about which you feel strongly.

What to Include Your persuasive essay should feature the following elements:

- a clear statement of your position on an issue that has more than one side
- persuasive evidence that supports your position
- language that appeals to both reason and emotion
- an appropriate organizational structure for an argument
- statements that identify and address reader concerns and counterarguments
- error-free writing, including proper sentence structure

To preview the criteria on which your persuasive essay may be judged, see the rubric on page 635.

 ## Writing Workshop: *Work in Progress*

If you have completed the Work in Progress assignments, you already have a wealth of ideas to use in your persuasive essay. Develop these ideas, or explore a new idea as you complete the Writing Workshop.

Using the Form

You may use elements of this form in these writing situations:

- editorials
- reviews
- advertisements
- problem-and-solution essays

Reading Writing Connection

To get the feel for persuasion, read "The Eternal Frontier" by Louis L'Amour, on page 438.

Prewriting

Choosing Your Topic

Use one of these strategies to find an issue that matters to you:

- **Round Table** With a group, hold a roundtable discussion of problems in your school. Raise as many different issues as possible. Jot down topics that spark strong feelings in you. Choose from among these subjects for your essay topic.

- **Quicklist** Fold a piece of paper in thirds lengthwise. In the first column, write issues and ideas that interest you. In the second column, write a descriptive word for each. In the third column, give an example supporting that description. Make sure each issue has an opposing side. Choose the topic that interests you most.

Work in Progress
Review the work you did on pages 595 and 613.

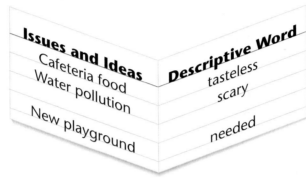

Issues and Ideas
Cafeteria food
Water pollution
New playground

Descriptive Word
tasteless
scary
needed

Examples
macaroni and cheese
streams polluted by fertilizer runoff
child hurt on slide

Narrowing Your Topic

Once you have chosen an issue to write about, narrow your focus. For example, the topic "violence in the media" includes violence on news reports, in movies, and on television. To write an effective persuasive essay, you might focus only on violence in television shows.

Gathering Details

Gather evidence to support your position. Conduct research either in the library, on the Internet, or by interviewing experts on your topic. Gather the following types of support:

Facts: statements that can be proved true

Statistics: facts presented in the form of numbers

Anecdotes: brief stories that illustrate a point

Quotes from Authorities: statements of leading experts

Anticipate counterarguments. Make a list of the arguments people might have against your position. For each, identify a response that you can use to address the issues in your essay.

Drafting

Shaping Your Writing

Develop and support your thesis statement. To keep your position clearly before your readers, review your notes and develop a thesis statement—one strong sentence that sums up your argument. Include this statement in your introduction.

Organize to emphasize your arguments. As you draft, present the supporting evidence you have gathered, starting with your least important points and building toward your most important ones. Address opposing concerns and counterarguments directly—do not avoid them. Consider organizing as shown in the pyramid.

Introduction and thesis

- First set of arguments
  - Supporting details
- Concerns and counterarguments
- Statements proving opposition is weak or incorrect
- Strongest argument
  - Supporting details

Conclusions

Providing Elaboration

Choose precise words. Forceful language helps convey your point and builds support for your position. Use precise, lively words that will stir readers' emotions and appeal to their sense of reason.

> **Vague:**   a *good* candidate
> **Precise:**   a *trustworthy* or *intelligent* candidate

Appeal to your audience. Use words that your audience will know. If you are writing for teenagers, use informal language. If you are writing to a government official, use formal, serious language.

To read the complete student model, see page 634.

Student Model: Using Language That Appeals to Your Audience

To you, voting may seem ~~unimportant~~, just a ~~chore~~ that you
like just a waste of time   *mere piece of paper with boxes on it*

have to go through to ~~choose~~ which person you want for that
mark

particular job.

> By using informal language, the writer appeals to teenage readers.

Pat Mora

On Supporting a Point

Pat Mora

When I was a university administrator, a friend mentioned that her daughter, Gabriela, wanted writing advice. I've always liked to write letters, so I wrote a persuasive essay as a letter to Gabi. The letter/essay became part of my collection *Nepantla: Essays from the Land in the Middle.* From the time I was in high school, I was intrigued by essays, perhaps because I like seeing how writers express their beliefs convincingly.

> *"I write because I'm a reader."*
> —— *Pat Mora*

Professional Model:

from *"To Gabriela, A Young Writer"*

I know that the society we live in and that the movies, television programs, and commercials we see, all affect us. It's not easy to learn to judge others fairly, not because of the car they drive, the house they live in, the church they attend, the color of their skin, the language they speak at home. It takes courage to face the fact that we all have ten toes, get sleepy at night, get scared in the dark. Some families, some cities, some states, and even some countries foolishly convince themselves that they are better than others. And then they teach their children this ugly lie. It's like a weed with burrs and stickers that pricks people.

How are young women who are African American, Asian American, American Indian, Latinas, or members of all the other ethnic groups supposed to feel about themselves? Some are proud of their cultural roots. . . .

I played with different human similarities. Humans have arms and eyes. There's something so basic about the words "ten toes," though.

The right comparison, or metaphor, is like a shortcut to the reader's feelings and imagination. We all know the discomfort of stickers.

Here and throughout, I'm building my argument by using lists of examples to support my thesis. I'm building a case.

Revising

Revising Your Overall Structure

Highlight main points. To check your organization, first highlight each main point. Then, use one or more of these strategies:

- If a reader needs to know one main point to understand a second one, make sure the first main point comes before the second.
- If one main point means the same as another, combine them, or combine the paragraphs in which they appear.
- If one main point is stronger than the others, move it to the end of your essay.

To read the complete student model, see page 634.

Student Model: Revising to Highlight Main Points

Vote because you can. Remind yourself that not everyone is as lucky. In many countries, voting is not an option. The leaders take control rather than being voted into a leadership role. Often leaders who are not elected can be corrupt or tyrannical, because the people can't remove them from power. We are citizens of a free country in which we have the right to vote. Whether or not the system works perfectly, it is better than a system with no voting. ∨

> This point is stronger than the others. Moving it to the end of the essay gives it more impact.

Peer Review: Read your draft to a group of peers. Ask whether the order of points was logical. Consider their responses as you revise.

Revising Your Sentences

Combine sentences to show connections. To improve your writing, combine short, choppy sentences to stress the connections you see.

Similar Ideas: The town permits skating on the lake. We don't have the money to open a rink.

Combined: The town permits skating on the lake, **and** we don't have the money to open a rink.

Opposing Ideas: The food is better heated. Most classrooms do not have microwave ovens.

Combined: The food is better heated, *but* most classrooms do not have microwave ovens.

Integrating Grammar Skills

Revising Fragments and Run-On Sentences

The most basic sentence contains a single **independent clause**—a group of words including a subject and a verb and expressing a complete idea. A **fragment** is a group of words that does not express a complete thought. It is often missing a subject, a verb, or both. A **run-on sentence** occurs when two or more independent clauses are joined without proper punctuation.

Prentice Hall Writing and Grammar Connection: Chapter 21, Sections 2 and 4

> **Fragments:** I'll give my report today. As long as you give yours, too.
> **Corrected:** I'll give my report today as long as you give yours, too.

Run-ons contain at least two clauses, as the example shows.

> **Run-on:** <u>We dove into the water,</u> <u>we swam fast.</u>

Run-ons can be corrected in the following ways:

- Use punctuation to correctly indicate where each idea ends.

    Corrected: We dove into the water. We swam fast.

- Use a comma and a coordinating conjunction such as *and, or, so,* or *but* to set equal ideas.

    Corrected: We dove into the water, and we swam fast.

- Use a semicolon and a subordinating conjunction to show the relationship between ideas.

    Corrected: We dove into the water; then, we swam fast.

Common Subordinating Conjunctions				
after	as long as	even though	so that	until
although	because	if	though	when
as	before	since	unless	where

Fixing Sentence Errors To fix fragments and run-ons with sentence combining, use the following methods.

1. **To fix a fragment, first identify the incomplete sentence.** Then, make a complete sentence out of it.

2. **To fix a run-on, first identify the independent clauses in it.** Then follow the rules on this page.

Apply It to Your Editing

Choose a paragraph in your draft and circle any fragments or run-ons you find. Fix these sentence errors using one of the methods above.

Student Model:
Amanda Wintenburg
Daytona Beach, FL

Decide The Future

To you, voting may seem like just a waste of time, just a mere piece of paper with boxes on it, that you have to go through to mark which person you want for that particular job. But to me, it's something more, much more... it's your chance to decide the future. Everyone who is eligible should take advantage of the right to vote.

> In the opening paragraph, Amanda points out the two "sides" to the voting issue. She follows with her thesis statement.

I'm not the only one who thinks voting should be a top priority for people. For years, companies and organizations have supplied numerous reminders and reasons to explain when and why you vote. You've seen the commercials; they've all told us about it. Although there is no financial profit in convincing people to vote, money is being spent to make sure it happens. That should tell you something.

> This evidence supports the idea that voting matters.

Eenie, meenie, miney mo, . . . maybe you don't want to vote because you feel as if you don't know enough about the candidates to make an informed decision. However, newspapers, television broadcasts, performance records—all these fact-based sources of information are available to the interested voter who wants to make a responsible choice. Find out what the candidates have been doing and what they plan to do. Make your decision based on information.

> Here, Amanda identifies and addresses readers' concerns and counterarguments.

In many countries, voting is not an option. In countries with kings and queens, leaders are born into their positions. In other countries, the leaders take control rather than being voted into a leadership role. Often leaders who are not elected can be corrupt or tyrannical, because the people can't remove them from power. We are citizens of a free country in which we have the right to vote. Whether or not the system works perfectly, it is better than a system with no voting. Vote because you can. Remind yourself that not everyone is as lucky.

> Amanda reminds readers that not everyone has the right to vote. She uses language that appeals to both reason and emotion.

If you don't vote, you have less control over your own life. Voting is your chance to make your voice heard. It's your chance to decide the future.

Editing and Proofreading

Check your writing to correct errors in spelling, grammar, and punctuation.

Focus on End Marks: Be sure to use the correct end mark for each kind of sentence in your essay. Use a period at the end of a statement, a question mark at the end of a question, and an exclamation mark at the end of a statement that indicates strong feeling.

Publishing and Presenting

Consider one of the following ways to share your writing:

Give a speech. Use your persuasive essay as the basis for a speech that you give to your classmates.

Submit a newspaper article. Many local newspapers will publish well-written persuasive compositions if they appeal to the newspaper's audience. Submit your composition and see what happens.

Reflecting on Your Writing

Writer's Journal Jot down your thoughts on the experience of writing a persuasive essay. Begin by answering these questions:

- What part of the writing process seemed difficult to you? Explain.
- What did you learn about your subject as you wrote?

> *Prentice Hall Writing and Grammar Connection: Chapter 7*

Rubric for Self-Assessment

To assess your persuasive essay, use the following rubric:

Criteria	Rating Scale not very — very
Focus: How clearly is your position stated?	1 2 3 4 5
Organization: How organized is your argument or judgment?	1 2 3 4 5
Support/Elaboration: How persuasive is your evidence?	1 2 3 4 5
Style: How well do you balance language to appeal to reason and emotion?	1 2 3 4 5
Conventions: How correct is your grammar, especially your use of independent clauses?	1 2 3 4 5

Communications Workshop

Evaluating Advertisements

An **advertisement** is meant to persuade you to do something—perhaps purchase a product or vote for a political candidate. Evaluate the content, logic, and presentation of advertisements to make wise decisions.

Evaluating Content
Like all persuasive writing or speaking, an advertisement should be based on reliable information and logical reasoning.

Challenge the claims and the logic. Some claims may be technically true, but not as powerful as they appear at first. For example, stating that nine out of ten doctors recommend a medication may sound as if all doctors in the country had offered their opinions. However, this claim can be made even if only ten doctors have been interviewed.

Consider the sources. A company's own research may be slanted to favor its products. Facts from well-established groups are more likely to be reliable.

Evaluating Delivery
Advertisements often include speech, sound effects, music, or visual effects. Analyze the effect of these elements.

Analyze the entertainment effect. Dancing dogs, upbeat music, and bottles of ketchup that talk may be entertaining, but they do not give you the information you need about the product to make an informed decision.

Analyze the use of language. Advertisers may use specific types of language to appeal to certain groups of people. For example, formal, intellectual language may make people think they are smart if they buy the product. Advertisements aimed at teenagers may use informal language and popular slang.

Analyze the emotional effect. A car commercial may make it seem as if driving a particular car means you are adventurous and successful. Be aware that advertisers may try to sell a product by associating it with a feeling or quality.

Evaluating an Advertisement	
Product	
Facts	
Effects	
Persuasive techniques	
Questions, challenges, or affirmations	
Overall rating	

Activity ▸ *Media Evaluation* With others, watch several commercials on television. Individually, evaluate the content and delivery using a chart like the one shown. Compare your responses with your classmates'.

Crossroads: Classic Themes In Young Adult Literature

Anthology
Prentice Hall, 1984

Anthology Containing poems, plays, and short stories centered on the journey to adulthood, this anthology features work from the world's premier modern writers.  Gary Soto, Sandra Cisneros, Lois Lowry, J.R.R. Tolkien, and Nikki Giovanni are a few of the authors represented in this collection.

My Side of the Mountain

Jean Craighead George
Puffin, 1990

Novel Sam Gribley describes his year surviving on his own in a remote area of the Catskill Mountains. His diary of living off the land is marked by detailed  accounts of the animals, insects, plants, people, and books that help him survive.

The Summer of the Swans

Betsy Byars
Puffin Books, 1996

Novel Sara experiences an unforgettable summer that marks her entry into young womanhood. While changing and growing every day, she learns to cope 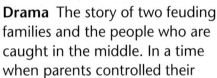 with her disabled brother and deal with the challenges of adolescence.

Romeo and Juliet

William Shakespeare
An Adapted Classic
Globe Fearon, 1996

Drama The story of two feuding families and the people who are caught in the middle. In a time when parents controlled their  children's lives, Romeo and Juliet made the mistake of falling in love. This poetic tragedy deals with the results of enmity and love.

These titles are available in the Penguin/Prentice Hall Literature Library.
Consult your teacher before using one.

Think About It Solving mathematical equations can be difficult and time consuming. However, it may be that many animals make calculations instinctively. This article suggests that animals can perform amazing feats of mathematics—a handy talent to have in the wild.

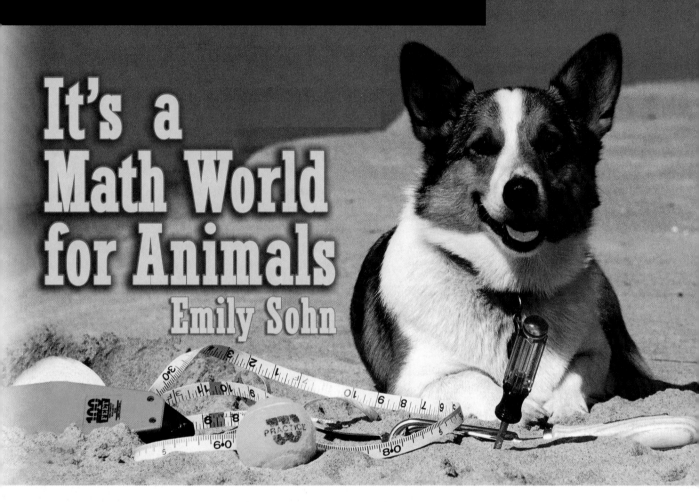

It's a Math World for Animals
Emily Sohn

Birds do it. Dogs do it. Even salamanders do it.

The ability to solve math problems is showing up in all sorts of unlikely creatures. From monkeys who know the difference between 2 and 3 to dogs who can calculate the fastest route, animal mathematicians are teaching scientists a few things about numbers.

A growing body of research suggests that nature probably discovered math long before people did. Studies of animal mathematicians might help explain how people learn to add, subtract, and multiply and indicate what types of math people can do without going to class.

Watching animals solve problems could also make math more fun for people who say they can't stand the subject.

A fetching dog

Mathematician Tim Pennings, for instance, was at the beach when he discovered that his dog Elvis could do a type of math called calculus.

"I would throw a ball into the water," Pennings says. "I noticed he'd run along the beach and then jump into the water and swim at an angle toward the ball."

That's a good strategy. Swimming is slow compared with running, so swimming all the way to the ball would take longer even if the route is more direct. On the other hand, running along the beach adds to the total distance Elvis must go to get to the ball. The best bet is a compromise between the two—running a certain distance along the beach before plunging into the water.

Pennings wondered if Elvis was instinctively taking the fastest possible route to the ball. First, he measured how fast Elvis runs and swims. Then, he threw a tennis ball into the water and let the little Welsh corgi go.

"I ran after Elvis with a screwdriver," says Pennings, who works at Hope College in Holland, Michigan. "Where he turned toward the water, I drove a screwdriver into the sand. While he was swimming to the ball, I ran and grabbed a tape measure and beat him to the ball."

Man and dog ran back and forth like this for more than 3 hours. After throwing out trials with bad tosses or high waves, Pennings had 35 sets of measurements. Then, he went home and did some calculations, using calculus to find the fastest route.

"I did all the math," Pennings says, "and I figured out that where Elvis jumps in is pretty much perfect. He kind of naturally knows the right spot to jump in."

It took the grown man about an hour to come up with the same solution that the 3-year-old dog could figure out in a fraction of a second. But is the dog really doing the math?

"Elvis is doing calculus in the sense that he somehow knows how to find the minimum time to get to the ball," Pennings says.

Pennings suspects that other creatures have naturally learned the most efficient ways to do things over millions of years of evolution. "There might be all sorts of things like that in nature," he says.

One interesting follow-up study would be to do a similar experiment with people of different ages, Pennings says. Results might show an innate ability to do math that gets better or worse as people grow up and go to school.

Number sense

Studying math skills in dogs to understand math in people might not be such a far-fetched idea. In fact, some research is showing that babies and animals actually have a lot in common when it comes to numbers.

Most animal math research has focused on primates. To test whether a monkey can tell the difference between numbers of objects, scientists measure how long an animal looks at things. A monkey will look longer at something that doesn't match what it expects to see.

Using this technique, researchers have shown that monkeys can add and substract small numbers of objects. If they are shown one apple slice and then another, for example, they know there should be a total of two. They will then look for a longer time at a pile of three or one than at a pile of two.

Recent evidence also shows that some primates know the difference between more and less. Cotton-top tamarins look longer at two Froot Loops than at one. Rhesus macaques look longer at three turnips than at two.

Likewise, 12-month-old babies look longer at a bigger pile of sugar cookies. Even though they can't talk or count, the babies seem to know how to go for more.

Most interesting of all, says cognitive scientist Claudia Uller, is that those skills fall apart at about the same number in both monkeys and babies.

"It's so incredible," says Uller, who is at the University of Louisiana at Lafayette. "It breaks down at around four. If you give babies two or three, they'll go for three. At three versus four, their choices are random. At four versus six, they're random." The same is true for monkeys and tamarins.

Because primates and people are so closely related, Uller wanted to try the same experiment with a completely different kind of animal: salamanders. Amazingly, she found the same results.

When shown test tubes holding different numbers of live fruit flies, red-backed salamanders looked at the tube that held more. But only up to a certain point. Just as in babies and monkeys, the system seemed to break down around four. Uller published her results recently in the journal *Animal Cognition.*

Her study is the first example that an animal other than a primate might be able to distinguish between more and less. Another scientist is now looking for the same phenomenon in fruit flies, Uller says. Further research could help explain the biology behind basic math skills.

A little training

The limits of animal math are still unclear. With a little training, rats can learn to press a lever a certain number of times, say exactly 45 times, to get a reward. When shown a pile of random objects, a famous parrot named Alex can tell you how many of them are red or green. The examples go on and on.

Widespread use of math in nature makes sense, experts say, considering the challenges to survival in the wild. By recognizing which bush offers more berries, for instance, or which pack of lions is more fearsome, an animal might improve its own chances of survival. The same was probably true of our ancestors.

So, maybe math is more than just a grade on your report card. At some point, your life might depend on it!

More to Explore

This article came from a Web site called *Science News for Kids*—a site from the publishers of *Science News Magazine.* It contains up-to-date articles covering all fields of science. The site provides useful information, hands-on activities, and Web resources.

Readings in Mathematics
Talk About It

Use these questions to guide a discussion.

1. What does Tim Pennings's research prove about animal instinct?

2. **(a)** What do some animals and human babies have in common, according to this article? **(b)** Does this fact surprise you? Explain.

3. The article shows that animals use mathematics in their daily lives. In a small group, consider the following questions:
   - What advantage does Elvis have by reaching the ball in the shortest amount of time?
   - Why is it important for animals to recognize different numbers?
   - What other situations might call for animals to use math effectively in the wild?

   Choose a point-person to share your group's ideas with the class.

Unit 5 Overview

Introduction
Exploring Drama

Part 1: Purpose for Reading

Part 2: Summarizing

Introduction:
Drama

From the Author's Desk

Laurence Yep

Laurence Yep
Talks About the Form

I can't see my readers' faces when they read one of my books; but I can watch the theater audience as they laugh or cry during one of my plays—hopefully at the places that I had intended.

▲ Laurence Yep, whose books have received many awards, has written plays, historical novels, mysteries, science fiction, and short stories.

Drama: The Magic of Playing "Pretend"

In my novels, I create a **character** by means of words printed on a page; but in my dramas live actors bring the characters to life by interpreting what I've written. **Drama** has an almost magical power because it taps into some of our earliest experiences—who hasn't played "pretend" as a child?

Good actors don't need **props** or **scenery**—movable items or painted backdrops representing places—because it's their voices and gestures that transport us across space and time. The different **casts,** or sets of actors, take audiences from China across the Pacific Ocean and to San Francisco. They make it possible for us to experience an earthquake or feel the wash of air from an airplane's propellers.

In a drama, as the **main character** grows as a person; the audience should identify with his or her emotions. When the character feels sad, they should feel sad; and when the character feels happy, they should feel happy as well.

◄ Critical Viewing Which details in this picture express the power of drama to transport audiences to new worlds? **[Interpret]**

The Climax: A Drama Reaches Completion

The character's development forms a kind of arc to the **climax** of the play, when there is some insight, revelation, or action that brings that development to completion. At the end of the play, the audience should feel joy or sorrow or even anger, but never boredom with what's happened to the character.

In writing a **script**—the text of a play, with dialogue and directions for actors—I keep in mind the quotation shown on this page. Spoken by the movie director Alfred Hitchcock, it tells me that I can only use the words and actions that are significant for a character's development. The rest have to be left out, even though some might be my favorite parts.

"What is drama, after all, but life with all the dull bits cut out."

from *Hitchcock*, by François Truffaut

—*Alfred Hitchcock*

The result: Drama is like a lens that brings a character's life into focus, a focus so sharp and intense that the action's lessons feel etched upon our souls.

More About the Author

Laurence **Yep** (b.1948)

Laurence Yep, who spent six years doing research for *Dragonwings,* has said, "Research is a lot like a treasure hunt for me." Like Windrider, the Chinese American aviator in *Dragonwings,* many of the characters in Yep's books are outsiders. Yep began writing about such characters early, selling his first story to a science-fiction magazine when he was eighteen. He was paid a penny a word.

Fast Facts

▶ As a young man, Yep worked long hours in his family's grocery in San Francisco.
▶ One of his high school English teachers first inspired him to write.
▶ He won the 2005 Laura Ingalls Wilder Medal for contributions to children's literature.

Learning About Drama

Elements of Drama

Drama is a story told in dialogue by performers in front of an audience. The following elements make drama come to life.

The **playwright** is the author of a play. **Actors** are the people who perform it.

Acts are the units of action in a drama. Acts are often divided into parts called **scenes.**

Characterization is the playwright's technique for creating believable characters.

Dramatic speech is important in drama because it advances the story's action. These are the most common types of speeches:

- **Dialogue** is conversation between or among characters.
- **Monologue** is a long speech that is spoken by a single character. It often reveals a character's private thoughts and feelings.

PEANUTS reprinted by permission of United Feature Syndicate, Inc.

Stage directions are the sets of bracketed information that describe the scenery and how the characters should move and speak. Some playwrights use abbreviations such as C, center stage; L, stage left; R, stage right; U, upstage or rear of stage; and D, downstage, or front of stage.

A **theater** is a place where plays are usually presented.

Set is the term used for the construction on stage that suggests the time and place of the action. **Scenery** is another word for set.

Props are the small movable items, such as a doctor's clipboard or a student's notebook, that the actors use to make their actions look realistic.

▶ Critical Viewing
What type of play would you expect to see in this type of setting? **[Speculate]**

Types of Drama

Comedy is a form of drama that has a happy ending, and often features normal characters in funny situations. Comedies can be written to entertain, but they can also point out the faults of a society.

Tragedy is often contrasted with comedy. The distinguishing feature of a tragedy is that the events lead to the downfall of the main character. This character can be an average person but is often a person of great significance, like a king or a heroic figure.

Drama is a word that is often used to describe plays that address serious subjects.

When you think of drama, you might think of stage plays and the exciting world of theater—actors, costumes, and lights. However, drama includes more than theater.

- **Screenplays** are the scripts for films. They include camera angles and can allow for more scene changes than a stage play.

- **Teleplays** are scripts written for television and often contain elements similar to a screenplay.

- **Radio plays** are written to be performed as radio broadcasts. They include sound effects and require no set, stage or directions that explain movement.

Check Your Understanding

Identify the *character, dialogue, stage directions, set, characterization,* and *props* in the following excerpt from *A Christmas Carol: Scrooge and Marley:*

[CRATCHIT *closes the door and returns to his workplace,* SCROOGE *is at his own counting table. He talks to* CRATCHIT *without looking up.*]

SCROOGE. It's less of a time of year for being merry, and more a time of year for being loony. . .if you ask me.

CRATCHIT. I must be going home. . .[*He snuffs out his candle and puts on his hat.*] I hope you have a. . .very very lovely day tomorrow, sir. . .

My novel *Dragonwings* tells about a boy named Moon Shadow who leaves China to join his father in San Francisco and becomes caught up in his father's dream to build an airplane. Twenty-two years passed between the time I published *Dragonwings* and when I dramatized the novel. This was an advantage because I could be more objective about what to cut—and I had to delete a lot.

The production was originally supposed to be performed at schools, so a 248-page novel had to fit into an hour-long play. I condensed whole sections of the book into a few narrative lines that an adult Moon Shadow says. In addition, I had to drop some of the novel's descriptive passages because special effects were impractical on our budget.

From Page to Stage: Some Characters Don't Survive

Because I only had five **actors,** there could never be more than five **characters** on stage at any one time. That meant cutting a number of characters, like Robin, Lefty, and Hand Clap. Also, I could no longer tell you what Moon Shadow felt and thought. On stage, it was the actor who had to convey all that with facial expressions and body language.

Dialogue in a Novel vs. Dialogue in a Play

I learned again how **dialogue** printed in a novel is different from dialogue spoken in a play. Spoken words have a certain rhythm that's created by contractions, run-on sentences, or dropped verbs or subjects. That's why, for the play, I had to revise some speeches to make them "sound" right.

It was both strange and wonderful to share a fantasy with that many people—the actors began to identify with their characters and say "I" instead of "he" or "she." When I work on a novel, my characters often seem to take on a life of their own, but I know it's all in my imagination.

In the scene that follows, after enduring an earthquake and many troubles, Moon Shadow is about to see if their airplane will really fly.

from the novel

Dragonwings
Laurence Yep

I do not know when I fell asleep, but it was already way past sunrise when I woke up. The light crept through the cracks in the walls and under the shutters and seemed to delight especially in dancing on my eyes. Father lay huddled, rolled up in his blanket. He did not move when the knock came at our door. I was still in my clothes because it was cold. I crawled out of the blankets and opened the side door.

▲ **Critical Viewing**
What historical period does this sepia photograph suggest? **[Infer]**

The fog lay low on the hill. Tendrils drifted in through the open doorway. At first I could not see anything but shadows, and then a sudden breeze whipped the fog away from the front of our barn. Hand Clap stood there as if he had appeared by magic. He bowed.

"There you are." He turned and called over his shoulder. "Hey, everybody, they're here."

I heard the clink of harness and the rattle of an old wagon trying to follow the ruts in the road. Toiling up the hill out of the fog was Red Rabbit, and behind him I saw Uncle on the wagon seat. The rest of the wagon was empty—I suppose to give Red Rabbit less of a load to pull. Behind the wagon came the Company, with coils of ropes over their shoulders and baskets of food. I ran down the hill, my feet pounding against the hard, damp earth. I got up on the seat and almost bowled Uncle over. For once Uncle did not worry about his dignity but caught me up and returned my hug.

"Ouch," he said, and pushed me away. He patted himself lightly on his chest. "I'm not as young as I used to be."

Then Hand Clap, Lefty, and White Deer crowded around.

"Am I ever glad you're here," I said. "Poor Father—"

Uncle held up his hands. "We know. That's why we came."

"But how? Why?" I was bursting with a dozen questions all at once.

"Why, to help you get that thing up to the top of the hill," Uncle said. "Why else would we close up our shop and take a boat and climb this abominable hill, all on the coldest, wettest day ever known since creation?"

"But you don't believe in flying machines."

"I still don't," Uncle said sternly. "But I still feel as if I owe you something for what was done to you by that man who once was my son[1]. I'll be there to haul your machine up the hill, and I'll be there to haul it back down when it doesn't fly."

"We were all getting fat anyway," White Deer said, "especially Uncle."

Laurence Yep
Author's Insight
Red Rabbit was named after the speedy horse ridden by Kuan Kung, the god of war.

Laurence Yep
Author's Insight
This is one of my favorite lines because Uncle acts like the elderly Chinese that I know.

Fiction
Prose In prose writing, the author combines dialogue with elements of description and narration.

---

1. man who was my son Black Dog, who robbed the narrator and his father.

from the dramatization of

Dragonwings
Laurence Yep

CAST OF CHARACTERS

RED RABBIT a horse that pulls the company's laundry wagon

UNCLE BRIGHT STAR another laundry owner

WHITE DEER the third laundry owner

MOON SHADOW the narrator of the story

MISS WHITLAW owner of a stable in San Francisco where the narrator and his father live

WINDRIDER Moon Shadow's father

Scene 9 *Piedmont, later that day outside the stable.*

MOON SHADOW: September twenty-second, Nineteen-ought-nine. Dear Mother. I have bad news. We are going to lose Dragonwings before father can fly it. Black Dog stole all we have, and the landlord will not give us an extension on our rent. So we'll have to move and leave Dragonwings behind. We have asked Miss Whitlaw for help, but her new house has taken up all of her money. And even if Uncle would speak to us, he has probably spent all he has on rebuilding his laundry.

[*UNCLE BRIGHT STAR and MISS WHITLAW enter from L.*]

MISS WHITLAW: I could have gotten down from the wagon by myself.

UNCLE BRIGHT STAR: Watch gopher hole.

MISS WHITLAW: I'm younger than you.

MOON SHADOW: Uncle, Miss Whitlaw!

MISS WHITLAW: How are you?

[*Shaking MOON SHADOW's hand. WINDRIDER enters from U. He now wears a cap.*]

Drama
Dialogue All the action is conveyed through characters' words and gestures.

Laurence Yep
Author's Insight
The friendly competition between Uncle Bright Star and Miss Whitlaw wasn't in the novel but was developed with the actors.

WINDRIDER: Come to laugh, Uncle?

UNCLE BRIGHT STAR: I came to help you fly your contraption.

MOON SHADOW: But you don't believe in flying machines.

UNCLE BRIGHT STAR: And I'll haul that thing back down when it doesn't fly. Red Rabbit and me were getting fat anyway. But look at how tall you've grown. And how thin. And ragged. [*Pause.*] But you haven't broken your neck which was more than I ever expected.

MISS WHITLAW: As soon as I told your uncle, we hatched the plot together. You ought to get a chance to fly your aeroplane.

UNCLE BRIGHT STAR: Flat purse, strong backs.

Laurence Yep
Author's Insight
The left-handed compliment—a compliment that is partly an insult—is typical of the Chinatown oldtimers.

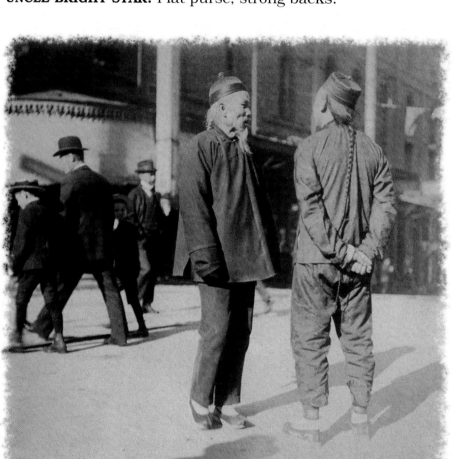

◄ Critical Viewing
What similarities and differences do you see between the setting of the photograph and the setting of the drama?
[Compare and Contrast]

WINDRIDER: We need to pull Dragonwings to the very top.

UNCLE BRIGHT STAR: That hill is a very steep hill.

WINDRIDER: It has to be that one. The winds are right.

UNCLE BRIGHT STAR: Ah, well, it's the winds.

WINDRIDER: Take the ropes. [*Pantomimes taking a rope over his shoulder as he faces the audience.*] Got a good grip?

OTHERS: [*Pantomiming taking the ropes.*] Yes, right, etc.

WINDRIDER: Then pull.

[*They strain. MOON SHADOW stumbles but gets right up. Stamping his feet to get better footing, he keeps tugging.*]

MOON SHADOW: [*Giving up.*] It's no good.

UNCLE BRIGHT STAR: Pull in rhythm. As we did on the railroad[1]. [*In demonstration, UNCLE BRIGHT STAR stamps his feet in a slow rhythm to set the beat and the others repeat. The rhythm picks up as they move.*]
Ngúng, ngúng.
Dew gùng.

OTHERS: Ngúng, ngúng.
Dew gùng.

UNCLE BRIGHT STAR: [*Imitating the intonation of the Cantonese.*] Púsh, púsh.
Wòrk, wòrk.

OTHERS: Púsh, púsh.
Wòrk, wòrk.

UNCLE BRIGHT STAR: Seen gà,
Gee gá.

[*High rising tone on the last syllable.*]

OTHERS: Seen gá,
Gee gá.

[*High rising tone on the last syllable.*]

---

1. railroad Uncle Bright Star had helped dig tunnels through the mountains for the railroad.

Drama
Stage Directions The information within these brackets describes actions, emotions, and gestures, and instructs the actors on using props.

Laurence Yep
Author's Insight
The accent marks over the English imitate the tones in Cantonese, a dialect of Chinese.

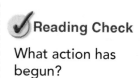Reading Check

What action has begun?

UNCLE BRIGHT STAR: Get rich,
Go hóme.

OTHERS: Get rìch,
Go hóme.

[*MOON SHADOW, WINDRIDER, UNCLE BRIGHT STAR and MISS WHITLAW arrive D.*]

MOON SHADOW: [*Panting.*] We made it. Tramp the grass down in front.

[*WINDRIDER stands C as the others stamp the grass. They can't help smiling and laughing a little.*]

WINDRIDER: That's enough.

MOON SHADOW: [To *MISS WHITLAW.*] Take that propeller.

[*MISS WHITLAW takes her place before the right propeller with her hands resting on the blade. MOON SHADOW takes his place beside the left propeller. WINDRIDER faces U., his back to the audience.*]

Laurence Yep
Author's Insight We needed to establish the hilltop was flat so I had them trample the grass; but the actors had such a good time doing it that I put it into the stage direction.

▼ **Critical Viewing**
Does this hill seem steep enough to launch *Dragonwings*? **[Deduce]**

MISS WHITLAW: Listen to the wind on the wings.

UNCLE BRIGHT STAR: It's alive.

WINDRIDER: All right.

[*MOON SHADOW and MISS WHITLAW pull down at the propellers and back away quickly. We hear a motor cough into life. Propellers begin to turn with a roar.*]

UNCLE BRIGHT STAR: [*Slowly turning.*] What's wrong? Is it just going to roll down the hill?

[*MISS WHITLAW crosses her fingers as they all turn to watch the aeroplane.*]

MISS WHITLAW: He's up!

[*WINDRIDER starts to do his flight ballet.*]

MOON SHADOW: [*Pointing.*] He's turning.

UNCLE BRIGHT STAR: He's really flying.

MISS WHITLAW: I never thought I'd see the day. A human up in the sky. Off the ground.

[*They turn and tilt their heads back.*]

MISS WHITLAW: [*Cont'd.*] Free as an eagle.

UNCLE BRIGHT STAR: [*Correcting her.*] Like dragon.

MOON SHADOW: Father, you did it. [*Wonderingly.*] You did it.

[*The aeroplane roars loudly overhead. MOON SHADOW as adult steps forward and addresses the audience.*]

MOON SHADOW: I thought he'd fly forever and ever. Up, up to heaven and never come down. But then some of the guy wires[2] broke, and the right wings separated. Dragonwings came crashing to earth. Father had a few broken bones, but it was nothing serious. Only the aeroplane was wrecked. Uncle took him back to the laundry to recover. Father didn't say much, just thought a lot—I figured he was busy designing the next aeroplane. But when Father was nearly well, he made me sit down next to him.

---

2. **guy wires** wires that help to steady the plane's two sets of wings.

Drama

Dialogue This brief exchange shows the enchanted nature of the moment.

Laurence Yep
Author's Insight
For several years, people believed the Wright Brothers had staged a hoax, and so some Americans did not believe they had flown until they put on a flying exhibition in Paris.

Laurence Yep
Author's Insight
This is another favorite line. Moon Shadow made sacrifices from duty, not because he believed his father would actually fly.

 Reading Check

What happened to Dragonwings?

WINDRIDER: Uncle says he'll make me a partner if I stay. So the western officials would have to change my immigration class. I'd be a merchant, and merchants can bring their wives here. Would you like to send for Mother?

MOON SHADOW: [*Going to WINDRIDER*] But Dragonwings?

WINDRIDER: When I was up in the air, I tried to find you. You were so small. And getting smaller. Just disappearing from sight. [*Handing his cap to MOON SHADOW.*] Like you were disappearing from my life. [*He begins his ballet again.*] I knew it wasn't the time. The Dragon King[3] said there would be all sorts of lessons.

[*MOON SHADOW turns to audience as an adult.*]

MOON SHADOW: We always talked about flying again. Only we never did. [*Putting on cap.*] But dreams stay with you, and we never forgot.

[*WINDRIDER takes his final pose. A gong sounds.*]

---

3. Dragon King In Chinese legends, most dragons are not evil creatures. Earlier in the story, Windrider relates a dream sequence in which he was given his name by the Dragon King and learned he had once been a flying dragon.

Drama
Monologue This speech reveals Windrider's private thoughts.

◀ **Critical Viewing** Do you think the dragon pictured is behaving like a king? Explain. **[Connect]**

Q. **What was the hardest part of adapting your novel as a drama?**

A. I had to think as a playwright rather than a novelist. In a book, I control what a reader hears and sees; but in a play I surrender most of that power to the actors. Setting up a scene was like creating the rules of a game that the actors would then play in their own way.

Q. **Which character in the play is your favorite?**

A. It's Moon Shadow. In creating him, I was also trying to imagine what it was like for my father when he came from China to America as a young boy. Like Moon Shadow, he hardly knew his father.

Q. **Would you like to act in your own play?**

A. I'm a terrible actor, and in college the most I did was act as a stage manager—and I didn't last long even in that job.

Student Corner

Q. **Why did you entitle the novel and play** *Dragonwings***?**
—Jamie Cappiello, Swiftwater, Pennsylvania

A. I was always fascinated by dragons because they were all around me in Chinatown where I went to school. Chinese dragons, unlike the dragons in the fantasy books I read, were good creatures—if a bit proud. I thought a Chinese would think about flight in terms of the greatest flying creature he knew—a dragon.

The Wright Brothers' first airplane was not much more than a pair of wings set on a wooden frame so I thought a Chinese might think of them as a dragon's wings.

 Writing Workshop: *Work in Progress*

Multimedia Report

For a multimedia report you may write, list four ideas in response to one of these general topics: locations around the world, nature and wildlife, sports and athletes. Save this Idea List in your writing portfolio.

Drama

Thinking About the Selections

1. **Respond:** Do you think Dragonwings is a good name for a plane? Why or why not?

2. **(a) Recall:** In the novel excerpt, how do Uncle and the others plan to get the flying machine up the hill? **(b) Compare:** In the play scene, what helps the audience understand how Dragonwings will be moved to the hilltop?

3. **(a) Recall:** What happens to Dragonwings? **(b) Infer:** How is Windrider changed by his flight? **(c) Interpret:** What does Moon Shadow mean when he says to the audience "dreams stay with you, and we never forget."

Drama Review

4. Explain the ways in which the **drama** enhances the emotion of the situation.

5. **(a)** In a chart like the one shown, list examples of **dialogue** and its uses. **(b)** Compare charts with a partner. How has your understanding grown or changed as a result of looking at someone else's responses?

To show action	To reveal thoughts and feelings	To describe setting
"Take that propeller."	"When I was up in the air, I tried to find you . . . Like you were disappearing from my life."	"That hill is a very steep hill."

Research the Author

Plan an **exhibit** of books, audiocassettes, and CDs of at least five Laurence Yep works. Follow these steps:

- Consult the library catalog for selections by Yep that will interest your classmates. Review each title to find key information such as characters, setting, and conflict.
- Display each item along with a short description.
- Prepare a brief overview to motivate and encourage others to read Yep's work.

QuickReview

Selections at a Glance

In the excerpt from the novel *Dragonwings* and in a scene from the play, a Chinese boy helps his father and others drag an airplane up a hill.

Go Online
Assessment

For: Self-test
Visit: www.PHSchool.com
Web Code: ema-6501

Drama: literature written to be performed before an audience

Dialogue: conversation that characters have with one another in a drama

Stage Directions: bracketed information in a drama that describes the scenery and how the characters should move and speak

Unit 5
Part 1
Purpose for Reading

Skills You Will Learn

Reading Skill: *Preview Text to Set a Purpose for Reading*
Literary Analysis: *Dialogue*

Reading Skill: *Adjust Your Reading Rate Based on Your Purpose for Reading*
Literary Analysis: *Stage Directions*

Reading Skill: *Analyze the Critic's Response*

Literary Analysis: *Comparing Characters*

Literature You Will Read

Reading: Purpose for Reading

> **Setting a purpose for reading** means determining the reasons you are reading.

Skills and Strategies You Will Learn in Part 1

In Part 1 you will learn

- to **preview a text** before reading to help set your **purpose for reading** (p. 662)
- to **adjust your reading rate** to suit your **purpose for reading** (p. 696)
- to **set a purpose** for **reading and analyzing a response** to a text (p. 732)

Using the Skills and Strategies in Part 1

Setting a purpose for reading gives you a focus as you read. For example, if your reading purpose is to learn about a subject, you pay more attention to details than if you are reading purely for entertainment. Use this chart to help guide your focus as you set a purpose for reading.

Purpose for Reading	Examples	Suggestions
to be entertained	• Popular magazines • Novels or short stories by your favorite author • Celebrity news	• Read at a comfortable rate. • Pay special attention to details that grab your interest.
to learn or gain understanding	• Textbooks • Informative Web sites • Assigned literature	• Preview the text • Read slowly and carefully. • Take notes.
to be inspired	• Self-help books or articles • Religious texts • Works of great literature • Biographies	• Preview • Read at a comfortable rate. • Reread or analyze parts that are meaningful to you.

Academic Vocabulary: Words for Setting a Purpose for Reading

The following words will help you write and talk about setting a purpose for reading for the selections in this unit.

Word	Definition	Example Sentence
reaction *n.*	an opposing action, a response	The editorial was a *reaction* to the new law.
involvement *n.*	participation	We welcomed his *involvement*.
conflict *n.*	opposition between or among different forces, clash	Bill's essay focused on the *conflict* between the main characters.
critique *n.*	an assessment, usually of a creative work	After reading a *critique* of the novel, Franz checked it out of the library.
assumption *n.*	the act of assuming or taking for granted	Our *assumption* was that the play was written long ago.

Vocabulary Skill: Suffixes

A **suffix** is a syllable, or a group of syllables, added to the end of a word that changes its meaning or part of speech.

In Part 1, you will learn
- the suffix *-ment* (p. 694)
- the suffix *-tion* (p. 730)

Suffix	Meaning of suffix	Examples
-ment	act or quality of; state of being	involvement, contentment
-tion	act or quality of; thing that is done; product or result of	reaction, participation, hesitation

Activity Use a dictionary to find out how to make nouns from these words, using either *-tion* or *-ment*. Use each new word in a sentence.

institute   participate   judge

enrich   graduate

These skills will help you become a better reader. Practice them with *A Christmas Carol: Scrooge and Marley,* Act I (p. 664).

Reading Skill

Setting a purpose gives you a focus as you read. You may set one or more of the purposes shown.

- to learn about a subject
- to take action or make a decision
- to be entertained
- to be inspired
- to gain understanding
- to complete a task

Preview a text before reading. Look at the title, the pictures, the captions, the organization, and the beginnings of passages. If you already have a purpose in mind, previewing will help you decide whether the text will fit your purpose. If you do not have a purpose in mind, previewing will help you determine a reason for reading it. Use a chart like the one shown to jot down notes on details you notice as you preview. Then, use your notes to set one or more purposes.

Element in Work	What Is Suggested About the Work?
Title	
Pictures	
Organization, Structure, Literary Form	
Beginnings of passages	

Literary Analysis

Dialogue is a conversation between characters. In a play, the characters are developed entirely through dialogue. Dialogue also advances the action of the plot and develops the conflict.

In the script of a dramatic work, you can tell which character is speaking by the name that appears before the character's lines. Look at this example:

Mrs. Perez. Come on, kids! We're leaving.
Jen. Wait for me!

Vocabulary Builder

A Christmas Carol: Scrooge and Marley, Act I

- **implored** (im plôrd´) *v.* begged (p. 666) *John implored us not to leave him alone.*

- **morose** (mə rōs´) *adj.* gloomy; ill-tempered (p. 668) *Her morose attitude left her with few friends.*

- **destitute** (des´ tə to͞ot´) *adj.* used as *n.,* people living in complete poverty (p. 671) *Please, donate food to the destitute.*

- **void** (void) *n.* emptiness (p. 676) *My friends could not fill the void created when Len left.*

- **conveyed** (kən vād´) *v.* made known; expressed (p. 678) *His tightly clenched fists conveyed anger.*

- **benevolence** (bə nev´ ə ləns) *n.* kindliness (p. 679) *The generous woman was known for her benevolence.*

Background

Economic and Social Change *A Christmas Carol* is set in England during the nineteenth century, a time of rapid industrial growth. In this booming economy, the wealthy lived in luxury, but the poor and the working class suffered. Charles Dickens's novel, from which this drama was adapted, shows sympathy for the situation of the poor and suggests a way in which it might be changed.

Connecting to the Literature

Reading/Writing Connection The character of Scrooge is so memorable that, over the years, his name has become part of everyday vocabulary. People use the word *scrooge* to refer to a selfish person who is concerned only with himself. List some ideas or associations that come to mind when you hear the word *scrooge*. Use at least three of these words: *acquire, appreciate, define, involve.*

Meet the Author

Israel **Horovitz** (b. 1939)

Israel Horovitz was born in Wakefield, Massachusetts. As a teenager, he did not like books by Charles Dickens. As he got older, however, he came to appreciate Dickens's style and stories. Now, Horovitz refers to Dickens as "a masterful storyteller." He imagines that if Dickens were alive today, the Englishman would be "our greatest television writer, or perhaps screenwriter."

Thoughts About *A Christmas Carol* As Horovitz adapted Dickens's novel into a play, he thought about which character was his favorite. The answer may surprise you: It is Scrooge, who reminds Horovitz of his own father.

Fast Facts

▶ Horovitz is married and has five children.
▶ He is the author of more than fifty plays and screenplays. He is also an actor.

Go Online
Author Link

For: More about Israel Horovitz
Visit: www.PHSchool.com
Web Code: eme-9502

A Christmas Carol: Scrooge and Marley

Israel Horovitz

from A Christmas Carol by Charles Dickens

The People of the Play

JACOB MARLEY, a specter

EBENEZER SCROOGE, not yet dead, which is to say still alive

BOB CRATCHIT, Scrooge's clerk

FRED, Scrooge's nephew

THIN DO-GOODER

PORTLY DO-GOODER

SPECTERS (VARIOUS), carrying money-boxes

THE GHOST OF CHRISTMAS PAST

FOUR JOCUND TRAVELERS

A BAND OF SINGERS

A BAND OF DANCERS

LITTLE BOY SCROOGE

YOUNG MAN SCROOGE

FAN, Scrooge's little sister

THE SCHOOLMASTER

SCHOOLMATES

FEZZIWIG, a fine and fair employer

DICK, young Scrooge's co-worker

YOUNG SCROOGE

A FIDDLER

MORE DANCERS

SCROOGE'S LOST LOVE

SCROOGE'S LOST LOVE'S DAUGHTER

SCROOGE'S LOST LOVE'S HUSBAND

THE GHOST OF CHRISTMAS PRESENT

SOME BAKERS

MRS. CRATCHIT, Bob Cratchit's wife

BELINDA CRATCHIT, a daughter

MARTHA CRATCHIT, another daughter

PETER CRATCHIT, a son

TINY TIM CRATCHIT, another son

SCROOGE'S NIECE, Fred's wife

THE GHOST OF CHRISTMAS FUTURE, a mute Phantom

THREE MEN OF BUSINESS

DRUNKS, SCOUNDRELS, WOMEN OF THE STREETS

A CHARWOMAN

MRS. DILBER

JOE, an old second-hand goods dealer

A CORPSE, very like Scrooge

AN INDEBTED FAMILY

ADAM, a young boy

A POULTERER

A GENTLEWOMAN

SOME MORE MEN OF BUSINESS

Act 1

THE PLACE OF THE PLAY   Various locations in and around the City of London, including Scrooge's Chambers and Offices; the Cratchit Home; Fred's Home; Scrooge's School; Fezziwig's Offices; Old Joe's Hide-a-Way.

THE TIME OF THE PLAY   The entire action of the play takes place on Christmas Eve, Christmas Day, and the morning after Christmas, 1843.

Scene 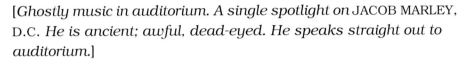 1

[*Ghostly music in auditorium. A single spotlight on* JACOB MARLEY, D.C. *He is ancient; awful, dead-eyed. He speaks straight out to auditorium.*]

MARLEY. [*Cackle-voiced*] My name is Jacob Marley and I am dead. [*He laughs.*] Oh, no, there's no doubt that I am dead. The register of my burial was signed by the clergyman, the clerk, the undertaker . . . and by my chief mourner . . . Ebenezer Scrooge . . . [*Pause; remembers*] I am dead as a doornail.

[*A spotlight fades up, Stage Right, on* SCROOGE, *in his countinghouse,*[1] *counting. Lettering on the window behind* SCROOGE *reads: "SCROOGE AND MARLEY, LTD." The spotlight is tight on* SCROOGE'*s head and shoulders. We shall not yet see into the offices and setting. Ghostly music continues, under.* MARLEY *looks across at* SCROOGE; *pitifully. After a moment's pause*]

I present him to you: Ebenezer Scrooge . . . England's most tightfisted hand at the grindstone, Scrooge! a squeezing, wrenching, grasping, scraping, clutching, covetous, old sinner! secret, and self-contained, and solitary as an oyster. The cold within him freezes his old features, nips his pointed nose, shrivels his cheek, stiffens his gait; makes his eyes red, his thin lips blue; and speaks out shrewdly in his grating voice. Look at him. Look at him . . .

[SCROOGE *counts and mumbles.*]

SCROOGE. They owe me money and I will collect. I will have them jailed, if I have to. They owe me money and I will collect what is due me.

---

1. **countinghouse** office for keeping financial records and writing business letters.

Reading Skill
Purpose for Reading
Based on the images, title, and other information you can quickly preview, what is your purpose for reading this play?

Reading Check

Where and when does this drama take place?

[MARLEY *moves towards* SCROOGE; *two steps. The spotlight stays with him.*]

MARLEY. [*Disgusted*] He and I were partners for I don't know how many years. Scrooge was my sole executor, my sole administrator, my sole assign, my sole residuary legatee,[2] my sole friend and my sole mourner. But Scrooge was not so cut up by the sad event of my death, but that he was an excellent man of business on the very day of my funeral, and solemnized[3] it with an undoubted bargain. [*Pauses again in disgust*] He never painted out my name from the window. There it stands, on the window and above the warehouse door: Scrooge and Marley. Sometimes people new to our business call him Scrooge and sometimes they call him Marley. He answers to both names. It's all the same to him. And it's cheaper than painting in a new sign, isn't it? [*Pauses; moves closer to* SCROOGE] Nobody has ever stopped him in the street to say, with gladsome looks, "My dear Scrooge, how are you? When will you come to see me?" No beggars <u>implored</u> him to bestow a trifle, no children ever ask him what it is o'clock, no man or woman now, or ever in his life, not once, inquire the way to such and such a place. [MARLEY *stands next to* SCROOGE *now. They share, so it seems, a spotlight.*] But what does Scrooge care of any of this? It is the very thing he likes! To edge his way along the crowded paths of life, warning all human sympathy to keep its distance.

[*A ghostly bell rings in the distance.* MARLEY *moves away from* SCROOGE, *now, heading* D. *again. As he does, he "takes" the light:* SCROOGE *has disappeared into the black void beyond.* MARLEY *walks* D.C., *talking directly to the audience. Pauses*]

The bell tolls and I must take my leave. You must stay a while with Scrooge and watch him play out his scroogey life. It is now the story: the once-upon-a-time. Scrooge is busy in his counting house. Where else? Christmas eve and Scrooge is busy in his counting-house. It is cold, bleak, biting weather outside: foggy withal: and, if you listen closely,

2. **my sole executor** (eg zek´ yōō tər), **my sole administrator, my sole assign** (ə sīn´), **my sole residuary legatee** (ri zij´ōō er´ē leg´ə tē´) legal terms giving one person responsibility to carry out the wishes of another who has died.
3. **solemnized** (säl´ əm nīzd´) *v.* honored or remembered. Marley is being sarcastic.

Literary Analysis
Dialogue What do these lines reveal about Marley's character?

Vocabulary Builder
implored (im plôrd´) *v.* begged

you can hear the people in the court go wheezing up and down, beating their hands upon their breasts, and stamping their feet upon the pavement stones to warm them . . .

[*The clocks outside strike three.*]

Only three! and quite dark outside already: it has not been light all day this day.

[*This ghostly bell rings in the distance again.* MARLEY *looks about him. Music in.* MARLEY *flies away.*]

Scene 2

[*N.B.* MARLEY's *comings and goings should, from time to time, induce the explosion of the odd flash-pot. I.H.*]

[*Christmas music in, sung by a live chorus, full. At conclusion of song, sound fades under and into the distance. Lights up in set: offices of Scrooge and Marley, Ltd.* SCROOGE *sits at his desk, at work. Near him is a tiny fire. His door is open and in his line of vision, we see* SCROOGE's *clerk,* BOB CRATCHIT, *who sits in a dismal tank of a cubicle, copying letters. Near* CRATCHIT *is a fire so tiny as to barely cast a light: perhaps it is one pitifully glowing coal?* CRATCHIT *rubs his hands together, puts on a white comforter[4] and tries to heat his hands around his candle.* SCROOGE's NEPHEW *enters, unseen.*]

SCROOGE. What are you doing, Cratchit? Acting cold, are you? Next, you'll be asking to replenish your coal from my coal-box, won't you? Well, save your breath, Cratchit! Unless you're prepared to find employ elsewhere!

NEPHEW. [*Cheerfully; surprising* SCROOGE] A merry Christmas to you, Uncle! God save you!

SCROOGE. Bah! Humbug![5]

NEPHEW. Christmas a "humbug," Uncle? I'm sure you don't mean that.

▼ **Critical Viewing**
How does this portrayal of Scrooge by actor George C. Scott compare with the image you picture as you read?
[**Compare and Contrast**]

✓ **Reading Check**

What was Marley's relationship to Scrooge?

---

4. comforter (kum′ fər tər) *n.* long, woolen scarf.
5. Humbug (hum′ bug′) *interj.* nonsense.

◀ Critical Viewing
Bob Cratchit heats
his hands over a
candle flame in his
office. What does this
action tell you about
the setting? **[Infer]**

SCROOGE. I do! Merry Christmas? What right do you have to be merry? What reason have you to be merry? You're poor enough!

NEPHEW. Come, then. What right have you to be dismal? What reason have you to be <u>morose</u>? You're rich enough.

SCROOGE. Bah! Humbug!

NEPHEW. Don't be cross, Uncle.

SCROOGE. What else can I be? Eh? When I live in a world of fools such as this? Merry Christmas? What's Christmas-time to you but a time of paying bills without any money; a time for finding yourself a year older, but not an hour richer. If I could work my will, every idiot who goes about with "Merry Christmas" on his lips, should be boiled with his own pudding, and buried with a stake of holly through his heart. He should!

NEPHEW. Uncle!

SCROOGE. Nephew! You keep Christmas in your own way and let me keep it in mine.

NEPHEW. Keep it! But you don't keep it, Uncle.

SCROOGE. Let me leave it alone, then. Much good it has ever done you!

Vocabulary Builder
morose (mə rōs´) *adj.*
gloomy; ill-tempered

NEPHEW. There are many things from which I have derived good, by which I have not profited, I daresay. Christmas among the rest. But I am sure that I always thought of Christmas time, when it has come round—as a good time: the only time I know of, when men and women seem to open their shut-up hearts freely, and to think of people below them as if they really were fellow-passengers to the grave, and not another race of creatures bound on other journeys. And therefore, Uncle, though it has never put a scrap of gold or silver in my pocket, I believe that it has done me good, and that it will do me good; and I say, God bless it!

[*The* CLERK *in the tank applauds, looks at the furious* SCROOGE *and pokes out his tiny fire, as if in exchange for the moment of impropriety.* SCROOGE *yells at him.*]

SCROOGE. [*To the clerk*] Let me hear another sound from you and you'll keep your Christmas by losing your situation. [*To the nephew*] You're quite a powerful speaker, sir. I wonder you don't go into Parliament.[6]

NEPHEW. Don't be angry, Uncle. Come! Dine with us tomorrow.

SCROOGE. I'd rather see myself dead than see myself with your family!

NEPHEW. But, why? Why?

SCROOGE. Why did you get married?

NEPHEW. Because I fell in love.

SCROOGE. That, sir, is the only thing that you have said to me in your entire lifetime which is even more ridiculous than "Merry Christmas"! [*Turns from* NEPHEW] Good afternoon.

NEPHEW. Nay, Uncle, you never came to see me before I married either. Why give it as a reason for not coming now?

SCROOGE. Good afternoon, Nephew!

NEPHEW. I want nothing from you; I ask nothing of you; why cannot we be friends?

SCROOGE. Good afternoon!

---

6. **Parliament** (pär′ lə mənt) national legislative body of Great Britain, in some ways like the United States Congress.

**Literary Analysis
Dialogue** How does this exchange between Scrooge and his nephew show the contrast between the two characters?

Reading Check

What invitation does Scrooge's nephew offer?

NEPHEW. I am sorry with all my heart, to find you so resolute. But I have made the trial in homage to Christmas, and I'll keep my Christmas humor to the last. So A Merry Christmas, Uncle!

SCROOGE. Good afternoon!

NEPHEW. And A Happy New Year!

SCROOGE. Good afternoon!

NEPHEW. [*He stands facing* SCROOGE.] Uncle, you are the most . . . [*Pauses*] No, I shan't. My Christmas humor is intact . . . [*Pause*] God bless you, Uncle . . . [NEPHEW *turns and starts for the door; he stops at* CRATCHIT's *cage.*] Merry Christmas, Bob Cratchit . . .

CRATCHIT. Merry Christmas to you sir, and a very, very happy New Year . . .

SCROOGE. [*Calling across to them*] Oh, fine, a perfection, just fine . . . to see the perfect pair of you: husbands, with wives and children to support . . . my clerk there earning fifteen shillings a week . . . and the perfect pair of you, talking about a Merry Christmas! [*Pauses*] I'll retire to Bedlam![7]

NEPHEW. [*To* CRATCHIT] He's impossible!

CRATCHIT. Oh, mind him not, sir. He's getting on in years, and he's alone. He's noticed your visit. I'll wager your visit has warmed him.

NEPHEW. Him? Uncle Ebenezer Scrooge? Warmed? You are a better Christian than I am, sir.

CRATCHIT. [*Opening the door for* NEPHEW; *two* DO-GOODERS *will enter, as* NEPHEW *exits*] Good day to you, sir, and God bless.

NEPHEW. God bless . . . [*One man who enters is portly, the other is thin. Both are pleasant.*]

CRATCHIT. Can I help you, gentlemen?

THIN MAN. [*Carrying papers and books; looks around* CRATCHIT *to* SCROOGE] Scrooge and Marley's, I believe. Have I the pleasure of addressing Mr. Scrooge, or Mr. Marley?

SCROOGE. Mr. Marley has been dead these seven years. He died seven years ago this very night.

7. **Bedlam** (bed´ ləm) hospital in London for the mentally ill.

Literary Analysis
Dialogue What can you infer about the nephew's character from his words to Cratchit?

PORTLY MAN. We have no doubt his liberality[8] is well represented by his surviving partner . . . [*Offers his calling card*]

SCROOGE. [*Handing back the card; unlooked at*] . . . Good afternoon.

THIN MAN. This will take but a moment, sir . . .

PORTLY MAN. At this festive season of the year, Mr. Scrooge, it is more than usually desirable that we should make some slight provision for the poor and <u>destitute</u>, who suffer greatly at the present time. Many thousands are in want of common necessities; hundreds of thousands are in want of common comforts, sir.

SCROOGE. Are there no prisons?

PORTLY MAN. Plenty of prisons.

SCROOGE. And aren't the Union workhouses still in operation?

THIN MAN. They are. Still. I wish that I could say that they are not.

SCROOGE. The Treadmill[9] and the Poor Law[10] are in full vigor, then?

THIN MAN. Both very busy, sir.

SCROOGE. Ohhh, I see. I was afraid, from what you said at first, that something had occurred to stop them from their useful course. [*Pauses*] I'm glad to hear it.

PORTLY MAN. Under the impression that they scarcely furnish Christian cheer of mind or body to the multitude, a few of us are endeavoring to raise a fund to buy the Poor some meat and drink, and means of warmth. We choose this time, because it is a time, of all others, when Want is

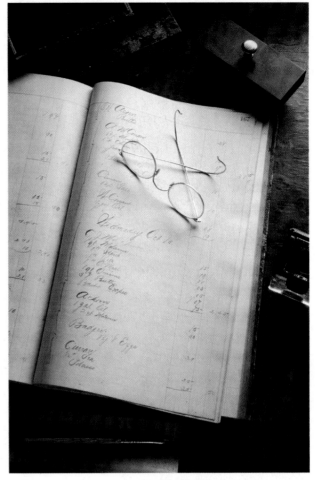

▲ **Critical Viewing**
Based on this photograph, how has bookkeeping changed since the time of the play? **[Draw Conclusions]**

Vocabulary Builder
destitute (des´ tə tōōt´) *adj.* used as *n.*, people living in complete poverty

✓ **Reading Check**

What do the thin man and the portly man want from Scrooge?

---

8. liberality (lib´ər al´i tē) generosity.
9. the Treadmill (tred´ mil´) kind of mill wheel turned by the weight of people treading steps arranged around it; this device was used to punish prisoners.
10. the Poor Law the original 16th-century Poor Laws called for overseers of the poor in each neighborhood to provide relief for the needy. The New Poor Law of 1834 made the workhouses in which the poor sometimes lived and worked extremely hard and unattractive.

keenly felt, and Abundance rejoices. [*Pen in hand; as well as notepad*] What shall I put you down for, sir?

SCROOGE. Nothing!

PORTLY MAN. You wish to be left anonymous?

SCROOGE. I wish to be left alone! [*Pauses; turns away; turns back to them*] Since you ask me what I wish, gentlemen, that is my answer. I help to support the establishments that I have mentioned: they cost enough: and those who are badly off must go there.

THIN MAN. Many can't go there; and many would rather die.

SCROOGE. If they would rather die, they had better do it, and decrease the surplus population. Besides—excuse me—I don't know that.

THIN MAN. But you might know it!

SCROOGE. It's not my business. It's enough for a man to understand his own business, and not to interfere with other people's. Mine occupies me constantly. Good afternoon, gentlemen! [SCROOGE *turns his back on the gentlemen and returns to his desk.*]

PORTLY MAN. But, sir, Mr. Scrooge . . . think of the poor.

SCROOGE. [*Turns suddenly to them. Pauses*] Take your leave of my offices, sirs, while I am still smiling.

[*The* THIN MAN *looks at the* PORTLY MAN. *They are undone. They shrug. They move to the door.* CRATCHIT *hops up to open it for them.*]

THIN MAN. Good day, sir . . . [*To* CRATCHIT] A merry Christmas to you, sir . . .

CRATCHIT. Yes. A Merry Christmas to both of you . . .

PORTLY MAN. Merry Christmas . . .

[CRATCHIT *silently squeezes something into the hand of the* THIN MAN.]

THIN MAN. What's this?

CRATCHIT. Shhhh . . .

[CRATCHIT *opens the door; wind and snow whistle into the room.*]

THIN MAN. Thank you, sir, thank you.

[CRATCHIT *closes the door and returns to his workplace.* SCROOGE *is at his own counting table. He talks to* CRATCHIT *without looking up.*]

SCROOGE. It's less of a time of year for being merry, and more a time of year for being loony . . . if you ask me.

CRATCHIT. Well, I don't know, sir . . . [*The clock's bell strikes six o'clock.*] Well, there it is, eh, six?

SCROOGE. Saved by six bells, are you?

CRATCHIT. I must be going home . . . [*He snuffs out his candle and puts on his hat.*] I hope you have a . . . very very lovely day tomorrow, sir . . .

SCROOGE. Hmmm. Oh, you'll be wanting the whole day tomorrow, I suppose?

CRATCHIT. If quite convenient, sir.

SCROOGE. It's not convenient, and it's not fair. If I was to stop half-a-crown for it, you'd think yourself ill-used, I'll be bound?

[CRATCHIT *smiles faintly.*]

CRATCHIT. I don't know, sir . . .

SCROOGE. And yet, you don't think me ill-used when I pay a day's wages for no work . . .

CRATCHIT. It's only but once a year . . .

▼ Critical Viewing
Compare this actor's portrayal of Cratchit with the one on page 668. Which looks more like your idea of Cratchit? Explain. **[Compare and Contrast]**

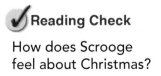

Reading Check

How does Scrooge feel about Christmas?

SCROOGE. A poor excuse for picking a man's pocket every 25th of December! But I suppose you must have the whole day. Be here all the earlier the next morning!

CRATCHIT. Oh, I will, sir. I will. I promise you. And, sir . . .

SCROOGE. Don't say it, Cratchit.

CRATCHIT. But let me wish you a . . .

SCROOGE. Don't say it, Cratchit. I warn you . . .

CRATCHIT. Sir!

SCROOGE. Cratchit!

[CRATCHIT *opens the door.*]

CRATCHIT. All right, then, sir . . . well . . . [*Suddenly*] Merry Christmas, Mr. Scrooge!

[*And he runs out the door, shutting same behind him.* SCROOGE *moves to his desk; gathering his coat, hat, etc. A* BOY *appears at his window. . . .*]

BOY. [*Singing*] "Away in a manger . . ."

[SCROOGE *seizes his ruler and whacks at the image of the* BOY *outside. The* BOY *leaves.*]

SCROOGE. Bah! Humbug! Christmas! Bah! Humbug! [*He shuts out the light.*]

A note on the crossover, following Scene 2:

[SCROOGE *will walk alone to his rooms from his offices. As he makes a long slow cross of the stage, the scenery should change. Christmas music will be heard, various people will cross by* SCROOGE, *often smiling happily.*

There will be occasional pleasant greetings tossed at him.

SCROOGE, *in contrast to all, will grump and mumble. He will snap at passing boys, as might a horrid old hound.*

In short, SCROOGE's *sounds and movements will define him in contrast from all other people who cross the stage: he is the misanthrope,*[11] *the malcontent, the miser. He is* SCROOGE.

This statement of SCROOGE's *character, by contrast to all other characters, should seem comical to the audience.*

> **Critical Viewing**
> Describe the tone of voice that each actor might use to play the scene pictured here. **[Speculate]**

Literary Analysis
Dialogue What do you learn about Scrooge through his words as he shuts out the light and through the description of him as he walks home?

---

11. **misanthrope** (mis´ən thrōp´) *n.* person who hates or distrusts everyone.

During SCROOGE's crossover to his rooms, snow should begin to fall. All passers-by will hold their faces to the sky, smiling, allowing snow to shower them lightly. SCROOGE, by contrast, will bat at the flakes with his walking-stick, as might an insomniac swat at a sleep-stopping, middle-of-the-night swarm of mosquitoes. He will comment on the blackness of the night, and, finally, reach his rooms and his encounter with the magical specter:[12] MARLEY, his eternal mate.]

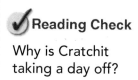

Reading Check

Why is Cratchit taking a day off?

---

12. specter (spek´ tər) *n.* ghost.

Scene 3

SCROOGE. No light at all . . . no moon . . . that is what is at the center of a Christmas Eve: dead black: <u>void</u> . . .

[SCROOGE *puts his key in the door's keyhole. He has reached his rooms now. The door knocker changes and is now* MARLEY's *face. A musical sound; quickly: ghostly.* MAR-LEY's *image is not at all angry, but looks at* SCROOGE *as did the old* MARLEY *look at* SCROOGE. *The hair is curiously stirred; eyes wide open, dead: absent of focus.* SCROOGE *stares wordlessly here. The face, before his very eyes, does deliquesce.*[13] *It is a knocker again.* SCROOGE *opens the door and checks the back of same, probably for* MARLEY's *pig-tail. Seeing nothing but screws and nuts,* SCROOGE *refuses the memory.*]

Pooh, pooh!

[*The sound of the door closing resounds throughout the house as thunder. Every room echoes the sound.* SCROOGE *fastens the door and walks across the hall to the stairs, trim-ming his candle as he goes; and then he goes slowly up the staircase. He checks each room: sitting room, bedrooms, slumber room. He looks under the sofa, under the table: nobody there. He fixes his evening gruel on the hob,*[14] *changes his jacket.* SCROOGE *sits near the tiny low-flamed fire, sipping his gruel. There are various pictures on the walls: all of them now show likenesses of* MARLEY. SCROOGE *blinks his eyes.*]

Bah! Humbug!

[SCROOGE *walks in a circle about the room. The pictures change back into their natural images. He sits down at the table in front of the fire. A bell hangs overhead. It begins to ring, of its own accord. Slowly, surely, begins the ringing of every bell in the house. They continue ringing for nearly half a minute.* SCROOGE *is stunned by the phenomenon. The bells cease their ringing all at once. Deep below* SCROOGE, *in the basement of the house, there is the sound of clanking, of*

---

13. deliquesce (del'i kwes') *v.* melt away.
14. gruel (groo̅' əl) **on the hob** (häb) thin broth warming on a ledge at the back or side of the fireplace.

Vocabulary Builder
void (void) *n.*
emptiness

Reading Skill
Purpose for Reading
Preview Scene 3. If your purpose were to find out what happens next to Scrooge, what details would you look for in the scene?

*some enormous chain being dragged across the floors; and
now up the stairs. We hear doors flying open.*]

Bah still! Humbug still! This is not happening! I won't
believe it!

[MARLEY'S GHOST *enters the room. He is horrible to look at:
pigtail, vest, suit as usual, but he drags an enormous chain
now, to which is fastened cash-boxes, keys, padlocks, led-
gers, deeds, and heavy purses fashioned of steel. He is
transparent.* MARLEY *stands opposite the stricken*
SCROOGE.]

How now! What do you want of me?

MARLEY. Much!

SCROOGE. Who are you?

MARLEY. Ask me who I was.

SCROOGE. Who were you then?

MARLEY. In life, I was your business partner: Jacob Marley.

SCROOGE. I see . . . can you sit down?

MARLEY. I can.

SCROOGE. Do it then.

MARLEY. I shall. [MARLEY *sits opposite* SCROOGE, *in the chair
across the table, at the front of the fireplace.*] You don't
believe in me.

SCROOGE. I don't.

MARLEY. Why do you doubt your senses?

SCROOGE. Because every little thing affects them. A slight dis-
order of the stomach makes them cheat. You may be an
undigested bit of beef, a blot of mustard, a crumb of
cheese, a fragment of an underdone potato. There's more of
gravy than of grave about you, whatever you are!

[*There is a silence between them.* SCROOGE *is made nervous
by it. He picks up a toothpick.*]

Humbug! I tell you: humbug!

[MARLEY *opens his mouth and screams a ghosty, fearful
scream. The scream echoes about each room of the house.*

Literary Analysis
Dialogue Based on
this dialogue, what is
Scrooge's attitude
toward Marley's
Ghost?

Reading Check

What does Scrooge
see in the door
knocker?

Bats fly, cats screech, lightning flashes. SCROOGE *stands and walks backwards against the wall.* MARLEY *stands and screams again. This time, he takes his head and lifts it from his shoulders. His head continues to scream.* MARLEY's *face again appears on every picture in the room: all screaming.* SCROOGE, *on his knees before* MARLEY.]

Mercy! Dreadful apparition,[15] mercy! Why, O! why do you trouble me so?

MARLEY. Man of the worldly mind, do you believe in me, or not?

SCROOGE. I do. I must. But why do spirits such as you walk the earth? And why do they come to me?

MARLEY. It is required of every man that the spirit within him should walk abroad among his fellow-men, and travel far and wide; and if that spirit goes not forth in life, it is con-demned to do so after death. [MARLEY *screams again; a tragic scream; from his ghosty bones.*] I wear the chain I forged in life. I made it link by link, and yard by yard. Is its pattern strange to you? Or would you know, you, Scrooge, the weight and length of the strong coil you bear yourself? It was full as heavy and long as this, seven Christmas Eves ago. You have labored on it, since. It is a ponderous chain.

[*Terrified that a chain will appear about his body,* SCROOGE *spins and waves the unwanted chain away. None, of course, appears. Sees* MARLEY *watching him dance about the room.* MARLEY *watches* SCROOGE; *silently.*]

SCROOGE. Jacob. Old Jacob Marley, tell me more. Speak comfort to me, Jacob . . .

MARLEY. I have none to give. Comfort comes from other regions, Ebenezer Scrooge, and is <u>conveyed</u> by other min-isters, to other kinds of men. A very little more, is all that is permitted to me. I cannot rest, I cannot stay, I cannot linger anywhere . . . [*He moans again.*] my spirit never walked beyond our countinghouse—mark me!—in life my spirit never roved beyond the narrow limits of our money-changing hole; and weary journeys lie before me!

---

15. apparition (ap´ ə rish´ ən) *n.* ghost.

Reading Skill
Purpose for Reading
What purpose for reading might Scrooge's question suggest to readers?

Vocabulary Builder
conveyed (kən vād´) *v.* made known; expressed

benevolence (bə nev´ ə ləns) *n.* kindliness

SCROOGE. But you were always a good man of business, Jacob.

MARLEY. [*Screams word "business"; a flash-pot explodes with him.*] BUSINESS!!! Mankind was my business. The common welfare was my business; charity, mercy, forbearance, <u>benevolence</u>, were, all, my business. [SCROOGE *is quaking.*] Hear me, Ebenezer Scrooge! My time is nearly gone.

SCROOGE. I will, but don't be hard upon me. And don't be flowery, Jacob! Pray!

MARLEY. How is it that I appear before you in a shape that you can see, I may not tell. I have sat invisible beside you many and many a day. That is no light part of my penance. I am here tonight to warn you that you have yet a chance and hope of escaping my fate. A chance and hope of my procuring, Ebenezer.

SCROOGE. You were always a good friend to me. Thank'ee!

MARLEY. You will be haunted by Three Spirits.

SCROOGE. Would that be the chance and hope you mentioned, Jacob?

MARLEY. It is.

SCROOGE. I think I'd rather not.

▲ **Critical Viewing**
How do the actors' gestures and positions reinforce the emotion of the scene? [**Connect**]

✔ **Reading Check**

Why does Marley visit Scrooge?

MARLEY. Without their visits, you cannot hope to shun the path I tread. Expect the first one tomorrow, when the bell tolls one.

SCROOGE. Couldn't I take 'em all at once, and get it over, Jacob?

MARLEY. Expect the second on the next night at the same hour. The third upon the next night when the last stroke of twelve has ceased to vibrate. Look to see me no more. Others may, but you may not. And look that, for your own sake, you remember what has passed between us!

[MARLEY *places his head back upon his shoulders. He approaches the window and beckons to* SCROOGE *to watch. Outside the window, specters fly by, carrying money-boxes and chains. They make a confused sound of lamentation.* MARLEY, *after listening a moment, joins into their mournful dirge. He leans to the window and floats out into the bleak, dark night. He is gone.*]

SCROOGE. [*Rushing to the window*] Jacob! No, Jacob! Don't leave me! I'm frightened!
[*He sees that* MARLEY *has gone. He looks outside. He pulls the shutter closed, so that the scene is blocked from his view. All sound stops. After a pause, he re-opens the shutter and all is quiet, as it should be on Christmas Eve. Carolers carol out of doors, in the distance.* SCROOGE *closes the shutter and walks down the stairs. He examines the door by which* MARLEY *first entered.*]
No one here at all! Did I imagine all that? Humbug! [*He looks about the room.*] I did imagine it. It only happened in my foulest dream-mind, didn't it? An undigested bit of . . . [*Thunder and lightning in the room; suddenly*]
Sorry! Sorry!

[*There is silence again. The lights fade out.*]

Scene 4

[*Christmas music, choral, "Hark the Herald Angels Sing," sung by an onstage choir of children, spotlighted,* D.C. *Above,* SCROOGE *in his bed, dead to the world, asleep, in his darkened room. It should appear that the choir is singing somewhere outside of the*

---

16. **scrim** (skrim) *n.* see-through fabric used to create special effects in the theater.

Reading Skill
Purpose for Reading
What questions do you have about what will happen to Scrooge? Read on to answer your questions.

house, of course, and a use of scrim[16] is thus suggested. When the singing is ended, the choir should fade out of view and MAR-LEY should fade into view, in their place.]

MARLEY. [*Directly to audience*] From this point forth . . . I shall be quite visible to you, but invisible to him. [*Smiles*] He will feel my presence, nevertheless, for, unless my senses fail me completely, we are—you and I—witness to the changing of a miser: that one, my partner in life, in business, and in eternity: that one: Scrooge. [*Moves to staircase, below* SCROOGE] See him now. He endeavors to pierce the darkness with his ferret eyes.[17] [*To audience*] See him, now. He listens for the hour.

[*The bells toll.* SCROOGE *is awakened and quakes as the hour approaches one o'clock, but the bells stop their sound at the hour of twelve.*]

SCROOGE. [*Astonished*] Midnight! Why this isn't possible. It was past two when I went to bed. An icicle must have gotten into the clock's works! I couldn't have slept through the whole day and far into another night. It isn't possible that anything has happened to the sun, and this is twelve at noon! [*He runs to window; unshutters same; it is night.*] Night, still. Quiet, normal for the season, cold. It is certainly not noon. I cannot in any way afford to lose my days. Securities come due, promissory notes,[18] interest on investments: these are things that happen in the daylight! [*He returns to his bed.*] Was this a dream?

[MARLEY *appears in his room. He speaks to the audience.*]

MARLEY. You see? He does not, with faith, believe in me fully, even still! Whatever will it take to turn the faith of a miser from money to men?

SCROOGE. Another quarter and it'll be one and Marley's ghosty friends will come. [*Pauses; listens*] Where's the chime for one? [*Ding, dong*] A quarter past [*Repeats*] Half-past! [*Repeats*] A quarter to it! But where's the heavy bell of the hour one? This is a game in which I lose my senses! Perhaps, if I allowed myself another short doze . . .

MARLEY. . . . Doze, Ebenezer, doze.

Literary Analysis

Dialogue What important information in Marley's opening speech will influence the rest of the play?

Reading Check

Why is Scrooge confused when he wakes up?

---

17. ferret eyes a ferret is a small, weasel-like animal used for hunting rabbits; this expression means to stare continuously, the way a ferret hunts.

18. promissory (pram´ i sôr´ ē) **notes** written promises to pay someone a certain sum of money.

[*A heavy bell thuds its one ring; dull and definitely one o'clock.*

There is a flash of light. SCROOGE *sits up, in a sudden. A hand draws back the curtains by his bed. He sees it.*]

SCROOGE. A hand! Who owns it! Hello!

[*Ghosty music again, but of a new nature to the play. A strange figure stands before* SCROOGE—*like a child, yet at the same time like an old man: white hair, but unwrinkled skin, long, muscular arms, but delicate legs and feet. Wears white tunic; lustrous belt cinches waist. Branch of fresh green holly in its hand, but has its dress trimmed with fresh summer flowers. Clear jets of light spring from the crown of its head. Holds cap in hand. The Spirit is called* PAST.]

Are you the Spirit, sir, whose coming was foretold to me?

PAST. I am.

MARLEY. Does he take this to be a vision of his green grocer?

SCROOGE. Who, and what are you?

PAST. I am the Ghost of Christmas Past.

SCROOGE. Long past?

PAST. Your past.

SCROOGE. May I ask, please, sir, what business you have here with me?

PAST. Your welfare.

SCROOGE. Not to sound ungrateful, sir, and really, please do understand that I am plenty obliged for your concern, but, really, kind spirit, it would have done all the better for my welfare to have been left alone altogether, to have slept peacefully through this night.

PAST. Your reclamation, then. Take heed!

SCROOGE. My what?

PAST. [*Motioning to* SCROOGE *and taking his arm*] Rise! Fly with me! [*He leads* SCROOGE *to the window.*]

SCROOGE. [*Panicked*] Fly, but I am a mortal and cannot fly!

PAST. [*Pointing to his heart*] Bear but a touch of my hand here and you shall be upheld in more than this!

Literary Analysis

Dialogue Based on this dialogue, how has Scrooge been affected by what has happened to him so far?

[SCROOGE *touches the spirit's heart and the lights dissolve into sparkly flickers. Lovely crystals of music are heard. The scene dissolves into another. Christmas music again*]

Scene 5

[SCROOGE *and the* GHOST OF CHRISTMAS PAST *walk together across an open stage. In the background, we see a field that is open; covered by a soft, downy snow: a country road.*]

SCROOGE. Good Heaven! I was bred in this place. I was a boy here!

[SCROOGE *freezes, staring at the field beyond.* MARLEY'S *ghost appears beside him; takes* SCROOGE'S *face in his hands, and turns his face to the audience.*]

MARLEY. You see this Scrooge: stricken by feeling. Conscious of a thousand odors floating in the air, each one connected with a thousand thoughts, and hopes, and joys, and care long, long forgotten. [*Pause*] This one—this Scrooge—before your very eyes, returns to life, among the living. [*To audience, sternly*] You'd best pay your most careful attention. I would suggest rapt.[19]

[*There is a small flash and puff of smoke and* MARLEY *is gone again.*]

PAST. Your lip is trembling, Mr. Scrooge. And what is that upon your cheek?

SCROOGE. Upon my cheek? Nothing . . . a blemish on the skin from the eating of overmuch grease . . . nothing . . . [*Suddenly*] Kind Spirit of Christmas Past, lead me where you will, but quickly! To be stagnant in this place is, for me, unbearable!

PAST. You recollect the way?

SCROOGE. Remember it! I would know it blindfolded! My bridge, my church, my winding river! [*Staggers about, trying to see it all at once. He weeps again.*]

PAST. These are but shadows of things that have been. They have no consciousness of us.

✓ Reading Check

Who appears to Scrooge during Scene 4?

---

19. rapt (rapt) *adj.* giving complete attention; totally carried away by something.

[*Four jocund travelers enter, singing a Christmas song in four-part harmony—"God Rest Ye Merry Gentlemen."*]

SCROOGE. Listen! I know these men! I know them! I remember the beauty of their song!

PAST. But, why do you remember it so happily? It is Merry Christmas that they say to one another! What is Merry Christmas to you, Mr. Scrooge? Out upon Merry Christmas, right? What good has Merry Christmas ever done you, Mr. Scrooge? . . .

SCROOGE. [*After a long pause*] None. No good. None . . . [*He bows his head.*]

PAST. Look, you, sir, a school ahead. The schoolroom is not quite deserted. A solitary child, neglected by his friends, is left there still.

[SCROOGE *falls to the ground; sobbing as he sees, and we see, a small boy, the young* SCROOGE, *sitting and weeping, bravely, alone at his desk: alone in a vast space, a void.*]

SCROOGE. I cannot look on him!

PAST. You must, Mr. Scrooge, you must.

SCROOGE. It's me. [*Pauses; weeps*] Poor boy. He lived inside his head . . . alone . . . [*Pauses; weeps*] poor boy. [*Pauses; stops his weeping*] I wish . . . [*Dries his eyes on his cuff*] ah! it's too late!

PAST. What is the matter?

SCROOGE. There was a boy singing a Christmas Carol outside my door last night. I should like to have given him something: that's all.

PAST. [*Smiles; waves his hand to* SCROOGE] Come. Let us see another Christmas.

[*Lights out on little boy. A flash of light. A puff of smoke. Lights up on older boy*]

SCROOGE. Look! Me, again! Older now! [*Realizes*] Oh, yes . . . still alone.

[*The boy—a slightly older* SCROOGE *—sits alone in a chair, reading. The door to the room opens and a young girl enters. She is much, much younger than this slightly older* SCROOGE. *She is,*

Literary Analysis
Dialogue How do these lines reveal that a change is taking place in Scrooge?

say, six, and he is, say, twelve. Elder SCROOGE *and the* GHOST OF CHRISTMAS PAST *stand watching the scene, unseen.*]

FAN. Dear, dear brother, I have come to bring you home.

BOY. Home, little Fan?

FAN. Yes! Home, for good and all! Father is so much kinder than he ever used to be, and home's like heaven! He spoke so gently to me one dear night when I was going to bed that I was not afraid to ask him once more if you might come home; and he said "yes" . . . you should; and sent me in a coach to bring you. And you're to be a man and are never to come back here, but first, we're to be together all the Christmas long, and have the merriest time in the world.

BOY. You are quite a woman, little Fan!

[*Laughing; she drags at boy, causing him to stumble to the door with her. Suddenly we hear a mean and terrible voice in the hallway, Off. It is the* SCHOOLMASTER.]

SCHOOLMASTER. Bring down Master Scrooge's travel box at once! He is to travel!

FAN. Who is that, Ebenezer?

BOY. O! Quiet, Fan. It is the Schoolmaster, himself!

[*The door bursts open and into the room bursts with it the* SCHOOLMASTER.]

SCHOOLMASTER. Master Scrooge?

BOY. Oh, Schoolmaster. I'd like you to meet my little sister, Fan, sir . . .

[*Two boys struggle on with* SCROOGE'S *trunk.*]

FAN. Pleased, sir . . . [*She curtsies.*]

SCHOOLMASTER. You are to travel, Master Scrooge.

SCROOGE. Yes, sir. I know sir . . .

[*All start to exit, but* FAN *grabs the coattail of the mean old* SCHOOLMASTER.]

BOY. Fan!

SCHOOLMASTER. What's this?

Reading Skill
Purpose for Reading
What questions do you have about Scrooge's family? Read on to see if they are answered.

✓ **Reading Check**

Where is Scrooge when his sister arrives to take him home?

FAN. Pardon, sir, but I believe that you've forgotten to say your goodbye to my brother, Ebenezer, who stands still now awaiting it . . . [*She smiles, curtsies, lowers her eyes.*] pardon, sir.

SCHOOLMASTER. [*Amazed*] I . . . uh . . . harumph . . . uhh . . . well, then . . . [*Outstretches hand*] Goodbye, Scrooge.

BOY. Uh, well, goodbye, Schoolmaster . . .

[*Lights fade out on all but* BOY *looking at* FAN; *and* SCROOGE *and* PAST *looking at them.*]

SCROOGE. Oh, my dear, dear little sister, Fan . . . how I loved her.

PAST. Always a delicate creature, whom a breath might have withered, but she had a large heart . . .

SCROOGE. So she had.

PAST. She died a woman, and had, as I think, children.

SCROOGE. One child.

PAST. True. Your nephew.

SCROOGE. Yes.

PAST. Fine, then. We move on, Mr. Scrooge. That warehouse, there? Do you know it?

SCROOGE. Know it? Wasn't I apprenticed[20] there?

PAST. We'll have a look.

[*They enter the warehouse. The lights crossfade with them, coming up on an old man in Welsh wig:* FEZZIWIG.]

SCROOGE. Why, it's old Fezziwig! Bless his heart; it's Fezziwig, alive again!

[FEZZIWIG *sits behind a large, high desk, counting. He lays down his pen; looks at the clock: seven bells sound.*]

Quittin' time . . .

FEZZIWIG. Quittin' time . . . [*He takes off his waistcoat and laughs; calls off*] Yo ho, Ebenezer! Dick!

Literary Analysis
Dialogue What surprising aspect of Scrooge's character does this scene reveal?

---

20. apprenticed (ə pren´ tist) *v.* receiving instruction in a trade as well as food and housing or wages in return for work.

[DICK WILKINS *and* EBENEZER SCROOGE—*a young man version—enter the room.* DICK *and* EBENEZER *are* FEZZIWIG's *apprentices.*]

SCROOGE. Dick Wilkins, to be sure! My fellow-'prentice! Bless my soul, yes. There he is. He was very much attached to me, was Dick. Poor Dick! Dear, dear!

FEZZIWIG. Yo ho, my boys. No more work tonight. Christmas Eve, Dick. Christmas, Ebenezer!
[*They stand at attention in front of* FEZZIWIG; *laughing*]
Hilli-ho! Clear away, and let's have lots of room here! Hilli-ho, Dick! Chirrup, Ebenezer!
[*The young men clear the room, sweep the floor, straighten the pictures, trim the lamps, etc. The space is clear now. A fiddler enters, fiddling.*]
Hi-ho, Matthew! Fiddle away . . . where are my daughters?

[*The fiddler plays. Three young daughters of* FEZZIWIG *enter followed by six young male suitors. They are dancing to the music. All employees come in: workers, clerks, housemaids, cousins, the baker, etc. All dance. Full number wanted here.*]

▲ **Critical Viewing**
Based on this photograph, what kind of a man does Fezziwig seem to be? **[Infer]**

 **Reading Check**

Who is Fezziwig?

Throughout the dance, food is brought into the feast. It is "eaten" in dance, by the dancers. EBENEZER dances with all three of the daughters, as does DICK. They compete for the daughters, happily, in the dance. FEZZIWIG dances with his daughters. FEZZIWIG dances with DICK and EBENEZER. The music changes: MRS. FEZZIWIG enters. She lovingly scolds her husband. They dance. She dances with EBENEZER, lifting him and throwing him about. She is enormously fat. When the dance is ended, they all dance off, floating away, as does the music. SCROOGE and the GHOST OF CHRISTMAS PAST stand alone now. The music is gone.]

PAST. It was a small matter, that Fezziwig made those silly folks so full of gratitude.

SCROOGE. Small!

PAST. Shhh!

[Lights up on DICK and EBENEZER]

DICK. We are blessed, Ebenezer, truly, to have such a master as Mr. Fezziwig!

YOUNG SCROOGE. He is the best, best, the very and absolute best! If ever I own a firm of my own, I shall treat my apprentices with the same dignity and the same grace. We have learned a wonderful lesson from the master, Dick!

DICK. Ah, that's a fact, Ebenezer. That's a fact!

PAST. Was it not a small matter, really? He spent but a few pounds[21] of his mortal money on your small party. Three or four pounds, perhaps. Is that so much that he deserves such praise as you and Dick so lavish now?

SCROOGE. It isn't that! It isn't that, Spirit. Fezziwig had the power to make us happy or unhappy; to make our service light or burdensome; a pleasure or a toil. The happiness he gave is quite as great as if it cost him a fortune.

PAST. What is the matter?

SCROOGE. Nothing particular.

PAST. Something, I think.

SCROOGE. No, no. I should like to be able to say a word or two to my clerk just now! That's all!

Literary Analysis
Dialogue What does this dialogue reveal about Scrooge's feelings for Fezziwig?

---

21. **pounds** (pŏundz) *n.* the money used in Great Britain at the time of the story.

[EBENEZER *enters the room and shuts down all the lamps. He*
stretches and yawns. The GHOST OF CHRISTMAS PAST *turns to*
SCROOGE *all of a sudden.*]

PAST. My time grows short! Quick!

[*In a flash of light,* EBENEZER *is gone, and in his place stands an*
OLDER SCROOGE, *this one a man in the prime of his life. Beside
him stands a young woman in a mourning dress. She is crying.
She speaks to the man, with hostility.*]

WOMAN. It matters little . . . to you, very little. Another idol
has displaced me.

MAN. What idol has displaced you?

WOMAN. A golden one.

MAN. This is an even-handed dealing of the world. There is
nothing on which it is so hard as poverty; and there is
nothing it professes to condemn with such severity as the
pursuit of wealth!

WOMAN. You fear the world too much. Have I not seen your
nobler aspirations fall off one by one, until the master-
passion, Gain, engrosses you? Have I not?

SCROOGE. No!

MAN. What then? Even if I have grown so much wiser, what
then? Have I changed towards you?

WOMAN. No . . .

MAN. Am I?

WOMAN. Our contract is an old one. It was made when we
were both poor and content to be so. You are changed.
When it was made, you were another man.

MAN. I was not another man: I was a boy.

WOMAN. Your own feeling tells you that you were not what you
are. I am. That which promised happiness when we were
one in heart is fraught with misery now that we are two . . .

SCROOGE. No!

WOMAN. How often and how keenly I have thought of this, I
will not say. It is enough that I have thought of it, and can
release you . . .

**Literary Analysis
Dialogue** What
personal change in
Scrooge does this
dialogue show?

Reading Check

What does the
woman tell Scrooge
about himself?

SCROOGE. [*Quietly*] Don't release me, madame . . .

MAN. Have I ever sought release?

WOMAN. In words. No. Never.

MAN. In what then?

WOMAN. In a changed nature; in an altered spirit. In every-thing that made my love of any worth or value in your sight. If this has never been between us, tell me, would you seek me out and try to win me now? Ah, no!

SCROOGE. Ah, yes!

MAN. You think not?

WOMAN. I would gladly think otherwise if I could, heaven knows! But if you were free today, tomorrow, yesterday, can even I believe that you would choose a dowerless girl[22]—you who in your very confidence with her weigh everything by Gain; or, choosing her, do I not know that your repentance and regret would surely follow? I do; and I release you. With a full heart, for the love of him you once were.

SCROOGE. Please, I . . . I . . .

MAN. Please, I . . . I . . .

WOMAN. Please. You may—the memory of what is past half makes me hope you will—have pain in this. A very, very brief time, and you will dismiss the memory of it, as an unprofitable dream, from which it happened well that you awoke. May you be happy in the life that you have chosen for yourself . . .

SCROOGE. No!

WOMAN. Yourself . . . alone . . .

SCROOGE. No!

WOMAN. Goodbye, Ebenezer . . .

SCROOGE. Don't let her go!

MAN. Goodbye.

SCROOGE. No!

Literary Analysis
Dialogue What do you learn about Scrooge's past from the dialogue here?

---

22. **a dowerless** (dou´ ər les) **girl** a girl without a dowry, the property or wealth a woman brought to her husband in marriage.

[*She exits.* SCROOGE *goes to younger man: himself.*]
You fool! Mindless loon! You fool!

MAN. [*To exited woman*] Fool. Mindless loon. Fool . . .

SCROOGE. Don't say that! Spirit, remove me from this place.

PAST. I have told you these were shadows of the things that have been. They are what they are. Do not blame me, Mr. Scrooge.

SCROOGE. Remove me! I cannot bear it!
[*The faces of all who appeared in this scene are now projected for a moment around the stage: enormous, flimsy, silent.*]
Leave me! Take me back! Haunt me no longer!

[*There is a sudden flash of light: a flare. The* GHOST OF CHRISTMAS PAST *is gone.* SCROOGE *is, for the moment, alone onstage. His bed is turned down, across the stage. A small candle burns now in* SCROOGE'S *hand. There is a child's cap in his other hand. He slowly crosses the stage to his bed, to sleep.* MARLEY *appears behind* SCROOGE, *who continues his long, elderly cross to bed.* MARLEY *speaks directly to the audience.*]

MARLEY. Scrooge must sleep now. He must surrender to the irresistible drowsiness caused by the recognition of what was. [*Pauses*] The cap he carries is from ten lives past: his boyhood cap . . . donned atop a hopeful hairy head . . . askew, perhaps, or at a rakish angle. Doffed now in honor of regret.[23] Perhaps even too heavy to carry in his present state of weak remorse . . .
[SCROOGE *drops the cap. He lies atop his bed. He sleeps. To audience*]
He sleeps. For him, there's even more trouble ahead. [*Smiles*] For you? The play house tells me there's hot cider, as should be your anticipation for the specter Christmas Present and Future, for I promise you both. [*Smiles again*] So, I pray you hurry back to your seats refreshed and ready for a miser—to turn his coat of gray into a blazen Christmas holly-red. [*A flash of lightning. A clap of thunder. Bats fly. Ghosty music.* MARLEY *is gone.*]

Reading Skill
Purpose for Reading
How does this speech by Marley influence your purpose for reading Act 2?

---

23. donned . . . regret To *don* and *doff* a hat means to put it on and take it off, *askew* means "crooked," and *at a rakish angle* means "having a dashing or jaunty look."

Apply the Skills

A Christmas Carol: Scrooge and Marley, Act I

Thinking About the Selection

1. **Respond:** In your opinion, what is the meanest thing Scrooge does in Act I? In a small group, share your responses. Then, as a group, choose one response to share with the class.
2. **(a) Recall:** What scenes from his past does Scrooge visit? **(b) Draw Conclusions:** How does each event contribute to his current attitude and personality?
3. **(a) Deduce:** What does Scrooge value in life? **(b) Draw Conclusions:** Do his values make Scrooge a happy man? Explain.
4. **(a) Connect:** What hints are given that Scrooge may change for the better? **(b) Speculate:** In the future, how might Scrooge's interactions with others differ from his interactions in the present?
5. **(a) Deduce:** What effects have Scrooge's past experiences had on the person he has become? **(b) Evaluate:** Based on Scrooge's past experiences, should he be excused for his current attitude and behavior? Explain.

Reading Skill

6. How did the title help you to get a sense of what this play would be about?
7. **(a)** What is your **purpose for reading** this play? **(b)** How might your purpose be different if you were reading a non-fiction play about life in the workhouses of Victorian England?

Literary Analysis

8. Complete a chart like the one shown by identifying important examples of dialogue. **(a)** For each line of **dialogue** in the first column, use the second column to tell what it means. **(b)** In the third column, tell why this dialogue is important to advancing the action of the play or developing characters.

What Does It Say?	What Does It Mean?	Why Is It Important?

QuickReview

Who's Who in the Play

Ebenezer Scrooge: a businessman

Jacob Marley: Scrooge's former business partner, now a ghost

Bob Cratchit: Scrooge's clerk

Go Online
—Assessment
For: Self-test
Visit: www.PHSchool.com
Web Code: ema-6502

Purpose for Reading: what the reader wants to get out of the text

Dialogue: conversation between or among characters

Vocabulary Builder

Practice Rewrite the following sentences so that they include a vocabulary word from the list on page 662 and convey the same basic meaning as those here.

1. Jack's gloomy expression showed that he lost the game.
2. Her sudden inheritance meant that she was no longer poor.
3. Thanks to Freddy's kind financial help, I am able to attend college.
4. The party helped to ease the emptiness I was feeling.
5. The grin on Dr. Jackson's face expressed his happiness.
6. We begged the guard not to close the gate.

Writing

Write a **letter** to Scrooge, telling him what he is missing in life by being cranky and negative with the people around him. Start your letter with a salutation, state your main points, and conclude with a closing and your signature. In the body of your letter, be sure to include strong support for the opinions you present.

(For a model of a friendly letter format, see page R22.)

For *Grammar, Vocabulary,* and *Assessment,*
see **Build Language Skills,** pages 694–695.

Extend Your Learning

Listening and Speaking Give an **oral summary** of the plot of Act I of *A Christmas Carol: Scrooge and Marley.* Identify the setting, describe the main characters, and explain the conflict and main events of the act. Conclude your summary by identifying the questions that need to be answered in Act II.

Research and Technology Prepare **costume plans** for this play. With a small group, research the clothing worn by the upper class during the Victorian period in England. Use the Internet and library resources to gather information, photos, sketches, and descriptions. Use the information to plan costumes for two different characters in *A Christmas Carol.* In your plan, show or describe the type of clothing, the color, and the fabric.

Build Language Skills

A Christmas Carol: Scrooge and Marley, Act I

Vocabulary Skill

Suffixes The **suffix** *-ment* means "the act or quality of." Adding *-ment* to a word creates a noun. When you add *-ment* to the verb *involve,* you create the noun *involvement,* meaning "the act of being involved." When you add *-ment* to *excite,* you create the noun *excitement,* meaning "the quality of being excited."

▶ **Example:** It required the *involvement* of the entire community to clean up after the hurricane.

Practice Add the suffix *-ment* to each word. Check your spelling in a dictionary. Use each new word in a sentence.

1. amuse
2. encourage
3. measure
4. arrange
5. judge

Grammar Lesson

Interjections **Interjections** are used to add emphasis to your writing. An interjection is a part of speech that expresses a feeling, such as pain or excitement. An interjection may be set off with a comma or an exclamation point. When writing dialogue, use interjections to make the language sound more realistic.

Pain: Ouch! I hit my toe.
Excitement: Wow, Melissa can certainly run fast!

The chart lists some common interjections.

Wow	Whew	Well	Hey
Huh	Oh	Oops	Boy
Hmmm	Yikes	Yuck	Ugh

MorePractice

For more on interjections, see the Grammar Handbook, p. R31.

Practice Add an interjection to help express emotion in each sentence.

1. That violinist plays well!
2. We did not expect you today.
3. Jim, you almost fell!
4. The cake tastes burnt.
5. Gina, come here.

𝒲𝒢 *Prentice Hall Writing and Grammar Connection: Chapter 18, Section 2*

Reading: Purpose for Reading

Directions: *Read the selection. Then, answer the questions.*

Scientists have found that, as many Americans age, some develop Alzheimer's (älts'hī'mərz) disease. Alzheimer's disease is a degenerative brain disease for which there is no cure.

Researchers at Case Western Reserve Medical School in Ohio studied the effects of involving people earlier in life in mind-stimulating games as a way to slow down Alzheimer's. Scientists found that people who had been involved in such games during their lifetimes were less likely to develop Alzheimer's. Activities that helped include playing bridge, chess or a musical instrument.

1. What is the most likely purpose a reader would have for reading this text?

A to be entertained

B to be totally persuaded

C to be informed

D to completely understand

2. If your purpose were to find other games that might be helpful in preventing Alzheimer's disease, which details would be most useful to you?

A Case Western Reserve Medical School

B a degenerative brain disease

C activities included playing bridge, chess or a musical instrument

D there is no cure for Alzheimer's

3. If your purpose were to find a researcher in the field of Alzheimer's disease, which would be most useful?

A researching other diseases

B contacting the department at Case Western Reserve Medical School

C learning which musical instrument people played

D learning the rules of bridge

4. Which section provides a description of Alzheimer's disease?

A paragraph 1

B paragraph 2

C sentence 4

D sentence 5

Timed Writing: Description [Cognition]

Review your favorite scene from *A Christmas Carol,* Act I. Write a description of the scene. Use details so that someone could draw the scene from your description. **(20 minutes)**

 ## Writing Workshop: *Work in Progress*

Multimedia Report

Good multimedia reports use authoritative sources. For each topic in your portfolio, list two print and two non-print sources that provide valuable information. Save the list in your writing portfolio.

These skills will help you become a better reader. Practice them with *A Christmas Carol: Scrooge and Marley,* Act II (p. 697).

Reading Skill

Setting a purpose for reading is deciding before you read what you want to get out of a text. The purpose you set will affect the way you read. **Adjust your reading rate** to suit your purpose. For example, if you are reading directions to perform a task, you will read more slowly and carefully than if you are reading to be entertained.

- As you read drama, slow down to read stage directions carefully. They may reveal action that is not shown in the dialogue.
- Speed up to read short lines of dialogue quickly to create the feeling of conversation.
- Slow down to read longer speeches by a single character so that you can reflect on the character's words and look for clues to the message.

> **Type of Reading Material**
>
> **+**
>
> **Purpose for Reading**
>
> **=**
>
> **Reading Rate**

Literary Skill

Stage directions are the words in a dramatic script that are not spoken by characters. When a play is performed, you can see the set, the characters, and the movements, and hear the sound effects. When you read a play, you get this information in the stage directions. Stage directions are usually written in italic type and set off by brackets or parentheses, as in this example.

> [*Jen bursts through the door, stage left. There is a crack of thunder. Then the lights go dark.*]

Vocabulary Builder

A Christmas Carol: Scrooge and Marley, Act II

- **astonish** (ə stän´ ish) *v.* amaze (p. 697) *The movie's unexpected ending will <u>astonish</u> you.*
- **compulsion** (kəm pul´ shən) *n.* a driving, irresistible force (p. 699) *She has a <u>compulsion</u> to eat chocolate.*
- **severe** (sə vir´) *adj.* harsh (p. 700) *Winters in Alaska can be <u>severe</u>.*
- **meager** (mē´ gər) *adj.* of poor quality; small in amount (p. 702) *The <u>meager</u> amount of food was not enough to feed the group.*
- **audible** (ô´ də bəl) *adj.* loud enough to be heard (p. 710) *The microphone will help to make her speech <u>audible</u>.*

A Christmas Carol: Scrooge and Marley

Israel Horovitz

from **A Christmas Carol** by Charles Dickens

Act 2

Scene 1

[*Lights. Choral music is sung. Curtain.* SCROOGE, *in bed, sleeping, in spotlight. We cannot yet see the interior of his room.* MARLEY, *opposite, in spotlight equal to* SCROOGE'S. MARLEY *laughs. He tosses his hand in the air and a flame shoots from it, magically, into the air. There is a thunder clap, and then another; a lightning flash, and then another. Ghostly music plays under. Colors change.* MARLEY'S *spotlight has gone out and now reappears, with* MARLEY *in it, standing next to the bed and the sleeping* SCROOGE. MARLEY *addresses the audience directly.*]

MARLEY. Hear this snoring Scrooge! Sleeping to escape the nightmare that is his waking day. What shall I bring to him now? I'm afraid nothing would astonish old Scrooge now. Not after what he's seen. Not a baby boy, not a rhinoceros, nor anything in between would <u>astonish</u> Ebenezer Scrooge just now. I can think of nothing . . . [*Suddenly*] that's it! Nothing! [*He speaks confidentially.*] I'll have the clock strike one and, when he awakes expecting my second messenger, there will be no one . . . nothing. Then I'll have the bell strike twelve. And then one again . . . and then nothing. Nothing . . . [*Laughs*] nothing will . . . astonish him. I think it will work.

Literary Analysis
Stage Directions
What sounds are used to establish this as a scary scene?

Vocabulary Builder
astonish (ə stän´ ish)
v. amaze

✓ **Reading Check**

How does Marley plan to surprise Scrooge?

[*The bell tolls one.* SCROOGE *leaps awake.*]

SCROOGE. One! One! This is it: time! [*Looks about the room*] Nothing!

[*The bell tolls midnight.*]

Midnight! How can this be? I'm sleeping backwards.

[*One again*]

Good heavens! One again! I'm sleeping back and forth! [*A pause.* SCROOGE *looks about.*] Nothing! Absolutely nothing!

[*Suddenly, thunder and lightning.* MARLEY *laughs and disappears. The room shakes and glows. There is suddenly springlike music.* SCROOGE *makes a run for the door.*]

MARLEY. Scrooge!

SCROOGE. What?

MARLEY. Stay you put!

SCROOGE. Just checking to see if anyone is in here.

[*Lights and thunder again: more music.* MARLEY *is of a sudden gone. In his place sits the* GHOST OF CHRISTMAS PRESENT—*to be called in the stage directions of the play,* PRESENT—*center of room. Heaped up on the floor, to form a kind of throne, are turkeys, geese, game, poultry, brawn, great joints of meat, suckling pigs, long wreaths of sausages, mince-pies, plum puddings, barrels of oysters, red hot chestnuts, cherry-cheeked apples, juicy oranges, luscious pears, immense twelfth cakes, and seething bowls of punch, that make the chamber dim with their delicious steam. Upon this throne sits* PRESENT, *glorious to see. He bears a torch, shaped as a Horn of Plenty.[1]* SCROOGE *hops out of the door, and then peeks back again into his bedroom.* PRESENT *calls to* SCROOGE.]

PRESENT. Ebenezer Scrooge. Come in, come in! Come in and know me better!

SCROOGE. Hello. How should I call you?

PRESENT. I am the Ghost of Christmas Present. Look upon me.

[PRESENT *is wearing a simple green robe. The walls around the room are now covered in greenery, as well. The room*

▶ **Critical Viewing**
Based on your knowledge of the play so far, who do you expect this character to be? Explain. **[Hypothesize]**

Reading Skill
Purpose for Reading At what rate would you read these stage directions? Why?

---

1. Horn of Plenty a horn overflowing with fruits, flowers, and grain, representing wealth and abundance.

seems to be a perfect grove now: leaves of holly, mistletoe and ivy reflect the stage lights. Suddenly, there is a mighty roar of flame in the fireplace and now the hearth burns with a lavish, warming fire. There is an ancient scabbard girdling the GHOST'S *middle, but without sword. The sheath is gone to rust.*]

You have never seen the like of me before?

SCROOGE. Never.

PRESENT. You have never walked forth with younger members of my family; my elder brothers born on Christmases past.

SCROOGE. I don't think I have. I'm afraid I've not. Have you had many brothers, Spirit?

PRESENT. More than eighteen hundred.

SCROOGE. A tremendous family to provide for! [PRESENT *stands*] Spirit, conduct me where you will. I went forth last night on <u>compulsion</u>, and learnt a lesson which is working now. Tonight, if you have aught to teach me, let me profit by it.

PRESENT. Touch my robe.

[SCROOGE *walks cautiously to* PRESENT *and touches his robe. When he does, lightning flashes, thunder claps, music plays. Blackout*]

Vocabulary Builder
compulsion (kəm puľ shən) *n.* driving, irresistible force

✓**Reading Check**

Who visits Scrooge in Scene 1?

Scene 2

[*PROLOGUE:* MARLEY *stands spotlit,* L. *He speaks directly to the audience.*]

MARLEY. My ghostly friend now leads my living partner through the city's streets.

[*Lights up on* SCROOGE *and* PRESENT]

See them there and hear the music people make when the weather is <u>severe</u>, as it is now.

[*Winter music. Choral group behind scrim, sings. When the song is done and the stage is re-set, the lights will fade up on a row of shops, behind the singers. The choral group will hum the song they have just completed now and mill about the streets,[2] carrying their dinners to the bakers' shops and restaurants. They will, perhaps, sing about being poor at Christmastime, whatever.*]

PRESENT. These revelers, Mr. Scrooge, carry their own dinners to their jobs, where they will work to bake the meals the rich men and women of this city will eat as their Christmas dinners. Generous people these . . . to care for the others, so . . .

[PRESENT *walks among the choral group and a sparkling incense[3] falls from his torch on to their baskets, as he pulls the covers off of the baskets. Some of the choral group become angry with each other.*]

MAN #1. Hey, you, watch where you're going.

MAN #2. Watch it yourself, mate!

[PRESENT *sprinkles them directly, they change.*]

MAN #1. I pray go in ahead of me. It's Christmas. You be first!

MAN #2. No, no, I must insist that YOU be first!

MAN #1. All right, I shall be, and gratefully so.

MAN #2. The pleasure is equally mine, for being able to watch you pass, smiling.

---

2. **mill about the streets** walk around aimlessly.
3. **incense** (in´ sens) *n.* any of various substances that produce a pleasant odor when burned.

Reading Skill
Purpose for Reading
At what rate would you read dialogue such as this? Why?

MAN #1. I would find it a shame to quarrel on Christmas Day . . .

MAN #2. As would I.

MAN #1. Merry Christmas then, friend!

MAN #2. And a Merry Christmas straight back to you!

[*Church bells toll. The choral group enter the buildings: the shops and restaurants; they exit the stage, shutting their doors closed behind them. All sound stops.* SCROOGE *and* PRESENT *are alone again.*]

SCROOGE. What is it you sprinkle from your torch?

PRESENT. Kindness.

SCROOGE. Do you sprinkle your kindness on any particular people or on all people?

PRESENT. To any person kindly given. And to the very poor most of all.

SCROOGE. Why to the very poor most?

PRESENT. Because the very poor need it most. Touch my heart . . . here, Mr. Scrooge. We have another journey.

[SCROOGE *touches the* GHOST'S *heart and music plays, lights change color, lightning flashes, thunder claps. A choral group appears on the street, singing Christmas carols.*]

Scene 3

[MARLEY *stands spotlit in front of a scrim on which is painted the exterior of* CRATCHIT'S *four-roomed house. There is a flash and a clap and* MARLEY *is gone. The lights shift color again, the scrim flies away, and we are in the interior of the* CRATCHIT *family home.* SCROOGE *is there, with the* SPIRIT (PRESENT), *watching* MRS. CRATCHIT *set the table, with the help of* BELINDA CRATCHIT *and* PETER CRATCHIT, *a baby, pokes a fork into the mashed potatoes on his highchair's tray. He also chews on his shirt collar.*]

SCROOGE. What is this place, Spirit?

PRESENT. This is the home of your employee, Mr. Scrooge. Don't you know it?

**Literary Analysis
Stage Directions**
What information in the stage directions here adds to the effectiveness of the scene?

Reading Check

What does the Ghost of Christmas Present show Scrooge?

SCROOGE. Do you mean Cratchit, Spirit? Do you mean this is Cratchit's home?

PRESENT. None other.

SCROOGE. These children are his?

PRESENT. There are more to come presently.

SCROOGE. On his <u>meager</u> earnings! What foolishness!

PRESENT. Foolishness, is it?

SCROOGE. Wouldn't you say so? Fifteen shillings[4] a week's what he gets!

PRESENT. I would say that he gets the pleasure of his family, fifteen times a week times the number of hours a day! Wait, Mr. Scrooge. Wait, listen and watch. You might actually learn something . . .

MRS. CRATCHIT. What has ever got your precious father then? And your brother, Tiny Tim? And Martha warn't as late last Christmas by half an hour!

[MARTHA *opens the door, speaking to her mother as she does.*]

MARTHA. Here's Martha, now, Mother! [*She laughs. The* CRATCHIT CHILDREN *squeal with delight.*]

BELINDA. It's Martha, Mother! Here's Martha!

PETER. Marthmama, Marthmama! Hullo!

BELINDA. Hurrah! Martha! Martha! There's such an enormous goose for us, Martha!

MRS. CRATCHIT. Why, bless your heart alive, my dear, how late you are!

MARTHA. We'd a great deal of work to finish up last night, and had to clear away this morning, Mother.

MRS. CRATCHIT. Well, never mind so long as you are come. Sit ye down before the fire, my dear, and have a warm, Lord bless ye!

BELINDA. No, no! There's Father coming. Hide, Martha, hide!

---

4. **Fifteen shillings** a small amount of money for a week's work.

Vocabulary Builder
meager (mē′ gər) *adj.* of poor quality; small in amount

Reading Skill
Purpose for Reading How does Mrs. Cratchit's use of language affect your reading rate? Explain.

702 ■ *Drama*

[MARTHA *giggles and hides herself.*]

MARTHA. Where? Here?

PETER. Hide, hide!

BELINDA. Not there! THERE!

[MARTHA *is hidden.* BOB CRATCHIT *enters, carrying* TINY TIM *atop his shoulder. He wears a threadbare and fringeless comforter hanging down in front of him.* TINY TIM *carries small crutches and his small legs are bound in an iron frame brace.*]

BOB AND TINY TIM. Merry Christmas.

BOB. Merry Christmas my love, Merry Christmas Peter, Merry Christmas Belinda. Why, where is Martha?

MRS. CRATCHIT. Not coming.

BOB. Not coming: Not coming upon Christmas Day?

MARTHA. [*Pokes head out*] Ohhh, poor Father. Don't be disappointed.

BOB. What's this?

MARTHA. 'Tis I!

BOB. Martha! [*They embrace.*]

TINY TIM. Martha! Martha!

MARTHA. Tiny Tim!

[TINY TIM *is placed in* MARTHA'S *arms.* BELINDA *and* PETER *rush him offstage.*]

BELINDA. Come, brother! You must come hear the pudding singing in the copper.

TINY TIM. The pudding? What flavor have we?

PETER. Plum! Plum!

TINY TIM. Oh, Mother! I love plum!

[*The children exit the stage, giggling.*]

▲ **Critical Viewing**
Based on this picture, how would you describe the relationship between Tiny Tim and his father? **[Infer]**

✓ **Reading Check**

Why does Martha hide?

MRS. CRATCHIT. And how did little Tim behave?

BOB. As good as gold, and even better. Somehow he gets thoughtful sitting by himself so much, and thinks the strangest things you ever heard. He told me, coming home, that he hoped people saw him in the church, because he was a cripple, and it might be pleasant to them to remember upon Christmas Day, who made lame beggars walk and blind men see. [*Pauses*] He has the oddest ideas sometimes, but he seems all the while to be growing stronger and more hearty . . . one would never know. [*Hears* TIM'S *crutch on floor outside door*]

PETER. The goose has arrived to be eaten!

BELINDA. Oh, mama, mama, it's beautiful.

MARTHA. It's a perfect goose, Mother!

TINY TIM. To this Christmas goose, Mother and Father I say . . . [*Yells*] Hurrah! Hurrah!

OTHER CHILDREN. [*Copying* TIM] Hurrah! Hurrah!

[*The family sits round the table.* BOB *and* MRS. CRATCHIT *serve the trimmings, quickly. All sit; all bow heads; all pray.*]

BOB. Thank you, dear Lord, for your many gifts . . . our dear children; our wonderful meal; our love for one another; and the warmth of our small fire—[*Looks up at all*] A merry Christmas to us, my dear. God bless us!

ALL. [*Except* TIM] Merry Christmas! God bless us!

TINY TIM. [*In a short silence*] God bless us every one.

[*All freeze. Spotlight on* PRESENT *and* SCROOGE]

SCROOGE. Spirit, tell me if Tiny Tim will live.

PRESENT. I see a vacant seat . . . in the poor chimney corner, and a crutch without an owner, carefully preserved. If these shadows remain unaltered by the future, the child will die.

SCROOGE. No, no, kind Spirit! Say he will be spared!

PRESENT. If these shadows remain unaltered by the future, none other of my race will find him here. What then? If he be like to die, he had better do it, and decrease the surplus population.

Literary Analysis
Stage Directions
Why is the pause in Bob's speech important here?

[SCROOGE *bows his head. We hear* BOB'S *voice speak* SCROOGE's name.]

BOB. Mr. Scrooge . . .

SCROOGE. Huh? What's that? Who calls?

BOB. [*His glass raised in a toast*] I'll give you Mr. Scrooge, the Founder of the Feast!

SCROOGE. Me, Bob? You toast me?

PRESENT. Save your breath, Mr. Scrooge. You can't be seen or heard.

MRS. CRATCHIT. The Founder of the Feast, indeed! I wish I had him here, that miser Scrooge. I'd give him a piece of my mind to feast upon, and I hope he'd have a good appetite for it!

▲ **Critical Viewing**
Why might a director stage the scene this way, with Tiny Tim standing on the table? **[Interpret]**

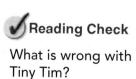**Reading Check**

What is wrong with Tiny Tim?

BOB. My dear! Christmas Day!

MRS. CRATCHIT. It should be Christmas Day, I am sure, on which one drinks the health of such an odious, stingy, unfeeling man as Mr. Scrooge . . .

SCROOGE. Oh, Spirit, must I? . . .

MRS. CRATCHIT. You know he is, Robert! Nobody knows it better than you do, poor fellow!

BOB. This is Christmas Day, and I should like to drink to the health of the man who employs me and allows me to earn my living and our support and that man is Ebenezer Scrooge . . .

MRS. CRATCHIT. I'll drink to his health for your sake and the day's, but not for his sake . . . a Merry Christmas and a Happy New Year to you, Mr. Scrooge, wherever you may be this day!

SCROOGE. Just here, kind madam . . . out of sight, out of sight . . .

BOB. Thank you, my dear. Thank you.

SCROOGE. Thank you, Bob . . . and Mrs. Cratchit, too. No one else is toasting me, . . . not now . . . not ever. Of that I am sure . . .

BOB. Children . . .

ALL. Merry Christmas to Mr. Scrooge.

BOB. I'll pay you sixpence, Tim, for my favorite song.

TINY TIM. Oh, Father, I'd so love to sing it, but not for pay. This Christmas goose—this feast—you and Mother, my brother and sisters close with me: that's my pay—

BOB. Martha, will you play the notes on the lute, for Tiny Tim's song.

BELINDA. May I sing, too, Father?

BOB. We'll all sing.

▼ **Critical Viewing**
Martha plays a lute like this one while her family sings. If this play were set in contemporary times, what instrument would Martha probably play? **[Analyze]**

[*They sing a song about a tiny child lost in the snow—probably from Wordsworth's poem.* TIM *sings the lead vocal; all chime in for the chorus. Their song fades under, as the* GHOST OF CHRISTMAS PRESENT *speaks.*]

PRESENT. Mark my words, Ebenezer Scrooge. I do not present the Cratchits to you because they are a handsome, or brilliant family. They are not handsome. They are not brilliant. They are not well-dressed, or tasteful to the times. Their shoes are not even waterproofed by virtue of money or cleverness spent. So when the pavement is wet, so are the insides of their shoes and the tops of their toes. These are the Cratchits, Mr. Scrooge. They are not highly special. They are happy, grateful, pleased with one another, contented with the time and how it passes. They don't sing very well, do they? But, nonetheless, they do sing . . . [*Pauses*] think of that, Scrooge. Fifteen shillings a week and they do sing . . . hear their song until its end.

SCROOGE. I am listening. [*The chorus sings full volume now, until . . . the song ends here.*] Spirit, it must be time for us to take our leave. I feel in my heart that it is . . . that I must think on that which I have seen here . . .

PRESENT. Touch my robe again . . .

[SCROOGE *touches* PRESENT'S *robe. The lights fade out on the* CRATCHITS, *who sit, frozen, at the table.* SCROOGE *and* PRESENT *in a spotlight now. Thunder, lightning, smoke. They are gone.*]

Scene 4

[MARLEY *appears* D.L. *in single spotlight. A storm brews. Thunder and lightning.* SCROOGE *and* PRESENT *"fly" past,* U. *The storm continues, furiously, and, now and again,* SCROOGE *and* PRESENT *will zip past in their travels.* MARLEY *will speak straight out to the audience.*]

MARLEY. The Ghost of Christmas Present, my co-worker in this attempt to turn a miser, flies about now with that very miser, Scrooge, from street to street, and he points out partygoers on their way to Christmas parties. If one were to judge from the numbers of people on their way to friendly

Literary Analysis
Stage Directions
What does the song—and the subject—add to the mood of the scene?

Reading Check

What does Scrooge observe the Cratchits doing?

**Reading Skill
Purpose for Reading**
Why is it important to
read Marley's lines
slowly?

gatherings, one might think that no one was left at home to give anyone welcome . . . but that's not the case, is it? Every home is expecting company and . . . [*He laughs.*] Scrooge is amazed.

[SCROOGE *and* PRESENT *zip past again. The lights fade up around them. We are in the* NEPHEW'S *home, in the living room.* PRESENT *and* SCROOGE *stand watching the* NEPHEW: FRED *and his wife, fixing the fire.*]

SCROOGE. What is this place? We've moved from the mines!

PRESENT. You do not recognize them?

SCROOGE. It is my nephew! . . . and the one he married . . .

[MARLEY *waves his hand and there is a lightning flash. He disappears.*]

FRED. It strikes me as sooooo funny, to think of what he said . . . that Christmas was a humbug, as I live! He believed it!

WIFE. More shame for him, Fred!

FRED. Well, he's a comical old fellow, that's the truth.

WIFE. I have no patience with him.

FRED. Oh, I have! I am sorry for him; I couldn't be angry with him if I tried. Who suffers by his ill whims? Himself, always . . .

SCROOGE. It's me they talk of, isn't it, Spirit?

FRED. Here, wife, consider this. Uncle Scrooge takes it into his head to dislike us, and he won't come and dine with us. What's the consequence?

WIFE. Oh . . . you're sweet to say what I think you're about to say, too, Fred . . .

FRED. What's the consequence? He don't lose much of a dinner by it, I can tell you that!

WIFE. Ooooooo, Fred! Indeed, I think he loses a very good dinner . . . ask my sisters, or your bachelor friend, Topper . . . ask any of them. They'll tell you what old Scrooge, your uncle, missed: a dandy meal!

FRED. Well, that's something of a relief, wife. Glad to hear it! [*He hugs his wife. They laugh. They kiss.*] The truth is, he misses much yet. I mean to give him the same chance every year, whether he likes it or not, for I pity him. Nay, he is my only uncle and I feel for the old miser . . . but, I tell you, wife: I see my dear and perfect mother's face on his own wizened cheeks and brow: brother and sister they were, and I cannot erase that from each view of him I take . . .

WIFE. I understand what you say, Fred, and I am with you in your yearly asking. But he never will accept, you know. He never will.

FRED. Well, true, wife. Uncle may rail at Christmas till he dies. I think I shook him some with my visit yesterday . . . [*Laughing*] I refused to grow angry . . . no matter how nasty he became . . . [*Whoops*] It was HE who grew angry, wife! [*They both laugh now.*]

SCROOGE. What he says is true, Spirit . . .

FRED AND WIFE. Bah, humbug!

FRED. [*Embracing his wife*] There is much laughter in our marriage, wife. It pleases me. You please me . . .

WIFE. And you please me, Fred. You are a good man . . . [*They embrace.*] Come now. We must have a look at the meal . . . our guests will soon arrive . . . my sisters, Topper . . .

FRED. A toast first . . . [*He hands her a glass.*] A toast to Uncle Scrooge . . . [*Fills their glasses*]

WIFE. A toast to him?

FRED. Uncle Scrooge has given us plenty of merriment, I am sure, and it would be ungrateful not to drink to his health. And I say . . . Uncle Scrooge!

Reading Check

What scenes does Christmas Present show Scrooge?

WIFE. [*Laughing*] You're a proper loon,[5] Fred . . . and I'm a
proper wife to you . . . [*She raises her glass.*] Uncle Scrooge!
[*They drink. They embrace. They kiss.*]

SCROOGE. Spirit, please, make me visible! Make me <u>audible</u>! I
want to talk with my nephew and my niece!

[*Calls out to them. The lights that light the room and* FRED *and
wife fade out.* SCROOGE *and* PRESENT *are alone, spotlit.*]

PRESENT. These shadows are gone to you now, Mr. Scrooge.
You may return to them later tonight in your dreams.
[*Pauses*] My time grows short, Ebenezer Scrooge. Look you
on me! Do you see how I've aged?

SCROOGE. Your hair has gone gray! Your skin, wrinkled! Are
spirits' lives so short?

PRESENT. My stay upon this globe is very brief. It ends
tonight.

SCROOGE. Tonight?

PRESENT. At midnight. The time is drawing near!

[*Clock strikes 11:45.*]

Hear those chimes? In a quarter hour, my life will have
been spent! Look, Scrooge, man. Look you here.

[*Two gnarled baby dolls are taken from* PRESENT'S *skirts.*]

SCROOGE. Who are they?

PRESENT. They are Man's children, and they cling to me,
appealing from their fathers. The boy is Ignorance; the girl
is Want. Beware them both, and all of their degree, but
most of all beware this boy, for I see that written on his
brow which is doom, unless the writing be erased. [*He
stretches out his arm. His voice is now amplified: loudly and
oddly.*]

SCROOGE. Have they no refuge or resource?

PRESENT. Are there no prisons? Are there no workhouses?
[*Twelve chimes*] Are there no prisons? Are there no workhouses?

---

5. a proper loon a silly person.

Vocabulary Builder
audible (ô′də bəl)
adj. loud enough to
be heard

Literary Analysis
Stage Directions
Why is the clock on
stage important to
the action?

[*A* PHANTOM, *hooded, appears in dim light,* D., *opposite.*]
Are there no prisons? Are there no workhouses?

[PRESENT *begins to deliquesce.* SCROOGE *calls after him.*]

SCROOGE. Spirit, I'm frightened! Don't leave me! Spirit!

PRESENT. Prisons? Workhouses? Prisons? Workhouses . . .

[*He is gone.* SCROOGE *is alone now with the* PHANTOM, *who is, of course, the* GHOST OF CHRISTMAS FUTURE. *The* PHANTOM *is shrouded in black. Only its outstretched hand is visible from under his ghostly garment.*]

SCROOGE. Who are you, Phantom? Oh, yes, I think I know you! You are, are you not, the Spirit of Christmas Yet to Come? [*No reply*] And you are about to show me the shadows of the things that have not yet happened, but will happen in time before us. Is that not so, Spirit? [*The* PHANTOM *allows* SCROOGE *a look at his face. No other reply wanted here. A nervous giggle here.*] Oh, Ghost of the Future, I fear you more than any Specter I have seen! But, as I know that your purpose is to do me good and as I hope to live to be another man from what I was, I am prepared to bear you company. [FUTURE *does not reply, but for a stiff arm, hand and finger set, pointing forward.*] Lead on, then, lead on. The night is waning fast, and it is precious time to me. Lead on, Spirit!

[FUTURE *moves away from* SCROOGE *in the same rhythm and motion employed at its arrival.* SCROOGE *falls into the same pattern, a considerable space apart from the* SPIRIT. *In the space between them,* MARLEY *appears. He looks to* FUTURE *and then to* SCROOGE. *He claps his hands. Thunder and lightning. Three* BUSINESSMEN *appear, spotlighted singularly: One is* D.L.; *one is* D.R.; *one is* U.C. *Thus, six points of the stage should now be spotted in light.* MARLEY *will watch this scene from his position,* C. SCROOGE *and* FUTURE *are* R. *and* L. *of* C.]

FIRST BUSINESSMAN. Oh, no, I don't know much about it either way, I only know he's dead.

SECOND BUSINESSMAN. When did he die?

FIRST BUSINESSMAN. Last night, I believe.

Literary Analysis
Stage Directions
Why does the stage direction that calls for Future to stretch out his arm add to the drama of the scene?

Reading Check

What warning does the Ghost of Christmas Present give Scrooge?

SECOND BUSINESSMAN. Why, what was the matter with him? I thought he'd never die, really . . .

FIRST BUSINESSMAN. [*Yawning*] Goodness knows, goodness knows . . .

THIRD BUSINESSMAN. What has he done with his money?

SECOND BUSINESSMAN. I haven't heard. Have you?

FIRST BUSINESSMAN. Left it to his Company, perhaps. Money to money; you know the expression . . .

THIRD BUSINESSMAN. He hasn't left it to me. That's all I know . . .

FIRST BUSINESSMAN. [*Laughing*] Nor to me . . . [*Looks at* SECOND BUSINESSMAN] You, then? You got his money???

SECOND BUSINESSMAN. [*Laughing*] Me, me, his money? Nooooo!

[*They all laugh.*]

THIRD BUSINESSMAN. It's likely to be a cheap funeral, for upon my life, I don't know of a living soul who'd care to venture to it. Suppose we make up a party and volunteer?

SECOND BUSINESSMAN. I don't mind going if a lunch is provided, but I must be fed, if I make one.

FIRST BUSINESSMAN. Well, I am the most disinterested among you, for I never wear black gloves, and I never eat lunch. But I'll offer to go, if anybody else will. When I come to think of it, I'm not all sure that I wasn't his most particular friend; for we used to stop and speak whenever we met. Well, then . . . bye, bye!

SECOND BUSINESSMAN. Bye, bye . . .

THIRD BUSINESSMAN. Bye, bye . . .

[*They glide offstage in three separate directions. Their lights follow them.*]

▲ Critical Viewing
How does the Ghost of Christmas Future differ from the Ghost of Christmas Present? [**Compare and Contrast**]

SCROOGE. Spirit, why did you show me this? Why do you show me businessmen from my streets as they take the death of Jacob Marley. That is a thing past. You are future!

[JACOB MARLEY *laughs a long, deep laugh. There is a thunder clap and lightning flash, and he is gone.* SCROOGE *faces* FUTURE, *alone on stage now.* FUTURE *wordlessly stretches out his arm-hand-and-finger-set, pointing into the distance,* U. *There, above them. Scoundrels "fly" by, half-dressed and slovenly. When this scene has passed, a woman enters the playing area. She is almost at once followed by a second woman; and then a man in faded black; and then, suddenly, an old man, who smokes a pipe. The old man scares the other three. They laugh, anxious.*]

FIRST WOMAN. Look here, old Joe, here's a chance! If we haven't all three met here without meaning it!

OLD JOE. You couldn't have met in a better place. Come into the parlor. You were made free of it long ago, you know; and the other two an't strangers [*He stands; shuts a door. Shrieking*] We're all suitable to our calling. We're well matched. Come into the parlor. Come into the parlor . . . [*They follow him* D. SCROOGE *and* FUTURE *are now in their midst, watching; silent. A truck comes in on which is set a small wall with fireplace and a screen of rags, etc. All props for the scene.*] Let me just rake this fire over a bit . . .

[*He does. He trims his lamp with the stem of his pipe. The* FIRST WOMAN *throws a large bundle on to the floor. She sits beside it crosslegged, defiantly.*]

FIRST WOMAN. What odds then? What odds, Mrs. Dilber? Every person has a right to take care of themselves. HE always did!

MRS. DILBER. That's true indeed! No man more so!

FIRST WOMAN. Why, then, don't stand staring as if you was afraid, woman! Who's the wiser? We're not going to pick holes in each other's coats, I suppose?

MRS. DILBER. No, indeed! We should hope not!

FIRST WOMAN. Very well, then! That's enough. Who's the worse for the loss of a few things like these? Not a dead man, I suppose?

Literary Analysis
Stage Directions If you were staging this play, how could you make people appear to "fly" by?

Reading Check

What does Scrooge think the spirit is showing him?

A Christmas Carol: Scrooge and Marley, Act II ■ 713

MRS. DILBER. [*Laughing*] No, indeed!

FIRST WOMAN. If he wanted to keep 'em after he was dead, the wicked old screw, why wasn't he natural in his lifetime? If he had been, he'd have had somebody to look after him when he was struck with Death, instead of lying gasping out his last there, alone by himself.

MRS. DILBER. It's the truest word that was ever spoke. It's a judgment on him.

FIRST WOMAN. I wish it were a heavier one, and it should have been, you may depend on it, if I could have laid my hands on anything else. Open that bundle, old Joe, and let me know the value of it. Speak out plain. I'm not afraid to be the first, nor afraid for them to see it. We knew pretty well that we were helping ourselves, before we met here, I believe. It's no sin. Open the bundle, Joe.

FIRST MAN. No, no, my dear! I won't think of letting you being the first to show what you've . . . earned . . . earned from this. I throw in mine.

[*He takes a bundle from his shoulder, turns it upside down, and empties its contents out on to the floor.*]

It's not very extensive, see . . . seals . . . a pencil case . . . sleeve buttons . . .

MRS. DILBER. Nice sleeve buttons, though . . .

FIRST MAN. Not bad, not bad . . . a brooch there . . .

OLD JOE. Not really valuable, I'm afraid . . .

FIRST MAN. How much, old Joe?

OLD JOE. [*Writing on the wall with chalk*] A pitiful lot, really. Ten and six and not a sixpence more!

FIRST MAN. You're not serious!

OLD JOE. That's your account and I wouldn't give another sixpence if I was to be boiled for not doing it. Who's next?

MRS. DILBER. Me! [*Dumps out contents of her bundle*] Sheets, towels, silver spoons, silver sugar-tongs . . . some boots . . .

OLD JOE. [*Writing on wall*] I always give too much to the ladies. It's a weakness of mine and that's the way I ruin myself.

Here's your total comin' up . . . two pounds-ten . . . if you asked me for another penny, and made it an open question, I'd repent of being so liberal and knock off half-a-crown.

FIRST WOMAN. And now do MY bundle, Joe.

OLD JOE. [*Kneeling to open knots on her bundle*] So many knots, madam . . . [*He drags out large curtains; dark*] What do you call this? Bed curtains!

FIRST WOMAN. [*Laughing*] Ah, yes, bed curtains!

OLD JOE. You don't mean to say you took 'em down, rings and all, with him lying there?

FIRST WOMAN. Yes, I did, why not?

OLD JOE. You were born to make your fortune and you'll certainly do it.

FIRST WOMAN. I certainly shan't hold my hand, when I can get anything in it by reaching it out, for the sake of such a man as he was, I promise you, Joe. Don't drop that lamp oil on those blankets, now!

OLD JOE. His blankets?

FIRST WOMAN. Whose else's do you think? He isn't likely to catch cold without 'em, I daresay.

OLD JOE. I hope that he didn't die of anything catching? Eh?

FIRST WOMAN. Don't you be afraid of that. I ain't so fond of his company that I'd loiter about him for such things if he did. Ah! You may look through that shirt till your eyes ache, but you won't find a hole in it, nor a threadbare place. It's the best he had, and a fine one, too. They'd have wasted it, if it hadn't been for me.

OLD JOE. What do you mean 'They'd have wasted it?'

FIRST WOMAN. Putting it on him to be buried in, to be sure. Somebody was fool enough to do it, but I took it off again . . .

[*She laughs, as do they all, nervously.*]

If calico[6] ain't good enough for such a purpose, it isn't good enough then for anything. It's quite as becoming to the body. He can't look uglier than he did in that one!

6. **calico** (kal′ i kō) *n.* coarse and cheap cloth.

Literary Analysis
Stage Directions
How do the stage directions help you picture the action in this scene?

Reading Check

Whose possessions are these people selling?

SCROOGE. [*A low-pitched moan emits from his mouth; from the bones.*] OOOOOOOooooOOOOOooooOOOOOOOO ooooOOOOOOooooOO!

OLD JOE. One pound six for the lot. [*He produces a small flannel bag filled with money. He divvies it out. He continues to pass around the money as he speaks. All are laughing.*] That's the end of it, you see! He frightened every one away from him while he was alive, to profit us when he was dead! Hah ha ha!

ALL. HAHAHAHAhahahahahahah!

SCROOGE. OOOoooOOOoooOOOoooOOOooo OOoooOOoooOOOooo! [*He screams at them.*] Obscene demons! Why not market the corpse itself, as sell its trimming??? [*Suddenly*] Oh, Spirit, I see it, I see it! This unhappy man—this stripped-bare corpse . . . could very well be my own. My life holds parallel! My life ends that way now!

[SCROOGE *backs into something in the dark behind his spotlight.* SCROOGE *looks at* FUTURE, *who points to the corpse.* SCROOGE *pulls back the blanket. The corpse is, of course,* SCROOGE, *who screams. He falls aside the bed; weeping.*]

Spirit, this is a fearful place. In leaving it, I shall not leave its lesson, trust me. Let us go!

[FUTURE *points to the corpse.*]

Spirit, let me see some tenderness connected with a death, or that dark chamber, which we just left now, Spirit, will be forever present to me.

[FUTURE *spreads his robes again. Thunder and lightning. Lights up, U., in the* CRATCHIT *home setting.* MRS. CRATCHIT *and her daughters, sewing*]

TINY TIM'S VOICE. [*Off*] And He took a child and set him in the midst of them.

SCROOGE. [*Looking about the room; to* FUTURE] Huh? Who spoke? Who said that?

Literary Analysis
Stage Directions
What is the effect of the spirit's silence?

▶ Critical Viewing
Why might a director choose to place the actors playing the Cratchits this way? What do their positions reveal about the family? **[Analyze]**

MRS. CRATCHIT. [*Puts down her sewing*] The color hurts my eyes. [*Rubs her eyes*] That's better. My eyes grow weak sewing by candlelight. I shouldn't want to show your father weak eyes when he comes home . . . not for the world! It must be near his time . . .

PETER. [*In corner, reading. Looks up from book*] Past it, rather. But I think he's been walking a bit slower than usual these last few evenings, Mother.

MRS. CRATCHIT. I have known him walk with . . . [*Pauses*] I have know him walk with Tiny Tim upon his shoulder and very fast indeed.

PETER. So have I, Mother! Often!

DAUGHTER. So have I.

MRS. CRATCHIT. But he was very light to carry and his father loved him so, that it was not trouble—no trouble.
[BOB, *at door*]
And there is your father at the door.

[BOB CRATCHIT *enters. He wears a comforter. He is cold, forlorn.*]

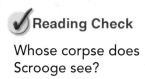

Reading Check

Whose corpse does Scrooge see?

PETER. Father!

BOB. Hello, wife, children . . .

[*The daughter weeps; turns away from* CRATCHIT.]

Children! How good to see you all! And you, wife. And look at this sewing! I've no doubt, with all your industry, we'll have a quilt to set down upon our knees in church on Sunday!

MRS. CRATCHIT. You made the arrangements today, then, Robert, for the . . . service . . . to be on Sunday.

BOB. The funeral. Oh, well, yes, yes, I did. I wish you could have gone. It would have done you good to see how green a place it is. But you'll see it often. I promised him that I would walk there on Sunday, after the service. [*Suddenly*] My little, little child! My little child!

ALL CHILDREN. [*Hugging him*] Oh, Father . . .

BOB. [*He stands*] Forgive me. I saw Mr. Scrooge's nephew, who you know I'd just met once before, and he was so wonderful to me, wife . . . he is the most pleasant-spoken gentleman I've ever met . . . he said "I am heartily sorry for it and heartily sorry for your good wife. If I can be of service to you in any way, here's where I live." And he gave me this card.

PETER. Let me see it!

BOB. And he looked me straight in the eye, wife, and said, meaningfully, "I pray you'll come to me, Mr. Cratchit, if you need some help. I pray you do." Now it wasn't for the sake of anything that he might be able to do for us, so much as for his kind way. It seemed as if he had known our Tiny Tim and felt with us.

MRS. CRATCHIT. I'm sure that he's a good soul.

BOB. You would be surer of it, my dear, if you saw and spoke to him. I shouldn't be at all surprised, if he got Peter a situation.

MRS. CRATCHIT. Only hear that, Peter!

MARTHA. And then, Peter will be keeping company with someone and setting up for himself!

PETER. Get along with you!

Reading Skill
Purpose for Reading
What plot information does this dialogue provide about a possible future for the Cratchits?

BOB. It's just as likely as not, one of these days, though there's plenty of time for that, my dear. But however and whenever we part from one another, I am sure we shall none of us forget poor Tiny Tim—shall we?—or this first parting that was among us?

ALL CHILDREN. Never, Father, never!

BOB. And when we recollect how patient and mild he was, we shall not quarrel easily among ourselves, and forget poor Tiny Tim in doing it.

ALL CHILDREN. No, Father, never!

LITTLE BOB. I am very happy, I am, I am, I am very happy.

[BOB *kisses his little son, as does* MRS. CRATCHIT, *as do the other children. The family is set now in one sculptural embrace. The lighting fades to a gentle pool of light, tight on them.*]

SCROOGE. Specter, something informs me that our parting moment is at hand. I know it, but I know not how I know it.

[FUTURE *points to the other side of the stage. Lights out on* CRATCHITS. FUTURE *moves slowing, gliding.* SCROOGE *follows.* FUTURE *points opposite.* FUTURE *leads* SCROOGE *to a wall and a tombstone. He points to the stone.*]

Am I that man those ghoulish parasites[7] so gloated over? [*Pauses*] Before I draw nearer to that stone to which you point, answer me one question. Are these the shadows of things that will be, or the shadows of things that MAY be, only?

[FUTURE *points to the gravestone.* MARLEY *appears in light well* U. *He points to grave as well. Gravestone turns front and grows to ten feet high. Words upon it:* EBENEZER

▼ **Critical Viewing**
Why do you think the sight of this tombstone scared Scrooge so much? **[Connect]**

✔ **Reading Check**

What has happened to Tiny Tim?

---

7. ghoulish parasites (gōōl´ ish par´ ə sĭts) man and women who stole and divided Scrooge's goods after he died.

SCROOGE: *Much smoke billows now from the grave. Choral music here.* SCROOGE *stands looking up at gravestone.* FUTURE *does not at all reply in mortals' words, but points once more to the gravestone. The stone undulates and glows. Music plays, beckoning* SCROOGE. SCROOGE *reeling in terror*]

Oh, no. Spirit! Oh, no, no!

[FUTURE'S *finger still pointing*]

Spirit! Hear me! I am not the man I was. I will not be the man I would have been but for this intercourse. Why show me this, if I am past all hope?

[FUTURE *considers* SCROOGE'S *logic. His hand wavers.*]

Oh, Good Spirit, I see by your wavering hand that your good nature intercedes for me and pities me. Assure me that I yet may change these shadows that you have shown me by an altered life!

[FUTURE'S *hand trembles; pointing has stopped.*]

I will honor Christmas in my heart and try to keep it all the year. I will live in the Past, the Present, and the Future. The Spirits of all Three shall strive within me. I will not shut out the lessons that they teach. Oh, tell me that I may sponge away the writing that is upon this stone!

[SCROOGE *makes a desperate stab at grabbing* FUTURE'S *hand. He holds firm for a moment, but* FUTURE, *stronger than* SCROOGE, *pulls away.* SCROOGE *is on his knees, praying.*]

Spirit, dear Spirit, I am praying before you. Give me a sign that all is possible. Give me a sign that all hope for me is not lost. Oh, Spirit, kind Spirit, I beseech thee: give me a sign . . .

[FUTURE *deliquesces, slowly, gently. The* PHANTOM'S *hood and robe drop gracefully to the ground in a small heap. Music in. There is nothing in them. They are mortal cloth. The* SPIRIT *is elsewhere.* SCROOGE *has his sign.* SCROOGE *is alone. Tableau. The lights fade to black.*]

Scene 5

[*The end of it.* MARLEY, *spotlighted, opposite* SCROOGE, *in his bed, spotlighted.* MARLEY *speaks to audience, directly.*]

Literary Analysis
Stage Directions
What action, described in the stage directions, gives Scrooge hope that he may change the future?

MARLEY. [*He smiles at* SCROOGE:] The firm of Scrooge and
Marley is doubly blessed; two misers turned; one, alas, in
Death, too late; but the other miser turned in Time's penul-
timate nick.[8] Look you on my friend, Ebenezer Scrooge . . .

SCROOGE. [*Scrambling out of bed; reeling in delight*] I will live in
the Past, in the Present, and in the Future! The Spirits of
all Three shall strive within me!

MARLEY. [*He points and moves closer to* SCROOGE'S *bed.*] Yes,
Ebenezer, the bedpost is your own. Believe it! Yes, Ebenezer, the room is your own. Believe it!

SCROOGE. Oh, Jacob Marley! Wherever you are, Jacob, know
ye that I praise you for this! I praise you . . . and
heaven . . . and Christmastime! [*Kneels facing away from*
MARLEY] I say it to ye on my knees, old Jacob, on my knees!
[*He touches his bed curtains.*] Not torn down. My bed curtains are not at all torn down! Rings and all, here they are!
They are here: I am here: the shadows of things that would
have been, may now be dispelled. They will be, Jacob! I
know they will be!

[*He chooses clothing for the day. He tries different pieces of
clothing and settles, perhaps on a dress suit, plus a cape of
the bed clothing: something of color.*]

I am light as a feather, I am happy as an angel, I am as
merry as a schoolboy. [*Yells out window and then out to
audience*] Merry Christmas to everybody! Merry Christmas
to everybody! A Happy New Year to all the world! Hallo here!
Whoop! Whoop! Hallo! Hallo! I don't know what day of the
month it is! I don't care! I don't know anything! I'm quite a
baby! I don't care! I don't care a fig! I'd much rather be a
baby than be an old wreck like me or Marley! (Sorry, Jacob,
wherever ye be!) Hallo! Hallo there!

[*Church bells chime in Christmas Day. A small boy, named*
ADAM, *is seen now* D.R., *as a light fades up on him.*]

Hey, you boy! What's today? What day of the year is it?

ADAM. Today, sir? Why, it's Christmas Day!

SCROOGE. It's Christmas Day, is it? Whoop! Well, I haven't
missed it after all, have I? The Spirits did all they did in one
night. They can do anything they like, right? Of course they
can! Of course they can!

**Reading Skill
Purpose for Reading**
Why might you read
this speech by
Scrooge quickly?

Reading Check

What promises does
Scrooge make?

---

8. **in Time's penultimate nick** just at the last moment.

Literature in Context Media Connection

The Many Faces of Scrooge

The part of Ebenezer Scrooge has been played by many different actors over the years.

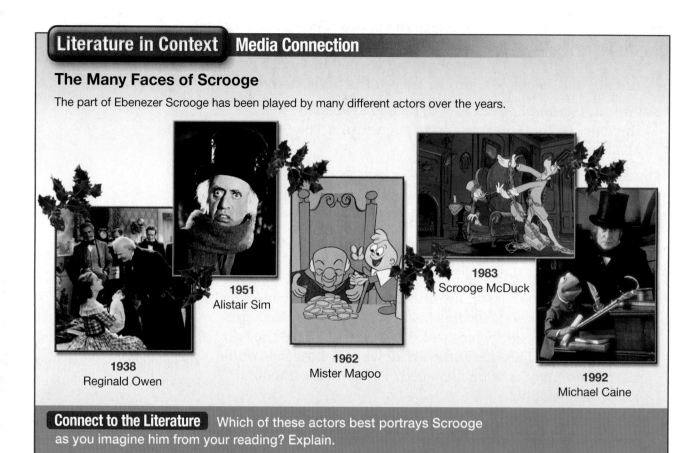

1951
Alistair Sim

1938
Reginald Owen

1962
Mister Magoo

1983
Scrooge McDuck

1992
Michael Caine

Connect to the Literature   Which of these actors best portrays Scrooge as you imagine him from your reading? Explain.

ADAM. Excuse me, sir?

SCROOGE. Huh? Oh, yes, of course, what's your name, lad?

[SCROOGE *and* ADAM *will play their scene from their own spotlights.*]

ADAM. Adam, sir.

SCROOGE. Adam! What a fine, strong name! Do you know the poulterer's[9] in the next street but one, at the corner?

ADAM. I certainly should hope I know him, sir!

SCROOGE. A remarkable boy! An intelligent boy! Do you know whether the poulterer's have sold the prize turkey that was hanging up there? I don't mean the little prize turkey, Adam. I mean the big one!

ADAM. What, do you mean the one they've got that's as big as me?

---

9. poulterer's (pōl′ tər ərz) *n.* British word for a store that sells poultry—chickens, turkeys, and geese.

SCROOGE. I mean, the turkey the size of Adam: that's the bird!

ADAM. It's hanging there now, sir.

SCROOGE. It is? Go and buy it! No, no, I am absolutely in earnest. Go and buy it and tell 'em to bring it here, so that I may give them the directions to where I want it delivered, as a gift. Come back here with the man, Adam, and I'll give you a shilling. Come back here with him in less than five minutes, and I'll give you half-a-crown!

ADAM. Oh, my sir! Don't let my brother in on this.

[ADAM *runs offstage.* MARLEY *smiles.*]

MARLEY. An act of kindness is like the first green grape of summer: one leads to another and another and another. It would take a queer man indeed to not follow an act of kindness with an act of kindness. One simply whets the tongue for more . . . the taste of kindness is too too sweet. Gifts—goods—are lifeless. But the gift of goodness one feels in the giving is full of life. It . . . is . . . a . . . wonder.

[*Pauses; moves closer to* SCROOGE, *who is totally occupied with his dressing and arranging of his room and his day. He is making lists, etc.* MARLEY *reaches out to* SCROOGE:]

ADAM. [*Calling, off*] I'm here! I'm here!

[ADAM *runs on with a man, who carries an enormous turkey.*]

Here I am, sir. Three minutes flat! A world record! I've got the poultryman and he's got the poultry! [*He pants, out of breath.*] I have earned my prize, sir, if I live . . .

[*He holds his heart, playacting.* SCROOGE *goes to him and embraces him.*]

SCROOGE. You are truly a champion, Adam . . .

MAN. Here's the bird you ordered, sir . . .

SCROOGE. Oh, my, MY!!! look at the size of that turkey, will you! He never could have stood upon his legs, that bird! He would have snapped them off in a minute, like sticks of sealingwax! Why you'll never be able to carry that bird to Camden-Town. I'll give you money for a cab . . .

MAN. Camden-Town's where it's goin', sir?

Literary Analysis
Stage Directions
What details here help show Scrooge's transformation?

Reading Check

What does Scrooge instruct Adam to do?

SCROOGE. Oh, I didn't tell you? Yes, I've written the precise address down just here on this . . . [*Hands paper to him*] Bob Cratchit's house. Now he's not to know who sends him this. Do you understand me? Not a word . . . [*Handing out money and chuckling*]

MAN. I understand, sir, not a word.

SCROOGE. Good. There you go then . . . this is for the turkey . . . [*Chuckle*] and this is for the taxi. [*Chuckle*] . . . and this is for your world-record run, Adam . . .

ADAM. But I don't have change for that, sir.

SCROOGE. Then keep it, my lad. It's Christmas!

ADAM. [*He kisses* SCROOGE'S *cheek, quickly.*] Thank you, sir. Merry, Merry Christmas! [*He runs off.*]

MAN. And you've given me a bit overmuch here, too, sir . . .

SCROOGE. Of course I have, sir. It's Christmas!

MAN. Oh, well, thanking you, sir. I'll have this bird to Mr. Cratchit and his family in no time, sir. Don't you worry none about that. Merry Christmas to you, sir, and a very happy New Year, too . . .

[*The man exits.* SCROOGE *walks in a large circle about the stage, which is now gently lit. A chorus sings Christmas music far in the distance. Bells chime as well, far in the distance. A gentlewoman enters and passes.* SCROOGE *is on the streets now.*]

SCROOGE. Merry Christmas, madam . . .

WOMAN. Merry Christmas, sir . . .

[*The portly businessman from the first act enters.*]

SCROOGE. Merry Christmas, sir.

PORTLY MAN. Merry Christmas, sir.

SCROOGE. Oh, you! My dear sir! How do you do? I do hope that you succeeded yesterday! It was very kind of you. A Merry Christmas.

PORTLY MAN. Mr. Scrooge?

SCROOGE. Yes, Scrooge is my name though I'm afraid you may not find it very pleasant. Allow me to ask your pardon. And will you have the goodness to—[*He whispers into the man's ear.*]

Reading Skill
Purpose for Reading
The positive change in Scrooge is becoming more noticeable. Will your reading rate change from here until the end of the act? Why or why not?

PORTLY MAN. Lord bless me! My dear Mr. Scrooge, are you serious!?!

SCROOGE. If you please. Not a farthing[10] less. A great many back payments are included in it, I assure you. Will you do me that favor?

PORTLY MAN. My dear sir, I don't know what to say to such munifi—

SCROOGE. [*Cutting him off*] Don't say anything, please. Come and see me. Will you?

PORTLY MAN. I will! I will! Oh I will, Mr. Scrooge! It will be my pleasure!

SCROOGE. Thank'ee, I am much obliged to you. I thank you fifty times. Bless you!

[*Portly man passes offstage, perhaps by moving backwards.* SCROOGE *now comes to the room of his* NEPHEW *and* NIECE. *He stops at the door, begins to knock on it, loses his courage, tries*

▲ **Critical Viewing**
How do the color and movement in this photo convey Scrooge's new attitude? **[Analyze Cause and Effect]**

✓ **Reading Check**
What does Scrooge whisper to the portly man?

---

10. farthing (fär´thiŋ) *n.* small British coin.

again, loses his courage again, tries again, fails again, and then backs off and runs at the door, causing a tremendous bump against it. The NEPHEW *and* NIECE *are startled.* SCROOGE, *poking head into room]*

Fred!

NEPHEW. Why, bless my soul! Who's that?

NEPHEW AND NIECE. [*Together*] How now? Who goes?

SCROOGE. It's I. Your Uncle Scrooge.

NIECE. Dear heart alive!

SCROOGE. I have come to dinner. May I come in, Fred?

NEPHEW. *May you come in???!!!* With such pleasure for me you may, Uncle!!! What a treat!

NIECE. What a treat, Uncle Scrooge! Come in, come in!

[*They embrace a shocked and delighted* SCROOGE: FRED *calls into the other room.*]

NEPHEW. Come in here, everybody, and meet my Uncle Scrooge! He's come for our Christmas party!

[*Music in. Lighting here indicates that day has gone to night and gone to day again. It is early, early morning.* SCROOGE *walks alone from the party, exhausted, to his offices, opposite side of the stage. He opens his offices. The offices are as they were at the start of the play.* SCROOGE *seats himself with his door wide open so that he can see into the tank, as he awaits* CRATCHIT, *who enters, head down, full of guilt.* CRATCHIT, *starts writing almost before he sits.*]

SCROOGE. What do you mean by coming in here at this time of day, a full eighteen minutes late, Mr. Cratchit? Hallo, sir? Do you hear me?

BOB. I am very sorry, sir. I am behind my time.

SCROOGE. You are? Yes, I certainly think you are. Step this way, sir, if you please . . .

BOB. It's only but once a year, sir . . . it shall not be repeated. I was making rather merry yesterday and into the night . . .

SCROOGE. Now, I'll tell you what, Cratchit. I am not going to stand this sort of thing any longer. And therefore . . .

[*He stands and pokes his finger into* BOB'S *chest.*]

Literary Analysis
Stage Directions
What do Scrooge's actions tell you about his feelings at this point?

Literary Analysis
Stage Directions
How could lighting be used to show the passage of time?

I am . . . about . . . to . . . raise . . . your salary.

BOB. Oh, no, sir, I . . . [*Realizes*] what did you say, sir?

SCROOGE. A Merry Christmas, Bob . . . [*He claps* BOB'S *back.*] A merrier Christmas, Bob, my good fellow! than I have given you for many a year. I'll raise your salary and endeavor to assist your struggling family and we will discuss your affairs this very afternoon over a bowl of smoking bishop.[11] Bob! Make up the fires and buy another coal scuttle before you dot another i, Bob. It's too cold in this place! We need warmth and cheer, Bob Cratchit! Do you hear me? DO . . . YOU . . . HEAR . . . ME?

[BOB CRATCHIT *stands, smiles at* SCROOGE: BOB CRATCHIT *faints. Blackout. As the main lights black out, a spotlight appears on* SCROOGE: C. *Another on* MARLEY: *He talks directly to the audience.*]

Literary Analysis
Stage Directions
What information here might be funny to audiences? Why?

MARLEY. Scrooge was better than his word. He did it all and infinitely more; and to Tiny Tim, who did NOT die, he was a second father. He became as good a friend, as good a master, as good a man, as the good old city knew, or any other good old city, town, or borough in the good old world. And it was always said of him that he knew how to keep Christmas well, if any man alive possessed the knowledge. [*Pauses*] May that be truly said of us, and all of us. And so, as Tiny Tim observed . . .

TINY TIM. [*Atop* SCROOGE'S *shoulder*] God Bless Us, Every One . . .

[*Lights up on chorus, singing final Christmas Song.* SCROOGE *and* MARLEY *and all spirits and other characters of the play join in. When the song is over, the lights fade to black.*]

---

11. **smoking bishop** hot sweet orange-flavored drink.

Apply the Skills

A Christmas Carol: Scrooge and Marley, Act II

Thinking About the Selection

1. **Respond:** Do you believe that people can change completely, as Scrooge does? In a small group, share your responses. As a group, choose one opinion to share with the class.

2. **(a) Recall:** In Scene 3, what does Scrooge learn about the Cratchit family? **(b) Analyze:** Why does Scrooge care about the fate of Tiny Tim? **(c) Draw Conclusions:** In what way is Scrooge changing?

3. **(a) Recall:** In Scene 4, what happens to Scrooge's belongings in Christmas Future? **(b) Draw Conclusions:** What does Scrooge learn from this experience?

4. **(a) Analyze:** Why is Scrooge happy at the end of the play? **(b) Evaluate:** How well does he live up to his promise to learn his "lessons"?

5. **Take a Position:** Do you think Cratchit and Scrooge's nephew do the right thing by forgiving Scrooge immediately? Explain.

Reading Skill

6. Which did you read more quickly: the dialogue or the stage directions? In your answer, explain how your **purpose** affected your reading rate.

7. When you read long speeches with difficult vocabulary, what happens to your reading rate? Explain.

Literary Analysis

8. Reread the **stage directions** at the beginning of Scene 1. Then, fill out a chart like the one shown to record the information the directions include.

Characters on Stage	Movement of Characters	Description of Lighting	Description of Sound	Other Special Effects

9. Which stage direction in Scene 4 is especially effective in making the scene mysterious? Explain.

QuickReview

Story at a Glance
Mean-spirited Scrooge faces the present and future consequences of his actions.

Go Online
—Assessment
For: Self-test
Visit: www.PHSchool.com
Web Code: ema-6503

Purpose for Reading: what the reader wants to get out of the text

Stage Directions: words in a script that describe the set, characters, movement, lighting, and sound effects

Vocabulary Builder

Practice Answer each question, then explain your answer.

1. If you were speaking to a large group of people, would you want your voice to be *audible*?
2. Would it *astonish* you if an elephant sang?
3. Would you take cover if a *severe* storm were approaching?
4. Can a family with a *meager* income build a large, fancy house?
5. Would a person with a *compulsion* to save money give away a million dollars?

Writing

Write a **tribute**, or expression of admiration, to the changed Scrooge. Your tribute may include brief stories that show how Scrooge has changed. As you draft, mention the new traits that make Scrooge worthy of this honor.

For *Grammar, Vocabulary,* and *Assessment,* see **Build Language Skills,** pages 730–731.

Extend Your Learning

Listening and Speaking Think about Scrooge's experiences with one of the ghosts in Act II of this play. Then, plan a **dramatic monologue** that presents Scrooge's thoughts.

- Speak as Scrooge from the first-person point of view, using the word *I.*
- Project your voice so that everyone can hear you.
- Pause when you need to collect your thoughts.
- Pace yourself to avoid rushing.

Present your monologue to the class.

Research and Technology With a group of classmates, create a **timeline** of the life of Charles Dickens. Use the Internet and library resources to gather information about major events in Dickens's life, his most important literary works, and his travels and speaking engagements. Include visuals, such as his picture, or quotations from his work.

Build Language Skills

A Christmas Carol: Scrooge and Marley, Act II

Vocabulary Skill: Suffixes

The **suffix** *-tion* creates a noun that names the "quality, act, or result" of the word it is added to. When you add *-tion* to the verb *react,* you create the noun *reaction,* or "the act of reacting." Adding *-tion* to the verb *participate* creates the noun *participation,* meaning "the act of participating."

➤ **Example:** Ms. Chang was proud of her students' **reaction** to the emergency.

Practice Use a dictionary to find the meaning of each word ending in *-tion.* Explain what act or quality is indicated in the word. Then, use each word in a sentence.

1. intention
2. accommodation
3. cancellation
4. detection

Grammar Lesson

Double Negatives **Double negatives** are two negative words used when only one is needed. Examples of negative words are *nothing, not, never,* and *no.* You can correct a double negative by revising the sentence.

This chart shows double negatives and ways to correct them.

Double Negative	Corrected Sentence
Coach never told us nothing about the other team.	Coach never told us anything about the other team.
Hilary does not have no cash now.	Hilary does not have any cash now.

Practice Correct the double negative in each sentence.

1. Emerging from the cave, we could not see nothing for a few minutes.
2. He could not do nothing to cheer her up.
3. Michael would not read nothing about the sad event.
4. Lucy does not want to visit nowhere but Seville.
5. We did not want to bid on no items at the auction.

𝑊𝐺 *Prentice Hall Writing and Grammar Connection: Chapter 21, Section 4*

Reading: Determining Your Reading Rate

Directions: *Read the following selection. Then, answer the questions.*

Mesophyll The bulk of most leaves consists of a specialized ground tissue known as mesophyll. These cells are crucial to two functions necessary for the plant's survival.

Photosynthesis Photosynthesis in most plants occurs in the mesophyll. Photosynthesis is necessary for the plant's survival. Palisade mesophyll are packed cells that absorb light that enters the leaf.

Transpiration Another important function of the mesophyll is transpiration. The surfaces of the spongy mesophyll cells are kept moist so that gases can enter and leave the cells easily.

1. What is the best way to preview this?
   A reading the text
   B reading the headings
   C rereading and taking notes
   D carefully reading each word

2. What can you learn from a close reading of the passage?
   A palisade mesophyll absorbs light
   B transpiration and photosynthesis are parts of mesophyll
   C mesophyll and photosynthesis are the same thing
   D transpiration is part of photosynthesis

3. What might be a purpose for reading this passage?
   A to be entertained
   B to find information for a history report
   C to understand something for science
   D to be persuaded of a theory

4. Which reading rate should be used?
   A You can skim and scan.
   B You should read the first paragraph slowly and scan the others.
   C You should slow down because the material is difficult.
   D You should scan the first paragraph and read the others slowly.

Timed Writing: Explanation [Connections]

Take a position on whether the change in Scrooge's personality will last. State your position and use specific examples from the text and from your experience to support your position. **(35 minutes)**

 ## Writing Workshop: *Work in Progress*

Multimedia Report

Multimedia reports "hook" their audiences by using visual and audio aids—photographs, charts, maps, and tape recordings—in creative ways. For each topic on your original list, jot down a creative idea for using a visual or audio aid. Save this list in your writing portfolio.

Reading Informational Materials

Literary Criticism

In Part 1, you are learning how to set a purpose for reading literature in order to give yourself a focus as you read. This skill is also useful in reading literary criticism. If you read the play *A Christmas Carol: Scrooge and Marley*, you may want to read reviews of performances of the play.

About Literary Criticism

Literary criticism is writing that analyzes and makes a judgment about a work of literature. The word *criticism* in this context can mean either a positive or negative judgment. A piece of writing of this kind is often called a *review*, and the writer is called a *critic*.

Most literary criticism contains these elements:

- A brief summary of the work
- A comparison or contrast to other works of literature or to other performances
- A judgment or recommendation

The following reviews focus on two different productions of *A Christmas Carol.*

Reading Skill

A critic's job is to analyze and judge a work, provide a summary, and give an opinion of the characterizations, setting, and plot. In some cases, the critic also responds to the quality of a dramatic production and its cast. Your **purpose** in reading criticism will sometimes be to deepen your understanding of a work. Another common purpose for reading criticism is to decide whether or not you want to read, view, or listen to the work being reviewed.

As you read literary criticism, **analyze the writer's response** to the work by using a graphic organizer like the one shown.

	TNT	Meadow Brook Theatre
Critic's summary		
Positive comments		
Negative comments		
Critic's overall opinion		

A Christmas Carol
TNT

(Sun., Dec. 5, 8 p.m. ET)
Picks & Pans: Television

Full text: COPYRIGHT 1999 Time, Inc.

So you muttered "humbug" when you spied yet another version of *A Christmas Carol* on the TV schedule. Don't feel guilty. It doesn't take a spiritual descendant of Ebenezer Scrooge to notice that the Charles Dickens classic has been adapted nearly to death. (Two years ago, there was even a Ms. Scrooge.)

> The newspaper or magazine where a review appears tells you something about the audience of the criticism. In this case, the audience is TV viewers.

But TNT's *Carol* would be worth watching if only for the lead performance of Patrick Stewart. The ex-skipper of *Star Trek: The Next Generation* has been giving staged, one-man readings of *A Christmas Carol* for 10 years, and his approach to Scrooge is consistently interesting and intelligent. Early on, Stewart seems to be speaking on the misanthropic diatribes straight from Scrooge's flinty heart, rather than reciting thoroughly familiar quotations. And when Scrooge offers a boy a one-shilling tip, Stewart has the reformed

> This paragraph reveals what the critic thinks is the strongest aspect of this performance.

People Weekly, Dec. 6, 1999

...this *Carol* feels more like Masterpiece Theatre than seasonal merchandise...

miser feel a pang of the old parsimony.

Filmed in England with a solid supporting cast (including Richard E. Grant as Bob Cratchit and Joel Grey as the Spirit of Christmas Past), this *Carol* feels more like Masterpiece Theatre than seasonal merchandise–except when the filmmakers embellish Scrooge's nocturnal visions with gratuitous special effects.

Bottom line: Old story well told.
–Terry Kelleher

> The review ends with a summary of the critic's opinion.

Toned-down *Christmas Carol* has more spirit

By John Sousanis

Special to *The Oakland Press*

Director Debra Wicks has tinkered with Meadow Brook's recipe for *A Christmas Carol* just enough to make the old holiday fruitcake seem fresh. To be sure, Wicks's changes are subtle. Meadow Brook is still producing the Charles Nolte adaptation of Charles Dickens's Christmas classic that has been a mainstay of local theater for most of the last two decades.

The audience still is serenaded by a band of merry carolers in the lobby before the show. With its giant revolving set pieces and big bag of special effects, the production's script, set and costumes are unchanged from these many Christmases past.

But ironically, Wicks has infused the show with new energy by calming everything down a bit. In prior productions, the play's singing Londoners seemed positively hopped up on Christmas cheer to the point where one feared for the life of anyone not bubbling over with the spirit of the season.

Against this unebbing Yuletide, it was easy to forgive Scrooge of all his bah-hum-bugging. If only he had seen fit to give Tiny Tim a good spanking, we might all have enjoyed Christmas a little more. But Wicks has introduced a modicum of restraint into the Happy English populace, reducing the play's saccharine content considerably and making *A Christmas Carol* a more palatable holiday treat for adults and children.

Peter Hicks's set design for the show is, as always, enormous and gorgeous: Scrooge's storefront on a busy London street revolves to reveal the interior of the businessman's office and home, then opens on itself, providing the frame for scenes from Scrooge's boyhood,

young adulthood and, of course, his potential end.

Meadow Brook's technical crew executes its stage magic without a hitch: Ghosts materialize and dematerialize in thick fogs and bolts of bright light, speaking to Scrooge in electronically altered voices and freezing the action onstage with a wave of their otherworldly hands.

The cast members take on multiple roles populating busy London in one scene, then visiting poor Scrooge in his dreams of Christmas Then, Now and Soon.

Standouts in the huge ensemble include John Biedenbach as Scrooge's put-upon assistant Bob Cratchit, Jodie Kuhn Ellison as Cratchit's fiercely loyal wife and Mark Rademacher, who pulls double duty as the Spirit of Christmas Present (the beefiest role in the play) and as a determined charity worker.

Scott Crownover, paying only passing attention to his English accent, takes an energetic turn as Scrooge's nephew, Fred, and Tom Mahard and Geoffrey Beauchamp have fun with a handful of roles they've been performing for years. Newcomer Sara Catheryn Wolf, fresh from three seasons at the Hilberry Theatre Company, provides an ethereal Spirit of Christmas Past.

The biggest change for longtime fans of the spectacle, however, is the replacement of Booth Coleman as Scrooge. Dennis Robertson's debut as the man in need of serious Christmas redemption is in perfect keeping with Wicks's toned-down production. If he's not quite as charismatic a miser as Coleman, Robertson is a much darker, even scarier Scrooge, which makes his ultimate transformation into an unabashed philanthropist that much more affecting.

All in all, *A Christmas Carol* is what it always has been: A well-produced, grand-scale event that is as much pageant as play. And like a beautifully wrapped gift under a well-decorated tree, it suits the season to a tee.

If you go, *A Christmas Carol* runs through December 24 at Meadow Brook Theatre, 127 Wilson Hall, Oakland University, Rochester Hills. Call 377-3300.

Reading: Purpose for Reading

Directions: *Choose the letter of the best answer.*

1. Which of the following purposes would not be supported by reading these reviews?

   A To be informed about performances of *A Christmas Carol*

   B To compare and contrast two different productions

   C To learn how to bring a literary work to the stage

   D To decide which production you would rather see

2. Which phrase from Sousanis's review best summarizes his opinion?

   A The production's script, set, and costumes are unchanged.

   B The cast members take on multiple roles.

   C If only he had seen fit to give Tiny Tim a good spanking.

   D It suits the season to a tee.

3. How does Kelleher generally feel about adaptations of *A Christmas Carol*?

   A The story has been done too many times.

   B The scriptwriter misunderstood the novel's message.

   C *A Christmas Carol* should be done every year.

   D Only the original should ever be performed.

Reading: Comprehension and Interpretation

Directions: *Write your answers on a separate piece of paper.*

4. Find one sentence from each review that supports this statement: The reviewer seems to think that the reader is already familiar with the plot of *A Christmas Carol.* [Applying]

5. What is Kelleher's overall judgment of *A Christmas Carol*? [Generating]

6. Is the Meadow Brook Theatre producing *A Christmas Carol* for the first time? How can you tell? [Integrating]

Timed Writing: Summary [Integrating]

Summarize Kelleher's review of the television version of *A Christmas Carol.* Include a brief overall statement of the review. Then expand by providing supporting details for your points, in some cases quoting from the critic. End with a statement that sums up the critic's opinion.

(30 minutes)

Character

A **character** is a person who takes part in a literary work.

- Like main characters in stories and novels, main characters in drama have traits that make them unique. These may include qualities such as dependability, intelligence, selfishness, and stubbornness.
- Like other fictional characters, those in dramas also have *motives*, or reasons, for behaving the way they do. For example, one character may be motivated by compassion, while another may be motivated by guilt.

When you read a drama, pay attention to what each character says and does and note the reactions these words and actions spark in others. Notice what these things reveal to you about the characters' traits and motives.

Comparing Characters

In drama, one way to develop a character is through a **foil**, another character whose behavior and attitude contrasts with those of the main character. With a foil, audiences can see *good* in contrast with *bad*, or *generousness* in contrast with *selfishness*.

These two excerpts from *A Christmas Carol: Scrooge and Marley* show how two employers react very differently to the idea of celebrating Christmas. As you read the two passages, use a character wheel like the one shown to analyze each character. Then, decide whether these characters might be classified as foils.

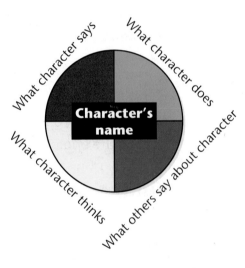

Vocabulary Builder

A Christmas Carol: Scrooge and Marley

- **snuffs** (snufs) *v.* extinguishes; puts out (p. 738) *Mr. Roth snuffs the candles before he leaves.*

- **fiddler** (fid′ lər) *n.* person who plays a fiddle, or violin (p. 739) *Gregory is a fiddler for a bluegrass band.*

- **suitors** (so͞ot′ ərz) *n.* men who court a woman or seek to marry her (p. 739) *Matt, one of Alice's many suitors, wants to take her to a movie.*

Build Understanding

Connecting to the Literature

Reading/Writing Connection In these passages, you will
see that two men treat their employees differently. In a few
sentences, identify several reasons that explain the contrast in
the way bosses treat those who work for them. Use at least
three of the following words: *establish, ignore, respond,
conclude, emphasize.*

Meet the Authors

Charles **Dickens** (1812–1870)

English author Charles Dickens's early life was difficult. When he
was just a boy, his father went to prison, and young Charles had
to work long hours pasting labels on bottles.

Writing As a young man, Dickens taught himself shorthand
and got a job as a court reporter. In his early twenties, Dickens
began to publish humorous stories. People liked his writing, and
he was able to earn a living as a writer. Some of his novels are
David Copperfield, Hard Times, and *Nicholas Nickleby.* One of his
most well-known pieces is *A Christmas Carol,* which was published in 1843.

Israel **Horovitz** (b. 1939)

Israel Horovitz is a well-known playwright who lives in New
York with his wife. Horovitz is the author of more than fifty
plays. His plays have introduced such actors as Al Pacino and
Richard Dreyfus. *A Christmas Carol: Scrooge and Marley* was
first produced in Baltimore, Maryland in 1978.

Finding Inspiration in Tragedy Shortly after the attacks
of September 11, 2001, Horovitz wrote a play about the
event. The play, "3 Weeks After Paradise," reflects his experiences during the tragedy and includes family photos and
films.

For: More about the authors
Go Online
Visit: www.PHSchool.com
Author Link **Web Code:** eme-9503

from A Christmas Carol
Scrooge and Marley, Act 1, Scene 2

CRATCHIT. I must be going home . . . [He <u>snuffs</u> out his candle and puts on his hat.] I hope you have a . . . very very lovely day tomorrow, sir . . .

SCROOGE. Hmmm. Oh, you'll be wanting the whole day tomorrow, I suppose?

CRATCHIT. If quite convenient, sir.

SCROOGE. It's not convenient, and it's not fair. If I was to stop half-a-crown for it, you'd think yourself ill-used, I'll be bound?

[CRATCHIT *smiles faintly.*]

CRATCHIT. I don't know, sir . . .

SCROOGE. And yet, you don't think me ill-used when I pay a day's wages for no work . . .

CRATCHIT. It's only but once a year . . .

SCROOGE. A poor excuse for picking a man's pocket every 25th of December! But I suppose you must have the whole day. Be here all the earlier the next morning!

CRATCHIT. Oh I will, sir. I will. I promise you. And, sir . . .

SCROOGE. Don't say it, Cratchit.

CRATCHIT. But let me wish you a . . .

SCROOGE. Don't say it, Cratchit. I warn you . . .

CRATCHIT. Sir!

SCROOGE. Cratchit!

[CRATCHIT *opens the door.*]

CRATCHIT. All right, then, sir . . . well . . . [*Suddenly*] Merry Christmas, Mr. Scrooge!

[*And he runs out the door, shutting same behind him.*]

Scrooge and Marley, Act 1, Scene 5

FEZZIWIG. Yo ho, my boys. No more work tonight. Christmas Eve, Dick. Christmas, Ebenezer!

[*They stand at attention in front of FEZZIWIG; laughing*] Hilli-ho! Clear away, and let's have lots of room here! Hilli-ho, Dick! Chirrup, Ebenezer!

[*The young men clear the room, sweep the floor, straighten the pictures, trim the lamps, etc. The space is clear now. A fiddler enters, fiddling.*]

Hi-ho, Matthew! Fiddle away . . . where are my daughters?

[*The fiddler plays. Three young daughters of FEZZIWIG enter followed by six young male suitors. They are dancing to the music. All employees come in: workers, clerks, housemaids, cousins, the baker, etc. All dance. Full number wanted here. Throughout the dance, food is brought into the feast. It is "eaten" in dance, by the dancers. EBENEZER dances with all*

Literary Analysis
Character What details here show how Fezziwig feels about the holiday?

Vocabulary Builder
fiddler (fid´ lər) *n.* person who plays a fiddle, or violin

suitors (sōōt´ ərz) *n.* men who court a woman or seek to marry her

three of the daughters, as does DICK. They compete for the daughters, happily, in the dance. FEZZIWIG dances with the daughters. FEZZIWIG dances with DICK and EBENEZER. The music changes: MRS. FEZZIWIG enters. She lovingly scolds her husband. They dance. She dances with EBENEZER, lifting him and throwing him about. She is enormously fat. When the dance is ended, they all dance off, floating away, as does the music.]

PAST. It was a small matter, that Fezziwig made those silly folks so full of gratitude.

SCROOGE. Small?

PAST. Shhh!?

[Lights up on *DICK and EBENEZER.*]

DICK. We are blessed, Ebenezer, truly, to have such a master as Mr. Fezziwig!

YOUNG EBENEZER. He is the best, best, the very and absolute best! If ever I own a firm of my own, I shall treat my apprentices with the same dignity and the same grace. We have learned a wonderful lesson from the master, Dick!

DICK. Ah, that's a fact, Ebenezer. That's a fact!

Thinking About the Selection

1. **(a) Recall:** What does Cratchit say to Scrooge as Cratchit leaves? **(b) Infer:** Why do you think he says this—against Scrooge's wishes? **(c) Generalize:** What do you think this shows about Cratchit?

2. **(a) Infer:** Do you think Scrooge will work on Christmas day? Why or why not? **(b) Make a Judgment:** Do you think that a boss should be required to give employees a day off for a holiday that is not celebrated by everyone? Explain.

3. **(a) Infer:** What kind of relationship do you think Fezziwig has with his daughters? **(b) Support:** What examples illustrate this opinion?

Apply the Skills

from *A Christmas Carol: Scrooge and Marley*

Comparing Characters

1. **(a)** How would you describe Scrooge? **(b)** What details from the play support your idea?

2. **(a)** How would you describe Fezziwig? **(b)** What details from the play support your idea?

3. Complete the chart below to compare each character's traits and motives.

4. **(a)** In what ways does Fezziwig act as a foil to Scrooge? **(b)** Why is Fezziwig's character important to the play?

QuickReview

Character: person who takes part in a literary work

Foil: a character whose behavior and attitudes contrast with those of another

Go Online
—Assessment
For: Self-test
Visit: www.PHSchool.com
Web Code: ema-6504

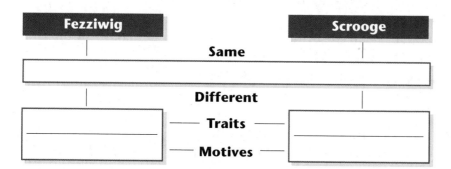

Writing to Compare Literary Works

Use the scenes presented here to compare and contrast Fezziwig and Scrooge. In an essay, discuss how each man's actions and words help the playwright make a point about Scrooge and his behavior. Consider these questions to get you started:

- Why does each man act as he does?
- Which character would audiences probably prefer? Why?
- What do audiences learn about Scrooge because of Fezziwig?
- How does Fezziwig help Scrooge to change?

Vocabulary Builder

Use each pair of words correctly in a sentence.

1. suitors; marriage
2. fiddler; dance
3. snuffs; light

Reading

Directions: *Read the selection. Then answer the questions.*

The Challenge of Studying Earth's Interior. We know many things about our planet, but the Earth's interior remains mysterious because scientists cannot study it directly. Holes have been drilled to depths of about eight miles, but scientists would have to drill five times deeper just to get through the Earth's outer layer! Other methods, such as studying meteorites or analyzing vibrations, have provided some information on the different layers.

Core Earth's center, or **core,** is divided into two regions with different physical properties. The outer core is 2,260 kilometers thick and the inner core is 1,220 kilometers thick.

Mantle The area between the core and the crust is called the **mantle.** This area is about 1,800 miles thick.

Crust Earth's outer layer, called the **crust,** reaches depths of 43 miles.

1. **What is the best way to preview this selection to determine if it includes the information you want to find?**
   A   Read the first sentence.
   B   Read the subheadings.
   C   Outline the passage.
   D   Read the last sentence.

2. **For what purpose might you read this passage?**
   A   to be entertained
   B   to form an opinion
   C   to gain information
   D   to take action

3. **What information would you most likely learn only through a close reading of the text?**
   A   Earth's interior consists of three parts.
   B   Studying Earth's interior is challenging.
   C   Earth's crust is 43 miles deep.
   D   We know many things about Earth.

4. **You should read this passage at about the same rate as you would read**
   A   a movie review.
   B   a mystery novel.
   C   an encyclopedia article.
   D   a letter to the editor.

5. **What is the least likely reason a reader would reread this text?**
   A   to look for the answer to a question about Earth's mantle
   B   to determine if the text contains information on Earth's crust
   C   to get an overall sense of the content
   D   to identify challenges of studying Earth's interior

Directions: *Choose the word that best completes each sentence.*

6. When you read you make _____ about details that the author doesn't provide.
   A assumptions
   B conflicts
   C involvements
   D reactions

7. Jorge's _____ in after-school acting classes paid off when he earned a part in the play.
   A involvement
   B initiation
   C destination
   D agreement

8. There was a _____ between the two main characters.
   A involvement   C conflict
   B critique   D focus

9. The school newspaper printed Mario's _____ of the new play.
   A reaction
   B critique
   C conflict
   D focus

10. My _____ to the play was more favorable than Mario's.
    A reaction
    B critique
    C conflict
    D focus

Directions: *Choose the best definition for each word.*

11. contentment
    A a sense of satisfaction
    B the ability to make others happy
    C one who puts others at ease
    D a reason to be happy

12. hesitation
    A the ability to wait
    B the act of waiting
    C one who is indecisive
    D the quality of uncertainty

13. amazement
    A one who shocks
    B the ability to astonish
    C capable of admiration
    D a result of a surprise

14. information
    A facts
    B shapes
    C delivery
    D action

15. requirement
    A asking again for information
    B able to provide what is necessary
    C something necessary
    D acting important

Research: Multimedia Report

Presentations that include videos, slides, photographs, maps, music, or sound effects capture your attention by providing interesting visual and auditory effects. A presentation that incorporates information from both print and nonprint sources like these is called a **multimedia report.** Follow the steps outlined in this workshop to create your own multimedia report.

Assignment Create a multimedia report about a topic that interests you and presents opportunities for audio and visual support.

What to Include Your multimedia report should feature the following elements:

- a focused topic that can be covered in the time and space allotted
- a clear and logical organization that presents a main idea
- well-integrated audio and visual features from a variety of sources
- use of formatting and presentation techniques for visual appeal
- effective pacing with smooth transitions between elements
- error-free writing, including correct usage of frequently confused words.

To preview the criteria on which your multimedia report may be judged, see the rubric on page 748.

Prewriting

Choosing Your Topic

Flip through magazines. Scan magazines that explore areas you find interesting, such as travel, science, or nature. Jot down areas that inspire you. Consider whether you will be able to find information in both print and nonprint sources, and then choose a topic.

Gathering Details

Research your topic, noting creative ways to engage your audience. Beyond typical print sources, use multimedia sources such as the Internet, videotaped documentaries, slides, charts, maps, photographs, music, and sound effects. Keep your content, audience, and purpose in mind as you make your selections.

Using the Form
You may use elements of this form in these types of writing:

- documentaries
- research reports
- biographies
- TV news reports

Work in Progress
Review the work you did on pages 657, 695, and 731.

Drafting

Shaping Your Writing

Write a script. Plan every word and action in your multimedia presentation by writing a script. Include any words that you will speak and any stage directions that make actions and effects clear.

Providing Elaboration

Incorporate your audio and visual aids. Audio, such as interviews or music, can set a mood and provide information. **Visual aids,** such as spreadsheets, maps, or charts, can organize large amounts of information, making it easier to read.

Use appropriate software to design additional information, and plan to display information on posters, on computer monitors, or as handouts.

Revising

Revising Your Paragraphs

Find the link between paragraphs. Read the final sentence of each paragraph. Then, read the opening sentence of the next paragraph. If one or both sentences clearly show the relationship between paragraphs, underline them. If you do not find a transition, add a word, phrase, or sentence to link them together.

To read the complete student model, see page 747.

Finding the Link Between Paragraphs

Several of the toothed whales shoot a jet of water at the ocean floor. They use this jet to stir up prey hiding in the sand. These whales also have very flexible necks that help them scan the ocean floor for food.

Other characteristics can help a whale live in a harsh environment. The bowhead has several interesting physical features that allow it to live in the Arctic all the time.

> The writers found a few places where they needed transitions. They added words and phrases there to glue their paragraphs together.

Integrating Grammar Skills

Revising to Avoid Common Usage Problems

Identifying Common Usage Problems   When you choose the wrong word in your writing, you can confuse readers or lead them to question the care you take with your work. The sets of words presented here are frequently confused:

- *Accept*, a verb, means "to take what is offered" or "to agree to."
- *Except*, a preposition, means "leaving out" or "other than."

*Prentice Hall Writing and Grammar Connection:
Chapter 21, Section 4*

Verb: She **accepted** her award graciously.
Preposition: Everyone **except** Anabelle went to the movie.

- *Affect*, a verb, means "to influence" or "to cause a change in."
- *Effect*, usually a noun, means "result."

Verb: Lack of sleep can **affect** your ability to concentrate.
Noun: What is the **effect** of getting too much sleep?

Fixing Common Usage Problems To fix a usage problem, first identify words that you often confuse. Then, correct it using one of the following methods.

1. **Identify the word's part of speech and its use in the sentence.**
2. **Determine the meaning you want to convey.**
3. **Consult a dictionary or a language handbook for clarification and choose the correct word.**

Apply It to Your Editing

Choose three paragraphs in your draft. Underline each sentence that contains one of the words discussed, or another word you suspect you may have used incorrectly. Fix any usage problems using one of the methods described.

Other Commonly Confused Words

advice: noun, "an opinion"
advise: verb, "to give an opinion"

in: preposition, refers to position
into: preposition, suggests motion

beside: preposition, "at the side of"
besides: preposition, "in addition to"

farther: adjective, refers to distance
further: adjective, "additional"
or "to a greater extent"

Student Model: Shane Larkin and Ian Duffy
Williamston, MI

Zia

Slide 1

Visual: Title and Author Slide: *Zia,* by Scott O'Dell

Script: This presentation is about the book *Zia* by Scott O'Dell. *Zia* is a sequel to the book *Island of the Blue Dolphins* and shares some of the same characters. Instead of dolphins, though, Zia and her brother see gray whales, like those heard here.

> The writers have chosen a topic that can be well covered in the time allotted to their report.

Slide 2

Visual: Whale

Sound: Whale song

Script: Reading this book got us very interested in the study of whales and how they adapt to the world around them.

> The writers' choice of visual is both dramatic and appropriate to their topic, audience, and purpose.

Slide 3

Visual: Setting Slide

Sound: Ocean waves crashing against beach

Script: The setting of *Zia* is the southern coast of California during the Spanish colonial era. The action takes place in several locations. This is a picture of the California coast.

> The writers use boldface heads and other appropriate formatting to present the organization of their report clearly.

Video 1: Video clip of whale scanning for food

Script: From reading this book and doing a small amount of research, we discovered many ways whales can adapt to these kinds of harsh environments. Several of the toothed whales shoot a jet of water at the ocean floor. They use this jet to stir up prey hiding in the sand. These whales also have very flexible necks that help them scan the ocean floor for food.

Slide 4

Visual: Arctic shoreline

Script: Other characteristics can help a whale live in a harsh environment. The bowhead, for instance, has several interesting physical features that allow it to live in the Arctic all the time.

Sound: Whale song

Script: We learned a lot about whales by reading *Zia* and doing our research, but this is only the beginning. This book has inspired us to continue our research to learn more about these amazing creatures and their adaptations to the environment.

Editing and Proofreading

Review your draft to eliminate errors in grammar, spelling, and punctuation.

Focus on Presentation Copies: To avoid distracting your audience with mistakes, run a spelling and grammar check on any visuals you present. Be careful, however, because spell checkers do not catch mistakes in homophones such as *there*, *their*, and *they're*. You must catch these errors yourself. In addition, check the layout of slides or handouts to be sure information is clear and error-free.

Publishing and Presenting

Consider one of the following ways to share your writing:
Present your report. Perform your multimedia report for your classmates. Ask them to evaluate what they see and hear.
Take a road trip. Present your report outside your school. Contact a local library, club, or elementary school that might be interested in your report.

Reflecting on Your Writing

Writer's Journal Jot down your thoughts on the experience of writing a multimedia report. Begin by answering these questions:
- If you had to create another multimedia report, what would you do differently? Why?
- In the process of writing, what did you learn about the topic you chose?

Prentice Hall Writing and Grammar Connection: Chapter 28

Rubric for Self-Assessment

To assess your multimedia report, use the following rubric:

Criteria	Rating Scale
	not very very
Focus: How clearly focused is your topic?	1 2 3 4 5
Organization: How logical is your organization?	1 2 3 4 5
Support/Elaboration: How effective are your audio and visual features?	1 2 3 4 5
Style: How smooth are the transitions between elements?	1 2 3 4 5
Conventions: How correct is your word usage?	1 2 3 4 5

Unit 5
Part
2

Summarizing

Reading: Summarizing

> A **summary** is a short statement that presents the main ideas and most important points expressed in a piece of writing.

Skills and Strategies You Will Learn in Part 2

In Part 2, you will learn

- to **summarize** a text (p. 752)
- to **distinguish between important and unimportant details** as you summarize (p. 752)
- to **read closely** to follow steps in a process (p. 780)

Using the Skills and Strategies in Part 2

In Part 2, you will learn to summarize by reading closely, reviewing main events, and then briefly restating these events in your own words. Summarizing as you read helps you focus on the most important ideas and events in a text.

Original: Few people would question that George Washington was the first president of the United States. The United States declared independence in 1776, George Washington was not sworn in as president until 1789. For more than 10 years someone else was in charge! John Hanson, Thomas Mifflin, John Hancock, and others were presidents before Washington. However, the history of the government of the United States officially begins in 1789, the year that the Articles of Confederation were replaced by the Constitution of the United States.

Summary: Although George Washington is commonly accepted as the first president of the United States, several men held the office of the president before him. However, they were elected before the official history of the United States began.

Academic Vocabulary: Words for Discussing Summarizing

The following words will help you write summaries as you read the selections in this unit.

Word	Definition	Example Sentence
chronological *adj.*	arranged in the order in which events occur	Summarize the plot in *chronological* order.
sequence *n.*	one thing after another in logical or chronological order	Teri explained the *sequence* of events in the story from beginning to end.
summarize *v.*	briefly state the most important events in a story	Karika *summarized* the plot in her book report.
characteristic *n.*	a quality that makes something recognizable	One *characteristic* of Mia's poetry is a regular rhyme scheme.
focus *v.*	look closely at	Today, we will *focus* on verbs.

Vocabulary Skill: Suffixes

A **suffix** is a letter, syllable, or group of syllables added to a word that contributes to its meaning and indicates the word's function.

In Part 2, you will learn
- the suffixes *-ize/-yze* (p. 778)

Word	Suffix	New Word	Part of Speech
energy	*-ize*	energize	verb

Activity Add to the chart the words *character, drama, summary,* and *analysis.* Then, complete each column for each word. Use a dictionary to help you add suffixes correctly.

These skills will help you become a better reader. Practice them with "The Monsters Are Due on Maple Street" (p. 754).

Reading Skill

A **summary** is a brief statement that presents only the main ideas and most important details. Summarizing helps you review and understand what you are reading.

To summarize, you must first **distinguish between important and unimportant details.** Ask yourself questions like the following:

- Is this detail necessary for my understanding of the literary work?
- Would the literary work hold together without this information?

As you read, pause periodically to recall and restate only the key events and important details.

Literary Analysis

A **character's motives** are the reasons for his or her actions. Motives are usually related to what a character wants, needs, or feels. For example, the desire to win might motivate an athlete to practice daily. Powerful motives include love, anger, fear, greed, and jealousy.

As you read, think about what motivates each of the characters. Use a graphic organizer like the one shown to explore each character's motives.

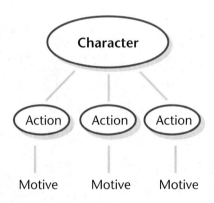

Vocabulary Builder

- **flustered** (flus´ tərd) *adj.* nervous; confused (p. 758) *The flustered bus driver took many wrong turns.*

- **sluggishly** (slug´ ish lē) *adv.* as if lacking energy (p. 758) *The tired hikers walked sluggishly down the trail.*

- **persistently** (pər sist´ ənt lē) *adv.* firmly and steadily (p. 760) *She taught the dog commands by persistently repeating them.*

- **defiant** (dē fī´ ənt) *adj.* boldly resisting (p. 761) *The defiant colonists demanded independence.*

- **metamorphosis** (met´ ə môr´ fə sis) *n.* change of form (p. 763) *The film showed the amazing metamorphosis of a caterpillar into a butterfly.*

Build Understanding • *The Monsters Are Due on Maple Street*

Background

The Cold War This screenplay was written during the Cold War (1946–1989), a period when the United States and the communist Soviet Union were engaged in a nuclear arms race. Fear led to suspicion, and many people in the United States were accused of being communist spies. In much the same way, Serling's characters suspect and accuse one another in "The Monsters Are Due on Maple Street."

Connecting to the Literature

Reading/Writing Connection The characters in this play start rumors because they are afraid and confused. Write several sentences about the reasons people start rumors and the damage rumors can do. Use at least three of the following words: *arouse, illustrate, impress, contribute, dispute.*

Meet the Author

Rod **Serling** (1924–1975)

Rod Serling once said that he did not have much imagination. This is an odd statement from a man who wrote more than 200 television scripts.

Quick Success Serling did not become serious about writing until college. Driven by a love for radio drama, he earned second place in a national script contest. Soon after, he landed his first staff job as a radio writer. Serling branched out into writing for a new medium—television—and rocketed to fame.

Fast Facts

▶ In the 1950s and 1960s, television censors banned scripts that appeared to question American society.

▶ Serling disguised his social criticism as science fiction in plays like "The Monsters Are Due on Maple Street."

Go **Online**
─Author Link

For: More about the author
Visit: www.PHSchool.com
Web Code: eme-9504

The Monsters Are Due On Maple Street

Rod Serling

CHARACTERS

NARRATOR	FIGURE ONE	FIGURE TWO

RESIDENTS OF MAPLE STREET

STEVE BRAND	WOMAN	MAN TWO
CHARLIE'S WIFE	DON MARTIN	PETE VAN HORN
MRS. GOODMAN	SALLY *(TOMMY'S*	CHARLIE
MRS. BRAND	*MOTHER)*	LES GOODMAN
TOMMY	MAN ONE	

Act 1

[*Fade in on a shot of the night sky. The various nebulae and planet bodies stand out in sharp, sparkling relief, and the camera begins a slow pan across the Heavens.*]

NARRATOR'S VOICE. There is a fifth dimension beyond that which is known to man. It is a dimension as vast as space, and as timeless as infinity. It is the middle ground between light and shadow—between science and superstition. And it lies between the pit of man's fears and the summit of his knowledge. This is the dimension of imagination. It is an area which we call The Twilight Zone.

[*The camera has begun to pan down until it passes the horizon and is on a sign which reads "Maple Street." Pan down until we are shooting down at an angle toward the street below. It's a tree-lined, quiet residential American street, very typical of the small town. The houses have front porches on which people sit and swing on gliders, conversing across from house to house.* STEVE BRAND *polishes his car parked in front of his house. His neighbor,* DON MARTIN, *leans against the fender watching him. A Good Humor man rides a bicycle and is just in the process of stopping to sell some ice cream to a couple of kids. Two women gossip on the front lawn. Another man waters his lawn.*]

✓ **Reading Check**

What is the fifth dimension?

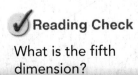

NARRATOR'S VOICE. Maple Street, U.S.A., late summer. A tree-lined little world of front porch gliders, hop scotch, the laughter of children, and the bell of an ice cream vendor.

[*There is a pause and the camera moves over to a shot of the Good Humor man and two small boys who are standing alongside, just buying ice cream.*]

NARRATOR'S VOICE. At the sound of the roar and the flash of light it will be precisely 6:43 P.M. on Maple Street.

[*At this moment one of the little boys, TOMMY, looks up to listen to a sound of a tremendous screeching roar from overhead. A flash of light plays on both their faces and then it moves down the street past lawns and porches and rooftops and then disappears.*

Various people leave their porches and stop what they're doing to stare up at the sky. STEVE BRAND, the man who's been polishing his car, now stands there transfixed, staring upwards. He looks at DON MARTIN, his neighbor from across the street.]

STEVE. What was that? A meteor?

DON. [*Nods*] That's what it looked like. I didn't hear any crash though, did you?

STEVE. [*Shakes his head*] Nope. I didn't hear anything except a roar.

MRS. BRAND. [*From her porch*] Steve? What was that?

STEVE. [*Raising his voice and looking toward porch*] Guess it was a meteor, honey. Came awful close, didn't it?

MRS. BRAND. Too close for my money! Much too close.

[*The camera pans across the various porches to people who stand there watching and talking in low tones.*]

NARRATOR'S VOICE. Maple Street. Six-forty-four P.M. on a late September evening. [*A pause*] Maple Street in the last calm and reflective moment . . . before the monsters came!

[*The camera slowly pans across the porches again. We see a man screwing a light bulb on a front porch, then getting down off the stool to flick the switch and finding that nothing happens.*

Another man is working on an electric power mower. He plugs in the plug, flicks on the switch of the power mower, off and on, with nothing happening.

Reading Skill
Summarize Do you think the flash of light is an important or unimportant detail? Explain.

Through the window of a front porch, we see a woman pushing her finger back and forth on the dial hook. Her voice is indistinct and distant, but intelligible and repetitive.]

WOMAN. Operator, operator, something's wrong on the phone, operator!

[MRS. BRAND *comes out on the porch and calls to* STEVE.]

MRS. BRAND. [*Calling*] Steve, the power's off. I had the soup on the stove and the stove just stopped working.

WOMAN. Same thing over here. I can't get anybody on the phone either. The phone seems to be dead.

[*We look down on the street as we hear the voices creep up from below, small, mildly disturbed voices highlighting these kinds of phrases:*]

VOICES.

Electricity's off.

Phone won't work.

Can't get a thing on the radio.

My power mower won't move, won't work at all.

Radio's gone dead!

[PETE VAN HORN, *a tall, thin man, is seen standing in front of his house.*]

VAN HORN. I'll cut through the back yard . . . See if the power's still on on Floral Street. I'll be right back!

[*He walks past the side of his house and disappears into the back yard.*
 The camera pans down slowly until we're looking at ten or eleven people standing around the street and overflowing to the curb and sidewalk. In the background is STEVE BRAND'S *car.*]

STEVE. Doesn't make sense. Why should the power go off all of a sudden, and the phone line?

DON. Maybe some sort of an electrical storm or something.

CHARLIE. That don't seem likely. Sky's just as blue as anything. Not a cloud. No lightning. No thunder. No nothing. How could it be a storm?

Literary Analysis
Character's Motives
Why do the characters come out of their homes?

Reading Check

What strange event occurs just before Maple Street loses electricity?

WOMAN. I can't get a thing on the radio. Not even the portable.

[*The people again murmur softly in wonderment and question.*]

CHARLIE. Well, why don't you go downtown and check with the police, though they'll probably think we're crazy or something. A little power failure and right away we get all <u>flustered</u> and everything.

STEVE. It isn't just the power failure, Charlie. If it was, we'd still be able to get a broadcast on the portable.

[*There's a murmur of reaction to this.* STEVE *looks from face to face and then over to his car.*]

STEVE. I'll run downtown. We'll get this all straightened out.

[*He walks over to the car, gets in it, turns the key. Looking through the open car door, we see the crowd watching him from the other side.* STEVE *starts the engine. It turns over* <u>sluggishly</u> *and then just stops dead. He tries it again and this time he can't get it to turn over. Then, very slowly and reflectively, he turns the key back to "off" and slowly gets out of the car.*

The people stare at STEVE. *He stands for a moment by the car, then walks toward the group.*]

STEVE. I don't understand it. It was working fine before . . .

DON. Out of gas?

STEVE. [*Shakes his head*] I just had it filled up.

WOMAN. What's it mean?

CHARLIE. It's just as if . . . as if everything had stopped. [*Then he turns toward* STEVE.] We'd better walk downtown.

[*Another murmur of assent at this.*]

Woman on telephone as seen through window, William Low, Courtesy of the artist.

▲ **Critical Viewing**
What impression does this illustration convey about life on Maple Street? [**Analyze**]

Vocabulary Builder
flustered (flus´ tərd) *adj.* nervous; confused

sluggishly (slug´ ish lē) *adv.* as if lacking energy

STEVE. The two of us can go, Charlie. [*He turns to look back at the car.*] It couldn't be the meteor. A meteor couldn't do this.

[*He and* CHARLIE *exchange a look, then they start to walk away from the group.*

We see TOMMY, *a serious-faced fourteen-year-old in spectacles who stands a few feet away from the group. He is halfway between them and the two men, who start to walk down the sidewalk.*]

TOMMY. Mr. Brand . . . you better not!

STEVE. Why not?

TOMMY. They don't want you to.

[STEVE *and* CHARLIE *exchange a grin, and* STEVE *looks back toward the boy.*]

STEVE. Who doesn't want us to?

TOMMY. [*Jerks his head in the general direction of the distant horizon*] Them!

STEVE. Them?

CHARLIE. Who are them?

TOMMY. [*Very intently*] Whoever was in that thing that came by overhead.

[STEVE *knits his brows for a moment, cocking his head questioningly. His voice is intense.*]

STEVE. What?

TOMMY. Whoever was in that thing that came over. I don't think they want us to leave here.

[STEVE *leaves* CHARLIE *and walks over to the boy. He kneels down in front of him. He forces his voice to remain gentle. He reaches out and holds the boy.*]

STEVE. What do you mean? What are you talking about?

TOMMY. They don't want us to leave. That's why they shut everything off.

STEVE. What makes you say that? Whatever gave you that idea?

WOMAN. [*From the crowd*] Now isn't that the craziest thing you ever heard?

Literary Analysis
Character's Motives
Why does Tommy warn Charlie and Steve not to leave?

**Reading Check**

What happens when Steve tries to start his car?

TOMMY. [_Persistently but a little intimidated by the crowd_] It's always that way, in every story I ever read about a ship landing from outer space.

WOMAN. [_To the boy's mother,_ SALLY, _who stands on the fringe of the crowd_] From outer space, yet! Sally, you better get that boy of yours up to bed. He's been reading too many comic books or seeing too many movies or something.

SALLY. Tommy, come over here and stop that kind of talk.

STEVE. Go ahead, Tommy. We'll be right back. And you'll see. That wasn't any ship or anything like it. That was just a . . . a meteor or something. Likely as not—[_He turns to the group, now trying to weight his words with an optimism he obviously doesn't feel but is desperately trying to instill in himself as well as the others._] No doubt it did have something to do with all this power failure and the rest of it. Meteors can do some crazy things. Like sunspots.

DON. [_Picking up the cue_] Sure. That's the kind of thing—like sunspots. They raise Cain[1] with radio reception all over the world. And this thing being so close—why, there's no telling the sort of stuff it can do. [_He wets his lips, smiles nervously._] Go ahead, Charlie. You and Steve go into town and see if that isn't what's causing it all.

[STEVE _and_ CHARLIE _again walk away from the group down the sidewalk. The people watch silently._

TOMMY _stares at them, biting his lips, and finally calling out again._]

TOMMY. _Mr. Brand!_

[_The two men stop again._ TOMMY _takes a step toward them._]

TOMMY. Mr. Brand . . . please don't leave here.

[STEVE _and_ CHARLIE _stop once again and turn toward the boy. There's a murmur in the crowd, a murmur of irritation and concern as if the boy were bringing up fears that shouldn't be brought up; words which carried with them a strange kind of validity that came without logic but nonetheless registered and had meaning and effect. Again we hear a murmur of reaction from the crowd._

TOMMY _is partly frightened and partly defiant as well._]

---

1. raise Cain badly disturb.

Vocabulary Builder
persistently (pər sist′ ənt lē) _adv._ firmly and steadily

Literary Analysis
Character's Motives
Why does Tommy's mother want him to stop talking?

Vocabulary Builder
defiant (dē fī′ ənt) _adj._ boldly resisting

TOMMY. You might not even be able to get to town. It was that way in the story. Nobody could leave. Nobody except—

STEVE. Except who?

TOMMY. Except the people they'd sent down ahead of them. They looked just like humans. And it wasn't until the ship landed that—

[*The boy suddenly stops again, conscious of the parents staring at them and of the sudden hush of the crowd.*]

SALLY. [*In a whisper, sensing the antagonism of the crowd*] Tommy, please son . . . honey, don't talk that way—

MAN ONE. That kid shouldn't talk that way . . . and we shouldn't stand here listening to him. Why this is the craziest thing I ever heard of. The kid tells us a comic book plot and here we stand listening—

[STEVE *walks toward the camera, stops by the boy.*]

STEVE. Go ahead, Tommy. What kind of story was this? What about the people that they sent out ahead?

TOMMY. That was the way they prepared things for the landing. They sent four people. A mother and a father and two kids who looked just like humans . . . but they weren't.

[*There's another silence as* STEVE *looks toward the crowd and then toward* TOMMY. *He wears a tight grin.*]

STEVE. Well, I guess what we'd better do then is to run a check on the neighborhood and see which ones of us are really human.

[*There's laughter at this, but it's a laughter that comes from a desperate attempt to lighten the atmosphere. It's a release kind of laugh. The people look at one another in the middle of their laughter.*]

CHARLIE. There must be somethin' better to do than stand around makin' bum jokes about it.

[*Rubs his jaw nervously*] I wonder if Floral Street's got the same deal we got. [*He looks past the houses.*] Where is Pete Van Horn anyway? Didn't he get back yet?

[*Suddenly there's the sound of a car's engine starting to turn over.*

Reading Skill
Summarize How do you know that Tommy's idea will be important to the story?

Reading Skill
Summarize Do you think Steve's comment will prove to be important as the story develops? Why or why not?

Reading Check

What does Tommy say about the people who were sent from outer space?

Overview of family walking dog on the street, William Low. Courtesy of the artist.

We look across the street toward the driveway of LES GOOD-MAN'S *house. He's at the wheel trying to start the car.*]

SALLY. Can you get it started, Les? [*He gets out of the car, shaking his head.*]

GOODMAN. No dice.

[*He walks toward the group. He stops suddenly as behind him, inexplicably and with a noise that inserts itself into the silence, the car engine starts up all by itself.* GOODMAN *whirls around to stare toward it.*

The car idles roughly, smoke coming from the exhaust, the frame shaking gently.

GOODMAN'S *eyes go wide, and he runs over to his car. The people stare toward the car.*]

MAN ONE. He got the car started somehow. He got his car started!

▲ **Critical Viewing**
How do the colors in this illustration contrast with the mood of the drama? Explain. [**Compare and Contrast**]

Reading Skill Summarize Why might this detail about a car starting be important?

[*The camera pans along the faces of the people as they stare, somehow caught up by this revelation and somehow, illogically, wildly, frightened.*]

WOMAN. How come his car just up and started like that?

SALLY. All by itself. He wasn't anywheres near it. It started all by itself.

[DON *approaches the group, stops a few feet away to look toward* GOODMAN'S *car and then back toward the group.*]

DON. And he never did come out to look at that thing that flew overhead. He wasn't even interested. [*He turns to the faces in the group, his face taut and serious.*] Why? Why didn't he come out with the rest of us to look?

CHARLIE. He always was an oddball. Him and his whole family. Real oddball.

DON. What do you say we ask him?

[*The group suddenly starts toward the house. In this brief fraction of a moment they take the first step toward performing a <u>metamorphosis</u> that changes people from a group into a mob. They begin to head purposefully across the street toward the house at the end.* STEVE *stands in front of them. For a moment their fear almost turns their walk into a wild stampede, but* STEVE'S *voice, loud, incisive, and commanding, makes them stop.*]

STEVE. Wait a minute . . . wait a minute! Let's not be a mob!

[*The people stop as a group, seem to pause for a moment, and then much more quietly and slowly start to walk across the street.* GOODMAN *stands alone facing the people.*]

GOODMAN. I just don't understand it. I tried to start it and it wouldn't start. You saw me. All of you saw me.

[*And now, just as suddenly as the engine started, it stops and there's a long silence that is gradually intruded upon by the frightened murmuring of the people.*]

GOODMAN. I don't understand. I swear . . . I don't understand. What's happening?

DON. Maybe you better tell us. Nothing's working on this street. Nothing. No lights, no power, no radio. [*And then meaningfully*] Nothing except one car—yours!

Vocabulary Builder
metamorphosis
(met′ə môr′fə sis) *n.*
change of form

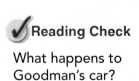

Reading Check

What happens to Goodman's car?

[*The people pick this up and now their murmuring becomes a loud chant filling the air with accusations and demands for action. Two of the men pass* DON *and head toward* GOODMAN, *who backs away, backing into his car and now at bay.*]

GOODMAN. Wait a minute now. You keep your distance—all of you. So I've got a car that starts by itself—well, that's a freak thing, I admit it. But does that make me some kind of a criminal or something? I don't know why the car works— it just does!

[*This stops the crowd momentarily and now* GOODMAN, *still backing away, goes toward his front porch. He goes up the steps and then stops to stand facing the mob.*
We see a long shot of STEVE *as he comes through the crowd.*]

STEVE. [*Quietly*] We're all on a monster kick, Les. Seems that the general impression holds that maybe one family isn't what we think they are. Monsters from outer space or something. Different than us. Fifth columnists[2] from the vast beyond. [*He chuckles.*] You know anybody that might fit that description around here on Maple Street?

GOODMAN. What is this, a gag or something? This a practical joke or something?

[*We see a close-up of the porch light as it suddenly goes out. There's a murmur from the group.*]

GOODMAN. Now I suppose that's supposed to incriminate me! The light goes on and off. That really does it, doesn't it? [*He looks around the faces of the people.*] I just don't understand this— [*He wets his lips, looking from face to face.*] Look, you all know me. We've lived here five years. Right in this house. We're no different from any of the rest of you! We're no different at all. Really . . . this whole thing is just . . . just weird—

WOMAN. Well, if that's the case, Les Goodman, explain why—

[*She stops suddenly, clamping her mouth shut.*]

GOODMAN. [*Softly*] Explain what?

STEVE. [*Interjecting*] Look, let's forget this—

CHARLIE. [*Overlapping him*] Go ahead, let her talk. What about it? Explain what?

Reading Skill
Summarize Briefly explain what has happened to Goodman and his car up to this point.

---

2. Fifth columnists people who help an invading enemy from within their own country.

WOMAN. [*A little reluctantly*] Well . . . sometimes I go to bed late at night. A couple of times . . . a couple of times I'd come out on the porch and I'd see Mr. Goodman here in the wee hours of the morning standing out in front of his house . . . looking up at the sky. [*She looks around the circle of faces.*] That's right, looking up at the sky as if . . . as if he were waiting for something. [*A pause*] As if he were looking for something.

[*There's a murmur of reaction from the crowd again.*

We cut suddenly to a group shot. As GOODMAN *starts toward them, they back away frightened.*]

GOODMAN. You know really . . . this is for laughs. You know what I'm guilty of? [*He laughs.*] I'm guilty of insomnia. Now what's the penalty for insomnia? [*At this point the laugh, the humor, leaves his voice.*] Did you hear what I said? I said it was insomnia. [*A pause as he looks around, then shouts.*] I said it was insomnia! You fools. You scared, frightened rabbits, you. You're sick people, do you know that? You're sick people—all of you! And you don't even know what you're starting because let me tell you . . . let me tell you—this thing you're starting—that should frighten you. As God is my witness . . . you're letting something begin here that's a nightmare!

Act 2

[*We see a medium shot of the* GOODMAN *entry hall at night. On the side table rests an unlit candle.* MRS. GOODMAN *walks into the scene, a glass of milk in hand. She sets the milk down on the table, lights the candle with a match from a box on the table, picks up the glass of milk, and starts out of scene.*

MRS. GOODMAN *comes through her porch door, glass of milk in hand. The entry hall, with table and lit candle, can be seen behind her.*

Outside, the camera slowly pans down the sidewalk, taking in little knots of people who stand around talking in low voices. At the end of each conversation they look toward LES GOODMAN'S *house. From the various houses we can see candlelight but no electricity, and there's an all-pervading quiet that blankets the whole area, disturbed only by the almost whispered voices of the people as they stand around. The camera pans over to one group where* CHARLIE *stands. He stares across at* GOODMAN'S *house.*

Reading Skill
Summarize In a few sentences, summarize the action of Act 1.

Literary Analysis
Character's Motives What emotions motivate Goodman to shout?

Reading Check

Why is the crowd following Goodman?

We see a long shot of the house. Two men stand across the street in almost sentry-like poses. Then we see a medium shot of a group of people.]

SALLY. [*A little timorously*] It just doesn't seem right, though, keeping watch on them. Why . . . he was right when he said he was one of our neighbors. Why, I've known Ethel Goodman ever since they moved in. We've been good friends—

CHARLIE. That don't prove a thing. Any guy who'd spend his time lookin' up at the sky early in the morning—well, there's something wrong with that kind of person. There's something that ain't legitimate. Maybe under normal circumstances we could let it go by, but these aren't normal circumstances. Why, look at this street! Nothin' but candles. Why, it's like goin' back into the dark ages or somethin'!

[STEVE *walks down the steps of his porch, walks down the street over to* LES GOODMAN'S *house, and then stops at the foot of the steps.* GOODMAN *stands there, his wife behind him, very frightened.*]

GOODMAN. Just stay right where you are, Steve. We don't want any trouble, but this time if anybody sets foot on my porch, that's what they're going to get—trouble!

STEVE. Look, Les—

GOODMAN. I've already explained to you people. I don't sleep very well at night sometimes. I get up and I take a walk and I look up at the sky. I look at the stars!

MRS. GOODMAN. That's exactly what he does. Why this whole thing, it's . . . it's some kind of madness or something.

STEVE. [*Nods grimly*] That's exactly what it is—some kind of madness.

CHARLIE'S VOICE. [*Shrill, from across the street*] You best watch who you're seen with, Steve! Until we get this all straightened out, you ain't exactly above suspicion yourself.

STEVE. [*Whirling around toward him*] Or you, Charlie. Or any of us, it seems. From age eight on up!

WOMAN. What I'd like to know is—what are we gonna do? Just stand around here all night?

▶ **Critical Viewing**
Why does night's darkness, shown in this illustration, make the people of Maple Street more fearful? **[Hypothesize]**

**Reading Skill
Summarize** Is Charlie's statement about candles important? Why or why not?

Streetlight, 1930, Constance Coleman Richardson, Indianapolis Museum of Art

CHARLIE. There's nothin' else we can do! [*He turns back looking toward* STEVE *and* GOODMAN *again.*] One of 'em'll tip their hand. They got to.

STEVE. [*Raising his voice*] There's something you can do, Charlie. You could go home and keep your mouth shut. You could quit strutting around like a self-appointed hanging judge and just climb into bed and forget it.

CHARLIE. You sound real anxious to have that happen, Steve. I think we better keep our eye on you too!

DON. [*As if he were taking the bit in his teeth, takes a hesitant step to the front*] I think everything might as well come out now. [*He turns toward* STEVE.] Your wife's done plenty of talking, Steve, about how odd you are!

CHARLIE. [*Picking this up, his eyes widening*] Go ahead, tell us what she's said.

Literary Analysis
Character's Motives
Why does Steve want Charlie to be quiet?

✓ Reading Check

Why does Goodman go out and stare at the sky early in the morning?

[*We see a long shot of* STEVE *as he walks toward them from across the street.*]

STEVE. Go ahead, what's my wife said? Let's get it all out. Let's pick out every idiosyncrasy of every single man, woman, and child on the street. And then we might as well set up some kind of kangaroo court.[3] How about a firing squad at dawn, Charlie, so we can get rid of all the suspects? Narrow them down. Make it easier for you.

DON. There's no need gettin' so upset, Steve. It's just that . . . well . . . Myra's talked about how there's been plenty of nights you spent hours down in your basement workin' on some kind of radio or something. Well, none of us have ever seen that radio—

[*By this time* STEVE *has reached the group. He stands there defiantly close to them.*]

CHARLIE. Go ahead, Steve. What kind of "radio set" you workin' on? I never seen it. Neither has anyone else. Who you talk to on that radio set? And who talks to you?

STEVE. I'm surprised at you, Charlie. How come you're so dense all of a sudden? [*A pause*] Who do I talk to? I talk to monsters from outer space. I talk to three-headed green men who fly over here in what look like meteors.

[STEVE'S *wife steps down from the porch, bites her lip, calls out.*]

MRS. BRAND. Steve! Steve, please. [*Then looking around, frightened, she walks toward the group.*] It's just a ham radio set, that's all. I bought him a book on it myself. It's just a ham radio set. A lot of people have them. I can show it to you. It's right down in the basement.

STEVE. [*Whirls around toward her*] Show them nothing! If they want to look inside our house—let them get a search warrant.

CHARLIE. Look, buddy, you can't afford to—

STEVE. [*Interrupting*] Charlie, don't tell me what I can afford! And stop telling me who's dangerous and who isn't and who's safe and who's a menace. [*He turns to the group and shouts.*] And you're with him, too—all of you! You're

Literary Analysis
Character's Motivation What do you think Steve is feeling at this point?

---

3. **kangaroo court** unofficial court that does not follow normal rules.

standing here all set to crucify—all set to find a scapegoat[4]—all desperate to point some kind of a finger at a neighbor! Well now look, friends, the only thing that's gonna happen is that we'll eat each other up alive—

[*He stops abruptly as* CHARLIE *suddenly grabs his arm.*]

CHARLIE. [*In a hushed voice*] That's not the only thing that can happen to us.

[*Cut to a long shot looking down the street. A figure has suddenly materialized in the gloom·and in the silence we can hear the clickety-clack of slow, measured footsteps on concrete as the figure walks slowly toward them. One of the women lets out a stifled cry. The young mother grabs her boy as do a couple of others.*]

TOMMY. [*Shouting, frightened*] It's the monster! It's the monster!

[*Another woman lets out a wail and the people fall back in a group, staring toward the darkness and the approaching figure.*

We see a medium group shot of the people as they stand in the shadows watching. DON MARTIN *joins them, carrying a shotgun. He holds it up.*]

DON. We may need this.

STEVE. A shotgun? [*He pulls it out of* DON'S *hand.*] Good Lord—will anybody think a thought around here? Will you people wise up? What good would a shotgun do against—

[*Now* CHARLIE *pulls the gun from* STEVE'S *hand.*]

CHARLIE. No more talk, Steve. You're going to talk us into a grave! You'd let whatever's out there walk right over us, wouldn't yuh? Well, some of us won't!

[*He swings the gun around to point it toward the sidewalk. The dark figure continues to walk toward them.*

The group stands there, fearful, apprehensive, mothers clutching children, men standing in front of wives. CHARLIE *slowly raises the gun. As the figure gets closer and closer he suddenly pulls the trigger. The sound of it explodes in the stillness. There is a long angle shot looking down at the figure, who suddenly lets out a small cry, stumbles forward onto his knees and then falls forward on his face.* DON, CHARLIE, *and* STEVE *race forward over*

---

4. **scapegoat** person or group blamed for the mistakes or crimes of others.

Literary Analysis
Character's Motivation What explains the characters' fearful actions here?

Literary Analysis
Character's Motives Why does Charlie pull the shotgun from Steve's hands?

Reading Check

What does Steve have in his basement?

to him. STEVE *is there first and turns the man over. Now the crowd gathers around them.*]

STEVE. [*Slowly looks up*] It's Pete Van Horn.

DON. [*In a hushed voice*] Pete Van Horn! He was just gonna go over to the next block to see if the power was on—

WOMAN. You killed him, Charlie. You shot him dead!

CHARLIE. [*Looks around at the circle of faces, his eyes frightened, his face contorted*] But . . . but I didn't know who he was. I certainly didn't know who he was. He comes walkin' out of the darkness—how am I supposed to know who he was? [*He grabs* STEVE.] Steve—you know why I shot! How was I supposed to know he wasn't a monster or something? [*He grabs* DON *now.*] We're all scared of the same thing. I was just tryin' to . . . tryin' to protect my home, that's all! Look, all of you, that's all I was tryin' to do. [*He looks down wildly at the body.*] I didn't know it was somebody we knew! I didn't know—

[*There's a sudden hush and then an intake of breath. We see a medium shot of the living room window of* CHARLIE'S *house. The window is not lit, but suddenly the house lights come on behind it.*]

Reading Skill
Summarize How do you know that Pete Van Horn's death is an important detail?

WOMAN. [*In a very hushed voice*] Charlie . . . Charlie . . . the lights just went on in your house. Why did the lights just go on?

DON. What about it, Charlie? How come you're the only one with lights now?

GOODMAN. That's what I'd like to know.

[*A pause as they all stare toward* CHARLIE.]

GOODMAN. You were so quick to kill, Charlie, and you were so quick to tell us who we had to be careful of. Well, maybe you had to kill. Maybe Peter there was trying to tell us something. Maybe he'd found out something and came back to tell us who there was amongst us we should watch out for—

[CHARLIE *backs away from the group, his eyes wide with fright.*]

CHARLIE. No . . . no . . . it's nothing of the sort! I don't know why the lights are on. I swear I don't. Somebody's pulling a gag or something.

[*He bumps against* STEVE, *who grabs him and whirls him around.*]

▲ Critical V
How does t
manipulate
photograph
communica
ideas of the
[Connect]

Reading
Who shoots
Horn?

The Monsters Are Due on Maple St

STEVE. *A gag?* A gag? Charlie, there's a dead man on the side-walk and you killed him! Does this thing look like a gag to you?

[CHARLIE *breaks away and screams as he runs toward his house.*]

CHARLIE. No! No! Please!

[*A man breaks away from the crowd to chase* CHARLIE.
    We see a long angle shot looking down as the man tackles CHARLIE *and lands on top of him. The other people start to run toward them.* CHARLIE *is up on his feet, breaks away from the other man's grasp, lands a couple of desperate punches that push the man aside. Then he forces his way, fighting, through the crowd to once again break free, jumps up on his front porch. A rock thrown from the group smashes a window alongside of him, the broken glass flying past him. A couple of pieces cut him. He stands there perspiring, rumpled, blood running down from a cut on the cheek. His wife breaks away from the group to throw her-self into his arms. He buries his face against her. We can see the crowd converging on the porch now.*]

VOICES.

It must have been him.

He's the one.

We got to get Charlie.

[*Another rock lands on the porch. Now* CHARLIE *pushes his wife behind him, facing the group.*]

CHARLIE. Look, look I swear to you . . . it isn't me . . . but I do know who it is . . . I swear to you, I do know who it is. I know who the monster is here. I know who it is that doesn't belong. I swear to you I know.

GOODMAN. [*Shouting*] What are you waiting for?

WOMAN. [*Shouting*] Come on, Charlie, come on.

MAN ONE. [*Shouting*] Who is it, Charlie, tell us!

DON. [*Pushing his way to the front of the crowd*] All right, Char-lie, let's hear it!

[CHARLIE'S *eyes dart around wildly.*]

CHARLIE. It's . . . it's . . .

MAN TWO. [*Screaming*] Go ahead, Charlie, tell us.

Literary Analysis
Character's Motives
What motivates Charlie to claim that he knows who the monster is? Explain.

CHARLIE. It's . . . it's the kid. It's Tommy. He's the one!

[*There's a gasp from the crowd as we cut to a shot of* SALLY *holding her son* TOMMY. *The boy at first doesn't understand and then, realizing the eyes are all on him, buries his face against his mother.*]

SALLY. [*Backs away*] That's crazy! That's crazy! He's a little boy.

WOMAN. But he knew! He was the only one who knew! He told us all about it. Well, how did he know? How could he have known?

[*The various people take this up and repeat the question aloud.*]

VOICES.

How could he know?

Who told him?

Make the kid answer.

DON. It was Charlie who killed old man Van Horn.

WOMAN. But it was the kid here who knew what was going to happen all the time. He was the one who knew!

[*We see a close-up of* STEVE.]

STEVE. Are you all gone crazy? [*Pause as he looks about*] Stop.

[*A fist crashes at* STEVE'S *face, staggering him back out of the frame of the picture.*

There are several close camera shots suggesting the coming of violence. A hand fires a rifle. A fist clenches. A hand grabs the hammer from VAN HORN'S *body, etc. Meanwhile, we hear the following lines.*]

DON. Charlie has to be the one—Where's my rifle—

WOMAN. Les Goodman's the one. His car started! Let's wreck it.

MRS. GOODMAN. What about Steve's radio—He's the one that called them—

MRS. GOODMAN. Smash the radio. Get me a hammer. Get me something.

STEVE. Stop—Stop—

CHARLIE. Where's that kid—Let's get him.

MAN ONE. Get Steve—Get Charlie—They're working together.

Reading Skill
Summarize What details show that Charlie finds it hard to say who to blame?

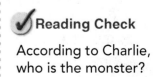

Reading Check

According to Charlie, who is the monster?

[*The crowd starts to converge around the mother, who grabs the child and starts to run with him. The crowd starts to follow, at first walking fast, and then running after him.*

We see a full shot of the street as suddenly CHARLIE'S *lights go off and the lights in another house go on. They stay on for a moment, then from across the street other lights go on and then off again.*]

MAN ONE. [*Shouting*] It isn't the kid . . . it's Bob Weaver's house.

WOMAN. It isn't Bob Weaver's house. It's Don Martin's place.

CHARLIE. I tell you it's the kid.

DON. It's Charlie. He's the one.

[*We move into a series of close-ups of various people as they shout, accuse, scream, interspersing these shots with shots of houses as the lights go on and off, and then slowly in the middle of this nightmarish morass of sight and sound the camera starts to pull away, until once again we've reached the opening shot looking at the Maple Street sign from high above. The camera continues to move away until we dissolve to a shot looking toward the metal side of a space craft, which sits shrouded in darkness. An open door throws out a beam of light from the illuminated interior. Two figures silhouetted against the bright lights appear. We get only a vague feeling of form, but nothing more explicit than that.*]

FIGURE ONE. Understand the procedure now? Just stop a few of their machines and radios and telephones and lawn mowers . . . throw them into darkness for a few hours, and then you just sit back and watch the pattern.

FIGURE TWO. And this pattern is always the same?

FIGURE ONE. With few variations. They pick the most dangerous enemy they can find . . . and it's themselves. And all we need do is sit back . . . and watch.

FIGURE TWO. Then I take it this place . . . this Maple Street . . . is not unique.

FIGURE ONE. [*Shaking his head*] By no means. Their world is full of Maple Streets. And we'll go from one to the other and let them destroy themselves. One to the other . . . one to the other . . . one to the other—

Reading Skill
Summarize Is the detail about lights going on and off in various homes important? Why or why not?

[*Now the camera pans up for a shot of the starry sky and over this we hear the* NARRATOR'S *voice.*]

NARRATOR'S VOICE. The tools of conquest do not necessarily come with bombs and explosions and fallout. There are weapons that are simply thoughts, attitudes, prejudices— to be found only in the minds of men. For the record, prejudices can kill and suspicion can destroy and a thoughtless frightened search for a scapegoat has a fallout all its own for the children . . . and the children yet unborn. [*A pause*] And the pity of it is . . . that these things cannot be confined to . . . The Twilight Zone!

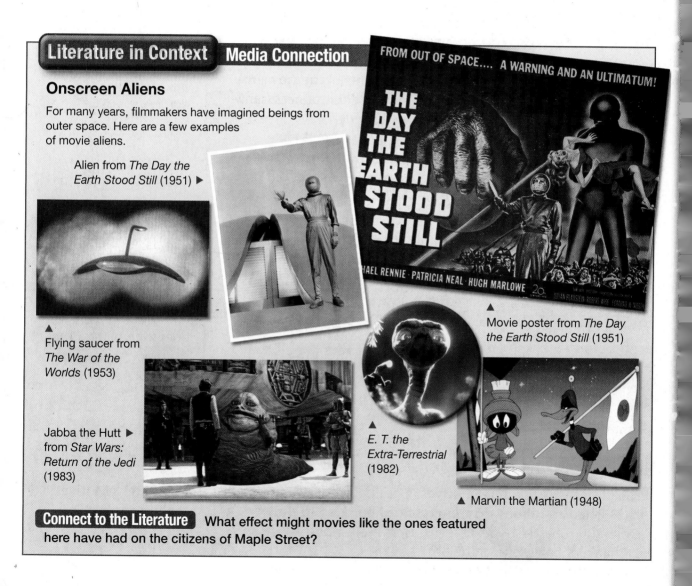

Literature in Context | Media Connection

Onscreen Aliens

For many years, filmmakers have imagined beings from outer space. Here are a few examples of movie aliens.

Alien from *The Day the Earth Stood Still* (1951) ▶

▲ Flying saucer from *The War of the Worlds* (1953)

FROM OUT OF SPACE.... A WARNING AND AN ULTIMATUM!

THE DAY THE EARTH STOOD STILL

MICHAEL RENNIE · PATRICIA NEAL · HUGH MARLOWE

▲ Movie poster from *The Day the Earth Stood Still* (1951)

Jabba the Hutt ▶ from *Star Wars: Return of the Jedi* (1983)

▲ E. T. the Extra-Terrestrial (1982)

▲ Marvin the Martian (1948)

Connect to the Literature What effect might movies like the ones featured here have had on the citizens of Maple Street?

Apply the Skills

The Monsters Are Due on Maple Street

Thinking About the Selection

1. **Respond:** If you were a resident of Maple Street, how would you have responded to the strange events?
2. **(a) Recall:** How do the people on Maple Street single out Les Goodman in Act I? **(b) Interpret:** What qualities of his cause the reaction? **(c) Deduce:** What does this suggest about what is really happening on Maple Street?
3. **(a) Recall:** Why does Charlie shoot Pete Van Horn? **(b) Infer:** What does the crowd's response to this shooting suggest about how clearly they are thinking?
4. **(a) Recall:** Who accuses Tommy after the shooting, and why? **(b) Connect:** Why are people prepared to believe such an accusation? **(c) Support:** How do the events of the play support this statement: "The tools of conquest do not necessarily come with bombs and explosions and fallout"?
5. **(a) Draw Conclusions:** Who are the monsters on Maple Street? **(b) Discuss:** Share your responses with a partner. Then, discuss how hearing someone else's responses did or did not change your answers.

Reading Skill

6. At the beginning of the play, the electricity goes off and phones and radios stop working. Are these important or unimportant details? Explain your answer.
7. **Summarize** the play using a chart like the one shown.

Important Details From Beginning	Important Details From Middle	Important Details From End
Summary:		

Literary Analysis

8. Explain the **character's motives** in each of these examples: **(a)** Pete Van Horn walks from his neighborhood to the next one. **(b)** Charlie shoots Pete Van Horn. **(c)** Goodman accuses Charlie of being one of the others.
9. What motivates the characters to finally turn on Tommy?

QuickReview

Screenplay at a Glance

Strange occurrences create suspicion and turn one neighbor against another.

Go Online
Assessment
For: Self-test
Visit: www.PHSchool.com
Web Code: ema-6505

Summarize: write a brief statement of the main points and important details in a work

Character's Motives: the reasons for his or her actions

Vocabulary Builder

Practice For each item, write a single sentence using both words.

1. flustered; teacher
2. sluggishly; engine
3. persistently; nagged
4. defiant; teenager
5. metamorphosis; tadpole

Writing

Write a **report** from the point of view of Figure One or Figure Two telling your leader what you learned during your visit to Maple Street. Include these elements:

- details about the people, events, and general atmosphere in the neighborhood
- recommendations for further action

For *Grammar, Vocabulary,* and *Assessment,* see **Build Language Skills,** pages 778–779.

Extend Your Learning

Listening and Speaking With a group, stage a **scene** from the screenplay.
- Select a scene with enough roles, and choose a director.
- Assign the roles.
- Practice performing the scene.
- Pay attention to the stage directions for movements and other special instructions.

After you rehearse, present the scene to your class.

Research and Technology Plan how you would prepare a **film version** of any scene from the screenplay or of the scene you presented in the previous activity.
- List the events that occur in the scene.
- Plan the camera angles that will best illustrate the action.
- Consider any special sound or lighting effects you would like to use.

If a camera is available and you have time, film the scene.

Build Language Skills

The Monsters Are Due on Maple Street

Vocabulary Skill

Suffixes The suffix *-ize* (*-yze*) means "make." This suffix forms verbs. Adding *-yze* to the noun *analysis* forms the verb *analyze*. When you add *-ize* to the noun *summary,* you create the verb *summarize,* meaning "make a summary."

▶ **Example:** To explain the plot, Julia had to *summarize* the main events.

Practice Use a dictionary to find the base of each italicized word. Explain how the suffix modifies the meaning of the original word. Then, answer each question using the italicized word in your answer.

1. How would you *familiarize* yourself with the characters in a play?
2. Do not *generalize* based on one example.
3. Why is it important to *synthesize* information from several sources?
4. What qualities *characterize* spring?
5. We have to *analyze* the way words are used for emotional effect.

Grammar Lesson

Sentence Functions and Endmarks Sentences are classified into four categories based on their function.

MorePractice

For more practice with sentence types, see the Grammar Handbook, p. R31.

Category	Function	Endmark	Example
Declarative	to make statements	.	Our cat chased a squirrel up a tree.
Interrogative	to ask questions	?	Where did I put my jacket?
Imperative	to give commands	. or !	Put your books away. Don't touch that stove!
Exclamatory	to call out or exclaim	!	That's a great idea!

Practice Add correct punctuation and indicate the function of the sentence. Write a related sentence that performs a different function.

1. Did you read this week's newspaper
2. Remember to call home when you arrive
3. We meet each morning at the bus stop
4. Watch out for that tree limb
5. This is the best sandwich I ever ate

*W*_G *Prentice Hall Writing and Grammar Connection: Chapter 21, Section 1*

Reading Skill: Summarize

Directions: *Choose the best answer to each question.*

   Callie awoke at 7 a.m. to the sound of the wind. She looked out and saw a blanket of snow on the ground, and more snow falling. She was worried about Willy, the lamb she was raising. Even in the barn, he could freeze in a blizzard like this one. Wrapped in an overcoat and scarf, Callie trudged through the snow to the barn. Inside, she found an empty cage. She looked but Willy was nowhere to be found. Running back to the house, Callie yelled for her mom and dad to help her search. When she reached the door, her dad opened it, holding Willy. He had brought Willy in during the night and had not seen Callie slip out earlier.

1. Which of these details should be included in a summary?

   A It was 7 a.m.

   B Callie heard a sound.

   C Callie wore an overcoat.

   D Callie worried that Willy would freeze.

2. What does not have to be included in a summary?

   A there was wind

   B Callie was raising Willy

   C Willy was a lamb

   D her dad had brought Willy in

3. Which is the best summary?

   A Callie woke up and went to the barn to see if her lamb was warm. She found the lamb with her dad.

   B While searching for her missing lamb, Callie worried that he would freeze.

   C Callie was worried that her lamb would freeze. After looking for the lamb, she discovered that her father had already brought the lamb in.

   D After finding the lamb's cage empty, Callie found that her father had brought the lamb in.

Timed Writing: Interpretation [Critical Stance]

Review "The Monsters Are Due on Maple Street." Determine whether the author's purpose is to entertain, to teach a lesson, or both. Then, explain whether you think the author was successful in achieving his purpose. State your position clearly and support it with specific examples from the play. **(45 minutes)**

 ## Writing Workshop: *Work in Progress*

Cause-and-Effect Essay

For a cause-and-effect essay you may write, make a list of three questions that spark your interest. Keep this question list in your writing portfolio.

Reading Informational Materials

Applications

In Part 2, you are learning how to summarize, which requires you to read closely. Reading closely is also important when you are filling out applications. If you want to act in plays—such as "The Monsters Are Due on Maple Street," which you may have read—you might need to fill out an application like the one in this lesson.

About Applications

The purpose of an **application** is to provide specific information requested by a group or organization that will then make a decision based on that information. At some point, you will probably fill out an application for one or more of the following reasons:

- to get a job
- to be admitted to a school
- to get a library card
- to open a savings account
- to join a club or sports leagues
- to get a driver's license

When preparing applications, read carefully to find out what information is needed, when and where the application should be turned in, and what, if any, other documents, payments, or paperwork should be included with the application.

Reading Skill

Reading an application involves **close reading**—carefully reading *every* word. The task is to follow each step on the application form. Start with the directions, and complete each one. If you have questions, call the organization and ask for clarification. Do not leave any section blank, unless it is marked as *optional*. Also, be sure to read the *fine print* carefully. It often includes information about rules or requirements.

Review your application, making sure it is completed thoroughly. Make sure that the information is legible, or readable. The checklist shown can help you in this process.

Checklist for Filling Out an Application	✓
Do I have the correct application?	
Have I followed all the directions step-by-step?	
Have I written or typed clearly?	
Have I signed the application, if requested?	
Have I checked the application for accuracy?	
Have I read the fine print?	
Have I submitted the application by the correct deadline?	
Have I sent any additional materials that must be submitted along with the application?	

The **Flat Rock** Playhouse

The Flat Rock Playhouse has grown in recent years from a traditional summer theater to a regional powerhouse. It boasts one of the largest Resident Contract Agreements with Actors' Equity Association, the union of actors and stage managers, in the southern region. Flat Rock Playhouse unites its seasonal talent pool with its year-round administrative and artistic staff, 70% of whom were formerly apprentices and interns. The Playhouse proudly trains and educates to nurture its own future.

A photograph showing actors on stage with spotlights immediately conveys some of the activities at The Flat Rock Playhouse.

Do you have a reputable Equity Apprenticeship in your background? Outside an education setting what steps have you taken to build a career? **Have you begun professional networking?** • How are you going to make the contacts necessary to get the job? • Do you have **acting professionals** on your reference list? • What do you know about marketing yourself in the theater business? Do you have a professionally photographed head shot? • Do you have a means to continually **update** your resume? • Do you know **how to find an agent?** Do you know how to get call backs at a cattle-call audition? • Would you feel comfortable in a **professional** environment? • Are you ready to join a union? **Are you a triple-threat talent?**

The questions imply that the program will teach these skills.

We will be attending SETC in March and will be happy to contact all serious applicants who have already initiated contact regarding their audition numbers. Applicants can, of course, call and set up personal auditions at the Playhouse if they are not attending SETC. However, if one's schedule or geographic distance from the Playhouse makes a personal audition impossible, one may send a video-taped audition consisting of two monologues and if applicable examples of singing and dance work. Also to expedite our selection and registration process, be sure to include two reference letters with the return correspondence. An application form and descriptive material about the program are subject to change due to variations in the talents and needs of each student class. Please complete and return the application at your earliest convenience if you wish to be considered among this year's candidates.

The directions tell you to submit the application promptly.

Read the title of the application to be sure it is the one you need.

This application supplies the address, phone number, and email address of the school, in case you have questions.

Apprentice Application Form for the Vagabond School of the Drama

TO ENROLL: PLEASE **PRINT** THIS FORM, COMPLETE IT, AND RETURN IT WITH A HEADSHOT OR SNAP SHOT, as well as any other information you deem necessary. Videotapes are welcome. Auditions and/or interviews by the Executive Director or his appointeee are required.

Read the directions closely to find out how to fill out the application. The directions may also describe other documents you have to provide.

Student Name		Social Security	
Address			
City	State		Zip
Home Phone	Work Phone	E-mail	
Age Date of Birth //	Weight Height	Hair Color	

Instruction

Song	Dance	Instruments

Theater Training
Parent/Guardian Name

Address			
City	State		Zip
Home Phone	Work Phone	E-mail	

Please provide a character reference

Name			
Address			
City	State		Zip
Home Phone	Work Phone	E-mail	

The Vagabond School of the Drama, Inc. is a not-for-profit educational institution that admits students of any race, creed, sex, national, or ethnic origin.

Reading: Reading Closely

Directions: *Choose the letter of the best answer to each question.*

1. In addition to the completed application form, what other materials does The Vagabond School of the Drama school require?

   A a check for $200

   B a headshot or snapshot

   C one letter of recommendation

   D the dates the applicant is available for an audition

2. Which part of the application specifically seeks to determine the applicant's experience?

   A "Videotapes are welcome."

   B "Return [this application] with a headshot or snap shot."

   C "Please provide a character reference."

   D "Instruction"

3. Which of the following are not required as part of the application process?

   A videotapes

   B auditions

   C character reference

   D headshots

Reading: Comprehension and Interpretation

Directions: *Write your answers on a separate sheet of paper.*

4. **(a)** What are three ways you can contact the Vagabond School of the Drama? **(b)** Where did you find this information? **[Knowledge]**

5. Why do you think this application form is designed with more space for the applicant's previous instruction in song, dance, and instrument than for the applicant's name? **[Generating]**

6. Explain the advantages of being a member of the Vagabond School of the Drama if you are looking for a career in acting. **[Applying]**

Timed Writing: Summary [Cognition]

Write a summary of the information about the Vagabond School of the Drama. Describe its mission or purpose, its history, its apprentice program, its location, and other important aspects of the school. **[20 minutes]**

Dramatic Speeches

Dramatic speeches are performed by actors in a drama or play. Whether spoken by a single character or as part of a larger scene, these speeches move the action of the story forward and help define the conflict within the plot. There are two main types of dramatic speeches:

- **Monologues** are long, uninterrupted speeches that are spoken by a single character. They reveal the private thoughts and feelings of the character.
- **Dialogues** are conversations between or among characters. They reveal characters' traits, develop conflict, and move the plot along.

Comparing Dramatic Speeches

The excerpt from *Grandpa and the Statue* and *My Head Is Full of Starshine* both contain dramatic speeches. *My Head Is Full of Starshine* is a monologue, and the excerpt from *Grandpa and the Statue* is a dialogue. As you read, consider these questions:

- How do you learn about the characters in each scene?
- How is other key information revealed?

Use a chart like the one shown to record information about the characters and how the playwright tells you about them.

	Grandpa and the Statue	My Head Is Full of Starshine
Main Characters		
Description of Characters		
How I Learned About Characters		

Vocabulary Builder

Grandpa and the Statue

- **peeved** (pēvd) *adj.* irritated; annoyed (p. 787) *I was peeved when my little brother took my new CD.*

My Head Is Full of Starshine

- **practical** (prak´ ti kəl) *adj.* level-headed; efficient; realistic (p. 791) *Chris is a practical person who saves some of his allowance for college.*

- **rummaging** (rum´ ij iŋ) *v.* searching through something (p. 791) *She was rummaging through her purse for her keys.*

- **potential** (pō ten´ shəl) *n.* possibility; capability (p. 791) *Her debating skills show that Wanda has great potential to be a politician someday.*

Build Understanding

Connecting to the Literature

Reading/Writing Connection Both of these dramatic speeches deal with relationships. As you may know, people do not have to be alike to become friends. In a few sentences, describe a friendship you have with a person who is different from you in some way. Use at least three of the following words: *appreciate, interpret, rely, select, react, appeal.*

Meet the Authors

Arthur **Miller** (1915–2005)

Arthur Miller is considered among the finest American playwrights. Most of his plays focus on the problems of ordinary people. Born in New York City during the Depression, Miller was unable to finish high school. In 1934, he convinced the University of Michigan to accept him as a student anyway.

Promising Playwright In 1947, Miller saw his first play *All My Sons* open on Broadway. *Death of a Salesman* (1949), perhaps his most famous play, won a Pulitzer Prize and made Miller internationally famous. *Grandpa and the Statue* was originally written as a radio drama in 1944.

Peg **Kehret** (b. 1936)

Before Peg Kehret began writing books for children, she wrote radio commercials, plays, and stories for magazines.

Animal Lover Kehret is a longtime volunteer for animal welfare causes and has won an award for her work with animals. For many years, she and her husband traveled to cities around the United States so that Kehret could attend speaking engagements at schools and libraries. The couple traveled in a motor home so that their pets could go with them.

Go Online
Author Link

For: More about the authors
Visit: www.PHSchool.com
Web Code: eme-9505

from
Grandpa
and the
Statue

ARTHUR MILLER

▲ Critical Viewing
What can you see in this photograph that you do not usually see in pictures of the Statue of Liberty?
[Analyze]

SHEEAN. [*Slight brogue*[1]] A good afternoon to you, Monaghan.

MONAGHAN. [*Grandfather*] How're you, Sheean, how're ya?

SHEEAN. Fair, fair. And how's Mrs. Monaghan these days?

MONAGHAN. Warm. Same as everybody else in summer.

SHEEAN. I've come to talk to you about the fund, Monaghan.

MONAGHAN. What fund is that?

SHEEAN. The Statue of Liberty fund.

MONAGHAN. Oh, that.

SHEEAN. It's time we come to grips with the subject, Monaghan.

MONAGHAN. I'm not interested, Sheean.

SHEEAN. Now hold up on that a minute. Let me tell you the facts. This here Frenchman has gone and built a fine statue of Liberty. It costs who knows how many millions to build. All they're askin' us to do is contribute enough to put up a base for the statue to stand on.

MONAGHAN. I'm not . . . !

---

1. brogue (brōg) *n.* Irish accent

SHEEAN. Before you answer me. People all over the whole United States are puttin' in for it. Butler Street is doin' the same. We'd like to hang up a flag on the corner saying—"Butler Street, Brooklyn, is one hundred per cent behind the Statue of Liberty." And Butler Street is a hundred per cent subscribed except for you. Now will you give us a dime, Monaghan? One dime and we can put up the flag. Now what do you say to that?

MONAGHAN. I'm not throwin' me good money away for somethin' I don't even know exists.

SHEEAN. Now what do you mean by that?

MONAGHAN. Have you seen this statue?

SHEEAN. No, but it's in a warehouse. And as soon as we get the money to build the pedestal they'll take it and put it up on that island in the river, and all the boats comin' in from the old country will see it there and it'll raise the hearts of the poor immigrants to see such a fine sight on their first look at this country.

MONAGHAN. And how do I know it's in this here warehouse at all?

SHEEAN. You read your paper, don't you? It's been in all the papers for the past year.

MONAGHAN. Ha, the papers! Last year I read in the paper that they were about to pave Butler Street and take out all the holes. Turn around and look at Butler Street, Mr. Sheean.

SHEEAN. All right. I'll do this: I'll take you to the warehouse and show you the statue. Will you give me a dime then?

MONAGHAN. Well . . . I'm not sayin' I would, and I'm not sayin' I wouldn't. But I'd be more likely if I saw the thing large as life, I would.

SHEEAN. [*Peeved*] All right, then. Come along.

[*Music up and down and out*]
[*Footsteps, in a warehouse . . . echo . . . they come to a halt.*]
Now then. Do you see the Statue of Liberty or don't you see it?

MONAGHAN. I see it all right, but it's all broke!

SHEEAN. *Broke!* They brought it from France on a boat. They had to take it apart, didn't they?

Literary Analysis
Dramatic Speeches
What characteristics of Monaghan do these lines of dialogue reveal?

Vocabulary Builder
peeved (pēvd) *adj.* irritated; annoyed

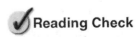Reading Check

What does Sheean want from Monaghan?

MONAGHAN. You got a secondhand statue, that's what you got, and I'm not payin' for new when they've shipped us something that's all smashed to pieces.

SHEEAN. Now just a minute, just a minute. Visualize what I'm about to tell you, Monaghan, get the picture of it. When this statue is put together it's going to stand ten stories high. Could they get a thing ten stories high into a four-story building such as this is? Use your good sense, now Monaghan.

MONAGHAN. What's that over there?

SHEEAN. Where?

MONAGHAN. That tablet there in her hand. What's it say? July Eye Vee (IV) MDCCLXXVI . . . what . . . what's all that?

SHEEAN. That means July 4, 1776. It's in Roman numbers. Very high class.

MONAGHAN. What's the good of it? If they're going to put a sign on her they ought to put it: Welcome All. That's it. Welcome All.

▲ Critical Viewing
Why might Monaghan be unwilling to contribute after seeing these pieces of the statue? **[Infer]**

SHEEAN. They decided July 4, 1776, and July 4, 1776, it's going to be!

MONAGHAN. All right, then let them get their dime from somebody else!

SHEEAN. Monaghan!

MONAGHAN. No, sir! I'll tell you something. I didn't think there was a statue but there is. She's all broke, it's true, but she's here and maybe they can get her together. But even if they do, will you tell me what sort of a welcome to immigrants it'll be, to have a gigantic thing like that in the middle of the river and in her hand is July Eye Vee MCDVC . . . whatever it is?

SHEEAN. That's the date the country was made!

MONAGHAN. The divil with the date! A man comin' in from the sea wants a place to stay, not a date. When I come from the old country I git off at the dock and there's a feller says to me, "Would you care for a room for the night?" "I would that," I sez, and he sez, "All right then, follow me." He takes me to a rooming house. I no sooner sign me name on the register—which I was able to do even at that time—when I look around and the feller is gone clear away and took my valise[2] in the bargain. A statue anyway can't move off so fast, but if she's going to welcome let her say welcome, not this MCDC. . . .

SHEEAN. All right, then, Monaghan. But all I can say is, you've laid a disgrace on the name of Butler Street. I'll put the dime in for ya.

▼ **Critical Viewing**
What tools and equipment might be needed to reassemble the statue? **[Draw Conclusions]**

2. valise (və lēs´) *n.* small suitcase.

MONAGHAN. Don't connect me with it! It's a swindle, is all it is. In the first place, it's broke; in the second place, if they do put it up it'll come down with the first high wind that strikes it.

SHEEAN. The engineers say it'll last forever!

MONAGHAN. And I say it'll topple into the river in a high wind! Look at the inside of her. She's all hollow!

SHEEAN. I've heard everything now, Monaghan. Just about everything. Good-bye.

MONAGHAN. What do you mean, good-bye? How am I to get back to Butler Street from here?

SHEEAN. You've got legs to walk.

MONAGHAN. I'll remind you that I come on the trolley.

SHEEAN. And I'll remind you that I paid your fare and I'm not repeating the kindness.

MONAGHAN. Sheean? You've stranded me!

[*Music up and down*]

Literary Analysis
Dramatic Speeches
List three adjectives you would use to describe Monaghan based on the dialogue you have read.

Thinking About the Selection

1. **(a) Explain:** Why does Monaghan not want to give Sheean a dime? **(b) Analyze:** Do you think Monaghan really believes the statue is broken? Explain.

2. **(a) Recall:** Why does Monaghan object to the Roman numbers on the tablet the statue holds? **(b) Connect:** Do you agree with him? Explain why or why not.

3. **(a) Infer:** Judging from the dialogue, how do you think that Sheean and Monaghan know each other? **(b) Speculate:** Do you think that they are good friends? Why or why not?

4. **(a) Summarize:** List at least three excuses that Monaghan gives for not paying his dime to Sheean. **(b) Predict:** Do you think Monaghan will ever give money for the pedestal? Why or why not?

My Head Is Full of Starshine

A Monologue
Peg Kehret

My friend, Pam, says my head is full of starshine. She laughs when she says it. What she really means is that she doesn't always understand the poems I write, but she's glad that I write them. She means she recognizes that I'm not like her, but it's OK for me to be different.

Pam is <u>practical</u>. Every night before she goes to sleep, Pam makes a list of what she needs to do the next day. She puts down items like return library books and hem dress for Margo's party on Saturday. When the list is made, she numbers the items in order of importance. If it's critical, it's Number One. Pam has never had to pay an overdue fine at the library and when Saturday arrives, her dress will not only be hemmed, it will be washed, ironed, and ready to wear.

I have a long history of library fines. Twenty cents here, fifty cents there. I'm always amazed to notice that a book is overdue. It just never seems like three weeks could go by so quickly. When Saturday comes, I'll be <u>rummaging</u> frantically through my closet, hoping to find something decent to wear to the party. But I wrote a birthday poem for Margo that I like a lot. It took me two days; I think Margo will like it, too.

My mother often wonders aloud why I can't be more like Pam. Just once, according to my mother, it would be nice to know more than twenty-four hours in advance that your child is performing in a school concert. I always forget to bring home the notices, or else I write something on the back and stick them in my desk. Either way, Mom doesn't get them in time to make plans.

On my last report card, Mr. Evans, my science teacher, wrote that I am not working up to my <u>potential</u>. He said I tend to daydream, instead of paying attention in class. I have to admit that's true, especially when we were learning about insects. Pam found the unit on insects fascinating. Too

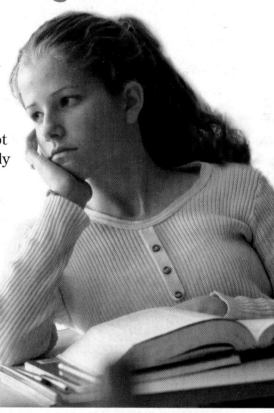

Vocabulary Builder
practical (prak´ ti kəl)
adj. level-headed; efficient; realistic

rummaging (rum´ ij iŋ)
v. searching through something

potential (pō ten´ shəl)
n. possibility; capability

fascinating, if you ask me. One day she sat beside me in the cafeteria and announced that ladybugs eat aphids, spider mites, white-flies and mealybugs.

I said, "Yuck."

Pam continued blissfully on, informing me that ladybugs eat several times their own weight in insects every day. I put down my peanut butter sandwich and told Pam that the conversation was not very appetizing, but she was so excited about ladybugs that she didn't even hear me. She just babbled on about how even the ladybug larvae eat insects and how a company in California collects the ladybugs and sells them to fruit growers, to eat the aphids off the fruit trees. I finally moved to a different table, but by then my appetite was gone.

Pam got an A in science. I only get As in English. Some kids moan and complain whenever they have to write an essay or a story, but I love assignments like that. I have a whole notebook full of ideas for stories and poems that I intend to write someday. I also have a list of good titles. My favorite title is "Magic Mud in Kansas City," but so far I haven't been able to think of a story to go with it.

I will, though. I always do. Usually it happens when I least expect it, like when I'm sitting in science class trying not to get sick as I listen to how certain animals eat their young. When Mr. Evans talks about gross things like that, I pretend my chair is a flying carpet, and I watch myself float out the window, up past the flagpole and over the trees. Sometimes I pretend that I fly beyond the moon, to a different galaxy, where I meet wonderful creatures with purple beards who ride on giant rabbits.

Maybe Pam is right. My head is full of starshine. Except for those library fines, I'm glad it is.

▼ **Critical Viewing**
Would you mind discussing a ladybug's diet while you ate your lunch? Explain. **[Connect]**

Literary Analysis
Dramatic Speech
What do the details in this paragraph tell you about the speaker?

Thinking About the Selection

1. **(a) Compare and Contrast:** How is Pam different from the speaker? **(b) Infer:** How does it make the speaker feel when Pam tells her that she has a head full of starshine? **(c) Infer:** What does this tell you about their friendship?

2. **(a) Analyze:** What do you think the last paragraph shows about the speaker's feelings about herself? **(b) Speculate:** How do you think an actor playing the role of the speaker could use body language and vocal tone to best express these feelings?

Apply the Skills

from *Grandpa and the Statue* • *My Head Is Full of Starshine*

Comparing Dramatic Speeches

1. **(a)** In a chart like the one shown, rewrite the lines of dialogue from *Grandpa and the Statue* as a monologue delivered by Sheean. **(b)** Rewrite the lines of the monologue *My Head Is Full of Starshine* as a dialogue between the speaker and Pam.

from **Grandpa and the Statue**	As a Monologue
SHEEAN. I've come to talk to you about the fund, Monaghan MONAGHAN. What fund is that? SHEEAN. The Statue of Liberty Fund. MONAGHAN. Oh, that.	

from **My Head Is Full of Starshine**	As a Dialogue
She means she recognizes that I'm not like her, but it's OK for me to be different.	

2. **(a)** Do you think you can learn more about a character from a monologue or from a dialogue? Explain. **(b)** Can you learn more about a character in a story told by a narrator? Explain.

Writing to Compare

Compare and contrast a dramatic speech in each selection. In an essay, discuss how these speeches shape your attitude toward these characters. Use these questions to get started:
- Which ideas in the speeches are familiar to you?
- With which ideas in the speeches do you agree or disagree?
- Which character do you know best? Why?

Vocabulary Builder

Practice Use the following word pairs correctly in sentences.

1. rummaging; messy
2. peeved; annoying
3. potential; success
4. practical; silly

QuickReview

Dramatic Speeches: speeches performed by actors in a drama, including *dialogue* and *monologue*

Go Online
—Assessment
For: Self-test
Visit: www.PHSchool.com
Web Code: ema-6506

Summarizing

Directions: *Read the selection. Then, answer the questions.*

[1] A strange orange glow shone through the cracks in the tool shed walls. Carrie was troubled by the spooky light she noticed as she opened the back door to let her cat out for the night. Miss Kitty, who usually sprang for freedom as soon as the door opened, hung back hesitantly.

[2] Creeping carefully but nervously toward the shed, Carrie had the feeling her curiosity might get her into trouble. Mom and Dad were scheduled to return soon from a meeting at school, and she knew she should wait and let them explore the cause of the light. Patience had never been one of her strongest virtues, though.

1. **Which detail is not important to add to a summary of paragraph 1?**
   A   an orange glow shone from shed
   B   Carrie was troubled by the light
   C   she opened the back door
   D   Miss Kitty usually sprang for freedom

2. **Which of the following is the best summary of paragraph 1?**
   A   A spooky light in the shed was frightening to Carrie and her cat.
   B   The light in the shed frightened Miss Kitty, who usually went out at night.
   C   When Carrie opened the door to let the cat out, she saw a light in the shed.
   D   Miss Kitty's behavior made it clear that something scary was in the shed.

3. **What key detail adds suspense to paragraph 2?**
   A   Carrie crept carefully.
   B   Mom and Dad were scheduled to return.
   C   She knew she should wait.
   D   Patience had never been one of her strongest virtues.

4. **What key detail should you include in a summary of paragraph 2?**
   A   Carrie is feeling nervous.
   B   Carrie is often curious.
   C   Carrie's parents are not at home.
   D   Carrie is not a patient person.

5. **Which is the best one-sentence summary of paragraph 2?**
   A   Carrie went to explore the light although she knew she should wait until her parents returned.
   B   Carrie was not able to wait until her parents returned.
   C   Carrie decided to go explore the strange orange glow.
   D   Carrie's curiosity was about to get her in trouble.

Assessment Practice

Vocabulary

Directions: *Select the best answer from the choices given.*

6. In the essay the _____ is on the problem, not the solution.
   A sequence
   B focus
   C chronology
   D summarization

7. The _____ of events in a story is the plot.
   A sequence
   B characteristic
   C detail
   D summarize

8. A _____ of science fiction is that it allows the author to build a new world.
   A characteristic
   B detail
   C sequence
   D summarized

9. When you _____ the story it helps you understand key ideas.
   A characterize
   B summarize
   C sequential
   D chronological

10. The _____ order of events is important in the plot of a mystery story.
    A sequence
    B focus
    C chronological
    D summary

Directions: *Choose the sentence that uses the underlined word correctly.*

11. A Make a <u>general</u> about friendship.
    B Make a <u>generalization</u> about friendship.
    C Make a <u>generality</u> about friendship.
    D Make a <u>generally</u> about friendship.

12. A <u>Familiar</u> yourself with the rules.
    B <u>Familiarity</u> yourself with the rules.
    C <u>Familiarize</u> yourself with the rules.
    D <u>Familiarly</u> yourself with the rules.

13. A The song is <u>popularize</u>.
    B The song is <u>popularity</u>.
    C The song is <u>popularly</u>.
    D The song is <u>popular</u>.

14. A They use <u>modernize</u> methods.
    B They use <u>modern</u> methods.
    C They <u>modern</u> methods.
    D They <u>modernizing</u> methods.

15. A This will <u>revolutionary</u> the system.
    B This will <u>revolutionize</u> the system.
    C This will <u>revolutionary</u> the system.
    D This <u>revolution</u> the system.

Plurals

Most plurals in the English language are formed according to spelling rules. You can spell the majority of plural nouns correctly if you understand and apply these rules.

Rules for Spelling Plurals

- Add -s to most nouns.
  novel/novels poem/poems dialogue/dialogues
- Add -es to nouns that end in *s, ss, sh, ch,* and *x.*
  pass/passes dash/dashes coach/coaches tax/taxes
- Change *y* to *i* and add -es to nouns that end in a consonant + *y.*
  memory/memories economy/economies
- Do not change the *y* and add -s to nouns that end in a vowel + *y.*
  play/plays key/keys
- For most nouns ending in *fe,* change the *fe* to *ve* and add -s.
  thief/thieves wife/wives

Irregular Plurals and Exceptions

- Some nouns have the same spelling in both forms.
  sheep/sheep
- Some nouns' base word spelling changes in the plural form.
  foot/feet mouse/mice
- Nouns that are not countable do not have plural forms.
  information/cash

Practice Write the singular form of each word on the Word List. Then write the plural form and explain which rule applies. Add another example for each rule or exception.

Word List

disks

characters

envelopes

boxes

classes

countries

biographies

plays

knives

information

Assessment Practice

Directions: *Choose the sentence in which the italicized word is spelled correctly.*

1. **A** The *keyes* were left in the door.
   B Sometimes the *key* are left beside the door.
   C Having extra *keys* is a good precaution.
   D Did we have a set of *keis* made?

2. **A** It is interesting to read about the *lives* of famous people.
   B Their *lifes* are different from mine.
   C It is difficult to imagine how busy their *livs* are.
   D The *lifs* of famous people aren't very private.

3. **A** The *musicianes* were well-known.
   B *Musicans* practice long hours.
   C Even after they are famous, *musicanes* must work hard.
   D *Musicians* can never forget to practice.

4. **A** We have to bake 10 *batchs* of cookies for the bake sale.
   B Several of these *batces* seem to have disappeared from the kitchen.
   C The *batcis* were all out on the table to cool.
   D Now there are extra *batches* to bake.

5. **A** We saw several *foxs* on our hike.
   B It is unusual to see *foxes* in these mountains.
   C *Foxis* tend to stay hidden from view.
   D The *foxxes* have learned to stay away from humans.

6. **A** The *Caies* are beautiful places to vacation.
   B You can snorkel at any of the *Cays*.
   C The water is calm at several of the *Cais*.
   D I intend to return to these *Cayes* next year.

7. **A** We are recording our *observationes* in science class.
   B Our *observation* are of the night sky.
   C We get to use the telescope at school for these *observationnes*.
   D Then we note our *observations* in the science log.

8. **A** I had to have *blood* taken as part of my physical examination.
   B I don't like having *bloods* taken.
   C Having *bloodes* taken scares me a little.
   D I know that taking *bloodds* is not dangerous.

9. **A** We have a lot of *homeworks* tonight.
   B I will be up for hours doing the *homeworkes*.
   C We were given *homework* in all of our classes.
   D The *homeworkks* not easy, either!

10. **A** I looked for the phone number in several *directorys*.
    B The *directoryes* were all new ones.
    C These *directores* are difficult to use.
    D In the *directories,* everything is by last name.

Exposition: Cause-and-Effect Essay

A **cause-and-effect essay** is expository writing that explains why something happens or what happens as a result of something else. A cause-and-effect essay might focus on causes, such as why the days get shorter in the fall, or on effects, such as what will happen if you do not wear sunscreen. Follow the steps in this workshop to write your own cause-and-effect essay.

Assignment Write a cause-and-effect essay about a question or issue that interests you.

What to Include Your essay should feature the following elements:
- a well-defined topic that can be covered in a few pages
- information gathered from reference materials and resources
- detailed, factual explanations of events or situations and the relationships among them
- a clear organization with transitions that indicate the relationships among details
- error-free writing, including correct subject-verb agreement

To preview the criteria on which your cause-and-effect essay may be judged, see the rubric on page 805.

Using the Form
You may use elements of this form in these types of writing:
- lab reports
- persuasive essays
- magazine articles
- speeches
- historical accounts

Writing Workshop: *Work in Progress*

If you have completed the Work-in-Progress assignments, you have ideas to use in your cause-and-effect essay. Continue to develop these ideas or explore a new idea as you complete the Writing Workshop.

Reading \ Writing
Connection

To get the feel for cause-and-effect writing, read "Life Without Gravity" by Robert Zimmerman on page 372.

Prewriting

Choosing Your Topic

To choose a good topic for your essay, use one of these strategies:

- **Brainstorming** Sometimes the best way to find a topic is to just start writing. Write for five minutes about whatever questions come to mind. Use phrases such as "What causes . . ." or "Why does . . ." to begin each question. Circle any questions that could make a good topic.

- **Imagine a Walk** Close your eyes and imagine yourself walking through a house, apartment, or other place you know well. Observe the objects, people, or activities that you "see" along the way. To find items that suggest cause-and-effect relationships, ask, "What caused this?" or "What effects does this have?" Jot down several ideas and then choose your topic from these items.

Work in Progress
Review the work you did on page 779.

Narrowing Your Topic

A topic with many causes and effects, such as the causes and effects of storms, is far too broad. Instead, narrow your topic to focus on a single cause or a single effect. For example, the effects of a tornado—a single cause—would be appropriate. Use a web like the one shown to narrow your topic. Write your topic in the center and surround it by subtopics. Then, note causes or effects connected to each subtopic. Consider whether any of the subtopics would make a good focus for your essay.

Gathering Details

Conduct research. Do research to fill in any gaps in your knowledge. Use library resources, online references, or interview an expert on the topic. Use a two-column chart to help you gather details. In one column, list the causes involved in your event or situation. In the other column, list the effects.

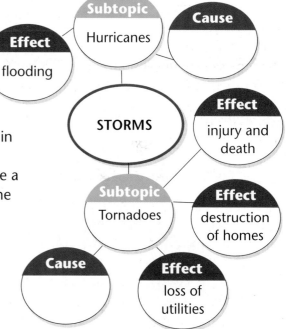

Drafting

Shaping Your Writing

Organize logically. Before you begin the body of your essay, decide how you want to organize your details. Use these suggestions:

- If you are writing about a single event with many causes, devote one paragraph to each cause and one paragraph to the effect.
- If you are writing about a single cause with many effects, devote a paragraph to each effect.
- If you are writing about a series of causes and effects, organize your paragraphs in chronological, or time, order.

Write a strong introduction. Your introduction is the first thing your audience will read. Include a sentence or two explaining the importance of your topic and then identify the main points you will make in your essay.

Providing Elaboration

Explain causes and effects. Prove the cause-and-effect relationships you describe. As you draft, explain the logic of each cause-and-effect relationship you present. Use specific statistics, dates, names, or places whenever possible.

Use the SEE Technique. For each main idea you identify, use the SEE technique to add depth to your essay. First, write a statement. Next, write a sentence that extends the idea. Finally, write a sentence that elaborates on the extension.

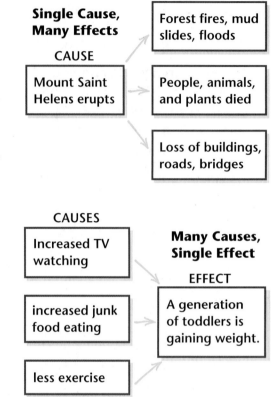

To read the complete student model, see page 804.

Student Model: Using SEE to Elaborate	
Statement:	Many people say that cell phones cause a disturbance.
Extension:	You cannot go on a train or be in a mall without constantly hearing phone rings and other people's conversations.
Elaboration:	The effect of this is that more people are stressed and being disturbed by cell phones.

Sarah states the main idea, extends it with examples, and elaborates on it by explaining the effect.

From the Author's Desk

Laurence Yep
on Showing Causes and Effects

Laurence Yep

I often get asked what caused me to write *Dragonwings*, and the passage that follows is from an article that I wrote about it. The revisions show how much work I do on a draft. Mark Twain once said, "The difference between the almost right word and the right word is . . . the difference between the lightning bug and the lightning." As you'll see, I tried to find the "right word" to show what inspired me to write this novel.

> *" . . . it takes me a minimum of seven drafts . . ."*
> ———Laurence Yep

Professional Model:

from "A Cord to the Past"

As a writer and as an individual, I have been drawn to the stories of those Chinese Americans who have learned to live with a kind of grace on the borderland between two cultures. . . . What first ~~attracted~~ ∧drew me to the story of Fung Joe Guey, the Chinese American aviator, was the scope of his mind. ∧Here was a Chinese American who ~~He~~ had built and flown his own airplane just six years after the Wright brothers had flown at Kitty Hawk. In fact, I did not incorporate all of his real mechanical achievements in the novel, *Dragonwings*—which included his own telephone system. When his ~~imaginary~~ ∧fictional counterpart, Windrider, dreams that he is a dragon, it was symbolic of Fung Joe Guey's own imagination: that ability to grasp with the mind and heart what he could not grasp with the hand.

I substituted "drew" for "attracted" because I wanted to indicate the effect of Fung Joe Guey's life on me, how compelled I was to write the story.

I reversed the word order to emphasize his specialness. The normal order would only make it a statement of fact.

I changed "imaginary" to "fictional" because I used "imagination" shortly afterwards. I didn't want to sound repetitive.

Revising

Revising Your Paragraphs

State main ideas clearly. Simply by starting a new paragraph, you signal readers that a new idea is coming up. Effective writers state the main idea in each paragraph clearly. To analyze the connections among your other sentences, use color-coding.

Reread each paragraph. Use two highlighters—one color to mark phrases that present causes and another to mark those that discuss effects. Evaluate the connections between the two. Go back and add transitions such as *because of* and *as a result* to help readers see cause-and-effect connections.

To read the complete student model, see page 804.

Student Model: Color-Coding Causes and Effects

Cell phones have caused a change in our economy. Although the cost of cell phones has gone down greatly over the years, they are still very expensive. As a result, for families that are not very wealthy, owning a cell phone might affect their income badly. However, loads of money is coming in to phone companies every month from cell phone bills.

> Sarah added a transition to make a better connection.

Peer Review: Ask a classmate to review your draft to help you determine whether you have logical cause-and-effect links.

Revising Your Sentences

Use the appropriate verb tense. Generally, you should use one verb tense consistently throughout your paper. However, to show the order of events, you may need to shift tenses. Review your draft to determine the tense of most of your verbs. Circle any verbs that are in a different tense. If these verbs do not show events happening at different times or show a recurring event, consider changing them.

> EVENTS AT DIFFERENT TIMES:
>   past
> Because I **missed** my math test
>   present
> yesterday, I **need to** take it today.
>
> EVENTS THAT RECUR:
>   past   present
> Last week, I **missed** French. Because I **leave** school early
>   present
> on Wednesdays, I **miss** one class every week.

Integrating Grammar Skills

Correcting Subject-Verb Agreement With Compound Subjects

Incorrect subject-verb agreement occurs whenever a subject disagrees with its verb in number.

Identifying Compound Subjects A compound subject consists of two subjects joined by a conjunction such as *and, or,* or *nor.* When the subjects joined are plural, they take a plural verb. When the subjects joined are singular, the following rules will help you make sure that a compound subject agrees with its verb.

Prentice Hall Writing and Grammar Connection: Chapter 24, Section 1

Two or more singular subjects joined by *and* take a plural verb.

> **Example:** *Swimming **and** tennis* **are** both fun sports.

Two or more singular subjects joined by *or* or *nor* take a singular verb.

> **Example:** *A swimming lesson **or** a tennis lesson* **is** good exercise.
> *Neither a swimming lesson **nor** a tennis lesson* **is** a waste of time.

When singular and plural subjects are joined by *or* or *nor*, the verb must agree with the closer subject.

> **Example:** Neither the *roast* **nor** the *potatoes* **are** cooking.
> Concert *tickets* **or** a fancy *dinner* **is** a great gift.

Fixing Subject-Verb Agreement To fix subject-verb agreement with compound subjects, first identify whether the subjects joined by *and, or,* or *nor* are singular or plural. Then use one of the following methods.

1. **If the subjects joined are plural, use a plural verb.**
2. **If the subjects are singular and joined by *and*, use a plural verb.** See the example above.
3. **If the subjects are singular and joined by *or* or *nor*, use a singular verb.** See the examples above.
4. **If singular and plural subjects are joined by *or* or *nor*, the verb agrees with the closer subject.** See examples above.

Apply It to Your Editing

Choose two paragraphs in your draft. Underline any subjects joined by *and, or,* or *nor.* Then, circle the verb for each. If the subject does not agree with its verb, fix the subject-verb agreement using one of the methods above.

Student Model: Sarah Langsam
South Orange, NJ

The Invention of Cell Phones

Imagine our world today without cell phones. This portable way of communicating is a part of many people's everyday lives. If we did not have cell phones, moms would not be able to call from the store, more kids might have trouble staying in touch, and emergencies would be harder to report.

Sarah defines her topic in the first paragraph.

However people did, and still do, manage without them. Cell phones weren't invented that long ago. In 1973, Dr. Martin Cooper invented the first portable handset and soon after created the first prototype of a cellular phone. Four years later, cell phones became available to the public and cell phone testing began.

Sarah uses facts in her explanation.

What effect has the invention of cell phones had on the world? With everything in life there are pros and cons. Today, most teenagers own cell phones. This means there is no excuse for not letting a parent or guardian know where you are or for not having your cell phone charged. And of course the most important thing is never to lose your phone.

Sarah restates her topic and begins to support it with examples.

Cell phones have caused a change in our economy. Although the cost of cell phones has gone down greatly over the years, they are still very expensive. As a result, for families that are not very wealthy, owning a cell phone might affect their income badly. However, loads of money is coming in to phone companies every month from cell phone bills.

Many people say that cell phones cause a disturbance. You cannot go on a train or shop in a mall without constantly hearing phone rings and listening to other people's conversations. The effect of this is that more people are stressed and being disturbed by cell phones. A teacher in school left her cell phone at school over the weekend. She was in the office on Monday recalling her story angrily, reporting that it was an awful experience and that she could not function without her phone.

Sarah gives an example to show that cell phones can be disturbing.

Although there are many negative aspects of cell phones, these items have also caused our world to be more secure. If you ask people why they first bought their cell phone, many will mention safety. Cell phones are very effective when people get into car accidents and can call "911" immediately. Parents can always know where their kids are.

The invention of cell phones has changed our lives immensely. There are positive and negative effects. However, despite the nuisance some cell phones present, I believe the safety issues cell phones solve can make us all feel a little more secure.

Sarah sums up the effects of cell phones in her conclusion.

Editing and Proofreading

Review your draft to eliminate errors.

Focus on Unnecessary Words: In good writing, saying something in a few words is more effective than saying it with a lot of words. Review your work to cut out these types of unnecessary language:

> **Repetition:** The hazy sky was heavy *and hazy.*
>
> **Filler Phrases:** It is, *in fact,* a surprise.

Publishing and Presenting

Consider one of the following ways to share your writing:
Present a diagram. On a posterboard or an overhead slide, create a diagram of the cause-and-effect chain in your essay. Read your essay aloud, pointing out appropriate parts of the diagram as you go.
Produce a talk show. Work with a partner, taking turns being a talk-show host and a guest expert. Answer questions about your topic. Then, ask questions about your partner's topic.

Reflecting on Your Writing

Writer's Journal Jot down your thoughts on the experience of writing a cause-and-effect essay. Begin by answering these questions:

- Which prewriting strategy was most useful for generating a topic?
- What was the most interesting thing you learned when writing?

> *Prentice Hall Writing and Grammar Connection: Chapter 9*

Rubric for Self-Assessment

To assess your cause-and-effect essay, use the following rubric:

Criteria	Rating Scale
	not very → *very*
Focus: How well is your topic defined?	1 2 3 4 5
Organization: How organized is your information from reference materials?	1 2 3 4 5
Support/Elaboration: How well do your facts explain the relationship between events?	1 2 3 4 5
Style: How smooth are the transitions between elements?	1 2 3 4 5
Conventions: How correct is your word usage?	1 2 3 4 5

Evaluating Media Messages

Every day you are bombarded with media messages—commercials, news, and announcements, to name just a few. It is important to **analyze media messages**—to actively and critically evaluate what you hear and see. Use these strategies in your analysis.

Analyzing Effects

Even when you are sitting passively, the sounds, images, and words in media messages affect you. Be aware of these effects.

Analyze images. First consider what you see. Ask yourself questions: Is it realistic or imaginary? Colorful or muted? Fast- or slow-paced? Is the focus on people, places, or things? Look carefully at what you see and ask yourself what the message behind the image is.

Analyze text. Consider what is not said, as well as what is. "Dentists recommend this toothpaste" does not tell you *how many* dentists recommend it.

Analyze sound. In addition to the words, notice the music and sound effects that you hear and the mood that they create.

Identifying Techniques

- **Slant and Bias** Beware of any message that presents only one side of an issue that has many different sides.
- **Bandwagon** Watch out for any message that suggests that everyone is doing something and that you will be unpopular if you do not do it.
- **Spokespersons** Just because a celebrity or an expert delivers a message does not make it sound. Ask yourself if the person has the knowledge or background to make the advice significant.
- **Purpose** Identify the *goal* of something you are watching. Some messages are attempts to sell you something. Others are attempts to convince you of the value of participating in some activity—such as watching more television!

Evaluation Form for Media Messages

Effects
What are the key images?
What are the key words?
What sounds do you hear?

Techniques
Is there a slant or bias?
Is there a bandwagon approach?
Who is the spokesperson?
What is the purpose?

How would you rate the credibility of this message?
___ Excellent ___Good ___Fair ___Poor

Give a reason for your rating: _____

Activity ▸ **Evaluate Media** With a partner, videotape a commercial aimed at young people. Together, write a short analysis of its message using the terms defined above as a guide. Present your analysis to the class.

A Tale of Two Cities

Charles Dickens
Pacemaker Classic, 1993

Novel This is a story of people caught in the French Revolution, a changing world where no one is safe in the relative quiet of England. The characters' lives are all changed by the time and place they live in. Some escape with their lives. Some face the guillotine.

Don't Tell Anyone

Peg Kehret
Puffin, 2000

Novel Megan loves animals and is determined to save the stray cats when their field is bulldozed. She is grateful for the stranger who offers to help rescue the cats. But Megan begins receiving threatening notes and her world becomes dangerous. Soon Megan has to save not only the cats, but herself.

The Mousetrap and Other Plays

Agatha Christie
Penguin Putnam, 2000

Plays The reader is front row center to murder as a homicidal maniac stalks the snowbound guests of an imposing manor. Or, witness the diabolical delight of a secret killer as a group of strangers gathers on an isolated island. All of these mysteries are solved to perfection by the Queen of Crime at her royal best.

A Christmas Carol and Other Christmas Stories

Charles Dickens
Signet, 1984

Short Stories *A Christmas Carol,* Dickens's most beloved story, is a heartwarming tale that continues to stir in everyone the same feelings of repentance, forgiveness, and love that transformed Scrooge. Dickens's other stories in this collection also evoke the gloom of those who isolate themselves from humanity and the joy of those who raise a wassail cup to goodwill toward men.

These titles are available in the Penguin/Prentice Hall Literature Library.
Consult your teacher before choosing one.

Think About It If you have never lived in a city, it might be hard to imagine a place without trees. In her writing, Sandra Cisneros captures the feelings of a young girl living in the city and her thoughts about the four trees outside of her urban home. The following selection is a portion of the book *The House on Mango Street,* which reveals a specific character in a city neighborhood through a collection of vignettes, or short descriptive works.

Four Skinny Trees

Sandra Cisneros

They are the only ones who understand me. I am the only one who understands them. Four skinny trees with skinny necks and pointy elbows like mine. Four who do not belong here but are here. Four raggedy excuses planted by the city. From our room we can hear them, but Nenny just sleeps and doesn't appreciate these things.

Their strength is secret. They send ferocious roots beneath the ground. They grow up and they grow down and grab the earth between their hairy toes and bite the sky with violent teeth and never quit their anger. This is how they keep.

Let one forget his reason for being, they'd all droop like tulips in a glass, each with their arms around the other. Keep, keep, keep, trees say when I sleep. They teach.

When I am too sad and too skinny to keep keeping, when I am a tiny thing against so many bricks, then it is I look at trees. When there is nothing left to look at on this street. Four who grew despite concrete. Four who reach and do not forget to reach. Four whose only reason is to be and be.

Meet the Author

Sandra Cisneros (b. 1954) was born and raised in Chicago. Because her parents were born in Mexico, she grew up speaking English and Spanish. She writes both poetry and fiction about subjects she knows best—memories of her childhood and her Mexican heritage.

Readings in Contemporary Fiction
Talk About It

Use these questions to guide a discussion of "Four Skinny Trees."

1. **(a)** Where are the "Four Skinny Trees" located? **(b)** How do you know the location of the trees?

2. **(a)** The speaker says that she can "hear" the trees from her room. What does this reveal about the speaker's feelings toward the trees? **(b)** What places or things in nature spark this feeling in you?

3. According to "Four Skinny Trees," what lessons can the trees teach? Break into small groups to consider the following questions:
   - To the speaker, what physical attributes of trees show strength?
   - What do these physical attributes suggest about the "personality" of the trees?
   - What is the ultimate lesson that the trees teach the speaker?
   - What message about our relationship to nature does this selection demonstrate? Do you agree with it?

   Choose a point-person to share your group's ideas with the class.

Themes in the Oral Tradition

Unit 6 Overview

Introduction
Exploring Themes
in the Oral Tradition

Part 1: Cause and Effect

Part 2: Comparison and
Contrast

Introduction:
Themes in the Oral Tradition

Jon
Scieszka

Jon Scieszka
Talks About Storytelling

I love to mess around with different forms of storytelling. Some of the oldest forms of storytelling—**myths**, **legends**, **fables**, and **fairy tales**—have been around since before writing even existed.

▲ Jon Scieszka entertains readers of all ages with his wild, zany, and hilarious versions of traditional fables and tales.

Stories in the Oral Tradition

These types of stories were told from person to person. They were stories good enough, wise enough, and entertaining enough to be retold for thousands of years. They are part of our **oral tradition** of storytelling. I'm always amazed that these stories are still with us. So of course these are the kind of stories I like to goof up most.

As a kid I found in these tales a whole crazy world of wolves eating grandmas, talking animals, gods and goddesses, heroes and fools. I think I knew even then that there was something old and powerful about these stories.

Now, I do research by reading collections of fairy tales like the one I quote from on the next page. I read collections like these to learn as many different variations of tales as I can, and to learn about the history of stories.

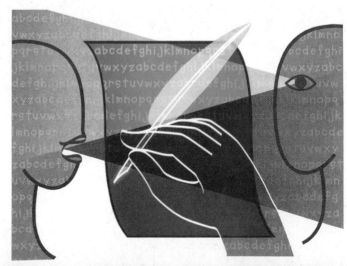

▶ Critical Viewing Which details in this picture suggest stories that are told from person to person as part of the oral tradition? **[Connect]**

Learning to Use Humor

Before I published any of my own stories, I taught elementary school in New York City. That's where I got to see what makes a story good enough to hook its audience. Telling stories to my students was how I also learned to use humor. I found humor kept my older listeners connected . . . and kept my first-grade listeners from rolling around on the floor and picking their noses.

When I took off from teaching to write my own stories, my idea was to use the old forms of storytelling, but to tweak and twist them in a new, funny way. In this way I see myself continuing the oral tradition—telling stories that entertain listeners of today but also connecting them with stories that have been told for ages.

Fairy tales had their origins in an adult oral storytelling culture, where tales were told to shorten the time devoted to . . . household chores that required physical concentration but left the mind open to wander and daydream . . . they were stories that made listeners sit up and pay attention . . .

from *The Annotated Brothers Grimm*
—Maria Tatar

Jon **Scieszka** (b. 1954)

Jon Scieszka, whose name is pronounced SHESS ka, says his "audience is hardcore silly kids, and there are a lot of 'em out there." Often working with illustrator Lane Smith, Scieszka goes all out to please this audience. In *The Stinky Cheese Man and Other Fairly Stupid Tales*, for example, he includes such tales as "Little Red Riding Shorts" and "The Not So Ugly Duckling." What prompts Scieszka to mess up stories everyone knows? He confesses, "I love to make kids laugh."

Fast Facts

▶ Before he began writing books, Scieszka worked as a house painter and lifeguard, as well as a teacher.

▶ One of his favorite books is also one of the first that he ever read, Dr. Seuss's *Green Eggs and Ham*. It showed him "that books could be goofy."

Learning About Themes in the Oral Tradition

Characteristics of the Oral Tradition

Gods and goddesses, talking animals, strange and wondrous events—these are some of the elements of myths, legends, folk tales, and other stories passed down through generations. Although writers retell these stories in print, most of these tales originated long before reading and writing began. They have survived by being handed down through the ages through what is called the **oral tradition**—the sharing of stories, cultures, and ideas by word of mouth. People used these traditional stories to communicate shared beliefs and to explain their world. Here are common characteristics you will see when studying the oral tradition.

Theme is a central idea, message, or insight that is revealed within a story. A **universal theme** is an idea that is repeated across many cultures and throughout many time periods.

A **moral** is a lesson about life that is taught by a story.

PEANUTS reprinted by permission of United Feature Syndicate, Inc.

Heroes and **heroines** are larger-than-life figures whose virtues and deeds are often celebrated in stories from the oral tradition.

Storytelling calls on the talents and personality of the teller to bring the narrative to life. Some stories in the oral tradition call on the reteller to use these common techniques:

- **Hyperbole:** using exaggeration or overstatement, either for comic effect or to express heightened emotion
- **Personification:** giving human characteristics to nonhuman subjects, such as animals or elements of nature
- **Allusion:** reference to a well-known person, place, event, literary work, or work of art

The Oral Tradition in Print

After generations of oral retellings, many stories have been written down for readers. Here are the categories of such stories.

- **Myths** are tales that explain the actions of gods, goddesses, and the heroes who interact with them. Every culture has its own collection of myths, or **mythology**, and these stories often attempt to explain the causes of natural phenomena.

- **Legends** are traditional stories about the past. They are based on real-life events but over generations of retellings, legends often twist fact into fiction and feature larger-than-life people.

- **Folk tales** tell stories about ordinary people. These stories reveal the traditions and values of a culture and teach a lesson.

- **Tall tales** are types of folk tales that often use **hyperbole**— deliberate overstatement—for comic effect. Tall tales often focus on a central hero who performs impossible feats.

- **Fables** are brief stories featuring animals that speak and act like humans. Fables often end with a moral that is directly stated.

- **Epics** are long narrative poems about a larger-than-life hero who engages in a dangerous journey, or **quest**, that is important to the history of a nation or culture.

Check Your Understanding

For each item, indicate which term best applies.

1. A story about the Greek god Zeus
   a. fable   **b.** myth

2. A narrative poem about the voyage of a great explorer
   a. legend   **b.** epic

3. A story in which a fox outsmarts a crow, then teases him
   a. fable   **b.** myth

▼ Critical Viewing
What kind of a story would you expect to be set in a place like this? **[Speculate]**

From the Author's Desk
Jon Scieszka Introduces His Work

I grew up watching cartoons and reading comic books at the same time I was reading history, science, and school books. And I think that the mix of comic book and cartoon style with more traditional kinds of storytelling is a big part of the **humor** in my writing.

Twisting Fairy Tales

When I first thought about twisting **fairy tales** for the book that eventually became *The Stinky Cheese Man,* I started by messing up the process of storytelling in as many different ways as possible. I wrote stories with no beginning, stories with no ending, stories with unexpected endings, stories that go backwards, and stories that go nowhere.

"The Other Frog Prince," for example, is a story with an unexpected ending. It's told in the classic form of a joke: The audience is expecting the story to go in one direction, but it suddenly turns in a completely opposite direction.

Fables: Annoying, Weird People Disguised as Animals

The idea for using **fables** to tell funny stories came to me one day when my daughter, Casey, was telling me stories about her friends and classmates. I had been reading Aesop's Fables. And it struck me that I could do the same thing as Aesop—write about all of those annoying, weird, mean kinds of people we all know . . . but change them into animals so they wouldn't know I was writing about them.

So the Squid character in *Squids Will Be Squids* is that irritating friend who never wants to do anything and never makes any suggestions of her own. Grasshopper is every one of us who ever put off doing homework. BeefSnakStik® is the guy who always thinks he's so great just because he's got a lot of stuff.

— THE END OF THE BEGINNING —

Grasshopper Logic

from Squids Will be Squids

JON SCIESZKA AND LANE SMITH

One bright and sunny day, Grasshopper came home from school, dropped his backpack, and was just about to run outside to meet his friends.

"Where are you going?" asked his mom.

"Out to meet some friends," said Grasshopper.

"Do you have any homework due tomorrow?" asked his mom.

"Just one small thing for History. I did the rest in class."

"Okay" said Mom Grasshopper. "Be back at six for dinner."

Grasshopper hung out with his friends, came home promptly at six, ate his dinner, then took out his History homework.

His mom read the assignment and freaked out.

"Rewrite twelve Greek myths as Broadway musicals. Write music for songs. Design and build all sets. Sew original costumes for each production."

"How long have you known about this assignment?" asked Mom Grasshopper, trying not to scream.

"I don't know," said Grasshopper.

▲ Critical Viewing
What emotion does the grasshopper in this illustration show? **[Draw Conclusions]**

Jon Scieszka
Author's Insight
This is a thinly disguised story of my son Jake. Only the character's name was changed to protect the not-so-innocent.

MORAL
There are plenty of things to say to calm a hopping mad Grasshopper mom. "I don't know" is not one.

THE OTHER FROG PRINCE

title

Myrmeleon formicarius

Pompilus viaticus

fly

fly

Bombus terrestris

Geometridæ

fly

hyssa

fly

Fla

fly

Locustidæ

fly

The Other Frog Prince

from The Stinky Cheese Man
and Other Fairly Stupid Tales

JON SCIESZKA AND LANE SMITH

Once upon a time there was a frog.

One day when he was sitting on his lily pad, he saw a beautiful princess sitting by the pond. He hopped in the water, swam over to her, and poked his head out of the weeds.

fly

◄ **Critical Viewing**
What symbol of royalty can you find in this illustration? **[Interpret]**

Themes in the Oral Tradition
Fable The frog speaks to the princess as though he is human.

Jon Scieszka
Author's Insight
In the original tale, the princess throws the frog against a wall to change him. I used the kiss version for a funnier ending. I added THE END after reading to my son's kindergarten class. Otherwise, they didn't know when these strange stories were finished.

"Pardon me, O beautiful princess," he said in his most sad and pathetic voice. "I wonder if you could help me."

The princess was about to jump up and run, but she felt sorry for the frog with the sad and pathetic voice.

So she asked, "What can I do to help you, little frog?"

"Well," said the frog. "I'm not really a frog, but a handsome prince who was turned into a frog by a wicked witch's spell. And the spell can only be broken by the kiss of a beautiful princess."

The princess thought about this for a second, then lifted the frog from the pond and kissed him.

"I was just kidding," said the frog. He jumped back into the pond and the princess wiped the frog slime off her lips.

The End.

duckbilled platypus
vs.
beefsnakstik®

from Squids Will be Squids

JON SCIESZKA AND LANE SMITH

"I have a bill like a duck and a tail like a beaver," bragged Duckbilled Platypus.

"So what?" said BeefSnakStik®. "I have beef, soy protein concentrate, and dextrose."

"I also have webbed feet and fur," said Duckbilled Platypus.

"Who cares?" said BeefSnakStik®. "I also have smoke flavoring, sodium erythorbate, and sodium nitrite.

"I am one of only two mammals in the world that lay eggs," said Duckbilled Platypus.

"Big deal," said BeefSnakStik®. "I have beef lips."

▲ **Critical Viewing**
How does the tie add humor to the picture? **[Interpret]**

Jon Scieszka
Author's Insight
All of the science in the book is accurate. The other mammal that lays eggs is the Echidna (a character in another fable).

MORAL
Just because you have a lot of stuff, don't think you're so special.

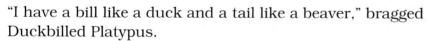

From the Author's Desk
Jon Scieszka's Insights Into His Work

Q. What would be another way to "twist" the Frog fairy tale?

A. I twisted it once by starting the story after "They lived happily ever after." It could be very funny to have both frog and princess turn into something else—like the pumpkin and the rat from Cinderella. Or maybe the frog could turn into something worse, like a sea cucumber, or a naked mole rat, or a fungus, or . . .

Q. Why did you choose a grasshopper to avoid doing homework?

A. In one of Aesop's classic fables, the Grasshopper is the guy who fools around all summer dancing and singing while the ants work hard storing food. I decided to use the same animal for the same kind of character who plays around first and works later. I just updated him with a modern problem.

Q. How important is the way your fables look on the page?

A. The illustrations and designs of my picture book stories are easily half of the story. The illustrations tell the reader right away that these stories are different. The design decisions (like the type growing larger) show more of the characters' personalities. I work closely with my illustrator and designer to make sure the three of us are all telling one story.

Student Corner

Q. Why would any princess even think about kissing a frog?
—Sam Brown, Warwick, New York

A. In most of the Frog Prince stories, the princess promises to be nice to the frog if he retrieves her favorite golden ball that she accidentally dropped in the water. I guess it just goes to show you never know what crazy thing you might promise when you lose something and panic.

 Writing Workshop: *Work in Progress*

Business Letter

For a business letter that you might write, imagine you are planning an elaborate party. Create a Wish List of five places where you would like to host a party. Keep the Wish List in your writing portfolio.

Learning About Themes in the Oral Tradition

Thinking About the Selections

1. **Respond:** Which tale is your favorite? Why?

2. **(a) Recall:** In "Grasshopper Logic," where is Grasshopper going? **(b) Infer:** Why does Grasshopper call his history assignment "small"? **(c) Generalize:** What makes the details of his assignment so funny?

3. **(a) Describe:** What tone of voice does the frog use with the princess? **(b) Compare:** Does the frog have the same attitude or tone of voice as BeefSnakStik®? Explain. **(c) Interpret:** What do you think makes these characters funny?

Oral Tradition Review

4. **(a)** Complete a chart like the one shown by listing examples of **hyperbole** and **personification** in each **fable**. **(b)** Compare your examples with a partner. How has your understanding of each fable grown or changed?

Fable	Hyperbole	Personification
Grasshopper Logic		
The Other Frog Prince		
duckbilled platypus vs. beefsnakstik®		

5. **(a)** What makes the moral of each fable funny? **(b)** What do you think is the **theme** or message of each fable? Explain.

Research the Author

Using the Internet and library resources, create a **bulletin board display** of Jon Scieszka's life and work. Follow these steps:

- Locate a Web page or home page for the writer on the Internet. Download information about his family, education, and other books.
- Include the names of the illustrators of Scieszka's books, along with examples of their work.
- Write a brief summary of the books you have chosen for the bulletin board.

QuickReview

Fables at a Glance

In "**Grasshopper Logic,**" a grasshopper annoys his mother over a homework assignment. In "**The Other Frog Prince,**" a frog strikes up a conversation with a princess. A talking beefstick describes what he's made of in "**duckbilled platypus vs. beefsnakstik®.**"

—Assessment

For: Self-test
Visit: www.PHSchool.com
Web Code: ema-6601

Fable: a brief story with animals that speak and act like humans

Theme: a central idea or insight in a story

Moral: a lesson about life

Hyperbole: using exaggeration for comic effect

Personification: giving human characteristics to nonhuman subjects

Unit 6
Part 1
Cause and Effect

Skills You Will Learn

Reading Skill: *Ask Questions to Analyze Cause-and-Effect Relationships*
Literary Analysis: *Myth*

Reading Skill: *Skimming and Scanning for Details That Show Cause and Effect*

Reading Skill: *Reread to Look for Connections*
Literary Analysis: *Legend and Fact*

Literary Analysis: *Comparing Treatment of Epic Conventions*

Literature You Will Read

Reading: Cause and Effect

> A **cause** is an event or a situation that produces a result. An **effect** is the result produced.

Skills and Strategies You Will Learn in Part 1

- to **ask questions to analyze cause-and-effect relationships**. (p. 826)
- to **reread to look for connections** among words and sentences. (p. 848)
- to **skim and scan** for **cause-and-effect** details. (p. 844)

Using the Skills and Strategies in Part 1

In Part 1, you will learn to ask questions that will help you find and evaluate cause-and-effect relationships. You will practice rereading to find cause-and-effect connections. You will also skim and scan to find details that support your ideas about cause and effect.

Use a chart like the one shown as you identify cause-and-effect relationships.

Ask Questions Like These	Reread For Clue Words Like These	
• What happened?	• because	• as a result of
• What will happen as a result of this?	• due to	• therefore
• Why did this happen?	• for this reason	

As you read the literature in this part, you will practice analyzing cause-and-effect relationships.

Academic Vocabulary: Words for Discussing Cause and Effect

The following words will help you write and talk about cause and effect as you read the selections in this unit.

Word	Definition	Example Sentence
effect *n.*	something that occurs as a direct result of an action	One *effect* of the storm was that houses flooded.
affect *v.*	have an effect on someone or something	Connotation *affects* the way a reader responds to a work.
consequence *n.*	something that follows as a result of something else	A *consequence* is the effect of an action or a series of actions.
occur *v.*	happen or come about	The reader expects unusual events to *occur* in a science-fiction novel.
alter *v.*	adjust or make changes to	To *alter* the plot, the writer added a character.

Vocabulary Skill: Denotation and Connotation

A word's **denotation** is its strict, literal meaning, or the definition you find in a dictionary. The **connotations** of a word are the meanings and feelings generally associated with the word.

Some words have positive connotations. Others have negative connotations. Some words are neutral.

Word	Denotation	Connotation	Sentence
alter	modify, adjust	NEUTRAL	The news *altered* her mood.
transform	change in form	POSITIVE	The news *transformed* her.

Activity Copy the chart. Add the following words and complete each section for each word.

1. thrifty   2. cheap   3. insinuate

These skills will help you become a better reader. Practice them with either "Icarus and Daedalus" (p. 828) or "Demeter and Persephone" (p. 835).

Reading Skill

A **cause** is an event, action, or feeling that produces a result. That result is called an **effect**. In some literary works, multiple causes result in a single effect. In other works, a single cause results in multiple effects. Effects can also become causes for events that follow. This linking of causes and effects propels the action forward.

As you read, **ask questions to analyze cause-and-effect relationships.** Ask yourself questions like these:

- What happened? Why?
- What will happen as a result of this?

Use a chart like the one shown to record your answers.

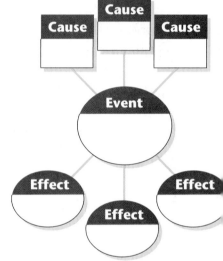

Literary Analysis

Since time began, people have tried to understand the world around them. Ancient peoples created **myths**—stories that explain natural occurrences and express beliefs about right and wrong.

Every culture has its own collection of myths, or *mythology*. In many of these myths, gods and goddesses have human traits, while human heroes possess superhuman traits. Myths explore universal themes and explain the world in human terms.

Vocabulary Builder

Icarus and Daedalus

- **vacancy** (vā´ kən sē) *n.* emptiness (p. 830) *The drummer quit, leaving a vacancy in the band.*

- **sustained** (sə stānd´) *adj.* supported (p. 831) *I felt sustained by the snack until dinner.*

Demeter and Persephone

- **defies** (dē fīz´) *v.* resists or opposes boldly or openly (p. 835) *She defies the law by driving too fast.*

- **intervene** (in´ tər vēn´) *v.* come between as an influence to modify, settle, or hinder some action or argument (p. 837) *My mother will intervene in the fight between my brothers.*

Build Understanding • *Icarus and Daedalus*

Background

Greek Mythology The ancient Greeks believed in a complex collection of gods and goddesses, ruled by Zeus. Zeus ruled with his wife, Hera, from atop Mount Olympus. Beneath Zeus in rank were many lesser gods and goddesses, each linked to ideas or qualities in nature. The ancient Greeks believed that the gods taught lessons to people who were too proud or arrogant. As you read this myth, consider the lesson that Daedalus needs to learn.

Connecting to the Literature

Reading/Writing Connection Some myths teach lessons about right and wrong. Think of a lesson that you have learned about the right way to live or act. Jot down three sentences that describe this lesson. Use at least three of these words: *adapt, complicate, eliminate, modify.*

Meet the Author

Josephine Preston Peabody (1874–1922)

Josephine Preston Peabody was born in Brooklyn, New York, and moved with her family to Massachusetts when she was ten years old. Since both of her parents loved literature and the theater, it is no surprise that Peabody learned to love reading and writing as a child. Her talent became obvious at an early age. She published a poem in *The Women's Journal* when she was fourteen and her first book—*Old Greek Folk-Stories told Anew*—when she was twenty-three. "Icarus and Daedalus" is from this collection.

A Teacher and Writer After attending Radcliffe College in Cambridge, Massachusetts, Peabody published her first book of poems in 1898. From 1901 to 1903, she taught English literature at Wellesley College. Peabody continued to write plays and poetry throughout her life.

Fast Facts

▶ Peabody married a Harvard professor named Lionel Marks in 1906.

▶ She was a supporter of women's right to vote.

Go Online
Author Link

For: More about the author
Visit: www.PHSchool.com
Web Code: eme-9602

Icarus and Daedalus

Josephine Preston Peabody

Among all those mortals who grew so wise that they learned the secrets of the gods, none was more cunning[1] than Daedalus (ded´ əl əs).

He once built, for King Minos of Crete,[2] a wonderful Labyrinth[3] of winding ways so cunningly tangled up and twisted around that, once inside, you could never find your way out again without a magic clue. But the king's favor veered[4] with the wind, and one day he had his master architect imprisoned in a tower. Daedalus managed to escape from his cell; but it seemed impossible to leave the island, since every ship that came or went was well guarded by order of the king.

At length, watching the sea-gulls in the air—the only creatures that were sure of liberty—he thought of a plan for himself and his young son Icarus (ik´ ə rəs), who was captive with him.

Little by little, he gathered a store of feathers great and small. He fastened these together with thread, molded them in with wax, and so fashioned two great wings like those of a bird. When they were done, Daedalus fitted them to his own shoulders, and after one or two efforts, he found that by waving his arms he could winnow[5] the air and cleave it, as a swimmer does the sea. He held himself aloft, wavered this way and that with the wind, and at last, like a great fledgling,[6] he learned to fly.

---

1. cunning (kun´ iŋ) *adj.* skillful; clever.
2. King Minos (mī´ nəs) **of Crete** King Minos was a son of the god Zeus. Crete is a Greek island in the eastern Mediterranean Sea, southeast of Greece.
3. Labyrinth (lab´ ə rinth´) *n.* maze.
4. veered (vird) *v.* changed directions.
5. winnow (win´ ō) *v.* beat, as with wings.
6. fledgling (flej´ liŋ) *n.* young bird.

Literary Analysis
Myth How does the first sentence indicate that the work is a myth?

Reading Skill
Cause and Effect Why does Daedalus make wings out of feathers?

Daedalus and Icarus, French colored engraving, 1660

▲ **Critical Viewing** Use the title of this myth, your knowledge of Greek mythology, and this illustration to predict what will happen to the two people in the story. **[Predict]**

Without delay, he fell to work on a pair of wings for the boy Icarus, and taught him carefully how to use them, bidding him beware of rash adventures among the stars. "Remember," said the father, "never to fly very low or very high, for the fogs about the earth would weigh you down, but the blaze of the sun will surely melt your feathers apart if you go too near."

For Icarus, these cautions went in at one ear and out by the other. Who could remember to be careful when he was to fly for the first time? Are birds careful? Not they! And not an idea remained in the boy's head but the one joy of escape.

The day came, and the fair wind that was to set them free. The father bird put on his wings, and, while the light urged them to be gone, he waited to see that all was well with Icarus, for the two could not fly hand in hand. Up they rose, the boy after his father. The hateful ground of Crete sank beneath them; and the country folk, who caught a glimpse of them when they were high above the treetops, took it for a vision of the gods—Apollo,[7] perhaps, with Cupid[8] after him.

At first there was a terror in the joy. The wide <u>vacancy</u> of the air dazed them—a glance downward made their brains reel.

---

7. Apollo (ə päl´ ō) *n.* the Greek god of music, poetry, and medicine; identified with the sun.
8. Cupid (kyōō´ pid) *n.* in Roman mythology, the god of love, son of Venus.

Literary Analysis
Myth What lesson does Daedalus try to teach Icarus?

Vocabulary Builder
vacancy (vā´ kən sē) *n.* emptiness

But when a great wind filled their wings, and Icarus felt himself <u>sustained</u>, like a halcyon bird[9] in the hollow of a wave, like a child uplifted by his mother, he forgot everything in the world but joy. He forgot Crete and the other islands that he had passed over: he saw but vaguely that wingèd thing in the distance before him that was his father Daedalus. He longed for one draft of flight to quench the thirst of his captivity: he stretched out his arms to the sky and made towards the highest heavens.

Alas for him! Warmer and warmer grew the air. Those arms, that had seemed to uphold him, relaxed. His wings wavered, drooped. He fluttered his young hands vainly—he was falling—and in that terror he remembered. The heat of the sun had melted the wax from his wings; the feathers were falling, one by one, like snowflakes; and there was none to help.

He fell like a leaf tossed down the wind, down, down, with one cry that overtook Daedalus far away. When he returned, and sought high and low for his poor boy, he saw nothing but the birdlike feathers afloat on the water, and he knew that Icarus was drowned.

The nearest island he named Icaria, in memory of the child; but he, in heavy grief, went to the temple of Apollo in Sicily, and there hung up his wings as an offering. Never again did he attempt to fly.

---

9. halcyon (hal′ sē ən) **bird** *n.* legendary sea bird, which the ancient Greeks believed could calm the sea by resting on it.

Vocabulary Builder
sustained (sə stānd′)
adj. supported

Reading Skill
Cause and Effect
What is the result of Icarus' flying too high?

Apply the Skills

Icarus and Daedalus

Thinking About the Selection

1. **Respond:** Do you think Icarus deserved his fate? Why or why not?
2. **(a) Recall:** Where is Daedalus when the story begins?
   (b) Analyze: In what ways does Daedalus show how clever he is?
3. **(a) Recall:** Who is Icarus? **(b) Infer:** What does Daedalus reveal about himself through his words to Icarus?
4. **(a) Recall:** Summarize the warning Daedalus gives to Icarus.
   (b) Infer: What do Icarus' actions reveal about his character?
5. **(a) Compare and Contrast:** Compare and contrast Icarus' experience of flying with Daedalus' experience. **(b) Evaluate:** What does the difference reveal about the characters? Explain.
6. **(a) Take a Position:** Does Daedalus share any responsibility for Icarus' fall? Why or why not? **(b) Discuss:** Share your answer with a classmate. How has your answer grown or changed?

Reading Skill

7. Answer these questions to analyze **cause-and-effect** relationships in the myth:
   (a) What happens to Icarus at the end of the myth? **(b)** Why does it happen?
   (c) What happens to Daedalus? **(d)** Why does it happen?
8. What effect does the sun have in the myth?

Literary Analysis

9. What superhuman qualities does Daedalus possess?
10. Complete a chart like the one shown to describe the lessons the **myth** teaches through each character.

Character	Lesson	How Taught
Icarus		
Daedalus		

QuickReview

Who's Who in the Story

King Minos: King of Crete

Daedalus: King Minos' master architect

Icarus: Daedalus' son

Go Online
—Assessment
For: Self-test
Visit: www.PHSchool.com
Web Code: ema-6602

Cause: why something happens

Effect: what happens

Myth: a story about gods and heroes that explains natural occurrences and teaches lessons about right and wrong

Vocabulary Builder

Practice For each item, write a single sentence using the words indicated.

1. vacancy; hole
2. sustained; noise

Writing

You may have wondered why leaves change colors in the fall or what causes an earthquake. Write a short **myth** that explains a natural phenomenon that fascinates you. The following tips will help you get started.

- Think of a natural phenomenon and a creative explanation for its occurrence.
- Decide on how many characters your myth will have. Limit the number to keep the story simple.
- Describe the traits of your characters through their appearances, actions, words, and the ways in which other characters relate to them.
- Plan the action of your story by identifying a problem and its solution.

For *Grammar, Vocabulary,* and *Assessment,* see **Build Language Skills,** pages 842–843.

Extend Your Learning

Listening and Speaking With a small group, conduct a **debate** about whether or not Daedalus shares any responsibility for Icarus' fall. Each side should prepare an argument and material to back up the argument.

- Before the debate, consider what the opposing arguments might be and prepare to counterattack these ideas.
- After the debate, poll your audience to see which side presented a more convincing argument.

Research and Technology Use the Internet and library resources to conduct research on how birds fly. Find out how a bird's wing structure and bone weight help make flight possible. Create a **poster** or **three-dimensional model** that explains your findings.

Build Understanding • *Demeter and Persephone*

Background

Seasonal Changes Ancient Greeks explained the changing seasons with the story of "Demeter and Persephone." Today, scientists explain these changes differently. The Earth completes one revolution around the sun during the course of a year. As the Earth travels, its tilt causes different parts of its surface to receive more of the sun's light. In regions getting more sunlight, it is summer. In areas getting less sunlight, it is winter.

Connecting to the Literature

Reading/Writing Connection Every season has unique qualities. Write three sentences describing what you like best about your favorite season. Use at least three of the following words: *appreciate, impress, specify, unify.*

Meet the Author

Anne Terry **White** (1896–1980)

Anne Terry White, who was born in Ukraine (then part of Russia), was one of the leading writers of nonfiction for children. She wrote her first two books: *Heroes of the Five Books,* a look at figures of the Old Testament, and *Three Children and Shakespeare,* a family discussion of four of Shakespeare's plays, to introduce her own children to great works of literature. In addition to writing books, White was an editor, a translator, and an authority on ancient Greece. She shares this knowledge in her retelling of the myth of Demeter and Persephone. White also explored science, biography, and other topics in her many books for children and young adults.

Fast Facts

▶ White wrote books about the stars, rocks, rivers, archaeology, and mountains in her "All About" series.

▶ She wrote a number of historical books, including biographies such as *George Washington Carver: The Story of a Great American.*

Review

For **Reading Skill, Literary Analysis,** and **Vocabulary Builder,** see page 826.

Go **O**nline
Author Link

For: More about the author
Visit: www.PHSchool.com
Web Code: eme-9603

Demeter and Persephone
Anne Terry White

Deep under Mt. Aetna, the gods had buried alive a number of fearful, fire-breathing giants. The monsters heaved and struggled to get free. And so mightily did they shake the earth that Pluto, the king of the underworld, was alarmed.

"They may tear the rocks asunder and leave the realm of the dead open to the light of day," he thought. And mounting his golden chariot, he went up to see what damage had been done.

Now the goddess of love and beauty, fair Aphrodite (af′ rə dīt′ ē), was sitting on a mountainside playing with her son, Eros.[1] She saw Pluto as he drove around with his coal-black horses and she said:

"My son, there is one who <u>defies</u> your power and mine. Quick! Take up your darts! Send an arrow into the breast of that dark monarch. Let him, too, feel the pangs of love. Why should he alone escape them?"

At his mother's words, Eros leaped lightly to his feet. He chose from his quiver[2] his sharpest and truest arrow, fitted it to his bow, drew the string, and shot straight into Pluto's heart.

The grim King had seen fair maids enough in the gloomy underworld over which he ruled. But never had his heart been touched. Now an unaccustomed warmth stole through his veins. His stern eyes softened. Before him was a

✓ Reading Check

Who is Pluto?

---

1. Eros (er′ äs) in Greek mythology, the god of love; identified by the Romans as Cupid.
2. quiver (kwiv′ ər) *n.* case for arrows.

blossoming valley, and along its edge a charming girl was gathering flowers. She was Persephone (pər sefʹ ə nē), daughter of Demeter (di mētʹ ər), goddess of the harvest. She had strayed from her companions, and now that her basket overflowed with blossoms, she was filling her apron with lilies and violets. The god looked at Persephone and loved her at once. With one sweep of his arm he caught her up and drove swiftly away.

"Mother!" she screamed, while the flowers fell from her apron and strewed the ground. "Mother!"

And she called on her companions by name. But already they were out of sight, so fast did Pluto urge the horses on. In a few moments they were at the River Cyane.[3] Persephone struggled, her loosened girdle[4] fell to the ground, but the god held her tight. He struck the bank with his trident.[5] The earth opened, and darkness swallowed them all—horses, chariot, Pluto, and weeping Persephone.

From end to end of the earth Demeter sought her daughter. But none could tell her where Persephone was. At last, worn out and despairing, the goddess returned to Sicily. She stood by the River Cyane, where Pluto had cleft the earth and gone down into his own dominions.

Now a river nymph[6] had seen him carry off his prize. She wanted to tell Demeter where her daughter was, but fear of Pluto kept her dumb. Yet she had picked up the girdle Persephone had dropped, and this the nymph wafted[7] on the waves to the feet of Demeter.

The goddess knew then that her daughter was gone indeed, but she did not suspect Pluto of carrying her off. She laid the blame on the innocent land.

"Ungrateful soil!" she said. "I made you fertile. I clothed you in grass and nourishing grain, and this is how you reward me. No more shall you enjoy my favors!"

That year was the most cruel mankind had ever known. Nothing prospered, nothing grew. The cattle died, the seed would not come up, men and oxen toiled in vain. There was too much sun. There was too much rain. Thistles[8] and weeds

Literary Analysis
Myths What details in this paragraph tell you the story is a myth?

Reading Skill
Cause and Effect What are the effects of Demeter's anger?

---

3. **River Cyane** (sī an) a river in Sicily, an island just south of Italy.
4. **girdle** (gʉrdʹ əl) *n.* belt or sash for the waist.
5. **trident** (trīdʹ ənt) *n.* spear with three points.
6. **river nymph** (nimf) goddess living in a river.
7. **wafted** (wäftʹ əd) *n.* carried.
8. **thistles** (thisʹ əlz) *n.* stubborn, weedy plants with sharp leaves and usually purplish flowers.

Demeter Mourning for Persephone, 1906, Evelyn de Morgan, The De Morgan Foundation, London

◀ **Critical Viewing**
What symbols in this painting convey Demeter's role as goddess of the harvest? [**Analyze**]

Vocabulary Builder
intervene (in tər vēn′)
v. come between as an influence to modify, settle, or hinder some action or argument

 **Reading Check**

Why does Demeter punish the earth?

were the only things that grew. It seemed that all mankind would die of hunger.

"This cannot go on," said mighty Zeus. "I see that I must <u>intervene</u>." And one by one he sent the gods and goddesses to plead with Demeter.

But she had the same answer for all: "Not till I see my daughter shall the earth bear fruit again."

Zeus, of course, knew well where Persephone was. He did not like to take from his brother the one joyful thing in his life,

but he saw that he must if the race of man was to be preserved. So he called Hermes[9] to him and said:

"Descend to the underworld, my son. Bid Pluto release his
bride. Provided she has not tasted food in the realm of the
dead, she may return to her mother forever."

Down sped Hermes on his winged feet, and there in the dim
palace of the king, he found Persephone by Pluto's side. She
was pale and joyless. Not all the glittering treasures of the
underworld could bring a smile to her lips.

"You have no flowers here," she would say to her husband
when he pressed gems upon her. "Jewels have no fragrance.
I do not want them."

When she saw Hermes and heard his message, her heart
leaped within her. Her cheeks grew rosy and her eyes spar-
kled, for she knew that Pluto would not dare to disobey his
brother's command. She sprang up, ready to go at once. Only
one thing troubled her—that she could not leave the underworld forever. For she had accepted a pomegranate[10] from
Pluto and sucked the sweet pulp from four of the seeds.

With a heavy heart Pluto made ready his golden car.[11] He
helped Persephone in while Hermes took up the reins.

"Dear wife," said the King, and his voice trembled as he
spoke, "think kindly of me, I pray you. For indeed I love you
truly. It will be lonely here these eight months you are away.
And if you think mine is a gloomy palace to return to, at least
remember that your husband is great among the immortals.
So fare you well—and get your fill of flowers!"

Straight to the temple of Demeter at Eleusis, Hermes drove
the black horses. The goddess heard the chariot wheels and,
as a deer bounds over the hills, she ran out swiftly to meet her
daughter. Persephone flew to her mother's arms. And the sad
tale of each turned into joy in the telling.

**Reading Skill
Cause and Effect**
When Persephone
eats four pomegranate
seeds, what is the
result?

**Literary Analysis
Myth** What human
traits does Pluto
display here?

---

9. Hermes (hʉr´ mēz) a god who served as a messenger.
10. pomegranate (päm´ ə gran´ it) *n.* round fruit with a red leathery rind and many seeds.
11. car (kär) *n.* chariot.

So it is to this day. One third of the year Persephone spends in the gloomy abode of Pluto—one month for each seed that she tasted. Then Nature dies, the leaves fall, the earth stops bringing forth. In spring Persephone returns, and with her come the flowers, followed by summer's fruitfulness and the rich harvest of fall.

Literature in Context   Mythology Connection

Gods and Goddesses

The ancient Greeks and Romans had different names for their gods and goddesses. In the diagram below, the Roman name for the god or goddess is given in parentheses. In their traditions, each god and goddess had control or power in a different area.

Poseiden (Neptune)
god of the sea

Zeus (Jupiter)
ruler of gods and men

Hera (Juno)
goddess of marriage

Demeter (Ceres)
goddess of agriculture

Hades (Pluto)
god of the underworld

Hermes (Mercury)
messenger of the gods

Aphrodite (Venus)
goddess of beauty

Ares (Mars)
god of war

Athena (Minerva)
goddess of wisdom

Persephone (Proserpina)
goddess of springtime

Connect to the Literature   Why do you think that ancient peoples told stories about gods and goddesses such as Demeter and Persephone?

Apply the Skills

Demeter and Persephone

Thinking About the Selection

1. **Respond:** For whom do you feel sorrier—Persephone or Pluto? Explain.
2. **(a) Recall:** Why did Pluto take Persephone to his kingdom? **(b) Analyze:** What does Pluto's nickname, "the grim King," suggest about his emotional outlook on the world?
3. **(a) Recall:** What does Demeter do when she discovers her daughter is lost? **(b) Make a Judgment:** Do you think her actions were justifiable? Why or why not? **(c) Discuss:** Share your answer with a classmate. How has your response grown or changed?
4. **(a) Recall:** How is Persephone reunited with her mother? **(b) Speculate:** How might their experiences in this myth change each of the three main characters?
5. **(a) Recall:** How does nature change as Persephone moves between Earth and the underworld? **(b) Synthesize:** How do the powerful emotions of the main characters account for the changing of the seasons?

Reading Skill

6. Answer these questions to analyze **cause-and-effect** relationships in the myth:
   (a) What happens to Persephone at the end of the myth?
   (b) Why does it happen?
   (c) What happens to Demeter? (d) Why does it happen?
7. Describe the effect of the giants struggling to get free at the beginning of the myth.

Literary Analysis

8. What human qualities does Pluto possess?
9. Complete a chart like the one shown to describe the lessons the **myth** teaches through each character.

Character	Lesson	How Taught
Demeter		
Persephone		
Pluto		

QuickReview

Who's Who in the Story

Zeus: King of the ancient Greek gods

Pluto: God of the underworld, brother of Zeus

Aphrodite: Goddess of love and beauty

Eros: Aphrodite's son

Demeter: Goddess of the harvest

Persephone: Demeter's daughter

For: Self-test
Visit: www.PHSchool.com
Web Code: ema-6603

Cause: why something happens

Effect: what happens

Myth: a story about gods and heroes that explains natural occurrences and teaches lessons about right and wrong

Vocabulary Builder

Practice Rewrite each of the following sentences so that it includes a vocabulary word from the "Demeter and Persephone" vocabulary list on page 826 and means the opposite.

1. Lori obeyed her mother by going to the movie.
2. Paul avoided getting involved in the disagreement between the teams.

Writing

You may have wondered why leaves change colors in the fall or what causes an earthquake. Write a short **myth** that explains a natural phenomenon that fascinates you. The following tips will help you get started.

- Think of a natural phenomenon and a creative explanation for its occurrence.
- Decide on how many characters your myth will have.
- Describe the traits of your characters through their appearances, actions, words, and the ways in which other characters relate to them.
- Plan the action of your story by identifying a problem and its solution.

For *Grammar, Vocabulary,* and *Assessment,* see **Build Language Skills,** pages 842–843.

Extend Your Learning

Listening and Speaking With a small group, conduct a **debate** about whether Demeter was justified in changing the weather on Earth. Each side should prepare an argument and material to back up the argument. Before the debate, consider the opposing arguments and prepare to counterattack these ideas. After, poll your audience to see which side was more convincing.

Research and Technology Use the Internet and library resources to learn about Earth and sun positions and how they affect the seasons. Create a **poster** or **three-dimensional model** that explains your findings.

Build Language Skills

Vocabulary Skill

Denotation and Connotation You can look up a word's **denotation**, or literal meaning, in a dictionary. A word's **connotations**, however, are the associations it has in our culture. Recognizing a word's connotations helps you understand its shades of meaning. For example, the denotation of *consequence* is "an effect" or "the result of an action." However, the connotations of *consequence* are negative. Consequence often suggests a punishment or other negative result.

Not all words have connotations. For example, *outcome, result,* and *effect* mean almost the same thing as *consequence* but they have no negative association.

> **Example:** The *consequence* of not studying for the test was a failing grade.

Practice The words in these pairs have close denotations. For each pair write a sentence explaining the difference in the connotation.

1. antique/old   **2.** disagree/debate   **3.** restrict/enclose

Grammar Lesson

Colon A *colon* looks like two periods, one above the other (:). Colons can be used to introduce lists of items. Do not use a colon directly between a verb or a preposition and its object.

Correct: The box contained many items: an alarm clock, a vase, and a book.
I need to shop for the following: pencils, paper, and a backpack.

Incorrect: The box contained: an alarm clock, a vase, and a book.
I need to shop for: pencils, paper, and a backpack.

Practice Write the following sentences on a sheet of paper. Insert colons where they are needed. If none is needed, write "none."

1. I can travel on any of the following days Mondays, Wednesdays, or Thursdays.

2. We are hoping for good weather, a smooth flight, and delicious food.

3. On the desk were piles of paper, scattered pens and pencils, and day-old pizza.

4. He found a number of things in the drawer two pens, a lock, and a nail.

MorePractice

For more practice with the use of a colon, see the Grammar Handbook, p. R31.

W͞G Prentice Hall Writing and Grammar Connection: Chapter 26, Section 3

Reading: Cause and Effect

Directions: *Read the selection. Then, answer the questions.*

Earth's rotation causes day and night. As Earth rotates eastward, the sun appears to move westward across the sky. It is day on the side of Earth facing the sun. Sunlight does not reach the side of Earth facing away from the sun, so it is night there. Each 24-hour cycle of day and night is called a day. In addition to rotating on its axis, Earth travels around the sun. One complete revolution of Earth around the sun is called a year.

1. What is the result of Earth's rotation?
   - A a day
   - B a year
   - C 24 hours
   - D day and night

2. What result belongs in the empty box?

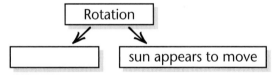

   - A sun moves
   - B seasons occur
   - C a year passes
   - D day and night

3. What is the cause of night's darkness?
   - A Sunlight reaches the side of Earth facing away from the sun.
   - B Sunlight cannot reach the side of Earth facing away from the sun.
   - C The sun sets in the west.
   - D The sun revolves.

4. Why doesn't sunlight reach one side of Earth?
   - A The Earth moves parallel to the sun.
   - B It is farther away than during daytime.
   - C Within 24 hours there must be night.
   - D It is faced away from the sun.

Timed Writing: Persuasion [Connections]

Review "Icarus and Daedalus" or "Demeter and Persephone." Then, think about this question: Do you believe that a single event can change a person's life? Write a brief essay explaining why or why not. Use examples from the selections to support your ideas.
(20 minutes)

 ## Writing Workshop: *Work in Progress*

Business Letter

In your letter provide details to support your request. Make a list of specific details that you will need to provide, such as the approximate date, time, and size of the party you plan to host.

Reading Informational Materials

Textbooks

In Part 1, you are learning how to identify cause-and-effect relationships in literature. This skill is also useful when reading textbooks. If you read "Demeter and Persephone," a myth explaining the seasons, you may use your understanding of cause-and-effect relationships to analyze and interpret explanations in a science textbook.

About Textbooks

A **textbook** is a nonfiction work that presents instructional information in a particular subject area. Textbooks have some common features and characteristics.

- **Purpose** The purpose of a textbook is to present information for students. New information is organized and developed around a clearly identified main concept, idea, or topic.

- **Structure** Most textbooks are organized into sections, chapters, or units. The table of contents lists titles of these parts and indicates on what page each one begins.

- **Text Format** Headings, type size, color, and boldfacing are used to highlight key terms or concepts. Information may also be presented visually in charts or diagrams.

Reading Skill

The information in a textbook is organized to help you learn facts, ideas, and concepts. When you need to locate specific information in a text that you have already read, **skim** and **scan**, instead of rereading every word. Skimming is glancing through a written work to get a general idea of what it is about. Scanning is quickly reading through a written work looking for key words or ideas.

Tips for Skimming and Scanning

Skim the table of contents to find the chapter you need.

Skim headings to identify the topics covered in a section of text.

Scan paragraphs looking for key words related to the question you need to answer.

Scan captions and labels of visual aids to see if the information you need is presented in a chart, diagram, or illustration.

The Seasons on Earth

from *Prentice Hall Science Explorer*

Most places outside the tropics and polar regions have four distinct seasons: winter, spring, summer, and autumn. But there are great differences in temperature from place to place. For instance, it is generally warmer near the equator than near the poles. Why is this so?

How Sunlight Hits Earth

Figure 1 shows how sunlight strikes Earth's surface. Notice that sunlight hits Earth's surface most directly near the equator. Near the poles, sunlight arrives at a steep angle. As a result, it is spread out over a greater area. That is why it is warmer near the equator than near the poles.

Earth's Tilted Axis

If Earth's axis were straight up and down relative to its orbit, temperatures would remain fairly constant year-round. There would be no seasons. Earth has seasons because its axis is tilted as it revolves around the sun.

Notice in Figure 2 that Earth's axis is always tilted at an angle of 23.5° from the vertical. As Earth revolves

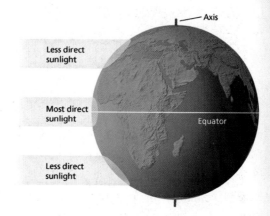

Figure 1 Sunlight Striking Earth's Surface
Near the equator, sunlight strikes Earth's surface more directly and is less spread out than near the poles.
Relating Cause and Effect Why is it usually colder near the poles than near the equator?

around the sun, the north end of its axis is tilted away from the sun for part of the year and toward the sun for part of the year.

Summer and winter are caused by Earth's tilt as it revolves around the sun. The change in seasons is not caused by changes in Earth's distance from the sun. In fact, Earth is farthest from the sun when it is summer in the Northern Hemisphere.

Reading Informational Materials

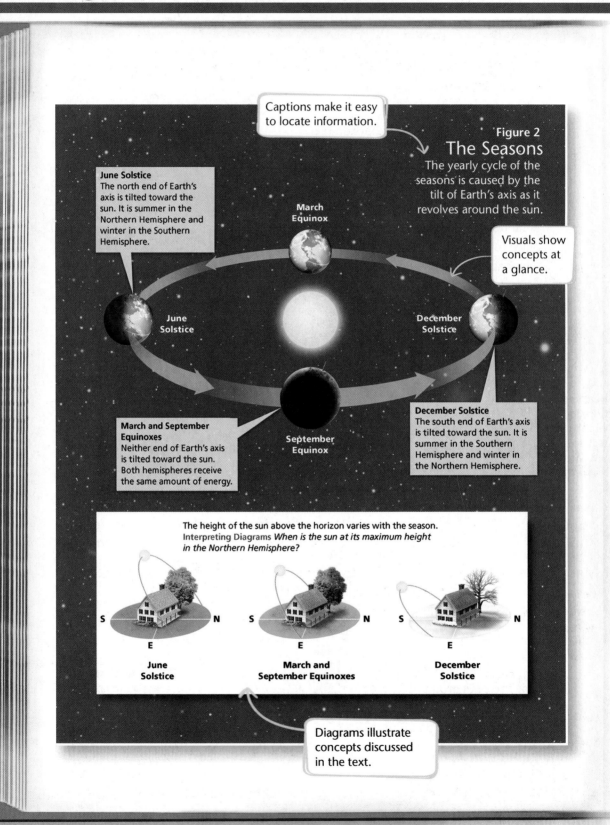

Captions make it easy to locate information.

Figure 2
The Seasons
The yearly cycle of the seasons is caused by the tilt of Earth's axis as it revolves around the sun.

Visuals show concepts at a glance.

June Solstice
The north end of Earth's axis is tilted toward the sun. It is summer in the Northern Hemisphere and winter in the Southern Hemisphere.

March Equinox

June Solstice

December Solstice

March and September Equinoxes
Neither end of Earth's axis is tilted toward the sun. Both hemispheres receive the same amount of energy.

September Equinox

December Solstice
The south end of Earth's axis is tilted toward the sun. It is summer in the Southern Hemisphere and winter in the Northern Hemisphere.

The height of the sun above the horizon varies with the season.
Interpreting Diagrams *When is the sun at its maximum height in the Northern Hemisphere?*

S   N
E
June
Solstice

S   N
E
March and
September Equinoxes

S   N
E
December
Solstice

Diagrams illustrate concepts discussed in the text.

Reading: Skim and Scan

Directions: *Choose the letter of the best answer to each question.*

1. What causes the yearly cycle of the seasons on Earth?

    A changes in Earth's distance from the sun

    B the difference in temperature between the equator and the poles

    C the tilt of Earth's axis

    D sunlight striking Earth's surface

2. Study the diagram in Figure 2. What is the season in the Southern Hemisphere during the December Solstice?

    A summer

    B autumn

    C winter

    D spring

3. Scan the paragraph titled "How Sunlight Hits Earth." Which word is a clue indicating a cause-and-effect relationship?

    A notice

    B directly

    C arrives

    D why

Reading: Comprehension and Interpretation

Directions: *Write your answer on a separate sheet of paper.*

4. Using Figure 2, describe the weather in the Northern Hemisphere during the June Solstice. **[Integrating]**

5. Explain why people living near the equator need lighter weight clothing than those living at the North Pole. **[Generating]**

Timed Writing: Explanation

Explain how the seasons of the year are caused by the tilt of the Earth's axis as it revolves around the sun. Include the reasons that the seasons in the Northern Hemisphere are different from the seasons in the Southern Hemisphere during the same times of year. **(15 minutes)** **[Interpretation]**

These skills will help you become a better reader.
Practice them with either "Tenochtitlan" (p. 850) or
"Popocatepetl and Ixtlaccihuatl" (p. 857).

Reading Skill

A **cause** is an event or situation that produces a result.
An **effect** is the result produced. In a story or an essay,
each effect may eventually become a cause for the next
event. This results in a cause-and-effect chain, which propels the
action forward.

As you read, think about the causes and effects of events. If you do
not clearly see the cause-and-effect relationships in a passage,
reread to look for connections among the words and sentences.

Some words that identify causes and effects are *because, due to, for
this reason,* and *as a result.* Notice the clue words in the cause-and-
effect chain shown.

> **Cause/Effect**
> *Because* the infant
> was crying, the
> mother woke up.

> **Effect/Cause**
> She tripped in the
> dark and made a
> small groan.

> **Cause/Effect**
> *As a result of* her
> groan, the father
> woke up.

Literary Analysis

A **legend** is a traditional story about the past. A **fact** is something
that can be proved to be true. Before legends were written down,
they were passed on orally. Legends are based on facts that have
grown into fiction in the many retellings over generations.

Every culture has its own legends to immortalize people who were
famous. Most legends include these elements:

- a human who is larger than life
- fantastic elements
- roots or basis in historical facts
- events that reflect the culture that created the story

Vocabulary Builder

Tenochtitlan: Inside the Aztec Capital

- **outskirts** (out´skʉrts´) *n.* part of a district far
  from the center of a city (p. 853) *The mall is
  on the outskirts of the city.*

- **reeds** (rēdz) *n.* tall, slender grasses that
  grow in marshy land (p. 853) *The reeds
  blew in the wind.*

- **goblets** (gäb´ lits) *n.* bowl-shaped drinking
  containers without handles (p. 853) *Please
  pour water into five goblets.*

Popocatepetl and Ixtlaccihuatl

- **decreed** (di krēd´) *v.* officially ordered
  (p. 861) *The Queen decreed the day a
  holiday.*

- **unanimous** (yo͞o nan´ ə məs) *adj.* based on
  complete agreement (p. 863) *Beth was
  elected president by a unanimous vote.*

- **routed** (rout´ əd) *v.* completely defeated
  (p. 864) *The king's men routed the invaders.*

Background

Origins of Mexico City Mexico City, the capital of Mexico, was built on the ruins of the ancient Aztec city of Tenochtitlan. The city itself sat on an island in the center of a lake called Texcoco. Over the years, the lake was slowly drained to make room for the growing city. Because Mexico City is located on a drained lakebed, the effects of earthquakes have been severe. The city is slowly sinking several inches a year. "Tenochtitlan: Inside the Aztec Capital" presents factual information about the people and activities of the legendary city.

Connecting to the Literature

Reading/Writing Connection This article describes a city that was designed as it grew. You may have played video games in which you designed a city or civilization. List some ideas that come to mind when you think about planning a city. Use three of the following words: *adapt, modify, detect, maximize, minimize.*

Meet the Author

Jacqueline **Dineen**

Jacqueline Dineen began her career as an editor for an educational publisher in London before she turned to writing children's books. She has written books on a variety of subjects, including science, history, and geography. Among them are *Lift the Lid on Mummies, The Early Inventions,* and *Food From the Sea.*

Text and Images In "Tenochtitlan: Inside the Aztec Capital," Dineen uses a skillful mix of description, eyewitness accounts, maps, photographs, and art to give readers a sense of what it took to build the city.

Fast Facts

▶ Dineen has written more than eighty books.
▶ She wrote a book called *Chocolate,* which is a history of chocolate for children.

Go Online
Author Link

For: More about the author
Visit: www.PHSchool.com
Web Code: eme-9604

TENOCHTITLAN:
INSIDE THE AZTEC CAPITAL
Jacqueline Dineen

The Lake City of Tenochtitlan

The city of Tenochtitlan[1] began on an island in the middle of a swampy lake. There the Aztecs built their first temple to Huitzilopochtli.[2] The place was given the name Tenochtitlan, which means "The Place of the Fruit of the Prickly Pear Cactus." Later on the name was given to the city that grew up around the temple. The Aztecs rebuilt their temples on the same site every 52 years, so the first temple eventually became the great Temple Mayor[3] that stood at the center of the city.

The city started as a collection of huts. It began to grow after 1385, while Acamapichtli[4] was king. The Aztecs were excellent engineers. They built three causeways over the swamp to link the city with the mainland. These were raised roads made of stone supported on wooden pillars. Parts of the causeways were bridges. These bridges could be removed to leave gaps and this prevented enemies from getting to the city. Fresh water was brought from the mainland to the city along stone aqueducts.[5]

from *THE AZTECS* by Jacqueline Dineen (Words of the Past), Heinemann Educational Books Ltd, an imprint of Reed Educational and Professional Publishing

▲ Critical Viewing
What features of the city described in the text are shown on this map? **[Connect]**

---

1. **Tenochtitlan** (tā nôch′ tēt län′) *n.* ancient Aztec capital located in what is now Mexico City.
2. **Huitzilopochtli** (wēt sē lō pōch′ tlē)
3. **Mayor** (mä yōr′) *adj.* (Sp.) main.
4. **Acamapichtli** (ä kä mä pēch′ tlē)
5. **aqueducts** (ak′ wə dukts′) *n.* large bridgelike structures made for bringing water from a distant source.

◀ **Critical Viewing**
Why do you think the Aztecs found many uses for Maguey cactus plants, like those in the photograph? **[Infer]**

Inside the City

The Spaniards' first view of Tenochtitlan was described by one of Cortés's[6] soldiers, Bernal Diaz: "And when we saw all those towns and level causeway leading into Mexico, we were astounded. These great towns and buildings rising from the water, all made of stone, seemed like an enchanted vision."

By that time Tenochtitlan was the largest city in Mexico. About 200,000 people lived there. The houses were one story high and had flat roofs. In the center of the city was a large square. The twin temple stood on one side, and the king's palace on another. Officials' houses made of white stone also lined the square. There were few roads. People traveled in canoes along canals.

Floating Gardens

Tenochtitlan was built in a huge valley, the Valley of Mexico, which was surrounded by mountains. Rivers flowed from the mountains into Lake Texcoco, where Tenochtitlan stood. The lake was linked to four other shallow, swampy lakes. The land around the lakes was dry because there was very little rain. The Aztecs dug ditches and piled up the earth to make islands in the shallow parts of the lake. These chinampas, or swamp gardens, could be farmed. The ditches carried water into larger canals that were used for irrigation[7] and as waterways to the city.

Literary Analysis
Legend and Fact
How might the Spaniards' reactions to their first sight of Tenochtitlan have sparked the beginning of a legend?

 **Reading Check**

Who built the city of Tenochtitlan?

---

6. Hernando Cortés (er nän´ dō kōr tes´) Spanish adventurer (1485–1547) who conquered what is now central and southern Mexico.
7. irrigation (ir´ ə gā´ shən) *n.* supplying water with ditches, canals, or sprinklers.

Texcoco and the lake to the south contained fresh water, but the northern lakes contained salt water, which was no good for irrigation. The Aztecs built an embankment[8] 10 miles long to keep out the salt water and also to protect the city from flooding.

Feeding the People

Archaeologists think that when Tenochtitlan was at its greatest, about one million people lived in the Valley of Mexico. That included Tenochtitlan and the 50 or 60 city-states on the mainland surrounding the lakes. Food for all these people had to come from farming.

Historians are not sure how many people in Tenochtitlan were farmers, but they think it may have been between one third and one half of the population. The rest were the nobility, craftspeople, and others. Each chinampa was only big enough to grow food for one family. Most people in Tenochtitlan depended on food from outside the city.

As the city grew, more and more land was drained for farming and for building. Farmers had no tools except simple hoes and digging sticks, but the loose soil was fertile and easy to turn. The main crop was corn, but farmers also grew tomatoes, beans, chili peppers, and prickly pears. They grew maguey cactus for its fibers and to make a drink called pulque. Cacao trees were grown in the hottest areas. The seeds were used for trading and to make a chocolate drink.

Inside an Aztec Home

There were big differences between a rich Aztec home and a poor one. The nobles' houses were like palaces. They were one story high and built around a courtyard. Each of the four sides contained four or five large rooms. The courtyards were planted with flower and vegetable gardens. Some houses on the island in the center of the city were built of adobe—bricks made from mud and dried in the sun. Adobe is still used for building in Mexico today. These grand houses and palaces were whitewashed so that they shone in the sun. The Spanish soldier Bernal Diaz described buildings that looked like "gleaming white towers and castles: a marvelous sight."

---

8. **embankment** (em bank´ mənt) *n.* wall of earth built to keep water back.

Reading Skill
Cause and Effect
Identify one effect of the city's growth.

There is very little evidence about the buildings in Tenochtitlan and hardly any about the poor people's houses. What we do know has been pieced together from scattered historical records such as documents that record the sale of building sites on the chinampa gardens. All of the poorer people's homes were built on the chinampas on the <u>outskirts</u> of the city. Because the chinampas would not take the weight of stone, houses had to be built of lighter materials such as wattle-and-daub. This was made by weaving <u>reeds</u> together and then plastering them with mud. We know that the outskirts of the city were divided into groups of houses inside walled areas, or compounds. A whole family lived in each compound. The family consisted of a couple, their married children, and their grandchildren. Every married couple in the family had a separate house of one or two rooms. All the houses opened onto an outdoor patio that belonged to the whole family.

Outside the house, the families often kept turkeys in pens. The turkeys provided eggs and meat. There was also a beehive for honey. Most families had a bathhouse in the garden.

Furniture and Decoration

Aztec houses were very plain inside. Everyone slept on mats of reeds that were spread on the dirt floor at night. Families had cooking pots and utensils made of clay. There were <u>goblets</u> for pulque and other drinks, graters for grinding chilis, and storage pots of various designs. Reed baskets were also used for storage. Households had grinding stones for grinding corn into flour. There was also a household shrine with statues of the gods.

The houses had no windows or chimneys, so they must have been dark and smoky from the cooking fire. There were no doors, just an open doorway. Even the palaces had open doorways with cloths hanging over them.

Vocabulary Builder
outskirts (out skʉrtz´) *n.* part of a district far from the center of a city

reeds (rēdz) *n.* tall, slender grasses that grow in marshy land

goblets (gäb´ lits) *n.* bowl-shaped drinking containers without handles

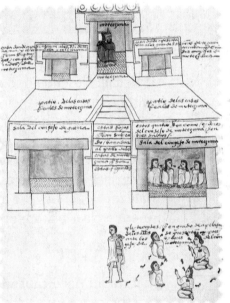

▲ Critical Viewing
What details in this drawing of Montezuma's palace suggest the Emperor's importance?
[Analyze]

Apply the Skills

Tenochtitlan: Inside the Aztec Capital

Thinking About the Selection

1. **Respond:** What questions do you still have after reading the article? Using a chart like the one shown, write your questions in the first column. Trade lists with a partner. In the second column of the chart, answer your partner's questions if you can. Then, discuss each chart. Finally, in the third column, explain how your understanding of the article has or has not changed based on the discussion.

My Questions	Answers to My Questions	How Has My Understanding Changed?

2. **(a) Recall:** Describe one way in which the Aztecs shaped their environment to suit their needs. **(b) Make a Judgment:** How did this improve their lives?
3. **(a) Recall:** Name one way in which the environment shaped the Aztecs' lives. **(b) Draw Conclusions:** How well did the Aztecs deal with that element? Explain.
4. **Analyze:** How does the author use factual information to present a clear picture of ancient Aztec life?

Reading Skill

5. What might have **caused** the Aztecs to remove the bridges from the causeways?
6. Reread the essay to find an **effect** for each of these causes:
   (a) The city of Tenochtitlan was built on a lake.
   (b) The city grew.
   (c) Aztec houses had no windows or chimneys.
   (d) The chinampas could not support the weight of stone houses.

Literary Analysis

7. Identify three **facts** from the article. Identify two statements that are predictions or assumptions made by archaeologists, which are likely but cannot be proved.
8. What facts in this article might be used to create an interesting **legend** about Tenochtitlan? Explain.

QuickReview

Article at a Glance
This nonfiction article describes the development and people of the ancient Aztec city of Tenochtitlan.

Go Online
Assessment
For: Self-test
Visit: www.PHSchool.com
Web Code: ema-6604

Cause: why something happens

Effect: what happens

Legend: traditional story about the past that is usually based on historical fact

Fact: something that can be proved to be true

Vocabulary Builder

Practice Answer each of the following questions.

1. What type of buildings would you find on the *outskirts* of a modern city?

2. Where do *reeds* grow?

3. What might you do with a set of *goblets*?

Writing

Write a short **description** of the city of Tenochtitlan.

- Using the article for reference, jot down details about the time, place, and overall environment of the city.
- List vivid verbs and adjectives that will make your details interesting to readers. Include words that will appeal to the senses of sight, sound, smell, touch, and taste.

Use your notes to create a descriptive word picture of the city of Tenochtitlan.

For *Grammar, Vocabulary,* and *Assessment,* see **Build Language Skills,** pages 868–869.

Extend Your Learning

Listening and Speaking Deliver a **persuasive speech** to convince authorities that building a city in the middle of a lake is a good idea.

- On a note card, write a short statement explaining your position.
- List the main points that support your position on additional cards. Use solid evidence, including facts, statistics, and quotes from other authorities. Jot down phrases that will remind you of your points, rather than writing complete sentences.
- Refer to your note cards as you deliver your speech.

Research and Technology The city of Tenochtitlan changed over the years. Use a range of resources to write a **brief report** on how Tenochtitlan developed. Your report should explain what became of the city and what is there today. It may also mention how the city was planned and the engineering used to build the city. Share your finished report with the class.

Legend

Background

Oral Tradition The oral tradition is the collection of songs, stories, and poems that are passed from generation to generation by word of mouth. People used the traditional stories to communicate shared beliefs and to explain their world. In "Popocatepetl and Ixtlaccihuatl," you will see how the storyteller shares Aztec beliefs through a tale about teenagers who fall in love.

Connecting to the Literature

Reading/Writing Connection "Popocatepetl and Ixtlacci-huatl" is a legend that has been passed down from one generation to the next. Think about family stories or fairy tales you were told as a child. In a few sentences, identify which stories were your favorites and why. As you write, consider the effect these stories have had on you. Use at least three of these words: *communicate, reinforce, illustrate, enrich, appreciate.*

Review

For **Reading Skill, Literary Analysis,** and **Vocabulary Builder,** see page 848.

Meet the Author

Juliet Piggott **Wood** (1924–1996)

Juliet Piggott Wood discovered her love for learning about different cultures while living in Japan, where her grandfather was a legal advisor to Prince Ito. Wood's interest in Japan inspired her to produce several books on Japanese history and folklore. Her fascination with one culture led to research about others. She went on to co-author a book retelling famous fairy tales from around the world.

Far and Wide In World War II, Wood served in England in the Women's Royal Naval Service. Her experience in that war may have influenced her to write about other military battles, especially the legendary Aztec battle described in her book on Mexican folk tales. Clearly a person with many talents, Wood expanded her nonfiction list with a work on famous regiments in Queen Alexandra's Royal Army Nursing Corps.

Go **Online**
Author Link

For: More about the author
Visit: www.PHSchool.com
Web Code: eme-9605

Popocatepetl
and Ixtlaccihuatl

—— MEXICAN LEGEND ——
JULIET PIGGOTT WOOD

Before the Spaniards came to Mexico and marched on the Aztec capital of Tenochtitlan[1] there were two volcanoes to the southeast of that city. The Spaniards destroyed much of Tenochtitlan and built another city in its place and called it Mexico City. It is known by that name still, and the pass through which the Spaniards came to the

---

1. Tenochtitlan (tä noch′ tēt län′) the Aztec capital, conquered by the Spanish in 1521.

ancient Tenochtitlan is still there, as are the volcanoes on each side of that pass. Their names have not been changed. The one to the north is Ixtlaccihuatl [ēs′ tlä sē′ wät′ əl] and the one on the south of the pass is Popoc-atepetl [pô pô kä te′ pet′ əl]. Both are snowcapped and beautiful, Popocatepetl being the taller of the two. That name means Smoking Mountain. In Aztec days it gushed forth smoke and, on occasion, it does so still. It erupted too in Aztec days and has done so again since the Spaniards came. Ixtlacci-huatl means The White Woman, for its peak was, and still is, white.

Perhaps Ixtlaccihuatl and Popocatepetl were there in the highest part of the Valley of Mexico in the days when the earth was very young, in the days when the new peo-ple were just learning to eat and grow corn. The Aztecs claimed the volcanoes as their own, for they possessed a legend about them and their creation, and they believed that legend to be true.

There was once an Aztec Emperor in Tenochtitlan. He was very powerful. Some thought he was wise as well, whilst oth-ers doubted his wisdom. He was both a ruler and a warrior and he kept at bay those tribes living in and beyond the mountains surrounding the Valley of Mexico, with its huge lake called Texcoco [tā skō′ kō] in which Tenochtitlan was built. His power was absolute and the splendor in which he lived was very great.

▲ **Critical Viewing** What does this photograph of the ruins of Tenochtitlan tell you about the Aztecs' stonework? **[Analyze]**

It is not known for how many years the Emperor ruled in Tenochtitlan, but it is known that he lived to a great age. However, it was not until he was in his middle years that his wife gave him an heir, a girl. The Emperor and Empress loved the princess very much and she was their only child. She was a dutiful daughter and learned all she could from her father about the art of ruling, for she knew that when he died she would reign in his stead in Tenochtitlan.

Her name was Ixtlaccihuatl. Her parents and her friends called her Ixtla. She had a pleasant disposition and, as a result, she had many friends. The great palace where she lived with the Emperor and Empress rang with their laughter when they came to the parties her parents gave for her. As well as being a delightful companion Ixtla was also very pretty, even beautiful.

Her childhood was happy and she was content enough when she became a young woman. But by then she was fully aware of the great responsibilities which would be hers when her father died and she became serious and studious and did not enjoy parties as much as she had done when younger.

Another reason for her being so serious was that she was in love. This in itself was a joyous thing, but the Emperor forbade her to marry. He wanted her to reign and rule alone when he died, for he trusted no one, not even his wife, to rule as he did except his much loved only child, Ixtla. This was why there were some who doubted the wisdom of the Emperor for, by not allowing his heiress to marry, he showed a selfishness and shortsightedness towards his daughter and his empire which many considered was not truly wise. An emperor, they felt, who was not truly wise could not also be truly great. Or even truly powerful.

The man with whom Ixtla was in love was also in love with her. Had they been allowed to marry their state could have been doubly joyous. His name was Popocatepetl and Ixtla and his friends all called him Popo. He was a warrior in the service of the Emperor, tall and strong, with a capacity for gentleness, and very brave. He and Ixtla loved each other very much and while they were content and even happy when they were together, true joy was not theirs because the Emperor continued to insist that Ixtla should not be married when the time came for her to take on her father's responsibilities.

Reading Skill
Cause and Effect
What causes Ixtla to be serious?

**Reading Check**

What does the Emperor forbid Ixtla to do?

▲ **Critical Viewing**
Why do you think
volcanoes like this
one inspired legends
among ancient
peoples? **[Speculate]**

   This unfortunate but moderately happy relationship
between Ixtla and Popo continued for several years, the couple
pleading with the Emperor at regular intervals and the
Emperor remaining constantly adamant. Popo loved Ixtla no
less for her father's stubbornness and she loved him no less
while she studied, as her father demanded she should do, the
art of ruling in preparation for her reign.

   When the Emperor became very old he also became ill. In
his feebleness he channeled all his failing energies towards
instructing Ixtla in statecraft, for he was no longer able to
exercise that craft himself. So it was that his enemies, the
tribes who lived in the mountains and beyond, realized that
the great Emperor in Tenochtitlan was great no longer, for
he was only teaching his daughter to rule and not ruling
himself.

   The tribesmen came nearer and nearer to Tenochtitlan until
the city was besieged. At last the Emperor realized himself
that he was great no longer, that his power was nearly gone
and that his domain was in dire peril.

Warrior though he long had been, he was now too old and too ill to lead his fighting men into battle. At last he understood that, unless his enemies were frustrated in their efforts to enter and lay waste to Tenochtitlan, not only would he no longer be Emperor but his daughter would never be Empress.

Instead of appointing one of his warriors to lead the rest into battle on his behalf, he offered a bribe to all of them. Perhaps it was that his wisdom, if wisdom he had, had forsaken him, or perhaps he acted from fear. Or perhaps he simply changed his mind. But the bribe he offered to whichever warrior succeeded in lifting the siege of Tenochtitlan and defeating the enemies in and around the Valley of Mexico was both the hand of his daughter and the equal right to reign and rule, with her, in Tenochtitlan. Furthermore, he <u>decreed</u> that directly he learned that his enemies had been defeated he would instantly cease to be Emperor himself. Ixtla would not have to wait until her father died to become Empress and, if her father should die

Reading Skill
Cause and Effect
What was one effect of the Emperor becoming old and ill?

Vocabulary Builder
decreed (di krēd´) v. officially ordered

✓ **Reading Check**

What is the reward for lifting the siege?

of his illness or old age before his enemies were vanquished, he further decreed that he who overcame the surrounding enemies should marry the princess whether he, the Emperor, lived or not.

Ixtla was fearful when she heard of her father's bribe to his warriors, for the only one whom she had any wish to marry was Popo and she wanted to marry him, and only him, very much indeed.

The warriors, however, were glad when they heard of the decree: there was not one of them who would not have been glad to have the princess as his wife and they all relished the chance of becoming Emperor.

And so the warriors went to war at their ruler's behest, and each fought trebly[2] hard for each was fighting not only for the safety of Tenochtitlan and the surrounding valley, but for the delightful bride and for the right to be the Emperor himself.

Even though the warriors fought with great skill and even though each one exhibited a courage he did not know he possessed, the war was a long one. The Emperor's enemies were firmly entrenched around Lake Texcoco and Tenochtitlan by the time the warriors were sent to war, and as battle followed battle the final outcome was uncertain.

The warriors took a variety of weapons with them; wooden clubs edged with sharp blades of obsidian,[3] obsidian machetes,[4] javelins which they hurled at their enemies from troughed throwing boards, bows and arrows, slings and spears set with obsidian fragments, and lances, too. Many of them carried shields woven from wicker and covered in tough hide and most wore armor made of thick quilted cotton soaked in brine.

The war was long and fierce. Most of the warriors fought together and in unison, but some fought alone. As time went on natural

---

2. trebly (treʹ blē) *adv.* three times as much; triply.
3. obsidian (əb sidʹ ē ən) *n.* hard, usually dark-colored or black, volcanic glass.
4. machetes (mə shetʹ ēs) *n.* large, heavy-bladed knives.

Literature in Context

Social Studies Connection

Tenochtitlan Archaeologists believe that, at one time, more than 200,000 people lived in Tenochtitlan, the Aztec capital city in the middle of the giant lake Texcoco. Approximately one half of the population were farmers. Much of the farming was done on small island gardens surrounding the city. People living in Tenochtitlan depended on food the farmers grew outside the city. They also depended on water from outside the city, which was carried to the city by a system of aqueducts.

Because of its location and dependence on outside food and water, the city would have been helpless in the face of a siege. With no way to get in or out to get food, a siege would soon lead to starvation.

Connect to the Literature

Based on the situation, do you think the rewards offered by the Emperor in this story were appropriate? Explain.

leaders emerged and, of these, undoubtedly Popo was the best. Finally it was he, brandishing his club and shield, who led the great charge of running warriors across the valley, with their enemies fleeing before them to the safety of the coastal plains and jungles beyond the mountains.

The warriors acclaimed Popo as the man most responsible for the victory and, weary though they all were, they set off for Tenochtitlan to report to the Emperor and for Popo to claim Ixtla as his wife at last.

But a few of those warriors were jealous of Popo. Since they knew none of them could rightly claim the victory for himself (the decision among the Emperor's fighting men that Popo was responsible for the victory had been <u>unanimous</u>), they wanted to spoil for him and for Ixtla the delights which the Emperor had promised.

These few men slipped away from the rest at night and made their way to Tenochtitlan ahead of all the others. They reached the capital two days later, having traveled without sleep all the way, and quickly let it be known that, although the Emperor's warriors had been successful against his enemies, the warrior Popo had been killed in battle.

It was a foolish and cruel lie which those warriors told their Emperor, and they told it for no reason other than that they were jealous of Popo.

When the Emperor heard this he demanded that Popo's body be brought to him so that he might arrange a fitting burial. He knew the man his daughter had loved would have died courageously. The jealous warriors looked at one another and said nothing. Then one of them told the Emperor that Popo had been killed on the edge of Lake Texcoco and that his body had fallen into the water and no man had been able to retrieve it. The Emperor was saddened to hear this.

After a little while he demanded to be told which of his warriors had been responsible for the victory but none of the fighting men before him dared claim the successful outcome of the war for himself, for each knew the others would refute him. So they were silent. This puzzled the Emperor and he decided to wait for the main body of his warriors to return and not to press the few who had brought the news of the victory and of Popo's death.

Then the Emperor sent for his wife and his daughter and told them their enemies had been overcome. The Empress was thoroughly excited and relieved at the news. Ixtla was only

Literary Analysis
Legend and Fact What does the account of the battle suggest about the Aztecs' attitudes toward war?

Vocabulary Builder
unanimous (yoō nan´ ə məs) *adj.* based on complete agreement

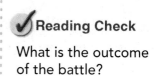

Reading Check

What is the outcome of the battle?

apprehensive. The Emperor, seeing her anxious face, told her quickly that Popo was dead. He went on to say that the warrior's body had been lost in the waters of Lake Texcoco, and again it was as though his wisdom had left him, for he spoke at some length of his not being able to tell Ixtla who her husband would be and who would become Emperor when the main body of warriors returned to Tenochtitlan.

But Ixtla heard nothing of what he told her, only that her beloved Popo was dead. She went to her room and lay down. Her mother followed her and saw at once she was very ill. Witch doctors were sent for, but they could not help the princess, and neither could her parents. Her illness had no name, unless it was the illness of a broken heart. Princess Ixtlaccihuatl did not wish to live if Popocatepetl was dead, and so she died herself.

The day after her death Popo returned to Tenochtitlan with all the other surviving warriors. They went straight to the palace and, with much cheering, told the Emperor that his enemies had been <u>routed</u> and that Popo was the undoubted victor of the conflict.

The Emperor praised his warriors and pronounced Popo to be the new Emperor in his place. When the young man asked first to see Ixtla, begging that they should be married at once before being jointly proclaimed Emperor and Empress, the Emperor had to tell Popo of Ixtla's death, and how it had happened.

Popo spoke not a word.

He gestured the assembled warriors to follow him and together they sought out the few jealous men who had given the false news of his death to the Emperor. With the army of

Vocabulary Builder
routed (rout´ əd) *v.* completely defeated

▼ **Critical Viewing**
In this manuscript, a human figure represents a corn plant growing. What does this tell you about the importance of corn in Aztec culture? **[Connect]**

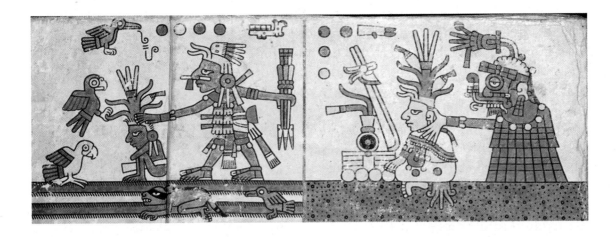

warriors watching, Popo killed each one of them in single combat with his obsidian studded club. No one tried to stop him.

That task accomplished Popo returned to the palace and, still without speaking and still wearing his stiff cotton armor, went to Ixtla's room. He gently lifted her body and carried it out of the palace and out of the city, and no one tried to stop him doing that either. All the warriors followed him in silence.

When he had walked some miles he gestured to them again and they built a huge pile of stones in the shape of a pyramid. They all worked together and they worked fast while Popo stood and watched, holding the body of the princess in his arms. By sunset the mighty edifice was finished. Popo climbed it alone, carrying Ixtla's corpse with him. There, at the very top, under a heap of stones, he buried the young woman he had loved so well and for so long, and who had died for the love of him.

That night Popo slept alone at the top of the pyramid by Ixtla's grave. In the morning he came down and spoke for the first time since the Emperor had told him the princess was dead. He told the warriors to build another pyramid, a little to the southeast of the one which held Ixtla's body and to build it higher than the other.

He told them too to tell the Emperor on his behalf that he, Popocatepetl, would never reign and rule in Tenochtitlan. He would keep watch over the grave of the Princess Ixtlaccihuatl for the rest of his life.

The messages to the Emperor were the last words Popo ever spoke. Well before the evening the second mighty pile of stones was built. Popo climbed it and stood at the top, taking a torch of resinous pine wood with him.

And when he reached the top he lit the torch and the warriors below saw the white smoke rise against the blue sky, and they watched as the sun began to set and the smoke turned pink and then a deep red, the color of blood.

So Popocatepetl stood there, holding the torch in memory of Ixtlaccihuatl, for the rest of his days.

The snows came and, as the years went by, the pyramids of stone became high white-capped mountains. Even now the one called Popocatepetl emits smoke in memory of the princess whose body lies in the mountain which bears her name.

Literary Analysis
Legend and Fact
What details about Popo make him larger than life?

Literary Analysis
Legend and Fact
Are the volcanoes real? How do you know?

Apply the Skills

Popocatepetl and Ixtlaccihuatl

Thinking About the Selection

1. **Respond:** What questions do you still have after reading the legend? Using a chart like the one shown, write your questions in the first column. Trade lists with a partner. In the second column of the chart, answer your partner's questions if you can. Then, discuss each chart. Finally, in the third column, explain how your understanding of the legend has or has not changed based on the discussion.

My Questions	Answers to My Questions	How Has My Understanding Changed?

2. **(a) Recall:** Why are Ixtla and Popo unable to marry?
   (b) Analyze: What qualities make the two well-matched?
3. **(a) Recall:** Why does Popo refuse to become emperor and rule in Tenochtitlan? **(b) Draw Conclusions:** Based on this legend, what traits do you think the Aztecs admired?
4. **(a) Interpret:** What lesson does the story suggest?
   (b) Evaluate: Can this lesson be applied in modern times? Explain.

Reading Skill

5. Reread the essay to find an **effect** for each of these **causes:**
   (a) The Emperor selfishly does not allow his daughter to marry.
   (b) The Emperor spends all his time teaching Ixtla statecraft.
   (c) The warriors lie to the Emperor about Popo's death.
   (d) Ixtla hears that Popo is dead.
6. According to the legend, what **causes** the volcano to smoke?

Literary Analysis

7. Identify two **facts** in this story. How do you know that they are facts?
8. Which events in this **legend** might have been based on historical events?
9. What details show Popo to be a larger-than-life hero?

QuickReview

Who's Who in the Legend

Emperor: an Aztec leader in Tenochtitlan

Ixtla: the Emperor's daughter

Popo: a warrior in love with Ixtla

Go Online
Assessment
For: Self-test
Visit: www.PHSchool.com
Web Code: ema-6605

Cause: why something happens

Effect: what happens

Legend: traditional story about the past that is usually based on historical fact

Fact: something that can be proved to be true

Vocabulary Builder

Practice Answer each question and then explain your answer.

1. If something is *decreed,* is it undecided?
2. If a vote is *unanimous,* does everyone agree?
3. If one's enemies have been *routed,* have they won?

Writing

Write a short **description** of the character of Ixtla.

- Using the legend for reference, jot down details about her appearance, emotional qualities, and actions.
- List vivid verbs and adjectives that will make your details interesting to readers. Include words that will appeal to the senses of sight and sound.

Use your notes to create a descriptive word picture of Ixtla.

For *Grammar, Vocabulary,* and *Assessment,*
see **Build Language Skills,** pages 868–869.

Extend Your Learning

Listening and Speaking Deliver a **persuasive speech** to convince the Emperor that Popo and Ixtla should be allowed to marry.

- On a note card, write a short statement explaining your position.
- List the main points that support your position on additional cards. Include solid evidence to appeal to the Emperor's emotions and reason. Jot down phrases that will remind you of your points, rather than using complete sentences.
- Refer to your note cards as you deliver your speech.

Research and Technology Write a **brief report** on the volcanoes in Mexico. Your report should include the names and locations of the major volcanoes, the type and appearance of each volcano, and human activity, if any, near or on each volcano. You may wish to include photos with captions. Share your report with the class.

Build Language Skills

Tenochtitlan: Inside the Aztec Capital •
Popocatepetl and Ixtlaccihuatl

Vocabulary Skill

Denotation and Connotation The **denotations**, or literal meanings, of *consequence* and *result* are very similar. They both refer to the outcome that follows a specific cause. However, *consequence* has a negative connotation because it has associations with actions or outcomes that follow a poor choice. *Result* does not have negative or positive connotations; it is neutral.

Practice Rewrite each sentence substituting a word with a positive connotation for the italicized word.

1. If you do not study, you must be prepared for the *consequences*.
2. Propaganda attempts to *sway* the reader's opinion.
3. Their *propaganda* didn't affect my opinion.
4. What could *crop up* that might alter these plans?

Grammar Lesson

Commas A *comma* signals a brief pause. A *semicolon* signals a stronger separation than a comma. The chart shows several uses of the comma.

MorePractice

For more about commas and semicolons, see the Grammar Handbook, p. R31.

Before a conjunction joining independent clauses	John thought he was late, and he rushed through the parking lot.
After an introductory phrase or clause	If you go to the play, how will you get your homework finished?
Between items in a series	It was a dark, cold, windy night.

Practice Punctuate each of the following sentences correctly with commas.

1. Children enjoy listening to a storyteller and they are encouraged to make up their own stories.
2. The semifinalists in the spelling bee are Joseph Israel Sarah and Lorna.
3. In the distance the child played innocently with her toys.
4. The flight lasted only twelve seconds and the plane traveled just 120 feet.

WG *Prentice Hall Writing and Grammar Connection: Chapter 26, Sections 2 and 3*

Reading: Cause and Effect

Directions: *Read the selection. Then, answer the questions.*

After a great start this season, the Mudville Tigers slumped during the finals. Ace pitcher Yasmin Jordan was unable to play past the first few games because of an injury. Her replacement, Samantha Jones, was equally gifted, but bad luck struck again, when heavy storms caused the cancellation of many practices. Cancelled practices led to more errors and more losses. As a result, team morale was low. By the time of the finals, the Tigers' spirit was gone, and they were playing poorly.

1. What caused Jordan to drop out of playing after the first few games?
   A bad weather
   B an argument with Jones
   C an injury
   D bad luck

2. What caused the cancellation of many practices for the Mudville Tigers?
   A low team morale
   B poor playing
   C a wrist injury
   D heavy storms

3. Which phrase in the story signals a cause-and-effect relationship?
   A As a result
   B After a great start
   C By the time of the finals
   D was equally gifted

4. Which cause led to low morale?
   A poor playing during the finals
   B more errors and more losses
   C injuries
   D a poor start to the season

Timed Writing: Explanation [Connections]

Review "Tenochtitlan: Inside the Aztec Capital" or "Popocatepetl and Ixtlaccihuatl." For one of the stories, describe and explain the culture of the people in the selection. Use specific facts and quotations from the work to support your ideas. **(40 minutes)**

 ## Writing Workshop: *Work in Progress*

Business Letter

Your interest in the information you request may be personal, but your letter should be formal and direct. Choose one of the locations from the Wish List in your portfolio and write a brief sentence stating your purpose for writing to that specific service provider.

Epic Conventions

An **epic** is story or long poem about the adventures of a larger-than-life hero. Epic tales usually focus on the hero's bravery, strength, and success in battle or adventure. In addition to telling the story of a hero, an epic is also a portrait of the culture that produced it. The following **epic conventions** are traditional characteristics of this form of literature:

- a dangerous journey, or *quest,* that the hero must take
- gods or powerful characters who help
- a setting covering several nations
- a serious, formal style

Comparing Treatment of Epic Conventions

Because epic tales have become an important part of the literature of different cultures, later generations often create new works inspired by these epics. For example, while one author may base a modern novel on the ancient Greek epic the *Odyssey,* another may use the same story as a basis for a humorous tale. As you read "Perseus" and "Percy-Us Brings the Gawgon's Head," determine which story is closer to the original epic and which is written to make you chuckle. Analyze the stories using a chart like this.

Epic Conventions	Perseus	Percy-Us
dangerous journey		
characters who help		
broad setting		
serious, formal style		

Vocabulary Builder

Perseus

- **cowered** (kou´ ərd) *v.* crouched down or huddled up, as from fear (p. 873) *Ron cowered when the barking dog saw him.*

- **hideous** (hid´ ē əs) *adj.* horrible to see; very ugly (p. 874) *The hideous monster frightened the moviegoers.*

- **pursuit** (pər soot´) *n.* the act of chasing (p. 876) *The man was in pursuit of his runaway cat.*

Percy-Us Brings the Gawgon's Head

- **knack** (nak) *n.* ability to do something easily (p. 877) *Larry has a knack for playing piano.*

- **reveling** (rev´ əl in) *n.* celebrating (p. 879) *The fans stopped their reveling at dawn.*

- **pathetic** (pə thet´ ik) *adj.* pitiful (p. 880) *The wet puppy gave me a pathetic look.*

- **petrified** (pe´ trə fīd´) *adj.* turned into stone (p. 880) *The petrified wood felt as heavy as a boulder.*

Build Understanding

Connecting to the Literature

Reading/Writing Connection Superheroes such as Spiderman and Wonder Woman are popular among children and adults alike. Write a few sentences explaining why you think people are interested in superheroes. Use at least three of the following words: *alter, assist, challenge, contrast, maximize.*

Meet the Authors

Alice **Low** (b. 1926)

Growing up in New York City, Alice Low was surrounded by creative people. Her mother wrote children's books and had friends in the fields of publishing and the arts. In addition, Low went to a school that emphasized the creative and performing arts.

Varied Interests Low has written children's books on topics ranging from Greek heroes to holidays. In addition to writing, she enjoys painting, ceramics, playing tennis, and traveling. About her writing, she has said, "Many a line has come to me on a tennis court or walk."

Lloyd **Alexander** (b. 1924)

The popular fantasy writer Lloyd Alexander grew up reading Greek and Celtic myths and the tales of King Arthur.

Writing From Life After years struggling as a writer, Alexander published his fourth novel *And Let the Credit Go.* The book was based on Alexander's own experiences. Once he realized that he could write about topics he loves, such as music and his cats, his career took off. Much later, Alexander began to write fantasy stories for children. He has said, ". . . years passed before I learned a writer could know and love a fantasy world as much as his real one."

Go **Online**
Author Link
For: More about the authors
Visit: www.PHSchool.com
Web Code: eme-9606

Perseus
Alice Low

◀ **Critical Viewing**
What details in this
painting suggest that
this story might be an
epic? **[Analyze]**

King Acrisius of Argos[1] had a beautiful daughter named
Danaë,[2] but he was not satisfied with her, for he wanted a
son. He visited the oracle at Delphi to find out if he would ever
have a male child. To his dismay he was told, "You shall never
have a son. Furthermore, your daughter shall give birth to a
son who shall take your life."

I must make certain that Danaë never has any children,
said the king to himself. And he shut his daughter away from
the world in a bronze house underground, so that no man
would ever fall in love with her and father her child. Nobody
could enter the house, for only a tiny section of the roof was
open to the surface of the earth, to let in light and air.

---

1. **Argos** (är´ gäs´) city-state in ancient Greece.
2. **Danaë** (dan´ ā ē´) Perseus' mother.

Poor Danaë! She was all alone, week after week, with just a patch of sky to look at. Then one day a strange thing occurred. Suddenly a shower of gold rained down into her house, and that shower changed into Zeus, who declared his love for her.

Within the year Danaë bore Zeus's son, whom she named Perseus. Danaë tried to hide Perseus from her father. At last, though, King Acrisius discovered him and said to Danaë, "One day this son of yours will kill me. I cannot kill him, for that would anger his father, Zeus. But I will have the two of you sealed in a chest and tossed into the sea. If you do not survive, that will be Poseidon's fault."

"Please, Father, spare us," cried Danaë. "I will keep Perseus by my side always and make certain that he will never harm you."

But Acrisius said, "The oracle at Delphi never lies, and I must protect myself."

He ordered carpenters to make a large wooden chest. When it was finished, he put Danaë and Perseus in it and had it thrown into the sea.

For a day and a night, Danaë <u>cowered</u> in the chest, holding Perseus in her arms as the waves tossed them to and fro. Then, suddenly, Danaë felt a bump, and the chest stopped moving. "We are on land," she said to Perseus. "But how can we ever get out of this sealed chest?"

Perseus was too young to understand her, and he cried and cried because he was hungry. Danaë tried to comfort him, but his wails continued, which was a good thing. A fisherman, passing by, heard the cries and broke open the chest. His name was Dictys, and he took Danaë and Perseus to his home, where he and his wife cared for them gladly, for they were childless.

Perseus grew into a strong young man and became a fisherman on that small island. He and his mother were content until Dictys's brother, Polydectes[3], who ruled the island, fell in love with Danaë and tried to force her to marry him. Perseus defended his mother so bravely that Polydectes decided he had to get rid of him.

Pretending he was going to marry another princess, Polydectes asked each guest to bring a wedding gift. Perseus said to Polydectes, "Alas, I am too poor to bring a gift for a ruler and his bride."

---

3. Polydectes (päl i dek´ tēz) the ruler of the island Perseus grew up on.

Literary Analysis
Epic Conventions
What aspect of Perseus' birth helps make him an epic hero?

Vocabulary Builder
cowered (kou´ ərd) *v.* crouched down or huddled up, as from fear

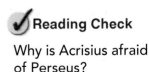**Reading Check**

Why is Acrisius afraid of Perseus?

And Polydectes said, "Then I shall tell you of a gift you can win for me, but I do not know if you are brave enough to get it."

"Tell me what it is, and I promise I shall get it for you," said Perseus. "I do not lack for bravery."

"Very well," said Polydectes. "I want you to bring me the head of Medusa, the horrible Gorgon."

Perseus was trapped by his bold promise, even though he knew that this feat was impossible for one man alone. Medusa was one of the three Gorgons—huge, <u>hideous</u> winged creatures. Their hair was made of snakes, and their faces were so ugly that anyone who looked at them immediately turned to stone.

Fortunately for Perseus, a goddess and a god overheard that conversation, and not long afterward they appeared to him and offered him their help.

First Athena flew down from Mount Olympus, holding her dazzling shield of brass. She gave it to the astonished Perseus, saying, "You must use this as a mirror when you slay Medusa. In this way you will not look at her directly, but only at her reflection, and so you will not be turned to stone."

Perseus thanked the wise goddess and then said, "But I do not know where Medusa lives. How shall I find her?"

At that moment, Perseus saw a bright light overhead. Hermes, the messenger of the gods, flew down and landed at his side. "I shall be your guide," he said, "and also help you overcome the terrible Medusa. Here is a sword that can never be broken, not even by the hard scales of Medusa's neck."

"This is indeed a wonderful gift," said Perseus. "Now I must be on my way to slay Medusa and bring back her head."

"Not yet," said Hermes. "There are three other things you must have first: winged sandals, a magic wallet, and a cap to make you invisible. These are guarded by the nymphs of the North, and only the Gray Women, who live in a dreary gray land, know where to find them. Follow me, and we will begin the long journey."

Hermes guided Perseus to the gray land, where it was always gray twilight. At last they found the shriveled old Gray Women, who had swanlike bodies and human heads, but only one eye among the three of them. Perseus and Hermes hid behind a rock and watched the Gray Women pass the eye around. Each had a turn to put it in the middle of her forehead.

"The next time the eye is passed around," said Hermes to Perseus, "you must grab it and not give it back until they tell you where to find the nymphs of the North."

Perseus waited for the right moment. Then he darted out and snatched the eye. The Gray Women ran around blindly, shouting, "Where is our eye? Who took it?"

"I took your eye," Perseus said, "and I will not give it back until you tell me how to find the nymphs of the North."

Of course the Gray Women were anxious to have their eye, and so they immediately gave Perseus detailed directions. He gave them back their eye and went on his way with Hermes.

Once more they traveled far and long, this time over the ocean to the north. The nymphs of the North received them warmly and gave Perseus the three magic gifts.

Perseus put on the cap of invisibility and the magic sandals and, holding the magic wallet, flew after Hermes to the island of the Gorgons. Beneath him he could see stones in the shapes of animals and men, and he shuddered, for he knew that they had once been alive—before they had looked at the fearful Gorgons. But he was confident, now that he was armed with Hermes' sword, Athena's shield, and the three magic gifts.

Perseus hovered over the Gorgons. Fortunately he remembered to look into the mirrorlike shield at their reflections. The three hideous, winged, snake-haired Gorgons were asleep.

But which one is Medusa? he thought. She is the only one I can kill, for the other two are immortal. Again Athena came to his aid, saying, "That one in the middle is Medusa. Strike now, while she is asleep."

Perseus flew within inches of Medusa, his sword held ready. Then, looking into the shield, he struck off Medusa's head with one well-aimed blow. He stuffed the head into his magic wallet, which grew large enough to hold the head with all its snakes still hissing and wriggling.

The other two Gorgons woke up when they heard the headless body of Medusa thrashing about. They flew into the air in

▲ **Critical Viewing**
Does this bust of Medusa meet your expectations of what a Gorgon should look like? Why or why not? **[Connect]**

✔ **Reading Check**

Why must Perseus avoid looking at the Gorgons directly?

pursuit of Perseus. But they could not see him, for he had on his cap of invisibility, and he flew away in his winged sandals, faster than the wind.

Now Perseus headed for home alone, for Hermes his mission accomplished, had left. On his way, Perseus slew a dangerous sea monster that was about to devour a lovely princess named Andromeda. Then Perseus took Andromeda home with him, for she had agreed to be his bride.

As soon as they reached home, Perseus strode into Polydectes' palace and said to the ruler, "I have brought you the head of Medusa."

But Polydectes refused to believe Perseus. "If you even had gone near Medusa, you would not be here to tell the tale. What a liar you are!"

Perseus could not stand to be taunted and mistrusted. And now he realized that this cruel ruler had sent him on the chase just to get rid of him. He pulled out Medusa's head to show it to Polydectes, who turned to stone the moment he saw it.

Kind Dictys became ruler of the island, and Perseus sailed to Argos with his mother, Danaë, and his wife, Andromeda. Danaë wanted to see her father, King Acrisius, again and to be reconciled with him. But Acrisius was attending games that were being held in another city.

Since Perseus wanted to take part in the games, he journeyed to that city. There he took his turn at throwing the discus. As the discus left his hand, a sudden wind blew it into the grandstand. It hit King Acrisius, who was a spectator, and killed him. Thus was fulfilled the prophecy of the oracle at Delphi, which had predicted that the king would be killed by his grandson.

Vocabulary Builder
pursuit (pər so͞ot′) *n.* the act of chasing

Thinking About the Selection

1. **Respond:** What do you admire most about the hero Perseus? Explain.

2. **(a) Recall:** Why does Perseus agree to give Polydectes the head of Medusa? **(b) Infer:** What does this reveal about Perseus? **(c) Analyze:** Why is this event important to the story?

3. **(a) Recall:** What event happens at the end of the story? **(b) Speculate:** How do you think Perseus and Danaë will react to this event? **(c) Support:** Do you think the ending of the story represents a sense of justice? Support your answer with details from the story.

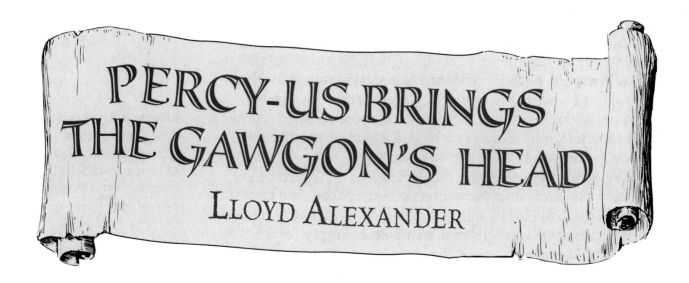

PERCY-US BRINGS THE GAWGON'S HEAD

LLOYD ALEXANDER

Percy-Us[1] put on the cap and sandals the nymphs of the Tulip Garden had given him. Next thing he knew, he was high in the air—a thrilling sensation, except he was flying upside down and backward. Kicking his heels and flapping his arms, it took him some time to get the <u>knack</u> of soaring through the clouds as if he were belly-flopping on a sled.

Since the cap made him invisible, flocks of birds kept bumping into him until he finally took it off.

Soon, Percy-Us saw the mountain range that Hermes had described and swooped down to land at the mouth of a cave, where The Gawgon[2] sat in a rocking chair.

"I've been expecting you, Percy-Us," said The Gawgon. The serpents that covered her head instead of hair had been snoozing; but now they perked up, darted out forked tongues, and fixed him with beady eyes.

Percy-Us made sure not to gaze directly at The Gawgon. Following the advice of Hermes, he used his polished shield as a mirror.

"Speak up. I can't hear you," said The Gawgon. "Stop mumbling into that shield. When you talk to people, it's polite to look at them. Don't you know anything at all about being a hero?"

Percy-Us, too clever to be caught in such a trap, only tightened his grip on the sword. The Gawgon kept on calmly rocking.

Vocabulary Builder
knack (nak) *n.* ability to do something easily

---

1. **Percy-Us** character based on Perseus in the epic tale "Perseus."
2. **The Gawgon** character based on Medusa, one of the Gorgons in the epic tale "Perseus."

"I assume you're here to cut my head off," The Gawgon said. "Very well, get on with it."

Holding up his shield, observing The Gawgon in its reflection, Percy-Us walked backward to her. When he was close enough, he swung his sword in a great, glittering sweep.

Percy-Us miscalculated. He had forgotten that everything reflected in a mirror was reversed. Instead of smiting The Gawgon, he nearly sliced off his own ear.

"Try again," The Gawgon suggested.

Percy-Us made another swipe with his sword, but eyes on the polished shield, he still got mixed up over which was left and which was right. He kept swinging at empty air until he was out of breath.

"This is getting tiresome," said The Gawgon, who kept on rocking while Percy-Us slashed around in all the wrong directions. "You'll do better if you can see what you're trying to chop off.

"Put down that shield and go straight about your business. Don't worry," she added, "you won't be turned to stone. I'll give you something to make you immune."

The Gawgon tossed Percy-Us a licorice gumdrop. "Here, eat this," she said as Percy-Us eyed it distrustfully. "Go on, it will protect you. Gawgons never lie."

Literary Analysis
Epic Conventions
How do the actions of Percy-Us differ from the actions of a typical epic hero?

▼ **Critical Viewing**
The Gawgon is actually an elderly woman. Why might a young boy—like the one shown on page 879—see an elderly woman as a powerful monster? **[Speculate]**

Percy-Us chewed up the gumdrop and took a quick peek at The Gawgon. He was glad to find he had not turned to stone.

"That should make things easier," The Gawgon said. "But, before you start chopping, let me review the situation. You need a present for a wedding you don't want to go to, for a king you don't like to begin with. So you blurt out the first thing that comes into your head and promise something you know perfectly well you can't deliver.

"Furthermore"—The Gawgon sharply eyed Percy-Us, who shuffled his feet uncomfortably— "what you promised was at the expense of an innocent bystander who never did you any harm. All for the sake of saving yourself embarrassment, making yourself a hero, and gaining the good opinion of that oaf Polly Deck-Tease.[3] Am I correct so far?"

Percy-Us sheepishly admitted she was.

"That strikes me as utterly selfish," The Gawgon said, "with no regard for anyone's feelings but your own. Stupid, into the bargain. What do you say to that?"

Percy-Us stuttered and stammered and came up with no answer. He finally admitted The Gawgon was right.

"Good," said The Gawgon. "Now you're beginning to think straight even if you can't smite straight. Nevertheless, I recognize you've gone to some effort. That's commendable; I give you credit. So, I'll tell you what I'm going to do."

The Gawgon explained her plan, to which Percy-Us heartily agreed. Hand in hand with The Gawgon, he soared into the air, and the two of them flew quickly to the palace of King Polly Deck-Tease.

While The Gawgon waited outside the door, Percy-Us strode into the great hall. The bride had not yet arrived, but the impatient Polly Deck-Tease and his warriors had already started feasting and <u>reveling</u>, gobbling refreshments by the handful.

"Aha!" shouted Polly Deck-Tease. "There you are! About time. You brought me The Gawgon's head?"

"Yes," Percy-Us replied, "I certainly did."

---

3. **Polly Deck-Tease** character based on Polydectes in the epic tale "Perseus."

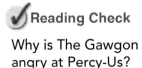

Vocabulary Builder
reveling (rev´ əl iŋ) v. celebrating

✓ **Reading Check**

Why is The Gawgon angry at Percy-Us?

"Let's have it, then," Polly Deck-Tease ordered. "So far, my only wedding presents are a lot of napkin rings."

Percy-Us tossed him the leather sack. Sucking his teeth in gleeful anticipation, Polly Deck-Tease opened it. His jaw dropped.

"Empty!" he burst out. "Nothing! What kind of joke is this? You broke your promise, you boasting, bragging, <u>pathetic</u> excuse for a hero! I don't like being disappointed, especially on my wedding day. You'll regret trifling with me. I'll have you diced up and deep-fried in boiling oil."

"I didn't break my promise," Percy-Us replied. "I told you I'd bring The Gawgon's head. So I did."

Having put on the cap of invisibility, The Gawgon stepped into the hall.

"And all the rest of her, too," said Percy-Us.

The Gawgon took off the cap and glared at the revelers. Instantly, they turned to stone. Polly Deck-Tease, shaking a fist, stood literally <u>petrified</u>. Some of the warriors had stayed seated, others climbed to their feet, still others held goblets in upraised hands, motionless as marble statues.

"Nice garden ornaments," The Gawgon said. "Someday, no doubt, they'll be in the British Museum."

Percy-Us, delighted everything had ended so well, flew The Gawgon to her cave, thanked her, and was about to leave when he stopped and turned back.

"For a Gawgon," he said, "you're not a bad sort."

"For a hero," said The Gawgon, "you're not a bad sort either."

Vocabulary Builder
pathetic (pə thet´ ik)
adj. pitiful

petrified (pe´ trə fīd´)
adj. turned into stone

Literary Analysis
Epic Conventions
What kind of language do Percy-Us and The Gawgon use?

Thinking About the Selection

1. **Respond:** What did you find most humorous about Percy-Us and The Gawgon?

2. **(a) Recall:** What does Polly Deck-Tease do when he discovers that the bag that Percy-Us has brought him is empty?
   (b) Interpret: What does this show about Polly Deck-Tease?
   (c) Make a Judgment: Do you think Percy-Us does the right thing by sparing the life of the Gawgon but helping to take the life of Polly Deck-Tease? Explain.

3. **Evaluate:** Do you think that Lloyd Alexander was successful in creating humor in his adaptation of this epic tale? Why or why not?

Apply the Skills

Perseus • Percy-Us Brings The Gawgon's Head

Comparing Treatment of Epic Conventions

1. Compare and contrast the scene in which the hero attempts to chop off the monster's head in each selection. Use a chart like the one shown.

	Perseus	Percy-Us
tools and weapons used		
attitude of the hero		
attitude of the monster		
outcome		

2. Explain how your experience of reading "Percy-Us Brings The Gawgon's Head" would have been different if you had not first read "Perseus."

Writing to Compare Literary Works

Both of these selections are based on a character in an epic written centuries ago. In an essay, compare and contrast the heroes Perseus and Percy-Us. Discuss how the characters are alike and different. Use these questions to get started:

- What traits does each character best demonstrate?
- What motivates each hero?
- How does each hero achieve his goal?
- Which character is more heroic? Why?

Vocabulary Builder

Practice For each item, write a sentence that correctly uses the given word pair.

1. knack; practice
2. hideous; frightening
3. reveling; joyful
4. pathetic; embarrass
5. pursuit; tired
6. cowered; coward
7. petrified; scared

QuickReview

Epics: stories or long poems about the adventures of larger-than-life heroes

Go Online
Assessment
For: Self-test
Visit: www.PHSchool.com
Web Code: ema-6606

Reading

Directions: *Questions 1–5 are based on the following selection.*

During summers off the coast of Alaska, long hours of sunshine warm the icy waters. Microscopic water plants begin to bloom, and tiny marine animals flock to the warming waters to feed on them. The tiny animals, in turn, lure giant humpback whales to the waters.

Because these whales have rows of filters in their mouths instead of teeth, the tiny creatures are a perfect food source. As water flows through the filters, the filters trap the small animals, which the whale eats.

Humpbacks also eat larger fish, such as sardines or mackerel. In fact, humpback whales spend most of their time eating because they need an enormous amount of food to remain active and warm. Each whale eats between 4,500 and 5,000 pounds of food each day!

As autumn nears, the days grow shorter, causing the water to cool. Food supplies are not as plentiful in the cooler water. Because of this, the humpback whales move to warmer waters near Hawaii. There they stay until summer days call them northward.

1. **What is the effect of longer hours of sunshine?**
   A Microscopic plants begin to bloom.
   B Whales create a bubble net.
   C Humpback whales return from Hawaii.
   D Sardines and mackerel are plentiful.

2. **Tiny marine creatures are a perfect food for humpback whales because**
   A they live in cold water.
   B these whales have filters in their mouths instead of teeth.
   C they are easy to catch.
   D most large fish do not eat them.

3. **Why do humpback whales spend so much time eating?**
   A Food takes a long time to consume.
   B Hunting takes a lot of energy.
   C They need a large amount of food to stay active and warm.
   D They need to eat as much as they can before the waters cool.

4. **What is the main reason humpback whales leave the waters of Alaska?**
   A The sun shines for more hours per day as autumn nears.
   B Fewer fish are in the water after the whales have been there.
   C The whales' food supply is not as plentiful in the cooler water.
   D The humpback whales always spend the winter near Alaska.

5. **Which is an effect of changing seasons?**
   A The whales move east.
   B The whales move.
   C The whales move to deeper water.
   D The whales move to shallower water.

Vocabulary

Directions: *Choose the sentence in which the word is used correctly.*

6. **effect**
   A The rain will effect our plans.
   B Procedural changes effect us.
   C The effect of the snow was that they had to reschedule their trip.
   D We need to effect the decision before it is final.

7. **consequence**
   A They consequence the rain by carrying an umbrella.
   B We will consequence the experiment in the hypothesis section.
   C To consequence the effect of that, you must look at all the possibilities.
   D It is not difficult to predict the consequence of forgetting to study.

8. **alter**
   A The stone was part of an ancient alter.
   B There are consequences of that alter.
   C Snow means we should alter our plans.
   D An alter method of defense is necessary.

9. **affect**
   A The rain will affect our plans.
   B The affect of the snow was that they had to reschedule their trip.
   C We weren't sure what the affect of adding another musician would be.
   D Despite the weather's affect we were determined to continue our journey.

10. **occur**
    A A hurricane is an unusual occur here.
    B Tryouts cannot occur until we decide on the play.
    C We occur a lot of expenses.
    D It was an occur that seemed unusual.

Directions: *Choose the word whose connotation best fits the sentence.*

11. He _____ kept his water canteen full in case the next water source was dry.
    A warily
    B slowly
    C cautiously
    D watchfully

12. Players on our lacrosse team _____ well; they always play as a team.
    A agree
    B cooperate
    C combine
    D ally

13. The fireman was honored for his _____ act.
    A foolhardy
    B courageous
    C brazen
    D reckless

14. Voting in an election is a _____ act.
    A dedicated
    B chauvinistic
    C zealous
    D patriotic

Workplace Writing: Business Letter

A **business letter** is a brief but formal written communication with a specific purpose. People write business letters to provide or request information, to express an opinion, or to complain. Follow the steps outlined in this workshop to write your own business letter.

Assignment Write a business letter requesting information from a company or an organization.

What to Include Your letter should feature these elements:
- standard business letter format
- a clear statement of your request
- details to support your request
- formal and polite language
- an appropriate organizational structure
- error-free writing, including the correct use of commas

To preview the criteria on which your business letter may be judged, see the rubric on page 888.

Prewriting

Choosing Your Topic

Use this strategy for choosing a topic:

Brainstorm With a partner, identify the types of companies or organizations from which you might request information. Think about local service providers, magazines, stores, or other businesses with which you interact on a regular basis.

Gathering Details

Organize the facts. Briefly, state your purpose for writing. Then, jot down your contact information to ensure that the recipient can respond to your letter. Use the library, Internet, or customer service department to locate the recipient's name, title, and business address. Use an organizer like this to keep track of your information.

Using the Form

You may use elements of this form in these types of writing:
- memos
- letters to the editor
- proposals
- letters of inquiry or complaint

Work in Progress

Review the work you did on pages 821, 843, and 869.

Company or Organization	Purpose for Writing	Contact Information	Details
Greenhaus Dance Company	to get information about the faculty	Name: Rita Moore Title: Director Address: 2 Main St., Chicago, IL 80808	I want to know the dance background of the various faculty members.

Drafting

Shaping Your Writing

Use an appropriate format. The standard form for a business letter has the following parts:
- **Heading:** your address and the date of the letter
- **Inside Address:** the name and address that shows where the letter will be sent
- **Greeting:** the recipient's name, *Dear Sir, Dear Madam,* or *To Whom It May Concern,* followed by a colon
- **Body:** your purpose for writing
- **Closing:** *Sincerely* or *Respectfully,* followed by a comma
- **Signature:** your full name and your signature above it

In **block format,** each part of the letter begins at the left margin. In **modified** block format, the heading, the closing, and the signature are indented to the center of the page. (See page R23.)

Providing Elaboration

Develop the body. Open with a brief introduction that clearly states your purpose. Then, develop your request, including supporting details. Use a polite tone. End by thanking the recipient.

Revising

Revising Your Overall Structure

Eliminate irrelevant details. The details you include in your business letter should support your main points. Delete any unnecessary information, including extra—but not key—details from your personal life. Also, revise any wordy or repetitive passages.

Revising Your Word Choice

Use formal language. The tone of your letter should be friendly, but serious and respectful. Replace any slang words in your draft.

Reading Writing Connection

To read the complete student model, see page 887.

Student Model: Revising to Eliminate Irrelevant Details

So, if you will, look at this once-in-a lifetime opportunity ~~and an excellent opportunity~~ to learn many different things that aren't taught in schools. ~~The gymnastics clubs and marching bands usually raise their own funds, and it takes a long time!~~

> Melissa removed a repetitive phrase and an unimportant detail from her letter.

Integrating Grammar Skills

Revising Incorrect Use of Commas

A **comma** is a punctuation mark used to indicate a brief pause. The following examples illustrate some common misuses of commas.

Prentice Hall Writing and Grammar Connection: Chapter 26, Section 2

Rule: Commas separate two adjectives in a series, but not the adjective from the noun.

> **Misused:** My favorite drink is a cool, refreshing, lemonade.
>
> **Correct:** My favorite drink is a cool, refreshing lemonade.

Rule: Commas do not separate parts of a compound subject.

> **Misused:** After dinner, my friend Annie, and her sister Emma, left.
>
> **Correct:** After dinner, my friend Annie and her sister Emma left.

Rule: Commas separate clauses that include both a subject and its verb, not parts of a compound verb.

> **Misused:** The candidate looked out at the audience, and laughed.
>
> **Correct:** The candidate looked out at the audience and laughed.

Rule: Commas do not separate parts of a compound object.

> **Misused:** He made a sundae with whipped cream, and sprinkles.
>
> **Correct:** He made a sundae with whipped cream and sprinkles.

Fixing Incorrect Use of Commas To fix comma errors, follow these rules:

1. **Add a comma or commas:**
   - before a conjunction that separates two independent clauses in a compound sentence.
   - to separate three or more words, phrases, or clauses.
   - to separate adjectives of equal rank.
   - to set off an introductory adverb clause.

2. **Eliminate the comma:**
   - if it comes directly between the subject and the verb of a sentence.
   - if it separates an adjective from the noun that follows it.
   - if it separates a compound subject, verb, or object.

Apply It to Your Editing

Reread each sentence in your letter, noting compound subjects, verbs, and objects. If necessary, revise the sentences using one of the methods above.

Student Model: Melissa Gornto
Durham, NC

Melissa Gornto
1436 Any Street
Durham, NC 27713

September 23, 2010

14th District Judicial Bar Board
Government Office Building, Office #33
67 Sherman Street
Durham, NC 27713

Dear Sir or Madam:

I am writing to you concerning financing for the trip that my classmates and I are taking to London. I see it as a great educational opportunity to learn about a different culture, history, and way of life. We do not know much about the British society, and this is a chance for us to find out the real information.

> Melissa uses block format in her business letter, setting all elements at the left margin.

> Melissa clearly states her purpose.

If you were to help us with the monetary grant, a weight would be lifted off our shoulders concerning the money issue. Using the money, we would be able to go to London, where we could see many things. We would be able to go to Buckingham Palace, Stonehenge, and Big Ben. This is also a great educational opportunity because it allows us to see the English way of life, including the exchange of money (the euro), and the difference in speech. They may speak English, but that doesn't mean the words have the same sound or definition. So, if you will, look at this as a once-in-a-lifetime opportunity to learn many different things that aren't taught in schools.

> By adding these details, Melissa supports her request with reasons.

Thank you for your time regarding this matter. Please take this trip into consideration and help us out. If you do, you won't have to worry about us not being grateful. This is an adventure my fellow classmates and I would love to go on. Once again, thank you for your time.

> Melissa uses friendly, yet formal language.

Sincerely,

Melissa Gornto

Melissa Gornto

Editing and Proofreading

A letter with mistakes makes a poor impression and may signal that the writer is not serious in his or her request. Review your draft to eliminate errors in grammar, spelling, or punctuation.

Focus on Spelling: Use the Internet or phone directories to verify that the name, title, and address of the recipient are spelled correctly. Carefully reread your letter to check for any other spelling errors.

Publishing and Presenting

Consider one of the following ways to share your writing:

Swap letters. Trade letters with a classmate. Read the letter carefully. Then, write a realistic response to the request for information.

Send your letter. Use e-mail or standard mail to send your request for information to the company or organization you have selected. If you send your letter by standard mail, sign it and neatly write the address on the envelope before mailing.

Reflecting on Your Writing

Writer's Journal Jot down your thoughts on the experience of writing a business letter. Begin by answering these questions:
- Which revision strategy was most useful? Why?
- In the process of writing, what did you learn about the business or organization you chose?

> *Prentice Hall Writing and Grammar Connection: Styles for Business and Friendly Letters, pages 758–759.*

Rubric for Self-Assessment

To assess your business letter, use the following rubric:

Criteria	Rating Scale (not very — very)				
Focus: How clearly have you stated your request?	1	2	3	4	5
Organization: How well have you organized your letter according to standard business format?	1	2	3	4	5
Support/Elaboration: How well do the details support your request?	1	2	3	4	5
Style: How formal and polite is the language?	1	2	3	4	5
Conventions: How correct is your grammar, especially your use of commas?	1	2	3	4	5

Skills You Will Learn

Reading Skill: *Use Prior Knowledge to Compare and Contrast*
Literary Analysis: *Cultural Context*

Reading Skill: *Comparison-and-Contrast Organization*

Reading Skill: *Use a Venn Diagram to Compare and Contrast*
Literary Analysis: *Folk Tales*

Literary Analysis: *Comparing Tone*

Literature You Will Read

Reading: Compare and Contrast

> When you **compare**, you tell how two or more things are alike.
> When you **contrast**, you tell how two or more things are different.

Skills and Strategies You Will Learn in Part 2

In Part 2, you will learn

- to **use your prior knowledge to compare and contrast** (p. 892)
- to **use a Venn diagram** to examine similarities and differences (p. 912)
- to recognize **comparison-and-contrast organization** (p. 908)

Using the Skills and Strategies in Part 2

In Part 2, you will learn to look for similarities and differences between something you are learning about and something you are familiar with. You will also practice using graphic organizers to structure details that are similar and those that are different.

The Venn diagram shows you how you can organize similarities and differences when you compare and contrast.

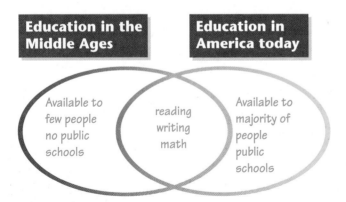

Education in the Middle Ages

Education in America today

Available to few people no public schools

reading writing math

Available to majority of people public schools

As you read the literature in this part, you will practice comparing and contrasting.

Academic Vocabulary: Words for Discussing Comparison and Contrast

The following words will help you write and talk about comparing and contrasting as you read the selections in this unit.

Word	Definition	Example Sentence
analyze *v.*	examine something in great detail	Serena helped her friend *analyze* the story and identify its theme.
characteristic *n.*	a quality that makes a person or thing recognizable	One *characteristic* of Mia's poetry is a regular rhyme scheme.
aspect *n.*	one feature or part of a whole	A familiar *aspect* of Asimov's writing is the set of laws for robots.
detail *n.*	an individual part of something, such as one item of information in a story	Every *detail* of the setting contributed to the spooky mood in the mystery story.
unique *adj.*	being the only one of its kind	The *unique* characteristic of O. Henry stories is the surprise ending.

Vocabulary Skill: Idioms

▶ An **idiom** is an expression unique to a language or culture that is not meant to be understood literally.

In Part 2 you will learn
- common idioms
- idiomatic expressions

Idiom I don't like it when my friends *talk behind my back.*

Meaning I don't like it when my friends talk about me when I'm not around.

Activity Work with a partner to write a definition for each of the following idioms. Then, use each in a sentence.

1. throw out
2. run into
3. pass the buck
4. teach an old dog new tricks
5. cut down

These skills will help you become a better reader. Practice
them with either "Sun and Moon in a Box" (p. 894) or
"How the Snake Got Poison" (p. 901).

Reading Skill

- A **comparison** tells how two or more things are
  alike.
- A **contrast** tells how two or more things are different.

By **using your prior knowledge to compare and contrast**, you
can understand an unfamiliar concept. For example, you may understand an ancient culture better if you look for ways in which it is similar to and different from your own culture. You might also find
similarities and differences between a story told long ago and one
that is popular today. To help you compare and contrast stories, ask
questions such as the following:

- What does this event bring to mind?
- Does this character make me think of someone I know or
  have read about?

Literary Analysis

Stories such as fables, folk tales, and myths are influenced by the
cultural context, or background, customs, and beliefs, of the people
who originally told them. Recognizing the cultural context will help
you understand and appreciate what you read. Use a chart like the
one shown to keep track of the cultural context of a literary work.

Story Title	
Time	Customs
Place	Beliefs

Vocabulary Builder

Sun and Moon in a Box

- **reliable** (ri lī′ ə bəl) *adj.* dependable (p. 896)
  *I did not ask Lisa for help because she is not
  <u>reliable</u>.*

- **relented** (ri lent′ əd) *v.* gave in (p. 897) *Larry
  finally <u>relented</u> and agreed to come with me.*

- **curb** (kʉrb) *v.* to check or control (p. 897)
  Anna could not <u>curb</u> her desire to eat candy.

How the Snake Got Poison

- **ornament** (or′ nə ment′) *v.* beautify (p. 901)
  I put lights in the tree to <u>ornament</u> the patio.

- **immensity** (i men′ sə tē) *n.* immeasurable
  largeness or vastness (p. 901) *The search
  team had to spread out because of the canyon's <u>immensity</u>.*

Background

Folk Tales Many cultures have folk tales that are similar to the folk tales of other cultures. Stories about creation, the discovery of fire, and the origin of the seasons come from many different lands and peoples. As you read folk tales from different cultures, you can see how each culture changes the story with its own values and customs.

Connecting to the Literature

Reading/Writing Connection You may have read a story about a character who plays tricks on others. Describe the behavior you would expect from such a tricky character. Use at least three of these words: *interact, convince, debate, exploit.*

Meet the Authors

Richard **Erdoes** (b. 1912)

Richard Erdoes was born in Frankfurt, Germany. He studied art and later worked as a caricaturist sketching humorous portraits for several German daily newspapers.

On the Move In 1939, when the Nazis occupied Austria, Erdoes fled to France. He moved to New York in 1940. There, he worked as an illustrator for newspapers and magazines. While working at *Life* magazine, Erdoes took pictures for an article on a Sioux reservation and his eyes were opened to the conditions there. Since then he has written more than twenty books on the American West.

Alfonso **Ortiz** (1939–1997)

Alfonso Ortiz was born in San Juan, a Tewa pueblo in northern New Mexico. He earned degrees in both sociology and anthropology, and spent many years of his life as a university professor.

An Advocate for Native Americans During his teaching career, Ortiz brought scholars from the community to the university to share their knowledge with students and teachers. He also worked with the Association on American Indian Affairs and served as president of the organization for fifteen years.

Go **O**nline
Author Link

For: More about the authors
Visit: www.PHSchool.com
Web Code: eme-9608

Sun and Moon in a Box

── Zuni Folk Tale ──

Alfonso Ortiz and Richard Erdoes

Coyote and Eagle were hunting. Eagle caught rabbits. Coyote caught nothing but grasshoppers. Coyote said: "Friend Eagle, my chief, we make a great hunting pair."

"Good, let us stay together," said Eagle.

They went toward the west. They came to a deep canyon. "Let us fly over it," said Eagle.

"My chief, I cannot fly," said Coyote. "You must carry me across."

Reading Skill
Compare and Contrast What does this comparison tell you about the two characters?

"Yes, I see that I have to," said Eagle. He took Coyote on his back and flew across the canyon. They came to a river. "Well," said Eagle, "you cannot fly, but you certainly can swim. This time I do not have to carry you."

Eagle flew over the stream, and Coyote swam across. He was a bad swimmer. He almost drowned. He coughed up a lot of water. "My chief," he said, "when we come to another river, you must carry me." Eagle regretted to have Coyote for a companion.

They came to Kachina Pueblo.[1] The Kachinas were dancing. Now, at this time, the earth was still soft and new. There was as yet no sun and no moon. Eagle and Coyote sat down and watched the dance. They saw that the Kachinas had a square box. In it they kept the sun and the moon. Whenever they wanted light they opened the lid and let the sun peek out. Then it was day. When they wanted less light, they opened the box just a little for the moon to look out.

"This is something wonderful," Coyote whispered to Eagle.

"This must be the sun and the moon they are keeping in that box," said Eagle. "I have heard about these two wonderful beings."

"Let us steal the box," said Coyote.

---

1. **Kachina Pueblo** (kə chē´ nə pweb´ lō) Native American village.

Literary Analysis
Cultural Context
What details show that this is a Native American story set in the Southwest?

✔ Reading Check

What do the Kachinas keep in the square box?

"No, that would be wrong," said Eagle. "Let us just borrow it."

When the Kachinas were not looking, Eagle grabbed the box and flew off. Coyote ran after him on the ground. After a while Coyote called Eagle: "My chief, let me have the box. I am ashamed to let you do all the carrying."

"No," said Eagle, "you are not <u>reliable</u>. You might be curious and open the box and then we could lose the wonderful things we borrowed."

For some time they went on as before—Eagle flying above with the box, Coyote running below, trying to keep up. Then once again Coyote called Eagle: "My chief, I am ashamed to let you carry the box. I should do this for you. People will talk badly about me, letting you carry this burden."

"No, I don't trust you," Eagle repeated. "You won't be able to refrain from opening the box. Curiosity will get the better of you."

"No," cried Coyote, "do not fear, my chief, I won't even think of opening the box." Still, Eagle would not give it to him, continuing to fly above, holding the box in his talons. But Coyote went on pestering Eagle: "My chief, I am really embarrassed. People will say: 'That lazy, disrespectful Coyote lets his chief do all the carrying.'"

Vocabulary Builder
reliable (ri lī′ ə bəl) *adj.*
dependable

Reading Skill
Compare and Contrast How do Coyote's and Eagle's feelings about responsibility differ?

▼ **Critical Viewing** Based on this photograph and what you have read, why is the coyote often characterized as sly and clever? **[Infer]**

"No, I won't give this box to you," Eagle objected. "It is too precious to entrust to somebody like you."

They continued as before, Eagle flying, Coyote running. Then Coyote begged for the fourth time: "My chief, let me carry the box for a while. My wife will scold me, and my children will no longer respect me, when they find out that I did not help you carry this load."

Then Eagle <u>relented</u>, saying: "Will you promise not to drop the box and under no circumstances to open it?"

"I promise, my chief, I promise," cried Coyote. "You can rely upon me. I shall not betray your trust."

Then Eagle allowed Coyote to carry the box. They went on as before, Eagle flying, Coyote running, carrying the box in his mouth. They came to a wooded area, full of trees and bushes. Coyote pretended to lag behind, hiding himself behind some bushes where Eagle could not see him. He could not <u>curb</u> his curiosity. Quickly he sat down and opened the box. In a flash, Sun came out of the box and flew away, to the very edge of the sky, and at once the world grew cold, the leaves fell from the tree branches, the grass turned brown, and icy winds made all living things shiver.

Then, before Coyote could put the lid back on the box, Moon jumped out and flew away to the outer rim of the sky, and at once snow fell down from heaven and covered the plains and the mountains.

Eagle said: "I should have known better. I should not have let you persuade me. I knew what kind of low, cunning, stupid creature you are. I should have remembered that you never keep a promise. Now we have winter. If you had not opened the box, then we could have kept Sun and Moon always close to us. Then there would be no winter. Then we would have summer all the time."

▲ **Critical Viewing** What details in this photograph show that Kachina dancers admired animals? **[Analyze]**

Vocabulary Builder
relented (ri lent´ əd) *v.* gave in

curb (kʉrb) *v.* check or control

Apply the Skills

Sun and Moon in a Box

Thinking About the Selection

1. **Respond:** As you were reading the story, did you think that Eagle should give the box to Coyote? Why or why not?
2. **(a) Support:** Make a two-column chart. In the first column, write sentences, or comments from other characters that give details about what Coyote is like. In the second column, explain what you think each detail reveals about Coyote.
   (b) Discuss: In a small group, discuss your lists. Then, choose the best details from each list to share with the class.
3. **(a) Recall:** What does Coyote say to Eagle when Eagle is carrying the box? **(b) Infer:** Why do you think he says this? **(c) Infer:** Why do you think Eagle finally agrees to give the box to Coyote?
4. **Make a Judgment:** In your opinion, does Eagle share any responsibility for the appearance of the first winter? Why or why not?

Reading Skill

5. Use a Venn diagram like the one shown to compare and contrast Eagle and Coyote. Think about how they look, their abilities, and how they react to responsibility.

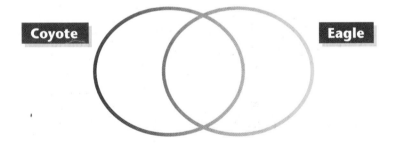

Literary Analysis

6. Describe where Coyote and Eagle are when they first see the box. How do these details help you understand the **cultural context** of the story?
7. What attitudes are expressed in the story about summer and winter? Why do you think ancient people felt this way about these seasons?

QuickReview

Story at a Glance
Earth is changed forever when Coyote and Eagle take a box from the Kachinas that contains the Sun and Moon.

Assessment
For: Self-test
Visit: www.PHSchool.com
Web Code: ema-6607

Compare: tell how two or more things are alike

Contrast: tell how two or more things are different

Cultural Context: the background, customs, and beliefs of the people who originally told a story

Vocabulary Builder

Practice **Analogies** show the relationships between pairs of words. Use a word from the vocabulary list on page 892 to complete each analogy. Your choice should make a word pair that matches the relationship between the first two words. Explain the relationship.

1. come in : go out : : _____ : stood firm

2. trick : fool : : _____ : control

3. famous : unknown : : _____ : undependable

Writing

Write a **plot summary** of "Sun and Moon in a Box."
- Take notes to describe each of the following: setting, major characters, main events, and final outcome.
- Use your notes to write your summary.
- Include one major event from the beginning, one from the middle, and one from the end.

For *Grammar, Vocabulary,* and *Assessment,* see **Build Language Skills,** pages 906–907.

Extend Your Learning

Listening and Speaking With a partner, find five unusual facts about an animal. Include these facts in a **story** about the animal that does not reveal the animal's name. Present the story to your classmates and have them guess the animal. Make your presentation entertaining and effective by using these ideas:
- Include dialogue.
- Use facial expressions and body movements.
- Include specific facts and details.

Research and Technology Use Internet and library resources to research the Zuni culture. Narrow your topic by finding one aspect of the culture that interests you. Then write a **feature article** based on this information. Here are some tips to help you:
- Start your article with a fact or detail that will grab the reader's attention.
- Use headings to emphasize main ideas.
- Be sure each paragraph has a main idea and supporting details.

Folk Tale

Background

Dialect is the form of a language that is spoken by people in a particular region or social group. It differs from standard English in pronunciation, grammar, word choice, and sentence structure. Dialect used in the retelling of a folk tale honors the oral tradition by helping the reader "hear" how the story was first told. The dialect in "How the Snake Got Poison" reflects its roots in African American folklore.

Connecting to the Literature

Reading/Writing Connection Dialect is an informal use of language. You use informal language on a regular basis when you talk to your friends. On the other hand, you speak more formally to teachers. Write a few sentences describing why you think people use different language for different situations. Use at least three of these words: *adapt, communicate, comprehend, interact*.

Review

For **Reading Skill, Literary Analysis,** and **Vocabulary Builder,** see page 892.

Meet the Author

Zora Neale **Hurston** (1891–1960)

Zora Neale Hurston grew up in the small town of Eatonville, Florida, the daughter of a preacher and a schoolteacher. In 1925, Hurston headed to New York and became part of the Harlem Renaissance, a creative movement among African Americans.

Hurston's Career Hurston collected folklore in the southern United States and in Jamaica, Haiti, Bermuda, and Honduras. Her first book, *Jonah's Gourd Vine,* was published in 1934. Although Hurston's writing was popular, she was not able to make a living from it and died penniless. In 1973, author Alice Walker found Hurston's grave and placed a gravestone on the site.

Fast Facts

▶ Hurston studied anthropology at Barnard College and Columbia University.
▶ When she was sixteen, she became a member of a traveling theatrical troupe.

Go Online
Author Link

For: More about the author
Visit: www.PHSchool.com
Web Code: eme-9609

HOW THE SNAKE GOT POISON

Zora Neale Hurston

Well, when God made de snake he put him in de bushes to <u>ornament</u> de ground. But things didn't suit de snake so one day he got on de ladder and went up to see God.

"Good mawnin', God."

"How do you do, Snake?"

"Ah[1] ain't so many, God, you put me down here on my belly in de dust and everything trods upon me and kills off my generations. Ah ain't got no kind of protection at all."

God looked off towards <u>immensity</u> and thought about de subject for awhile, then he said, "Ah didn't mean for nothin' to be stompin' you snakes lak dat. You got to have some kind of a protection. Here, take dis poison and put it in yo' mouf and when they tromps on you, protect yo'self."

So de snake took de poison in his mouf and went on back.

So after awhile all de other varmints went up to God.

"Good evenin', God."

"How you makin' it, varmints?"

"God, please do somethin' 'bout dat snake. He' layin' in de bushes there wid poison in his mouf and he's strikin' everything dat shakes de bushes. He's killin' up our generations. Wese skeered to walk de earth."

1. Ah dialect, or regional pronunciation, for "I."

Vocabulary Builder
ornament (ōr′ nə mənt)
v. beautify

immensity (i men′sə tē)
n. immeasurable largeness or vastness

✓ **Reading Check**

What is the snake's complaint?

So God sent for de snake and tole him:

"Snake, when Ah give you dat poison, Ah didn't mean for you to be hittin' and killin' everything dat shake de bush. I give you dat poison and tole you to protect yo'self when they tromples on you. But you killin' everything dat moves. Ah didn't mean for you to do dat."

De snake say, "Lawd, you know Ah'm down here in de dust. Ah ain't got no claws to fight wid, and Ah ain't got no feets to git me out de way. All Ah kin see is feets comin' to tromple me. Ah can't tell who my enemy is and who is my friend. You gimme dis protection in my mouf and Ah uses it."

God thought it over for a while then he says:

"Well, snake, I don't want yo' generations all stomped out and I don't want you killin' everything else dat moves. Here take dis bell and tie it to yo' tail. When you hear feets comin' you ring yo' bell and if it's yo' friend, he'll be keerful. If it's yo' enemy, it's you and him."

So dat's how de snake got his poison and dat's how come he got rattles.

Reading Skill
Compare and Contrast How does the varmints' problem compare with the snake's problem at the beginning of the story?

▼ **Critical Viewing** Does this snake look defenseless? Explain. **[Analyze]**

The Harlem Renaissance

During the 1920s and '30s in New York City, a talented group of African American writers, artists, and musicians took part in a cultural movement that became known as the Harlem Renaissance.

DUKE ELLINGTON AND HIS COTTON CLUB ORCHESTRA "BLACK AND TAN" with FREDI WASHINGTON

Music

COTTON CLUB

▲ Blues great Bessie Smith and musicians such as jazz legend Duke Ellington performed at the famous Cotton Club nightclub.

Literature

Arts

▲ Zora Neale Hurston, Countee Cullen (top right), and Langston Hughes (right) brought the African American experience to life through their writing.

Into Bondage, 1936 by Aaron Douglas, Corcoran Gallery of Art.

▲ The photographs of James Van Der Zee (top) and the paintings (left) of Aaron Douglas (center) captured the look and feel of the times.

Connect to the Literature How did works like Hurston's folk tale "How the Snake Got Poison" contribute to the Harlem Renaissance?

Apply the Skills

How the Snake Got Poison

Thinking About the Selection

1. **Respond:** This folk tale presents arguments from two conflicting sides. What would you have decided in this situation? Explain.
2. **(a) Recall:** Find three examples of dialect in the story.
   (b) Speculate: Why do you think Hurston chose to tell the story in dialect?
3. **(a) Recall:** In your notebook, describe the two arguments that the snake makes in the story. **(b) Analyze:** Tell whether you think each argument was effective and explain why you think so. **(c) Discuss:** Share your responses with a partner. Then discuss how looking at someone else's responses did or did not change your opinion.
4. **(a) Recall:** What is God's final decision? **(b)** How does this decision affect both the snake and the varmints?
5. **(a) Analyze:** Explain why the varmints and the snake did not work out their problems together. **(b) Apply:** What might this reveal about people and their ways of interacting? **(c) Apply:** How does this story illustrate the concept of "balance of nature"?

Reading Skill

6. Use a Venn diagram like the one shown to **compare and contrast** the snake and the varmints at the beginning of the story. Think about how they look and their abilities.

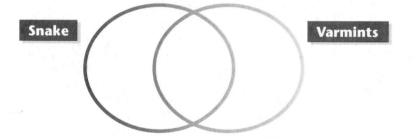

Literary Analysis

7. How does the author's use of dialect help you understand the **cultural context** of the story?
8. In the story, God says to the snake, "You got to have some kind of protection." What does this show about beliefs within the culture where the story originated?

QuickReview

Story at a Glance

God finds a way to help the snake protect himself against other creatures.

Go Online
Assessment
For: Self-test
Visit: www.PHSchool.com
Web Code: eme-6608

Compare: tell how two or more things are alike

Contrast: tell how two or more things are different

Cultural Context: the background, customs, and beliefs of the people who originally told a story

Vocabulary Builder

Practice Using a word from the vocabulary list on page 892, rewrite the following sentences to have the same meaning.

1. Wanda wanted to buy some posters to decorate her room.
2. Isaac studied the constellations in the great expanse of darkness.

Writing

Write a **plot summary** of "How the Snake Got Poison."
- Take notes to describe each of the following: setting, major characters, main events, and final outcome.
- Use your notes to write your summary.
- Include one major event from the beginning, one from the middle, and one from the end.

For *Grammar, Vocabulary,* and *Assessment,*
see **Build Language Skills,** pages 906–907.

Extend Your Learning

Listening and Speaking With a partner, find five unusual facts about an animal. Include these facts in a **story** about the animal that does not reveal the animal's name. Present the story to your classmates and have them guess the animal. Make your presentation entertaining and effective by using these ideas:
- Include dialogue.
- Use facial expressions and body movements.
- Include specific facts and details.

Research and Technology Use Internet and library resources to conduct research on the life of Zora Neale Hurston. Narrow your topic by finding one aspect of her life that interests you. Then, write a **feature article** based on this information. Use these tips:
- Start your article with a fact or detail that will grab the reader's attention.
- Use headings to emphasize main ideas.
- Be sure each paragraph has a main idea and supporting details.

Build Language Skills

Vocabulary Skill

Idioms and idiomatic expressions are commonly used in language. We are used to hearing them and forget that they do not make sense if we take them literally. For example, when someone asks you if you "need a hand," they are not asking if you require an extra hand to add to your arm. You are being asked if you would "like help."

▶ **Example:** Would you **like a hand** setting up the party?

Practice In a small group, list as many idioms and idiomatic expressions as you can think of. Then, share your list with other groups to create a master list.

Grammar Lesson

Capitalization **Capital letters** signal the beginning of a sentence or quotation and identify proper nouns and adjectives.

Proper nouns include the names of people, geographical locations, specific events and time periods, organizations, languages, and religions. Proper adjectives are derived from proper nouns, as in *France/French* and *Canada/Canadian.*

> **Sentence beginning:** My dog ran away.
> **Quotation:** I yelled, "Come back!"
> **Proper nouns:** Michael, Queen Elizabeth, Boston Marathon, Friday
> **Proper adjectives:** Mexican, Jeffersonian, Irish

MorePractice

For more on capitalization, see the Grammar Handbook, p. R31.

Practice Rewrite the following sentences, adding the missing capitals.

1. did you last visit cleveland in april or may?
2. we visited the cayman islands after the meeting of the women's sports foundation.
3. jason said, "let's do everything we can to save the alaskan wilderness."
4. my brother charles, who lives in new zealand, visited us for thanksgiving.
5. ms. hanks said, "Chris, have you studied the life of king richard I of england?"

W͟G Prentice Hall Writing and Grammar Connection: Chapter 27

Reading: Compare and Contrast

Directions: *Read the selection. Then answer the questions.*

Even though they are sisters, my friends Rose and Ashley are very different. Ashley is a quiet, calm person who enjoys reading novels. She and I both love to take hikes in the hills around our town. Her room is always neat.

On the other hand, when I walk into Rose's room, I have to push books and clothing aside just to sit on her bed. One of her walls is painted pink and another yellow. Rock music is usually blaring from her stereo, and she talks nonstop.

Even though Rose and Ashley are as different as day and night, they have a few similarities. They both like our math class and, like me, they both love to go to the movies. They are good friends!

1. How are Ashley and the narrator alike?
   A They both like their math class.
   B They both take hikes.
   C They both collect artwork.
   D They both read long books.

2. How are the three girls alike?
   A They all like to go to the movies.
   B They all like rock music.
   C They all like to hike.
   D They are all very calm.

3. How are Rose and Ashley different?
   A Ashley is less athletic.
   B Ashley is more creative.
   C Rose is neater.
   D Rose is more outgoing.

4. Both Rose and Ashley
   A like rock music.
   B like to take hikes.
   C enjoy math.
   D are talkative.

Timed Writing: Interpretation [Interpretation]

Review "Sun and Moon in a Box" or "How the Snake Got Poison." Interpret what the tale reveals about the people who originally told it. Use details from the text to support your ideas. **(25 minutes)**

 ## Writing Workshop: *Work in Progress*

Research Report

For a research report you may write, list six ideas in response to one or more of the following topics: science, technology, society, or the environment. Save this list in your writing portfolio.

Reading Informational Materials

Editorials

In Part 2, you are learning how to compare and contrast when reading literature. Comparing and contrasting is also useful when you are reading editorials, brief works generally found in newspapers that give an opinion on a specific issue. If you read "How the Snake Got Poison," a folk tale written from the perspective of a snake, you may also want to read other types of writing that express viewpoints about the lives of animals.

About Editorials

Editorials are articles that reflect the writer's opinion on a current issue—a topic on which there is more than one possible point of view. Editorial writers create strong arguments by supporting their opinions with facts, statistics, and examples. The purpose of an editorial is to persuade readers to believe in the writer's point of view or to take a certain action. People who are interested in current events or those who simply enjoy reading newspapers are especially likely to read editorials.

Editorials are often published in newspapers, but they may also be printed in magazines and online. The editorial "Zoos: Joys or Jails?" appeared on a Web site by and for teens.

Reading Skill

The writer of this editorial emphasizes her argument and addresses counterarguments, by using **comparison-and-contrast organization.** She logically connects details so that readers can notice similarities and differences.

Use a chart like the one shown to keep track of the comparisons presented in the editorial. Use the information in your completed chart to analyze the effectiveness of the writer's argument.

Animals in Zoos	Animals in the Wild

Zoos: Joys or Jails?

Rachel F., San Diego, CA

The title of the editorial briefly presents two sides of the issue.

Imagine your family lives in a luxurious mansion where all your needs are provided for. There are gardens and daily walks and all your favorite foods.

Suddenly, you're taken from your home and shipped to a place where people come from far and wide to ogle at you, thinking they are learning about your lifestyle. Sometimes, your captors force you to perform for thousands of people.

The writer makes a comparison to emphasize her point of view.

Your life has changed drastically. Welcome to the zoo!

Although the circumstances and reasons for animals being in zoos vary, its concept has faults many don't notice during their visit with the animals. Animals in many zoos are kept in areas that are much smaller than their natural habitats. As a result, animals behave differently than they would in their natural surroundings. Animals like big cats are accustomed to roaming territories of up to 10 square miles.

The most important point is presented first and is backed up with statistics.

One of the best aspects of the zoo is its emphasis on education. Signs tell visitors about

The writer acknowledges opposing arguments and then counters them with strong evidence.

the animals and their behavior in the wild, but notice how the majority say the animals were born in the zoo. Unfortunately, the adaptive behavior due to small cages gives visitors a skewed perception of how the animals actually behave in the wild. Although the idea of education to protect and preserve animals is excellent, is the zoo really setting a good example of treatment or representing the natural actions of these creatures?

Some advocates say that zoos protect and save endangered species. Despite today's advanced breeding techniques, animals raised in the zoo or other places of captivity are not learning the survival techniques they would in the wild. These animals would be very vulnerable if released and would encounter difficulties coping. Would it not be more beneficial to raise them in

Reading Informational Materials

their natural habitat?

In this way scientists wouldn't face as many risks in reintroducing captive animals raised into the wild.

Helping endangered species in the wild gives them a better chance for survival and reproduction. Scientists should only revert to the zoo if the necessary funding or habitat for breeding is not available.

Animals are not just brought to the zoo to protect their species, but also to provide entertainment. Many animals' lives will include performing for visitors. Four shows are performed every day at the San Diego Zoo. The zoo should be reserved for education and protecting endangered species, not an amusement park where animals are trained to perform.

Although the zoo is trying to be helpful in providing shows about the animals, it is harming those it intends to protect. The zoo has good intentions in its educational purposes, and in breeding endangered species, but animals shouldn't perform or be treated in a manner that could change their behaviors from how they act in the wild.

Though zoos are meant to be a joy to viewers and teach lessons about our earth, the zoo jails its inhabitants and passes on faulty knowledge. The wild animals in our world are a wonder, and they must be preserved. At the zoo they are treated with care, but they should be treated with reverence.

Next time you visit a zoo, look at the enclosure of the tigers and watch the seals balance a ball on their noses, and then think about what you are really learning from your day at the zoo.

The editorial concludes with a strong, memorable sentence.

Reading: Compare and Contrast

Directions: *Choose the letter of the best answer to each question about the editorial.*

1. What comparison does the writer make between animals' habitats in zoos and in the wild?

   A Habitats are smaller in zoos.

   B Habitats are bigger in zoos.

   C Habitats are less dangerous in zoos.

   D Habitats are more dangerous in zoos.

2. According to the writer, where do animals learn survival techniques?

   A in zoos

   B in the wild

   C from predators

   D from humans

3. What is the writer's main argument?

   A Zoos are educational.

   B Animals are better off in zoos.

   C Animals are better off in the wild.

   D Zoo animals do not like to perform.

Reading: Comprehension and Interpretation

Directions: *Write your answers on a separate piece of paper.*

4. What does the writer say are two major mistakes that zoos make? **[Knowledge]**

5. Which do you think the writer would consider more educational— a zoo exhibit that features lions or a film that shows lions in their natural habitat? Support your answer. **[Generating]**

6. Which of the writer's arguments against zoos do you think is the strongest? Explain. **[Evaluating]**

Timed Writing: Editorial [Critical Stance]

Write a brief editorial about an issue of importance to you and for which there is more than one "side." The issue may concern your school, neighborhood, or the nation. Clearly present your argument and back it up with facts, anecdotes, descriptions, or examples. End your editorial with a thought-provoking sentence. **(25 minutes)**

These skills will help you become a better reader. Practice them with either "The People Could Fly" (p. 914) or "All Stories Are Anansi's" (p. 921).

Reading Skill

When you **compare and contrast**, you recognize similarities and differences. You can compare and contrast elements in a literary work by **using a Venn diagram** to examine character traits, situations, and ideas.

- First, reread the text to locate the details you will compare.
- Then, write the details on a diagram like this one.

Recording these details will help you understand the similarities and differences in a literary work. You can also use a Venn diagram to compare and contrast elements of two different literary works.

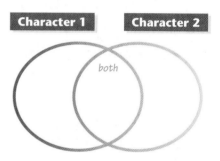

Character 1   Character 2

both

Literary Analysis

A **folk tale** is a story that is composed orally and then passed from person to person by word of mouth. Though they originate in this **oral tradition,** most folk tales are eventually collected and written down. Similar folk tales are told by different cultures throughout the world, using common character types, plot elements, and themes. Folk tales often teach a lesson about life and present a clear separation between good and evil. Folk tales are part of the oral tradition that also includes fairy tales, legends, myths, fables, tall tales, and ghost stories.

Vocabulary Builder

The People Could Fly

- **scorned** (skôrnd) *adj.* looked down upon (p. 915) *Scorned by my friends for being afraid to ride the rollercoaster, I cried.*

- **croon** (kroon) *v.* sing or hum quietly and soothingly (p. 915) *When you croon that lullaby, I get sleepy.*

- **shuffle** (shuf´ əl) *v.* walk with dragging feet (p. 917) *We heard the man shuffle down the hallway.*

All Stories Are Anansi's

- **yearned** (yʉrnd) *v.* wanted very much (p. 921) *I yearned for some hot chocolate on that cold winter night.*

- **gourd** (gôrd) *n.* a fruit; the dried shell is used as a cup (p. 921) *We drank water from a gourd.*

- **acknowledge** (ak näl´ ij) *v.* recognize and admit (p. 925) *I acknowledge that you were right and I was wrong.*

Background

African American Folk Tales "The People Could Fly" is a freedom tale, a kind of folk tale that enslaved Africans told to keep their hopes alive, despite the hardships they faced. Like many freedom tales, "The People Could Fly" contains images of freedom and escape as well as many references to the original storytellers' native Africa.

Connecting to the Literature

Reading/Writing Connection Folk tales such as this one have been told for years within families and from one generation of people to the next. List three reasons that families tell stories to each other. Use at least three of these words: *appreciate, attach, establish, create, define.*

Meet the Author

Virginia **Hamilton** (1936–2002)

"I started writing as a kid," Virginia Hamilton once said. "It was always something I was going to do." The author of countless novels, stories, and collections of African American folk tales, Hamilton has been called "America's most honored writer of books for children."

Stories of the Past Hamilton was raised in a house of gifted storytellers. She described her childhood as ideal, saying "I heard 'tells' every day of my life from parents and relatives." Some of those stories were about slavery, and most were about the past. As a result, the past came to play an important role in Hamilton's writing. She developed a unique style, combining elements of history, myth, legend, and dream to bring her stories to life.

Fast Facts

▶ As a child, Hamilton was a cheerleader and captain of the girls' basketball team. She also ran track and sang in her school choir.

▶ Her book *M.C. Higgins, the Great* won the Newbery medal in 1975.

Go Online
Author Link

For: More about the author
Visit: www.PHSchool.com
Web Code: eme-9610

From *The People Could Fly* by Virginia Hamilton, illustrated by Leo and Diane Dillon

THE PEOPLE COULD FLY

African American Folk Tale

VIRGINIA HAMILTON

They say the people could fly. Say that long ago in Africa, some of the people knew magic. And they would walk up on the air like climbin up on a gate. And they flew like blackbirds over the fields. Black, shiny wings flappin against the blue up there.

Then, many of the people were captured for Slavery. The ones that could fly shed their wings. They couldn't take their

▲ Critical Viewing
What are some reasons why a person might wish to fly?
[Speculate]

wings across the water on the slave ships. Too crowded, don't you know.

The folks were full of misery, then. Got sick with the up and down of the sea. So they forgot about flyin when they could no longer breathe the sweet scent of Africa.

Say the people who could fly kept their power, although they shed their wings. They kept their secret magic in the land of slavery. They looked the same as the other people from Africa who had been coming over, who had dark skin. Say you couldn't tell anymore one who could fly from one who couldn't.

One such who could was an old man, call him Toby. And standin tall, yet afraid, was a young woman who once had wings. Call her Sarah. Now Sarah carried a babe tied to her back. She trembled to be so hard worked and <u>scorned</u>.

The slaves labored in the fields from sunup to sundown. The owner of the slaves callin himself their Master. Say he was a hard lump of clay. A hard, glinty[1] coal. A hard rock pile, wouldn't be moved. His Overseer[2] on horseback pointed out the slaves who were slowin down. So the one called Driver[3] cracked his whip over the slow ones to make them move faster. That whip was a slice-open cut of pain. So they did move faster. Had to.

Sarah hoed and chopped the row as the babe on her back slept.

Say the child grew hungry. That babe started up bawling too loud. Sarah couldn't stop to feed it. Couldn't stop to soothe and quiet it down. She let it cry. She didn't want to. She had no heart to <u>croon</u> to it.

"Keep that thing quiet," called the Overseer. He pointed his finger at the babe. The woman scrunched low. The Driver cracked his whip across the babe anyhow. The babe hollered like any hurt child, and the woman fell to the earth.

The old man that was there, Toby, came and helped her to her feet.

"I must go soon," she told him.

"Soon," he said.

Sarah couldn't stand up straight any longer. She was too weak. The sun burned her face. The babe cried and cried,

Literary Analysis
Folk Tales How does the use of informal language suggest that this story has been passed on orally?

Vocabulary Builder
scorned (skôrnd) *adj.* looked down upon

croon (kro͞on) *v.* sing or hum quietly and soothingly

 **Reading Check**

What special gift do some of the people in this tale have?

"Pity me, oh, pity me," say it sounded like. Sarah was so sad and starvin, she sat down in the row.

"Get up, you black cow," called the Overseer. He pointed his hand, and the Driver's whip snarled around Sarah's legs. Her sack dress tore into rags. Her legs bled onto the earth. She couldn't get up.

Toby was there where there was no one to help her and the babe.

"Now, before it's too late," panted Sarah. "Now, Father!"

"Yes, Daughter, the time is come," Toby answered. "Go, as you know how to go!"

He raised his arms, holding them out to her. *"Kum . . . yali, kum buba tambe,"* and more magic words, said so quickly, they sounded like whispers and sighs.

The young woman lifted one foot on the air. Then the other. She flew clumsily at first, with the child now held tightly in her arms. Then she felt the magic, the African mystery. Say she rose just as free as a bird. As light as a feather.

The Overseer rode after her, hollerin. Sarah flew over the fences. She flew over the woods. Tall trees could not snag her. Nor could the Overseer. She flew like an eagle now, until she was gone from sight. No one dared speak about it. Couldn't believe it. But it was, because they that was there saw that it was.

Say the next day was dead hot in the fields. A young man slave fell from the heat. The Driver come and whipped him. Toby come over and spoke words to the fallen one. The words of ancient Africa once heard are never remembered completely. The young man forgot them as soon as he heard them. They went way inside him. He got up and rolled over on the air. He rode it awhile. And he flew away.

Another and another fell from the heat. Toby was there. He cried out to the fallen and reached his arms out to them. *"Kum kunka yali, kum . . . tambe!"* Whispers and sighs. And they too rose on the air. They rode the hot breezes. The ones flyin were black and shinin sticks, wheelin above the head of the Overseer. They crossed the rows, the fields, the fences, the streams, and were away.

"Seize the old man!" cried the Overseer. "I heard him say the magic *words.* Seize him!"

Reading Skill
Compare and Contrast How does the Overseer's treatment of Sarah compare with Toby's treatment of her?

▼ **Critical Viewing** Based on this story, what do these manacles symbolize or represent? **[Connect]**

Literary Analysis
Folk Tale What message do you think this story had for enslaved Africans?

The one callin himself Master come runnin. The Driver got his whip ready to curl around old Toby and tie him up. The slaveowner took his hip gun from its place. He meant to kill old, black Toby.

But Toby just laughed. Say he threw back his head and said, "Hee, hee! Don't you know who I am? Don't you know some of us in this field?" He said it to their faces. "We are ones who fly!"

And he sighed the ancient words that were a dark promise. He said them all around to the others in the field under the whip,

"... buba yali ... buba tambe. ..."

There was a great outcryin. The bent backs straightened up. Old and young who were called slaves and could fly joined hands. Say like they would ring-sing.[4] But they didn't <u>shuffle</u> in a circle. They didn't sing. They rose on the air. They flew in a flock that was black against the heavenly blue. Black crows or black shadows. It didn't matter, they went so high. Way above the plantation, way over the slavery land. Say they flew away to *Free-dom*.

Vocabulary Builder
shuffle (shuf´əl) *v.*
walk with dragging
feet

And the old man, old Toby, flew behind them, takin care of them. He wasn't cryin. He wasn't laughin. He was the seer.[5] His gaze fell on the plantation where the slaves who could not fly waited.

"Take us with you!" Their looks spoke it but they were afraid to shout it. Toby couldn't take them with him. Hadn't the time to teach them to fly. They must wait for a chance to run.

"Goodie-bye!" The old man called Toby spoke to them, poor souls! And he was flyin gone.

So they say. The Overseer told it. The one called Master said it was a lie, a trick of the light. The Driver kept his mouth shut.

Reading Skill
**Compare and
Contrast** How is
Toby's position now
different from his
position at the
beginning of the
story?

The slaves who could not fly told about the people who could fly to their children. When they were free. When they sat close before the fire in the free land, they told it. They did so love firelight and *Free-dom*, and tellin.

They say that the children of the ones who could not fly told their children. And now, me, I have told it to you.

---

4. ring-sing joining hands in a circle to sing and dance.
5. seer (sē´ ər) *n.* one who has supposed power to see the future; prophet.

Apply the Skills

The People Could Fly

Thinking About the Selection

QuickReview

Story at a Glance
Enslaved Africans find freedom with the help of an old man.

1. **Respond:** Who do you think is the most important character in the story, Toby or the narrator? Explain your answer.
2. **(a) Describe:** What words would you use to describe the living conditions of many African Americans during the time this story originated? **(b) Support:** Describe three details that help you understand these living conditions.
3. **(a) Infer:** What are the "magic words" Toby says? **(b) Interpret:** Why do you think the author includes these words in the story?
4. **(a) Recall:** What happens when Toby says the "magic words"? **(b) Draw Conclusions:** To what do you think "flying" really refers?
5. **(a) Recall:** Who is called Master? **(b) Contrast:** Who is the real "master" in the story? **(c) Evaluate:** Do you think this folk tale inspires hope? Explain.

┌Go ●nline
└──Assessment
For: Self-test
Visit: www.PHSchool.com
Web Code: ema-6609

Reading Skill

6. **Compare and contrast** the personalities of Toby and the Overseer. How are they similar? How are they different?
7. Use a Venn diagram to compare and contrast "The People Could Fly" with another story you have read in this book. In your diagram, include details about setting, plot, and characters.

Compare: tell how two or more things are alike

Contrast: tell how two or more things are different

Literary Analysis

8. Give examples of the elements of **folk tales** that you find in this story. Use a chart like the one shown.

Elements:	Good	Evil	Lesson	Theme
Examples:				

Folk tale: a story composed orally and then passed from person to person by word of mouth

Vocabulary Builder

Practice Rewrite each sentence so that it includes a word from the vocabulary list on page 912 and conveys the same basic meaning.

1. When you do that dance, you have to drag your feet in time to the music.

2. The man freely spoke his mind even though he was looked down upon.

3. The mother will quietly sing a lullaby to her baby.

Writing

Write a **review** of "The People Could Fly" in which you tell other readers whether or not they will enjoy the folk tale.

- Give your opinions about the characters, the use of description and dialogue, and the plot.
- Support your points with details from the story.

For *Grammar*, *Vocabulary*, and *Assessment*, see **Build Language Skills,** pages 928–929.

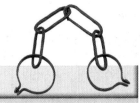

Extend Your Learning

Listening and Speaking Prepare a **television news report** on the amazing events that took place in the story.

- Organize your information to make the report straightforward and clear.
- Include facts about when and where the incidents took place, using details from the story.
- "Interview" a guest who witnessed the people flying and include quotations from him or her.
- Present your news report to a small group.

Research and Technology Slave songs are part of the African American oral tradition. These songs were often coded to give slaves directions to help them escape to the north. Conduct **research** on coded slave songs, such as "Wade in the Water" or "Follow the Drinking Gourd." Present the lyrics of the song with an explanation of the coded words.

Build Understanding • *All Stories Are Anansi's*

Background

Trickster in Folktales "All Stories Are Anansi's" is a trickster tale. Typically, the trickster is an animal character, such as a spider, a fox, or a coyote, that tries to fool others. In some tales, he succeeds. In others, he is fooled himself. In American, African, and West Indian folklore, tricksters take advantage of larger and stronger animals through cunning or magic.

Connecting to the Literature

Reading/Writing Connection "All Stories Are Anansi's" is a folktale about a spider that uses its brain to outwit other animals. Jot down two animals that would be good at tricking others, and tell what characteristics would make them good tricksters. Use at least three of these words: *demonstrate, exhibit, display, identify, require.*

Review

For **Reading Skill, Literary Analysis,** and **Vocabulary Builder,** see page 912.

Meet the Author

Harold **Courlander** (1908–1996)

Harold Courlander is best known for his collections of folk tales from around the world. He once told an interviewer that his interest in folk tales arose from the rich multicultural environment in which he lived in Detroit.

World Traveler During Courlander's career, he published more than thirty-five books. As he traveled around the world, he made sound recordings of the music and stories of African, African American, and Native American cultures. About his work, Courlander has said, "I think of myself primarily as a narrator. I have always had a special interest in using fiction and nonfiction narration to bridge communication between other cultures and our own."

Fast Facts

▶ For five years, Courlander worked as a farmer. He was also a historian and a United Nations press officer.

▶ During World War II, Courlander worked for an aircraft manufacturer in Eritrea, Africa (now Ethiopia).

Go Online **Author Link**

For: More about the author
Visit: www.PHSchool.com
Web Code: eme-9611

ALL STORIES ARE ANANSI'S

African Folk Tale
Harold Courlander

In the beginning, all tales and stories belonged to Nyame (nē ä´ mē), the Sky God. But Kwaku Anansi (kwä´ kōō ə nän´ sē), the spider, <u>yearned</u> to be the owner of all the stories known in the world, and he went to Nyame and offered to buy them.

The Sky God said: "I am willing to sell the stories, but the price is high. Many people have come to me offering to buy, but the price was too high for them. Rich and powerful families have not been able to pay. Do you think you can do it?"

Anansi replied to the Sky God: "I can do it. What is the price?"

"My price is three things," the Sky God said. "I must first have Mmoboro (mō bô´ rō), the hornets. I must then have Onini (ō nē´ nē), the great python. I must then have Osebo (ō sä´ bō), the leopard. For these things I will sell you the right to tell all stories."

Anansi said: "I will bring them."

He went home and made his plans. He first cut a <u>gourd</u> from a vine and made a small hole in it. He took a large calabash[1] and filled it with water. He went to the tree where the hornets lived. He poured some of the water over himself,

Vocabulary Builder
yearned (yʉrnd) *v.* wanted very much

gourd (gôrd) *n.* a fruit; the dried shell is used as a cup

---

1. calabash (kal´ ə bash´) *n.* large fruit that is dried and made into a bowl or cup.

so that he was dripping. He threw some water over the hornets, so that they too were dripping. Then he put the calabash on his head, as though to protect himself from a storm, and called out to the hornets: "Are you foolish people? Why do you stay in the rain that is falling?"

The hornets answered: "Where shall we go?"

"Go here, in this dry gourd," Anansi told them.

The hornets thanked him and flew into the gourd through the small hole. When the last of them had entered, Anansi plugged the hole with a ball of grass, saying: "Oh, yes, but you are really foolish people!"

He took the gourd full of hornets to Nyame, the Sky God. The Sky God accepted them. He said: "There are two more things."

Anansi returned to the forest and cut a long bamboo pole and some strong vines. Then he walked toward the house of Onini, the python, talking to himself. He said: "My wife is stupid. I say he is longer and stronger. My wife says he is shorter and weaker. I give him more respect. She gives him less respect. Is she right or am I right? I am right, he is longer. I am right, he is stronger."

When Onini, the python, heard Anansi talking to himself, he said: "Why are you arguing this way with yourself?"

The spider replied: "Ah, I have had a dispute with my wife. She says you are shorter and weaker than this bamboo pole. I say you are longer and stronger."

Literary Analysis
Folk Tale What lesson does the hornets' experience teach?

Onini said: "It's useless and silly to argue when you can find out the truth. Bring the pole and we will measure."

So Anansi laid the pole on the ground, and the python came and stretched himself out beside it.

"You seem a little short," Anansi said.

The python stretched further.

"A little more," Anansi said.

"I can stretch no more," Onini said.

"When you stretch at one end, you get shorter at the other end," Anansi said. "Let me tie you at the front so you don't slip."

He tied Onini's head to the pole. Then he went to the other end and tied the tail to the pole. He wrapped the vine all around Onini, until the python couldn't move.

"Onini," Anansi said, "it turns out that my wife was right and I was wrong. You are shorter than the pole and weaker. My opinion wasn't as good as my wife's. But you were even more foolish than I, and you are now my prisoner."

Anansi carried the python to Nyame, the Sky God, who said: "There is one thing more." Osebo, the leopard, was next. Anansi went into the forest and dug a deep pit where the leopard was accustomed to walk. He covered it with small branches and leaves and put dust on it, so that it was

Reading Skill
Compare and Contrast What word does Anansi use to describe both the hornets and the python after he catches them?

Reading Check

How does Anansi catch the hornets and the python?

▼ **Critical Viewing** Why might storytelling be a popular pastime in a landscape such as this? **[Infer]**

impossible to tell where the pit was. Anansi went away and hid. When Osebo came prowling in the black of night, he stepped into the trap Anansi had prepared and fell to the bottom. Anansi heard the sound of the leopard falling, and he said: "Ah, Osebo, you are half-foolish!"

When morning came, Anansi went to the pit and saw the leopard there.

"Osebo," he asked, "what are you doing in this hole?"

"I have fallen into a trap," Osebo said. "Help me out."

"I would gladly help you," Anansi said. "But I'm sure that if I bring you out, I will have no thanks for it. You will get hungry, and later on you will be wanting to eat me and my children."

"I swear it won't happen!" Osebo said.

"Very well. Since you swear it, I will take you out," Anansi said.

He bent a tall green tree toward the ground, so that its top was over the pit, and he tied it that way. Then he tied a rope to the top of the tree and dropped the other end of it into the pit.

"Tie this to your tail," he said.

Osebo tied the rope to his tail.

"Is it well tied?" Anansi asked.

"Yes, it is well tied," the leopard said.

"In that case," Anansi said, "you are not merely half-foolish, you are all-foolish." And he took his knife and cut the other rope, the one that held the tree bowed to the ground. The tree straightened up with a snap, pulling Osebo out of the hole. He hung in the air head downward, twisting and turning. And while he hung this way, Anansi killed him with his weapons.

Literary Analysis
Folk Tales How do Anansi's actions make him a trickster?

▶ **Critical Viewing** What characteristic of the leopard does Anansi use in his trick? **[Connect]**

Then he took the body of the leopard and carried it to Nyame, the Sky God, saying: "Here is the third thing. Now I have paid the price."

Nyame said to him: "Kwaku Anansi, great warriors and chiefs have tried, but they have been unable to do it. You have done it. Therefore, I will give you the stories. From this day onward, all stories belong to you. Whenever a man tells a story, he must <u>acknowledge</u> that it is Anansi's tale."

In this way Anansi, the spider, became the owner of all stories that are told. To Anansi all these tales belong.

Vocabulary Builder
acknowledge (ak näl´ ij) v. recognize and admit

Apply the Skills

All Stories Are Anansi's

Thinking About the Selection

1. **Respond:** Which of Anansi's accomplishments impressed you the most? Why?
2. **(a) Infer:** What can you infer about the hornets, the python, and the leopard from the fact that they listen to Anansi?
   (b) Interpret: In what way do these animals resemble humans in their behavior?
3. **(a) Infer:** What is Anansi's attitude toward the other animals?
   (b) Support: What details reveal this attitude?
4. **(a) Recall:** What does the Sky God ask Anansi to do?
   (b) Draw Conclusions: Why is Anansi able to do what warriors and chiefs have failed to do? **(c) Apply:** What qualities or characteristics are revealed by his success?
5. **(a) Interpret:** How would you describe Anansi's personal code of behavior? **(b) Evaluate:** Do you approve or disapprove of Anansi's behavior? Explain.

Reading Skill

6. **Compare and contrast** the hornets, the python, and the leopard. How are they similar? How are they different?
7. Use a Venn diagram to compare and contrast "All Stories Are Anansi's" with another story you have read in this book. In your diagram, include details about setting, plot, and characters.

Literary Analysis

8. Give examples of the elements of **folk tales** that you find in this story. Use a chart like the one shown.

Elements:	Good	Evil	Lesson	Theme
Examples:				

QuickReview

Who's Who in the Folk Tale
Nyame the Sky God
Anansi the spider
Mmoboro the hornets
Onini the great python
Osebo the leopard

Go Online
Assessment
For: Self-test
Visit: www.PHSchool.com
Web Code: ema-6610

Compare: tell how two or more things are alike

Contrast: tell how two or more things are different

Folk tale: a story composed orally and then passed from person to person by word of mouth

Vocabulary Builder

Practice For each item, write a single sentence correctly using the words indicated.

1. yearned; warmth
2. gourd; dip
3. acknowledge; right

Writing

Write a **review** of "All Stories Are Anansi's" in which you tell other readers whether or not they will enjoy the folk tale.

- Give your opinions about the characters, the use of description and dialogue, and the plot.
- Support your points with details from the story.

For *Grammar, Vocabulary,* and *Assessment,* see **Build Language Skills,** pages **928–929.**

Extend Your Learning

Listening and Speaking Prepare a **television news report** about Anansi's amazing deeds.

- Organize your information to make the report straightforward and clear.
- Include facts about when and where the incidents took place, using details from the story.
- Present your news report to a small group.

Research and Technology Use library and Internet resources to **research** tropical spiders of western Africa. Find out the following information:

- types of spiders
- physical features
- food
- life cycle
- where they live
- behavior

Prepare written descriptions and drawings of the spiders with captions. Then, share your findings with the class.

Build Language Skills

The People Could Fly • All Stories Are Anansi's

Vocabulary Skill

Idioms are part of our language and are often confusing. When people "show up" at your house, it means that they "arrive," but when they "show off," it means that they brag. Other idioms such as "turn in," "turn out," and "turn into" also use the second word to change the meaning of the phrase.

▶ **Example:** The fairy godmother tapped the frog, who *turned into* a handsome prince.

Practice Supply a definition for each of these idioms. Then, use each in a sentence.

1. swallow your pride
2. go over
3. showdown
4. get over it
5. blow up

Grammar Lesson

Abbreviations An *abbreviation* is a shortened form of a word or phrase, such as *Dr.* for *Doctor* or *Rd.* for *Road.* Most abbreviations end with a period and are useful when taking notes or writing lists.

Instance	Example	Abbreviation
Common Titles	Captain	Capt.
Academic Degrees	Master of Business Administration	M. B. A.
States	Maryland	Md.
Addresses	Street	St.
Traditional Measurements	foot	ft.
Metric Measurements	centimeter	cm

Practice Match each abbreviation with its long form.

1. qt.
2. blvd.
3. oz.
4. ml
a. ounce
b. quart
c. boulevard
d. milliliter

More Practice

For more practice with abbreviations, see the Grammar Handbook, p. R31.

W *Prentice Hall Writing and Grammar Connection: Abbreviations Guide, pages 774–777.*

Reading: Compare and Contrast

Directions: *Read the selection. Then answer the questions.*

At Camp Earth last summer, I made two close friends. All of us enjoy acting, and we met working on the camp play.

Other than acting, Doug and Jamal have different interests. Jamal, who is thirteen, is athletic and musical. Jamal hopes to be on a U.S. Olympic team someday.

Doug, on the other hand, has no tremendous interest in sports. His idea of fun is participating on the school's debating team and working on humanitarian projects.

Although they are different, I cherish my friendship with each.

1. What is one similarity between Jamal, Doug, and the author?
   A They share a love of team sports.
   B They have been friends for a long time.
   C They share an interest in acting.
   D They hope to become writers.

2. A difference between Jamal and Doug is
   A Jamal loves sports; Doug does not.
   B Doug is the narrator's friend, but Jamal is not.
   C Doug is a talented actor, while Jamal gives weak performances.
   D Jamal has applied for the summer Olympics, though Doug has not.

3. According to the passage,
   A the narrator does not have much in common with either boy.
   B the narrator has qualities in common with both boys.
   C the narrator has most in common with Jamal.
   D the narrator has nothing in common with Doug.

4. Which two boys are most similar?
   A Doug and Jamal
   B Doug and narrator
   C Jamal and narrator
   D not enough information

Timed Writing: Description [Interpretation]

Review "The People Could Fly" or "All Stories Are Anansi's" and write a vivid description of a person, place, or object in the story. Give a main impression supported by strong sensory details. **(50 minutes)**

 ## Writing Workshop: *Work in Progress*

Research Report

Choose two ideas from the list in your portfolio. For each topic, jot down three different types of resources that are likely to provide enough information for an in-depth report. Save this work in your writing portfolio.

Tone

The **tone** of a literary work is the writer's attitude toward his or her subject and characters. The tone can often be described by a single adjective, such as *formal, playful,* or *respectful.* Factors that contribute to the tone include word choice, details, sentence structure, rhythm, and rhyme.

Comparing Tone

The poem "The Fox Outwits the Crow" and the fable "The Fox and the Crow" have similar characters, settings, and plots, but the authors who wrote them have different attitudes toward their subjects. To determine the tone of each selection, notice the words and phrases that the authors use to express their ideas. In a chart like the one shown, identify specific words and phrases and label them with such adjectives as *serious, formal, funny, personal,* or *playful.*

	Word/phrase	Description
Title:	as I am a fox	formal
Title:		

Vocabulary Builder

The Fox Outwits the Crow

- **whiff** (hwif) *n.* smell; scent (p. 932) *As we walked past the bakery, I got a whiff of cinnamon.*
- **hors d'oeuvres** (ôr′ dʉrv′) *n.* savory foods served as appetizers (p. 932) *We served cheese, crackers, and green grapes as hors d'oeuvres.*
- **malice** (mal′ is) *n.* ill will (p. 932) *The people felt malice for the cruel dictator.*

The Fox and the Crow

- **glossy** (glôs′ ē) *adj.* smooth and shiny (p. 934) *I chose a glossy finish for my photos.*
- **surpass** (sər pas′) *v.* be superior to (p. 934) *Chuck's performance must surpass Lee's for him to make the team.*
- **flatterers** (flat′ ər ərz) *n.* those who praise a person insincerely (p. 934) *The queen's flatterers praised every decision, comment, and action she made.*

Build Understanding

Connecting to the Literature

Reading/Writing Connection In the fable "The Fox and the Crow," one character flatters another. Write briefly about the reasons why someone might use flattery and the ways a person might react to being flattered. Use at least three of these words: *react, respond, rely, maximize.*

Meet the Authors

William **Cleary** (b. 1926)

William Cleary is a writer, composer, filmmaker, and poet who lives in Burlington, Vermont. He has written twelve books on spirituality, published five collections of religious music, and composed a musical comedy that was performed at the 1988 Seoul Olympics. He has retold eighty of Aesop's fables in verse.

Aesop (about 620–560 B.C.)

People have enjoyed Aesop's fables for centuries. However, very little is known about the origin of the fables—including who actually wrote them.

Many Theories Aesop may have been an enslaved person who lived on the Greek island of Samos, a spokesman who defended criminals in court, or an advisor for one of the Greek kings. The most widely held theory, however, is that Aesop was not an actual person at all. Rather, because certain stories in ancient Greece were told over and over, people invented an imaginary author for them.

Go Online
Author Link

For: More about the authors
Visit: www.PHSchool.com
Web Code: eme-9612

The Fox Outwits the Crow
William Cleary

One day a young crow snatched a fat piece of cheese
From the porch of a house made of stone,
Then she flew to the top of a Juniper Tree
To enjoy her good fortune alone.

    But a fox passing by got a <u>whiff</u> of the cheese,
    The best of his favorite <u>hors d'oeuvres</u>,
    So he called to the crow, *Hey, you glamorous thing,*
    Does your voice match your beautiful curves?

The crow was so pleased by the flattering words
She quickly took out a libretto,[1]
How fondly that fox will listen, she thought,
To hear how I caw in falsetto.[2]

    She opened her mouth—and the cheese tumbled out,
    Which the fox gobbled up full of <u>malice</u>
    While he chuckled to think how that dim-witted crow
    Could believe she was MARIA CALLAS.[3]

MORAL: Attending to flattery comes at a high price.

---

1. libretto (li bret´ ō) *n.* the text of an opera for the musical theater.
2. falsetto (fôl set´ ō) *n.* an artificially high voice.
3. Maria Callas (kal´ əs) (1923–1977) U.S. opera singer.

Vocabulary Builder
whiff (hwif) *n.* smell; scent

hors d'oeuvres (ôr dʉrv´) *n.* savory foods served as appetizers

malice (mal´ is) *n.* ill will

Literary Analysis
Tone What details indicate that Cleary's attitude is playful?

Thinking About the Selection

1. **Respond:** What is the most amusing part of the poem? Why?

2. **(a) Recall:** What does the crow think after the fox flatters her?
   (b) Analyze: What does this show about her?

3. **(a) Recall:** To what does the poet compare the crow's voice?
   (b) Support: Why is this an amusing comparison?

4. **(a) Connect:** How do the characters' actions support the moral? **(b) Evaluate:** Is this an easy or difficult lesson to learn? Why?

▶ **Critical Viewing**
What details in this illustration reflect the tone of the poem? **[Analyze]**

The Fox and the Crow

Aesop

A Fox once saw a Crow fly off with a piece of cheese in its beak and settle on a branch of a tree. "That's for me, as I am a Fox," said Master Reynard,[1] and he walked up to the foot of the tree.

"Good day, Mistress Crow," he cried. "How well you are looking today: how <u>glossy</u> your feathers; how bright your eye. I feel sure your voice must <u>surpass</u> that of other birds, just as your figure does; let me hear but one song from you that I may greet you as the Queen of Birds."

The Crow lifted up her head and began to caw her best, but the moment she opened her mouth the piece of cheese fell to the ground, only to be snapped up by Master Fox. "That will do," said he. "That was all I wanted. In exchange for your cheese I will give you a piece of advice for the future—

MORAL: Do not trust <u>flatterers</u>."

---

1. Master Reynard (ren′ ərd) the fox in the medieval beast epic *Reynard the Fox*; therefore, a proper name for the fox in other stories.

Vocabulary Builder

glossy (glôs′ ē) *adj.* smooth and shiny

surpass (sər pas′) *v.* be superior to

flatterers (flat′ ər ərz) *n.* those who praise a person insincerely

Thinking About the Selection

1. **Respond:** Do you agree with the moral of the fable? Why or why not?

2. **(a) Recall:** How does the Fox persuade the Crow to drop the piece of cheese? **(b) Infer:** How does the Fox's attitude change when he gets the cheese?

3. **(a) Draw Conclusions:** What human character traits do the animal characters in the fable represent? **(b) Support:** What details in the fable support your answer?

4. **Evaluate:** Is the moral of "The Fox Outwits the Crow" and "The Fox and the Crow" relevant to today's world? Explain.

Apply the Skills

The Fox Outwits the Crow • The Fox and the Crow

Comparing Tone

1. Compare and contrast the tone of the fable "The Fox and the Crow" with that of the poem "The Fox Outwits the Crow" by completing a diagram like the one shown.

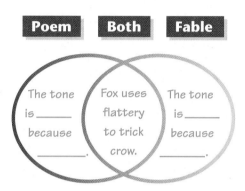

2. Which tone do you think is better suited to teaching a moral? Explain your answer.

Writing to Compare

Compare your reaction to "The Fox and the Crow" and "The Fox Outwits the Crow," based on the author's tone. In an essay, discuss how the tone of each influenced your attitude. Use these questions to get started:

- How are the characters presented?
- What details help you see whether the writer establishes a personal relationship with readers?
- How do you think the writer wants readers to react to the story?

Vocabulary Builder

Practice For each item, write a sentence correctly using the word pairs given.

1. malice; surprise
2. surpass; compete
3. hors d'oeuvres; fancy
4. whiff; aroma
5. glossy; polish
6. flatterers; trust

QuickReview

Tone: the writer's attitude toward the subject and characters

Go **O**nline
—Assessment

For: Self-test
Visit: www.PHSchool.com
Web Code: ema-6611

Reading

Directions: *Read the selection. Then answer the questions.*

Painting and collage are popular kinds of artwork.

Materials required for creating a painting include brushes, paints, and paper or canvas. Some artists paint landscapes, still lifes, or portraits. Oil paint, water color, and tempera are types of paint that are commonly used. They are applied to a surface, with brushes of various sizes.

To make a collage, artists use paper, which is torn or cut into small pieces, brushes, and glue. Some collages represent realistic subjects, such as flowers, people, or landscapes. Collage artists brush glue onto a small area of paper, which may or may not have an image painted on it. Then they apply bits of torn paper to the sticky surface.

1. **Which of these is a way in which painting and collage are alike?**
   A Both are colorful.
   B Both are made in similar ways.
   C Both are types of artwork.
   D Both are difficult to complete.

2. **Unlike a painting, a collage**
   A does not show realistic subjects.
   B is made using torn or cut paper.
   C requires the use of brushes.
   D presents a variety of abstract designs.

3. **Which of the following does not belong in the shaded area?**
   A paint
   B paper
   C water color
   D landscapes

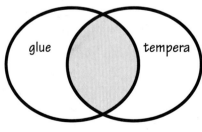

Collages   Paintings

4. **What do paintings and collages have the most in common with?**
   A a piece of sheet music
   B a short story
   C a clay sculpture
   D a poetry reading

5. **What is the best title for this selection?**
   A Paint and Paper: Art in the 1900s
   B Techniques for Creating Collages
   C Paint and Collage Art
   D Reflections of an Artist

Directions: *Choose the word that best completes each sentence.*

6. **They have to _____ the bone fragments in order to determine the age of the fossil.**
   - A detail
   - B aspect
   - C analyze
   - D characteristic

7. **I think there are too many _____ in that story; I am overwhelmed with information.**
   - A details
   - B aspects
   - C analyzed
   - D characteristics

8. **Each _____ of the play's set was carefully selected by the director.**
   - A details
   - B aspect
   - C analysis
   - D unique

9. **The _____ design was exciting to work with.**
   - A analyze
   - B unique
   - C characteristic
   - D analytical

10. **A _____ of a good leader is the ability to remain calm and rational in emergencies.**
    - A detail
    - B unique
    - C characteristic
    - D analysis

Directions: *Choose the best definition for each italicized expression or word.*

11. **We will *go over* the test tomorrow.**
    - A take to another place
    - B cover
    - C review
    - D give to the students

12. **The pumpkin will *turn into* a coach.**
    - A move around
    - B become
    - C move sharply to the right
    - D move 90 degrees.

13. **We are going to *call on* Mr. Smith.**
    - A ask a question
    - B go to visit
    - C choose to answer
    - D phone

14. **Are you *coming down with* a cold.**
    - A getting sick
    - B feeling better
    - C having to rest
    - D not feeling poorly

15. **Should we *throw out* the old basketballs?**
    - A rotating motion with your arm
    - B propel forward
    - C give away to charity
    - D put in the trash

Vowel Sounds in Unstressed Syllables

In many words, the vowel sound in certain syllables is not clear. These indistinct vowel sounds, which come in syllables that are not stressed or accented, can make it hard to spell some words.

That Troublesome "Uh" Sound Most people do not have trouble spelling words like "reward" or "inherit," where the vowel in each syllable has a recognizable sound. Many words, though, have at least one syllable in which the vowel sound is not clear. The *e* in *category,* for example, sounds the same as the first *i* in *medicine.* This "uh" sound may be spelled by any vowel, and it may occur in more than one syllable, as in *abandon.* Study the word list, noting the spelling of vowels in unstressed syllables.

WORD FACTORY

Just use any vowel for that uh sound and get that word into production!

Word List
medicine
multiply
evidence
category
discipline
episode
cemetery
oxygen
abandon
article

Practice Each of the following contains the letters of a Word List word, plus one additional letter representing the "uh" sound. Eliminate the extra letter and unscramble the remaining letters to correctly spell the word.

1. ygertocai
2. aygexon
3. iclatere
4. ndaoaabn
5. cndeeiiam

6. pimlltuay
7. disapeeo
8. deeevince
9. sciidlpneii
10. eeceytrm

A. Directions: *Write the letter of the sentence in which the underlined word is spelled correctly.*

1. **A** On one <u>epasode</u> of the travel show, the host visited New Orleans.
   B Every <u>cematery</u> he toured had at least one famous person buried in it.
   C One, a pirate, is said to have hidden <u>treasire</u> nearby.
   D No one could <u>answer</u> the question if this was a true story.

2. **A** Mom told Susie, "Take your <u>medasin</u> like a good girl."
   B "We don't want the germs in your body to <u>multiply</u>."
   C "You will get more <u>oxigen</u> if I open the window a little."
   D "Don't worry—I won't <u>ebandon</u> you when you're sick."

3. **A** The contestant on the game show had a wonderful <u>memary</u>.
   B He could <u>anser</u> all kinds of questions.
   C No <u>category</u> of question could stump him.
   D He could <u>multeply</u> large numbers.

4. **A** The old <u>sematery</u> stood at the top of a hill.
   B As years went by, the townspeople began to <u>abanden</u> it.
   C It was as if an <u>epesode</u> in the town's history no longer existed
   D Finally an <u>article</u> in the paper stirred the town's interest.

B. Directions: *Write the letter of the correctly spelled word to fill in the blank.*

1. People need _____ to survive.
   A oxigen
   B oxagen
   C oxegen
   D oxygen

2. What _____ do these reports fit into?
   A category
   B catagory
   C catigory
   D catygory

3. The rings of a tree are _____ of its age.
   A eviadence
   B evadence
   C evidance
   D evidence

4. Most people hate to take _____.
   A medasin
   B medisin
   C medicine
   D medicin

5. Self-_____ is an asset for an athlete.
   A discipline
   B discapline
   C disoplane
   D discipliane

6. They buried their dog in a pet _____.
   A sematery
   B cematery
   C cemetery
   D cematary

Research: Research Report

A **research report** analyzes information gathered from reference materials, observations, interviews, or other sources to present a clear and accurate picture of a topic or to answer a question. Follow the steps outlined in this workshop to write your own research report.

Assignment Write a research report about a contemporary issue that interests you or affects you in some way.

What to Include Your research report should feature the following elements:
- an overall focus or main idea to be analyzed
- information gathered from multiple sources
- a thesis statement giving the writer's viewpoint or perspective
- a clear organization and smooth transitions
- facts and details to support each main point
- visuals or media to support key ideas
- accurate, complete citations identifying sources according to an accepted format
- error-free writing, including the correct use of personal pronouns

To preview the criteria on which your research report may be judged, see the rubric on page 949.

Using the Form
You may use elements of this form in these types of writing:
- news articles
- lab reports
- persuasive essays
- biographies

 Writing Workshop: *Work in Progress*

If you have completed the Work-in-Progress assignments, you already have in your portfolio numerous ideas to use in your research report. You may continue to develop these ideas, or you may choose to explore a new idea as you complete the Writing Workshop.

Prewriting

Choosing Your Topic

To choose the right topic to research, use this strategy:

Newswatch and Notebook Browse Look through recent magazines or newspapers, listen to the news, and review your notebooks. List current events, issues, or subjects of interest and the questions they spark in you. Choose your topic from among these ideas.

Narrowing Your Topic

After you choose your topic, make sure it is narrow enough to cover in a short report. For example, "illiteracy" is too broad a topic for a research paper. You can narrow the topic by asking focused questions such as "How serious a problem has illiteracy become in America?"

Gathering Details

Use a variety of primary and secondary sources. Use both *primary sources* (firsthand or original accounts, such as interview transcripts and newspaper articles) and *secondary sources* (accounts that are not original, such as encyclopedia entries) in your research. Cross-check information from the Internet or an interview whenever possible by consulting printed sources.

Take notes. Use one or more of these strategies to take notes:

- Use index cards, writing one note per card and noting the source and page number.
- Photocopy articles and copyright pages; then highlight relevant information.
- Print articles from the Internet, or copy them directly into a "notes" folder.

You will use these notes to help you write original text. Copying directly from sources without citing them is *plagiarism,* a practice that has serious academic consequences.

Work in Progress
Review the work you did on pages 907 and 929.

Note Card

Education
Papp, p.5

Only the upper classes could read.

Most of the common people in Shakespeare's time could not read.

Source Card

Papp, Joseph
and Kirkland, Elizabeth

Shakespeare Alive!

New York: Bantam Books, 1988

Drafting

Shaping Your Writing

Develop a main idea or thesis. Review your prewriting notes to determine the overall focus of your report. Then, write a single sentence expressing your main idea. This sentence is called a thesis statement. As you draft, refer to your thesis statement to help keep your report focused.

▶ **Example:** Whales are among the most intelligent mammals on Earth.

Make an outline. Group your prewriting notes by category. Use Roman numerals (I, II, III) to number your most important points. Under each Roman numeral, use capital letters (A, B, C) for the supporting details. Use your outline as a guide to develop your draft by turning your notes into complete sentences.

Outline Format

Thesis Statement

I. First main point

    A. First supporting detail

    B. Second supporting detail

II. Second main point

    A. First supporting detail

    B. Second supporting detail

Providing Elaboration

Include visuals to support key ideas. Using charts or other visual aids allows you to present detailed information that might otherwise interrupt the flow of the report. In your writing, explain what the chart proves and direct readers to reference these aids as needed.

Find points for clarification. As you use language you learned during the research stage, define the words for your readers. In addition, add details to elaborate or clarify facts that your audience might find unrealistic or surprising.

To read the complete student model, see page 946.

Student Model: Finding Points for Clarification

A chicken egg should take about twenty-one days to incubate, or take form. During that time, the eggs must be kept warm. In addition, the eggs must be rotated, or turned, every eight to twelve hours. If they remain in one position for longer than that, the chick can become stuck to one side and may not form properly.

These additional details help clarify the writer's ideas.

Jon Scieszka

Jon
Scieszka

On Using Research in Fiction

Here's an early draft of the beginning of a *Time Warp Trio* novel. The Time Warp guys can travel anywhere in time. So to make their adventures come alive, I have to know every detail I can about the place and time they travel to—in this case, Italy hundreds of years ago.

I read everything I can find for at least a month before I start writing. I want to know what kind of food people of that time and place ate, how they brushed their teeth, what they wore for underwear.

"I do research . . . to learn about the history of stories."

———— Jon Scieszka

Professional Model:

from *Da Wild, Da Crazy, Da Vinci*

"Ready! . . . Aim! . . ."

"Wait," yelled Sam. He fixed his glasses to ~~get~~ take a better look ~~around.~~ "~~I think~~ We're supposed to be in Italy."

All of the Time Warp books start in the middle of some action. I figured these would be two great action words that everyone knows.

Fred, Sam, and I were standing with our backs to a steep, sandy hill. ~~In front of us sat~~ It looked like it could be Italy. But there was a ~~scary~~ strange-looking invention sitting in front of us—a wooden, flying-saucer-shaped thing, about as big as an ice cream truck.

The challenge in writing history-based fiction is to introduce the real history in a natural way. This tank really was one of Italian artist Leonardo da Vinci's inventions.

~~But that~~ The size wasn't the scary part. The scary part was the guns sticking out of it. The even scarier part was knowing the word that usually comes after "Ready! Aim!"

"You're ~~both~~ lucky we didn't end up in a giant toilet," said Fred. "But now you better figure out what to do about those guns pointed our way."

My characters set up the history for me. Here Fred mentions an invention we find out about later—the flush toilet.

Revising

Revising Your Overall Structure

Analyze Your Organization. After drafting, look over your draft and analyze your organization to see if it matches your outline. Stop at the end of each paragraph and refer to your outline. Follow these steps:

1. Mark each paragraph with the Roman numeral and capital letter from your outline and write a word or phrase to identify the subject of the paragraph.

2. If all the paragraphs with the same Roman numeral are not next to each other, decide whether the change is an improvement. If it is not, correct it.

Peer Review: Ask a classmate to read your report to determine if the organization of your draft is clear. If your reader finds areas that require transitions, consider revising your draft by adding a word, phrase, or sentence that shows the connection between your paragraphs. Use transitions such as *at first, finally,* or *as a result.*

Revising Your Sentences

Vary sentence length. To add interest to your writing, vary the length of your sentences. Look over your draft and underline your sentences in alternating colors so you can easily see differences in length. Then, review your color coding. Combine short, choppy sentences or break up longer sentences if there are too many of either.

To read the complete student model, see page 946.

Student Model: Revising to Vary Sentence Length

An incubator performs these same functions. The temperature inside the incubator is measured and regulated that by a thermostat. ~~The thermostat~~ tells the heater when to turn on and when to turn off. In this way, the temperature of the eggs is kept at a constant 99 degrees.

Laura combines two sentences to vary sentence length.

Integrating Grammar Skills

Revising to Correct Use of Pronoun Case

Many pronouns change form according to usage. *Case* is the relationship between a pronoun's form and its use.

Prentice Hall Writing and Grammar Connection: Chapter 23

Personal Pronouns	
Nominative Case	**Objective Case**
I, we	me, us
you	you
he, she, it, they	him, her, it, them

Using Personal Pronouns Personal pronouns in the **nominative case** may be the subject of a verb or a predicate nominative—a noun or pronoun that renames the subject.

> **Subject:** <u>She</u> plays soccer. Cassie and <u>I</u> play soccer, too.

> **Predicate Nominative:** Two of Beckham's biggest fans are Jenna and <u>I</u>.

Personal pronouns in the **objective case** have three uses: as a direct object, as an indirect object, and as the object of a preposition.

> **Direct Object:** Jason invited Raf and <u>me</u> to the game.

> **Indirect Object:** Paul had given <u>him</u> two extra tickets.

> **Object of a Preposition:** All three of <u>us</u> were grateful to <u>him</u>.

Fixing Incorrect Use of Personal Pronouns Mistakes with pronouns usually occur when the subject or object is compound.

1. **To test a pronoun in a compound subject, use just the pronoun with the verb in the sentence.** For example, in the sentence, "Cassie and me play soccer," "me play" clearly sounds wrong. The nominative case *I* is needed.

2. **To test a pronoun in a compound object, use the pronoun by itself after the verb or preposition.** For example, in the sentence, "Jason invited Raf and I to the game," "Jason invited I" sounds wrong. The objective case *me* is needed.

Apply It to Your Editing

Choose two paragraphs in your draft. Underline every sentence that contains a pronoun as part of a compound subject or a compound object. Use one of the methods above to identify and correct any pronouns used incorrectly.

Writing Workshop

Student Model: Laura Agajanian
Santa Clara, CA

Hatching Chirpers

A hen's egg is an amazing thing. Sitting in the nest, it seems as if it is an inanimate, or lifeless, object, but it contains everything that is needed to make a chick. In order for the chick to grow inside the egg, however, the right external conditions are needed. Under normal circumstances, these conditions are provided by the hen. They can also be reproduced and regulated in an incubator. My investigation was to discover whether the hen or the incubator would more efficiently and effectively provide the right external conditions. My hypothesis is that an incubator can provide the right external conditions more effectively and efficiently. Let's find out.

A chicken egg should take about twenty-one days to incubate, or take form. During that time, the eggs must be kept warm. The ideal temperature is between 99 and 100 degrees Fahrenheit. In addition, the eggs must be rotated, or turned, every eight to twelve hours. If they remain in one position for longer than that, the chick can become stuck to one side of the egg and may not form properly (Johnson 14–16).

Usually, the temperature and the turning are handled by the hen that sits on the nest. She regulates the temperature of the eggs by getting off the nest or standing above the eggs if the eggs begin to get too warm. When they have had some time to cool, she gets back on the nest. The hen turns the eggs by poking at them with her beak until each egg rolls a little to one side, eventually turning from its original position (Scott).

An incubator performs these same functions. The temperature inside the incubator is measured and regulated by a thermostat that tells the heater when to turn on and when to turn off. In this way, the temperature of the eggs is kept at a constant 99 degrees. The eggs sit on a device that rolls them every eight hours. This device is controlled by an electronic timer. It is dependable because it is automatic and does not require a person to push a button for the eggs to turn. It is more efficient than a hen, because all the eggs get turned equally and consistently (*Little Giant* 2–6).

In the first paragraph, the writer identifies her main topic, the question she is investigating. In this science report, she provides a hypothesis—a proposition that the research will prove or disprove. This statement gives her perspective or viewpoint on the topic.

Accurate facts and details gathered through the formal research process are presented. Since these are specific statistics that a reader might want to check, the writer gives the source.

The report is organized to give balanced information about both methods being investigated— natural hatching and incubation.

Based on the fact that conditions in the incubator are more consistent and controlled, I concluded that an incubator sets the ideal conditions more efficiently, and I hypothesized that it would hatch eggs more effectively. To test my hypothesis, I observed four hens sitting on a total of twenty-four eggs and placed twenty-four eggs in an incubator. Each egg was marked with a small x so that I could observe how frequently and completely each egg was turned. Chart A shows specific observations over a twenty-five day period.

Detailed information that would interrupt the flow of the report is presented in a separate chart for readers to reference as needed.

Chart A

Day	Incubator Observations	Nest Observations
Day 1	**6:45 AM:** After placing the turner in the incubator, I put the 24 eggs on the turner. The temperature leveled off at 100 degrees. The eggs have warmed up quickly. **5:33 PM:** The turner is working efficiently—eggs are tilted appropriately.	**7:10 AM:** After placing the 24 eggs on the nests in the cage, I put food and water in the cage. Then, I placed the hens in the cage. **6:01 PM:** All hens are on the eggs.
Day 5	X marks on the eggs show that eggs have made a complete turn.	X marks on the eggs show that the eggs were not turned completely since I last checked.
Day 10	The turner seems to be tilting the eggs efficiently—X marks show a complete turn.	X marks show that 18 eggs were turned, but 6 were not.
Day 15	The temperature of the eggs is at a steady 100 degrees.	Two hens have moved off the nest for a brief time. Temperature of the eggs right now is 97 degrees.
Day 25	The incubator has hatched thirteen out of the twenty-four eggs.	The hens have hatched ten out of the twenty-four eggs.

In general, the incubator eggs received much more consistent attention to their condition. The machine did not need to stop to eat or exercise, as the hens did. The marks on the eggs showed that the eggs under the hens did not always get completely turned. Sometimes, some of the eggs were turned and some were not. In addition, the hens sometimes left the nest for as long as an hour. When the temperature of the eggs was measured after a hen had been gone a long time, the egg temperature was sometimes as low as 97 degrees.

After twenty-five days, the hens had hatched ten out of the twenty-four eggs, and the incubator had hatched thirteen. The difference between the two numbers is not great enough to say that one way of incubating is more effective than the other. The incubator is definitely more efficient at delivering ideal conditions than the hens were. However, since the increased efficiency does not result in a higher number of hatches, maybe "ideal" conditions are not required for a successful hatch.

> The writer concludes by explaining whether the research did or did not support her original hypothesis.

Bibliography

Johnson, Sylvia A. *Inside an Egg.* Minneapolis: Lerner Publications Company, 1982.

Kruse Poultry Feed. *Care and Feeding of Baby Chicks.*

Little Giant Instruction Manual for Still Air Incubator and Automatic Egg Turner. Miller Mfg. Co., So. St. Paul, MN, 1998.

Scott, Wyatt. Personal Interview. 1 Dec. 2000.

Selsam, Millicent E. *Animals as Parents.* Canada: George J. McLeod Limited, 1965.

> In the bibliography, the writer lists all the works from which she gathered information used in her report. Some teachers prefer a "Works Cited" list, which lists only the sources that are actually cited, or noted, in your research report.

Editing and Proofreading

Set aside time to review your draft to eliminate errors in grammar, spelling, and punctuation.

Focus on Citations: Cite the sources for quotations, factual information, and ideas that are not your own. Citations in the body of your report appear in parentheses directly after the information cited. Include the author's last name and the relevant page number. (For more information, see Citing Sources, page R25.)

Publishing and Presenting

Create a reference list. Following the format that your teacher prefers, create a bibliography or works cited list of the information that you used to write your research report. (For more information, see Citing Sources, page R25.)

Give an oral presentation. Use your research report as the basis for an oral presentation on your topic. Keep your audience in mind as you prepare your presentation and revise accordingly.

Reflecting on Your Writing

Writer's Journal Jot down your thoughts on the experience of writing a research report. Begin by answering these questions:

- Which revising strategy did you find most effective? Explain.
- What did you learn about the topic you chose?

> *Prentice Hall Writing and Grammar Connection: Chapter 11*

Rubric for Self-Assessment

To assess your research report, use the following rubric:

Criteria	Rating Scale
	not very · · · · very
Focus: How clearly stated is the main idea?	1 2 3 4 5
Organization: How effective is your organization of information?	1 2 3 4 5
Support/Elaboration: How convincing are your supporting facts and details?	1 2 3 4 5
Style: How smooth are your transitions?	1 2 3 4 5
Conventions: According to an accepted format, how complete and accurate are your citations?	1 2 3 4 5

Conducting an Interview

In your research, you may at some time find it necessary to interview someone in order to get the information you need. Follow these steps to conduct a successful interview.

Preparing for the Interview

- **Identify your purpose.** It is important that you know what kind of information you would like to get from the interview. Do background research on your topic to focus on an area to ask about.

- **Create questions.** Use your research to draw up a list of questions for the interview. You will use this list at the interview, but you can also ask other questions that come to mind as you listen. You may need to ask follow-up questions to clarify points and get examples.

Conducting the Interview

Listen carefully. Listening is more than just hearing. Sometimes you think you know what someone is going to say, so you do not really hear what they *are* saying. Break this habit by making sure you understand what someone is saying before you move on to your next question. If you are listening to acquire new information or to evaluate a point of view, pay close attention to both main points and details.

Eliminate barriers to listening. Avoid distractions when listening. Sit close to the speaker and stay focused on what he or she is saying, not on other things that are going on in the room.

Take notes. Taking notes is a further step—beyond listening actively—that will help you remember what a speaker says. Do not write down every word. Instead, try to capture the speaker's main points and a few supporting details. Later, review your notes to be sure you understand them.

> **Six Rules for Listening Effectively**
>
> 1. Pay attention and concentrate on what is being said.
> 2. Do not look around. Focus your eyes and ears on the speaker.
> 3. Concentrate on what the speaker is saying. Do not be distracted by his or her manner of speaking.
> 4. Block out any distractions, such as noises or concerns you might have.
> 5. Put away anything that may distract you.
> 6. Keep a pencil and paper handy to take notes.

Activity ▸ **Conduct an Interview** Practice your skills by interviewing a community member, friend, or relative on a subject about which he or she is knowledgeable. You may want to record your interview so that you can review it for ways in which you can improve your skills.

The Prince and the Pauper

Mark Twain
Globe Fearon, 1993

Novel *The Prince and the Pauper* is set in England in the 1500s. The story is inspired by historical facts. Join two boys who decide to switch identities. Although they look exactly alike, one is a street kid and one the prince who will inherit the English throne. Neither is prepared for the surprises of someone else's world!

Destiny

Vicki Grove
Puffin Books, 2000

Novel Destiny, the main character in the novel, works for Mrs. Peck, a former Latin teacher, who has a great interest in Greek mythology. As the stories of war and magical intervention unfold, Destiny finds herself learning a great deal about modern life and herself. The novel interweaves Greek myths and modern life in a mixture that is fun, frightening, and fascinating.

The Gawgon and the Boy

Lloyd Alexander
Dutton Children's Books, 2001

Novel David thinks that having to be tutored by Aunt Annie might be the worst arrangement in the world. The aged Aunt Annie seems as frightening as a monstrous, snake-haired Gorgon. Soon, though, David has good reasons to change his mind. The Gawgon and the boy rescue King Tut's treasure, scale mountains, outwit master criminals, and fool the gods.

Myths and Legends From Ancient Greece and Around the World

Prentice Hall Literature Library
Prentice Hall, 2000

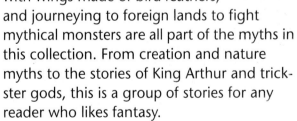

Anthology Driving a chariot that pulls the sun across the sky, flying with wings made of bird feathers, and journeying to foreign lands to fight mythical monsters are all part of the myths in this collection. From creation and nature myths to the stories of King Arthur and trickster gods, this is a group of stories for any reader who likes fantasy.

These titles are available in the Penguin/Prentice Hall Literature Library.
Consult your teacher before choosing one.

Think About It At some point in our lives, we all wish for supernatural powers—the power to be invisible, the power to read people's minds, or even the power to fly. Judith Ortiz Cofer recalls a time in her childhood when all she wanted to do was climb to the top of her building, break away from gravity, and fly wherever she wanted.

Volar: To Fly

Judith Ortiz Cofer

At twelve I was an avid consumer of comic books—*Supergirl* being my favorite. I spent my allowance of a quarter a day on two twelve-cent comic books or a double issue for twenty-five. I had a stack of *Legion of Super Heroes* and *Supergirl* comic books in my bedroom closet that was as tall as I. I had a recurring dream in those days: that I had long blond hair and could fly. In my dream I climbed the stairs to the top of our apartment building as myself, but as I went up each flight, changes would be taking place. Step by step I would fill out: my legs would grow long, my arms harden into steel, and my hair would magically go straight and turn a golden color. . . . Once on the roof, my parents safely asleep in their beds, I would get on tip-toe, arms outstretched in the position for flight and jump out my fifty-story-high window into the black lake of the sky. From up there, over the rooftops, I could see everything, even beyond the few blocks of our barrio; with my X-ray vision I could look inside the homes of people who interested me. Once I saw our landlord, whom I knew my parents feared, sitting in a treasure-room dressed in an ermine coat and a large gold crown. He sat on the floor counting his dollar bills. I played a trick on him. Going up to his building's chimney, I blew a little puff of my super-breath into his fireplace, scattering his stacks of money so that he had to start counting all over again. I could more or less program my Supergirl dreams in those days by focusing on the object of my current obsession. This way I "saw" into the private lives of my neighbors, my teachers, and in the last days of my childish fantasy and the beginning of adolescence, into the secret room of the boys I liked. In the mornings I'd wake up in my tiny bedroom with the incongruous—at least in our tiny apartment—white "princess" furniture my mother had chosen for me, and find myself back in my body: my tight curls still clinging to my head, skinny arms and legs . . .

   In the kitchen my mother and father would be talking softly over a café con leche. She would come "wake me" exactly forty-five minutes after they had gotten up. It was their time together at the beginning of each day and even at an early age I could feel their disappointment

if I interrupted them by getting up too early. So I would stay in my bed recalling my dreams of flight, perhaps planning my next flight. In the kitchen they would be discussing events in the barrio. Actually, he would be carrying that part of the conversation; when it was her turn to speak she would, more often than not, try shifting the topic toward her desire to see her *familia* on the Island: *How about a vacation in Puerto Rico together this year, Querido? We could rent a car, go to the beach. We*

could . . . And he would answer patiently, gently, *Mi amor, do you know how much it would cost for the all of us to fly there? It is not possible for me to take the time off . . . Mi vida, please understand. . . .* And I knew that soon she would rise from the table. Not abruptly. She would . . . look out the kitchen window. The view was of a dismal alley that was littered with refuse thrown from windows. The space was too narrow for anyone larger than a skinny child to enter safely, so it was never cleaned. My mother would check the time on the clock over her sink, the one with a prayer for patience and grace written in Spanish. A birthday gift. She would see that it was time to wake me. She'd sigh deeply and say the same thing the view from her kitchen window always inspired her to say: *Ay, si yo pudiera volar.**

---

* Oh, if only I could fly.

Meet the Author

Judith Ortiz Cofer (b. 1952) was born in Puerto Rico, but moved to Paterson, New Jersey, with her family when she was very young. Much of her writing—which includes fiction, nonfiction, and poetry—addresses the difference in the cultures of the two countries.

Readings in Nonfiction
Talk About It

Use the following questions to guide a discussion of "Volar: To Fly."

1. **(a)** What does the writer dream about at night? **(b)** What do you think these dreams say about her?

2. **(a)** Why does the writer wait in bed until her mother comes to wake her? **(b)** What reasons does her father give for not visiting Puerto Rico? **(c)** Do you think these are good reasons? Explain.

3. In this essay both daughter and mother long to fly, but for different reasons. In a small group, share your responses to the following questions:
   - Why does the writer wish to fly? Give some examples from her dreams.
   - Why does the writer's mother wish to fly? What details support your opinion?
   - If you were able to fly, where would you go? Why?

   Choose a point-person to share your group's ideas with the class.

RESOURCES

GLOSSARY

High-utility words and academic vocabulary appear in green.

A

acknowledge (ak näl´ ij) *v.* recognize and admit

acquainted (ə kwānt´ əd) *adj.* familiar

adequate (ad´ i kwət) *adj.* enough

affect (ə fekt´) *v.* to have an effect on someone or something

affects (ə fekts´) *v.* produces an effect upon; causes a change

ajar (ə jär´) *adj.* slightly open

almanac (ôl´mə nak´) *n.* a yearly publication that includes details about events or activities

alter (ôl´tər) *v.* adjust or make changes to

analyze (an´ə līz´) *v.* examine something in great detail

anonymous (ə nän´ ə məs) *adj.* unacknowledged; by someone whose name is withheld or unknown

anticipate (an tis´ə pāt´) *v.* to consider something before it happens

antidote (an´ tə dōt´) *n.* remedy; cure

apparent (ə par´ ənt) *adj.* seeming

aptitude (ap´ tə tōōd) *n.* talent; ability

arid (ar´ id) *adj.* dry and barren

aspect (as´pekt´) *n.* one feature or part of a whole

assumption (ə sump´shən) *n.* the act of assuming or taking for granted

astonish (ə stän´ ish) *v.* amaze

audible (ô´də bəl) *adj.* loud enough to be heard

awe (ô) *n.* mixed feelings of fear and wonder

B

background (bak ground´) *n.* a person's experience or knowledge; the information that helps you understand an event or situation

banish (ban´ish) *v.* send away; exile

bellow (bel´ ō) *v.* roar deeply

benevolence (bə nev´ ə ləns) *n.* kindliness

bigots (big´ əts) *n.* narrow-minded, prejudiced people

blander (bland´ ər) *adj.* more tasteless

bound (bound) *v.* tied

brawny (brôn´ ē) *adj.* strong and muscular

burrow (bʉr´ ō) *v.* dig a hole for shelter

C

cattails (kat´ tālz) *n.* tall reeds with furry, brown spikes, found in marshes and swamps

characteristic (kar´ək tər is´tik) *n.* a quality that makes a person or thing recognizable

check (chek) *v.* to confirm that something is true or accurate

chronological (krän´ə läj´i kəl) *adj.* arranged in the order in which events occur

clarify (klar´ə fī´) *v.* to make clear

coax (kōks) *v.* use gentle persuasion

communal (kə myōōn´ əl) *adj.* shared by all

compelled (kəm peld´) *v.* forced

compulsion (kəm pul´ shən) *n.* driving, irresistible force

conclude (kən klōōd´) *v.* to form an opinion or make a judgment, based on evidence presented

conflict (kän´flikt´) *n.* opposition between or among different forces; clash

consequence (kän´si kwens´) *n.* something that follows as a result of something else

consolation (kän´ səl ā´ shən) *n.* something that comforts a disappointed person

conspired (kən spīrd´) *v.* planned together secretly

context (kän´tekst´) *n.* the parts of a sentence or paragraph immediately next to or surrounding a specific word

contraption (kən trap´ shən) *n.* device or machine regarded as strange

conveyed (kən vād´) *v.* made known; expressed

conviction (kən vik´ shən) *n.* belief

coveted (kuv´ it id) *v.* wanted; desired

cowered (kou´ ərd) *v.* crouched down or huddled up, as from fear

credible (kred´ə bəl) *adj.* easy to believe

critique (kri tēk´) *n.* an assessment, usually of a creative work

croon (krōōn) *v.* sing or hum quietly and soothingly

crouches (krouch´ iz) *v.* stoops or bends low

crucial (krōō´ shəl) *adj.* important; critical

culprit (kul´ prit) *n.* guilty person

curb (kʉrb) *v.* check or control

D

deceive (dē sēv´) v. make someone believe something that is not true

decreed (di krēd´) v. officially ordered

defiant (dē fī´ ənt) adj. boldly resisting

defies (dē fīz´) v. resists or opposes boldly or openly

dejectedly (dē jek´ tid lē) adv. sadly; showing discouragement

deluge (del´ yōōj´) n. a great flood

desolate (des´ ə lit) adj. lonely; solitary

destination (des´ tə nā´ shən) n. place to which something is being sent

destiny (des´ tə nē) n. fate; preplanned course of events

destitute (des´ tə tōōt´) adj. used as n., people living in complete poverty

detail (di tāl´, dē´tāl´) n. an individual part of something

detect (dē tekt´) v. notice or discover something

devastated (dev´ ə stā´ tid) v. destroyed; completely upset

devastating (dev´ ə stāt´ iŋ) adj. destructive; overwhelming

diplomats (dip´lə mats´) n. government representatives who work with other nations

dislodge (dis läj´) v. force from a position or place

dispelled (di speld´) v. driven away; made to disappear

distinct (di stiŋkt´) adj. separate and different

distract (di strakt´) v. draw attention away in another direction

diversions (də vʉr´ zhənz) n. amusements

E

effect (e fekt´) n. something that occurs as a direct result of an action

elaboration (ē lab´ ə rā´ shən) n. adding of more details

elective (ē lek´ tiv) n. optional course

emerged (ē mʉrjd´) v. came into view; became visible

eminent (em´ ə nənt) adj. distinguished or outstanding

emphasize (em´fə sīz´) v. stress the importance of something

emulate (em´ yōō lāt´) v. copy or be like someone

envisioned (en vizh´ ənd) v. pictured in one's mind

epidemic (ep´ ə dem´ ik) n. outbreak of a contagious disease

establish (ə stab´lish) v. determine; make sure of

evading (ē vād´ iŋ) v. avoiding

evaluate (ē val´yōō āt´) v. to examine something in order to gain information or make a judgment

evidently (ev´ ə dent´ lē) adv. clearly; obviously

exertion (eg zʉr´ shən) n. physical work

expense (ek spens´) n. financial cost

exquisite (eks´ kwiz it) adj. beautiful in a delicate way

exultant (eg zult´ 'nt) adj. expressing great joy or triumph

F

feeble (fē´ bəl) adj. weak; infirm

fiddler (fid´ lər) n. person who plays a fiddle, or violin

flatterers (flat´ ər ərz) n. those who praise a person insincerely

fluent (flōō´ ənt) adj. able to write or speak easily and smoothly

flushed (flusht) v. drove from hiding

flustered (flus´ tərd) adj. nervous; confused

focus (fō´kəs) v. look closely at

formidable (fôr´ mə də bəl) adj. impressive

frontier (frun tir´) n. the developing, often uncivilized, region of a country; any new field of learning

fundamental (fun´ də ment´ 'l) adj. basic; forming a foundation

G

gauge (gāj) v. estimate or judge

glossy (glôs´ ē) adj. smooth and shiny

goblets (gäb´ lits) n. bowl-shaped drinking containers without handles

gourd (gôrd) n. a fruit; the dried shell is used as a cup

groves (grōvz) n. small groups of trees

gumption (gump´ shən) n. courage; enterprise

H

haunches (hônch´ iz) n. upper legs and hips of an animal

hideous (hid´ē əs) adj. horrible to see; very ugly

highlight (hī´ līt´) v. draw attention to something

hindered (hin´ dərd) adj. held back

hors d'oeuvres (ôr´ dʉrv´) n. savory foods served as appetizers

huddled (hud´ 'ld) v. crowded or nestled close together

I

identify (ī den´tə fī´) v. to recognize something and be able to say what it is

ignorant (ig´ nə rənt) adj. not knowing facts or information

ignored (ig nôrd´) v. paid no attention to

immensely (i mens´ lē) adv. a great deal; very much

immensity (i men´sə tē) *n.* immeasurable largeness or vastness

impetus (im´ pə təs) *n.* driving force

implored (im plôrd´) *v.* begged

impromptu (im prämp´ tōō) *adj.* unscheduled; unplanned

improvising (im´ prə vīz´ iŋ) *v.* making up or inventing on the spur of the moment

incessantly (in ses´ənt lē) *adv.* without stopping

indicate (in´di kāt´) *v.* to point something out or point to something

indispensable (in´ di spen´ sə bəl) *adj.* absolutely necessary

infer (in fʉr´) *v.* make a logical assumption based on evidence or reasoning

initiation (i nish´ ē ā´ shən) *n.* process by which one becomes a member of a group

insignificant (in´sig nif´ə kənt) *adj.* having little or no meaning

interplanetary (in´ tər plan´ ə ter´ ē) *adj.* between planets

intersection (in´ tər sek´ shən) *n.* the place where two or more roads meet or cross

intervene (in tər vēn´) *v.* come between as an influence to modify, settle, or hinder some action or argument

intricate (in´ tri kit) *adj.* complex; detailed

intrigue (in´ trēg´) *n.* curiosity and interest

investigate (in ves´tə gāt´) *v.* to examine in order to gain information

involvement (in välv´ mənt) *n.* participation in

irrelevant (i rel´ə vənt) *adj.* not having a connection with

J

justifies (jus´ tə fīz´) *v.* excuses

K

knack (nak) *n.* ability to do something easily

L

laborious (lə bôr´ ē əs) *adj.* taking much work or effort

legislation (lej´ is lā´ shən) *n.* law

loathed (lō*th*d) *v.* hated

luminous (lōō´ mə nəs) *adj.* giving off light

M

maestro (mīs´ trō) *n.* great musician

malice (mal´ is) *n.* ill will

malicious (mə lish´ əs) *adj.* spiteful; hateful

meager (mē´ gər) *adj.* of poor quality; small in amount

meek (mēk) *adj.* timid; not showing anger

metamorphosis (met´ə môr´fə sis) *n.* change of form

Millennium (mi len´ ē əm) *n.* any period of one thousand years; when capitalized, the year 2000 or, some people say, the year 2001

morose (mə rōs´) *adj.* gloomy; ill-tempered

mortality (môr tal´ ə tē) *n.* the condition of being mortal, or having to die eventually

murmuring (mʉr´ mər iŋ) *v.* making low, indistinct, continuous sounds

N

neglected (ni gleckt´ əd) *v.* failed to take care of

O

object (äb´jikt) *n.* a thing that can be seen or touched

occur (ə kʉr´) *v.* happen or come about

ominous (äm´ ə nəs) *adj.* threatening

optimist (äp´ tə mist) *n.* someone who takes the most hopeful view of matters

ornament (ôr´ nə mənt) *v.* beautify

outskirts (ʊut skʉrtz´) *n.* part of a district far from the center of a city

P

parallel (par´ ə lel´) *adv.* extending in the same direction and at the same distance apart

paraphrase (par´ə frāz´) *v.* restate something in your own words

passage (pas´ij) *n.* a section of a piece of writing

pathetic (pə thet´ ik) *adj.* pitiful

paupers (pô´ pərz) *n.* people who are very poor

peeved (pēvd) *adj.* irritated; annoyed

perilous (per´ ə ləs) *adj.* dangerous

permanent (pʉr´mə nənt) *adj.* lasting for all time

perpetual (pər pech´ ōō əl) *adj.* constant; unending

persistently (pər sist´ ənt lē) *adv.* firmly and steadily

perspective (pər spek´tiv) *n.* an assessment of a situation, especially from one person's point of view

petrified (pe´ trə fīd´) *adj.* turned into stone

plausible (plô´ zə bəl) *adj.* seemingly true; acceptable

proposal (prə pōz´ əl) *n.* plan; offer

plot (plät) *n.* the sequence of events in a story

pondered (pän´ dərd) *v.* thought about deeply; meditated

porridge (pôr´ij) *n.* soft food made of cereal boiled in water or milk

potential (pō ten´ shəl) *n.* possibility; capability

practical (prak´ ti kəl) *adj.* level-headed; efficient; realistic

predict (prē dikt´) v. to say what is going to happen in the future, based on available information or past experience

preliminary (prē lim´ ə ner´ ē) adj. coming before or leading up to the main action

presumptuous (prē zump´ choo əs) adj. overconfident; arrogant

previous (prē´ vē əs) adj. occurring before in time order

prior (prī´ ər) adj. coming before in time; earlier

profound (prō found´) adj. deeply or intensely felt

profusely (prō fyoos´ lē) adv. freely; plentifully

promote (prə mōt´) v. encourage; contribute to the growth of

proposal (prə pōz əl) n. plan; offer

pungent (pun´ jənt) adj. sharp-smelling

pursuit (pər soot´) n. the act of chasing

Q

quest (kwest) n. a long search for something

R

radiant (rā´ dē ənt) adj. shining brightly

rancid (ran´ sid) adj. spoiled and smelling bad

rash (rash) adj. thoughtless; reckless

reaction (rē ak´ shən) n. an opposing action; a response

reassuring (rē´ ə shoor´ iŋ) adj. having the effect of restoring confidence

recall (ri kôl´) v. to call back; remember

reeds (rēdz) n. tall, slender grasses that grow in marshy land

refer (ri fur´) v. consult a source in order to find information; mention a source of information

refugee (ref yoo jē´) n. person who flees home or country to seek shelter from war or cruelty

relented (ri lent´ əd) v. gave in

relevant (rel´ ə vənt) adj. having a logical connection with

reliable (ri lī´ ə bəl) adj. dependable

remote (ri mōt´) adj. far away from everything else

reproach (ri prōch´) n. disgrace; blame

resilient (ri zil´ yənt) adj. springing back into shape

restate (rē stāt´) v. say something again; summarize

resumed (ri zoomd´) v. began again; continued

reveal (ri vēl´) v. to make known

reveling (rev´ əl iŋ) n. celebrating

revived (ri vīvd´) v. came back to consciousness

routed (rout´ əd) v. completely defeated

rummaging (rum´ ij iŋ) v. searching through something

S

sage (sāj) n. very wise person

scorned (skôrnd) adj. looked down upon

scowl (skoul) v. make an unpleasant expression by contracting the eyebrows and lowering the corners of the mouth

sensitive (sen´ sə tiv) adj. easily hurt

sequence (sē´ kwəns) n. one thing after another in logical or chronological order

severe (sə vir´) adj. harsh

shuffle (shuf´ əl) v. walk with dragging feet

significance (sig nif´ ə kəns) n. meaning; importance

significant (sig nif´ ə kənt) adj. having an important meaning

simultaneously (sī´ məl tā´ nē əs lē) adv. at the same time

sinewy (sin´ yoo ē) adj. tough and strong

slackening (slak´ ən iŋ) v. easing; becoming less active

sluggishly (slug´ ish lē) adv. as if lacking energy

snuffs (snufs) v. extinguishes; puts out

solemn (säl´ əm) adj. serious; somber

spectators (spek´ tāt´ erz) n. onlookers

spigot (spig´ ət) n. faucet; spout

spines (spīnz) n. backbones

sputters (sput´ ərz) v. makes hissing or spitting sounds

strategy (strat´ ə jē) n. set of plans used to gain success or achieve an aim

strive (strīv) v. struggle

stutter (stut´ ər) v. to speak in a hesitant or faltering way

subject (sub´ jikt) n. the main idea or topic

suitors (soot´ ərz) n. men who court a woman or seek to marry her

summarize (sum´ ə rīz´) v. briefly state the most important events in a story

summoned (sum´ ənd) v. called together

supple (sup´ əl) adj. able to bend easily; flexible

surpass (sər pas´) v. be superior to

sustained (sə stānd′) *adj.* supported

swerve (swɐrv) *n.* curving motion

T

tentatively (ten′ tə tiv lē) *adv.* hesitantly; with uncertainty

thrive (thrīv) *v.* do well

timid (tim′ id) *adj.* showing shyness

tolerant (täl′ ər ənt) *adj.* accepting; free from bigotry or prejudice

torrent (tôr′ ənt) *n.* flood

transfixed (trans fikst′) *adj.* rooted to the spot

transform (trans fôrm′) *v.* change the shape or structure of

transformation (trans′fər mā′shən) *n.* change

tumultuously (tōō mul′chōō əs lē) *adv.* noisily and violently

twine (twīn) *n.* strong string or cord of two or more strands twisted together

U

ultimate (ul′ tə mit) *adj.* final

unanimous (yōō nan′ ə məs) *adj.* based on complete agreement

uncanny (un kan′ ē) *adj.* strange; eerie

unique (yōō nēk′) *adj.* being the only one of its kind

unravel (un rav′ əl) *v.* become untangled or separated

utter (ut′ ər) *v.* speak

V

vacancy (vā′ kən sē) *n.* emptiness

valid (val′id) *adj.* justifiable, or logically correct

venerable (ven′ ər ə bəl) *adj.* worthy of respect or reverence by reason of age; impressive on account of age

verify (ver′ə fī′) *v.* to check whether or not something is true based on examination; to prove to be true

vital (vīt′ 'l) *adj.* extremely important or necessary

void (void) *n.* emptiness

vowed (voud) *v.* promised solemnly

W

weasel (wē′ zəl) *n.* a small mammal that eats rats, mice, birds, and eggs

whiff (hwif) *n.* smell; scent

whimper (hwim′ pər) *v.* make low, crying sounds

withered (with′ ərd) *adj.* dried up

writhing (rīth′ iŋ) *adj.* squirming, often in response to pain

Y

yearned (yɐrnd) *v.* wanted very much

Using a Dictionary

Use a **dictionary** to find the meaning, the pronunciation, and the part of speech of a word. Consult a dictionary also to trace the word's *etymology*, or its origin. Etymology explains how words change, how they are borrowed from other languages, and how new words are invented, or "coined."

Here is an entry from a dictionary. Notice what it tells about the word *anthology*.

anthology (an thäl′ə jē) *n., pl.* **–gies** [Gr. *anthologia*, a garland, collection of short poems < *anthologos*, gathering flowers < *anthos*, flower + *legein*, to gather] a collection of poems, stories, songs, excerpts, etc., chosen by the compiler

Dictionaries provide the *denotation* of each word, or its objective meaning. The symbol < means "comes from" or "is derived from." In this case, the Greek words for "flower" and "gather" combined to form a Greek word that meant a garland, and then that word became an English word that means a collection of literary flowers—a collection of literature like the one you are reading now.

Activity: Use a dictionary to learn about the origins of these words. Then, write a sentence explaining how each word's origin contributes to its meaning.
1. literature
2. author
3. language

Using a Thesaurus

Use a **thesaurus** to increase your vocabulary. In a thesaurus, you will find synonyms, or words that have similar meanings, for most words. Follow these guidelines to use a thesaurus:

- Do not choose a word just because it sounds interesting or educated. Choose the word that expresses exactly the meaning you intend.
- To avoid errors, look up an unfamiliar word in a dictionary to check its precise meaning and to make sure you are using it properly.

Here is an entry from a thesaurus. Notice what it tells about the word *book*.

book *noun*

A printed and bound work: tome, volume. *See* **WORDS.**

book *verb* 1. To register in or as if in a book: catalog, enroll, inscribe, list, set down, write down. *See* **REMEMBER**. 2. To cause to be set aside, as for one's use, in advance: bespeak, engage, reserve. *See* **GET**.

If the word can be used as different parts of speech, as *book* can, the thesaurus entry provides synonyms for the word as each part of speech. Many words also have *connotations*, or emotional associations that the word calls to mind. A thesaurus entry gives specific synonyms for each connotation of the word.

Activity: Look up the word *story* in a thesaurus. Then, answer the questions.

1. What are two synonyms for this word?
2. In what way do the connotations of the synonyms differ?

The History of the English Language

Old English English began about the year 500 when Germanic tribes from the middle of Europe traveled west and settled in Britain. These peoples—the Angles, Saxons, and Jutes—spoke a Germanic language that combined with Danish and Norse when Vikings attacked Britain and added some Latin elements when Christian missionaries arrived. The result was Old English.

Middle English The biggest change in English took place after the Norman Conquest of Britain in 1066. The Normans spoke a dialect of Old French, and Old English changed dramatically when the Normans became the new aristocracy. From about 1100 to 1500, the people of Britain spoke what we now call Middle English.

Modern English During the Renaissance (1300–1600) with its emphasis on reviving classical culture, Greek and Latin languages exerted a strong influence on the English language. In addition, Shakespeare added about two thousand words to the language. Grammar, spelling, and pronunciation continued to change. Modern English was born.

Old Words, New Words

Modern English has a larger vocabulary than any other language in the world. Here are the main ways that new words enter the language:

- **War**—Conquerors introduce new terms and ideas—and new vocabulary, such as *anger* from Old Norse.

- **Immigration**—When large groups of people move from one country to another, they bring words with them, such as *boycott*, from Ireland.

- **Travel and Trade**—Those who travel to foreign lands and those who do business in faraway places bring new words back with them, such as *shampoo*, from the Hindi language of Northern India.

- **Science and Technology**—In our time, the amazing growth of science and technology adds many new words to English, such as *Internet*.

- **Other Languages**—Sometimes borrowed words keep basically the same meanings they have in their original languages. Examples include *pajamas* (Hindi), *sauna* (Finnish), and *camouflage* (French). Sometimes borrowed words take on new meanings. *Sleuth*, for example, an Old Norse word for *trail*, has come to mean the person who follows a trail—a detective.

- **Mythology**—Some of the days of the week are named after Norse gods—Wednesday was Woden's Day, Thursday was Thor's Day. Greek and Roman myths have given us many words, such as *martial* (from Mars) and *herculean* (from Hercules).

Activity: Look up the following words in a dictionary. Describe the ways in which you think these words entered American English.

sabotage   burrito   moccasin   megabyte

TIPS FOR IMPROVING READING FLUENCY

When you were younger, you learned to read. Then, you read to expand your experiences or for pure enjoyment. Now, you are expected to read to learn. As you progress in school, you are given more and more material to read. The tips on these pages will help you improve your reading fluency, or your ability to read easily, smoothly, and expressively.

Keeping Your Concentration

One common problem that readers face is the loss of concentration. When you are reading an assignment, you might find yourself rereading the same sentence several times without really understanding it. The first step in changing this behavior is to notice that you do it. Becoming an active, aware reader will help you get the most from your assignments. Practice using these strategies:

- Cover what you have already read with a note card as you go along. Then, you will not be able to reread without noticing that you are doing it.

- Set a purpose for reading beyond just completing the assignment. Then, read actively by pausing to ask yourself questions about the material as you read.

- Use the Reading Skill instruction and notes that appear with each selection in this textbook.

- Stop reading after a specified period of time (for example, 5 minutes) and summarize what you have read. To help you with this strategy, use the Reading Check questions that appear with each selection in this textbook. Reread to find any answers you do not know.

Reading Phrases

Fluent readers read phrases rather than individual words. Reading this way will speed up your reading and improve your comprehension. Here are some useful ideas:

- Experts recommend rereading as a strategy to increase fluency. Choose a passage of text that is neither too hard nor too easy. Read the same passage aloud several times until you can read it smoothly. When you can read the passage fluently, pick another passage and keep practicing.

- Read aloud into a tape recorder. Then, listen to the recording, noting your accuracy, pacing, and expression. You can also read aloud and share feedback with a partner.

- Use the *Prentice Hall Listening to Literature* CDs to hear the selections read aloud. Read along silently in your textbook, noticing how the reader uses his or her voice and emphasizes certain words and phrases.

Understanding Key Vocabulary

If you do not understand some of the words in an assignment, you may miss out on important concepts. Therefore, it is helpful to keep a dictionary nearby when you are reading. Follow these steps:

- Before you begin reading, scan the text for unfamiliar words or terms. Find out what those words mean before you begin reading.
- Use context—the surrounding words, phrases, and sentences—to help you determine the meanings of unfamiliar words.
- If you are unable to understand the meaning through context, refer to the dictionary.

Paying Attention to Punctuation

When you read, pay attention to punctuation. Commas, periods, exclamation points, semicolons, and colons tell you when to pause or stop. They also indicate relationships, between groups of words. When you recognize these relationships, you will read with greater understanding and expression. Look at the chart below.

Punctuation Mark	Meaning
comma	brief pause
period	pause at the end of a thought
exclamation point	pause that indicates emphasis
semicolon	pause between related but distinct thoughts
colon	pause before giving explanation or examples

Using the Reading Fluency Checklist

Use the checklist below each time you read a selection in this textbook. In your Language Arts journal or notebook, note which skills you need to work on and chart your progress each week.

Reading Fluency Checklist

- ☐ Preview the text to check for difficult or unfamiliar words.
- ☐ Practice reading aloud.
- ☐ Read according to punctuation.
- ☐ Break down long sentences into the subject and its meaning.
- ☐ Read groups of words for meaning rather than reading single words.
- ☐ Read with expression (change your tone of voice to add meaning to the word).

Reading is a skill that can be improved with practice. The key to improving your fluency is to read. The more you read, the better your reading will become.

LITERARY TERMS

ALLITERATION *Alliteration* is the repetition of initial consonant sounds. Writers use alliteration to draw attention to certain words or ideas, to imitate sounds, and to create musical effects.

ALLUSION An *allusion* is a reference to a well-known person, event, place, literary work, or work of art. Allusions allow the writer to express complex ideas without spelling them out. Understanding what a literary work is saying often depends on recognizing its allusions and the meanings they suggest.

ANALOGY An *analogy* makes a comparison between two or more things that are similar in some ways but otherwise unalike.

ANECDOTE An *anecdote* is a brief story about an interesting, amusing, or strange event. Writers tell anecdotes to entertain or to make a point.

ANTAGONIST An *antagonist* is a character or a force in conflict with a main character, or protagonist.

See *Conflict* and *Protagonist*.

ATMOSPHERE *Atmosphere*, or *mood*, is the feeling created in the reader by a literary work or passage.

AUTHOR'S ARGUMENT An *author's argument* is the position he or she puts forward, supported by reasons.

AUTHOR'S PURPOSE An *author's purpose* is his or her main reason for writing. For example, an author may want to entertain, inform, or persuade the reader. Sometimes an author is trying to teach a moral lesson or reflect on an experience. An author may have more than one purpose for writing.

AUTOBIOGRAPHY An *autobiography* is the story of the writer's own life, told by the writer. Autobiographical writing may tell about the person's whole life or only a part of it.

Because autobiographies are about real people and events, they are a form of nonfiction. Most autobiographies are written in the first person.

See *Biography, Nonfiction,* and *Point of View*.

BIOGRAPHY A *biography* is a form of nonfiction in which a writer tells the life story of another person. Most biographies are written about famous or admirable people. Although biographies are nonfiction, the most effective ones share the qualities of good narrative writing.

See *Autobiography* and *Nonfiction*.

CHARACTER A *character* is a person or an animal that takes part in the action of a literary work. The main, or *major*, character is the most important character in a story, poem, or play. A *minor* character is one who takes part in the action but is not the focus of attention.

Characters are sometimes classified as flat or round. A *flat character* is one-sided and often stereotypical. A *round character*, on the other hand, is fully developed and exhibits many traits—often both faults and virtues. Characters can also be classified as dynamic or static. A *dynamic character* is one who changes or grows during the course of the work. A *static character* is one who does not change.

See *Characterization, Hero/Heroine,* and *Motive*.

CHARACTERIZATION *Characterization* is the act of creating and developing a character. Authors use two major methods of characterization—*direct* and *indirect*. When using *direct* characterization, a writer states the *characters' traits,* or characteristics.

When describing a character indirectly, a writer depends on the reader to draw conclusions about the character's traits. Sometimes the writer tells what other participants in the story say and think about the character.

See *Character* and *Motive*.

CLIMAX The *climax*, also called the turning point, is the high point in the action of the plot. It is the moment of greatest tension, when the outcome of the plot hangs in the balance.

See *Plot*.

COMEDY A *comedy* is a literary work, especially a play, which is light, often humorous or satirical, and ends happily. Comedies frequently depict ordinary characters faced with temporary difficulties and conflicts. Types of comedy include *romantic comedy*, which involves problems between lovers, and the *comedy of manners*, which satirically challenges social customs of a society.

CONCRETE POEM A *concrete poem* is one with a shape that suggests its subject. The poet arranges the letters, punctuation, and lines to create an image, or picture, on the page.

CONFLICT A *conflict* is a struggle between opposing forces. Conflict is one of the most important elements of stories, novels, and plays because it causes the action. There are two kinds of conflict: external and internal. An *external conflict* is one in which a character struggles against some outside force, such as another person. Another kind of external conflict may occur between a character and some force in nature.

An *internal conflict* takes place within the mind of a character. The character struggles to make a decision, take an action, or overcome a feeling.

See *Plot*.

CONNOTATIONS The *connotation* of a word is the set of ideas associated with it in addition to its explicit meaning. The connotation of a word can be personal, based on individual experiences. More often, cultural connotations—those recognizable by most people in a group—determine a writer's word choices.

See also *Denotation*.

COUPLET A *couplet* is two consecutive lines of verse with end rhymes. Often, a couplet functions as a stanza.

CULTURAL CONTEXT The *cultural context* of a literary work is the economic, social, and historical environment of the characters. This includes the attitudes and customs of that culture and historical period.

DENOTATION The *denotation* of a word is its dictionary meaning, independent of other associations that the word may have. The denotation of the word *lake*, for example, is "an inland body of water." "Vacation spot" and "place where the fishing is good" are connotations of the word *lake*.

See also *Connotation*.

DESCRIPTION A *description* is a portrait, in words, of a person, place, or object. Descriptive writing uses images that appeal to the five senses —sight, hearing, touch, taste, and smell.

See *Images*.

DEVELOPMENT See *Plot*.

DIALECT *Dialect* is the form of a language spoken by people in a particular region or group. Dialects differ in pronunciation, grammar, and word choice. The English language is divided into many dialects. British English differs from American English.

DIALOGUE A *dialogue* is a conversation between characters. In poems, novels, and short stories, dialogue is usually set off by quotation marks to indicate a speaker's exact words.

In a play, dialogue follows the names of the characters, and no quotation marks are used.

DICTION *Diction* is a writer's word choice and the way the writer puts those words together. Diction is part of a writer's style and may be described as formal or informal, plain or fancy, ordinary or technical, sophisticated or down-to-earth, old-fashioned or modern.

DRAMA A *drama* is a story written to be performed by actors. Although a drama is meant to be performed, one can also read the script, or written version, and imagine the action. The *script* of a drama is made up of dialogue and stage directions. The *dialogue* is the words spoken by the actors. The *stage directions*, usually printed in italics, tell how the actors should look, move, and speak. They also describe the setting, sound effects, and lighting.

Dramas are often divided into parts called *acts*. The acts are often divided into smaller parts called *scenes*.

DYNAMIC CHARACTER See *Character*.

ESSAY An *essay* is a short nonfiction work about a particular subject. Most essays have a single major focus and a clear introduction, body, and conclusion.

There are many types of essays. An *informal essay* uses casual, conversational language. A *historical essay* gives facts, explanations, and insights about historical events. An *expository essay* explains an idea by breaking it down. A *narrative essay* tells a story about a real-life experience. An *informational* essay explains a process. A *persuasive essay* offers an opinion and supports it. A *humorous essay* uses humor to achieve the author's purpose. A *reflective essay* addresses an event or experience and includes the writer's personal insights about the event's importance.

See *Exposition, Narration,* and *Persuasion.*

EXPOSITION In the plot of a story or a drama, the *exposition,* or introduction, is the part of the work that introduces the characters, setting, and basic situation.

See *Plot.*

EXPOSITORY WRITING *Expository writing* is writing that explains or informs.

EXTENDED METAPHOR In an *extended metaphor,* as in a regular metaphor, a subject is spoken or written of as though it were something else. However, extended metaphor differs from regular metaphor in that several connected comparisons are made.

See *Metaphor.*

EXTERNAL CONFLICT See *Conflict.*

FABLE A *fable* is a brief story or poem, usually with animal characters, that teaches a lesson, or moral. The moral is usually stated at the end of the fable.

See *Irony* and *Moral.*

FANTASY A *fantasy* is highly imaginative writing that contains elements not found in real life. Examples of fantasy include stories that involve supernatural elements, stories that resemble fairy tales, stories that deal with imaginary places and creatures, and science-fiction stories.

See *Science Fiction.*

FICTION *Fiction* is prose writing that tells about imaginary characters and events. Short stories and novels are works of fiction. Some writers base their fiction on actual events and people, adding invented characters, dialogue, settings, and plots. Other writers rely on imagination alone.

See *Narration, Nonfiction,* and *Prose.*

FIGURATIVE LANGUAGE *Figurative language* is writing or speech that is not meant to be taken literally. The many types of figurative language are known as *figures of speech.* Common figures of speech include metaphor, personification, and simile. Writers use figurative language to state ideas in vivid and imaginative ways.

See *Metaphor, Personification, Simile,* and *Symbol.*

FIGURE OF SPEECH See *Figurative Language.*

FLASHBACK A *flashback* is a scene within a story that interrupts the sequence of events to relate events that occurred in the past.

FLAT CHARACTER See *Character.*

FOIL A *foil* is a character whose behavior and attitude contrast with those of the main character.

FOLK TALE A *folk tale* is a story composed orally and then passed from person to person by word of mouth. Folk tales originated among people who could neither read nor write. These people entertained one another by telling stories aloud—often dealing with heroes, adventure, magic, or romance. Eventually, modern scholars collected these stories and wrote them down.

Folk tales reflect the cultural beliefs and environments from which they come.

See *Fable, Legend, Myth,* and *Oral Tradition.*

FOOT See *Meter.*

FORESHADOWING *Foreshadowing* is the author's use of clues to hint at what might happen later in the story. Writers use foreshadowing to build their readers' expectations and to create suspense.

FREE VERSE *Free verse* is poetry not written in a regular, rhythmical pattern, or meter. The poet is free to write lines of any length or with any number of stresses, or beats. Free verse is therefore less constraining than *metrical verse,* in which every line must have a certain length and a certain number of stresses.

See *Meter.*

GENRE A *genre* is a division or type of literature. Literature is commonly divided into three major genres: poetry, prose, and drama. Each major genre is, in turn, divided into lesser genres, as follows:

1. *Poetry:* lyric poetry, concrete poetry, dramatic poetry, narrative poetry, epic poetry

2. *Prose:* fiction (novels and short stories) and nonfiction (biography, autobiography, letters, essays, and reports)

3. *Drama:* serious drama and tragedy, comic drama, melodrama, and farce

See *Drama, Poetry,* and *Prose.*

HAIKU The *haiku* is a three-line Japanese verse form. The first and third lines of a haiku each have five syllables. The second line has seven syllables. A writer of haiku uses images to create a single, vivid picture, generally of a scene from nature.

HERO/HEROINE A *hero* or *heroine* is a character whose actions are inspiring or noble. Often heroes and heroines struggle to overcome the obstacles and problems that stand in their way. Note that the term *hero* was originally used only for male characters, while heroic female characters were always called *heroines.* However, it is now acceptable to use *hero* to refer to females as well as to males.

HISTORICAL CONTEXT The *historical context* of a literary work includes the actual political and social events and trends of the time. When a work takes place in the past, knowledge about that historical time period can help the reader understand its setting, background, culture, and message, as well as the attitudes and actions of its characters. A reader must also take into account the historical context in which the writer was creating the work, which may be different from the time period of the work's setting.

HUMOR *Humor* is writing intended to evoke laughter. While most humorists try to entertain, humor can also be used to convey a serious theme.

IDIOM An *idiom* is an expression that has a meaning particular to a language or region. For example, in "Seventh Grade," Gary Soto uses the idiom "making a face," which means to contort one's face in an unusal, usually unattractive way.

IMAGERY See *Images.*

IMAGES *Images* are words or phrases that appeal to one or more of the five senses. Writers use images to describe how their subjects look, sound, feel, taste, and smell. Poets often paint images, or word pictures, that appeal to your senses. These pictures help you to experience the poem fully.

INTERNAL CONFLICT See *Conflict.*

IRONY *Irony* is a contradiction between what happens and what is expected. There are three main types of irony. *Situational irony* occurs when something happens that directly contradicts the expectations of the characters or the audience. *Verbal irony* is something contradictory that is said. In *dramatic irony*, the audience is aware of something that the character or speaker is not.

JOURNAL A *journal* is a daily, or periodic, account of events and the writer's thoughts and feelings about those events. Personal journals are not normally written for publication, but sometimes they do get published later with permission from the author or the author's family.

LEGEND A *legend* is a widely told story about the past—one that may or may not have a foundation in fact. Every culture has its own legends—its familiar, traditional stories.

See *Folk Tale, Myth,* and *Oral Tradition.*

LETTERS A *letter* is a written communication from one person to another. In personal letters, the writer shares information and his or her thoughts and feelings with one other person or group. Although letters are not normally written for publication, they sometimes do get published later with the permission of the author or the author's family.

LIMERICK A *limerick* is a humorous, rhyming, five-line poem with a specific meter and rhyme scheme. Most limericks have three strong stresses in lines 1, 2, and 5 and two strong stresses in lines 3 and 4. Most follow the rhyme scheme *aabba.*

LYRIC POEM A *lyric poem* is a highly musical verse that expresses the observations and feelings of a single speaker. It creates a single, unified impression.

MAIN CHARACTER See *Character.*

MEDIA ACCOUNTS *Media accounts* are reports, explanations, opinions, or descriptions written for television, radio, newspapers, and magazines. While some media accounts report only facts, others include the writer's thoughts and reflections.

METAPHOR A *metaphor* is a figure of speech in which something is described as though it were something else. A metaphor, like a simile, works by pointing out a similarity between two unlike things.

See *Extended Metaphor* and *Simile*.

METER The *meter* of a poem is its rhythmical pattern. This pattern is determined by the number of *stresses*, or beats, in each line. To describe the meter of a poem, read it emphasizing the beats in each line. Then, mark the stressed and unstressed syllables, as follows:

Mў fáth | er wás | the first | to héar |

As you can see, each strong stress is marked with a slanted line (´) and each unstressed syllable with a horseshoe symbol (˘). The weak and strong stresses are then divided by vertical lines (|) into groups called *feet*.

MINOR CHARACTER See *Character*.

MOOD See *Atmosphere*.

MORAL A *moral* is a lesson taught by a literary work. A fable usually ends with a moral that is directly stated. A poem, novel, short story, or essay often suggests a moral that is not directly stated. The moral must be drawn by the reader, based on other elements in the work.

See *Fable*.

MOTIVATION See *Motive*.

MOTIVE A *motive* is a reason that explains or partially explains a character's thoughts, feelings, actions, or speech. Writers try to make their characters' motives, or motivations, as clear as possible. If the motives of a main character are not clear, then the character will not be believable.

Characters are often motivated by needs, such as food and shelter. They are also motivated by feelings, such as fear, love, and pride. Motives may be obvious or hidden.

MYTH A *myth* is a fictional tale that explains the actions of gods or heroes or the origins of elements of nature. Myths are part of the oral tradition. They are composed orally and then passed from generation to generation by word of mouth. Every ancient culture has its own mythology, or collection of myths. Greek and Roman myths are known collectively as *classical mythology*.

See *Oral Tradition*.

NARRATION *Narration* is writing that tells a story. The act of telling a story is also called narration. Each piece is a *narrative*. A story told in fiction, nonfiction, poetry, or even in drama is called a narrative.

See *Narrative, Narrative Poem*, and *Narrator*.

NARRATIVE A *narrative* is a story. A narrative can be either fiction or nonfiction. Novels and short stories are types of fictional narratives. Biographies and autobiographies are nonfiction narratives. Poems that tell stories are also narratives.

See *Narration* and *Narrative Poem*.

NARRATIVE POEM A *narrative poem* is a story told in verse. Narrative poems often have all the elements of short stories, including characters, conflict, and plot.

NARRATOR A *narrator* is a speaker or a character who tells a story. The narrator's perspective is the way he or she sees things. A *third-person narrator* is one who stands outside the action and speaks about it. A *first-person narrator* is one who tells a story and participates in its action.

See *Point of View*.

NONFICTION *Nonfiction* is prose writing that presents and explains ideas or that tells about real people, places, objects, or events. Autobiographies, biographies, essays, reports, letters, memos, and newspaper articles are all types of nonfiction.

See *Fiction*.

NOVEL A *novel* is a long work of fiction. Novels contain such elements as characters, plot, conflict, and setting. The writer of novels, or novelist, develops these elements. In addition to its main plot, a novel may contain one or more subplots, or independent, related stories. A novel may also have several themes.

See *Fiction* and *Short Story*.

NOVELLA A fiction work that is longer than a short story but shorter than a novel.

ONOMATOPOEIA *Onomatopoeia* is the use of words that imitate sounds. *Crash, buzz, screech, hiss, neigh, jingle,* and *cluck* are examples of onomatopoeia. *Chickadee, towhee,* and *whippoorwill* are onomatopoeic names of birds.

Onomatopoeia can help put the reader in the activity of a poem.

ORAL TRADITION *Oral tradition* is the passing of songs, stories, and poems from generation to generation by word of mouth. Folk songs, folk tales, legends, and myths all come from the oral tradition. No one knows who first created these stories and poems.

See *Folk Tale, Legend,* and *Myth.*

OXYMORON An *oxymoron* (pl. *oxymora*) is a figure of speech that links two opposite or contradictory words, to point out an idea or situation that seems contradictory or inconsistent but on closer inspection turns out to be somehow true.

PERSONIFICATION *Personification* is a type of figurative language in which a nonhuman subject is given human characteristics.

PERSPECTIVE See *Narrator* and *Point of View.*

PERSUASION *Persuasion* is used in writing or speech that attempts to convince the reader or listener to adopt a particular opinion or course of action. Newspaper editorials and letters to the editor use persuasion. So do advertisements and campaign speeches given by political candidates.

See *Essay.*

PLAYWRIGHT A *playwright* is a person who writes plays. William Shakespeare is regarded as the greatest playwright in English literature.

PLOT *Plot* is the sequence of events in which each event results from a previous one and causes the next. In most novels, dramas, short stories, and narrative poems, the plot involves both characters and a central conflict. The plot usually begins with an *exposition* that introduces the setting, the characters, and the basic situation. This is followed by the *inciting incident,* which introduces the central conflict. The conflict then increases during the *development* until it reaches a high point of interest or suspense, the *climax.* The climax is followed by the *falling action,* or end, of the central conflict. Any events that occur during the *falling action* make up the *resolution* or *denouement.*

Some plots do not have all of these parts. Some stories begin with the inciting incident and end with the resolution.

See *Conflict.*

POETRY *Poetry* is one of the three major types of literature, the others being prose and drama. Most poems make use of highly concise, musical, and emotionally charged language. Many also make use of imagery, figurative language, and special devices of sound such as rhyme. Major types of poetry include *lyric poetry, narrative poetry,* and *concrete poetry.*

See *Concrete Poem, Genre, Lyric Poem,* and *Narrative Poem.*

POINT OF VIEW Point of view is the perspective, or vantage point, from which a story is told. It is either a narrator outside the story or a character in the story. *First-person point of view* is told by a character who uses the first-person pronoun "I."

The two kinds of *third-person point of view,* limited and omniscient, are called "third person" because the narrator uses third-person pronouns such as he and she to refer to the characters. There is no "I" telling the story.

In stories told from the *omniscient third-person point of view,* the narrator knows and tells about what each character feels and thinks.

In stories told from the *limited third-person point of view,* the narrator relates the inner thoughts and feelings of only one character, and everything is viewed from this character's perspective.

See *Narrator.*

PROBLEM See *Conflict.*

PROSE *Prose* is the ordinary form of written language. Most writing that is not poetry, drama, or song is considered prose. Prose is one of the major genres of literature and occurs in fiction and nonfiction.

See *Fiction, Genre,* and *Nonfiction.*

PROTAGONIST The *protagonist* is the main character in a literary work. Often, the protagonist is a person, but sometimes it can be an animal.

See *Antagonist* and *Character.*

REFRAIN A *refrain* is a regularly repeated line or group of lines in a poem or a song.

REPETITION *Repetition* is the use, more than once, of any element of language—a sound, word, phrase, clause, or sentence. Repetition is used in both prose and poetry.

See *Alliteration, Meter, Plot, Rhyme,* and *Rhyme Scheme.*

RESOLUTION The *resolution* is the outcome of the conflict in a plot.

See *Plot.*

RHYME *Rhyme* is the repetition of sounds at the ends of words. Poets use rhyme to lend a songlike quality to their verses and to emphasize certain words and ideas. Many traditional poems contain *end rhymes*, or rhyming words at the ends of lines.

Another common device is the use of *internal rhymes*, or rhyming words within lines. Internal rhyme also emphasizes the flowing nature of a poem.

See *Rhyme Scheme.*

RHYME SCHEME A *rhyme scheme* is a regular pattern of rhyming words in a poem. To indicate the rhyme scheme of a poem, one uses lowercase letters. Each rhyme is assigned a different letter, as follows in the first stanza of "Dust of Snow," by Robert Frost:

The way a crow	*a*
Shook down on me	*b*
The dust of snow	*a*
From a hemlock tree	*b*

Thus, the stanza has the rhyme scheme *abab.*

RHYTHM *Rhythm* is the pattern of stressed and unstressed syllables in spoken or written language.

See *Meter.*

ROUND CHARACTER See *Character.*

SCENE A *scene* is a section of uninterrupted action in the act of a drama.

See *Drama.*

SCIENCE FICTION *Science fiction* combines elements of fiction and fantasy with scientific fact. Many science-fiction stories are set in the future.

SENSORY LANGUAGE *Sensory language* is writing or speech that appeals to one or more of the five senses.

See Images.

SETTING The *setting* of a literary work is the time and place of the action. The setting includes all the details of a place and time—the year, the time of day, even the weather. The place may be a specific country, state, region, community, neighborhood, building, institution, or home. Details such as dialects, clothing, customs, and modes of transportation are often used to establish setting. In most stories, the setting serves as a backdrop—a context in which the characters interact. Setting can also help to create a feeling, or atmosphere.

See *Atmosphere.*

SHORT STORY A *short story* is a brief work of fiction. Like a novel, a short story presents a sequence of events, or plot. The plot usually deals with a central conflict faced by a main character, or protagonist. The events in a short story usually communicate a message about life or human nature. This message, or central idea, is the story's theme.

See *Conflict, Plot,* and *Theme.*

SIMILE A *simile* is a figure of speech that uses *like* or *as* to make a direct comparison between two unlike ideas. Everyday speech often contains similes, such as "pale as a ghost," "good as gold," "spread like wildfire," and "clever as a fox."

SOUND DEVICES *Sound devices* are techniques used by writers to give musical effects to their writing. Some of these include *onomatopoeia, alliteration, rhyme, meter,* and *repetition.*

SPEAKER The *speaker* is the imaginary voice a poet uses when writing a poem. The speaker is the character who tells the poem. This character, or voice, often is not identified by name. There can be important differences between the poet and the poem's speaker.

See *Narrator*.

SPEECH A *speech* is a work that is delivered orally to an audience. There are many kinds of speeches suiting almost every kind of public gathering. Types of speeches include *dramatic*, *persuasive*, and *informative*.

STAGE DIRECTIONS *Stage directions* are notes included in a drama to describe how the work is to be performed or staged. Stage directions are usually printed in italics and enclosed within parentheses or brackets. Some stage directions describe the movements, costumes, emotional states, and ways of speaking of the characters.

STAGING *Staging* includes the setting, lighting, costumes, special effects, and music that go into a stage performance of a drama.

See *Drama*.

STANZA A *stanza* is a group of lines of poetry that are usually similar in length and pattern and are separated by spaces. A stanza is like a paragraph of poetry—it states and develops a single main idea.

STATIC CHARACTER See *Character*.

SURPRISE ENDING A *surprise ending* is a conclusion that is unexpected. The reader has certain expectations about the ending based on details in the story. Often, a surprise ending is *foreshadowed*, or subtly hinted at, in the course of the work.

See *Foreshadowing* and *Plot*.

SUSPENSE *Suspense* is a feeling of anxious uncertainty about the outcome of events in a literary work. Writers create suspense by raising questions in the minds of their readers.

SYMBOL A *symbol* is anything that stands for or represents something else. Symbols are common in everyday life. A dove with an olive branch in its beak is a symbol of peace. A blindfolded woman holding a balanced scale is a symbol of justice. A crown is a symbol of a king's status and authority.

SYMBOLISM *Symbolism* is the use of symbols. Symbolism plays an important role in many different types of literature. It can highlight certain elements the author wishes to emphasize and also add levels of meaning.

THEME The *theme* is a central message in a literary work. A theme can usually be expressed as a generalization, or a general statement, about human beings or about life. The theme of a work is not a summary of its plot. The theme is the writer's central idea.

Although a theme may be stated directly in the text, it is more often presented indirectly. When the theme is stated indirectly, or implied, the reader must figure out what the theme is by looking at what the work reveals about people or life.

TONE The *tone* of a literary work is the writer's attitude toward his or her audience and subject. The tone can often be described by a single adjective, such as *formal* or *informal, serious* or *playful, bitter,* or *ironic*. Factors that contribute to the tone are word choice, sentence structure, line length, rhyme, rhythm, and repetition.

TRAGEDY A *tragedy* is a work of literature, especially a play, that results in a catastrophe for the main character. In ancient Greek drama, the main character is always a significant person—a king or a hero—and the cause of the tragedy is a tragic flaw, or weakness, in his or her character. In modern drama, the main character can be an ordinary person, and the cause of the tragedy can be some evil in society itself. The purpose of tragedy is not only to arouse fear and pity in the audience, but also, in some cases, to convey a sense of the grandeur and nobility of the human spirit.

TURNING POINT See *Climax*.

UNIVERSAL THEME A *universal theme* is a message about life that is expressed regularly in many different cultures and time periods. Folk tales, epics, and romances often address universal themes like the importance of courage, the power of love, or the danger of greed.

WORD CHOICE See *Diction*.

TIPS FOR DISCUSSING LITERATURE

As you read and study literature, discussions with other readers can help you understand and enjoy what you have read. Use the following tips.

- ## Understand the purpose of your discussion.

  Your purpose when you discuss literature is to broaden your understanding of a work by testing your own ideas and hearing the ideas of others. Keep your comments focused on the literature you are discussing. Starting with one focus question will help to keep your discussion on track.

- ## Communicate effectively.

  Effective communication requires thinking before speaking. Plan the points that you want to make and decide how you will express them. Organize these points in logical order and use details from the work to support your ideas. Jot down informal notes to help keep your ideas focused.

  Remember to speak clearly, pronouncing words slowly and carefully. Also, listen attentively when others are speaking, and avoid interrupting.

- ## Consider other ideas and interpretations.

  A work of literature can generate a wide variety of responses in different readers. Be open to the idea that many interpretations can be valid. To support your own ideas, point to the events, descriptions, characters, or other literary elements in the work that led to your interpretation. To consider someone else's ideas, decide whether details in the work support the interpretation he or she presents. Be sure to convey your criticism of the ideas of others in a respectful and supportive manner.

- ## Ask questions.

  Ask questions to clarify your understanding of another reader's ideas. You can also use questions to call attention to possible areas of confusion, to points that are open to debate, or to errors in the speaker's points. To move a discussion forward, summarize and evaluate conclusions reached by the group members.

  When you meet with a group to discuss literature, use a chart like the one shown to analyze the discussion.

Work Being Discussed:	
Focus Question:	
Your Response:	Another Student's Response:
Supporting Evidence:	Supporting Evidence:

TYPES OF WRITING

Narration

Whenever writers tell any type of story, they are using **narration.** While there are many kinds of narration, most narratives share certain elements, such as characters, a setting, a sequence of events, and, often, a theme.

Autobiographical writing tells the story of an event or person in the writer's life.

Biographical writing is a writer's account of another person's life.

Short story A short story is a brief, creative narrative—a retelling of events arranged to hold a reader's attention. A few types of short stories are realistic stories, fantasy, science-fiction stories, and adventure stories.

Description

Descriptive writing is writing that creates a vivid picture of a person, place, thing, or event. Descriptive writing includes descriptions of people or places, remembrances, observations, vignettes, and character profiles.

Persuasion

Persuasion is writing or speaking that attempts to convince people to accept a position or take a desired action. Forms of persuasive writing include persuasive essays, advertisements, persuasive letters, editorials, persuasive speeches, and public-service announcements. Problem-and-solution essays may also contain elements of persuasion.

Expository Writing

Expository writing is writing that informs or explains. The information you include in expository writing is factual. Effective expository writing reflects a well-thought-out organization—one that includes a clear introduction, body, and conclusion. Here are some types of exposition.

Comparison-and-Contrast essay A comparison-and-contrast essay analyzes the similarities and differences between two or more things.

Cause-and-Effect essay A cause-and-effect essay explains the reasons why something happened or the results an event or situation will probably produce. You may examine several causes of a single effect or several effects of a single cause.

Problem-and-Solution essay The purpose of a problem-and-solution essay is to describe a problem and offer one or more solutions to it. An effective problem-and-solution essay describes a clear set of steps to achieve a result and explains and defends the proposed solution. Elements of problem-and-solution writing may be found in advice columns, memos, and proposals.

How-to essay A how-to essay explains how to do or make something. The process is broken down into steps and the steps are explained in order.

Summary A summary is a brief statement that includes only the main ideas and significant supporting details presented in a piece of writing. A summary should be written in your own words.

Research Writing

Writers often use outside research to gather information and explore subjects of interest. The product of that research is called **research writing.** Good research writing does not simply repeat information. It guides readers through a topic, showing them why each fact matters and creating an overall picture of the subject. Here are some types of research writing.

Research report A research report presents information gathered from reference books, observations, interviews, or other sources.

Biographical report A biographical report examines the high points and achievements in the life of a notable person. It includes dates, details, and main events in the person's life as well as background on the period in which the person lived.

Multimedia report A multimedia report presents information through a variety of media, including text, slides, photographs, prerecorded music and sound effects, and digital imaging.

A **response to literature** discusses and interprets what is of value in a book, short story, essay, article, or poem. You take a careful, critical look at various important elements in the work.

In addition to the standard literary essay, here are some other types of responses to literature.

Literary criticism Literary criticism is the result of literary analysis—the examination of a literary work or a body of literature. In literary criticism, you make a judgment or evaluation by looking carefully and critically at various important elements in the work. You then attempt to explain how the author has used those elements and how effectively they work together to convey the author's message.

Book or movie reviews A book review gives readers an impression of a book, encouraging them either to read it or to avoid reading it. A movie review begins with a basic response to whether or not you enjoyed the movie and then explains the reasons why or why not.

Letter to an author People sometimes respond to a work of literature by writing a letter to the writer. It lets the writer know what a reader found enjoyable or disappointing in a work. You can praise the work, ask questions, or offer constructive criticism.

Comparisons of works A comparison of works highlights specific features of two or more works by comparing them.

Creative Writing

Creative writing blends imagination, ideas, and emotions, and allows you to present your own unique view of the world. Poems, plays, short stories, dramas, and even some cartoons are examples of creative writing. Here are some types of creative writing.

Lyric poem A lyric poem uses sensory images, figurative language, and sound devices to express deep thoughts and feelings about a subject. Writers give lyric poems a musical quality by employing sound devices, such as rhyme, rhythm, alliteration, and onomatopoeia.

Narrative poem A narrative poem is similar to a short story in that it has a plot, characters, and a theme. However, a writer divides a narrative poem into stanzas, usually composed of rhyming lines that have a definite rhythm, or beat.

Song lyrics Song lyrics, or words to accompany a song, contain many elements of poetry—rhyme, rhythm, repetition, and imagery. In addition, song lyrics convey emotions, as well as interesting ideas.

Drama A drama or a dramatic scene is a story that is intended to be performed. The story is told mostly through what the actors say (dialogue) and what they do (action).

Practical and Technical Documents

Practical writing is fact-based writing that people do in the workplace or in their day-to-day lives. A business letter, memorandum, school form, job application, and a letter of inquiry are a few examples of practical writing.

Technical documents are fact-based documents that identify the sequence of activities needed to design a system, operate a tool, follow a procedure, or explain the bylaws of an organization. You encounter technical writing every time you read a manual or a set of instructions.

In the following descriptions, you'll find tips for tackling several types of practical and technical writing.

Business letter A formal letter that follows one of several specific formats. (See page R23.)

News release A news release, also called a press release, announces factual information about upcoming events. A writer might send a news release to a local newspaper, local radio station, TV station, or other media that will publicize the information.

Guidelines Guidelines give information about how people should act or provide tips on how to do something.

Process explanation A process explanation is a step-by-step explanation of how to do something. The explanation should be clear and specific and might include diagrams or other illustrations to further clarify the process.

WRITING LETTERS

Writing Friendly Letters

A friendly letter is much less formal than a business letter. It is a letter to a friend, a family member, or anyone with whom the writer wants to communicate in a personal, friendly way. Most friendly letters are made up of five parts:

- the heading
- the salutation, or greeting
- the body
- the closing
- the signature

The purpose of a friendly letter is often one of the following:

- to share personal news and feelings
- to send or to answer an invitation
- to express thanks

Model Friendly Letter

In this friendly letter, Betsy thanks her grandparents for a birthday present and gives them some news about her life.

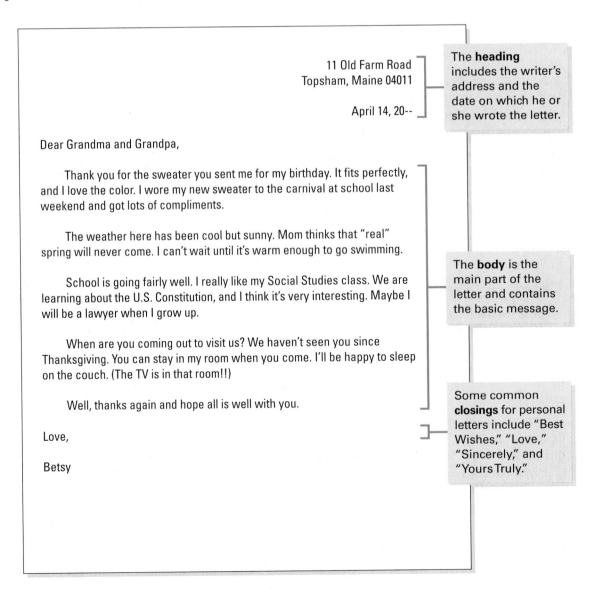

11 Old Farm Road
Topsham, Maine 04011

April 14, 20--

> The **heading** includes the writer's address and the date on which he or she wrote the letter.

Dear Grandma and Grandpa,

Thank you for the sweater you sent me for my birthday. It fits perfectly, and I love the color. I wore my new sweater to the carnival at school last weekend and got lots of compliments.

The weather here has been cool but sunny. Mom thinks that "real" spring will never come. I can't wait until it's warm enough to go swimming.

School is going fairly well. I really like my Social Studies class. We are learning about the U.S. Constitution, and I think it's very interesting. Maybe I will be a lawyer when I grow up.

When are you coming out to visit us? We haven't seen you since Thanksgiving. You can stay in my room when you come. I'll be happy to sleep on the couch. (The TV is in that room!!)

Well, thanks again and hope all is well with you.

Love,

Betsy

> The **body** is the main part of the letter and contains the basic message.

> Some common **closings** for personal letters include "Best Wishes," "Love," "Sincerely," and "Yours Truly."

Formatting Business Letter

Business letters follow one of several acceptable formats. In **block format,** each part of the letter begins at the left margin. A double space is used between paragraphs. In **modified block format,** some parts of the letter are indented to the center of the page. No matter which format is used, all letters in business format have a heading, an inside address, a salutation or greeting, a body, a closing, and a signature. These parts are shown and annotated on the model business letter below, formatted in modified block style.

Model Business Letter

In this letter, Yolanda Dodson uses modified block format to request information.

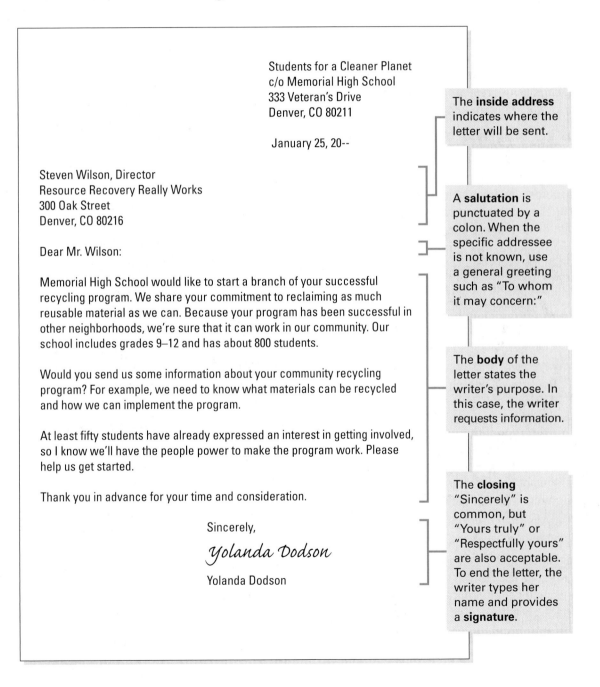

Students for a Cleaner Planet
c/o Memorial High School
333 Veteran's Drive
Denver, CO 80211

January 25, 20--

Steven Wilson, Director
Resource Recovery Really Works
300 Oak Street
Denver, CO 80216

Dear Mr. Wilson:

Memorial High School would like to start a branch of your successful recycling program. We share your commitment to reclaiming as much reusable material as we can. Because your program has been successful in other neighborhoods, we're sure that it can work in our community. Our school includes grades 9–12 and has about 800 students.

Would you send us some information about your community recycling program? For example, we need to know what materials can be recycled and how we can implement the program.

At least fifty students have already expressed an interest in getting involved, so I know we'll have the people power to make the program work. Please help us get started.

Thank you in advance for your time and consideration.

Sincerely,

Yolanda Dodson

Yolanda Dodson

The **inside address** indicates where the letter will be sent.

A **salutation** is punctuated by a colon. When the specific addressee is not known, use a general greeting such as "To whom it may concern:"

The **body** of the letter states the writer's purpose. In this case, the writer requests information.

The **closing** "Sincerely" is common, but "Yours truly" or "Respectfully yours" are also acceptable. To end the letter, the writer types her name and provides a **signature**.

USING THE INTERNET

Keyword Search

Before you begin a search, narrow your subject to a keyword or a group of **keywords.** These are your search terms, and they should be as specific as possible. For example, if you are looking for information about your favorite musical group, you might use the band's name as a keyword. You might locate such information as band member biographies, the group's history, fan reviews of concerts, and hundreds of sites with related names containing information that is irrelevant to your search. Depending on your research needs, you might need to narrow your search.

How to Narrow Your Search

If you have a large group of keywords and still don't know which ones to use, write out a list of all the words you are considering. Then, delete the words that are least important to your search, and highlight those that are most important.

Use **search connectors** to fine-tune your search:

AND: narrows a search by retrieving documents that include both terms. For example: *baseball AND playoffs*

OR: broadens a search by retrieving documents including any of the terms. For example: *playoffs OR championships*

NOT: narrows a search by excluding documents containing certain words. For example: *baseball NOT history*

Tips for an Effective Search

1. Search engines can be case-sensitive. If your first attempt at searching fails, check your search terms for misspellings and try again.

2. Present in order, from the most important to the least important keyword.

3. Avoid opening the link to every single page in your results list. Search engines present pages in descending order of relevancy. The most useful pages will be located at the top of the list.

4. Some search engines provide helpful tips for specializing your search.

Tips for Evaluating Internet Sources

Consider who constructed and who now maintains the Web page. Determine whether this author is a reputable source. Often, the URL endings indicate a source.

- Sites ending in *.edu* are maintained by educational institutions.
- Sites ending in *.gov* are maintained by government agencies (federal, state, or local).
- Sites ending in *.org* are normally maintained by nonprofit organizations and agencies.
- Sites with a *.com* ending are commercially or personally maintained.

Other Ways to Search

How you search should be tailored to what you are hoping to find. If you are looking for data and facts, use reference sites before you jump onto a simple search engine. For example, you can find reference sites to provide definitions of words, statistics about almost any subject, biographies, maps, and concise information on many topics. Useful online reference sites include online libraries, online periodicals, almanacs and encyclopedias.

You can also use other electronic sources such as CD-ROMs. Ask a reference librarian to help you locate and use the full range of electronic resources.

Respecting Copyrighted Material

Because the Internet is a growing medium, issues of copyright and ownership arise almost daily. Laws that govern the use and reuse of material are posted online and may change the way that people can access or reprint material. Text, photographs, music, and fine art printed online may not be reproduced without acknowledged permission of the copyright owner.

CITING SOURCES AND PREPARING MANUSCRIPT

Proofreading and Preparing Manuscript

Before preparing a final copy, proofread your manuscript. The chart shows the standard symbols for marking corrections to be made.

Proofreading Symbols	
insert	$\wedge$
delete	✎
close space	⌒
new paragraph	¶
add comma	⌃
add period	⊙
transpose (switch)	∾
change to cap	a̲
change to lowercase	⫽

- Choose a standard, easy-to-read font.
- Type or print on one side of unlined 8 1/2" x 11" paper.
- Set the margins for the side, top, and bottom of your paper at approximately one inch. Most word-processing programs have a default setting that is appropriate.
- Double-space the document.
- Indent the first line of each paragraph.
- Number the pages in the upper right corner.

Follow your teacher's directions for formatting formal research papers. Most papers will have the following features:

- Title page
- Table of Contents or Outline
- Works-Cited List

Avoiding Plagiarism

Whether you are presenting a formal research paper or an opinion paper on a current event, you must be careful to give credit for any ideas or opinions that are not your own. Presenting someone else's ideas, research, or opinion as your own—even if you have phrased it in different words—is *plagiarism,* the equivalent of academic stealing, or fraud.

Do not use the ideas or research of others in place of your own. Read from several sources to draw your own conclusions and form your own opinions. Incorporate the ideas and research of others to support your points. Credit the source of the following types of support:

- Statistics
- Direct quotations
- Indirectly quoted statements of opinions
- Conclusions presented by an expert
- Facts available in only one or two sources

Crediting Sources

When you credit a source, you acknowledge where you found your information and you give your readers the details necessary for locating the source themselves. Within the body of the paper, you provide a short citation, a footnote number linked to a footnote, or an endnote number linked to an endnote reference. These brief references show the page numbers on which you found the information. Prepare a reference list at the end of the paper to provide full bibliographic information on your sources. These are two common types of reference lists:

- A **bibliography** provides a listing of all the resources you consulted during your research.
- A **works-cited list** indicates the works you have referenced in your paper.

The chart on the next page shows the Modern Language Association format for crediting sources. This is the most common format for papers written in the content areas in middle school and high school. Unless instructed otherwise by your teacher, use this format for crediting sources.

MLA Style for Listing Sources

Book with one author	Pyles, Thomas. *The Origins and Development of the English Language.* 2nd ed. New York: Harcourt Brace Jovanovich, Inc., 1971.
Book with two or three authors	McCrum, Robert, William Cran, and Robert MacNeil. *The Story of English.* New York: Penguin Books, 1987.
Book with an editor	Truth, Sojourner. *Narrative of Sojourner Truth.* Ed. Margaret Washington. New York: Vintage Books, 1993.
Book with more than three authors or editors	Donald, Robert B., et al. *Writing Clear Essays.* Upper Saddle River, NJ: Prentice Hall, Inc., 1996.
Single work from an anthology	Hawthorne, Nathaniel. "Young Goodman Brown." *Literature: An Introduction to Reading and Writing.* Ed. Edgar V. Roberts and Henry E. Jacobs. Upper Saddle River, NJ: Prentice-Hall, Inc., 1998. 376–385. [Indicate pages for the entire selection.]
Introduction in a published edition	Washington, Margaret. Introduction. *Narrative of Sojourner Truth.* By Sojourner Truth. New York: Vintage Books, 1993, pp. v–xi.
Signed article in a weekly magazine	Wallace, Charles. "A Vodacious Deal." *Time* 14 Feb. 2000: 63.
Signed article in a monthly magazine	Gustaitis, Joseph. "The Sticky History of Chewing Gum." *American History* Oct. 1998: 30–38.
Unsigned editorial or story	"Selective Silence." Editorial. *Wall Street Journal* 11 Feb. 2000: A14. [If the editorial or story is signed, begin with the author's name.]
Signed pamphlet or brochure	[Treat the pamphlet as though it were a book.]
Pamphlet with no author, publisher, or date	*Are You at Risk of Heart Attack?* n.p. n.d. [n.p. n.d. indicates that there is no known publisher or date.]
Filmstrips, slide programs, videocassettes, DVDs, and other audiovisual media	*The Diary of Anne Frank.* Dir. George Stevens. Perf. Millie Perkins, Shelly Winters, Joseph Schildkraut, Lou Jacobi, and Richard Beymer. Twentieth Century Fox, 1959.
Radio or television program transcript	"Nobel for Literature." Narr. Rick Karr. *All Things Considered.* National Public Radio. WNYC, New York. 10 Oct. 2002. Transcript.
Internet	*National Association of Chewing Gum Manufacturers.* 19 Dec. 1999 <http://www.nacgm.org/consumer/funfacts.html> [Indicate the date you accessed the information. Content and addresses at Web sites change frequently.]
Newspaper	Thurow, Roger. "South Africans Who Fought for Sanctions Now Scrap for Investors." *Wall Street Journal* 11 Feb. 2000: A1+ [For a multipage article, write only the first page number on which it appears, followed by a plus sign.]
Personal interview	Smith, Jane. Personal interview. 10 Feb. 2000.
CD (with multiple publishers)	Simms, James, ed. *Romeo and Juliet.* By William Shakespeare. CD-ROM. Oxford: Attica Cybernetics Ltd.; London: BBC Education; London: HarperCollins Publishers, 1995.
Signed article from an encyclopedia	Askeland, Donald R. "Welding." *World Book Encyclopedia.* 1991 ed.

GUIDE TO RUBRICS

What is a rubric?

A rubric is a tool, often in the form of a chart or a grid, that helps you assess your work. Rubrics are particularly helpful for writing and speaking assignments.

To help you or others assess, or evaluate, your work, a rubric offers several specific criteria to be applied to your work. Then the rubric helps you or an evaluator indicate your range of success or failure according to those specific criteria. Rubrics are often used to evaluate writing for standardized tests.

Using a rubric will save you time, focus your learning, and improve the work you do. When you know what the rubric will be before you begin writing a persuasive essay, for example, as you write you will be aware of specific criteria that are important in that kind of an essay. As you evaluate the essay before giving it to your teacher, you will focus on the specific areas that your teacher wants you to master—or on areas that you know present challenges for you. Instead of searching through your work randomly for any way to improve it or correct its errors, you will have a clear and helpful focus on specific criteria.

How are rubrics constructed?

Rubrics can be constructed in several different ways.

- Your teacher may assign a rubric for a specific assignment.
- Your teacher may direct you to a rubric in your textbook.
- Your teacher and your class may construct a rubric for a particular assignment together.
- You and your classmates may construct a rubric together.
- You may create your own rubric with criteria you want to evaluate in your work.

How will a rubric help me?

A rubric will help you assess your work on a scale. Scales vary from rubric to rubric but usually range from 6 to 1, 5 to 1, or 4 to 1, with 6, 5, or 4 being the highest score and 1 being the lowest. If someone else is using the rubric to assess your work, the rubric will give your evaluator a clear range within which to place your work. If you are using the rubric yourself, it will help you make improvements to your work.

What are the types of rubrics?

- A **holistic rubric** has general criteria that can apply to a variety of assignments. See p. R29 for an example of a holistic rubric.
- An **analytic rubric** is specific to a particular assignment. The criteria for evaluation address the specific issues important in that assignment. See p. R28 for examples of analytic rubrics.

Sample Analytic Rubrics

Rubric With a 4-point Scale

The following analytic rubric is an example of a rubric to assess a persuasive essay. It will help you evaluate focus, organization, support, elaboration, and style conventions.

	Focus	Organization	Support/Elaboration	Style Conventions
4	Demonstrates highly effective word choice; clearly focused on task.	Uses clear, consistent organizational strategy.	Provides convincing, well-elaborated reasons to support the position.	Incorporates transitions; includes very few mechanical errors.
3	Demonstrates good word choice; stays focused on persuasive task.	Uses clear organizational strategy with occasional inconsistencies.	Provides two or more moderately elaborated reasons to support the position.	Incorporates some transitions; includes few mechanical errors.
2	Shows some good word choices; minimally stays focused on persuasive task.	Uses inconsistent organizational strategy; presentation is not logical.	Provides several reasons, but few are elaborated; only one elaborated reason.	Incorporates few transitions; includes many mechanical errors.
1	Shows lack of attention to persuasive task.	Demonstrates lack of organizational strategy.	Provides no specific reasons or does not elaborate.	Does not connect ideas; includes many mechanical errors.

Rubric With a 6-point Scale

The following analytic rubric is an example of a rubric to assess a persuasive essay. It will help you evaluate presentation, position, evidence, and arguments.

	Presentation	Position	Evidence	Arguments
6	Essay clearly and effectively addresses an issue with more than one side.	Essay clearly states a supportable position on the issue.	All evidence is logically organized, well presented, and supports the position.	All reader concerns and counterarguments are effectively addressed.
5	Most of essay addresses an issue that has more than one side.	Essay clearly states a position on the issue.	Most evidence is logically organized, well presented, and supports the position.	Most reader concerns and counterarguments are effectively addressed.
4	Essay adequately addresses issue that has more than one side.	Essay adequately states a position on the issue.	Many parts of evidence support the position; some evidence is out of order.	Many reader concerns and counterarguments are adequately addressed.
3	Essay addresses issue with two sides but does not present second side clearly.	Essay states a position on the issue, but the position is difficult to support.	Some evidence supports the position, but some evidence is out of order.	Some reader concerns and counterarguments are addressed.
2	Essay addresses issue with two sides but does not present second side.	Essay states a position on the issue, but the position is not supportable.	Not much evidence supports the position, and what is included is out of order.	A few reader concerns and counterarguments are addressed.
1	Essay does not address issue with more than one side.	Essay does not state a position on the issue.	No evidence supports the position.	No reader concerns or counterarguments are addressed.

Sample Holistic Rubric

Holistic rubrics such as this one are sometimes used to assess writing assignments on standardized tests. Notice that the criteria for evaluation are focus, organization, support, and use of conventions.

Points	Criteria
6 Points	• The writing is strongly focused and shows fresh insight into the writing task. • The writing is marked by a sense of completeness and coherence and is organized with a logical progression of ideas. • A main idea is fully developed, and support is specific and substantial. • A mature command of the language is evident, and the writing may employ characteristic creative writing strategies. • Sentence structure is varied, and writing is free of all but purposefully used fragments. • Virtually no errors in writing conventions appear.
5 Points	• The writing is clearly focused on the task. • The writing is well organized and has a logical progression of ideas, though there may be occasional lapses. • A main idea is well developed and supported with relevant detail. • Sentence structure is varied, and the writing is free of fragments, except when used purposefully. • Writing conventions are followed correctly.
4 Points	• The writing is clearly focused on the task, but extraneous material may intrude at times. • Clear organizational pattern is present, though lapses may occur. • A main idea is adequately supported, but development may be uneven. • Sentence structure is generally fragment free but shows little variation. • Writing conventions are generally followed correctly.
3 Points	• Writing is generally focused on the task, but extraneous material may intrude at times. • An organizational pattern is evident, but writing may lack a logical progression of ideas. • Support for the main idea is generally present but is sometimes illogical. • Sentence structure is generally free of fragments, but there is almost no variation. • The work generally demonstrates a knowledge of writing conventions, with occasional misspellings.
2 Points	• The writing is related to the task but generally lacks focus. • There is little evidence of organizational pattern, and there is little sense of cohesion. • Support for the main idea is generally inadequate, illogical, or absent. • Sentence structure is unvaried, and serious errors may occur. • Errors in writing conventions and spellings are frequent.
1 Point	• The writing may have little connection to the task and is generally unfocused. • There has been little attempt at organization or development. • The paper seems fragmented, with no clear main idea. • Sentence structure is unvaried, and serious errors appear. • Poor word choice and poor command of the language obscure meaning. • Errors in writing conventions and spelling are frequent.
Unscorable	The paper is considered unscorable if: • The response is unrelated to the task or is simply a rewording of the prompt. • The response has been copied from a published work. • The student did not write a response. • The response is illegible. • The words in the response are arranged with no meaning. • There is an insufficient amount of writing to score.

Student Model

This persuasive essay, which would receive a top score according to a persuasive rubric, is a response to the following writing prompt, or assignment:

Most young people today spend more than 5 hours a day watching television. Many adults worry about the effects on youth of seeing too much television violence. Write a persuasive piece in which you argue against or defend the effects of television watching on young people. Be sure to include examples to support your views.

Until the television was invented, families spent their time doing different activities. Now most families stay home and watch TV. Watching TV risks the family's health, reduces the children's study time, and is a bad influence on young minds. Watching television can be harmful.

> The writer clearly states a position in the first paragraph.

The most important reason why watching TV is bad is that the viewers get less exercise. For example, instead of watching their favorite show, people could get exercise for 30 minutes. If people spent less time watching TV and more time exercising, then they could have healthier bodies. My mother told me a story about a man who died of a heart attack because he was out of shape from watching television all the time. Obviously, watching TV puts a person's health in danger.

> Each paragraph provides details that support the writer's main point.

Furthermore, watching television reduces children's study time. For example, children would spend more time studying if they didn't watch television. If students spent more time studying at home, then they would make better grades at school. Last week I had a major test in science, but I didn't study because I started watching a movie. I was not prepared for the test and my grade reflected my lack of studying. Indeed, watching television is bad because it can hurt a student's grades.

Finally, watching TV can be a bad influence on children. For example, some TV shows have inappropriate language and too much violence. If children watch programs that use bad language and show violence, then they may start repeating these actions because they think the behavior is "cool." In fact, it has been proven that children copy what they see on TV. Clearly, watching TV is bad for children and it affects their behavior.

In conclusion, watching television is a bad influence for these reasons: It reduces people's exercise time and students' study time and it shows children inappropriate behavior. Therefore, people should take control of their lives and stop allowing television to harm them.

> The conclusion restates the writer's position.

GRAMMAR, USAGE, AND MECHANICS HANDBOOK

Parts of Speech

Nouns

A **noun** is the name of a person, place, or thing. A **common noun** names any one of a class of people, places, or things. A **proper noun** names a specific person, place, or thing.

Common Nouns	Proper Nouns
writer	Francisco Jiménez
city	Los Angeles

Use *apostrophes* with nouns to show ownership. Add an apostrophe and *s* to show the **possessive case** of most singular nouns. Add just an apostrophe to show the possessive case of plural nouns ending in *s* or *es*. Add an apostrophe and *s* to show the possessive case of plural nouns that do not end in *s* or *es*.

Exercise A Classifying Nouns Identify the underlined nouns in the following sentences as common or proper.

1. The <u>Milky Way</u> is one of several hundred million <u>galaxies</u>.
2. The <u>sun</u>, the closest star to the <u>Earth</u>, is a typical star.
3. <u>Supergiants</u> are the largest known <u>stars</u>.
4. A <u>committee</u> of astronomers gave numbers to some stars.
5. In the second century A.D., <u>Ptolemy</u> compiled the first catalog of stars.

Exercise B Using Apostrophes to Form Possessives of Nouns The first ten of the following nouns are singular. The last ten are plural. Make two columns on your paper, labeled Singular and Plural. Then, write the correct possessive form for each word in the appropriate column.

1. trainer	11. gymnasts
2. team	12. softballs
3. racket	13. athletes
4. swimmer	14. feet
5. muscle	15. goals
6. toss	16. trophies
7. track	17. coaches
8. champion	18. skis
9. game	19. teeth
10. skate	20. races

Pronouns

A **pronoun** is a word that stands for a noun or for a word that takes the place of a noun.

A **personal pronoun** refers to (1) the person speaking, (2) the person spoken to, or (3) the person, place, or thing spoken about.

	Singular	Plural
First Person	I, me, my, mine	we, us, our, ours
Second Person	you, your, yours	you, your, yours
Third Person	he, him, his, she, her, hers, it, its	they, them, their, theirs

A **demonstrative pronoun** directs attention to a specific person, place, or thing.

These are the juiciest pears I have ever tasted.

An **interrogative pronoun** is used to begin a question.

Who is the author of "Jeremiah's Song"?

An **indefinite pronoun** refers to a person, place, or thing, often without specifying which one.

Many of the players were tired.

Everyone bought something.

Exercise C Classifying Pronouns Label the underlined pronouns in the following sentences as *personal, demonstrative, interrogative,* or *indefinite* and as *singular* or *plural.*

1. <u>Who</u> designated stars by Greek letters?
2. Johann Bayer listed <u>them</u> in a star atlas in 1603; it included <u>many</u> that Ptolemy had not cataloged.
3. John Flamsteed listed <u>these</u> stars according to <u>their</u> constellations.

4. <u>Most</u> of our modern catalogs are not like <u>those</u> used earlier; instead, <u>they</u> use copies of photographs.

5. <u>Which</u> of the charts includes the southern sky?

Verbs

A **verb** is a word that expresses time while showing an action, a condition, or the fact that something exists.

An **action verb** indicates the action of someone or something.

A **linking verb** connects the subject of a sentence with a noun or a pronoun that renames or describes the subject.

A **helping verb** can be added to another verb to make a single verb phrase.

Exercise D Recognizing and Classifying Verbs
Write the verbs in the following sentences. Label each one *action* or *linking*. Include and identify all helping verbs.

1. Many stars vary their brightness when they expand and contract.

2. They can become very brilliant and then fade within days.

3. Some stars' cycles will last for years.

4. Most variations in brightness may be invisible to the human eye.

5. Scientists say that even the sun has a cycle of brightness.

Adjectives

An **adjective** describes a noun or a pronoun or gives a noun or a pronoun a more specific meaning. Adjectives answer the questions *what kind, which one, how many,* or *how much.*

The articles *the, a,* and *an* are adjectives. *An* is used before a word beginning with a vowel sound.

A noun may sometimes be used as an adjective.

family home   *science* fiction

Adverbs

An **adverb** modifies a verb, an adjective, or another adverb. Adverbs answer the questions *where, when, in what way,* or *to what extent.*

Exercise E Recognizing Adjectives and Adverbs
Label the underlined words in the following sentences as *adjectives* or *adverbs.* Then, write the word each one modifies.

1. The star called Rigel in the constellation Orion has a <u>bluish-white</u> tint.

2. Orion is located <u>almost squarely</u> on the celestial equator.

3. The stars form a picture of Orion, a hunter from <u>Greek</u> mythology.

4. He is standing with an <u>uplifted</u> club.

5. Three bright stars <u>accurately</u> represent his belt.

6. To the south, <u>three fainter</u> stars form his sword.

7. Another constellation, Pleiades, is a <u>loose</u> group of almost 3,000 stars.

8. The cluster was <u>initially</u> named by the Greeks after the mythological "Seven Sisters."

9. Observers can <u>sometimes</u> see up to twelve of the stars without a telescope.

10. Pleiades lies <u>375</u> light-years from our solar system.

Prepositions

A **preposition** relates a noun or a pronoun following it to another word in the sentence.

The ball rolled <u>under</u> the table.

Exercise F Recognizing Prepositions Write the prepositions in the following sentences, and then write the object of the preposition.

1. Tycho Brahe, a Danish astronomer, made measurements of the solar system.

2. This data was the most reliable until the invention of the telescope in the seventeenth century.

3. Brahe studied law and philosophy at universities in Copenhagen and Leipzig.

4. At night, he was busy with his observations of the stars.

5. Johannes Kepler, his assistant until 1601, used Brahe's data to formulate his three laws of planetary motion.

Conjunctions

A **conjunction** connects other words or groups of words.

A **coordinating conjunction** connects similar kinds or groups of words.

Correlative conjunctions are used in pairs to connect similar words or groups of words.

both Grandpa *and* Dad   *neither* they *nor* I

Exercise G Identifying Conjunctions Write the conjunctions in the following sentences, and label them coordinating or correlative.

1. Both North Star and Pole Star are names for the star that roughly marks the direction of the North Pole.

2. Pole Star has been used by sailors, for they needed to find their direction when sailing at night.

3. It is used today for determining latitudes and other measurements.

4. Not only is Polaris the current North Star, but it also is part of the Little Dipper constellation.

5. Polaris is very accurate, but in the future, other stars will point more accurately to the North Pole.

Interjections

An **interjection** is a word that expresses feeling or emotion and functions independently of a sentence.

"Ah!" says he—

Exercise H Recognizing Interjections Write an interjection that replaces the feeling shown in parentheses in the following sentences.

1. __(surprise)__! Did you see that meteor shower last night?

2. __(hesitation)__, I was not sure what that was.

3. __(disappointment)__, did that happen while I was sleeping?

4. __(amazement)__! I could not believe my eyes.

5. __(agreement)__, it is a natural event.

Cumulative Review: Parts of Speech

Exercise I Identifying Parts of Speech Write the part of speech of the underlined words in the following paragraph. Be as specific as possible.

These large comets <u>were</u> first <u>explained</u> by Tycho Brahe. Sir Isaac Newton and <u>Edmond</u> <u>Halley</u> made important observations about comets. The <u>American</u> astronomer Fred Whipple first described a comet as a "dirty <u>snowball</u>," a combination of ice and dust. <u>Gee</u>, that may not sound very scientific, <u>but</u> it is true. <u>Many</u> of the different comets pass <u>by</u> the Earth. Some are <u>easily</u> visible to the human eye.

Exercise J **Revising Sentences** Revise each sentence according to the directions in parentheses.

1. Halley's Comet is a famous comet. (Add an adverb that modifies *famous*.)

2. Halley's Comet was discovered by Edmond Halley. (Replace *Halley's Comet* with a pronoun.)

3. Before he made his discovery, people believed that comets traveled at random, with no set path. (Replace *he* with a proper noun.)

4. Halley believed, however, that comets traveled regular patterns. (Add a preposition before *regular*.)

5. Halley's Comet takes a time—approximately seventy-seven years—to travel its orbit. (Add an adjective to modify *time* and another adjective to modify *orbit*.)

Exercise K **Writing Application** Write a short narrative about a trip into outer space. Underline at least one noun, pronoun, verb, adjective, adverb, preposition, conjunction, and interjection. Then, label the part of speech of each as specifically as possible.

Phrases, Clauses, and Sentences

Sentences

A **sentence** is a group of words with two main parts: a complete subject and a complete predicate. Together, these parts express a complete thought.

We read that story last year.

A **fragment** is a group of words that does not express a complete thought.

"Not right away."

Subject

The **subject** of a sentence is the word or group of words that tells whom or what the sentence is about. The simple subject is the essential noun, pronoun, or group of words acting as a noun that cannot be left out of the complete subject. A **complete subject** is the **simple subject** plus any modifiers. In the following example, the complete subject is underlined. The simple subject is italicized.

<u>Pony express *riders*</u> carried packages more than 2,000 miles.

A **compound subject** is two or more subjects that have the same verb and are joined by a conjunction.

Neither the horse nor the driver looked tired.

Predicate

The **predicate** of a sentence is the verb or verb phrase that tells what the complete subject of the sentence does or is. The **simple predicate** is the essential verb or verb phrase that cannot be left out of the complete predicate. A **complete predicate** is the simple predicate plus any modifiers or complements. In the following example, the complete predicate is underlined. The simple predicate is italicized.

Pony express riders <u>*carried* packages more than 2,000 miles</u>.

A **compound predicate** is two or more verbs that have the same subject and are joined by a conjunction.

She *sneezed and coughed* throughout the trip.

Complement

A **complement** is a word or group of words that completes the meaning of the predicate of a sentence. Five different kinds of complements can be found in English sentences: *direct objects, indirect objects, objective complements, predicate nominatives,* and *predicate adjectives.*

A **direct object** is a noun, pronoun, or group of words acting as a noun that receives the action of a transitive verb.

We watched the *liftoff.*

An **indirect object** is a noun, pronoun, or group of words that appears with a direct object and names the person or thing that something is given to or done for.

> He sold the *family* a mirror.

An **objective complement** is an adjective or noun that appears with a direct object and describes or renames it.

> I called Meg my *friend.*

A **subject complement** is a noun, pronoun, or adjective that appears with a linking verb and tells something about the subject. A subject complement may be a *predicate nominative* or a *predicate adjective.*

A **predicate nominative** is a noun or pronoun that appears with a linking verb and renames, identifies, or explains the subject.

> Kiglo was the *leader.*

A **predicate adjective** is an adjective that appears with a linking verb and describes the subject of a sentence.

> Roko became *tired.*

Exercise A **Identifying Complements** Write the complements in the following sentences, and label each *direct object, indirect object, predicate noun,* or *predicate adjective.*

1. Australia's mountains are not high.
2. In fact, Australia is almost the world's flattest landmass.
3. Australians gave the interior the name *Outback.*
4. The Central-Eastern Lowlands is an area extending from the Great Dividing Range to the Great Western Plain.
5. The Nullarbor Plain seems strange with its caverns and tunnels.

Simple Sentence

A **simple sentence** consists of a single independent clause.

Compound Sentence

A **compound sentence** consists of two or more independent clauses joined by a comma and a coordinating conjunction or by a semicolon.

Complex Sentence

A **complex sentence** consists of one independent clause and one or more subordinate clauses.

Compound-Complex Sentence

A **compound-complex sentence** consists of two or more independent clauses and one or more subordinate clauses.

Exercise B **Recognizing Sentence Structure** Label each sentence *simple, compound,* or *complex.*

1. Kangaroos' powerful hind legs are used for hopping, and their thick, long tails are used for balancing.
2. The large red or gray kangaroo may stand as tall as seven feet.
3. Wallabies and kangaroo rats are smaller animals that are also members of the kangaroo family.
4. Although it does not bark, the dingo is a dog-like animal.
5. Rabbits, foxes, and cats were introduced into Australia by Europeans.

Declarative Sentence

A **declarative sentence** states an idea and ends with a period.

Interrogative Sentence

An **interrogative sentence** asks a question and ends with a question mark.

Imperative Sentence

An **imperative sentence** gives an order or a direction and ends with either a period or an exclamation mark.

Exclamatory Sentence

An **exclamatory sentence** conveys a strong emotion and ends with an exclamation mark.

Exercise C Recognizing Subjects, Predicates, and Sentence Types

Copy these sentences, underlining each simple subject once and each simple predicate twice. Then, identify each sentence as *declarative, interrogative, imperative,* or *exclamatory.*

1. Look at this globe. Here is Australia down in the Southern Hemisphere.
2. Wow! What a surprise that is!
3. Aborigines first migrated there and remained undisturbed until the seventeenth century.
4. Did not the first European settlers arrive at Botany Bay in 1788?
5. Were they British convicts? Please answer the question.

Phrases

A **phrase** is a group of words, without a subject and a verb, that functions in a sentence as one part of speech.

A **prepositional phrase** is a group of words that includes a preposition and a noun or a pronoun that is the object of the preposition.

near the town   with them

An **adjective phrase** is a prepositional phrase that modifies a noun or a pronoun by telling *what kind* or *which one.*

Mr. Sanderson brushed his hands over the shoes *in the window.*

An **adverb phrase** is a prepositional phrase that modifies a verb, an adjective, or an adverb by point-ing out *where, when, in what manner,* or *to what extent.*

Bring your saddle *to the barn.*

An **appositive phrase** is a noun or a pronoun with modifiers, placed next to a noun or a pronoun to add information and details.

The story, *a tale of adventure,* takes place in the Yukon.

A **participial phrase** is a participle modified by an adjective or an adverb phrase or accompanied by a complement. The entire phrase acts as an adjective.

Running at top speed, he soon caught up with them.

An **infinitive phrase** is an infinitive with modifiers, complements, or a subject, all acting together as a single part of speech.

At first I was too busy enjoying my food *to notice the other guests.*

Exercise D Recognizing Phrases Identify the underlined phrases as *prepositional, appositive,* or *participial.*

1. The climate of Australia varies <u>from region to region.</u>
2. The southern states—<u>warm, temperate regions</u>—have four seasons.
3. <u>Located in the Southern Hemisphere,</u> Australia has seasons opposite those in the Northern Hemisphere.
4. Queensland, <u>on the north coast,</u> experiences a great deal of rain.
5. However, <u>in the drier grasslands,</u> unpredictable rainfall must be supplemented by irrigation.
6. The deserts, <u>making up most of central and western Australia,</u> receive even less rainfall.
7. <u>Applying many modern irrigation techniques,</u> Australia has increased its agricultural production.

8. The Australian Alps, <u>a mountain range in New South Wales</u>, receives heavy snowfall.

9. <u>Lying in the temperate zone</u>, Tasmania has heavy rainfall and frequent winter storms.

10. Hot and dry winds are common <u>in the southern states</u>.

Clauses

A **clause** is a group of words with its own subject and verb.

An **independent clause** can stand by itself as a complete sentence.

"I think it belongs to Rachel."

A **subordinate clause** has a subject and a verb but cannot stand by itself as a complete sentence; it can only be part of a sentence.

"Although it was late"

Exercise E **Recognizing Clauses** Identify the underlined clauses as *independent* or *subordinate*. Identify the subordinate clauses as *adjective* or *adverb*.

1. The platypus is an aquatic mammal of the Monotreme order <u>that has a bill like a duck.</u>

2. The spiny anteater is also categorized as a Monotreme <u>because it is an egg-laying mammal</u>.

3. While the kangaroo is a marsupial, <u>it is still a type of mammal</u>.

4. Possums and koalas are marsupials <u>that live in trees</u>.

5. Marsupials are animals that give birth to live young <u>even though the young are then nourished in an external pouch</u>.

Cumulative Review: Phrases, Clauses, Sentences

Exercise F **Varying Sentences** Rewrite the following sentences according to the instructions in parentheses.

1. Australia has two species of crocodiles. (Start with "Actually.")

2. The larger crocodile lives in the northern coastal swamps and can grow to be twenty feet long. (Revise the sentence so that it begins with "Living in the northern coastal swamp.")

3. Smaller species of crocodiles can be found living contentedly in inland fresh water. (Revise sentence to begin with "In inland fresh water.")

4. More than 370 species of lizards are living in Australia. (Invert the subject-verb order.)

5. About 100 species of venomous snakes live in Australia. (Start with "Australia" as the subject, and change the verb as necessary.)

Exercise G **Combining Sentences** Rewrite the following sentences according to the instructions in parentheses.

1. Australian waters contain hundreds of sharks. Some are a danger to humans. (Combine into a compound sentence.)

2. Edible shellfish are abundant. Oysters, abalone, and crayfish have been exploited. (Combine by turning one sentence into a subordinate clause.)

3. Seals live around the southern coast. They also inhabit the surrounding islands. (Combine by making a compound verb.)

4. The waters around Australia support many fish. There are also many aquatic mammals. (Combine sentences by creating a compound direct object.)

5. The Queensland lungfish breathes with a single lung. It does this instead of using gills. (Combine by changing one sentence into a phrase.)

Exercise H Identifying and Revising Sentence Problems Label the error in each item as a *fragment, run-on, double negative, misplaced modifier,* or *common usage problem.* Then, correct the errors.

1. Believe the Aborigines were always in Australia.

2. By taking advantage of low sea levels that allowed land travel, researchers think the Aborigines migrated to Australia.

3. Tasmania was once part of Australia, a rise in sea level made Tasmania an island.

4. The Aborigines did not have no domesticated animals other than the dingo.

5. There most recent history features the use of tools.

Exercise I Writing Application Write a short description of a place you have visited. Vary the length and structure of your sentences. Circle at least three phrases and three clauses. Try to avoid fragments, run-ons, double negatives, misplaced modifiers, and the common usage problems you have studied.

Using Verbs, Pronouns, and Modifiers

Principal Parts

A **verb** has four **principal parts:** the *present,* the *present participle,* the *past,* and the *past participle.*

Regular verbs form the past and past participle by adding *-ed* to the present form.

Present: walk

Present Participle: (am) walking

Past: walked

Past Participle: (have) walked

Irregular verbs form the past and past participle by changing form rather than by adding *-ed.*

Present: go

Present Participle: (am) going

Past: went

Past Participle: (have) gone

Exercise A Recognizing the Principal Parts of Verbs Identify the principal part used to form the underlined verbs in the following sentences as *present, present participle, past,* or *past participle.*

1. Steve is <u>buying</u> my birthday presents at the local shopping center.

2. He <u>has found</u> some of the lowest prices at one of the stores.

3. Last year, I think I <u>paid</u> too much for his gift.

4. First, I put it in layaway, and I <u>went</u> back to get it a week later.

5. This year, I hope to enter the stores only once because I <u>am going</u> to make a list.

Verb Tense

A **verb tense** tells whether the time of an action or condition is in the past, the present, or the future. Every verb has six tenses: *present, past, future, present perfect, past perfect,* and *future perfect.*

The **present tense** shows actions that happen in the present.

The **past tense** shows actions that have already happened.

The **future tense** shows actions that will happen.

The **present perfect tense** shows actions that begin in the past and continue to the present.

The **past perfect tense** shows a past action or condition that ended before another past action.

The **future perfect tense** shows a future action or condition that will have ended before another begins.

Exercise B **Recognizing Verb Tense** Identify the tense of each underlined verb or verb phrase in the following sentences. Then, write the principal part used to form the tense.

1. For our vacation, I have been making a list of things that I think I will need.

2. It seems as though summer has taken a long time to arrive.

3. I am looking forward to a shopping trip with my mom and my best friend.

4. I had been hoping we would go this weekend, and we are!

5. We will go to the outlet center that has opened several miles away.

6. Before the outlets opened, the location had been mainly farmland.

7. We were sorry to see the farms go, but we are happy now to buy some of our favorite brands at discounted prices.

8. By the time we finish, we will have shopped for hours.

9. Nowadays, you will find outlet centers just off interstate highways all across the country.

10. Discount stores have found success in Canada and Western Europe, as well.

Pronoun Case

The **case** of a pronoun is the form it takes to show its use in a sentence. There are three pronoun cases: *nominative, objective,* and *possessive.*

The **nominative case** is used to name or rename the subject of the sentence. The nominative case pronouns are *I, you, he, she, it, we, you, they.*

As the subject: *She* is brave.

Renaming the subject: The leader is *she.*

The **objective case** is used as the direct object, indirect object, or object of a preposition. The objective case pronouns are *me, you, him, her, it, us, you, them.*

As a direct object: Tom called *me.*

As an indirect object: My friend gave *me* advice.

As an object of a preposition: My sister went shopping without *me.*

The **possessive case** is used to show ownership. The possessive pronouns are *my, your, his, her, its, our, their, mine, yours, his, hers, its, ours, theirs.*

Exercise C **Identifying Pronoun Case** Identify the case of each personal pronoun in the following sentences as *nominative, objective,* or *possessive.*

1. Most of us shop at our local supermarkets.

2. I remember my great-grandmother telling me that she grew up in a town without a supermarket.

3. Her times were very different from ours.

4. Before the Great Depression of the 1930s, most people bought their food and household items in many different shops.

5. For example, a person would buy his or her meat at a butcher shop, bread at a bakery, and milk and cheese at a dairy.

6. When supermarkets arrived on the scene, combining self-service with lower prices, they experienced immediate growth.

7. In addition, the spread of the automobile meant that shoppers could drive to a store and fill their cars with packaged groceries.

8. Now, in one place, we can buy all our food, cleaning products, greeting cards, batteries, and much, much more.

9. You can see how the supermarket got its name!

10. The theory of supermarkets has spread to other types of stores; it is called "low-cost mass distribution."

Subject-Verb Agreement

To make a subject and a verb agree, make sure that both are singular or both are plural. Two or more singular subjects joined by *or* or *nor* must have a singular verb. When singular and plural subjects are joined by *or* or *nor*, the verb must agree with the closest subject.

> *He is* at the door.
>
> They *drive* home every day.
>
> Both *pets are* hungry.
>
> Either the *chairs* or the *table is* on sale.

Exercise D **Revising to Eliminate Errors in Agreement** Revise the following sentences, eliminating errors in agreement. If a sentence has no errors, write *correct*.

1. A common sight in stores are the "sale" sign.

2. There is chains in many types of businesses.

3. Each town and city have its own branches of certain fast-food restaurants, banks, movie theaters, gas stations, and supermarkets.

4. The products or services of each branch of a particular chain is almost always the same.

5. The chicken burrito that a person buys for his or her lunch at one fast-food restaurant will be just like the chicken burrito sold at another branch of the same chain.

6. Each of us probably has our own favorites.

7. Developers of the first chain stores were not sure that they would be successful.

8. However, the lower prices and convenience has made chains very popular.

9. Usually in charge of a chain store is managers rather than an individual owner.

10. Managers make the day-to-day decisions concerning their particular stores.

Pronoun-Antecedent Agreement

Pronouns must agree with their antecedents in number and gender. Use singular pronouns with singular antecedents and plural pronouns with plural antecedents. Many errors in pronoun-antecedent agreement occur when a plural pronoun is used to refer to a singular antecedent for which the gender is not specified.

> Incorrect: Everyone did their best.
>
> Correct: Everyone did his or her best.

The following indefinite pronouns are singular: *anybody, anyone, each, either, everybody, everyone, neither, nobody, no one, one, somebody, someone.*

The following indefinite pronouns are plural: *both, few, many, several.*

The following indefinite pronouns may be either singular or plural: *all, any, most, none, some.*

Exercise E **Revising Sentences to Eliminate Errors in Agreement** Each sentence below contains one error in pronoun-antecedent agreement. Rewrite each sentence correctly, underlining the pronoun that you have changed and its antecedent.

1. Anybody can bring their dog to the party.

2. Either Curtis or Tim will bring their city map today.

3. It is the statue or that tall tree that is casting their shadow over the sidewalk.

4. Both Tom and Joe had his hair cut.

5. The taxicab and the delivery truck made its way through the busy traffic.

Modifiers

The **comparative** and **superlative** degrees of most adjectives and adverbs of one or two syllables can be formed in either of two ways: Use –*er* or *more* to form a comparative degree and –*est* or *most* to form the superlative degree of most one- and two-syllable modifiers.

More and *most* can also be used to form the comparative and superlative degrees of most one- and two-syllable modifiers. These words should not be used when the result sounds awkward, as in "A greyhound is *more* fast than a beagle."

Exercise F **Writing Sentences With Modifiers**
Write sentences according to the instructions. Be careful to use the correct forms of modifiers, and make sure your comparisons are complete and logical.

1. Using the comparative form of *expensive*, write a sentence about a shoe store.

2. Using the superlative form of *comfortable*, write a sentence about a new pair of shoes.

3. Using the superlative form of *friendly*, write a sentence about the salesperson.

4. Using the comparative form of *few*, write a sentence about job opportunities at this shoe store.

5. Using the comparative form of *far*, write a sentence about the distance of the store from your home.

6. Using the positive form of *good*, write a sentence about transportation into town.

7. Using the comparative form of *bad*, write about the service in another shoe store.

8. Using the superlative form of *much* as an adverb, describe the variety of styles in the shoe store.

9. Using the comparative form of *quickly*, write about a decision concerning a pair of shoes.

10. Using the superlative form of *good*, describe a purchase.

Cumulative Review: Using Verbs, Pronouns, and Modifiers

Exercise A **Revising to Eliminate Various Usage Errors** Rewrite the following paragraph, correcting errors in agreement and in the usage of verbs, pronouns, and modifiers.

As usual, my parents, brothers, sister, and me had different ideas about where we should go this summer. Each of my two brothers has their own favorite place for fishing, while my sister was insisting on the beach. My parents and me have different ideas. My father thinks that us should see someplace new; he wanted to camp and fish at the shore. His idea is not the most popularest since the rest of us want to be closer to stores, movies, and other conveniences. My mother wants to visit a city because you can do so much there. I think we should of drawn straws instead of arguing for so long.

Writing Application Describe a store in which you like to shop. Use a consistent verb tense, and check carefully for problems in agreement or in the usage of verbs, pronouns, and modifiers.

Glossary of Common Usage

accept, except

Accept is a verb that means "to receive" or "to agree to." *Except* is a preposition that means "other than" or "leaving out." Do not confuse these two words.

Aaron sadly *accepted* his father's decision to sell Zlateh.

Everyone *except* the fisherman and his wife had children.

affect, effect

Affect is normally a verb meaning "to influence" or "to bring about a change in." *Effect* is usually a noun, meaning "result."

among, between

Among is usually used with three or more items. *Between* is generally used with only two items.

bad, badly

Use the predicate adjective *bad* after linking verbs such as *feel, look,* and *seem.* Use *badly* whenever an adverb is required.

Mouse does not feel *bad* about tricking Coyote.

In the myth, Athene treats Arachne *badly.*

beside, besides

Beside means "at the side of" or "close to." *Besides* means "in addition to."

can, may

The verb *can* generally refers to the ability to do something. The verb *may* generally refers to permission to do something.

different from, different than

Different from is generally preferred over *different than.*

farther, further

Use *farther* when you refer to distance. Use *further* when you mean "to a greater degree or extent" or "additional."

fewer, less

Use *fewer* for things that can be counted. Use *less* for amounts or quantities that cannot be counted.

good, well

Use the predicate adjective *good* after linking verbs such as *feel, look, smell, taste,* and *seem.* Use *well* whenever you need an adverb.

hopefully

You should not loosely attach this adverb to a sentence, as in *"Hopefully, the rain will stop by noon."* Rewrite the sentence so *hopefully* modifies a specific verb. Other possible ways of revising such sentences include using the adjective *hopeful* or a phrase like "everyone *hopes* that."

its, it's

The word *its* with no apostrophe is a possessive pronoun. The word *it's* is a contraction for *it is.* Do not confuse the possessive pronoun *its* with the contraction *it's,* standing for "it is" or "it has."

lay, lie

Do not confuse these verbs. *Lay* is a transitive verb meaning "to set or put something down." Its principal parts are *lay, laying, laid, laid. Lie* is an intransitive verb meaning "to recline." Its principal parts are *lie, lying, lay, lain.*

leave, let

Be careful not to confuse these verbs. *Leave* means "to go away" or "to allow to remain." *Let* means "to permit."

like, as

Like is a preposition that usually means "similar to" or "in the same way as." *Like* should always be followed by an object. Do not use *like* before a subject and a verb. Use *as* or *that* instead.

loose, lose

Loose can be either an adjective (meaning "unattached") or a verb (meaning "to untie"). *Lose* is always a verb (meaning "to fail to keep, have, or win").

many, much

Use *many* to refer to a specific quantity. Use *much* for an indefinite amount or for an abstract concept.

of, have

Do not use *of* in place of *have* after auxiliary verbs like *would, could, should, may, might,* or *must.*

raise, rise

Raise is a transitive verb that usually takes a direct object. *Rise* is intransitive and never takes a direct object.

set, sit

Set is a transitive verb meaning "to put (something) in a certain place." Its principal parts are *set, setting, set, set. Sit* is an intransitive verb meaning "to be seated." Its principal parts are *sit, sitting, sat, sat.*

than, then

The conjunction *than* is used to connect the two parts of a comparison. Do not confuse *than* with the adverb *then,* which usually refers to time.

that, which, who

Use the relative pronoun *that* to refer to things or people. Use *which* only for things and *who* only for people.

their, there, they're

Their is a possessive adjective and always modifies a noun. *There* is usually used either at the beginning of a sentence or as an adverb. *They're* is a contraction for "they are."

to, too, two

To is a preposition that begins a prepositional phrase or an infinitive. *Too,* with two o's, is an adverb and modifies adjectives and other adverbs. *Two* is a number.

when, where, why

Do not use *when, where,* or *why* directly after a linking verb such as *is.* Reword the sentence.

Faulty:	Suspense is *when* an author increases the reader's tension.
Revised:	An author uses suspense to increase the reader's tension.
Faulty:	A biography is *where* a writer tells the life story of another person.
Revised:	In a biography, a writer tells the life story of another person.

who, whom

In formal writing, remember to use *who* only as a subject in clauses and sentences and *whom* only as an object.

Capitalization and Punctuation Rules

Capitalization

1. Capitalize the first word of a sentence.
   Young Roko glances down the valley.
2. Capitalize all proper nouns and adjectives.
   Mark Twain   Amazon River   Thanksgiving Day

   Montana   October   Italian
3. Capitalize a person's title when it is followed by the person's name or when it is used in direct address.

   Doctor   General Khokhotov   Mrs. Price
4. Capitalize titles showing family relationships when they refer to a specific person, unless they are preceded by a possessive noun or pronoun.

   Granny-Liz   Margie's mother
5. Capitalize the first word and all other key words in the titles of books, periodicals,

poems, stories, plays, paintings, and other works of art.

from *Tom Sawyer*   "Grandpa and the Statue"

"Breaker's Bridge"   "The Spring and the Fall"

6. Capitalize the first word and all nouns in letter salutations and the first word in letter closings.

Dear Willis,   Yours truly,

Exercise B **Proofreading to Correct Errors in Capitalization** Revise the following sentences, adding the missing capital letters.

1. castles in europe developed from the ancient roman idea of walled cities.

2. from spain to transylvania, castles were almost always built for defensive purposes.

3. the word castle also refers to large residences like william randolph hearst's castle in san simeon, california.

4. the area of nairnshire in northern scotland is well known for cawdor castle.

5. segovia, spain, located on the eresma river, is known for the alcazar, a famous castle.

6. in torun, poland, there are the ruins of a castle of ancient knights.

7. the wittelsbach family, a german dynasty, took their name from their castle in bavaria.

8. one wittelsbach was count otto vi, who served the emperor frederick I; he was made a duke in 1180.

9. in 1020 bishop werner built habsburg castle on the aare river.

10. later divided into the austrian and spanish branches, the habsburg family ruled in europe for hundreds of years.

11. a result of world war I was the banishment of emperor charles I.

12. in england, king george III bought buckingham palace but sometimes lived at saint james's palace.

13. another castle, balmoral castle, is the british royal residence in scotland.

14. in central japan, the city of osaka features a park built on the site of a sixteenth-century castle.

15. on an island near tokyo, iwatsuki is a castle town that was founded in 1458.

Punctuation

End Marks

1. Use a **period** to end a declarative sentence, an imperative sentence, and most abbreviations.

2. Use a **question mark** to end a direct question or an incomplete question in which the rest of the question is understood.

3. Use an **exclamation mark** after a statement showing strong emotion, an urgent imperative sentence, or an interjection expressing strong emotion.

Commas

1. Use a comma before the conjunction to separate two independent clauses in a compound sentence.

2. Use commas to separate three or more words, phrases, or clauses in a series.

3. Use commas to separate adjectives of equal rank. Do not use commas to separate adjectives that must stay in a specific order.

4. Use a comma after an introductory word, phrase, or clause.

5. Use commas to set off parenthetical and nonessential expressions.

6. Use commas with places and dates made up of two or more parts.

7. Use commas after items in addresses, after the salutation in a personal letter, after the closing in all letters, and in numbers of more than three digits.

Semicolons

1. Use a semicolon to join independent clauses that are not already joined by a conjunction.

2. Use a semicolon to join independent clauses or items in a series that already contain commas.

The Pengelly family had no say in the choosing of Lob; he came to them in the second way. . . .

Colons

1. Use a colon before a list of items following an independent clause.

2. Use a colon in numbers giving the time, in salutations in business letters, and in labels used to signal important ideas.

Exercise B **Proofreading Sentences to Correct Errors in End Marks, Commas, Semicolons, and Colons** Proofread the following sentences, inserting end marks, commas, semicolons, and colons where necessary. Eliminate unnecessary punctuation. Some items are questions.

1. There is an old palace located in the heart of Venice Italy

2. Called the Doges' Palace it was the residence of the elected rulers

3. The waterfront portion was built in 1340 the great balcony was added in 1404

4. Whose paintings cover the inner waiting room the Hall of the Cabinet, and the Hall of the Senate

5. Many rooms and ceilings were decorated by these Italian painters Tintoretto Bellini and Tiepolo

6. The palace contained offices meeting rooms and law courts

7. It also served as a prison: and it even held the famous Casanova

8. Wow You mean the notorious Italian adventurer

9. The Doges' Palace is connected to the New Prisons by a small stone bridge the Bridge of Sighs

10. Do you know the origin of the bridge's name

Quotation Marks

1. A **direct quotation** represents a person's exact speech or thoughts and is enclosed in quotation marks.

2. An **indirect quotation** reports only the general meaning of what a person said or thought and does not require quotation marks.

3. Always place a comma or a period inside the final quotation mark of a direct quotation.

4. Place a question mark or an exclamation mark inside the final quotation mark if the end mark is part of the quotation; if it is not part of the quotation, place it outside the final quotation mark.

Exercise C **Revision Practice: Dialogue** Write the following sentences as a dialogue, inserting the proper capitalization and punctuation and beginning a new paragraph with each new speaker.

stan i just read a book about castles but i am confused about the difference between a castle and a palace said rebecca

from what i remember from history class replied stan castles used to be the same as fortresses

kate added oh like the tower of london where they kept prisoners

right you must have read shakespeares richard III exclaimed stan

richard put prisoners in the tower added kate

thats true said stan however british royalty lived in the tower of london until the time of queen elizabeth I

wait a second kate said i saw the movie elizabeth but i do not remember the name of her castle

stan replied as time went on, castle came to mean the same thing as a large mansion

i think i see said kate some palaces were originally fortresses and were rebuilt as luxurious resorts

buckingham palace was built only as a residence but never to be a safe place during battle said stan

Titles

1. Underline or italicize the titles of long written works, movies, television and radio shows, lengthy works of music, paintings, and sculptures.
2. Use quotation marks around the titles of short written works, episodes in a series, songs, and titles of works mentioned as parts of collections.

Hyphens

Use a **hyphen** with certain numbers, after certain prefixes, with two or more words used as one word, and with a compound modifier that comes before a noun.

Apostrophes

1. Add an **apostrophe** and *s* to show the possessive case of most singular nouns.
2. Add an apostrophe to show the possessive case of plural nouns ending in *s* and *es*.
3. Add an apostrophe and *s* to show the possessive case of plural nouns that do not end in *s* or *es*.
4. Use an apostrophe in a contraction to indicate the position of the missing letter or letters.

Cumulative Review: Capitalization and Punctuation

Exercise D **Proofreading Sentences for All the Rules of Punctuation** Proofread the following sentences. Correct all punctuation errors. In the first sentence, the guide's words are directly quoted. Some items are questions.

1. Did you hear the guide say Windsor Castle is the primary residence of British kings and queens
2. Begun in 1474 Saint Georges Chapel was completed by King Henry VIII in 1528
3. Tradition says that the Round Tower is built on the site where King Arthurs Knights of the Round Table met
4. Valuable paintings statues and decorations are found in these state apartments Saint George's Hall the Waterloo Chamber and the Throne Room
5. Old Windsor was home to the Anglo Saxon kings in fact William the Conqueror built a castle nearby
6. Is that where Edward III met with the Knights of the Garter

7. Leading from Home Park to Great Park the tree lined road is more than three miles long

8. Did you know there was a very destructive fire there in 1992

9. What I cannot believe it

10. An article in the International Herald Tribune said it destroyed Saint Georges Hall and the Waterloo Chamber

Exercise E **Proofreading a Page to Correct Punctuation Errors** Proofread these paragraphs, supplying missing punctuation and correcting errors in usage of end marks, commas, semicolons, quotation marks, hyphens, and apostrophes.

Neuschwanstein Castle in Germany is one of the worlds best known castles? With it's turrets and tall archways; it looks like a medieval castle As a friend of mine who visited it exclaimed This castle is a real fairy-tale fantasy come true

It sits high on a hilltop overlooking the Alps, and a deep gorge. The castle was built between—1869 and 1886—for King Ludwig II. The room's feature murals and detailed carvings. The woodcarving in Ludwigs bedroom took four-teen carpenters 4 1/2 years to complete Do you think you can pronounce Neuschwanstein.

Writing Application Write a brief dialogue in which you and a friend discuss your dream castle or palace. Be sure to follow all the rules of capitalization and punctuation.

INDEX OF SKILLS

Boldface numbers indicate pages where terms are defined.

Reading Skills and Strategies

Vocabulary

Critical Thinking

Critical Viewing

Research the Author

Listening and Speaking

Research and Technology

INDEX OF FEATURES

Boldfaced numbers indicate pages where terms are defined.

INDEX OF AUTHORS AND TITLES

Nonfiction selections and informational text appear in red. Page numbers in italic text refer to biographical information.

ACKNOWLEDGMENTS

Brandt & Hochman Literary Agents, Inc. "The Third Wish" from *Not What You Expected: A Collection of Short Stories* by Joan Aiken. Copyright © 1974 by Joan Aiken. Reprinted by permission of Brandt & Hochman Literary Agents, Inc.

Brooks Permissions "Jim" by Gwendolyn Brooks from *Bronzeville Boys And Girls.* Copyright © 1956 by Gwendolyn Brooks. Used with permission.

Carnegie Mellon University Press "How I Learned English" from *Falling Deeply Into America* by Gregory Djanikian. Copyright 1989 by Gregory Djanikian. By permission of Carnegie Mellon University Press.

ClearyWorks "The Fox Outwits the Crow" by William Cleary from *www.clearyworks.com.* Used with permission of William Cleary, Burlington, Vermont.

Cobblestone Publishing "The Rhythms of Rap" by Kathiann M. Kowalski from *Odyssey's* March 2002 issue: *Music: Why Do We Love It?,* Copyright © 2002, Carus Publishing Company. Published by Cobblestone Publishing, 30 Grove Street, Suite C, Peterborough, NH 03458. All rights reserved. Reprinted by permission of the publisher.

Don Congdon Associates, Inc. "All Summer In A Day" by Ray Bradbury, published in *The Magazine of Fantasy and Science Fiction, March 1, 1954.* Copyright © 1954, renewed 1982 by Ray Bradbury. From "No Gumption" by Russell Baker. Copyright © by Russell Baker. Reprinted by permission of Don Congdon Associates, Inc.

The Emma Courlander Trust "All Stories Are Anansi's" from *The Hat-Shaking Dance And Other Ashanti Tales From Ghana* by Harold Courlander with Albert Kofi Prempeh Copyright © 1957, 1985 by Harold Courlander. Reprinted by permission of The Emma Courlander Trust.

Curtis Brown, Ltd. "Two Haiku" ("O foolish ducklings…" and "After the moon sets…") first appeared in Cricket Songs: Japanese Haiku, published by Harcourt. Copyright © 1964 by Harry Behn. "Suzy and Leah" from *American Girl Magazine,* by Jane Yolen. Copyright © 1993 by Jane Yolen. "Dragonwings" by Laurence Yep from *Theatre For Young Audiences: Around The World In 21 Plays.* Copyright © 1993 by Laurence Yep. First published by Dramatists Play Service, Inc. Reprinted by permission of Curtis Brown, Ltd. All rights reserved.

Dell Publishing, a division of Random House, Inc. "The Luckiest Time of All" from *The Lucky Stone* by Lucille Clifton. Copyright © 1979 by Lucille Clifton. Used by permission of Dell Publishing, a division of Random House, Inc.

Dial Books for Young Readers "The Three-Century Woman" copyright © 1999 by Richard Peck, from *Past Perfect, Present Tense* by Richard Peck. Used by permission of Dial Books for Young Readers, A Division of Penguin Young Readers Group, A Member of Penguin Group (USA) Inc., 345 Hudson Street, New York, NY 10014. All rights reserved.

Dutton Children's Books "Percy-Us Brings the Gawgon's Head" from *The Gawgon and the Boy* by Lloyd Alexander. Copyright © 2001 by Lloyd Alexander. Used by permission of Dutton Children's Books, A division of Penguin Young Readers Group, A Member of Penguin Group (USA) Inc. All rights reserved.

Farrar, Straus & Giroux, LLC "Seal" from *Laughing Time: Collected Nonsense* by William Jay Smith. Copyright © 1990 by William Jay Smith. "Train Tune" by Louise Bogan from *The Blue Estuaries.* Copyright © 1923 through 1968 by Louise Bogan.

Joanna Farrell "Popocatepetl and Ixtlaccihuatl by Juliet Piggott from *Mexican Folktales.* Copyright © 1973 by Juliet Piggott. Reprinted by permission of Mrs. J.S.E. Farrell.

Golden Books "The Bride of Pluto"(retitled "Demeter and Persephone") from *The Golden Treasury of Myths and Legends* by Anne Terry White, illustrated by Alice and Martin Provensen, copyright © 1959, renewed 1987 by Random House, Inc. Used by permission of Golden Books, a division of Random House, Inc.

June Hall Literary Agency "One" by James Berry from *When I Dance.* Text copyright © 1991, 1988 by James Berry. Illustrations copyright © 1991 by Karen Barbour. All rights reserved. Reproduced by permission of PFD (www.pfd.co.uk) on behalf of James Berry.

Harcourt, Inc. "Fog" from *Chicago Poems* by Carl Sandburg, copyright © 1916 by Holt, Rinehart and Winston and renewed 1944 by Carl Sandburg. "Seventh Grade" from *Baseball in April and Other Stories,* copyright © 1990 by Gary Soto. From "In Search of Our Mother's Gardens" by Alice Walker from *In Search Of Our Mother's Gardens: Womanist Prose.* Copyright © 1983 by Alice Walker. Reprinted by permission of Harcourt, Inc.

Harcourt Education Limited "Tenochtitlan: Inside the Aztec Capital" by Jacqueline Dineen from *The Aztecs.* Copyright © 1992 by Heinemann Educational Publishers. Reprinted by permission of Harcourt Education.

HarperCollins Publishers, Inc. "Sarah Cynthia Sylvia Stout Would Not Take the Garbage Out" from *Where the Sidewalk Ends* by Shel Silverstein. Copyright © 1974 by Evil Eye Music, Inc. From *An American Childhood* by Annie Dillard. Copyright © 1987 by Annie Dillard. "How the Snake Got Poison" from *Mules and Men* by Zora Neale Hurston. Copyright 1935 by Zora Neale Hurston. Copyright renewed 1963 by John C. Hurston and Joel Hurston. Reprinted by permission of HarperCollins Publishers Inc.

Harvard University Press "I'm Nobody" by Emily Dickinson. Reprinted by permission of the publishers and the Trustees of Amherst College from *The Poems Of Emily Dickinson,* Thomas H. Johnson, ed., Cambridge, Mass.: The Belknap Press of Harvard University Press, Copyright © 1951, 1955, 1979 by the President and Fellows of Harvard College.

John Hawkins & Associates, Inc. "My Furthest-Back Person - The African" by Alex Haley, published July 16, 1972, by *The New York Times Magazine.* Copyright © 1972 by Alex Haley. Used by permission.

Estate of Helmut Hirnschall "I am a Native of North America" by Chief Dan George from *My Heart Soars.* Copyright © 1974 by Clarke Irwin. Used by permission.

Edward D. Hoch "Zoo" by Edward D. Hoch, copyright © 1958, by King Size Publications, Inc.; copyright © 1986 renewed by Edward D. Hoch. Reprinted by permission of the author.

The Barbara Hogenson Agency, Inc. "The Night the Bed Fell" from *My Life and Hard Times* by James Thurber. Copyright © 1933, 1961 by James Thurber. Reprinted by arrangement with Rosemary Thurber and The Barbara Hogensen Agency. All rights reserved.

Henry Holt and Company, Inc. "Stopping by Woods on a Snowy Evening" from *The Poetry Of Robert Frost* edited by Edward Connry Lathem. Copyright 1923, 1969 by Henry Holt and Company, copyright 1951 by Robert Frost. From *Letters from Rifka* by Karen Hesse. Copyright © 1992 by Karen Hesse. Reprinted by permission of Henry Holt and Company, Inc. All rights reserved.

Information Please "Fall of the Hindenburg" from *Infoplease.com.* © Pearson Education, publishing as Infoplease.com. Reprinted by permission.

Japan Publications, Inc. "On sweet plum blossoms," "Has spring come indeed?" and "Temple bells die out" by Basho from *One Hundred Famous Haiku* by Daniel C. Buchanan. Copyright © 1973. Reprinted by permission.

Stanleigh Jones "He-y, Come on Ou-t!" by Shinichi Hoshi translated by Stanleigh Jones from *The Best Japanese Science Fiction Stories.* Copyright © 1989 by John L. Apostolou and Martin H. Greenberg. All rights reserved. Reprinted by permission of the author.

The Estate of Barbara Jordan "All Together Now" by Barbara Jordan from *Sesame Street Parents.*

Kinseido "Conversational Ballgames" by Nancy M. Sakamoto from *Polite Fictions: Why Japanese And Americans Seem Rude To Each Other.* Copyright © 1982.

Alfred A. Knopf Children's Books "People Could Fly" from *The People Could Fly: American Black Folktales* by Virginia Hamilton, copyright © 1985 by

Virginia Hamilton. Used by permission of Alfred A. Knopf Children's Books, a division of Random House, Inc.

Alfred A. Knopf, Inc. "Mother to Son" from *The Collected Poems of Langston Hughes* by Langston Hughes, copyright © 1994 by The Estate of Langston Hughes. Used by permission of Alfred A. Knopf, a division of Random House, Inc.

Barbara S. Kouts Literary Agency "The Bear Boy" by Joseph Bruchac from *Flying with the Eagle, Racing the Great Bear*. Copyright © 1993 by Joseph Bruchac. Used with permission.

Little, Brown and Company, Inc. "The Real Story of a Cowboy's Life" from *The West* by Geoffrey C. Ward. Copyright © 1996 by The West Book Project, Inc. By permission of Little, Brown and Company, Inc.

Liveright Publishing Corporation "in Just-" by E. E. Cummings, copyright 1923, 1951, © 1991 by the Trustees for the E.E. Cummings Trust. Copyright © 1976 by George James Firmage, from *Complete Poems, 1904-1962* by E.E. Cummings, edited by George J. Firmage. Used by permission of Liveright Publishing Corporation.

Gina Maccoby Literary Agency "mk" from *Open Your Eyes* by Jean Fritz. Copyright © Jean Fritz, 2003. Reprinted by permission of The Gina Maccoby Literary Agency. All rights reserved.

Naomi Long Madgett "Life" by Naomi Long Madgett from *One and the Many*, copyright © 1956; *Remembrances of Spring: Collected Early Poems*, copyright © 1993 Michigan State University Press. Reprinted by permission of the author.

Meriwether Publishing Ltd., Publisher "My Head is Full of Starshine" from *Acting Natural* by Peg Kehret © 1991 Meriwether Publishing Ltd. Used by permission.

Eve Merriam "Onomatopoeia" from *It Doesn't Always Have To Rhyme* by Eve Merriam. Copyright © 1964, 1992 Eve Merriam. Reprinted by permission of Marian Reiner, Literary Agent.

William Morris Agency "A Christmas Carol: Scrooge and Marley" by Israel Horovitz. Copyright 1979 by Israel Horovitz. All rights reserved. Israel Horovitz's adaptation of Charles Dickens' *A Christmas Carol: Scrooge and Marley* was first presented at Center Stage in Baltimore, Maryland, in December 1978. Reprinted by permission. CAUTION: Professionals and amateurs are hereby warned that *A Christmas Carol: Scrooge and Marley*, being fully protected under the copyright Laws of the United States of America, the British Empire, including the Dominion of Canada, and all other countries of the Universal Copyright and Berne Conventions, are subject to royalty. All rights, including professional, amateur, motion picture, recitation, lecturing, public reading, radio and television broadcasting, and the rights of translation into foreign languages, are strictly reserved. Particular emphasis is laid on the question of readings, permission for which must be secured in writing. All inquiries for *A Christmas Carol: Scrooge and Marley* should be addressed to the William Morris Agency, 1325 Avenue of the Americas, New York, NY 10019.

William Morrow & Company, Inc. "Winter" from *Cotton Candy On A Rainy Day* by Nikki Giovanni. Copyright © 1978 by Nikki Giovanni. Reprinted by permission of HarperCollins Publishers, Inc. William Morrow.

National Geographic Magazine "Yao Ming: NBA Giant Is Big in U.S., Bigger in China" by Brian Handwerk from *National Geographic News*. © 2004 National Geographic Society. All rights reserved. Reprinted by permission.

Naomi Shihab Nye "The Rider" by Naomi Shihab Nye from *Invisible*. Reprinted by permission of the author, Naomi Shihab Nye, 2004.

Harold Ober Associates, Inc. "Stolen Day" by Sherwood Anderson from *This Week Magazine*. Reprinted by permission.

ODYSSEY Magazine (Cobblestone Publishing) "A Special Gift—The Legacy of 'Snowflake Bentley'" by Barbara Eaglesham from *Odyssey Magazine*. From Odyssey's December 2002 issue: Chilly Science: Ice and Snow, Copyright © 2002, Carus Publishing Company. Published by Cobblestone Publishing, 30 Grove Street, Suite C, Peterborough, NH 03458. All rights reserved. Reprinted by permission of the publisher.

The Estate of Raymond R. Patterson "Martin Luther King" by Raymond Richard Patterson. Used by permission of the family of Raymond R. Patterson.

Pearson Prentice Hall (formerly Prentice-Hall, Inc.-Secondary) "Keeping it Quiet" from *Prentice Hall Science Explorer Sound and Light*. Copyright © 2005 by Pearson Education, Inc., publishing as Pearson Prentice Hall. "The Seasons on Earth" from *Prentice Hall Science Explorer Astronomy*. Copyright © 2005 by Pearson Education, Inc., publishing as Pearson Prentice Hall. Used by permission.

People Weekly Syndication, Time Inc. "Picks & Pans: A Christmas Carol (TNT)" by Terry Kelleher from *People Weekly, December 6th, 1999, Vol.52*. Copyright © 1999 by People Weekly. Registered trademarks of Time, Inc. All rights reserved Time Inc. Reprinted by permission.

Perseus Books, LLC "Alligator" by Bailey White from *Mama Makes Up Her Mind And Other Dangers Of Southern Living*. Copyright © 1993 by Bailey White. All rights reserved. Reprinted by permission of DaCapo, a member of Perseus Books, L.L.C.

Pinata Books "The Desert Is My Mother/El regalo de la flor de Nochebuena" by Pat Mora from *My Own True Name*. Text © 2000 by Pat Mora. All rights reserved.

Joel Poiley "Bernie Williams: Yankee Doodle Dandy" by Joel Poiley from *Boy Scouts Of America*. Joel Poiley is a freelance writer based in Florida. Copyright © Joel Poiley.

G.P. Putnam's Sons "Rodney" by Jacqueline Woodson from *Locomotion*. Text copyright © 2003 by Jacqueline Woodson. All rights reserved. "Two Kinds" from *The Joy Luck Club* by Amy Tan, copyright © 1989 by Amy Tan. Used by permission of G.P. Putnam's Sons, a division of Penguin Group (USA) Inc. "How I Got My Name" by Jacqueline Woodson from *Locomotion*. Text copyright © 2003 by Jacqueline Woodson. All rights reserved.

Random House, Inc. "Melting Pot" from *Living Out Loud* by Anna Quindlen, copyright © 1987 by Anna Quindlen. Used by permission of Random House, Inc.

Marian Reiner, Literary Agent "Weather" by Eve Merriam from *Catch A Little Rhyme*. Copyright © 1966 by Eve Merriam. Copyright © renewed 1994 by Dee Michel and Guy Michel. All rights reserved. Used by permission of Marian Reiner.

Wendy Rose "Loo-Wit" by Wendy Rose from *The Halfbreed Chronicles and Other Poems*. Copyright © 1985 by Wendy Rose. Reprinted by permission.

Science Service "It's a Math World for Animals" by Emily Sohn from *Science Service for Kids*, October 8, 2003. Copyright © 2003 Science Service. All rights reserved. Reprinted with permission from Science News for Kids, copyright © 2003 by Science Service.

Scribner, an imprint of Simon & Schuster Adult Publishing Group "Rattlesnake" from *Cross Creek* by Marjorie Kinnan Rawlings. Copyright © 1942 by Marjorie Kinnan Rawlings; copyright renewed © 1970 by Norton Baskin and Charles Scribner's Sons. Reprinted with permission of Scribner, an imprint of Simon & Schuster Adult Publishing Group. All rights reserved.

Simon & Schuster Books for Young Readers, an imprint of Simon & Schuster Children's Book Division "Perseus" by Alice Low from *The Macmillan Book Of Greek Gods And Heroes*. Copyright © 1985 by Macmillan Publishing Company, a division of Macmillan, Inc. All rights reserved. "Papa's Parrot" by Cynthia Rylant from *Every Living Thing*. Copyright © 1985 by Cynthia Rylant. "The Fox and the Crow" from the *Fables of Aesop*. Reprinted with permission of Simon & Schuster Books for Young Readers, an imprint of Simon & Schuster Children's Book Division.

Simon & Schuster, Inc. "A Day's Wait" by Ernest Hemingway from *Winner Take Nothing*. Copyright 1933 Charles Scribner's Sons. Copyright renewed © 1961 by Mary Hemingway. All rights reserved. Reprinted by permission.

The Society of Authors "The Highwayman" from *Collected Poems* by Alfred Noyes. Used by permission of The Society of Authors as the Literary

Representative of the Estate of Alfred Noyes.

Susan Solt "Forsythia" by Mary Ellen Solt from *Concrete Poetry: A World View.* Copyright © 1968 by Hispanic Arts, Indiana University. Copyright © 1970 by Indiana University Press. All rights reserved. Reprinted by permission of the author.

John Sousanis "Toned-down 'Christmas Carol' has more spirit" by John Sousanis, from *The Oakland Press,* November 29, 2000, Vol. 156, No. 280. John Sousanis is a Detroit area writer and editor. Copyright © 2000 The Oakland Press. Reprinted by permission of John Sousanis.

Piri Thomas "Amigo Brothers" by Piri Thomas from *Stories from El Barrio.* Copyright © 1978 by Piri Thomas. Reprinted by permission of the author.

The University of Georgia Press "Volar: To Fly" from *The Latin Deli: Prose and Poetry.* Copyright by Judith Ortiz Cofer. Reprinted by permission of the author and The University of Georgia Press.

University of Notre Dame Press "from Barrio Boy" by Ernesto Galarza. Copyright © 1971 by University of Notre Dame Press, Notre Dame, Indiana 46556. Reprinted by permission.

U.S. National Archives & Records Administration "NARA: U.S. National Archives & Records Administration" by Staff from *www.archives.gov.* Courtesy of the National Archives. Reprinted by permission.

The Vagabond School of the Drama "The Flat Rock Playhouse Apprentice Showcase and Apprentice Application Form" by Staff. *www.flatrockplayhouse.org.* Reprinted by permission.

Viking Penguin, A Division of Penguin Young Readers Group, A Member of Penguin Group (USA) From "What Makes a Rembrandt a Rembrandt?" by Richard Mühlberger. Copyright © 1993 by The Metropolitan Museum of Art. "Sun and Moon in a Box (Zuni)", from *American Indian Trickster Tales* by Richard Erdoes and Alphonso Ortiz, copyright © 1998 by Richard Erdoes & The Estate of Alphonso Ortiz. "The Other Frog Prince" by Jon Scieszka and Lane Smith from *The Stinky Cheese Man & Other Fairly Stupid Tales.* Text Copyright © Jon Scieszka, 1992. Illustrations Lane Smith © 1992. "Grasshopper Logic" from *Squids will be Squids: Fresh Morals, Beastly Fables* by Jon Scieszka, copyright © 1998 Jon Scieszka, text. Illustrations by Lane Smith © 1998. "Duckbilled Platypus vs. Beefsnakstik®" from *Squids will be Squids: Fresh Morals, Beastly Fables* by Jon Scieszka, copyright © 1998 Jon Scieszka, text. Illustrations by Lane Smith © 1998. Used by permission of Viking Penguin, A Division of Penguin Young Readers Group, A Member of Penguin Group (USA). All rights reserved.

Writers & Artists Agency From "The Monsters are Due on Maple Street" by Rod Serling. Copyright © 1960 by Rod Serling; Copyright © 1988 by Carolyn Serling, Jodi Serling and Anne Serling.

Laurence Yep "Ribbons" by Laurence Yep from *American Girl Magazine, January/February 1992.* Reprinted by permission of the author.

The Young Authors Foundation, Inc. "Zoos: Joys or Jails?" by Rachel F. from *teenink.com.* Copyright 2003 by Teen Ink, The 21st Century and The Young Authors Foundation, Inc. All rights reserved.

Robert Zimmerman "Life Without Gravity" by Robert Zimmerman originally published in *Muse Magazine, April 2002.* © 2002 Carus Publishing Company. All rights reserved. Author Zimmerman owns the rights. Reprinted by permission of the author.

Note: Every effort has been made to locate the copyright owner of material reproduced in this component. Omissions brought to our attention will be corrected in subsequent editions.

MAP AND ART CREDITS

All graphic organizers: In-House Pros; All maps by Mapping Specialist, except where noted; Illustrative "Literature in Context": Keithley and Associates; "More About the Author" illustration: Joseph Adolphe; "Writing Workshop" illustration: Marc Clamens

PHOTO CREDITS

Cover and Title page: Grevy's Zebra, Endangered Species Series, 1983, Andy Warhol, The Andy Warhol Foundation, Inc./Art Resource, NY, ©2005 Andy Warhol Foundation for the Visual Arts/Artists Rights Society (ARS), New York, Courtesy Ronald Feldman Fine Arts, New York; **vii:** Alan Briere/SuperStock; **viii-ix:** Images.com/CORBIS; **ix:** b. ©Hulton Getty/Archive Photos; **x-xi:** The Bridgeman Art Library, London/New York; **xi:** b. SuperStock; **xii-xiii:** Isy Ochoa/SuperStock; **xiii:** b. Royalty-Free/CORBIS; **xiv-xv:** Peter Sickles/SuperStock; **xvi-xvii:** Alexandra Day/CORBIS; **xvii:** b. Ralph A. Clevenger/CORBIS; **xviii-xix:** Images.com/CORBIS; **xix:** b. Corel Professional Photos CD-ROM™; **xx:** Joseph Sohm; ChromoSohm Inc./CORBIS; **xxviii:** Bob Daemmrich/The Image Works; **xxix:** Animals Animals; **1:** Images.com/CORBIS **2:** b. © Janusz Kapusta/Stock Illustration Source, Inc.; **2:** t. Prentice Hall **3:** t. © Sandra Templeton/Stock Illustration Source, Inc.; **4:** PEANUTS reprinted by permission of United Feature Syndicate, Inc.; **5:** Bettmann/CORBIS; **7:** G.G. Kopilak/SuperStock; **11:** Courtesy of the Library of Congress; **12:** t. Bettmann/CORBIS; **12:** m. Photofest; **12:** b. Bettmann/CORBIS; **14:** Ian Shaw/Getty Images; **17:** Bettmann/CORBIS; **18:** b. Bettmann/CORBIS; **18:** t. Bettmann/CORBIS; **21:** Images.com/CORBIS; **25:** Courtesy of Cynthia Rylant; **26:** John Arsenault/Getty Images; **26:** inset James Gritz/Getty Images; **28:** Stephen Oliver/© Dorling Kindersley; **28:** Corel Professional Photos CD-ROM™; **28:** Corel Professional Photos CD-ROM™; **29:** Corel Professional Photos CD-ROM™; **31:** James Gritz/Getty Images; **32:** Reprinted by permission of The Gina Maccoby Literary Agency. Copyright©1982 by Jean Fritz; **33:** Reprinted by permission of The Gina Maccoby Literary Agency. Copyright © 1982 by Jean Fritz; **34:** Hulton-Deutsch Collection/CORBIS; **36:** Reprinted by permission of The Gina Maccoby Literary Agency. Copyright ©1982 by Jean Fritz; **38:** Reprinted by permission of The Gina Maccoby Literary Agency. Copyright©1982 by Jean Fritz; **40-41:** James Randklev; Visions of America/CORBIS; **43:** Reprinted by permission of The Gina Maccoby Literary Agency. Copyright©1982 by Jean Fritz; **47:** © Dorling Kindersley; **48:** © Dorling Kindersley; **51:** Rollie McKenna; **52:** Annie Griffiths Belt/DRK Photo; **55:** Yuri Dojc/Getty Images; **57:** Annie Griffiths Belt/DRK Photo; **59:** Yuri Dojc/Getty Images; **60:** Christopher Felver/CORBIS; **61:** ©Tom & Dee Ann McCarthy/PhotoEdit; **62:** Royalty-Free/CORBIS; **65:** ©Tom & Dee Ann McCarthy/PhotoEdit; **69:** t. Courtesy of the Library of Congress; **69:** b. ©Hulton Archive/Archive Photos/Getty Images; **70:** John Lei/Omni-Photo Communications, Inc.; **72:** ©Richard Hutchings/PhotoEdit **75:** Oscar Burriel/Photo Researchers, Inc.; **76:** Getty Images; **87:** Images.com/CORBIS; **91:** AP/Wide World Photos; **92:** Kim Zumwalt/Getty Images; **94-95:** Paul A. Souders/CORBIS; **96:** NASA; **98:** Images.com/CORBIS; **101:** Kim Zumwalt/Getty Images; **102:** Prentice Hall; **103:** George Kadish, courtesy of United States Holocaust Memorial Museum Photo Archives; **105:** Main Commission for the Investigation of Nazi War Crimes, courtesy of United States Holocaust Memorial Museum Photo Archives; **107:** Shraga Wainer, courtesy of United States Holocaust Memorial Museum Photo Archives; **108:** Hikaru Iwasaki/United States Holocaust Memorial Museum; **110:** ©Hulton Getty/Archive Photos; **113:** George Kadish, courtesy of United States Holocaust Memorial Museum Photo Archives; **117:** Photo: Daniel Cima ©; **118:** ©Dale Sanders/Masterfile; **119:** CORBIS; **121:** Copyright© by Julia Alvarez. Reprinted by permission of Susan Bergholz Literary Services, NY. All Rights reserved.; **123:** Copyright© by Julia Alvarez. Reprinted by permission of Susan Bergholz Literary Services, NY. All Rights reserved.; **124:** Alex Gotfryd/CORBIS; **125:** Betty Press/Panos Pictures; **130:** © 1998 ABC, Inc. All rights reserved.; **132-133:** ©Faith Ringgold, 1986, The Purple Quilt (detail), 91" x 72", acrylic on canvas with pieced fabric borders; **135:** © 1998 ABC, Inc. All rights reserved.; **143:** t. AP/Wide World Photos; **143:** b. CORBIS; **144:** Sunday Afternoon, Ralph Fasanella; **147:** Culver Pictures, Inc.; **154:** Lynn Saville/Prentice Hall; **157:** Prentice Hall **164-165:** Joseph

Sohm; ChromoSohm Inc./CORBIS; **166:** Snow Crystals by W.A. Bentley and W.J. Humphreys, Dover Publications; **167:** Snow Crystals by W.A. Bentley and W.J. Humphreys, Dover Publications; **168-169:** The Bridgeman Art Library, London/New York; **170:** t. Miriam Berkley/Authorpix; **170:** b. ©Images.com/CORBIS; **171:** Spot on the Spot; **172:** PEANUTS reprinted by permission of United Feature Syndicate, Inc.; **173:** Joseph Sohm/CORBIS; **175:** Morning at the Jackson Ave. Ferry, Gilbert Fletcher, Courtesy of the artist; **176:** Disequilibrium, 1987, Catherine Redmond, Courtesy of the artist; **180:** Four Piece Orchestra, 1944, Ben Shahn, ©Estate of Ben Shahn/Licensed by VAGA, New York, NY; **182:** Getty Images; **187:** The Bridgeman Art Library, London/New York; **191:** Prentice Hall; **192:** Jack Parsons/Omni-Photo Communications, Inc.; **193:** Copyright ©Pres. and Fellows of Harvard College 1995. All rights reserved. Peabody Museum - Harvard University. Photograph by Hillel Burger.; **194:** Pearson Education/PH School Division; **195:** r. Corel Professional Photos CD-ROM™; **195:** m. Jack Parsons/Omni-Photo Communications, Inc.; **195** l. Silver Burdett Ginn; **197:** Copyright ©Pres. and Fellows of Harvard College 1995. All rights reserved. Peabody Museum - Harvard University. Photograph by Hillel Burger.; **198:** Underwood & Underwood/CORBIS; **199:** Clem Haagner/Photo Researchers, Inc.; **202-203:** E. Hanumantha Rao/Photo Researchers, Inc.; **205:** ©Joel Simon/Stone, **208:** R. Dev/Photo Researchers, Inc.; **210-211:** Paolo Koch/Photo Researchers, Inc.; **215:** Clem Haagner/Photo Researchers, Inc.; **219:** ©Gunter Ziesler/Peter Arnold, Inc.; **220:** Luxner News Inc.; **223:** AP/Wide World Photos; **224:** Thom Lang/CORBIS; **225:** Royalty-Free/CORBIS; **227:** ©Judith Miller & Dorling Kindersley/ ©Dorling Kindersley; **229:** ©Judith Miller & Dorling Kindersley/ ©Dorling Kindersley; **230:** Frank Capri/Getty Images; **231:** Bettmann/CORBIS; **234:** Courtesy of Amy Tan; **236:** David Young-Wolff/PhotoEdit; **238:** Chinese Girl Under Lanterns, Winson Trang, Courtesy of the artist; **242:** Portrait, Pamela Chin Lee, Courtesy of the artist; **245:** David Young-Wolff/PhotoEdit; **249:** t. Courtesy of Gary Soto; **249:** b. CORBIS; **250:** r. David Young-Wolff/PhotoEdit; **250:** l. Mary Kate Denny/PhotoEdit/PhotoEdit; **252:** Bob Daemmrich/The Image Works; **254:** Macduff Everton/CORBIS; **256:** SuperStock; **258:** John Cancalosi/Stock, Boston/PictureQuest; **260:** SuperStock; **269:** The Bridgeman Art Library, London/New York; **274:** Alan Briere/SuperStock; **276:** b. Hideki Fujii/Getty Images; **276:** m.b. Getty Images; **276:** m.t. Corel Professional Photos CD-ROM™; **276:** t. Corel Professional Photos CD-ROM™; **278:** Star map courtesy of Robert Dixon, Dynamic Astronomy, 6th ed., Prentice Hall, 1992; **279:** Pal Hermansen/Tony Stone Images; **281:** Alan Briere/SuperStock; **282:** Photo Courtesy Suzie Dod Thomas; **283:** ©David Madison 1997; **285:** ©2004 JupiterImages and its Licensors. All Rights Reserved.; **286:** Jeff Greenberg/Stock, Boston; **288:** ©David Madison 1997; **291:** ©David Madison 1997; **293:** ©David Madison 1997; **297:** David Young-Wolff/Getty Images; **301:** Getty Images; **306:** Prentice Hall; **307:** ©1990 Terry Heffernan; **309:** Three Studies of a Dancer in Fourth Position, c. 1879/80, Edgar Degas, Charcoal and pastel with stumping, with touches of brush and black wash on greyish-tan laid paper with blue fibers (discolored from pinkish-blue). c. 1879/80, 48 x 61.5 cm. Bequest of Adele R. Levy, 1962.703. Photograph ©1994, The Art Institute of Chicago. All rights reserved.; **313** l. Royalty-Free/CORBIS; **313:** r. Stockbyte; **314:** Madame X, 1993, Hung Liu, Courtesy Steinbaum Krauss Gallery, New York, New York; **316:** ©1990 Terry Heffernan; **319:** © 1990 Terry Heffernan; **323:** Japan Foreign-Rights Center; **323:** Bettmann/CORBIS; **325:** Nighthawks, 1942, Edward Hopper, oil on canvas, 84.1 x152.4 cm., Friends of American Art Collection 1942.51. photograph ©1998, The Art Institute of Chicago. All Rights Reserved.; **328:** ©David Schmidt/Masterfile; **331:** Buddy Mays/CORBIS; **332:** Custom Medical Stock Photo, Inc.; **338:** Michael Newman/PhotoEdit Inc.; **341:** Miriam Berkley/Authorpix; **349:** David Young-Wolf/PhotoEdit; **350:** m. Foodpix via Getty Images; **350:** t. Foodpix via Getty

Images; **350:** b. Corel Professional Photos CD-ROM™; **351:** AP/Wide World Photos; **352-353:** Isy Ochoa/SuperStock; **354:** t. Prentice Hall; **354:** b ©Laura Tedeschi/Stock Illustration Source, Inc.; **355:** ©Royalty-Free/CORBIS; **356:** PEANUTS reprinted by permission of United Feature Syndicate, Inc.; **357:** Réunion des Musées Nationaux/Art Resource, NY; **359:** The Night Watch (detail), Rembrandt Harmensz, Courtesy of Rijksmuseum; **360-361:** The Night Watch, Rembrandt Harmensz, Courtesy of Rijksmuseum; **362:** t. The Night Watch (detail), Rembrandt Harmensz, Courtesy of Rijksmuseum; **362:** b. The Night Watch (detail), Rembrandt Harmensz, Courtesy of Rijksmuseum; **364:** Rijksmuseum-Stichting; **367:** Isy Ochoa/SuperStock; **371:** Photo Courtesy of Robert Zimmerman; **372:** Space Adventures; **373:** NASA/Roger RessmeyerCORBIS; **374:** NASA Glenn Research Center (NASA-GRC); **375:** NASA; **377:** NASA; **378:** Courtesy of Nancy Masterson Sakamoto; **379:** Royalty-Free/CORBIS; **381:** R.W. Jones/CORBIS; **382:** Michael Newman/PhotoEdit; **385:** R.W. Jones/CORBIS; **389:** Bettmann/CORBIS; **390-391:** Corel Professional Photos CD-ROM™; **392:** Buffalo, 1992, Courtesy of the artist Jaune Quick-to-See Smith; **395:** Corel Professional Photos CD-ROM™; **396:** AP/Wide World Photos; **397:** Corel Professional Photos CD-ROM™; **399:** From the collection of the Old State House Museum; **401:** Corel Professional Photos CD-ROM™; **403:** Corel Professional Photos CD-ROM™; **407:** Ted StreshinskyCORBIS; **408:** Mark Peterson/CORBIS; **411:** t. © Joel Poiley; **411:** b. Yvonne Hemsey/Getty Images; **412:** David Bergman/CORBIS; **415:** Photo by Tasos Katopodis; **416:** Saturday Evening Post Cover,1937, Illustrated by Frances Tipton Hunter, ©1937 SEPS: Licensed by Curtis Publishing Co., Indianapolis, IN; **418:** Reprinted by permission of Don Congdon Associates, Inc. Copyright ©1982 by Russell Baker; **419:** Reprinted by permission of Don Congdon Associates, Inc. Copyright ©1982 by Russel Baker; **421:** Saturday Evening Post Cover, March 28, 1931, ©The Curtis Publishing Company, Illustrator: Norman Rockwell, Printed by permission of the Norman Rockwell Family Trust Copyright ©1931 the Norman Rockwell Family Entities; **423:** b. Saturday Evening Post Cover, September 2, 1939, © The Curtis Publishing Company, Illustrator: Norman Rockwell. Printed by permission of the Norman Rockwell Family Trust Copyright ©1939 the Norman Rockwell Family Entities; **423:** t. Saturday Evening Post Cover, August 10, 1935, Illustrated by G. Brehm, ©1935 SEPS: Licensed by Curtis Publishing Co., Indianapolis, IN; **433:** Isy Ochoa/SuperStock; **437:** Globe Photos; **438-439:** t. NASA; **438:** NASA; **439:** t.r. NASA; **441:** NASA; **442:** Getty Images; **443:** Hulton-Deutsch Collection/CORBIS; **445:** Bettmann/CORBIS; **447:** Bettmann/CORBIS; **451:** Seth Resnick/CORBIS; **453:** Kansas State Historical Society; **455:** Getty Images; **457:** Kansas State Historical Society; **458:** AP/Wide World Photos; **459:** S. Dimmitt/Photo Researchers, Inc.; **461:** Chas. & Elizabeth Schwartz Trust/Animals Animals; **463:** ©Tom Bean/Stone; **465:** S. Dimmitt/Photo Researchers, Inc.; **469:** b(1). Breck P. Kent/Animals Animals; **469:** b(2). Zig Leszczynski/Animals Animals; **469:** b(4). Zig Leszczynski/Animals Animals; **469:** b(3). Brian Kenney; **473:** t. Spencer; **473:** b. Bettmann/CORBIS; **474-475:** Carl & Ann Purcell/CORBIS; **476:** Renee Lynn/Photo Researchers, Inc.; **479:** My Life and Hard Times Copyright ©1933 by James Thurber. Copyright ©renewed 1961 by James Thurber. Reprinted by arrangement with Rosemary A. Thurber and The Barbara Hogenson Agency.; **480:** "Briggs Suffocating" by James Thurber, Barbara Hogenson Agency, Photo by Eric H. Antoniou; **481:** "Briggs and Rex", by James Thurber, Barbara Hogenson Agency, Photo by Eric H. Antoniou; **488:** Tom Stewart/CORBIS; **491:** Prentice Hall; **498:** AP/Wide World Photos; **500:** David Shadrack Smith ©NGT&F; **502-503:** Peter Sickles/SuperStock; **504:** t. Cheron Bayna; **504:** b ©Images.com/CORBIS; **505:** Getty Images; **506:** CALVIN AND HOBBES ©1992 Watterson. Reprinted with permission of UNIVERSAL PRESS SYNDICATE. All rights reserved.; **507:** IFA Bilderteam/eStock Photography, LLC; **509:** Getty Images; **510:** t. T. Wiewandt/Getty Images; **511:** Richard Cummins/CORBIS; **512:** Bob Krist/CORBIS; **515:** Peter Sickles/SuperStock; **519:** b. Yosa Buson, Heibonsha/Pacific Press Service; **519:** t. photo by James Evans; **519:** m. Oscar/CORBIS; **520-521:** Jeff Greenberg/Omni-Photo Communications, Inc.; **522:** b. ©Martin Harvey/Peter Arnold, Inc.; **522:** t. ©Martin Harvey/Peter Arnold, Inc.; **523:** Christie's Images/CORBIS; **525:** ©Martin Harvey/Peter Arnold, Inc.; **526:** t. ©Jan Cobb; **526:** b. Snark/Art Resource, NY; **527:** ©Ed Reschke/Peter Arnold, Inc.; **528:** Rights and Permissions will add this to their acknowledgements; **529:** Gary Conner/PhotoEdit; **531:** ©Ed Reschke/Peter Arnold, Inc.; **535:** b. Patricia Allen-Wolk; **535:** t. Courtesy of Detroit Free Press;

535: m. Time Life Pictures/Getty Images; **536:** Royalty-Free/CORBIS; **537:** The Newark Museum/Art Resource, NY; **538-539:** Roger Werth/Woodfin Camp & Associates; **541:** The Newark Museum/Art Resource, NY; **542:** t. Time Life Pictures/Getty Images; **542:** m. Getty Images; **542:** b. Time Life Pictures/Getty Images; **543:** ©Alamy Images; **544:** fine Art Photographic Library, London/Art Resource, NY; **545:** fine Art Photographic Library, London/Art Resource, NY; **546:** Kim Sayer/CORBIS; **547:** SIME s.a.s/eStock Photography, LLC; **549:** Kim Sayer/CORBIS; **553:** Image courtesy of The Advertising Archives; **554:** The Advertising Archive Ltd./The Picture Desk; **557:** b. Courtesy of Gregory Djanikian; **557:** t. Time Life Pictures/Getty Images; **557:** m. Getty Images; **558:** ©Herman Eisenbeiss/Photo Researchers, Inc.; **563:** Corel Professional Photos CD-ROM™; **564:** Corel Professional Photos CD-ROM™; **565:** ©2002 Jeff Schultz/Alaska Stock.com; **567:** Patrik Giardino/CORBIS; **577:** Peter Sickles/SuperStock; **581:** t. AP/Wide World Photos; **581:** b. gezette.de Buro fur Fotografie; **581:** m. Photo by Bachrach; **582:** Illustration from "Where the Sidewalk Ends" ©1974 by Evil Eye Music, Inc. Used by permssion of HarperCollins Publishers; **583:** Illustration from "Where the Sidewalk Ends" ©1974 by Evil Eye Music, Inc. Used by permssion of HarperCollins Publishers; **584:** Alan Schein Photography/CORBIS; **585:** Royalty-Free/CORBIS; **588:** t. William Shakespeare (detail), attributed to John Taylor, by courtesy of the National Portrait Gallery, London; **588:** b. ©G. Paul Bishop 1955; **588:** m. Photo by Bachrach. Used by permission of Marian Reiner; **589:** Larry Lipsky/Tom Stack & Associates; **590:** ©Alamy Images; **591:** W.A. Sharmann; Milepost 92 1/2/CORBIS; **593:** ©Alamy Images; **597:** b. The Granger Collection, New York; **597:** t. Bettmann/CORBIS; **597:** m. William E. Stafford; **598-599:** Corel Professional Photos CD-ROM™; **600:** Getty Images; **601:** Animals Animals; **603:** Animals Animals; **604:** m. Bettmann/CORBIS; **604:** t. ©Nancy Crampton; **604:** b. Time Life Pictures/Getty Images; **605:** Pearson Education/PH School Division; **606:** You Are Old, Father William, 1865, Sir John Tenniel, The Granger Collection, New York; **608-609:** ©R.G.K. Photography/Stone/Getty; **611:** Pearson Education/PH School Division; **615:** Tim Mosenfelder/CORBIS; **619:** b. Courtesy of the Library of Congress; **619:** t. Bettmann/CORBIS; **620:** La Bonne Aventure (Good Fortune),1939, René Magritte, Gouache on paper, 33.5 x 40.7 cm., Museum Boymans-Van Beuningen, Rotterdam, ©2000 C. Herscovici, Brussels/Artists Rights Sociey (ARS), New York; **622:** John Lei/Stock, Boston; **628:** Royalty-Free/CORBIS; **631:** Cheron Bayna; **638:** Photo by Tim Pennings **639:** Photo by Tim Pennings; **640:** Photo by Tim Pennings; **642-643:** Alexandra Day/CORBIS; **644:** t. Prentice Hall; **644:** b. ©Images.com/CORBIS; **645:** ©Getty Images; **646:** PEANUTS reprinted by permission of United Feature Syndicate, Inc.; **647:** Terry W. Eggers/CORBIS; **649:** Bettmann/CORBIS; **651:** Gary Torrisi; **652:** b. Bancroft Library, University of California; **652:** t. Gary Torrisi; **653:** Gary Torrisi; **654:** b. Terry W. Eggers/CORBIS; **654:** t. Gary Torrisi; **655:** Gary Torrisi; **656:** t. Gary Torrisi; **656:** b. Paul Van Reil/Robert Harding World Imagery; **659:** Alexandra Day/CORBIS; **663:** AP/Wide World Photos; **664:** border John Warden/Index Stock Photography, Inc.; **667:** CBS/The Kobal Collection; **668:** Charles Janasz as Bob Cratchit in the Guthrie Theatre's 1992 production of A Christmas Carol adapted by Barbara Field. Photo credit: Michal Daniel.; **671:** Jeffrey Coolidge/Getty Images; **672:** Mary Evans Picture Library; **673:** Bob Davis as Bob Cratchit, Kevin James Kelly as Charles Dickens and Richard Ooms as Ebenezer Scrooge in the Guthrie Theatre's 1994 production of A Christmas Carol adapted by Barbara Field. Photo credit: Michal Daniel.; **675:** Bob Davis as Bob Cratchit and Nathaniel Fuller in the Guthrie Theatre's 1994 production of A Christmas Carol adapted by Barbara Field. Photo credit: Michal Daniel.; **679:** ©Michal Daniel, 2003; **683:** David Buffington/Getty Images; **685:** Getty Images; **687:** ©Michal Daniel, 2003; **690:** ©The Trustees of The British Museum; **697:** border John Warden/Index Stock Photography, Inc.; **699:** Jim Baker as Ghost of Christmas Present in the Guthrie Theatre's 1975 production of A Christmas Carol adapted by Barbara Field. Photo credit: Michal Daniel.; **703:** ©Michal Daniel, 2003; **705:** The Guthrie Theatre; **706:** David Toase/Getty Images; **709:** Foodpix; **712:** Photo ©Michal Daniel, 2000; **717:** The Cratchit family and Ebenezer Scrooge in the Guthrie Theatre's 1994 production of A Christmas Carol adapted by Barbara Field.Photo credit: Michal Daniel.; **719:** Gary Braasch/CORBIS; **722:** m. Photofest; **722:** l(2). Renown/The Kobal Collection; **722:** l(1). Photofest; **722:** r(2). Photofest; **722:** r(1). Photofest; **725:** Ebenezer Scrooge celebrating in the Guthrie Theatre's 1994 production of A Christmas Carol adapted by Barbara Field. Photo credit: Michal Daniel.; **727:** The Guthrie Theatre; **729:** Photo ©Michal Daniel, 2000; **733:** Photofest; **737:** b. AP/Wide World Photos; **737:** t. Bettmann/CORBIS; **738:** border John Warden/Index Stock Photography, Inc.; **738:** CBS/The Kobal Collection; **739:** border John Warden/Index Stock Photography, Inc.; **739:** ©Michal Daniel, 2003; **740:** border John Warden/Index Stock Photography, Inc.; **740:** ©Michal Daniel, 2003; **747:** t. ©Doug Perrine/Seapics.com; **747:** b. ©Visuals Unlimited; **749:** Alexandra Day/CORBIS; **753:** Bettmann/CORBIS; **754-755:** Jean-Pierre Pieuchot/Getty Images; **758:** *Woman on telephone as seen through window,* William Low, Courtesy of the artist.; **762:** *Overview of family walking dog on the street,* William Low, Courtesy of the artist.; **767:** *Streetlight,* 1930, Constance Coleman Richardson, ©Indianapolis Museum of Art, Gift of Mrs. James W. Fesler; **770-771:** Donald Carroll/Getty Images; **775:** t.l. Getty Images; **775:** t.m. John Springer Collection/CORBIS; **775:** t.r. The Granger Collection, New York; **775:** b.m. Photofest; **775:** b.r. Photofest; **775:** b.l. Photofest; **777:** *Overview of family walking dog on the street* (detail), William Low, Courtesy of the artist; **781:** Flat Rock Playhouse, The State Theatre of North Carolina, YouTheatre production of Alice's Adventures In Wonderland; **785:** t. AP/Wide World Photos; **785** b. Courtesy of Peg Kehret; **786:** David Nieves/ Hudson Valley Aerial Photography; **788:** Courtesy of the Library of Congress; **789:** Musée Bartholdi, Colmar, reprod. C. Kempf"; **791:** Rob Lewine/CORBIS; **792:** Ralph A. Clevenger/CORBIS; **798:** Charles Gupton/CORBIS; **801:** Prentice Hall; **808:** Getty Images; **809:** AP/Wide World Photos **810-811:** Images.com/CORBIS; **812:** . Prentice Hall; **812:** b. ©Images.com/CORBIS; **813:** Courtesy of the Springville Museum of Art, Springville, Utah; **814:** PEANUTS reprinted by permission of United Feature Syndicate, Inc.; **815:** Images.com/CORBIS; **823:** Images.com/CORBIS; **827:** Courtesy of the Library of Congress; **829:** Daedalus and Icarus: French colored engraving, 1660, The Granger Collection, New York; **830-831:** Brian Parker/Tom Stack & Associates; **831:** Getty Images; **833:** Getty Images; **835:** George Lepp/CORBIS; **837:** *Demeter Mourning for Persephone,* 1906, Evelyn de Morgan, The De Morgan Foundation, London, UK/Bridgeman Art Library, London/New York; **838-839:** George Lepp/CORBIS; **839:** t(2). The Granger Collection, New York; **839:** t(1). The Granger Collection, New York; **839:** t(5). The Granger Collection, New York; **839:** t(3). The Granger Collection, New York; **839:** b(4).: The Granger Collection, New York; **839:** b(2). The Granger Collection, New York; **839:** b(5). Massimo Listri/CORBIS; **839:** b(1). Andrea Jemolo/CORBIS; **839:** t(4). Andrea Jemolo/CORBIS; **839:** b(3). Mimmo Jodice/CORBIS; **841:** George Lepp/CORBIS; **850:** Educational and Professional Publishing.; **851:** Werner Forman Archive/Art Resource, NY; **853:** The Bodleian Library, University of Oxford, MS. Arch. Selden, A.1, fol. 69r; **855:** Werner Forman Archive, Liverpool Museum, Liverpool/Art Resource NY; **856:** By permission of Mrs. J.S.E. Farrell; **857:** *The Volcanos,* 1905, Jose Maria Velasco, Galeria Arvil, Mexico. Courtesy of CDS Gallery, New York. Private Collection; **858:** Erich Lessing/ART RESOURCE, N Y; **860-861:** Robert Frerck/Odyssey Productions/Chicago; **862:** ©Charles & Josette Lenara/CORBIS; **864:** Werner Forman Archive, Liverpool Museum, Liverpool/Art Resource NY; **867:** Werner Forman Archive, Liverpool Museum, Liverpool/Art Resource NY; **871:** b. Alexander Limont; **871:** t. Courtesy of Alice Low; **872:** *Andromeda Liberated,* Pierre Mignard, Erich Lessing/Art Resource, NY; **875:** Araldo de Luca/CORBIS; **877:** Pearson Education/PH School Division; **878:** James L. Amos/CORBIS; **879:** Ronnie Kaufman/CORBIS; **889:** Images.com/CORBIS; **893:** b. AP/Wide World Photos; **893:** t. ©Bassouls Sophie/CORBIS Sygma; **894-895:** Ron Sanford/CORBIS; **896:** Darren Bennett/Animals Animals; **897:** Phil Lauro/Index Stock Photography, Inc.; **899:** Ron Sanford/CORBIS; **900:** The Granger Collection, New York; **902:** ©The Stock Market/Paul Loven; **903:** t.m. The Granger Collection, New York; **903:** t.l. Hulton Archive/Getty Images Inc.; **903:** m.r. The Granger Collection, New York; **903:** m.m. Bettmann/CORBIS; **903:** t.r Bettmann/CORBIS; **903:** b.l. Portrait of Langston Hughes (1902-1967) c. 1925, Winold Reiss, National Portrait Gallery, Washington, DC, USA/Art Resource, NY; **903:** b.r. Aaron Douglas (1899-1979). Artist., 1953, Betsy Graves Reyneau, National Portrait Gallery, Smithsonian Institution/Art Resource, NY; **903:** m.l. The Granger Collection, New York; **903:** b.m. Aaron Douglas, Into Bondage, 1936, 60 3/8 x 60 1/2, oil on canvas. In the collection of the Corcoran Gallery of Art, Washington, DC. Museum Purchase and Partial Gift of Thurlow Tibbs Jr., The Evans-Tibbs Collection. 1996.9; **905:** ©The Stock Market/Paul Loven; **909:** Ralph A. Clevenger/CORBIS; **910:** Buddy Mays/CORBIS; **913:** Prentice Hall; **914:** From THE PEOPLE COULD FLY by Virginia Hamilton, illustrated by Leo and Diane Dillon. Illustrations copyright ©1985 by Leo and Diane Dillon. Reprinted by permission of Alfred A. Knopf, Inc.; **916:** The Bridgeman Art Library, London/New York; **919:** The Bridgeman Art Library, London/New York; **920:** ©1966 by Michael Courlander; **921:** Getty Images; **922-923:** Les Pickett; Papilio/CORBIS; **924-925:** Corel Professional Photos CD-ROM™; **927:** Getty Images; **931:** t. Copyright 2004 The Burlington Free Press / Peter Huoppi; **931:** *Aesop,* c. 1639-1640. Oil on canvas, Diego Rodriguez Velazquez, Scala/Art Resource, NY; **933:** Felix Lorioux (1872-1964), "The Crow and the Fox", illustration for 'Fables' by Jean de La Fontaine (1621-95), color engraving. Private Collection/Bridgeman Art Library, London/New York; **934:** The Fox and the Crow, illustration by Arthur Rackham from 'Aesop's Fables', published by Heinemann, 1912/The Bridgeman Art Library, London/New York; **940:** Image Source/SuperStock; **943:** Prentice Hall; **952-953** Reuters/CORBIS; **953:** *Supergirl Archives Volume 1* ©2001 DC Comics. All rights Reserved. Used with Permission.; **954:** Paul Edmondson/CORBIS; **955:** Miriam Berkley/Authorpix

STAFF CREDITS

ADDITIONAL CREDITS